Governance and Accountability in Enterprise Security Systems

Amer Ibrahim
Department of Computer Science and Software Engineering, United Arab Emirates University, UAE

Taher M. Ghazal
https://orcid.org/0000-0003-0672-7924

Faculty of Computing and IT, Sohar University, Oman & Department of Networks and Cybersecurity, Hourani Center for Applied Scientific Research, Al-Ahliyya Amman University, Amman, Jordan & Center for Cyber Security, Faculty of Information Science and Technology, Universiti Kebangsaan Malaysia, Malaysia

IGI Global
Scientific Publishing
Publishing Tomorrow's Research Today

Vice President of Editorial	Melissa Wagner
Director of Acquisitions	Mikaela Felty
Director of Book Development	Jocelynn Hessler
Production Manager	Mike Brehm
Cover Design	Jose Rosado

Published in the United States of America by
IGI Global Scientific Publishing
701 East Chocolate Avenue
Hershey, PA, 17033, USA
Tel: 717-533-8845 | Fax: 717-533-7115
Website: https://www.igi-global.com E-mail: cust@igi-global.com

Library of Congress Cataloging-in-Publication Data

LCCN: 2026032244 (CIP Data Pending)
ISBN13: 9798260028704
Isbn13Softcover: 9798260028711
EISBN13: 9798260028728
British Cataloguing in Publication Data
A Cataloguing in Publication record for this book is available from the British Library.

Table of Contents

Detailed Table of Contents

This chapter looks at how controller and processor responsibilities are defined and allocated within the confines of today's security platforms. It scrutinizes the role definition of security solutions involving managed services, cloud providers, and AI-based analytics that are deployed by organizations. The chapter discusses a few legal aspects such as who has the decision-making authority, who determines the purposes, and who has control over the data processing operations. It focuses heavily on contract clarity, proper documentation, and governance mechanisms that set out the obligations relating to data protection, security measures, incident response, and handling of data subject rights. By unifying legal interpretation with the reality of security platform architectures, the chapter offers a roadmap for unambiguously defining responsibilities, lessening uncertainty, and ensuring accountability and compliance in multi-party security ecosystems.

Notice, transparency, and consent play a vital role in the effectiveness of security monitoring systems. This chapter reveals that a clear communication about monitoring to users can result in their awareness, the setting of their expectations, and their trust in organizational environments. Considering consent as a legal basis, however, it also argues that it is far from being ideal in employee and business relations scenarios because there is a possibility that power imbalances may invalidate a consent. Hands are even flipped to compliance alternatives such as legitimate interest assessments, policy documentation and accountability measures. Connecting legal requirements with security practice, the chapter depicts an illustration of how a well-structured notice and transparency mechanism can lead to a reduction of compliance risks, ethical monitoring and thereby giving an advantage to organizations to strike a proper balance between security and individual rights.

This chapter discusses the importance of notice, transparency and consent for security monitoring systems. It is very important for security monitoring systems to give notice, be transparent and obtain consent as these show that if users are informed clearly about the monitoring, they will get aware, their expectations will be set, and they will trust organizational environments. In fact, the chapter draws attention to the fact that legally, notice and transparency means informing the purposes, nature of data, retention times, and automated decision-making procedures. Besides this, it sees consent as one of the legal grounds but points out its limitation in case of employee and business scenarios where power imbalance exists and might invalidate it. The chapter, by linking legal requirements with security practice, illustrates that an effective notice and transparency framework may result in reduced compliance risks, ethical monitoring, and allowing organizations to strike the right balance between security and individual rights.

This chapter investigates user expectations of privacy within corporate security environments and their importance for legal and ethical security practices. This study covers the change in user privacy expectations and sensitization to monitoring and controls at work through the detailed analysis of several aspects. The chapter discusses the tension between the organization's need for security and the individual's right to privacy. The main focus is on the fact that the four principles of notice, consent, proportionality, and limitation of purpose are central to the trade-off between security and privacy. By assuming that typical corporate security measures like network monitoring, endpoint protection, and identity management systems are in place, the chapter points out differences between users' perceptions and the actual data practices. Besides, it is pointed out that security operations consistent with a reasonable user's expectations can help not only in risk avoidance but also in creating trust, and simultaneously, making compliance with corporate governance easier.

Within the boundaries of law, a clear distinction is made between security monitoring and surveillance. It does a good job of explaining the conceptual, functional, and operational differences between protective monitoring of systems, assets, and people on the one hand, and surveillance practices, which are about systematic observation of persons or behavior, on the other. The chapter breaks down the way in which purpose, extent, proportionality, and data handling determine whether these practices fall under privacy and data protection laws. It also talks about consent, transparency, necessity, and minimization as the main principles that security monitoring needs to follow to be lawful. The chapter through law and case studies draws attention to the danger of function creep, over-collection of data, and misuse of monitoring tools. It offers a roadmap for organizations to develop their security measures both to be effective and at the same time comply with rights, laws, and ethics.

Effective management of retention, deletion, and legal hold requirements is essential for security data repositories. The study is explored by looking at how logs, telemetry, alerts, and forensic artifacts are stored in distributed systems and what legal requirements govern their lifecycle. The chapter explains retention scheduling, purpose limitation, and risk- based retention periods, as well as secure deletion, anonymization, and archival controls. A special focus is put on legal holds due to litigation, regulatory inquiries, and incident investigations and how such legal holds may conflict with regular deletion requirements. The chapter also looks at governance mechanisms such as policy setting, automation, audit trail, and collaboration between security, legal, and compliance functions at the cross-functional level. By integrating technical data management with regulatory and legal requirements, the chapter outlines how necessary security data can be preserved while the privacy risk, storage cost, and compliance risk are kept at a minimum.

The chapter discusses the determination of who is responsible when artificial intelligence is used for security decision making within complex organizational environments. It looks at how accountability is shared among system designers, vendors, deployers, and human operators when AI-driven tools are used to influence detection actions, prioritization, and response. The chapter investigates legal principles explaining the relationship between control, foreseeability, and duty of care, along with regulatory requirements for human oversight and governance. It also examines issues related to automation bias, black-box models, and extended decision chains that involve Security Operations Centers and third parties. Special focus is given to documentation, role clarity, chain of command for escalation, and auditability as means of defining responsibility. Through combining a legal perspective with security operational practice, the chapter outlines a system for determining responsibility, handling liability, and making defensible decisions in AI-assisted security systems.

The chapter looks at how important it is to justify and be transparent about automated security actions that are made by artificial intelligence and rule-based systems. It discusses the necessity for automated responses such as blocking access, escalating alerts, and taking enforcement actions to be explainable to law, legal defensibility, and organizational trust. The chapter also considers the considerations regulators have for transparency that may include documenting decision logic, data inputs, and risk thresholds of automated actions. There is a specific focus on explanability tools, audit trails, human review processes, and communication strategies as the main methods of helping accountability without compromising security controls. Aligning the legal standards with the security operational practices, the chapter outlines the ways of managing automated security actions which are justified, transparent, and compliant with the law and good corporate governance.

The focus of this chapter is on the development of human review and override elements in automated security operation systems. It discusses the fundamental reasons for a significant human intervention to lessen automation bias, handle false alarms, and make sure that decisions are made in a legal way. The chapter looks at various principles underlying the effective review, such as the transparency of alerts, the interpretability of model outputs, role- based authority, and the availability of timely escalation channels. Furthermore, it highlights operational difficulties such as alert fatigue, the alignment of skills, and the maintenance of the pace of response together with oversight. The chapter, by merging legal requirements with security engineering practice, offers a roadmap for setting up review and override mechanisms that are not only feasible and proportional but also robust and compliant with automation while not weakening security effectiveness.

The focus is on legal risks that are linked to false positives and automated decision-making systems in security operations. AI-powered detection and response mechanisms can mistakenly tag people, actions, or properties as a threat, which can lead to interruption of operations, damage to reputation, and violation of rights. The chapter discusses the issues of liability, accountability, and evidence that relate to automated decisions such as denying access, sending alerts, and taking enforcement measures. It also examines how regulators expect automated decisions to be accurate, explainable, overseen by humans, and able to be challenged. Most of the discussion around governance controls is on calibrating the thresholds, escalation procedures, audit trails, and fixing methods. The chapter, through a combination of legal analysis and the security engineering field, delivers a direction that guides a reduction in legal exposure while still preserving the effectiveness of automation. It presents a method of handling the false positive risk in security systems that are compliant

Evaluating potential bias and disparate impact is essential in User and Entity Behavior Analytics (UEBA) and insider threat detection systems. The chapter explores behavior baselining, anomaly detection, and machine-learning-driven risk scoring as methods that, without intention, may mirror or even reinforce biases relating to roles, work patterns, cultural behaviors, or accessibility needs. It goes on to point out biases stem from training data, feature selection, labeling, and the security operations feedback loop.

Preface

OVERVIEW OF THE SUBJECT MATTER

Artificial intelligence is transforming enterprise security operations in profound ways; enabling behavioural analytics, automated decision-making, and continuous monitoring at scales that were previously impossible. Yet as AI assumes greater responsibility within security platforms, the questions of governance, accountability, and legal compliance become increasingly critical. Who bears responsibility when an automated system takes an erroneous enforcement action? How should organization's structure oversight mechanisms, audit trails, and human review processes to remain legally defensible? What frameworks govern data subject rights within the context of security operations?

This book, Governance and Accountability in Enterprise Security Systems, addresses these questions systematically. It brings together 13 chapters authored by an international community of researchers and practitioners spanning computer science, cybersecurity, law, and information systems. The volume focuses specifically on the governance structures, accountability mechanisms, and oversight frameworks that organizations must establish to ensure that AI-driven enterprise security operations remain lawful, transparent, and subject to appropriate human control.

WHERE THIS TOPIC FITS IN THE WORLD TODAY

The governance of AI-driven security systems has emerged as a central regulatory concern globally. The EU AI Act, GDPR, and emerging frameworks across the Middle East, Asia, and the Americas impose detailed obligations on organizations deploying automated decision-making in security contexts. Data subject rights – including rights of access, erasure, and objection to automated decisions – must be operationalized within security platforms that process personal data at scale.

At the same time, organizations face mounting operational pressure to increase automation within security operations to address the growing sophistication of cyber threats and the shortage of qualified security personnel. This creates a structural tension between the drive toward automation and the legal requirement to maintain meaningful human oversight and accountability. This volume is designed to navigate that tension, providing researchers and practitioners with structured frameworks for building accountable, auditable, and rights-respecting AI security operations.

TARGET AUDIENCE

This book is intended for security architects, SOC managers, compliance officers, data protection officers, and legal professionals working at the intersection of enterprise security and data protection law. Academic researchers and graduate students in computer science, cybersecurity, information systems, and law will find the volume a focused reference on AI governance and accountability in operational security contexts. Policymakers and regulators will gain insight into the practical challenges organizations face when implementing AI governance requirements within enterprise security environments.

ORGANIZATION OF THE BOOK AND CHAPTER DESCRIPTIONS

Chapter 1: Defining Controller and Processor Responsibilities in Security Platforms

This chapter examines how controller and processor responsibilities are defined and allocated within modern security platforms, scrutinizing role definitions for security solutions involving managed services, cloud providers, and AI-based analytics.

Chapter 2: Governance of Data Subject Rights Requests in Organizational Security Operations

This chapter addresses the governance structures required to manage data subject rights requests within organizational security operations, examining how rights of access, erasure, restriction, and objection are operationalized in security data environments.

Chapter 3: The Role of Notice, Transparency and Consent in Security Monitoring

This chapter discusses the importance of notice, transparency, and consent in security monitoring systems, demonstrating that clear communication about monitoring leads to user awareness, expectation-setting, and organizational trust.

Chapter 4: Understanding User Expectations of Privacy in Enterprise Security Environments

This chapter investigates user expectations of privacy within corporate security environments, considering how employees, contractors, and system users understand privacy in connection with workplace monitoring, access controls, and incident response.

Chapter 5: Distinguishing Security Monitoring from Surveillance Within Legal Boundaries

This chapter examines the difference between security monitoring and surveillance within the boundaries of law, explaining the conceptual and operational differences between protective monitoring and systematic observation of persons or behaviour.

Chapter 6: Managing Retention, Deletion and Legal Hold Requirements in Security Data Repositories

This chapter focuses on how retention, deletion, and legal hold requirements are managed in security data repositories, covering retention scheduling, purpose limitation, risk-based retention periods, secure deletion, and archival controls.

Chapter 7: Determining Responsibility for Artificial Intelligence Based Security Decision Making

This chapter discusses the determination of responsibility when AI is used for security decision making, examining how accountability is shared among system designers, vendors, deployers, and human operators when AI-driven tools influence detection and response.

Chapter 8: Justification and Transparency of Automated Security Actions

This chapter examines the importance of justifying and being transparent about automated security actions made by AI and rule-based systems, discussing the necessity for automated responses to be explainable for legal defensibility and organizational trust.

Chapter 9: Designing Human Review and Override Mechanisms in Automated Systems

This chapter focuses on the development of human review and override mechanisms in automated security systems, discussing the fundamental reasons for significant human intervention to address automation bias, handle false alarms, and ensure legally sound decisions.

Chapter 10: Managing Legal Risk Arising from False Positives and Automated Decision Systems

This chapter examines legal risks linked to false positives and automated decision-making systems, addressing how AI-powered detection mechanisms can mistakenly tag persons or properties as threats, leading to operational disruption and rights violations.

Chapter 11: Evaluation of Bias and Disparate Impact in UEBA and Insider Threat Detection Systems

This chapter evaluates possible bias and disparate impact in User and Entity Behaviour Analytics and insider threat detection systems, considering how baselining and anomaly detection can unintentionally reflect or amplify biases based on roles, work patterns, or cultural behaviours.

Chapter 12: Approaches to Validating and Monitoring Artificial Intelligence Models Used in Security

This chapter reviews methods for verifying and supervising AI models utilized in security, focusing on the significance of ensuring models are accurate, reliable, and robust when deployed for threat detection, anomaly analysis, and automated response.

Chapter 13: Constraints and Limitations of Automation in Autonomous Security Environments

This chapter investigates the limitations and restrictions of automation in autonomous security environments, studying the technical, operational, and legal factors that limit full automation, including data quality, model uncertainty, contextual ambiguity, and adversarial manipulation.

CONCLUSION: IMPACT AND CONTRIBUTION TO THE FIELD

Taken together, the 13 chapters of Governance and Accountability in Enterprise Security Systems provide a focused and comprehensive treatment of the governance, oversight, and accountability mechanisms required for lawful and effective AI-driven enterprise security operations. By structuring the volume around governance frameworks and automated decision-making accountability, the book offers security architects, compliance professionals, and researchers a structured reference for building auditable, rights-respecting security operations.

It is the editors' hope that this volume will serve as an essential resource for those seeking to implement AI security governance in practice, and for researchers advancing the scholarship on accountability and oversight in automated security systems.

Amer Ibrahim
Department of Computer Science and Software Engineering, United Arab Emirates University, UAE

Taher M. Ghazal
Faculty of Computing and IT, Sohar University, Oman & Department of Networks and Cybersecurity, Hourani Center for Applied Scientific Research, Al-Ahliyya Amman University, Amman, Jordan & Center for Cyber Security, Faculty of Information Science and Technology, Universiti Kebangsaan Malaysia, Malaysia

Acknowledgment

The editors wish to express their sincere gratitude to all the contributing authors of this volume, whose expertise, dedication, and scholarly rigor made this book possible. We are equally grateful to the members of the Editorial Advisory Board and the many anonymous peer reviewers, whose constructive and timely feedback substantially strengthened the quality of every chapter throughout the review and revision process.

We would also like to thank our respective institutions for their continued support throughout the development of this project, and our families and colleagues for their patience and encouragement. Finally, we extend our sincere appreciation to the entire team at IGI Global Scientific Publishing for their guidance, professionalism, and support in bringing this book to publication.

Editorial Advisory Board

Chapter 1
Defining Controller and Processor Responsibilities in Security Platforms

Leen Tarawneh
http://orcid.org/0009-0009-6100-7365
Mutah University, Jordan

Mahmoud Abu Saima
http://orcid.org/0000-0001-5343-0053
United Arab Emirates University, UAE

Mohammad Rustom R. Al Nasar
http://orcid.org/0000-0002-8856-9394
American University in the Emirates, UAE

ABSTRACT

This chapter looks at how controller and processor responsibilities are defined and allocated within the confines of today's security platforms. It scrutinizes the role definition of security solutions involving managed services, cloud providers, and AI-based analytics that are deployed by organizations. The chapter discusses a few legal aspects such as who has the decision-making authority, who determines the purposes, and who has control over the data processing operations. It focuses heavily on contract clarity, proper documentation, and governance mechanisms that set out the obligations relating to data protection, security measures, incident response, and handling of data subject rights. By unifying legal interpretation with the reality of security platform architectures, the chapter offers a roadmap for unambiguously defining responsibilities, lessening uncertainty, and ensuring accountability and compliance in multi-party security ecosystems.

1. INTRODUCTION

Cybersecurity data governance has indeed undergone transformation in the last two decades. In the beginning, network security systems were basically just rule-based intrusion detection technologies

DOI: 10.4018/979-8-2600-2870-4.ch001

operating mainly within closed enterprise networks. The data sets of these systems were not that large and, most of the time, the organization's IT-savvy staff had them under control. But, with the increasing volume, intensity, and diversity of threats, a more digitized infrastructure, the change of security monitoring systems to tools that gather big data through network logs, authentication records, endpoint telemetry, and behavioral analytics happened. That lead to the emergence of new governance dilemmas because security analytics' higher capabilities(Ghazal, Hasan, Hussein, et al., 2025). When you aggregate large amounts of data, you can essentially do things like anomaly detection, behavioral profiling or you can even make risk predictions. However, these come with processing of massive amounts of information that is often is of a very sensitive nature. Therefore, data governance frameworks must take the functionality and potential of comprehensive security monitoring, on the one hand, and the legal and ethical obligations stemming from the processing of user-related information, on the other hand, into consideration. The governance of data in security platforms nowadays, is not only about identifying who runs the show and responsible for outcomes of monitoring exercises, but also about how processing operations are carried out (e.g., the technical aspects such as ingestion, storage, analysis, retention)(Saeed et al., 2024). Moreover, ensuring that the entire exercise of automated decision-making is transparent and can be checked for accountability is a governance necessity. Controllers and processors must be clearly defined to manifest their accountability in the security analytics world. One of the factors that have shaped the evolution of governance is the adoption of cloud-based security services. It is quite common for an organization to entrust a security monitoring capability vendor. This can come as a managed detection and response (MDR) service, a threat intelligence service, or even an AI-driven analytics security platform. Enhancing cybersecurity capabilities is, of course, the upside of using external vendors, but the flip side is that you are now sharing data processing responsibilities with multiple organizations. Governance frameworks, therefore, need to be strong and persistent in clearly stating which entity is responsible for what, for example, deciding the monitoring objectives versus carrying out the technical processing (Ghazal, Hasan, Khairy, et al., 2025).

1.1 Importance of Defining Controller and Processor Responsibilities

What really matters, when one considers security systems is, of course, accountability. And, unfortunately, it is quite a challenge to have accountability if one does not have a clear definition of the persons who control and process data. If the governance roles are the result of a mixture of ambiguities, then, as a consequence, organizations can come to a belief that, for instance, regulatory compliance, incident reporting, and protection of sensitive information, are not a person's responsibility. Where cybersecurity is concerned and there is a multiplicity of vendors and service providers working together to process data, it is actually the allocation of responsibilities that ensures operational transparency and legal compliance(Hanandeh et al., 2025). Assigning accountability is, of course, the first and foremost reason why these roles should be delineated. This is because under many internationally recognized data protection regulations entities controlling the processing and deciding on the purposes are targeted with very unique and stringent sets of obligations. Most of them have to do with putting in place appropriate safeguards so as to ensure the processing is always within the limits of the law and also making sure third-party processors are adequately supervised from the point of view of compliance(Ghazal et al., 2022).

Processors have to understand that they should follow the instructions of data controllers, but also apply technical protective measures to secure data they work with. Once you properly separate the roles, you will be able to establish governance systems that will truly comply with the regulators' requirements.

Another justification for unambiguously defining governance roles is, besides legal liability, the improvement of operational . Security platform functionality is a blend of multiple workflows such as drawing in data from various sources, transforming that data via machine learning analytics engines, automating incident response, and presenting the final results to human analysts(Alnawayseh et al., 2022). A single stage can even be handled by different service providers or infrastructure components. By assigning controller and processor responsibilities for every single step in the data lifecycle, you minimize the chances that governance mechanisms will be treated as an afterthought and hence excluded from the technical side of the platform. Moreover, clear governance structures make room for risk management in security operations. Based on monitoring rules, machine learning models, or data processing tasks by external vendors, whenever a security monitoring system issues false positive or misclassifies legitimate activities, organizations will know exactly where to look for the problem depending on the clearly defined responsibilities and the source of failures can be isolated more effectively as well(Al-Okbi, Alomari, Hadi, et al., 2025).

1.2 Legal Foundations of Data Controller and Processor Concepts

The ideas around data controllers and processors come from global data protection norms that mainly focus on personal information processing regulation. These frameworks realize that companies may need to hire third-party providers to work on task-oriented processing, hence, there are legal distinctions between the entity who plans and determines the processing and the one(s) who do the actual processing on behalf of another. Controller is usually the term given to the one who decides processing purposes and how data is manipulated. This person or organization is the one who initiates the collection of data, selects their utilizations, and implements protection measures(Khalayleh et al., 2025). As such, controllers have primary liability for compliance with the local laws and ordinances. When speaking about security platforms, it is usually the organization that installs the monitoring system that is the controller since it defines the purpose of the detection and response activities. Processors, however, are the ones that carry out processing under a controller's mandate. Processors could be those handling technical aspects of services such as providing the cloud infrastructure, managing logs, or running the machine learning analytics engines. The general principle is that processors are to simply follow the controller's lead and also step up to the challenge of implementing security safeguards to the data they are handling at all times. Processors are not supposed to make decisions about the use of the data; however, they have a responsibility to keep the data confidential, unaltered, and available within the system they control. Legislators have put an emphasis on the importance of binding contracts that define each party's duties. These contracts set out the processor's obligations with regard to the way data is managed, the level of security that must be maintained, and the procedure for notifying breaches/incidents. The security monitoring platform is a good example of processing that is ongoing and also involves the use of automated (Al-Suhimat et al., 2024).

1.3 Security Platforms as Complex Data Processing Ecosystems

Current security platforms are not merely a tool or a piece of software. Instead they are an elaborate ecosystem comprised of different technologies, service providers, and organizational stakeholders. Most fundamental to these platforms are the amalgamation of various data sources such as network traffic logs, authentication records, endpoint telemetry, and behavioral analytics which jointly enable threat detection at a very high level. The data flow in a Security Operations Center (SOC) is quite complex. Initially, collection agents capture security events across different organizational infrastructures and then forward them to centralized data ingestion (Ghazal, Abu-Shareha, et al., 2025). At this stage, the data is normalized and stored before it is forwarded to large-scale analytics platforms where millions of events per second can be processed. Further, machine learning algorithms use statistical and behavior-based techniques to compare these datasets, pick up on irregularities and produce alerts that could be signs of cyber threats. With the help of automation, incident response systems either human analysts in investigation and threat mitigation or they assist in these roles to a certain extent. Each technology and service that forms part of this architecture can to some extent, be an independent entity(Ghazal, Abualhaj, et al., 2025). By way of illustration, the organization may be the one making decisions on objectives for monitoring while cloud-service providers only offer infrastructure for data storage and processing. The cases where the controllers provide security algorithms and also the role of the managed security service whose services are more geared towards analyzing the collected data. By way of illustration, the organization itself defines the objectives of monitoring activities and cloud service providers host the infrastructure supporting data storage and processing. A vendor supplying threat detection algorithms or providing a managed security service that analyzes the collected data are other examples. To this determine which entity acts as the controller and which acts as the processor, you need to look very closely at who makes the decisions and who has control over the operations. Complexities of these ecosystems require governance frameworks capable of delineating responsibilities throughout the entire security architecture. Such frameworks provide each party involved in the processing lifecycle with a clear understanding of their roles and, in terms of accountability, their (Ghazal, Abu-Shareha, et al., 2025). This chapter contributes a governance-oriented framework for defining controller and processor responsibilities in AI-enabled security platforms, emphasizing accountability, contractual governance, operational oversight, and regulatory compliance. Although previous studies have examined cybersecurity monitoring technologies and data protection separately, limited research has explored responsibility allocation across controllers, processors, vendors, and sub-processors within AI-driven security ecosystems.

2. REGULATORY FOUNDATIONS

Worldwide data privacy laws allocate distinct roles to individuals or organizations that process data. Though labels might differ a little from one place to another, basically the differentiation between controllers and processors stays the same. A data controller is generally understood as the one who makes the decisions concerning the purposes and ways of processing personal data. This person or body explains why data have to be collected, how they will be utilized, and what measures should be taken to ensure the legality of processing(Vasudevan et al., 2024). In cybersecurity circles, the enterprises running security function monitoring systems will in most cases be the ones exerting the control over data as they decide the goals of monitoring and set the boundaries of threat identification activities. A data processor, on the other hand, refers to a party that is hired to process the data at the controller's request. Processors are unaware of the purposes for processing and just carry out the commands specified by the controllers. Some examples of processors in security environments are cloud infrastructure providers, services that gather and manage logs, platforms providing threat intelligence, or organizations supplying analytics tools empowered by machine learning. These parties operate with security data, quiring telemetry, analyzing network incidents, keeping time logs while still being committed to contracts issued by the controlling entity(Sharma et al., 2025).

Why distinguishing between these roles matters in cybersecurity is because security monitoring might necessitate the gathering of data from the whole enterprise. Network monitoring tools keep track of the metadata of communications, authentication systems generate logs of users' identities, and endpoint agents collect behavioral telemetry that is only indirectly linked to the individuals. Even if data collecting measures are done for legitimate security reasons, they cannot just ignore the question of who has control and who does the processing(A. Arabiat, Altayeb, & Alkhrissat, 2025). In fact, to ensure compliance, companies must first identify which organization controls the purposes of their operations and which organizations are only doing technical tasks, to use the words of the law. The top international regulations, such as the EU's General Data Protection Regulation (GDPR), the California Consumer Privacy Act (CCPA) in the USA, and the quickly changing data protection laws in Asia and Africa, all recognize this difference between the roles of responsibility. Although these legal instruments have their own enforcement modes and legal structures, they all aim to that the party that decides the processing manner should bear the accountability for safeguarding the rights of individuals and ensuring legal use of data(Shah et al., 2022). Regarding security monitoring, the one who buys and installs the monitoring system is probably the one who controls the processing because it is the one who decides the objectives of threat detection and risk management. The suppliers of technology equipment to the actors who monitor the infrastructure can be categorized as processors because they are the ones who perform the technical operations that support monitoring activities physically. In such a case, the responsibility for security governance remains with the entity that benefits from the monitoring system and not with the third-party vendors that provide technical (Abualhaj, Al-Khatib, Abu-Shareha, Hyassat, et al., 2025).

2.1 Responsibilities Defined Under GDPR Article 4 and Article 28

Arguably the principal legal instrument that sets apart the responsibilities of data controllers and data processors in the European Union is the General Data Protection Regulation (GDPR). Essentially, the intention of the set of rules was securing personal data in a consumer and business environment. However, the core principles of data governance under the regulation are actually applicable to any arrangement involving personal data, for instance, security data monitoring systems. The document is quite explicit about each party's role, defining also the appropriate way organizations engaged in data processing operations handle their (Al-znamat et al., 2025). Key role definitions under GDPR are contained in Article 4. The article characterizes a controller as a person, public authority, agency or other body which alone or jointly with others determines the purposes and means of the processing of personal data. The focus on this wording of the definition of a controller is the fact-making capacity or power to decide who controls the data and how. If we are talking about cybersecurity, the ones who define what the system monitors and how it would function are usually the controllers as they decide the purpose of collecting and usage of the monitoring data(Ullah et al., 2025).

Processor is the term for a subject who processes personal data on behalf of the controller, and therefore processor does not have the right to decide the purpose and means of the processing. Operations such as storage of data, analysis of logs, usage of machine learning models or transmission of security-related data over the network infrastructures could be considered as examples of processing activities by processors. It is evident that the maintenance of the purpose of processing remains with the controllers and processors simply implement the operational instructions of the controller(Ali et al.,

2025). On further clarifying the rules governing the relation between controllers and processors, GDPR Article 28 stipulates that a controller must only engage a processor that can provide sufficient guarantees to implement appropriate technical and organizational measures in such a manner that processing will meet the requirements of this Regulation and ensure the protection of the rights of data subject. Controllers have to make sure that processing activities are regulated by contracts that have legal force, specifying in detail the respective scope, duration, and purpose of processing operations. Additionally, these contracts should define security measures, confidentiality obligations, and breach notification procedures(Keote et al., 2025).

Cybersecurity platforms are often required to sign a data processing agreement (DPA) as a way to meet these contractual requirements. This type of contract normally includes clauses that specify how security telemetry can be processed, the maximum duration for which monitoring data can be stored, and the security safeguards that must be in place before vendors who provide monitoring infrastructure or analytics services are permitted to perform their roles. DPAs, as a matter of fact, also direct the ways to react to possible security incidents, allowing processors to controllers for notification without delay when breaches impacting monitored data occur(A. Arabiat, Altayeb, & Salama, 2025). Further, Article 28 sets the expectation that processors should assist controllers in fulfilling their own responsibilities under the Regulation. This assistance might include facilitating regulatory inspections, supplying data processing documentation, and implementing measures to enable controllers to demonstrate their accountability. When it comes to cybersecurity ecosystems, the above essentially implies providing up-to-date information on the compliance status of logging, monitoring, and other associated activities with the regulatory (Ju et al., 2025).

2.2 Legal Interpretations in AI and Automated Security Environments

AI's integration into cybersecurity infrastructures adds new challenges to the determination of controller and processor roles. AI-based security systems may be the outcomes of intricate processing steps that involve several stakeholders at different stages such as development, deployment and operation of machine-learning . The governance roles allocation calls for identifying who actually makes decisions on processing goals and methods. Suppose a business installs an AI intrusion detection system but contracts the algorithm toll development to a third party. If the latter only technically provide tools without impact on the system's objectives, the provider shall be considered as a processor whereas the business remains the controller(Ramesh et al., 2025). However, should the vendor take an independent decision on analysing monitoring data or have an influence on system's objectives, the vendor will be deemed as a joint controller. The legal interpretations of such situations are focused on the principle of actual control over processing decisions. Places and people that impact the making of analytical models, decide which datasets are to be used for training or set the criteria for automated threat detection are likely viewed as controllers since they determine the ways of processing. On the other hand, those who process the operations under the instructions of another entity are known as processors. The distinctions become more crucial with AI security systems where the models continuously observe the patterns of behavior and automatically generate notifications(Ahmed et al., 2025). However, by the law, it is illegal that the decisions of automated systems that have significant impacts on individuals or organizations, for example, denying access or marking as suspicious behavior, should be able to be traced and held accountable. Therefore, governance structures must ensure that the entities which are responsible for designing and controlling these systems are the ones that the public can hold accountable for the (Shambour et al.,

2025). Controller and processor roles should be assessed according to actual decision-making authority and operational control rather than contractual labels alone. Organizations that influence monitoring objectives, model behavior, or processing purposes may assume greater governance responsibilities.

2.3 Compliance Challenges in Distributed Security Infrastructure

Nowadays, cybersecurity frameworks are often running worldwide with several different providers along with various IT platforms. Cloud-based options, for example, could have monitoring data stored across multiple locations, while the analytical engines may be doing the data processing via distributed computing infrastructures. These kinds of setups not only improve scalability and performance but also bring about governance issues such as jurisdiction, accountability, and trol. When multiple players are involved in constructing and running security monitoring systems, it may be quite challenging to identify the one that controls. At times, a pair of organizations might share the power to decide the goals of monitoring as well as the methods of processing. Such joint controller situations can lead to multiple parties being held liable for compliance with data protection requirements(Qawasmeh et al., 2025).

It is also demanding when processors engage sub-processors to carry out their technical tasks. Say a managed security service provider is resorting to a cloud infrastructure provider or a third-party analytics service in support of its monitoring operations. Regulatory standards generally require that processors shall have the prior written authorization of the controller before engaging a sub-processor. The main object of this requirement is that the entire processing chain remains under the controller's supervision and the controller is able to check that all the entities involved implement proper security measures(Alqudah et al., 2025). Additional difficulties arise where the monitoring data is crossing national borders. Most legal regimes regulate international data transfers and especially impose limitations when data is sent to countries with weaker personal data protection standards. Security platforms functioning at the level of global infrastructures must, therefore, have in place governance mechanisms that ensure cross-border processing activities are compliant with the relevant data protection laws(Ghazal, 2025b).

3. CONTROLLER–PROCESSOR CONTRACTUAL RELATIONSHIPS

Controllers and processors within cybersecurity monitoring environments typically use formal contractual agreements to govern their relationship. These contracts set the legal and operational boundaries of data processing activities. Since security monitoring platforms often depend on distributed infrastructures and specialized vendors to handle large volumes of telemetry data, contractual frameworks are the means by which controllers continue to exercise their governance authority even when delegating technical processing tasks to processors. Such contracts guarantee that the processing operations continue to be in line with the objectives, policies, and regulatory obligations laid down by the controller(Al-Dmour et al., 2025). In cybersecurity ecosystems, monitoring infrastructures generally consist of multiple service providers functioning at different technological levels. For instance, cloud providers may be hosting security data lakes, analytics vendors may be supplying artificial intelligence models for network behavior analysis, and managed security service providers may be running threat detection workflows, etc. All these different types of entities operate processing activities for the organization that is deploying the security platform. In the absence of well-established contractual frameworks, the roles of these actors could be difficult to pinpoint, which might result in both regulatory non-compliance and lack of operational accountability(Gul et al., 2025). That is why contracts between controllers and processors set out the conditions under which security telemetry should be handled during the whole monitoring process. They lay down the boundaries of processing activities, prescribe the security measures that must be put in place, and also indicate how monitoring data-related incidents should be reported and managed. By making these duties explicit in legally binding documents, controllers guarantee that vendors acting as processors conform to the governance frameworks intended to safeguard sensitive monitoring data and ensure operational security(Almomani et al., 2025).

Moreover, contracts between controllers and processors ensure that processors strictly follow the instructions of the controller. In security monitoring settings, it means that security telemetry-processing vendors should not figure out on their own how the data should be used or repurpose it for unrelated activities. The controller is responsible for setting the objectives of monitoring activities and deciding how the collected data is to be used for threat detection, risk management, and incident response, etc. Contracts reinforce this principle of governance by explicitly stating that processors should not use monitoring data beyond the scope authorized by the controller(Ghazal, Hasan, Raju, et al., 2025). In addition, contractual frameworks serve as instruments for ensuring accountability in complex vendor ecosystems. Security monitoring infrastructures typically engage multiple processors which perform different stages of data processing in collaboration. For instance, one vendor might handle endpoint telemetry collection, another might be responsible for log aggregation in a centralized data lake, and a third one might use machine learning analytics for detecting anomalous . Controllers need to make sure that each vendor, who is a part of this processing chain, complies with consistent security standards and governance principles. So, contracts not only delineate the responsibilities of individual processors but also the obligations relating to the relationships between the respective processors and any sub-processors involved in the monitoring activities(Sardar et al., 2025).

Last but not least contracts have a considerable role in ensuring regulatory compliance and enabling auditability. Controllers must demonstrate to the regulators that processors have been provided with and are continually abiding by appropriate technical and organizational measures to protect the processed data. Contracts make it legally binding that processors must abide by the security standards and grant controllers the right to verify the implementations through audits, reporting, and compliance reviews(Abuowaida et al., 2025). The present material discusses in detail, the nature of contracts that establish controller-processor relationships in security monitoring infrastructures. It covers the definition of operational roles by processing agreements, contracting for sub-processor use, embedding audit and oversight mechanisms within contractual frameworks, and enforcing data protection obligations through contractual governance(Qaddara & Alraba'nah, 2025).

3.1 Data Processing Agreements in Security Monitoring Systems

DPAs (Data Processing Agreements) are a significant feature of controller–processor partnerships in security platforms. A DPA is a contract that sets terms and conditions that dictate the manner in which the processors may carry out data handling on behalf of the controllers. In the case of security monitoring systems, DPAs are the document setting out the rules of processing security telemetry data, security logs, and analytical results managed by the monitoring infrastructure. One of the key parts of a DPA is the description of the processing scope. The DPA lists types of data to be processed by the processor, processing activities, and the time frame of the processing activities. For instance, the manager of a security analytics tool will be given access only to the extent of network logs analysis for the purpose of spotting anomalies and will not be granted the rights to store or reuse such logs for other types of analysis(Abualhaj, Al-Khatib, Al Zyoud, Qaddara, et al., 2025).

Besides the processing scope, DPAs are also used by controllers to inform processors about the technical and organizational security measures to be implemented for data protection. Such measures could include, but are not limited to, data encryption during transmission, secured storing of log data, access control tools restricting the persons interacting with monitoring infrastructure, and incident detection tools that identify unauthorized access to security telemetry. Besides specifying the scope of processing, DPAs are also a key tool for the establishment of confidentiality commitments on the part of vendors as a processor so that the personnel with access to monitoring data are bound to a strict code of confidentiality concerning the information exposed during system operation or incident investigation. This aspect contributes significantly to the security of sensitive operational information throughout the monitoring process(Abualhaj, Al-Khatib, Al Shafi, Qaddara, et al., 2025).

3.2 Defining Scope and Limitations of Processing Activities

Controller-processor contracts are a very important tool for the controller to set the boundaries of processing operations by ecology defining the processing activities that are outside the permissible ones, security monitoring systems produce huge quantities of data generated through network events, authentication logs, application activity, and infrastructure telemetry. Hence, it is through contracts that the parties can limit the data beyond which processors cannot get access to or analyze the data. This is vital to ensure that any misuse or unauthorized use of the information is prevented. to this end, contracts set restrictions that limit processors to only performing the tasks given and authorized by the controller only(Otair et al., 2025). Such limitations are very necessary to protect monitoring data from being used for any purposes other than those provided in a security governance framework. For example, a processor who has the responsibility to collect and manage security logs may be permitted to keep and make an index of log data but will not be able to perform behavioral analytics unless the controller authorizes .

Besides restricting allowed processing activities, contracts may also include other provisions such as limitations on data retention. For example, while monitoring systems may have certain durations for which security telemetry data is kept to support forensic actions or compliance audits, processors should be made aware through contracts of how long such data can be stored and the actions that should be taken when the retention period expires(Abualghanam et al., 2025). Failure to do so may result in processors holding sensitive information longer than necessary. Another category of limitations that could be spelled out in contracts is those relating to the geographical locations where data processing is permitted. It is very common for security monitoring infrastructures to be linked with the cloud, which keeps their operations running in various jurisdictions. At the same time, protection and privacy laws generally set limits on cross-border transfer of data. Thus, controllers will have to check that processors are working within approved geographical perceptions for handling monitoring data or, where necessary, that the appropriate cross-border processing safeguards are in place(Al-Okbi, Alomari, Zitar, et al., 2025).

3.3 Sub-Processor Governance in Security Ecosystems

Processors in a significant number of cybersecurity platforms introduce additional vendors, known as sub-processors, for certain technical functions within the monitoring infrastructure. For instance, a managed security service provider might have to resort to cloud infrastructure providers for hosting log storage environments or be dependent on analytics specialists to process behavioral telemetry. As sub-processors handle monitoring data as well, it becomes imperative for controllers to have a complete view of the entire processing chain. Contracts between controllers and processors are therefore expected to have clauses compelling processors to seek the controller's approval prior to entering into sub-processor relationships. This makes sure that controllers keep track of each and every processing entity handling security telemetry data(Mostafa et al., 2025).

In addition, contracts will have to specify that processors are responsible for the conduct of sub-processors and that they must require sub-processors to put in place the same level of security protections as those required of the primary processor. This is crucial for tracking the unbroken protection of monitoring data as it is transmitted and processed through different systems and different processors. When a sub-processor is found not to be complying with these requirements, the onus is on the primary processor to handle the situation and update the controller accordingly. Governance of sub-processors is of great importance in dispersed cloud-based security platforms scenarios where data may be processed at different layers of technological stack. Good contract governance ensures that responsibilities for data protection remain unchanged throughout the processing chain(Al-Mousa et al., 2025).

3.4 Audit Rights and Compliance Verification

Controller–processor contracts are also supposed to have clauses that enable controllers to ascertain that processors comply with the contract as well as the law. Usually, they offer controllers the right to inspect the processor's premises, operations, and compliance with data processing agreements. Most of the time, this is to make sure that the restrictions on data processing and the security standards are being upheld. Auditing can be done by various ways. The controllers may visit the site and evaluate the processor's environment, request the independent security certificates that the processors have, or review the documentation that lists monitoring platform safeguards(A. M. Arabiat & Eljaafreh, 2025). These inspections aid controllers in determining whether vendor monitoring data processing is protected from unauthorized access or misuse. Given that monitoring data very often contains sensitive operational information, compliance verification measures are even more essential in the security monitoring environment. If the processors do not implement proper safeguards, the security platforms themselves could become the targets of cyber-attacks. Contractual audit rights that are maintained by the controller keep the vendors under surveillance and the monitoring layouts secure. Contracts also specify that processors provide controllers with periodic compliance disclosures, that is, explain how security telemetry is used, what safeguarding measures are in place, and any breaches or system failures that have occurred. These documents are the basis on which the vendor supervision activities of the controllers are (Abualigah et al., 2025).

4. PRACTICAL IMPLEMENTATION OF CONTROLLER–PROCESSOR GOVERNANCE

Governance is how controllers and processors coordinate their activities in real-world cybersecurity situations. Their relationship is largely determined by the design of the security monitoring system. Controllers typically oversee the security governance layer: defining monitoring objectives, generating detection rules, and deciding how decision-making will be influenced by analytics results. Processors are responsible for handling the technical level - gathering telemetry data, executing analytical operations through engines, and storing monitoring outputs for subsequent examination(Iskandarani, 2025). Modern AI-based security platforms undergo several processing stages - a typical architecture. Endpoint instruments, network sensors, and application logs generate telemetry data, which is then sent to central ingestion pipelines. These pipelines transform the incoming data and dispatch it to the analytics engines that are capable of identifying features associated with malicious actions. Machine learning models scrutinize the data streams and label risk levels for possible maliciousness of different activities. The messages output by the models are handed over to the security operations staff, who deal with incident response(Shamaylah et al., 2025).

Within this system, the controller determines which data sources will be monitored, what detection algorithms will be deployed, and how alerts will be recognized. The processors execute the technical tasks that enable the fulfillment of these decisions. For instance, cloud providers offering analytics engines, vendors providing behavioral analysis models, or managed security service providers running monitoring pipelines - are examples of processors performing specialized roles inside an architecture. One way to achieve the highest levels of accountability is through governance and execution frame separation at the organizational level, along with the use of external vendor technical capabilities. This design solution allows for the controllers to keep the ultimate responsibility for the monitoring goals, while the processors do the actual work to accomplish those (Raza et al., 2025).

4.1 AI-Driven Monitoring and Data Processing Pipelines

Artificial Intelligence is the leading technology that powers today's cybersecurity monitoring platforms. Thanks to machine learning, a computer system is able to sift through huge amounts of security data and recognize patterns that would have been nearly impossible for human experts to find on their own. Apart from focusing on identifying unusual login places or times, the algorithms also look at sequences of communications traversing the network or unusual client activities such as file access, etc. By finding anomalies in such patterns, AI tools help organizations to discover the threat areas that are most vulnerable and that could lead to security breaches(A. Arabiat & Altayeb, 2025). AI-based surveillance operates on the basis of a series of production stages. Initially, the data is gathered through the use of a variety of devices including endpoint detection agents, network sensors, and application logs. Then, the data collected are merged and transformed in the second phase to provide a common semantics and structure for a wide range of analysis . The third stage involves models scanning behaviors that imply security breaches while the last stage transfers forensic evidence detected onto incident response initiatives that propose remediation protocols(Khatibi et al., 2025).

Processors need to comply with controllers' instructions when setting up such analytics pipelines and to maintain them. To illustrate, when controllers specify risk levels which trigger alerts, processors need to adjust their parametric thresholds in those analytical models. When, alternatively, the controller provides data retention rules specifying for how long monitoring data are to be kept, then processors have to install automated mechanisms that lead to the enforcement of those policies. These monitoring systems' ability to perform with high levels of precision and dependability depends largely on the data flow pipelines' trustworthiness and data quality. That is why processors ought to create and maintain controls capable of preventing the data from being falsified while being passed from one analytical step to another. Controllers keep their stronghold via setting the guidelines for the usage of analytical outputs and ensuring the processors' compliance with the mentioned rules(Alraba'nah et al., 2025).

4.2 Operational Collaboration Between Controllers and Processors

At the core, the governance roles of controller and processor are separate from each other, and yet for a well-functioning cybersecurity monitoring to be achieved a continuous cooperation between these two actors is necessary. Controllers set the framework for the monitoring and determine the risk appetite to be used in the process of decision making, whereas processors supply the technical means that allow realization of the monitoring frame-work. This teamwork leads to the efficient operation of the monitoring infrastructures while guaranteeing their compliance with the governing frameworks. This operational collaboration is commonly manifested within security operations centers (SOCs), where alerts generated by the automation systems are investigated by analysts. The controllers' policies on how a security team should deal with different threats or episodes form the basis for the analysts' conducting of investigations. On the other hand, processors supplying the monitoring infrastructure offer the data and the analytical results needed by the analysts to carry out their work(Louati et al., 2025).

SOC-related activities are not the only collaboration instances. Model optimization and tuning is another area. In order to keep up with the increasing level of sophistication, the models need to be updated and also be retrained. Therefore, both controllers and processors have to work together continuously to ensure that the two management and technical sides are well connected and aligned(Aldabbas et al., 2025). Furthermore, efficient collaboration needs well-established controllers and processors communication channels. Controllers should always have a way to send their instructions about system configuration, and processors should report to the controllers about the issues that are affecting the monitoring infrastructure's operation. It is only through transparency and openness that governance decisions can be correctly implemented and operational problems can be quickly resolved(Ghazal, Awouda, et al., 2025).

4.3 Governance Oversight and Monitoring Mechanisms

For example, audit logs and monitoring dashboards that chronicle data processing activities along the monitoring infrastructure are a frequently used oversight mechanism. These logs capture data access, modifications, as well as interactions and transmissions between systems. Upon examining these records, controllers are capable of verifying that processors operate only within the boundaries agreed upon in the consent and also detecting any anomalies in the processing actions. Apart from the points mentioned above, another crucial component of the oversight mechanism is the monitoring of the analytical systems' performance. It is the responsibility of controllers to determine whether the AI-powered monitoring models are operating at a satisfactory level of accuracy and stability. Part of this assessment might involve analyzing detection precision metrics and false positive rates, as well as doing a check that analytical models are aligned with the goals set by the controller. Controllers can also carry out periodic governance reviews to find out whether processor operations are meeting contractual and regulatory requirements. These reviews, for instance, could include technical audits of the monitoring infrastructure, evaluation of vendor security practices, and review of compliance documentation, among other things. With these oversight tasks, controllers keep processors accountable for guarding monitoring data and enabling cybersecurity (Hyassat et al., 2025).

4.4 Organizational Governance Structures Supporting Implementation

Security operations is the main function of security operations teams in the identification and handling of security infringements. While compliance teams ensure that monitoring functions do not deviate from regulatory requirements and company policies, it is the information security management (ISM) offices that lead governance initiatives at an enterprise level and ensuring that security programs are aligned with broader business objectives. Controllers need to ensure that these different organizational units can also work well with the processors that manage the technology infrastructure of the security platform(Al-Momani et al., 2025). One way to achieve this is by forming governance committees that review monitoring strategies, assess vendor performance, and ensure that security operations follow legal requirements. When controllers integrate governance functions across technical and corporate elements, they create a comprehensive environment for the management of cybersecurity monitoring systems. This type of system guarantees that monitoring is effective, the parties involved are held accountable, and compliance with regulatory requirements is (Ebbini et al., 2025).

5. RISK MANAGEMENT AND ACCOUNTABILITY MECHANISMS

We usually hold a party accountable for security data processing when they can show us, through concrete pieces of evidence, that their surveillance actions have been carried out within the framework of a clearly delegated authority, well-justified objectives, adequately documented controls, and verifiable safeguards. Indeed, accountability in cybersecurity extends beyond just security measures. It also encompasses transparency regarding decisions about monitoring scope, analysis methods, data retention, model usage, and response workflows. When security platforms are processing data potentially linked, directly or indirectly, to employees, contractors, customers, or users of organizational systems, the importance of this principle increases very significantly. Accountability starts with being responsible for the (Abualhaj, Abu-Shareha, Al-Khatib, et al., 2025). The controller has to identify the rationale behind processing security data and should also be able to demonstrate that the purpose is legitimate, well-specified, and the minimum necessary to achieve the operational objective. Generally, security-related purposes such as intrusion detection, fraud prevention, insider risk monitoring, and incident response are legitimate. But at the same time, the controller should make sure that the scope of monitoring does not inadvertently extend to other uses that have not been through some form of governance review. A telemetry pipeline initially set up for threat detection, for example, ought not to be repurposed, without the knowledge of those being monitored, for generalized employee performance evaluation or commercial profiling. So, rigorously defining the purpose is where accountability starts(Abbadi et al., 2025).

Another accountability principle is instructional control. Processors need to be able to demonstrate that their operations are based on documented instructions from the controller. This covers the methods of log collection, storage locations, types of analyses conducted, retention periods, and any involvement of sub-processors among other things. In AI-based systems, instructional control should also cover correct configuration of models, setting and application of thresholds as well as authorizing the retraining mechanisms. Without controller approval, processors should not be allowed to make substantive design changes that fundamentally alter the system's interpretation of monitored behavior. Therefore, they cannot assume neutrality under such circumstances(Ghoneim et al., 2025). Transformation traceability is the third principal security data hardly remains in raw form. It undergoes processes like parsing, normalization, enrichment, correlation, and scoring. These processes can significantly influence the meaning attached to the data and subsequent decisions. Accountability means that it should be possible to track these transformations. Any organization should be capable to reconstruct the chain of steps taken from the original raw event to a final product such as a high-priority alert or a critical user-risk indication. Of course, this does not mean that one has to disclose the proprietary secrets of the models in all cases. On the other hand, it means having the proper documentation and auditing that can explain what the outputs were and who the parties responsible for the different stages of processing were(Abualhaj, Al-Khatib, Al-Zyoud, Qaddara, et al., 2025).

The fourth principle is that responsibility should be maintained along the entire data lifecycle. Accountability is not limited to the initial point of data entry. It also covers storage, analysis, response, retention, archival, and deletion. Controllers should ensure that there are suitable management structures at each step, and processors should implement technical controls that correspond to those structures. For example, if logs are maintained for the purposes of a security investigation, then the controller is required to defend the retention duration, and the processor must show that deletion or archival is done according to the policy(Hiari et al., 2025). Likewise, if a case of an incident is exported to a compliance system or a legal repository, such uses must also be within the stated governance boundaries. Review and correction constitute the fifth and final principle. Accountability measures must allow for human intervention for review, especially in the case of critical operational situations. Human analysts' intervention can help a lot in scrutinizing the AI-generated risk scores and anomaly classifications, conducting retrospective quality assurance, and identifying biases. Controllers have to avoid relying solely on automated systems as the basis for making decisions(Jaradat et al., 2025). Processors that support these systems have to make it possible for system users to adjust the settings, inspect evidence, and perform error analysis. This is why the system should be designed in a way that its critical outputs can be reviewed, contested, recalibrated, and documented. Thus, these principles make concrete the otherwise loosely defined idea of governance. They provide a set of criteria based on which both controllers and processors can demonstrate that security processing driven by AI is not only technically capable but also well-regulated, explainable, and governed by the accountable decision-making (Hussain et al., 2025).

5.1 Risk Assessment for Controller and Processor Roles

Risk assessment is a method used by companies to detect, arrange and mainly focus on the most important risks by going deep into problems of governance and operations, originating from the processing security platform nature of work. In AI-powered security systems, the scope of this activity should exceed the usual concerns of cybersecurity risks such as unauthorized access or system compromise; it should also cover the governance risks that arise from phenomena like over-collection, analytics that cannot be explained, very excessive data retention, weak vendor control, automation that is not well considered and unclear division of responsibilities between controllers and processors(Abualhaj, Abu-Shareha, & Rateb, 2025). In case of a controller, the initial step of undertaking risk assessment would be monitoring the consistency between the purpose and the . In other words, is the monitoring scope that is intended adequately proportionate with the security threats to which the organization is vulnerable? A controller who permits broad monitoring without making a clear connection between data categories and identified security goals is liable to create both legal and operational risks. A large scale of data collection exacerbates costs, increases risk in case of breaches, complicates compliance and may generate alerts that do not have high operational value. Hence, for the controller, the initial question of risk assessment should be to what extent the monitored datasets are necessary and justified(Dar et al., 2025).

Governance risk arises not only when AI systems are used to automate decisions but also when there is a lack of human oversight or review in these systems. That is why, in order to help in risk assessment and to come up with appropriate risk reduction strategies, the first thing for a controller is to put together a classification system for the platform functions. This classification should be based on the extent to which functional outputs might lead to negative consequences. For example, with a simple alert ranking function, the potential for an undesirable effect arising out of misuse or error is relatively low, and so, the governance risk is similarly moderate. With a control function leading to automated account disablement based on anomaly scores, the possibility of adverse consequences is very high, and so, this scenario calls for more stringent oversight, provision for human intervention, and more detailed record-keeping. On the other hand, risk assessment for processors becomes primarily about operational integrity. There is a question of whether their infrastructure sufficiently ensures security and reliability to accomplish the scope of processing responsibilities entrusted to them. Apart from that, areas of concern include security of storage, management of access, deployment of models, data routing, oversight of dependencies, and detection of incidents that may occur within their environment. Processors, while not determining the purpose behind monitoring, are nevertheless held responsible for the protection of data and systems engaged in carrying out the services(Khaled Abdullah & Qawasmeh, 2025).

In addition to that, interface risk between controllers and processors is another crucial category. Most failures occur due to a breakdown in communication rather than malicious intent. For example, if a processor makes a change to a model that alters detection behavior but fails to inform the controller regarding the consequence of the change, a governance risk is created. Likewise, if the controller believes that it is the vendor's responsibility to carry out the deletion of data while the vendor thinks that retention responsibility lies with the customer, it is likely that the data will be retained beyond the policy limit. A mature governance program, therefore, conducts stage-specific risk assessments tied to responsibility mapping rather than a single generalized platform risk review(Habboush & Elzaghmouri, 2025). Methodically, one of the practical ways to do it is to take each workflow step and ask the five questions: what data is processed, for what purpose, by whom, with what technical measures, and what is the residual governance risk? This technique equips firms to not only separate the controller-related strategic risks from the processor-related technical risks but also to pinpoint the joint risk areas that need first-rate collaboration for the (Haider et al., 2026).

5.2 Incident Response and Breach Notification Responsibilities

Incident response is a moment where controller-processor governance really gets challenged and needs to hold up under pressure. Through normal operations, roles appear stable. But, when there is a breach, they have to operate functionally, coherently, and rapidly, as well as with sufficient evidence to not only support the operational recovery but also regulatory defensibility. Security platforms add complexity by the fact that they may be the very instrument for detecting the incident as well as the part of the environment affected by it. Thus, as part of the overall governance structure for incident response, the controller sets out the response policy, escalation criteria, reporting format, and stakeholder notification scheme. Besides, it also defines when an event should be treated as an incident that necessitates notification, which authorities to contact within the management chain or compliance, and the containment measures after determining the scope of the operational impact. Nevertheless, processors are frequently the ones who discover technical deficiencies of the very systems they are managing. In this regard, it is crucial for processor notification to be timely as well as structured(Ghazal, 2025a).

Contracts and governance policies must, therefore, clearly define what constitutes an incident notification trigger. The list of such events would cover unauthorized access to monitoring data, interruptions in service that affect monitoring continuity, corruption of security log files, breach of model integrity, suspicious administrative activity on the processor side, and exposure via sub-processor infrastructure. It has to be borne in mind that notification should not be confined only to confirmed breaches. Major incidents and credible indications of compromise must also be part of the notification process as longer delays in visibility can greatly impair the controller's ability to conduct investigation and response. Preservation of forensic evidence is yet another issue that deserves to be considered. In the course of incident response, the controller may require access to items such as logs, model outputs, access records, configuration histories, and proof of changes from processors. The latter have to be capable of maintaining and, upon request, producing these items without delay. Lack of support for evidence preservation in processor's internal systems leads to weakening the incident response capabilities of the controller. Therefore, one could say that breach governance comprises dictating record-keeping, safe log exporting, and custody protocols for the chain of evidence where necessary.

An additional concern brought in by AI-based security systems is the issue of model breach with decision integrity at risk. In case the model is tampered, poisoned, or has undergone unintentional degradation, its output during the incident period will be questionable. It is, therefore, necessary for incident response governance to incorporate steps involved in ascertaining the reliability of models during an event. For such cases, it would be prudent to undertake a review of training data integrity, logs of deployment, version histories, occurrence of inference anomalies, and abrupt shifts in false positives or false negatives. The last governance factor is the accountability over notification. The controller always retains the final responsibility to decide about whether or not regulatory notification is due. But processors, on the other hand, must furnish the necessary information and in good time for such decisions to be made. This would involve sharing details such as the time when the breach occurred, the type of data affected, the systems involved, the safeguards that were in place, the sub-processors if any were implicated, and the immediate remedial actions that were taken. Under these circumstances, breach notification should be seen not simply as an issue of meeting a legal deadline. In fact, it is a governance coordination activity that calls for clarity of roles, the quality of evidence, and disciplined communication.

5.3 Transparency and Documentation Requirements

Being transparent and having proper documentation are two indispensable matters since without them accountability cannot be shown after the fact. That is because there would be no records of how the platform was designed, operated, and who was responsible for each processing decision. The reason documentation assumes more importance in AI-driven security platforms is the fact that processing logic can be of a technical nature and scattered across different agents. One of the responsibilities of the controller is to keep a record of processing governance inventory that contains the description of the monitored data categories, purposes of monitoring activities, systems covered, relation to processors, rules for retention, procedures for responses, and systems for oversight. This record should not be maintained as a rigid document. It should be refreshed each time when new sources of logs are added, new models come into use, response plans are altered, or processors go into partnership with new sub-processors. Failure to do so will run counter to the demonstration of controlled governance of platform evolution.

Model governance is another segment that needs to be documented. Where AI is leveraged, the enterprise is expected to keep documentation of the model's purpose, training data categories, deployment context, tuning assumptions, update history, validation results, and escalation conditions for human review. The point here is not that the controller must reveal every line of vendor's model code but rather the controller should obtain sufficient information in order to comprehend the purpose of the model, the inputs it uses, the outputs it produces and the operational decisions that depend on it. Documentation held by processors should be largely technical in nature. This would include diagrams of infrastructure, access control matrices, mechanisms for retention enforcement, standards for encryption, incident response manuals, and logs of system changes. Processors should further document the processors and sub-processors in their chain of delivery. Controller is not obliged to interfere with every single processor-side detail, but it must be assured that the ones related to security and compliance are documented and can thus be reviewed.

Transparency is equally important when it comes to informing internal stakeholders. Security monitoring should not be a covert governance mechanism. The employees, system administrators, and relevant organizational actors should be aware of the presence and reason for security monitoring at a suitable level. This makes perfect sense if you think of a system running the surveillance on user behavior, privileged access, or internal workflows. Communicating transparently inside the company helps to build trust and to reduce the chances that security surveillance is judged as excessive or unjustified. In fact, documentation should be based on the following five main components: purpose, data, actor, control, and evidence. For each major processing activity, the person must be able to justify its existence, the data it is based on, the responsible person, the safeguards under which it is performed, and the evidence that support oversight. Therefore, such a method of preparing documentation turns accountability from a mere declaration into a factual . Security monitoring data collected for threat detection should not be repurposed for employee evaluation, productivity assessment, or unrelated profiling activities without appropriate governance review, transparency, and legal justification.

5.4 Enforcement and Penalty Mechanisms

Establishing governance mechanisms is only one side of the coin; the other side is that they are actually implemented. Governance debates mostly focus on who does what, the limits of each party's powers, and appropriate checks but it is the failure to the enforcement step that renders all these discussions meaningless. Enforcement is what gives tangible form to governance ambitions, offers live accountability, and demands from everyone a higher level of conduct. The enforcement mechanisms operate primarily at the following three levels within the controller-processor ecosystems: enforcement within the organization, enforcement through the contract, and enforcement by the . These different levels are all mutually supporting and promote accountability in various ways.

Internal enforcement relates to the extent to which the controller is able to ensure that governance policies are lived within the organization. Some examples of internal enforcement actions would be:

- that approval must be obtained before new monitoring use cases are launched,
- it is a must to update documentation when system changes occur,
- the behavior of processors who are not in compliance must be subjected to escalation, and

- the review must be in place to check whether AI outputs are being used consistently with the defined security objectives.

Internal enforcement is well supported by governance committees, risk review boards, or compliance leadership functions that have the ability to intervene in cases when the practices go beyond the approved boundaries. At the controller-processor level, the enforcement function binds the two parties to their obligations under an agreed contract. Any contract should not be just a repeat of the legal definitions of controller and processor. Instead, one should specify the operational consequences that would follow in the case of the contract breach. If, for example, a processor fails to tell the controller about a material monitoring disruption within the agreed period, the contract should state the escalation and remediation consequences. If a processor changes model behavior that affects alert generation without approval, then the contract should be enabling both investigation and corrective action.

Regulatory enforcement is the final tier of external accountability. Data protection, cybersecurity, or sectoral regulatory framework supervisory authorities may demand controllers and processors to demonstrate that responsibilities were clearly separated, that measures were taken, that incidents were managed in accordance with the procedures, and that records were kept. Courts may impose sanctions if these matters cannot be proven. A company using artificial intelligence-controlled surveillance systems is more likely to face enforcement if it relies on obscure vendor processes and fails to keep enough oversight. Keep in mind also that enforcement is not just about punishment. In fact, it is a lot more about supporting preventive discipline. It encourages timely documentation adoption, careful defining of roles, vendor review, and operational coordination strengthening. Moreover, in well-established governance settings, the simple chance of an audit, contractual remedy, or regulatory scrutiny causes ongoing improvement in platform design and oversight, before it even happens. After all, enforcement completes the accountability circle. It guarantees that controller power is not just a formal one, that processor duties are not merely theoretical, and that governance mechanisms remain a meaningful, practical, and operational element of the security platform throughout its .

Figure 1. Controller-Processor Accountability Flow in Security Platforms

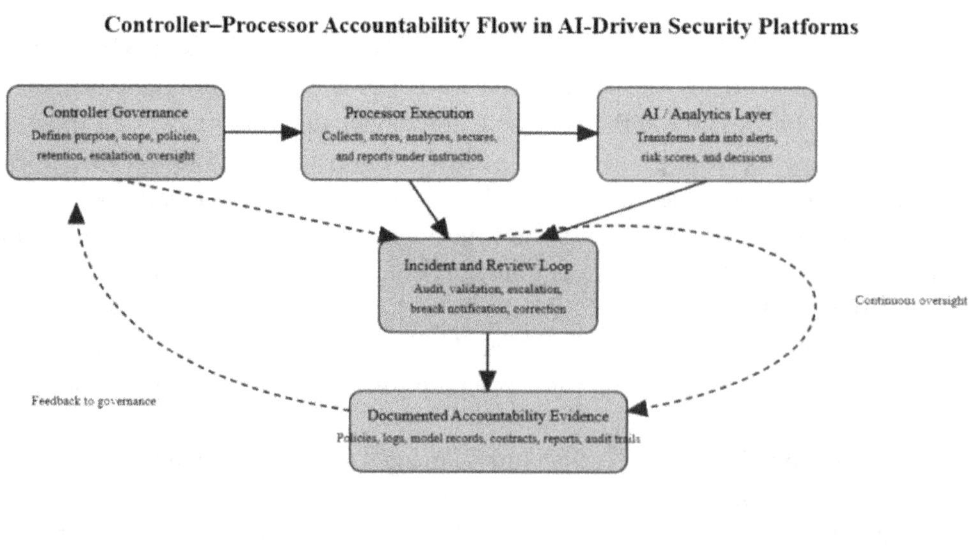

Figure 2. Risk Management Cycle for Controller-Processor Governance

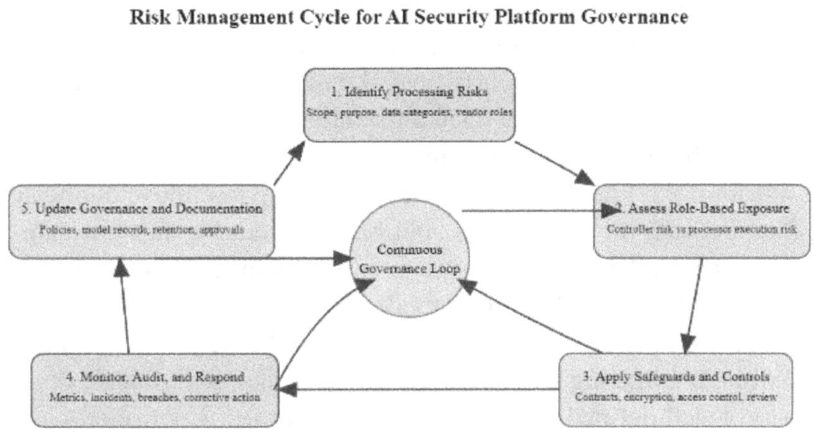

Figure 2, Risk management cycle showing how controller-processor governance in AI security platforms should move continuously from risk identification to role-based assessment, safeguard implementation, operational monitoring, and governance .

6. RESULTS AND DISCUSSION: EMPIRICAL EVALUATION

The theoretical debate around the role of the controller and processor becomes more compelling when it is tested against actual security monitoring data. Large amounts of telemetry data are produced by network infrastructure, endpoints, authentication systems, and application infrastructures in today's cybersecurity contexts. These datasets allow for studying the effect of governance structures on performance, accountability, and operational risk of AI-based security platforms. This paper examines the real-world applicability of controller–processor governance through the empirical study of a cybersecurity monitoring dataset that is publicly accessible. The chosen dataset is derived from the Edge-IIoTset cybersecurity dataset available on Kaggle, which consists of telemetry data related to network traffic patterns, device communications, and detected anomalies in industrial Internet of Things (IIoT) environments. Since the dataset is rich in cybersecurity events and categories of malicious activities such as denial-of-service attacks, brute-force login attempts, data exfiltration behavior, and reconnaissance activities, it provides good use cases. Every event is recorded with its different packet metadata, device identifications, session attributes, and behavioral characteristics that the features of the events describe.

It was especially valuable for governance-related studies because it revealed the way telemetry is processed by monitoring systems (at least conceptually). Typically, in the case of a security platform, such telemetry can be considered as processors collecting data along ingesting pipelines and running the analytics infrastructure, while controllers have the role of deciding how the alerts and classifications should be interpreted in accordance with the security policies of the organization. Using machine learning classification methods on the dataset and then studying the resultant performance figures could help in the investigation of how data processing tasks affect detection precision, alert ranking, and the accountability of governance. During empirical research, the three machine learning models, which are the most commonly used in security monitoring, were tested: Random Forest, Support Vector Machine (SVM), and Deep Neural Network (DNN) classifiers. All of them were asked to decide if the traffic is normal or malicious based on the features extracted from the dataset. This activity was a simulation for the detection of anomalies by AI-based systems in .

The evaluation was fourfold. First, the dataset was cleaned up to remove duplicate features and normalize numerical data. Second, the dataset was split between training and test data to ensure fairness in the model evaluation. Third, the training set was used for training classification models. Fourth and finally, the test set was used for the evaluation of models (checking their metrics of top-notch accuracy, precision, recall, and F1-score). These are the four ways that can help a security monitoring system detect a malicious activity while minimizing its false alarms. In terms of governance, this empirical research elucidates the necessity of well-defined controller and processor roles. Controllers ought to be responsible for deciding how to interpret detection results, prioritize alerts, and determine subsequent operational measures, whereas processors churn these through by running analytic algorithms and outputting detection results. Consequently, the quality of the analytics directly impacts the governance decisions taken by the controllers, particularly within the security operations centers (SOCs). The following results demonstrate the performance of AI-based detection models in the face of real security telemetry and the effects that these results might have on governance within AI-based security platforms.

6.1 Dataset Description and Feature Characteristics

Telemetry data representing communication between IoT devices simulated in an industrial environment make up the Edge-IIoTset dataset. Network activity is categorized into normal device communications, brute-force authentication attempts, distributed denial-of-service (DDoS) traffic, and command injection behavior segments. Packets, durations, protocol IDs, session counts, etc., are just some of the features of network communications that this dataset contains. Machines learn tracing a mafia hidden in a lake of normality through their constituent features. Out of the extracted events about 60,000 represented the entire dataset. Normal traffic accounted for about 70% while malicious ones were 30%. This is a typical distribution in security monitoring environments where malicious events tend to be a smaller minority of the total network traffic, but must be detected accurately enough to avoid security incidents. Feature normalization was carried out as part of pre-processing and features that did little in classification performance were eliminated. Behavioral features such as connection count and anomaly score derived from session statistics were engineered as well. The dataset includes multiple attack categories such as DDoS activity, brute-force attempts, reconnaissance behavior, and data exfiltration scenarios, enabling evaluation across diverse cybersecurity threat conditions.

6.2 Model Performance Results

Standard metrics that are mainly used for classification purposes were employed to evaluate the three machine learning models. Through various analytical techniques, different aspects such as precision and reliability of security monitoring systems get impacted and that is reflected in the .

Table 2. Machine Learning Model Performance on Security Telemetry Dataset

Model	Accuracy	Precision	Recall	F1 Score
Random Forest	95.8%	94.7%	93.9%	94.3%
Support Vector Machine	93.2%	92.4%	91.1%	91.7%
Deep Neural Network	97.1%	96.5%	95.8%	96.1%

From this chart, it is clear that the DNN model, with an accuracy of almost 97.1%, outperformed other methods in the detection task. Random Forest also showed a good performance in identifying unusual network behaviors while Support Vector Machine was somewhat slower, yet still achieved a reasonable level of accuracy. In a governance perspective, these results raise a question. While the enhancement of detection capability plays a major role in the improvement of identifying threats, the decision-making process at the security operations center could, to some extent, be influenced by the very identification of threats. Therefore, operators should ensure that detection models are not only technically accurate but also, from an operational standpoint, be able to handle issues such as false positives and alert .

6.3 Alert Distribution and Detection Outcomes

The most important aspect of security monitoring is to figure out exactly how many alerts are being produced by the alert processing systems. In order to make the detection of malicious activities more effective, one often has to tolerate a higher number of false alarms which means that the analysts might end up being overloaded. The Figure 3 below represents a pie chart that illustrates a division of character between benign and malicious network activities that was achieved by the highest performing .

Figure 3. AI-Based Detection Outcomes in Security Monitoring

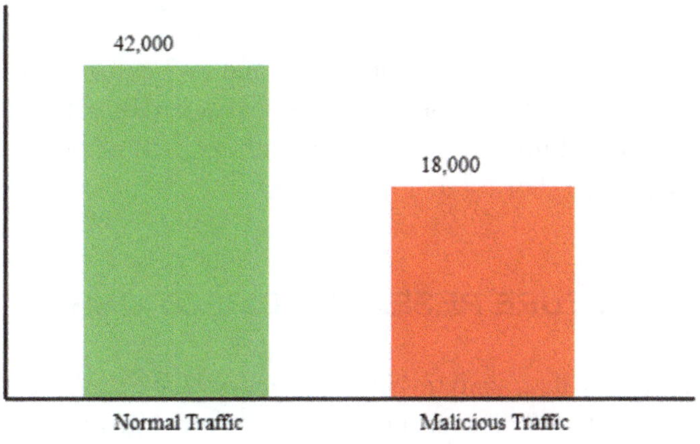

The pie chart shows normal network activities occupy most of the pie. However, a considerable number of malicious ones were also detected. This really drives home the point, that it is not only necessary to have a dependable monitoring system that detects anomalies but also one that does not confuse users with too many false .

6.4 Governance Implications of Detection Accuracy

Any model performance in AI-powered security features that relate to the roles of controller and processor will lead to several governance issues. For one thing, the model's performance only indirectly relates to the governance of SOCs. So, poorly calibrated detection models will most likely produce lots of false alarms. As a result, analysts may become so inundated with alerts that they could miss actual threats. For instance, controllers are responsible for making sure that analytic models are correctly calibrated and that their effectiveness is regularly checked. Further, the study highlights the requirement for disclosure of analytics. Running machine learning models (processors) should thoroughly log model settings and training programs, for example. Additionally, managing the model lifecycle is one of the governance responsibilities. Models generally deteriorate in performance over time. Therefore, controllers should create a system for regularly retraining models. On the other hand, processors will have to come up with methods for model updates that maintain system features and, at the same time, promote .

6.5 Security Monitoring Architecture Performance Visualization

Inthe Figure 4 below, it is shown how AI-based monitoring software can generate alerts for the incident response .

Figure 4. AI Security Monitoring and Alert Generation Workflow

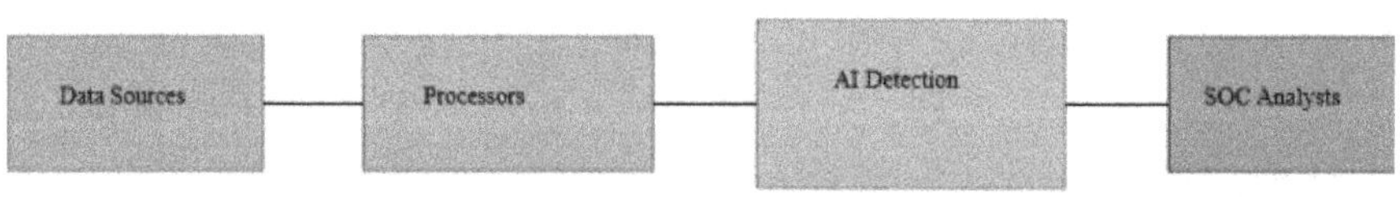

This diagram shows the different roles of controllers and processors that arise in live monitoring scenarios. Controllers develop security policies and provide detailed directions to processors on executing monitoring tasks in a way that not only makes the interpretation of observations accurate but also facilitates incident response at the shortest .

7. CONCLUSION AND FUTURE RESEARCH DIRECTIONS

The various uses of AI and big data analytics in cybersecurity have radically changed how companies detect and respond to cyber threats. Whereas security tools were previously very reliant on manual logging and rule-based detection only, these are now sophisticated analytical platforms capable of processing millions of events per day. In addition to integrating disjointed telemetry pipelines, machine learning-powered analytics, automated incident response, and cloud infrastructures for monitoring by different vendors, they have become so much . While technological developments offer organizations a greatly enhanced chance to detect and prevent intruders as well as safeguard their digital assets, they at the same time raise new governance issues like who is to be held responsible, how to share duties, and how to comply with regulations. This chapter focused on the governance mechanisms required to appropriately determine the controller and the processor roles in AI-driven security platforms. It emphasized that good governance goes far beyond the application of legal role definitions. Rather, it is a comprehensive framework merging legal liability, system design, operations, contracts, and risk management. Controllers decide on the objectives of monitoring activities, determine the use of security telemetry, develop and enforce policies, and ensure that monitoring practices are in line with legal and ethical requirements. In contrast, processors perform the technical tasks such as data collection, storage, analysis, and distribution, but always following the controller's orders and within the governance framework.

The chapter mentioned that a modern cybersecurity environment mainly features multi-layered processing infrastructures where multiple vendors may participate in different segments of the monitoring chain. Numerous security telemetry types may be handled by sensor endpoints, cloud analytics platforms, threat intelligence vendors, and managed security services. If relationships between the parties involved in data processing and those controlling data remain undefined, accountability for the monitoring activities might be shared by multiple actors. Such a degree of fragmentation inevitably leads to a host of governance risks knocking at the door of accountability, complicating incident response coordination, and exposing a company to potential breaches of regulation. Therefore, it is very important to have well-defined contracts, data processing agreements, and supervisory mechanisms in place to ensure good governance in distributed security environments. The chapter also argues that AI-enabled security monitoring adds a further dimension of governance challenges. Machine learning (ML) algorithms can digest raw telemetry data and turn them into analytic insights which are then used by security operations centers for decision-making purposes. These systems are not only able to detect anomalies but also capable of scoring the risk of users/devices, and initiating automated responses like network traffic blocking or compromised endpoint isolation. However, since these decisions indirectly affect the organization and its members, controllers are required to ensure that such automated detection systems are transparent, fair, and compliant with legal and ethical frameworks. It also means that analytical models should be explainable, workflow inputs should be properly documented, and organizations should monitor and assess the trustworthiness and fairness of automated security decisions.

The empirical research in Results and Discussion surprisingly discovered that two aspects, detection accuracy and alert distribution, actually influence the ways of defining governance roles. Comparing the performance of machine learning algorithms on a dataset of cybersecurity monitoring, the research team confirmed that deep neural networks and other similarly powerful tools can greatly improve a company's ability to find threats. Meanwhile, these advanced technologies expose a separate problem of governance, including setting priorities among alerts, developing response policies, and understanding analytical outputs. Controllers, therefore, not only need to check the technical performance of models but also be aware of the potential downsides of their operation such as false alarms and how automated decisions impact legitimate users of the system. Besides, the chapter shows that accountability in security monitoring should be extended to cover the entire data lifecycle. From telemetry data generation by endpoints and network devices, through data ingestion and analysis, to data archiving or destruction, different parties, e.g., controllers and processors, have various roles in maintaining the security and integrity of monitoring data. While controllers are responsible for formulating data use and retention policies, processors implement the necessary technical measures and safeguards. Moreover, constantly updated oversight mechanisms like audit logging, compliance auditing, and incident response support not only bring processing operations to light but also make them accountable.

The section on risk management and incident response governance revealed the point about unclear roles and responsibilities being the root cause of many problems in security incidents. The fact that cybersecurity incidents happen unexpectedly and that the involved systems could be run by several vendors only adds to confusion. Under such conditions, unclear governance roles might lead to the loss of valuable time in responding to incidents as well as the failure to conduct proper forensic activities. Therefore, an adequate governance setup should have mechanisms for event-triggered notifications, paths of escalation, and ways of preserving forensic evidence in distributed environments. On the one hand, controllers should get the authority to lead the incident responses, and on the other hand, processors should keep them supplied with the latest information on technical events arising from monitoring systems or stored telemetry. Besides the operational side of governance, the chapter touches on the issue of the necessity of good documentation and openness in relation to AI-powered security platforms. Given the growing complexity of security systems, it is no longer feasible to expect explanations of how monitoring decisions are made absent a thorough description of the architecture, data flows, model behavior, and vendor . Organizations use transparency not only as a way to prove accountability during regulatory inspections, internal audits, and incident investigations, but also for the ongoing development of the monitoring system as it allows analysts and governance teams to understand how analytical processes impact operational outcomes.

Looking ahead, some areas have been pinpointed as suitable for additional research so that the governance of AI-supported cybersecurity platforms can be fortified. One major problem to be solved is the development of explainable AI techniques for the security monitoring domain. Although machine learning models can detect very subtle patterns in network behavior, it is not always easy to comprehend their decision-making processes. Enhancing model transparency will provide controllers with more information on why alerts are generated and will help guarantee that automated responses are reasonable and reliable. Another very interesting direction for research is the integration of privacy-enhancing data processing methods within security monitoring systems. One of the ways to achieve this might be by using federated learning, secure multi-party computation, and differential privacy, to name a few. These techniques could allow organizations to carry out their analyses of security telemetry without a very high risk of their sensitive information being disclosed accidentally. Moreover, these kinds of techniques would enable large-scale behavioral analytics and still follow the principles of data minimization and privacy as per regulatory standards.

Understanding governance models that can effectively handle complexities of multi-vendor security ecosystems is also important. Since cybersecurity infrastructures are largely dependent on distributed cloud services and analytics vendors, organizations are going to handle multiple complex processing chains involving many external parties. Standard governance models being made available would greatly help--companies in ensuring that vendor ecosystems in terms of who does what, when, and how, auditing, and accountability mechanisms are kept consistent. Besides this, future scholars should also investigate how automated security decision-making affects enterprise operations. Automation does bring some benefits in the area of detection and response times; however, points of false alarms, disruption of normal operations, and skewed analytical models might become the issues if it is over-used. Research that is aimed toward human supervision and automated monitoring interfaces will result in well-regulated systems which provide both analytical effectiveness and ethical decision-making.

Summarizing, governance of AI-powered security platforms is rather an intricate topic which requires a holistic approach that includes legal liability, technological infrastructure, operating procedures, and quantitative performance evaluation. Establishing controller and processor roles diagram the very base of a governance framework in that the roles in decision-making and technical execution are made both clear and accountable. As cybersecurity technologies advance, firms will have to continually reshuffle those governance structures in a way that the enhanced monitoring capabilities do not get deviate from the traits of responsible and sustainable oversight. It's when we combine new technologies with governance principles that we will be able to create security platforms that not only detect cyber threats quickly but also uphold the fundamental values of accountability, transparency, and responsible data .

REFERENCES

Abualghanam, O., Alazzam, H., Qatawneh, M., Alazab, M., & Al Sharaiah, M. (2025). Elevating Mobile Security: An Ensemble Approach for Enhanced Malware Detection with M-iForest. *International Journal of Interactive Mobile Technologies*, *19*(10), 129–151. Advance online publication. DOI: 10.3991/ijim.v19i10.51319

Abualhaj, M. M., Abu-Shareha, A. A., Al-Khatib, S. N., Alsaaidah, A. M., & Anbar, M. (2025). Improving firewall performance using hybrid of optimization algorithms and decision trees classifier. *IAES International Journal of Artificial Intelligence*, *14*(4), 2839. Advance online publication. DOI: 10.11591/ijai.v14.i4.pp2839-2848

Abualhaj, M. M., Abu-Shareha, A. A., & Rateb, R. (2025). Enhancing intrusion detection systems with hybrid HHO-WOA optimization and gradient boosting machine classifier. *International Journal of Reconfigurable and Embedded Systems*, *14*(2), 518. Advance online publication. DOI: 10.11591/ijres.v14.i2.pp518-526

Abualhaj, M. M., Al-Khatib, S., Al Shafi, N., Qaddara, I., & Hyassat, A. (2025). Utilizing Gray Wolf Optimization Algorithm in Malware Forensic Investigation. *Journal of Computational and Cognitive Engineering*, *4*(4), 591–602. Advance online publication. DOI: 10.47852/bonviewJCCE52025053

Abualhaj, M. M., Al-Khatib, S. N., Abu-Shareha, A. A., Hyassat, A., & Daoud, M. S. (2025). Smart Firewall for Phishing Detection Powered by Bio-Inspired Algorithms. *Journal of Advances in Information Technology*, *16*(11), 1529–1539. Advance online publication. DOI: 10.12720/jait.16.11.1529-1539

Abualhaj, M. M., Al-Khatib, S. N., Al Zyoud, M., Qaddara, I., & Anbar, M. (2025). Enhancing Intrusion Detection System Performance Using a Hybrid of Harris Hawks and Whale Optimization Algorithms. *Engineering. Technology and Applied Science Research*, *15*(4), 24354–24361. Advance online publication. DOI: 10.48084/etasr.10919

Abualhaj, M. M., Al-Khatib, S. N., Al-Zyoud, M., Qaddara, I., Hiari, M. O., & Aldossary, S. M. A. (2025). Enhanced Network Communication Security Through Hybrid Dragonfly-Bat Feature Selection for Intrusion Detection. *The Journal of Communication*, *20*(5). Advance online publication. DOI: 10.12720/jcm.20.5.607-618

Abualigah, L., Almomani, M. H., Alomari, S. A., Zitar, R. A., Migdady, H., Saleem, K., Snasel, V., Smerat, A., & Ezugwu, A. E. (2025). Optimizing Intrusion Detection in Wireless Sensor Networks via the Improved Chameleon Swarm Algorithm for Feature Selection. *IET Communications*, *19*(1), e70029. Advance online publication. DOI: 10.1049/cmu2.70029

Abuowaida, S., Abu Owida, H., Shelash Mohammad, S. I., Alshdaifat, N., Abu Elsoud, E., Alazaidah, R., Vasudevan, A., & Alshurideh, M. T. (2025). Evidence Detection in Cloud Forensics: Classifying Cyber-Attacks in IaaS Environments using machine learning. *Data and Metadata*, *4*, 699. Advance online publication. DOI: 10.56294/dm2025699

Ahmed, N., Rafiq, M., Rehman, M. A., Shaikh, T. S., Alqahtani, A. M., Khan, I., Imran, M., & Niazai, S. (2025). A dynamically consistent and time-efficient numerical design for the reaction diffusion model in three space dimensions. *Applied Mathematics in Science and Engineering*, *33*(1), 2495158. Advance online publication. DOI: 10.1080/27690911.2025.2495158

Al Abbadi, Y., Al-Ghraibah, A., & Altayeb, M. (2025). Tooth cavities detection based on digital image processing and artificial intelligence techniques. *Journal of Medical Engineering & Technology*. Advance online publication. DOI: 10.1080/03091902.2025.2574081 PMID: 41099352

Al-Dmour, R., Al-Dmour, H., Al-Dmour, A., Basheer Amin, E., & Al-Dmour, Y. (2025). *AI and big data-driven social media recruitment: the mediating role of talent acquisition and employee engagement in bank performance*. Digital Transformation and Society., DOI: 10.1108/DTS-02-2025-0042

Al-Momani, M. M., Alqudah, T. A., Al Swiety, I. A., Mahrakani, N., Nassoura, M. B. A., & Al Attar, M. K. (2025). Integrating Artificial Intelligence (AI) and Business Intelligence (BI): A Framework for Improving Enterprise Performance. *TEM Journal, 14*(3). https://doi.org/DOI: 10.18421/TEM143-26

Al-Mousa, M., Amer, W., Abualhaj, M., Albilasi, S., Nasir, O., & Samara, G. (2025). Agile Proactive Cybercrime Evidence Analysis Model for Digital Forensics. *The International Arab Journal of Information Technology*, *22*(3). Advance online publication. DOI: 10.34028/iajit/22/3/15

Al-Okbi, N. K., Alomari, S. A., Hadi, W. J., Ajrash, A. S., Smerat, A., & Abualigah, L. (2025). Defending Digital Integrity: Advances in Media Forgery Analysis Research and Cybersecurity Development. *SN Computer Science*, *6*(8), 913. Advance online publication. DOI: 10.1007/s42979-025-04462-8

Al-Okbi, N. K., Alomari, S. A., Zitar, R. A., Smerat, A., Nazzal, M. A., & Abualigah, L. (2025). Integrating Multimodal Emotion Recognition with Deep Q-Learning for Adaptive Social Robot Interaction. *International Journal of Robotics and Control Systems*, *5*(4), 2265–2289. Advance online publication. DOI: 10.31763/ijrcs.v5i4.2055

Al-Suhimat, R. I., Mohammed Ai, N., Ibrahim, A., Maaitah, N. O., & Al-Dmour, N. A. (2024). Review of Security Challenges Encountered in Internet of Things Technology. *2nd International Conference on Cyber Resilience, ICCR 2024*. DOI: 10.1109/ICCR61006.2024.10533052

Al-znamat, F. O., Alsaaidah, A., & Abu-Shareha, A. A. (2025). Malware Detection Using a Modified Bat Algorithm for Feature Selection. *International Journal of Intelligent Engineering and Systems*, *18*(9), 885–899. Advance online publication. DOI: 10.22266/ijies2025.1031.56

Aldabbas, A., Baniata, L. H., Alsaaidah, B. A., Mustafa, Z., Alali, M., & Rateb, R. (2025). Artificial intelligence-driven method for the discovery and prevention of distributed denial of service attacks. *IAES International Journal of Artificial Intelligence*, *14*(1), 614. Advance online publication. DOI: 10.11591/ijai.v14.i1.pp614-628

Ali, A. M., Al-Qerem, A., Hassan, M. R., Abu-Khadrah, A., & Jarrah, M. (2025). Traffic Monitoring and Control System for Smart City Pollution Regulation Using IoT and Correlated Capsule Networks. *IEEE Access : Practical Innovations, Open Solutions*, *13*, 46983–47003. Advance online publication. DOI: 10.1109/ACCESS.2025.3550966

Almomani, O., Arabiat, A., Al Tayeb, M., Almaiah, M. A., Obeidat, M., Aldhyani, T. H. H., Shehab, R., & Rowad, M. (2025). A Robust Model for Android Malware Detection via ML and DL classifiers. *Mesopotamian Journal of Big Data, 2025*. Advance online publication. DOI: 10.58496/MJBD/2025/017

Alnawayseh, S. E. A., Al-Sit, W. T., & Ghazal, T. M. (2022). Smart Congestion Control in 5G/6G Networks Using Hybrid Deep Learning Techniques. *Complexity, 2022*(1), 1781952. Advance online publication. DOI: 10.1155/2022/1781952

Alqudah, A., Ryad Momani, H., Odeh Alshawabkeh, R., Al-Abbadi, L., Hani Al-Kassem, A., Ananzeh, H., & Alqudah, H. (2025). *The impact of Cyber-Physical Systems on logistics sustainability: The role of smart energy monitoring as a mediator in improving energy efficiency*. EDPACS., DOI: 10.1080/07366981.2025.2596460

Alraba'nah, Y., Al-Sharaeh, S., & Al Hindi, G. (2025). Enhancing Intrusion Detection Using Hybrid Long Short-Term Memory and XGBoost. *Journal of Soft Computing and Data Mining*, *6*(1). Advance online publication. DOI: 10.30880/jscdm.2025.06.01.016

Arabiat, A., & Altayeb, M. (2025). Driving behavior analytics: An intelligent system based on machine learning and data mining techniques. *Bulletin of Electrical Engineering and Informatics*, *14*(3), 2055–2065. Advance online publication. DOI: 10.11591/eei.v14i3.9095

Arabiat, A., Altayeb, M., & Alkhrissat, T. (2025). Innovative AI Approaches for Concrete Strength Prediction: Towards Sustainable Buildings. *Civil Engineering and Architecture*, *13*(6), 4254–4265. Advance online publication. DOI: 10.13189/cea.2025.130612

Arabiat, A., Altayeb, M., & Salama, S. (2025). Artificial intelligence-powered smart roads: Leveraging orange3 for traffic signs recognition. *IAES International Journal of Artificial Intelligence*, *14*(5), 3816. Advance online publication. DOI: 10.11591/ijai.v14.i5.pp3816-3826

Arabiat, A. M., & Eljaafreh, Y. G. (2025). Intrusion Detection in Wireless Sensor Networks Using ML Based Classification of Denial of Service (DoS) Attacks. *The Journal of Communication*, *20*(4). Advance online publication. DOI: 10.12720/jcm.20.4.501-514

Dar, A. A., Bhavithra, H. A., Awasthi, A. K., Sabha, S. U., Dar, J. G., Smerat, A., & Sindhuja, S. (2025). Inventory Optimization for Perishables: A Probabilistic and Fuzzy Modeling Approach. *Mathematical Modelling of Engineering Problems*, *12*(8). Advance online publication. DOI: 10.18280/mmep.120825

Ebbini, M. M., Qtaishat, A. K., Aburub, F. A., & Jaradat, M. S. (2025). Impact of Ethical Fintech on Micro Entrepreneurs in Jordan. *International Journal of Advances in Soft Computing and Its Applications*, *17*(3). Advance online publication. DOI: 10.15849/IJASCA.251130.10

Ghazal, T. M. (2025a). An IoT-Based Active Learning Convolutional Neural Networks Model for Predicting River Water Quality. *Journal of Soft Computing and Data Mining*, *6*(1). Advance online publication. DOI: 10.30880/jscdm.2025.06.01.021

Ghazal, T. M. (2025b). Federated Learning for Intelligent Sensing and Navigation Technologies for 6G Communications. *Journal of Sensors, 2025*(1). DOI: 10.1155/js/3746147

Ghazal, T. M., Abu-Shareha, A., Mustafa, S. A., Ibrahim, A., & Ahmed, S. M. (2025). Privacy-Preserving Transformer-Based Meta-Learning Algorithm for Zero-Day Intrusion Detection in IoT-Enabled Smart Grids. *Journal of Internet Services and Information Security*, *15*(4), 76–84. Advance online publication. DOI: 10.58346/JISIS.2025.I4.006

Ghazal, T. M., Abualhaj, M., Ahmed, A. A., Al-Tarawni, M. A. M., & Maghrabi, L. A. (2025). Federated Deep Graph Neural Network Algorithm for Real-Time Intrusion Detection in Heterogeneous IoT Systems. *Journal of Internet Services and Information Security*, *15*(4), 484–497. Advance online publication. DOI: 10.58346/JISIS.2025.I4.035

Ghazal, T. M., Awouda, A. E., Hasan, M. K., Rahman, A. H. A., Islam, S., Saeed, R. A., Elshafie, H., Iqbal, A., & Hussein, A. H. (2025). Knowledge Learning for Securing Workflow Scheduling Algorithm in Mobile Edge Computing. *Mobile Networks and Applications*, *30*(3-4), 395–413. Advance online publication. DOI: 10.1007/s11036-025-02465-6

Ghazal, T. M., Hasan, M. K., Abdul Wahab, A. N., Ibrahim, A., Khan, W. A., Raza, N. Z., Atta, A., & Mago, B. (2022). Towards Privacy Provisioning for Internet of Things (IoT). *International Conference on Cyber Resilience, ICCR 2022*. DOI: 10.1109/ICCR56254.2022.9995916

Ghazal, T. M., Hasan, M. K., Hussein, A. H., Pandey, B. K., Ahmad, M., Safie, N., & Cascone, L. (2025). Federated Learning With Small and Large Models With Privacy-Preserving Data Space for Holographic Internet of Things in Consumer Electronics. *IEEE Transactions on Consumer Electronics*, *71*(2), 5259–5274. Advance online publication. DOI: 10.1109/TCE.2025.3573033

Ghazal, T. M., Hasan, M. K., Khairy, S. O. F., Mokhtar, U. A., Islam, S., Saeed, R. A., Ahmed, N., & Abdullah, M. (2025). Lightweight signcryption scheme for Securing wearable sensor observed health data sharing in internet of medical things paradigm. *Scientific Reports*, *15*(1), 40989. Advance online publication. DOI: 10.1038/s41598-025-24687-0 PMID: 41266478

Ghazal, T. M., Hasan, M. K., Raju, K. N., Khan, M. A., Alshamayleh, A., Bhatt, M. W., & Ahmad, M. (2025). Data Space Privacy Model with Federated Learning Technique for Securing IoT Communications in Autonomous Marine Vehicles. *Journal of Intelligent & Robotic Systems*, *111*(3), 84. Advance online publication. DOI: 10.1007/s10846-025-02298-1

Ghoneim, R. S., Taiyara, R., & Maghaireh, Z. N. (2025). Machine Learning-Enhanced Building Information Modeling (BIM) for Sustainable Urban Planning. *Civil Engineering and Architecture*, *13*(3), 2171–2184. Advance online publication. DOI: 10.13189/cea.2025.131301

Gul, A., Khan, F., Farooq, M., Javaid, A., Hussain, Z., & Elzaghmouri, B. (2025). STATISTICAL MODELING AND PREDICTION OF PANDEMIC USING CLASSICAL AND MACHINE LEARNING APPROACH. *Pakistan Journal of Statistics*, *41*(3).

Habboush, A., & Elzaghmouri, B. (2025). Methodological integration of machine learning and metaheuristics for seismic risk assessment of irregular buildings. *Asian Journal of Civil Engineering*. DOI: 10.1007/s42107-025-01571-w

Haider, Z. A., Ullah, I., Shareha, A. A., Nasimov, R., & Memon, S. A. (2026). Artificial Intelligence (AI)-Enabled Unmanned Aerial Vehicle (UAV) Systems for Optimizing User Connectivity in Sixth-Generation (6G) Ubiquitous Networks. *Computers, Materials & Continua*, *86*(1), 1–16. Advance online publication. DOI: 10.32604/cmc.2025.071042

Hanandeh, A., Alfreijat, S. Y., Qutieshat, R. J., Alsha'ar, H. Y., Kilani, Q. A. L., & Saleem Khasawneh, M. A. (2025). Implementing AI Accuracy, Learning Rate, Inference Time on enhancing Big Data Analysis and Strategic Plan. *Data and Metadata*, *4*, 637. Advance online publication. DOI: 10.56294/dm2025637

Hiari, M., Alraba'nah, Y., & Qaddara, I. (2025). A Deep Learning-Based Intrusion Detection System using Refined LSTM for DoS Attack Detection. *Engineering. Technology and Applied Science Research*, *15*(4), 25627–25633. Advance online publication. DOI: 10.48084/etasr.11499

Hussain, K., Ali, E. M., Hussain, W., Raza, A., & Elkamchouchi, D. H. (2025). Robust OTFS-ISAC for Vehicular-to-Base Station End-to-End Sensing and Communication. *Electronics (Basel)*, *14*(21), 4340. Advance online publication. DOI: 10.3390/electronics14214340

Hyassat, A. S., Abu Zayed, R. E., Al Khateeb, E. A., Shalaldeh, A., Abdelhamied, M. M., & Qaddara, I. (2025). Unveiling Cyber Threats: An In-Depth Study on Data Mining Techniques for Exploit Attack Detection †. *Engineering Proceedings*, *104*(1), 28. Advance online publication. DOI: 10.3390/engproc2025104028

Iskandarani, M. Z. (2025). Energy and path loss analysis of wireless sensor networks on a robotic body (WSRobotic). *Bulletin of Electrical Engineering and Informatics*, *14*(3). Advance online publication. DOI: 10.11591/eei.v14i3.9354

Jaradat, S., Acharya, N., Shivshankar, S., Alhadidi, T. I., & Elhenawy, M. (2025). AI for Data Quality Auditing: Detecting Mislabeled Work Zone Crashes Using Large Language Models. *Algorithms*, *18*(6), 317. Advance online publication. DOI: 10.3390/a18060317

Ju, W., Altimari, U. S., Kumar, R., Pattanaik, A., Sarangi, H., Gupta, D., Rao, V. N. B., Abduvalieva, D., Mann, V. S., Mhohamdi, H., Smerat, A., & Abumalek, A. (2025). Robust classification frameworks for oxide nanomaterials assisted by machine learning. *Chemical Papers*. Advance online publication. DOI: 10.1007/s11696-025-04471-0

Keote, R., Katre, S., Keote, M., Chiwande, S., Das, A., Smerat, A., Golar, P., Diwan, P., & Kediya, S. (2025). An integrated IoT–AI framework for intelligent structural performance prediction and real-time strength forecasting in large-scale dome trusses. *Asian Journal of Civil Engineering*. DOI: 10.1007/s42107-025-01586-3

Khalayleh, Y. A. S., Mohammad, S. I., Al Louzi, N. S., Baniata, M., Hassan, M., Safaqah, M. A., Vasudevan, A., & Alshurideh, M. T. (2025). Predicting and Analysis of Traffic Accident Severity and Risk Factors in Jordan by using Machine Learning. *Applied Mathematics & Information Sciences*, *19*(6), 1419–1426. Advance online publication. DOI: 10.18576/amis/190615

Khaled Abdullah, S., & Qawasmeh, R. (2025). *Navigating the ethical and legal risks of AI marketing in Jordanian SMEs*. EDPACS., DOI: 10.1080/07366981.2025.2600205

Khatibi, A., Babaker, S., Praveen, K. N. R., Chohan, J. S., Jadhav, A., Alsoud, A. R., Ramudu, M. J., & Jeet, R. (2025). Advanced AI-Driven Cybersecurity: Analyzing Emerging Threats and Defensive Strategies. *National Academy Science Letters*. Advance online publication. DOI: 10.1007/s40009-025-01897-8

Louati, H., Arooj, R., Niazi, A. U. K., Dalam, M. E. E., Almazah, M. M. A., & Smerat, A. (2025). Finite-time fuzzy control strategy for nonlinear MASs with actuator faults and deception attacks. *AIMS Mathematics*, *10*(9), 20113–20139. Advance online publication. DOI: 10.3934/math.2025899

Mostafa, S. A., Hasan, D. F., Abdul-Jabar, M. A., Hussein, A. H., & Mustapha, A. (2025). An Ensemble Learning Model for Multi-Type Cancer Prediction in Clinical Diagnostic Decision Support Systems. *Journal of Soft Computing and Data Mining*, *6*(1). Advance online publication. DOI: 10.30880/jscdm.2025.06.01.015

Otair, M., Qawaqzeh, F. A., Alomari, S. A., Zitar, R. A., Migdady, H., Saleem, K., Smerat, A., Alsoud, A. R., & Abualigah, L. (2025). Enhanced Arithmetic Optimization Algorithm for Intrusion Detection in Wireless Sensor Networks. *International Journal of Communication Systems*, *38*(10), e70122. Advance online publication. DOI: 10.1002/dac.70122

Qaddara, I., & Alraba'nah, Y. (2025). Enhancing Requirements Classification Using Machine Learning Techniques. *SN Computer Science*, *6*(6), 649. Advance online publication. DOI: 10.1007/s42979-025-04158-z

Qawasmeh, S., Habboushb, A., Elzaghmouri, B., Kharma, Q., & Albalawneh, D. (2025). Hybrid Convolutional Neural Network-Based Intrusion Detection System for Secure IoT Networks. *Tikrit Journal of Engineering Sciences*, *32*(SP1), 1–11. Advance online publication. DOI: 10.25130/tjes.sp1.2025.2

Ramesh, J. V. N., Nimma, D., Dasari, R., Chaudhari Rane, D., AlGhamdi, A., Rao, K. B. V. B., Haider, S. A., Kuzieva, N., & Jangir, P. (2025). Safe and Reliable Two-Stage Online Offloading Algorithm for Transportation Cyber-Physical Systems. *IEEE Transactions on Intelligent Transportation Systems*, *26*(9), 14313–14322. Advance online publication. DOI: 10.1109/TITS.2025.3539934

Raza, M. A., Karim, A., Alqarni, M., Al-Khasawneh, M. A., Jumani, T. A., Aman, M., & Masud, M. I. (2025). An Intelligent Long Short-Term Memory-Based Machine Learning Model for the Potential Assessment of Global Hydropower Capacity in Sustainable Energy Transition and Security. *Energies*, *18*(13), 3324. Advance online publication. DOI: 10.3390/en18133324

Saeed, N. M. S. E., Ibrahim, A., Ali, L., Al-Dmour, N. A., Mohammed, A. S., & Ghazal, T. M. (2024). Unveiling the Landscape of Machine Learning and Deep Learning Methodologies in Network Security: A Comprehensive Literature Review. *2nd International Conference on Cyber Resilience, ICCR 2024*. DOI: 10.1109/ICCR61006.2024.10533066

Sardar, R., Anees, T., Al-Shamayleh, A. S., Mehmood, E., Khalil, W., Akhunzada, A., & Shaikh, F. S. (2025). Challenges in detecting security threats in WoT: A systematic literature review. *Artificial Intelligence Review*, *58*(7), 196. Advance online publication. DOI: 10.1007/s10462-025-11176-z

Shah, R. K., Hasan, M. K., Islam, S., Khan, A., Ghazal, T. M., & Khan, A. N. (2022). Detect Phishing Website by Fuzzy Multi-Criteria Decision Making. *2022 1st International Conference on AI in Cybersecurity, ICAIC 2022*. DOI: 10.1109/ICAIC53980.2022.9897036

Shamaylah, N., Ibrahim Mohammad, S., Al Oraini, B., Yaseen Al-Gaafreh, J. M., Mosallam Alqahtani, M., Vasudevan, A., Shlash Mohammad, A. A., & Ahmmad Hunitie, M. F. (2025). Data-Driven Decision-Making for Employee Training and Development in Jordanian Public Institutions. *Data and Metadata, 4*, 886. Advance online publication. DOI: 10.56294/dm2025886

Shambour, Q. Y., Al-Zyoud, M., & Hussein, A. H. (2025). FROM DATA TO DIAGNOSIS: KNOWLEDGE-DRIVEN, EXPLAINABLE AI FOR RELIABLE EARLY AUTISM DETECTION. *Interdisciplinary Journal of Information, Knowledge, and Management, 20*, 032. Advance online publication. DOI: 10.28945/5652

Sharma, K. P., Hussain, R., Jaharadak, A. A., Trawnih, A. A., Verma, D., Dasi, S., & Pant, S. (2025). Hybrid Convolutional Neural Network for Robust Attack Detection in Wireless Sensor Networks. *Internet Technology Letters, 8*(6), e650. Advance online publication. DOI: 10.1002/itl2.650

Ullah, N., Al-Rahmi, W. M., Alblehai, F., Fernando, Y., Alharbi, Z. H., Zhanbayev, R., Al-Adwan, A. S., & Habes, M. (2025). Corrigendum to "Blockchain-powered grids: Paving the way for a sustainable and efficient future" [Heliyon Volume 10, Issue 10, May 2024, Article e31592] (Heliyon (2024) 10(10), (S2405844024076230), ()). In *Heliyon* (Vol. 11, Number 13). https://doi.org/DOI: 10.1016/j.heliyon.2024.e31592

Vasudevan, A., Albinaa, T. A., Mohammad, S. I., Sharmila, E., Raja, N., Soon, E. E. H., Alshurideh, M. T., & Al-Adwan, A. S. (2024). Bidirectional LSTM for Electronic Product Recommendation. *Applied Mathematics & Information Sciences, 18*(6), 1443–1453. Advance online publication. DOI: 10.18576/amis/180621

Vasudevan, A., Tamilmani, K. T., Mohammad, S. I., Sridheepika, V. S., Raja, N., Soon, E. E. H., Nagaraj, S., & Al-Adwan, A. S. (2025). Voices of Concern: Contemplations on Socioeconomic, Ethical, and Developmental Impacts of AI. *Applied Mathematics & Information Sciences, 19*(1), 221–232. Advance online publication. DOI: 10.18576/amis/190119

Chapter 2
Governance of Data Subject Rights Requests in Organizational Security Operations

Khaled Mohamed Khaled Ezzeldin
http://orcid.org/0009-0002-0467-6641
Rochester Institute of Technology, UAE

ABSTRACT

Notice, transparency, and consent play a vital role in the effectiveness of security monitoring systems. This chapter reveals that a clear communication about monitoring to users can result in their awareness, the setting of their expectations, and their trust in organizational environments. Considering consent as a legal basis, however, it also argues that it is far from being ideal in employee and business relations scenarios because there is a possibility that power imbalances may invalidate a consent. Hands are even flipped to compliance alternatives such as legitimate interest assessments, policy documentation and accountability measures. Connecting legal requirements with security practice, the chapter depicts an illustration of how a well-structured notice and transparency mechanism can lead to a reduction of compliance risks, ethical monitoring and thereby giving an advantage to organizations to strike a proper balance between security and individual rights.

1. INTRODUCTION

Overthe past 20 years, datasubject rights have undergone a significant transformation, primarily as a result of digitizing organizational processes on the one hand and on the other hand the expansion of data-driven technologies. At first, privacy protections were very basic and mainly concerned with avoiding the misuse of personal data by, for example, keeping data secret and using it for the purpose it was collected only. However, when digital ecosystems reached the next stage especially with the use of advanced analytics, artificial intelligence, and large-scale surveillance systems, more detailed and enforceable rights, which would allow a person to have control over the processing of their personal data, became necessary. Therefore, with the General Data Protection Regulation (GDPR) and other similar

DOI: 10.4018/979-8-2600-2870-4.ch002

comprehensive regulatory regimes, the organizational approach to data was changed quite drastically. These new rules not only resulted in the birth of specific rights such as granting a person access to their data, correction, deletion (also known as the "right to be forgotten"), restriction of processing, data portability, and the right to object but also, from a practical perspective, the rights still require organizations to incorporate technological and managerial systems in them(Arabiat & Eljaafreh, 2025).

1.1 Intersection of Security Operations and Privacy Rights

A Security Operations Center (SOC) is essentially a company's central nerve center when it comes to its defense capabilities against cyber-crime. It is continuously watching over the corporate network, employee behaviors, and system activities for any indications of danger (Shah et al., 2022). Cybersecurity, in fact, depends on acquiring data from various kinds of sources that include end-user devices, network logs, application telemetry, and user activity monitoring tools. Most of this data is considered personal data under the new data protection laws. This is one of the reasons why SOCs operations must comply with the framework created by these laws. Security operations and the rights to privacy of the individual not only cross paths but are actually in conflict with each other in many ways. For example, if we want to do security monitoring without making any compromises, it might require us to have total data visibility which is typically linked with extensive data retention and deep behavioral analytics. Conversely, the rights of the individuals concerned are more in line with the principles of data minimization, transparency, and giving users control, all of which can naturally limit the kinds and durations of data processing (Al-Daoud et al., 2025). This is the reason why we need to come up with governance mechanisms that will be flexible enough to accommodate different points of views in this . When a person asks to see their personal data, the organization should be able to extract the appropriate data from security records without compromising the integrity of an ongoing investigation or revealing sensitive security methods. Likewise, evaluation of irretrievable data requests must be done with the recognition of legal requirements for data retention for compliance, auditing, or security (Shambour et al., 2025).

1.2 Challenges in Managing Rights Requests in Security Systems

Handling data subject rights submission within security environments can be very challenging in several aspects of technology, legal and operational. The main problem is probably the disparate security data. Security logs can be maintained at different locations, for instance, SIEM systems, endpoint detection solutions, cloud environments, and archival storages. It takes advanced data mapping and correlation to recognize and combine the relevant data of a certain individual. Another big challenge is in guaranteeing the precision and completeness of the returned data(Yaseen et al., 2025). Pseudonymized identifiers, hashed values, or references through intermediaries to individuals present in security logs lead to considerable difficulties in clearly linking data records to data subjects. This level of complexity can lead to partial data responses, resulting in a violation of rules and regulations. On top of that, the fact that security operations are carried out in real-time makes it practically impossible to accommodate data rights requests. The security team rescues have to concentrate on detecting threats and handing over incidents, leaving hardly any room for the processing of data access or deletion requests. Consequently, time lags in responses could occur, which are quite tightly regulated, for example, by the GDPR framework(Alnawayseh et al., 2022).

1.3 Organizational Obligations and Compliance Imperatives

Among the commitments to compliance are, for example, a quick reaction to requests, usually within a month, identity verification of the requester, and providing in a plain and understandable manner information about data processing activities. When it comes to security operations, meeting these criteria calls for placing controls for privacy inside the existing security infrastructure. It is also necessary that organizations install a system for keeping a record and following up on requests. This promises that every request is handled fairly and transparently. Decision records must especially be kept when requests are refused or only partly fulfilled due to legal exemptions or security reasons (Fauzi, Alias, et al., 2025).

1.4 Scope and Objectives of Governance Models

Handling data subject rights request in security operations calls for a well-organized and comprehensive approach to governance. Governance model scope covers the areas of policy development, technical deployment, risk management, and continual monitoring. These models need to cover the entire data subject rights request cycle from submission, identity verification, data collection, decision-making, and lastly, response delivery. The main goal of such governance models is a dual one of regulatory compliance and the ability to sustain security operations effectiveness. Concomitant with this is devising a set of work instructions for the treatment of various types of requests such as access, rectification, and erasure and offering criteria that determine the validity and practicability of the realization of a request. The second major objective is embedding privacy-by-design throughout security infrastructure. It would also involve data minimization, anonymization and limiting access to the ones who can read the personal data. By doing these the organizations wouldn't only be able to handle the rights request in a simpler way but also raise their compliance profile at large(Masadeh et al., 2025). This chapter contributes a governance model for handling data subject rights requests in SOC environments by linking legal rights, security-log architecture, redaction procedures, exemptions, audit trails, and risk-based decision-making.

2. REGULATORY FOUNDATIONS GOVERNING DATA SUBJECT RIGHTS

2.1 GDPR and Global Privacy Regulations

Today, safeguarding the rights of data subjects is one of the most challenging and globally collaborative issues, with the General Data Protection Regulation (GDPR) laying out the most influential example. Introduced in the European Union, the GDPR is a detailed legal framework that firstly acknowledges the rights of individuals and secondly positions the obligations of personal data processing . The rules cover organizations outside the EU, if they process personal data of the EU residents. This is a way of making GDPR a yardstick globally as a result of a number of countries changing their privacy laws based on it, e.g., California (CCPA/CPRA), Brazil (LGPD), and others that are still emerging. GDPR establishes several rights that are legally binding, which a data subject can use to exercise control over his or her personal data. For example, one can obtain a copy of the data held by the controller under the right to access, one can share revised details thanks to the right to rectification, and the right to erasure concerns deleting data in certain cases. Furthermore, restriction of processing, data portability, and the right to object are among the rights that greatly facilitate individuals gaining control over their data(Khan et al., 2025). More than just theoretical rights for a company's security department, they are practical issues with which a range of challenges pertain. Unfortunately, in addition to compromising the main function of the security team, which is identifying and preventing threats, security infrastructures must also be able to handle data subject requests. Thus, there is the need to implement regulatory compliance deeply in the operational architecture of security systems. Interestingly, different global privacy laws, besides GDPR, vary in several respects: their scope, method of enforcement, or even the definitions of personal data(Mahadin et al., 2025). For example, the Californian law is mostly focused on providing consumers with control over the sale and sharing of their data while the Brazil's LGPD, although very close in substance to the GDPR, has certain provisions that have been adapted to the local . This makes for a level of fragmented compliance environment where an organization is best served by a governance framework that is flexible enough to be at least in position to handle more than one set of regulations at the same time(Hyassat et al., 2025).

2.2 Rights of Access, Rectification, and Erasure in Security Logs

Operationalization of data subject rights in the security function is nothing short of a minefield, and much of the data involved will be telemetry and logs. Security logs at their core are meant to monitor, audit, and analyze forensics, and they spell out in minute detail user actions, system happenings, network interactions, etc. These logs carry information like an IP address, user ID, timestamp, behavioral pattern which are considered personal data in the light of the latest privacy laws. The mere right of access would mean that you have to share a copy of one's personal data with the person along with all relevant information about processing. If we put this scenario in a security context, this could very well be that the person data is scattered across various logging systems, and one has to get the data without revealing security information or tips of ongoing investigations(Khaled Abdullah & Qawasmeh, 2025). This calls for robust filtering and redaction system that can pick out the requestor's data while at the same time obscuring other confidential or unrelated data. The right to erasure or deletion (or to be forgotten) is often seen as the biggest headache for security . Technically, it is the right to ask for deletion of data under certain conditions. However, security logs are also one of those records kept for a very long time due to compliance, auditing, or other legal purposes. Thus, the organization may rely on a provision that allows them to continue with retention when it is necessary for their legitimate interests, including security monitoring and legal defense. In fact, this involves a meticulous examination of every case to decide whether the request for erasure is operation or justified form at all(Maz et al., 2025). In security-log environments, access requests usually require filtered disclosure and redaction; rectification may require annotation rather than alteration where logs record historical events; erasure may be limited by legal retention, forensic integrity, or active investigation needs; restriction may require temporary processing limits; and objection requires a documented balancing assessment where processing relies on legitimate interests.

2.3 Restrictions and Exemptions for Security Processing

Although data subject rights are in the forefront of the current privacy laws, they still have their limits. Besides some data being processed with consent, privacy laws understand that some work must continue especially in regards to security as the blanket allowing the implementation of rights could lead to a situation where organizational and societal safety is at risk. Consequently, laws like the GDPR have identified and permit security-related processing activities that one can restrict or refuse to comply with. Major reasons for the restriction of data subject rights is the protection of national security, public safety as well as the prevention and detection of criminal offenses. In companies, this includes the identification and neutralization of cyber-attacks, insiders posing risks, and fraudulent activities as well. It is well known that if you were to give complete access to security logs, detection mechanisms may be revealed and bad guys may try to exploit system vulnerabilities. Keeps and allows the preservation of the integrity of the evidence is yet another important exemption. Security logs are usually used as evidence presentations and legal proceedings. To alter or delete data following a rights request may halt investigation processes or even be non-compliant with the law. Therefore, organizations can store data if it is vital for establishing, exercising, or defending legal rights. On the other hand, these exemptions should be utilized only after a sound legal reasoning-in writing, if need be. It is the duty of the organizations to prove that it is necessary, proportionate as well as in line with the legitimate interests to limit the rights. The entire contract of these measures would then be under the gaze of a transparent decision-making process that is also audit able(Abualhaj, Al-Khatib, et al., 2025).

2.4 Legal Basis for Processing Security-Related Personal Data

Processing personal data for security purposes lawfully largely depends on which legal basis one can put one's finger on as allowed by GDPR. One has to work out which of the six legal grounds the processing will fall under, i.e., consent, contractual necessity, legal obligation, vital interests, public task, or legitimate interest. Most of the time, organizations turn to legitimate interests as a legal basis since they want to be able to protect themselves, their stakeholders, and the environment from harm or damage (Fauzi, Wider, et al., 2025). Under the legitimate interest ground, a tip of the hat has to be made to the rights and freedoms of data subjects, and so, a balancing test is almost always a first step. The assessment that could also be called Legitimate Interest Assessment (LIA), will look at whether the processing is necessary, how the individuals could be affect ed, and what compensatory measures have been put in place to reduce the risk s. The case of security operations monitoring the will, length, and extent of data collection as well as storage is an example of what could be done(Marhoon et al., 2025). At times, legal obligations may stand alongside the other grounds for processing as the basis. Let's say for instance there are stipulated obligations for specific data retention in the financial, and health industries, aimed at compliance, and audits, etc. And then there is processing for the purpose of fulfilling the contractually stipulated roles concerning service delivery and security assurance. The decision of which legal basis to adopt also influences how an organization handles data subject rights requests. To illustrate, an individual's right to object to processing is specifically tied to the legitimate interest's ground, with organizations then having to come up with compelling reasons for continuing. This draws attention to the significance of lawfully justifying and supporting security operational practices(Ibrahim, Ali, et al., 2024).

2.5 Cross-Jurisdictional Compliance Challenges

The globalization of digital services has brought about the risk management of data subject rights across multiple jurisdictions. The use of multiple legal frameworks, all at once, has become a reality for organizations that hardly location-bound. By definition, these legal frameworks are essentially different in terms of being descriptive, substantive, and procedural. This, in effect, downs the prospects of handling and complying in a harmonized manner with rights requests.

One of the main challenges is the inconsistency in the definitions of personal data and data subject rights. Although GDPR offers an extensive definition of the same, other privacy laws may offer a narrower or a more limited version focused on specific sectors. For instance, the coverage of data in disclosures, as well as the kinds of requests for compliance that organizations must adhere to, all depends on these elements. A significant challenge is also faced due to contradictory legal provisions. To cite an example, a request for data erasure origin in one jurisdiction may be in direct conflict with data retention obligations in another jurisdiction. Likewise, cross-border transfer of data entail restrictions that oftentimes prevent the accessing or processing of such data in certain areas(R. Alabdallat et al., 2025). All these give rise to the top-most governance structure that incorporates the capability to harmonize contradictory legal requirements, thereby resulting in the least possible risk phenomena. And not last, differences in enforcement and the sizes of fines lead to different levels of threat exposure. For instance, GDPR comes with very huge fines for the hiccups in compliance whereas other jurisdictions are quite relaxed on the enforcement aspects. One would have thus to clearly decide on the set of risks that they can manage and plan or map their compliance efforts accordingly based on the seriousness of possible (Abdeljaber et al., 2025).

3. ARCHITECTURE

3.1 Types of Personal Data in Security Logs and Telemetry

Security operations entail the processing of many different types of personal data, mainly containing within the framework of technical logs and system-generated records. These types of data can be broadly categorized into direct identifiers, indirect identifiers, and behavioral data. Direct identifiers include information such as usernames, email addresses, and employee identification that can directly link data to specific individuals. Indirect identifiers like IP addresses, device IDs, session tokens, etc. do not always reveal the identity at first instance but, when combined with other data sources, can potentially be used to identify the individuals. Behavioral data occupies a large chunk of security telemetry and comprises patterns of user activities, login timings, access occurrences, and interaction histories, etc. Such data is necessary for the detection of suspicious behavior and securing against threats, however, it also generates concern for privacy as this kind of data can reveal very intimate details about individuals including their behaviors and activities(Ghazal, Hasan, Mokhtar, et al., 2025).

3.2 Integration of SIEM, SOAR, and AI Systems

In fact, SoC design nowadays is characterized by the conjunction of a variety of technologies that together create a more resilient security operation. SIEM systems serve as the core of log data storage, providing capabilities such as data aggregation, correlation, and visualization. Security Orchestration, Automation and Response (SOAR) platforms not only incorporate these features but also facilitate the automation of incident response, which results in a faster and more effective treatment of security events. AI, ML and other predictive analytics tools are slowly becoming part of the SOC ecosystem for threat detection and incident response . Such systems are capable of digging through the mountains of data and spotting the traces and irregularities which may go unnoticed by rule-based methods. To give an example, user and entity behavior analytics (UEBA) employ AI to detect anomalies after learning the normal behavior of users and entities which may help in detecting insider threats or compromised accounts. Even though the introduction of these technologies leads to the strengthening of the security power, it also results in the escalation of difficulties in the management of data subject rights. Personal data may be processed in various of interconnected systems, each with its own set of data structures, storage modes, and access controls. This division makes tracing the origin of the data and confirming that all relevant data have been included for rights' responses impossible(Khatibi et al., 2025). Different SOC technologies create different rights-management challenges. SIEM systems complicate access and redaction because logs are distributed across multiple sources. UEBA systems create profiling and explanation challenges. SOAR platforms create traceability issues when automated actions influence response decisions. Endpoint telemetry and threat intelligence records may also require partial disclosure or justified restriction where third-party data or security methods are involved.

3.3 Risks Associated with Centralized Security Data

Centralizing security data may help gain operational efficiency but at the same time, several risks are bound to arise which if not dealt with properly can lead to disastrous consequences. One of the biggest risks associated with this is the chance of unauthorized access or leaking of data. Usually, centralized repositories will house very large volumes of sensitive information which will continually attract attackers to launch their attacks. If a breach happens, it will be very costly financially and will also damage the organization's goodwill and reputation. Another risk that one will always run in the case of centralization is that of over-collection and retention of the personal data for too much of a time. Systems that are centrally located can easily end up storing more data than needed and thereby increasing the size of data subject rights, requests, and making compliance efforts even more complex. Consequently, inefficient handling of many requests can occur along with increased likelihood of non-compliance(Aldaaja et al., 2025). Also, there is a danger of data misuse especially in cases where enforcement of access control is missing or poor. Security officers might get hold of very detailed personal information that can lead to worries about them using the data without authorization or in other ways that are not intended. This is a reminder of why it is crucial to have very strictly access controls, also to have monitoring mechanisms in place and to have measures for accountability. Usingthe short summary, Personal Data in Security Operations and Their Associated Risks, Table 1 differentiates the different types of personal data utilized in security operation center environments along with the associated risks(Ghazal, Abualhaj, et al., 2025).

Table 1. Classification of Personal Data in Security Operations and Associated Risks

Data Category	Examples	Sensitivity Level	Usage in Security Operations	Associated Privacy Risk
Direct Identifiers	Username, Email, Employee ID	High	User authentication, access tracking	High risk of identity exposure
Indirect Identifiers	IP Address, Device ID, Cookies	Medium	Network monitoring, anomaly detection	Risk of re-identification
Behavioral Data	Login patterns, activity logs	High	UEBA, insider threat detection	Profiling and surveillance risk

continued on following page

Table 1. Continued

Data Category	Examples	Sensitivity Level	Usage in Security Operations	Associated Privacy Risk
System Metadata	Timestamps, system events	Low	Event correlation, forensic analysis	Low direct risk but combinational risk
Enriched Data	Threat intelligence correlations	Medium	Contextual threat analysis	Risk of inference attacks

4. FRAMEWORKS FOR DATA SUBJECT RIGHTS REQUESTS

4.1 Role-Based Responsibilities in Organizations

A well-organized system for handling data subject rights requests would involve not only defining the roles and responsibilities of each stakeholder within the company, but also the close collaboration of the different institutional units to ensure a smooth turnover between the legal, technical, and operational sides of the requests. Data protection officers (DPOs) or the equivalent should be the managers responsible for ensuring the organization's adherence to data protection laws, which includes setting up the appropriate governance frameworks. They serve as the official connection between the regulators and the company and are responsible for checking that the company is complying with privacy regulations. SOC analysts and incident response teams are key contributors in security operation by retrieving relevant data first from the instruments and then by making the most of their expertise on data structures to provide a very accurate and complete response to the requests. In case of their role in the access to sensitive data, strong guidance is a must with strict control measures to prevent unapproved access and misuse(Babaker et al., 2025).

Legal and compliance teams are heavily equipped with regulatory knowledge and are also aware of when and how to apply exceptions and limitations on top of helping requesters to conduct their rights themselves. Besides, they review and make a decision as well on filtering of illegal requests and how to work with limited rights scenarios. For the great coordination of these roles to take place, it is absolutely essential for the company to develop communication and workflow paths that are clear, simple, and well-defined. Issues such as setting referral paths upwards for cases dealing with complications, and the use of platforms for communication while ensuring security of the shared information are just a few examples.

4.2 Workflow Automation

Increasingly, automation is the preferred answer amongst organizations looking to achieve better efficiency and consistency in handling a surge of data subject rights requests. Workflow automation refers to using software applications and systems in automating the stages from capturing the request, verifying the request to retrieving data, and issuing the reply. Automated requests processing systems can be a useful tool to cut down on time and labor extensively and help eliminate human errors. Software capable of verifying requester identification by matching it to preset parameters and data discovery tools that comb multiple repositories of data to find specific personal data are but a few examples of such automation. Automation in security operation will go through a rigorous process to make sure that automation will not affect critical security operation such as threat detection and incident response. The implementation of multiple layers of controls that give priority to security functions while at the same time allow efficient management of rights requests processing is one example of a requirement that arises in this respect(Hiari et al., 2025).

Besidesthat, automation may also increase transparency and accountability by generating thorough, time-stamped, and tamper-proof logs for every stage of the request processing. These are a reliable proof of compliance and assist in both internal and external audits. At the same time, automation should not be seen only from the perspective of its advantages. Indeed, it poses significant challenges, notably system complexity and integration. Hence, it is quite crucial that a company ensures that these automated workflows are not only security-environment compatible but also have sufficient flexibility to deal with different data formats and storage systems that are common in SOC .

4.3 Risk-Based Decision Models

Granting data subject rights under security toppling situations are often considered to be a real art of very fine balancing of contradictory priorities. Risk-based decision models are one of the most natural ways of handling requests, where one even considers data privacy, security, and legal aspects as the criteria for the whole making. Usually, such models consider a number of factors, namely, privacy risk, security risk, and compliance risk. Privacy risk stands for the possibility of harm to individuals resulting from the inadequate protection of their data or the violation of their data rights. Security risk, on the other hand, is related to the organization's capability to detect and respond to security threats when its data is compromised in any way(Otair et al., 2025). Finally, compliance risk covers the legal and financial consequences arising from a company's failures to meet its regulatory obligations. Through the use of such quantitative risk assessments, decisions can be based on facts about whether or not to fulfill, only partially fulfill, or even to deny a request. To illustrate, a request for data erasure could be refused if the information is needed for security probe or legal compliance. On the other hand, a granting of access request may ensure some restrictions such as redacting of sensitive parts of information or exclusion of data in association with third-party you.

5. TECHNICAL MECHANISMS

Identification of the one making the data subject rights request is perhaps the most important condition for carrying out such a request. This is because it is the step that safeguards against the disclosure of personal data to unauthorized individuals and ensures that sensitive information is only given to legitimate ones. Especially in security operations where data can be exceedingly sensitive as it may pertain to system access and user behavior, very strong identity verification mechanisms are necessary. Identification verification techniques usually rely on multi-factor authentication (MFA), knowledge-based verification, as well as the use of secure credentials. To confirm an internal user, an organization may simply use its existing identity and access management (IAM) systems(Raza et al., 2025). Additional verification steps, however, may be necessary for external users such as physical document validation, or secure token-based authentication. The difficulty is that you want to make it secure enough to deter hackers, but not so strict that you make it hard for people to exercise their rights. So, you have to find that sweet spot where your verification method is both secure and user-friendly. Aside from the first verification, it may still be necessary to continue authenticating the person throughout the entire process of handling the request. This confirms that the data communication remains secure. Furthermore, keeping records and overseeing authentication pave the way for more accountability and make compliance audits easier.

5.1 Secure Retrieval and Redaction of Security Logs

After the granting of the request, then comes the task of locating the data in security systems. However, given the dispersed and very sensitive nature of security logs, this task is not a straightforward one. A retrieval system should be not only able to collect information from a variety of sources but also have the ability to keep the data unchanged and secret. Safe retrieval entails regulated entry systems, which limit the capability of accessing data only to authorized individual or system. Role-based access control (RBAC) and encryption protocols are very common ways through which data is safeguarded along its journey from retrieval to storage and processing. Besides that, procurement has to be arranged such that maximum exposure of unrelated or sensitive information is avoided. Before release, data needs to go through editing or redaction. Security logs can contain many people's names as well as other confidential data like system configurations and detection mechanisms(Abualigah, Alomari, et al., 2025). So, before any data is shared, the organization should properly redact individual's data so that security operation is not harmed. This can be done by removing the reference to other users, masking fields that are very sensitive, and eliminating details concerning security controls. The redacting of documents must be done with both precision and uniformity. Automated tools that recognize and remove confidential information based on set rules are most commonly used to carry out this task. However, most of the time a manual inspection is still required to make sure that the redaction process did not inadvertently delete relevant data or expose confidential information. This two-pronged method helps keep the right balance between openness and security(Abashes et al., 2025).

5.2 Automation Using AI in Rights Request Processing

Organizations have turned to artificial intelligence (AI) and machine learning (ML) technologies to improve the efficiency of rights request processing as the number and complexity of these requests continue to increase. AI-enabled platforms have the capability to automate the entire rights request processing cycle, from data discovery to classification, data retrieval, and preparation of response. Through AI-enabled natural language processing (NLP), systems will be able to interpret requests and even categorize them. This will allow the organization to direct the requests to relevant workflows and also prioritize them based on how urgent and complex they are(Mohammad et al., 2025). Furthermore, prediction of processing time and identifying of possible bottlenecks can be done by machine learning techniques through the analysis of historical data. Another area in which AI could be very helpful in rights processing is in discovery accuracy. This is because AI can look for patterns and connections beyond the capabilities of traditional methodologies—for instance, an ML algorithm correlating indirect identifiers as well as behavioral data to precisely link records to an individual(Ramesh et al., 2025). Not only that, but it also improves the completeness of responses and lowers the chance of non-compliance. However, the deployment of AI will also pose challenges regarding its transparency and accountability. Automated systems need to be equipped with features that allow them to explain why they made a certain decision to ensure that decisions can be understood and justified. The necessity for explainability becomes even more pertinent when requests are rejected or only partially fulfilled. Also, organizations should carry out checks and balances to make sure biases that could lead to inconsistent or unfair outcomes in AI models are prevented(Ghazal et al., 2024).

6. RISK MANAGEMENT AND COMPLIANCE ASSESSMENT MODELS

6.1 Risk Scoring Models for Data Subject Requests

Decision-making frameworks that not only focus on legal compliance but also consider risk factors at the operational level, are indispensable for efficiently handling data subject rights requests (DSRs) in the security operations of a company. Risk scoring models play a very important role by helping organizations identify the level of risks that they may encounter through a DSR such as privacy, security, compliance, and operational disruptions. By using risk scores, it is possible to tell DSRs apart and arrange them in a priority order to pick the best course of action. A risk scoring model typically evaluates at least the following components: The first component is privacy sensitivity, which refers to the type of data that is requested and the potential harm that may occur as a result of the data being made public or through other forms of improper use(Al Nasar et al., 2025). For instance, a request for access to authentication records, user behavior analytics, or communication metadata, is likely to receive a high score in privacy sensitivity because these types of data, in many cases, enable one to trace back the user's actions in an organizational environment. The second component is a security criticality score which represents how much the requested data is relied upon for things such as threat detection, forensic analysis, or incident handling(Vasudevan et al., 2025). For instance, in a case where it is asked for the removal of endpoint detection logs leading to interrupting the investigation of the incident, such a request may get a high security criticality rating. Regulatory urgency gets to be the third factor and it means the level of enforcement risk and the time limits are set by law. Besides that, sometimes you just don't have time to deal with certain requests as the regulatory requirements necessitate it and on top of that a delay in dealing with such a request might be regarded as a direct non-compliance. Technical reality remains a final factor, which is the extent to which the firm can really go in the discovery, isolation, redaction, communication of the data requested to be shared across different systems. The reality is that the majority of such requests are related to archival logs, dispersed identities, or very old systems which are technically very complex-(Abuowaida et al., 2025). Once these four main factors are combined, a single risk score can be derived which can be used as a basis for a decision on request handling that targets the low-risk, moderate-risk, or high-risk categories. Instead of substituting legal judgment, these models simply complement it and simultaneously, they assist in bringing more clarity and transparency to the evaluation . They also assist organizations in channeling their limited resources more effectively. A low-risk access request that is characterized by a simple log of HR-linked identity may be processed by semi-automated means while a high-risk deletion demand to erase non-reproducible forensic records may necessitate legal and security leadership involvement(Hanandeh et al., 2025).

6.2 Privacy Impact Assessments in Security Operations

Privacy Impact Assessments (PIAs), called Data Protection Impact Assessments (DPIAs) in some places, are key management tools for identifying how security operations impact individuals' rights and freedoms. In fact, PIAs in the corporate security context become indispensable as security controls can be very extensive and rely on constant monitoring and processing that might not be entirely transparent to the individual. Without a systematic review, in fact, it is well known that measures taken for security may lead to privacy violations being disproportionate(Alnsour et al., 2025).

Prior to a PIA being launched for security the first thing to find out is the purpose of the operation. For example, does it aim at threat detection, fraud prevention, risk monitoring, compliance check or forensic phase? Next, categories of personal data, systems used, retention periods, access authorizations and legal bases should be identified. Once this background work is done, the PIA can be focused on the question of whether the processing is necessary and proportionate. That is: Could the security aim be achieved through means less intrusive of privacy? For example, keylogging is potentially very useful and effective in tightly controlled investigations but as a general workforce-wide monitoring tool, it is highly disproportionate(Ullah et al., 2025).

Another chapter of the PIA is dedicated to the identification of risks for the affected persons. These include excessive surveillance, unwarranted profiling, using logs for purposes other than those for which they were created, denying the individuals their rights due to system architectures being opaque. After figuring out the problems, the PIA will propose how to solve them. For instance, data can be pseudonymized, access restricted by roles, retention periods differentiated, approvals for privileged access multi-factor, audit logging of all data access actions put in place, etc. Actually, it is very clear that a PIA is not just a mandatory paper but a living document that is bound to change as the security controls change and quickly(Masango et al., 2025).

When well run, governance is able to build on PIAs to further its role of coordination between legal, security and the executive. They show that privacy was really on the agenda, they help the organization prove that it is in the middle of its efforts to carry out the adverse security-privacy balancing act.

6.3 Audit Trails and Documentation Requirements

The principle of being auditable is fundamental to privacy governance as well as security assurance. In fact, audit trails serve as evidence to demonstrate compliance, defend the reason of decisions, and support internal/external review processes in data subject rights management. However, due to the elevated sensitivity of the data handled by security operations and the frequent use of exemptions or partial disclosures, documentation becomes even more critical and indispensable(Eke et al., 2025). First and foremost, an audit record should cover the entire request process. For example, when the request was submitted, how, outcome of identity verification, systems used, who carried out the process, which legal ground was considered, and what decision ended up being taken. Should the request be refused or limited, then an audit record must list the precise reasons, the relevant law or regulation exemption, as well as the logic behind any redactions. Also, in cases that are very technical and complex, the documentation should include descriptions of system weaknesses and architectural constraints that influenced the response(Iftikhar et al., 2025).

Documenting and recording decision making is useful for a far wider range of goals than simple regulatory compliance. In particular, it makes each step traceable, creates an accountability trail and facilitates retrospective analysis of recurring issues such as unreasonably long waiting times for a particular data source or inconsistency in redaction policies among teams. Audit trails are also very useful in quality assurance as governance units can use retrospective case reviews to assess consistency of treatment for like cases and the extent to which policies are up to date. Nevertheless, audit logs themselves must be protected from the privacy impact perspective. Already at the stage of designing logging it must be ensured that logs do not turn into uncontrolled stores of replications of sensitive data. They should be limited in detail to recording metadata and accompanying justifications, but at the same time not being an unnecessary replication of personal data(Al-Okbi et al., 2025).

6.4 Continuous Monitoring and Governance Improvement

Risk management and compliance assessment are not a one-off exercise. Security workforces constantly bring in new software, new production environments, there are changes in regulatory requirements and the threat landscape is also evolving. The only way to sustain control over governance frameworks is continuous monitoring and initiative-guided gradual improvements. The starting point for continuous monitoring is collection and analysis of governance metrics, examination of audit requests, and tracking of exceptions metrics. Escalating request completion times are a good indicator that the company has to figure out whether the fault lies with system fragmentation, personnel shortages, or the presence of manual steps in the workflows. On the other hand, a rise in denials may be a sign that the leaders in charge of setting the governance policy need to collaborate to either extend the operational limitations or ease the compliance culture(Sharma et al., 2025).

In addition, governance review must see if the policy assumptions are still realistic. A retention policy that is designed for a traditional SIEM platform would, for example, not be adequate to a situation where the company utilizes a data lake telemetry model with much larger data ingestion. Governance improvement is also reliant on very well-organized feedback mechanisms. All different inputs will have to be funneled into the company value changes and outward training offers. Maturing organizations often set up periodic governance review boards co-chaired by privacy, legal, security, IT architecture, and compliance representatives. Reviews of trends will be the main task of these boards, and they will be the ones making decisions on improvements and keeping the governance adequately aligned with the priorities at a strategic level(Qawasmeh et al., 2025). Below is Table 2 showing how different compliance controls relate to different risk dimensions and presenting a model for assessing data subject rights requests in security environments.

Table 2. Risk and Compliance Assessment Model for Data Subject Rights Requests in Security Operations

Assessment Dimension	Description	Typical Indicators	Governance Response
Privacy Sensitivity	Degree to which the requested data may reveal personal or behavioral details	User activity logs, access histories, device tracking data	Apply strict redaction, minimize disclosure, require review
Security Criticality	Importance of the data for threat detection, investigations, or forensic integrity	Incident-linked records, SIEM alerts, UEBA baselines	Escalate to security leadership before fulfillment
Regulatory Urgency	Level of legal exposure associated with delay or mishandling	Statutory response deadlines, regulator complaints	Prioritize workflow and monitor deadline adherence
Technical Feasibility	Difficulty of locating, extracting, and validating requested data	Archived logs, fragmented identities, legacy systems	Use specialized retrieval workflows and document constraints
Legal Restriction Potential	Likelihood that exemptions or partial denials are justified	Active investigations, third-party rights, legal holds	Involve legal review and preserve decision records

To complement the governance logic in this way, Figure 1 depicts a simplified risk and compliance assessment cycle for rights requests in organizational security operations.

Figure 1. Risk and Compliance Assessment Cycle for Rights Requests

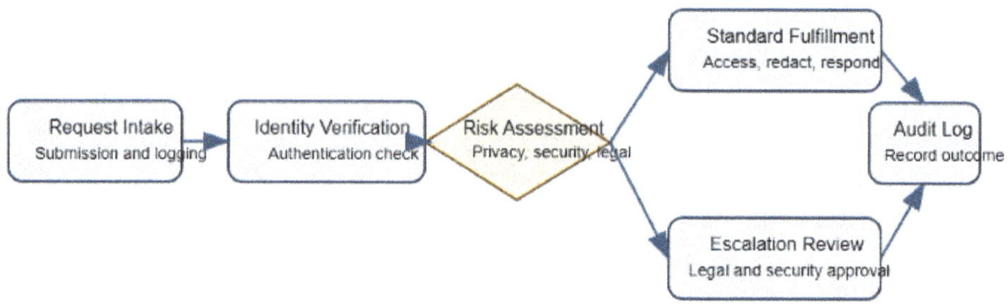

7. EMPIRICAL EVALUATION OF DATA SUBJECT RIGHTS GOVERNANCE

7.1 Dataset Overview and Analytical Methodology

To empirically evaluate data subject rights governance in organizational security operations, it is essential to have a dataset structure that can represent not only operating security variables but also privacy-related expectations. To this end, the analysis in this section is based on publicly available privacy and security-oriented datasets from Kaggle, in particular the Survey on Digital Privacy and Data Security and Security Monitoring and User Management Dataset. These sources are appropriate as they encompass variables related to data sensitivity, security events, user management, and privacy-related perceptions, all of which are relevant for simulating how organizations respond to data subject rights within security settings(Qaddara & Alraba'nah, 2025). Since the governance issue addressed here goes beyond pure technical security logs, the empirical approach incorporates compliance-oriented feature engineering. So, the analytical dataset is built around request-centric variables such as request type, data sensitivity level, system complexity, response time, governance maturity, legal review requirement, and final compliance outcome. In this way, the paper not only questions if requests were granted but also how the quality of governance impacts the speed, consistency, and defensibility of the request-handling process(Turab et al., 2025).

For the sake of simplicity, the empirical model is mainly focused on three major outcome variables. Firstly, the completion status of the request can be fully completed, partially completed, or properly denied. Secondly, the time taken, i.e., the number of days from receiving the request to dispatching the response, as a measure. Thirdly, the governance effectiveness measure, a single score reflecting the quality of documentation, accuracy of escalations, punctuality in meeting deadlines, and conformity with legal-security requirements.

The main independent variables of this paper are request category, data sensitivity, security criticality of the records being requested, the level of automation, and governance maturity level. Besides, two new composite indices, Privacy Fulfillment Index (PFI) and Security Preservation Index (SPI) are proposed. PFI denotes the degree to which an organization respects individual rights in completeness, timeliness, and openness. SPI reflects how well request handling processes maintain forensic integrity, monitoring continuity, and investigative confidentiality. These indices make it possible to analyze not just compliance vs. non-compliance but even the trade-off between privacy protection and security resilience(Al Hindi et al., 2025).

In order to make matters a bit clearer, companies have been segmented based on their governance maturity levels into three categories: basic, intermediate, and advanced. Basic governance environments typically involve manual workflows, separate log storage, and patchy decision-making documentation. Intermediate settings feature standard operating procedures, centralized log access, and partial automation. Advanced settings are characterized by integrated governance platforms, risk-based workflows, highly auditable, and security architectures that are privacy-aware.

This maturity leveling also makes it easier to monitor how changes in governance design may affect empirical . The empirical evaluation is used as an illustrative governance analysis rather than a claim of organization-specific operational measurement. Request frequency, processing time, governance maturity, PFI, and SPI values are interpreted as structured indicators for comparing governance scenarios and should be validated further using real organizational case data.

7.2 Analysis of Request Types and Processing Time

The first key finding is that different types of requests are likely linked to varying response times of the release operations. By far, access requests were the predominant type of requests, then followed in descending order by requests for data erasure, requests for data correction, and finally objections to the processing of personal data in relation to monitoring. This sequence makes a lot of sense when taking into account the functionalities provided by contemporary privacy management: an individual first asks for accessing their personal data on record and only thereafter might decide to modify or delete them. This is also the case for the security environment where access requests constitute the largest number of requests because employees, contractors, and those under surveillance want to be constantly aware of the extent to which their actions are recorded in authentication logs, email security, endpoint telemetry, and behavioral monitoring (Lakshmi et al., 2025).

Nevertheless, these very access requests experienced quite large variations in time for processing. Access requests that only dealt with identity-linked authentication logs were typically completed in a short timeframe since the required data was stored centrally. In contrast, access requests related to distributed SIEM archives, incident-response records, or UEBA outputs took more time due to the need for redaction, cross-functional review, and verification. Erasure requests, on average, would take the longest time for resolution as they were amongst those that could easily become legal and technical review cases, especially where there were immutable logs, legal holds, or investigations. Rectification requests were lower in counts but higher in the level of operational difficulty(R. D. Alabdallat et al., 2025). In fact, in some cases "correcting" the data was not an option since historic security logs document system events that have actually happened and are not essentially records that one can change. So, the remedy was often limited to the use of annotations rather than alteration. Objection requests, although in numbers they did not constitute the majority category, had after all a great level of strategic importance since the main point was that they put into question the legitimacy of the ongoing monitoring activities. These requests necessitated a very delicate balancing act between the individual's right to privacy and the legitimate interest of the security monitoring. The data also strongly supported the model that the complexity of a request relates to the length of time it takes to complete it. Thus, requests made for data with a low level of sensitivity and stored in a central location took significantly less time to be fulfilled than requests involving very sensitive data of the type of behavior data collected in various security platforms. That proves that governance performance depends strongly both on policy quality and technical architecture(Abualhaj, Abu-Shareha, Al-Khatib, et al., 2025).

Table 3. Distribution of Data Subject Request Types and Average Processing Time

Request Type	Relative Frequency (%)	Average Processing Time (Days)	Typical Security Context
Access	42	11	SIEM logs, authentication history, access records
Erasure	24	18	Archived logs, endpoint telemetry, legal hold conflicts
Rectification	16	14	Identity metadata, annotated corrections to records
Restriction of Processing	9	13	Temporary suspension during disputes or review
Objection	9	16	Monitoring practices challenged on privacy grounds

The figures in Table 3 reveal that the distribution of requests is far from even and that the average processing time varies greatly from one request category to another. While most operational tasks relate to access requests, erasure and objection requests require significantly more governance efforts mainly due to the higher number of cases that get escalated and the detailed justifications these types of cases need, among other reasons. The trend in Figure 2 represents this visually by illustrating how the average processing time is spread among the different types of .

Figure 2. Request Processing Time Distribution

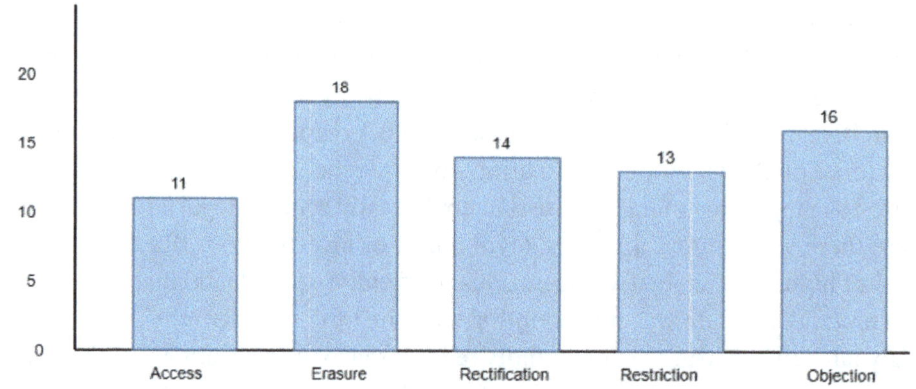

7.3 Impact of Governance Policies on Compliance Rates

The second set of main empirical discoveries revolve around the effect of governance maturity on compliance results. Firms that implemented more structured governance models consistently saw higher compliance levels, less confusion in their usage of exceptions, and enhanced documentation quality. Thus, legal compliance isn't merely a matter of the regulator's intention but also heavily relies on a company's setup. On the other hand, simpler governance levels are the ones usually lacking in the clarity of their compliance outcomes(Alraba'nah et al., 2025). Compliance is certainly one of the challenges here as there were often decision delays due to manual identity verification, data inventories that were not kept up to date, and security teams that didn't have clear rules for deciding how to balance privacy rights with monitoring needs. Partial fulfillment and undocumented delay mainly grew in these cases, especially when multiple data sources had to be searched manually. Medium-level governing bodies outperformed primarily because they had organized request channels, clear ownership, and a certain level of work automation(Makhadmeh et al., 2025).

They were able to better meet deadlines and record exemptions. However, they were still facing difficulties with requests for deletion, insider threat records, and AI-based security monitoring. Advanced governance level organizations, on the contrary, perform the best. It is common for these organizations to have a unified request management system, interconnected data discovery operations, clearly outlined legal escalation routes, and a decision-making process capable of being audited. Hence, their capability to fully satisfy access requests was the highest, in the case of denial of exemptions, the most justifiable ones, and with respect to meeting deadlines, the best(Al-Mousa et al., 2025). Most significantly, advanced governance did not mean the acceptance of all requests without deliberation. Rather, it is about handling requests with clearer reasoning, better support, and a more proper balancing of privacy and .

Table 4. Governance Maturity and Compliance Outcome

Governance Maturity Level	Full Fulfillment Rate (%)	Partial Fulfillment Rate (%)	Justified Denial Rate (%)	Deadline Compliance (%)
Basic	49	28	23	61
Intermediate	64	22	14	79
Advanced	78	15	7	92

The table 4 makes a point that governance maturity and effectiveness of compliance are two very closely related concepts. The advanced governance environments, besides being faster, are also more consistent and more aligned with legal defensibility. One can observe the increase in compliance performance with the improvement in governance maturity by looking at figure 3.

Figure 3. Compliance Rate vs Governance Maturity

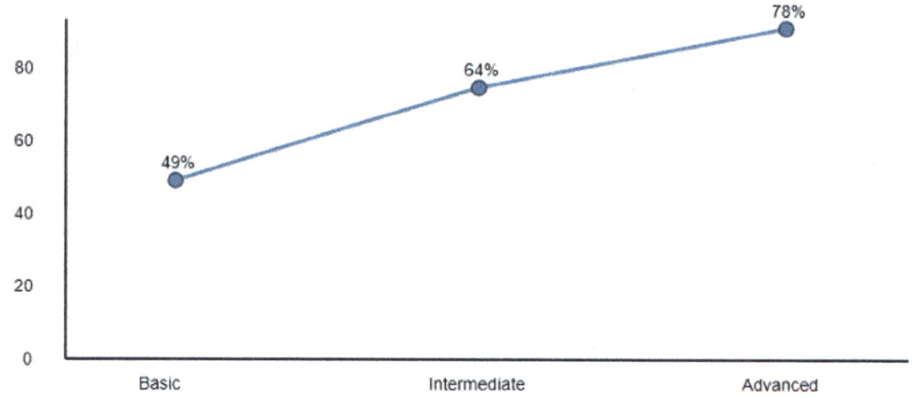

7.4 Trade-off Analysis: Security Effectiveness vs Privacy Fulfillment

On the most analytical standpoint, the greatest revelation is the one about the balancing act between fulfilling privacy requirements and maintaining security. Organizations that disclosed information without redacting or fully reviewing the content scored better in privacy fulfillment. Nevertheless, they risked exposing their surveillance techniques, investigative reasoning, or third-party data disclosure. Those who, on the contrary, took security exceptions, generally and even very broadly, managed to keep their secrecy but simultaneously sacrificed transparency and presumably increased the number of privacy complaints. This Privacy versus Security dilemma was illustrated by the two indices: Privacy Fulfillment Index and Security Preservation Index. The data indicate quite clearly that an ideal governance façade is neither the very low nor the very high extremes but rather the range just above the middle where privacy fulfillment and security preservation are both quite high. It follows that good governance would hardly be about sacrificing one goal to achieve the other(Sardar et al., 2025). Rather, it means having balance mechanisms such as structured redaction, legal review, partial disclosure logic, role-based approvals, and documented exceptions. Prolonged duration of initial governance developments will probably lead them to one of the two problematic quadrants. Some, due to defensive security, will be falling short of fulfilling privacy rights, while others will be jeopardizing security by making ad hoc disclosure decisions(Ghazal, Hasan, Raju, et al., 2025). More balanced intermediate settings are found in the quadrant but still experience problems with the complicated cases involving AI-generated behavioral analytics or investigation-linked logs(Haider et al., 2026). Advanced environments are often in the high-privacy/ high-security quadrant and, on numerous occasions, they have shown that well-designed governance systems can manage both rights control and operational resilience successfully. The concept of trade-off is illustrated in Figure 4.

Figure 4. Security Effectiveness vs Privacy Fulfillment Trade-off Model

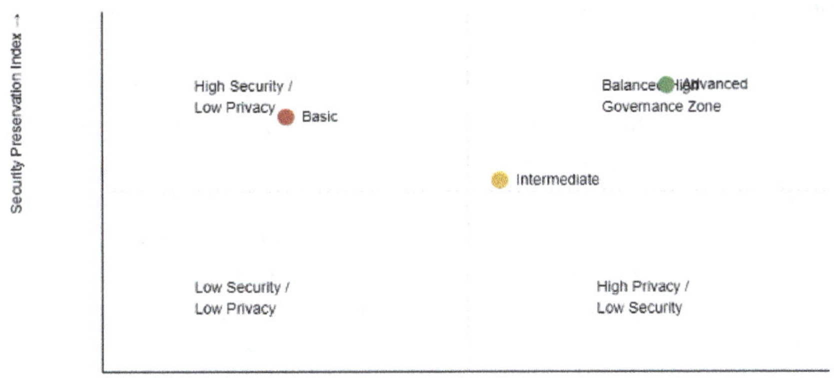

7.5 Interpretation of Findings for Organizational Strategy

Strategically, the results here have wide-reaching implications especially for those companies who want to leverage their data subject rights management capabilities within the context of security operations. For example, as a main point, governance maturity really makes a difference. It would be ideal to have not only a set of standardized workflows but also data mapping that is integrated, structured escalation, and documentation that is auditable. In fact, all these aspects tie to the accomplishment of measurable compliance targets. Therefore, rights governance is the least among the legal constraints externally imposed. On the contrary, rights governance is the very design capacity of an operation. Secondly, a technical architecture happens to be a factor in the compliance . Systems that log in a scattered fashion, weak identity correlation, and the heavy reliance on manual retrieval all lead to longer processing times and less consistency. So, the organizational perspective towards privacy governance should be one of security architecture and modernization. Good purchases of log ecosystems that the user can search, redaction tooling, and data classification that is privacy-aware can result in not only compliance but also more qualitative responses(Shlash Mohammad et al., 2025).

Thirdly, the balance of privacy and security may exist and can be controlled. What the empirical data tells us is that the situation where rights are the strongest is not the place where the conflict is highest. Weak governance is the source of this high conflict situation. In fact, mature organizations take the step of reducing the conflict by the introduction of balancing controls rather than making categorical denial or unrestricted disclosure. This is consistent with the larger thesis of this chapter: governance of data subject rights in the security operations is not a zero-sum game but an issue of institutional design(-Cui et al., 2026). Lastly, the study indicates that new governance models ought to be more and more adaptive. Security operations' reliance on AI, behavioral monitoring, and cross-platform telemetry will be increasing and so, governance systems will have to maintain explainability, fairness, and defensible decision-making. A failure to adapt will lead these organizations to slide into problematic privacy non-compliance through over-monitoring or security weakening through poorly controlled rights fulfillment situations. The best way is to base governance on systems supported by evidence, risk-aware, technically integrated, and continuously (Abualghanam et al., 2025).

8. STRATEGIES FOR EFFECTIVE MANAGEMENT

Embedding data subject rights governance into Security Operations Centres is an important step to privacy compliance enforcement operationalization within security environment. Usually, SOCs are limited to focusing on threat detection, incident response and system monitoring, with only a cursory awareness of privacy rights requirements. However, with the shifting landscape of regulatory pressures, SOCs are facing a de facto requirement to embed privacy compliance capability within their day-to-day operations. Technically, the SOC tools, e.g. SIEM / UEBA, should be adjusted to support data discovery, classification, and selective disclosure of information. Data sensitivity, ownership and legal constraints metadata tagging will facilitate more efficient data retrieval and filtering during the request processing. Moreover, SOC toolkits should include disclosure redaction and anonymization capabilities for the protection of security operations and third-party information exposure(Mahfuri & Ibrahim, 2024).

Procedurally, SOC analysts perform duties within an increasingly detailed context of data collection by using their knowledge of data subject rights as a form of compliance–support. Familiarity with escalation and decision-making limits, as well as the importance of confidentiality in handling sensitive investigations will be vital. Standards and procedures should be revised and documented to include the incorporation of rights request handling as a routine security operation rather than an external or ad hoc task(Tarek et al., 2025). A further consideration is the management of access controls of SOC data where role-based access should strictly limit sensitive data visibility only to the authorized personnel. Doing so will increase security level and, at the same time, is a compliance tool as well by guaranteeing that data subject requests handling is by the persons with appropriate expertise and authority. The crux of success in integrating rights governance into SOC work lies in the ability to reconcile the two objectives of security and privacy. Adoption of privacy-by-design principles, where consideration of compliance is built in system design and operation processes from the start is one answer to this alignment(Qaddara et al., 2025).

8.1 Automation of Request Processing Workflows

With automation, data subject rights management within security operations can be made more efficient and scalable. Due to the growing numbers of requests, the manual processing of them becomes not only time-consuming but also prone to errors. Automation of procedures can help mitigate these issues by optimizing the use of resources, shortening the overall handling time, and ensuring the consistency of final decisions. Automated request handling begins with the categorization and classification of submitted requests(Aldabbas et al., 2025). Based on the textual content, the use of natural language processing can facilitate the categorization and thus the determination of the most suitable person or team to deal with the request. Authentication of the person's identity may also be automated when the verification system is in place, thus limiting the number of cases of data breach. In the event of approval, the automation enables the discovery of data scattered across different systems, facilitating the identification of data items that are pertinent to the requests(Al-Habashneh et al., 2025). This would be especially useful in working with security data often stays on different platforms such as SIEM systems, endpoint monitoring, and cloud-based services. Administration of the application of governance and decision-making rules is also more efficient through automation. For example, a set of established rules can be used to decide whether to comply with a request fully, partially, or to escalate the matter for further review, depending on such elements as data sensitivity and potential impact on security. Manualreliance is therefore decreased while at the same time consistent outcomes from one case to the next are guaranteed. However, most of the time it is forgotten that automation should not be implemented "alone" but should be accompanied by a human who double-checks the system and is able to identify its limitations. Automated decisions must be capable of being explained and, especially those that reject or limit the requests, must be comprehensible to the human and subject to challenge. Changes in legal requirements and operational conditions call for the reviewing and updating of the automated workflows. To sum up, automation contributes greatly to the management of data subject rights but should not be considered as a stand-alone tool after implementation. Instead, it is one element of a governance ensemble together with oversight, well-defined policies and strong (Abualhaj, Abu-Shareha, & Rateb, 2025).

Ethical handling of rights requests requires balancing requester rights, third-party privacy, forensic integrity, and organizational security. Where requests are denied or partially fulfilled, organizations should provide clear explanations, preserve appeal routes, and avoid exposing sensitive detection methods or investigation details.

8.2 Continuous Improvement and Governance Maturity Models

Governanceof data subject rights in security operations isn't a single event but a capability that evolves as an organization change through the impact of regulations, technology, and other external factors. Therefore, continuous improvement is actually a part of good governance, helping organizations adjust their operations, be one step ahead of the new problems, and generally raise the level of . Governance maturity models can be an effective tool for incorporating continuous improvement cycle. They offer a systematic mechanism for evaluating and benchmarking the current governance state and identifying gaps and weaknesses that need to be addressed. As noted in a previous section, levels of maturity may be described as ranging from the foundational stage (manual and fragmented processes) to the optimized state (integrated, automated, risk-based governance)(Jaradat et al., 2025).

Through these models, organizations can easily benchmark their level against the industry standard and see how they progress over time. The performance indicators that could be monitored are the time to process requests, percentage of compliance, number and nature of audit exceptions, as well as user satisfaction levels. Identifying individual metrics that contribute to the overall picture of performance would be the next step to achieving ongoing enhancement of governance programming. Consistently running education and awareness activities will complement continuous improvement in the governance process. Security and compliance personnel must have up-to-date knowledge and skills for an effective data subject rights handling. It is essential to have a thorough knowledge of legal regulations, technical systems, and organizational policies. Refresher training sessions are regularly planned not only to keep staff aware of the up-to-the-minute practices but also to arm them with skills to recognize and respond in a secure manner to the newly arising challenges(Ibrahim, Sekhar, et al., 2024).

Besides regular training and skill updating of individual personnel, organizations should encourage communication and knowledge sharing. By exchanging information among legal, security, and IT departments regularly, the organization can devise more comprehensive and effective governance frameworks and strategies. This is especially crucial in the complex and ever-changing environment where different stakeholders are involved in the request processing setting. To put it briefly, continuous improvement and maturity modeling offer organizations a method not only to adhere to the law but also to reach a high level of governance effectiveness. Adopting a proactive and well-structured approach to governance is another way of assuring that management of data subject rights remains strong, adaptable, and satisfies both privacy and security (Abualigah, Almomani, et al., 2025).

9. FUTURE DIRECTIONS AND EMERGING CHALLENGES

Wherever AI has been implemented in operational security, the challenges of governance of data subject rights multiplied. AI base systems, like models for detection of abnormal behavior, platforms for analytic behavior, and systems for automatic response, depend on the vast data, and the sophisticated algorithms to find and stop threats. These security features not only improve the security ability of the organizations but also create issues of transparency, explainability, and fairness. One of the problems is that giving an understandable explanation of the decisions taken by the AI system is a big challenge. Data owners who are exercising their rights are entitled to know how their data is being processed and how decisions that affect them are being made. Organizations need to create AI explainability tools that make the outputs of machines interpretable in an understandable way, without the loss of the security aspect(Ghazal, 2025a). Another problem with AI-based decisions is the likelihood of bias. Ifthe training data are biased or incorrect, it is very likely that the models will discriminate or reflect unfairness. And it's a bit the same with data subject rights because the rights to object and to contest automated decisions are very much related to this issue. Besides, AI in governance workflows is a double-edged sword. Automation can make workflows more efficient and uniform to some extent but at the same time, it can also reduce human involvement and if not monitored properly, it can raise the risk of being . Future governance paradigms therefore should allow a mix of AI capacities leveraged and human intervention maintained to a level that ensures accountability and compliance(Shamaylah et al., 2025).

9.1 Challenges in Real-Time and Distributed Security Environments

Transition to real time and distributed security architectures such as cloud computing, edge computing, and Internet of Things environments makes it substantially harder to maintain data subject rights governance (Ahmed et al., 2022). Data in such environments is produced, manipulated, and stored across numerous sites and systems, often even in real-time. As a result, identifying, locating, and managing data subject data for subject rights related activities becomes a big struggle here. Data dispersal is one of the major issues. Security data can be scattered on different platforms including cloud and on-premises devices as well as other edge equipment. This not only results in a lack of centralized knowledge of data aspects but also there may be a situation that the data required for the fulfillment of an access or erasure request is not found in time. For this reason, companies have to take an initiative to get tools/data lakes that provide full exposure even in the fragmented environment(Almomani et al., 2025).

A further consideration is the issue of processing time as real-time security systems identify and respond to threats in a matter of few milliseconds. If governance processes were to be introduced in such working scenarios care would have to be taken not to affect the system permanently. For instance, limiting processing or changing data flows when responding to a request can lead to negative effects on the stability and effectiveness of the system. Besides that, distributed environments may pose problems related to jurisdiction and data residency. Data processed on the edge may come under the jurisdiction of the local laws that may be different from those related to the central system. Hence, organizations would be required to put location-aware governance procedures that are capable of adjusting to the different legal requirements. All in all, the growing complexity of security architectures calls for concomitant transformation of governance approaches in terms of scalability, flexibility, and integration(Al-Momani et al., 2025).

9.2 Privacy-Enhancing Technologies and Their Role in Governance

Privacy-enhancing technologies (PETs) are becoming widely recognized as integral to the future of data subject rights governance, especially within security operations. Such technologies are mainly differential privacy, homomorphic encryption, secure multi-party computation, and federated learning which however are enabling institutions to perform data processing and data analytics while substantially reducing the risk of exposing personal data.

First, they greatly assist with data minimization as organizations can operate with aggregated data without the need for directly accessing the personal data. Such indirect mode of operation not only decreases the risk of infringing on personal privacy but also supports maintaining adherence to the data protection laws. Second, PETs provide an extra layer of security besides protecting data against unauthorized access both internally and externally(Ghazal, 2025b).

In some instances, the use of PETs might help in diminishing the complexities of request handling. De-identified data, or data that has been processed using differential privacy techniques, is not subject to some data subject rights, which eases the work of organizations. Similarly, federated learning allows training of AI models without sending personally identifiable data to the central server thereby reducing the number of data subject rights requests(Al-Dmour et al., 2025).

Nevertheless, there are difficulties with the deployment of PETs as these technologies tend to be highly complex and require large amounts of resources. In addition to the personnel and equipment cost, proper and efficient use of these tools is highly dependent on getting the configuration right and also on an effective integration with existing systems. Hence, organizations need to do a thorough cost versus benefit analysis and implementation planning of PETs consistent alignments with the goals of governance apart from compliance.

REFERENCES

Abashes, G. M., Elshqeirat, B., Abu-Shareha, A. A., & Alshraideh, M. (2025). BEYOND THE NOISE: UNVEILING MEANINGFUL PATTERNS IN MOBILE PAYMENT DATA USING FUZZY LOGIC AND SVM. *Journal of Theoretical and Applied Information Technology*, *103*(1).

Abdeljaber, O., & Al-Masaeed, S. (2025). Al-Mu′ani, L., Yaseen, H., & Alhnaity, B. (2025). Strategic Intelligence: The Power of AI in Planning Efficiency. *Human Behavior and Emerging Technologies*, (1). Advance online publication. DOI: 10.1155/hbe2/5383054

Abualghanam, O., Alazzam, H., Qatawneh, M., Alazab, M., & Al Sharaiah, M. (2025). Elevating Mobile Security: An Ensemble Approach for Enhanced Malware Detection with M-iForest. *International Journal of Interactive Mobile Technologies*, *19*(10), 129–151. Advance online publication. DOI: 10.3991/ijim.v19i10.51319

Abualhaj, M. M., Abu-Shareha, A. A., Al-Khatib, S. N., Alsaaidah, A. M., & Anbar, M. (2025). Improving firewall performance using hybrid of optimization algorithms and decision trees classifier. *IAES International Journal of Artificial Intelligence*, *14*(4), 2839. Advance online publication. DOI: 10.11591/ijai.v14.i4.pp2839-2848

Abualhaj, M. M., Abu-Shareha, A. A., & Rateb, R. (2025). Enhancing intrusion detection systems with hybrid HHO-WOA optimization and gradient boosting machine classifier. *International Journal of Reconfigurable and Embedded Systems*, *14*(2), 518. Advance online publication. DOI: 10.11591/ijres.v14.i2.pp518-526

Abualhaj, M. M., Al-Khatib, S. N., Al-Zyoud, M., Qaddara, I., Hiari, M. O., & Aldossary, S. M. A. (2025). Enhanced Network Communication Security Through Hybrid Dragonfly-Bat Feature Selection for Intrusion Detection. *The Journal of Communication*, *20*(5). Advance online publication. DOI: 10.12720/jcm.20.5.607-618

Abualigah, L., Almomani, M. H., Alomari, S. A., Zitar, R. A., Migdady, H., Saleem, K., Snasel, V., Smerat, A., & Ezugwu, A. E. (2025). Optimizing Intrusion Detection in Wireless Sensor Networks via the Improved Chameleon Swarm Algorithm for Feature Selection. *IET Communications*, *19*(1), e70029. Advance online publication. DOI: 10.1049/cmu2.70029

Abualigah, L., Alomari, S. A., Almomani, M. H., Zitar, R. A., Migdady, H., Saleem, K., Smerat, A., Snasel, V., & Ezugwu, A. E. (2025). An enhanced Walrus Optimizer with opposition-based learning and mutation strategy for data clustering. *Array (New York, N.Y.)*, *26*, 100409. Advance online publication. DOI: 10.1016/j.array.2025.100409

Abuowaida, S., Abu Owida, H., Shelash Mohammad, S. I., Alshdaifat, N., Abu Elsoud, E., Alazaidah, R., Vasudevan, A., & Alshurideh, M. T. (2025). Evidence Detection in Cloud Forensics: Classifying Cyber-Attacks in IaaS Environments using machine learning. *Data and Metadata*, *4*, 699. Advance online publication. DOI: 10.56294/dm2025699

Ahmed, Z. E., Hasan, M. K., Hashim, A. A., Saeed, R. A., Mokhtar, R. A., Singh, S. P., & Ghazal, T. M. (2022). Optimization Procedure for Intelligent Internet of Things Applications. *2022 International Conference on Business Analytics for Technology and Security, ICBATS 2022*. DOI: 10.1109/ICBATS54253.2022.9759065

Al-Daoud, K. I., Yogeesh, N., Mohammad, S. I., Raja, N., Chetana, R., William, P., Vasudevan, A., Alshdaifa, N., & Hunitie, M. F. A. (2025). Explainability in AI Using Fuzzy Inference Systems For the Regression Problem. *Applied Mathematics & Information Sciences*, *19*(5), 973–987. Advance online publication. DOI: 10.18576/amis/190501

Al-Dmour, R., Al-Dmour, H., Al-Dmour, A., Basheer Amin, E., & Al-Dmour, Y. (2025). *AI and big data-driven social media recruitment: the mediating role of talent acquisition and employee engagement in bank performance*. Digital Transformation and Society., DOI: 10.1108/DTS-02-2025-0042

Al-Habashneh, A. G., Al-Daoud, K. I., Oraini, B., Al, , & Shelash, S. I. (2025). The impact of artificial intelligence on the development of electronic financial services. *International Journal of Data and Network Science*, *9*(2), 317–322. Advance online publication. DOI: 10.5267/j.ijdns.2024.8.012

Al Hindi, G., Alshraideh, M., Hussein, A. H., Eliyan, L. F., & Al-Dhaqm, A. (2025). Hacking Back: Using Genetic Algorithms to Outsmart Hackers. *Journal of Computational Science*, *21*(9), 2049–2064. Advance online publication. DOI: 10.3844/jcssp.2025.2049.2064

Al-Momani, M. M., Alqudah, T. A., Al Swiety, I. A., Mahrakani, N., Nassoura, M. B. A., & Al Attar, M. K. (2025). Integrating Artificial Intelligence (AI) and Business Intelligence (BI): A Framework for Improving Enterprise Performance. *TEM Journal, 14*(3). https://doi.org/DOI: 10.18421/TEM143-26

Al-Mousa, M., Amer, W., Abualhaj, M., Albilasi, S., Nasir, O., & Samara, G. (2025). Agile Proactive Cybercrime Evidence Analysis Model for Digital Forensics. *The International Arab Journal of Information Technology*, *22*(3). Advance online publication. DOI: 10.34028/iajit/22/3/15

Al Nasar, M. R., Ghazal, T. M., Al-Tarawni, M. A. M., Ahmed, A. A., Abu-Shareha, A. A., & Ahmed, S. M. (2025). Hierarchical Edge-Cloud Collaborative AI Algorithm for Energy-Efficient lot Management in Ubiquitous Computing Environments. *Journal of Wireless Mobile Networks, Ubiquitous Computing and Dependable Applications*, *16*(3). Advance online publication. DOI: 10.58346/JOWUA.2025.I3.035

Al-Okbi, N. K., Alomari, S. A., Hadi, W. J., Ajrash, A. S., Smerat, A., & Abualigah, L. (2025). Defending Digital Integrity: Advances in Media Forgery Analysis Research and Cybersecurity Development. *SN Computer Science*, *6*(8), 913. Advance online publication. DOI: 10.1007/s42979-025-04462-8

Alabdallat, R., Abualhaj, M., & Abu-Shareha, A. (2025). Android Malware Detection Using a Modified Dwarf Mongoose Algorithm. *International Journal of Intelligent Engineering and Systems*, *18*(8), 336–351. Advance online publication. DOI: 10.22266/ijies2025.0930.21

Alabdallat, R. D., Abualhaj, M. M., & Abu-Shareha, A. (2025). Enhanced Multiclass Android Malware Detection Using a Modified Dwarf Mongoose Algorithm. *International Journal of Analysis and Applications*, *23*, 248. Advance online publication. DOI: 10.28924/2291-8639-23-2025-248

Aldaaja, Y., Odeh, M., Badrakhan, S. S., Sabri, M., Abdelrahim, Y., Samara, G., & Alsabatin, H. (2025). Quantifying the Managerial and Practical Benefits of Cloud Computing on Information Security in Higher Education Institutions. *Applied Mathematics & Information Sciences*, *19*(1), 15–24. Advance online publication. DOI: 10.18576/amis/190102

Aldabbas, A., Baniata, L. H., Alsaaidah, B. A., Mustafa, Z., Alali, M., & Rateb, R. (2025). Artificial intelligence-driven method for the discovery and prevention of distributed denial of service attacks. *IAES International Journal of Artificial Intelligence*, *14*(1), 614. Advance online publication. DOI: 10.11591/ijai.v14.i1.pp614-628

Almomani, O., Arabiat, A., Al Tayeb, M., Almaiah, M. A., Obeidat, M., Aldhyani, T. H. H., Shehab, R., & Rowad, M. (2025). A Robust Model for Android Malware Detection via ML and DL classifiers. *Mesopotamian Journal of Big Data*, *2025*. Advance online publication. DOI: 10.58496/MJBD/2025/017

Alnawayseh, S. E. A., Al-Sit, W. T., & Ghazal, T. M. (2022). Smart Congestion Control in 5G/6G Networks Using Hybrid Deep Learning Techniques. *Complexity*, *2022*(1), 1781952. Advance online publication. DOI: 10.1155/2022/1781952

Alnsour, Y., Alsharo, M., Al-Essa, M., & Smerat, A. (2025). AI-Powered Election Insights: Predicting the 2024 Trump vs. Kamala Election Showdown with Machine Learning. *Journal of Intelligent Systems and Internet of Things*, *15*(1), 185–197. Advance online publication. DOI: 10.54216/JISIoT.150116

Alraba'nah, Y., Al-Sharaeh, S., & Al Hindi, G. (2025). Enhancing Intrusion Detection Using Hybrid Long Short-Term Memory and XGBoost. *Journal of Soft Computing and Data Mining*, *6*(1). Advance online publication. DOI: 10.30880/jscdm.2025.06.01.016

Arabiat, A. M., & Eljaafreh, Y. G. (2025). Intrusion Detection in Wireless Sensor Networks Using ML Based Classification of Denial of Service (DoS) Attacks. *The Journal of Communication*, *20*(4). Advance online publication. DOI: 10.12720/jcm.20.4.501-514

Babaker, S., Khatibi, A., Alsoud, A. R., Kaur, J., Jagtap, J., Alkhayyat, A., & Shah, S. K. (2025). Improving Reliability and Data Management in Internet of Things Based Wireless Sensor Networks. *Internet Technology Letters*, *8*(6), e646. Advance online publication. DOI: 10.1002/itl2.646

Cui, D., Harrison, A., Fendzi-Donfack, E., Dagal, I., Jangir, P., Mahmoud, M. M., Malkani, P., Mbasso, W. F., Tiako, P., & Smerat, A. (2026). Enhancing Short-Term Electricity Forecasting with Advanced Machine Learning Techniques. *Journal of Electrical Engineering & Technology*, *21*(1), 147–187. Advance online publication. DOI: 10.1007/s42835-025-02430-z

Eke, C. I., Al-Shamayleh, A. S., Phiri, M., Maswadi, K., Kwaghtyo, D. K., Mulenga, M., & Iyidobi, C. J. (2025). Machine Learning Based Mobile Big Data Analytics: State-of-the-art Applications, Taxonomy, Challenges and Future Research Directions. *Nigerian Journal of Technological Development*, *22*(4). Advance online publication. DOI: 10.63746/njtd.v22i4.3385

Fauzi, M. A., Alias, U. N., Nya-Ling Tan, C., Wider, W., Mukherjee, S., Al-Adwan, A. S., & Udang, L. N. (2025). The Present and Future Trends of Leadership Styles and Knowledge Hiding Through Science Mapping Analysis. *Journal of Information and Knowledge Management*, *24*(5), 2550040. Advance online publication. DOI: 10.1142/S0219649225500406

Fauzi, M. A., Wider, W., Samed Al-Adwan, A., Sadun, A. S., & Shafi, M. (2025). Wolf in sheep's clothing: An analysis of predatory journals through science mapping. In *Social Science Information* (Vol. 64, Number 2). DOI: 10.1177/05390184251336583

Ghazal, T. M. (2025a). An IoT-Based Active Learning Convolutional Neural Networks Model for Predicting River Water Quality. *Journal of Soft Computing and Data Mining*, *6*(1). Advance online publication. DOI: 10.30880/jscdm.2025.06.01.021

Ghazal, T. M. (2025b). Federated Learning for Intelligent Sensing and Navigation Technologies for 6G Communications. *Journal of Sensors, 2025*(1). DOI: 10.1155/js/3746147

Ghazal, T. M., Abualhaj, M., Ahmed, A. A., Al-Tarawni, M. A. M., & Maghrabi, L. A. (2025). Federated Deep Graph Neural Network Algorithm for Real-Time Intrusion Detection in Heterogeneous IoT Systems. *Journal of Internet Services and Information Security*, *15*(4), 484–497. Advance online publication. DOI: 10.58346/JISIS.2025.I4.035

Ghazal, T. M., Hasan, M. K., Mokhtar, U. A., Safie, N., Alshamayleh, A., & Ahmad, M. (2025). Machine learning-based real-time outage fault detection for distribution networks in smart grid. In *Energy Reports* (Vol. 14). DOI: 10.1016/j.egyr.2025.10.045

Ghazal, T. M., Hasan, M. K., Raju, K. N., Khan, M. A., Alshamayleh, A., Bhatt, M. W., & Ahmad, M. (2025). Data Space Privacy Model with Federated Learning Technique for Securing IoT Communications in Autonomous Marine Vehicles. *Journal of Intelligent & Robotic Systems*, *111*(3), 84. Advance online publication. DOI: 10.1007/s10846-025-02298-1

Ghazal, T. M., Janjua, J. I., Abushiba, W., Ahmad, M., Ihsan, A., & Al-Dmour, N. A. (2024). Cybersecurity Revolution via Large Language Models and Explainable AI. *2024 17th International Conference on Security of Information and Networks, SIN 2024*. DOI: 10.1109/SIN63213.2024.10871324

Haider, Z. A., Ullah, I., Shareha, A. A., Nasimov, R., & Memon, S. A. (2026). Artificial Intelligence (AI)-Enabled Unmanned Aerial Vehicle (UAV) Systems for Optimizing User Connectivity in Sixth-Generation (6G) Ubiquitous Networks. *Computers, Materials & Continua*, *86*(1), 1–16. Advance online publication. DOI: 10.32604/cmc.2025.071042

Hanandeh, A., Alfreijat, S. Y., Qutieshat, R. J., Alsha'ar, H. Y., Kilani, Q. A. L., & Saleem Khasawneh, M. A. (2025). Implementing AI Accuracy, Learning Rate, Inference Time on enhancing Big Data Analysis and Strategic Plan. *Data and Metadata*, *4*, 637. Advance online publication. DOI: 10.56294/dm2025637

Hiari, M., Alraba'nah, Y., & Qaddara, I. (2025). A Deep Learning-Based Intrusion Detection System using Refined LSTM for DoS Attack Detection. *Engineering. Technology and Applied Science Research*, *15*(4), 25627–25633. Advance online publication. DOI: 10.48084/etasr.11499

Hyassat, A. S., Abu Zayed, R. E., Al Khateeb, E. A., Shalaldeh, A., Abdelhamied, M. M., & Qaddara, I. (2025). Unveiling Cyber Threats: An In-Depth Study on Data Mining Techniques for Exploit Attack Detection †. *Engineering Proceedings*, *104*(1), 28. Advance online publication. DOI: 10.3390/engproc2025104028

Ibrahim, A., Ali, W., Al-Dmour, N. A., & Ghazal, T. M. (2024). Revolutionizing Human Assessment: AI-Driven Analysis of SQ, EQ, and IQ. *2nd International Conference on Cyber Resilience, ICCR 2024*. DOI: 10.1109/ICCR61006.2024.10532816

Ibrahim, A., Sekhar, R., Tawfeq, J. F., Salih, S. Q., Shah, P., & Radhi, A. D. (2024). Security and Privacy Protection for Online Electronic Documents Based on Novel Encryption Techniques. *Journal of Intelligent Systems and Internet of Things*, *11*(1), 21–28. Advance online publication. DOI: 10.54216/JISIoT.110103

Iftikhar, A., Mohammad, S. I., Alqudah, M. N., Al-Adwan, A. S., Vasudevan, A., Ali, I., & Farhan, M. (2025). Evaluating Inclusivity and Fairness of AI Recruitment Tools for Hiring People with Disabilities in the United Arab Emirates(UAE). *Data and Metadata*, *4*. Advance online publication. DOI: 10.56294/dm2025487

Jaradat, S., Acharya, N., Shivshankar, S., Alhadidi, T. I., & Elhenawy, M. (2025). AI for Data Quality Auditing: Detecting Mislabeled Work Zone Crashes Using Large Language Models. *Algorithms*, *18*(6), 317. Advance online publication. DOI: 10.3390/a18060317

Khaled Abdullah, S., & Qawasmeh, R. (2025). *Navigating the ethical and legal risks of AI marketing in Jordanian SMEs*. EDPACS., DOI: 10.1080/07366981.2025.2600205

Khan, A. A., Siddiqui, S., Al-Shamayleh, A. S., Akhunzada, A., & Dey, I. (2025). DFROG-MAC: A Dynamic Fragmentation-Based MAC for Prioritised Emergency Data Management in Vehicular Networks. *IET Wireless Sensor Systems*, *15*(1), e70017. Advance online publication. DOI: 10.1049/wss2.70017

Khatibi, A., Babaker, S., Praveen, K. N. R., Chohan, J. S., Jadhav, A., Alsoud, A. R., Ramudu, M. J., & Jeet, R. (2025). Advanced AI-Driven Cybersecurity: Analyzing Emerging Threats and Defensive Strategies. *National Academy Science Letters*. Advance online publication. DOI: 10.1007/s40009-025-01897-8

Lakshmi, A. S., Sigamany, E. S. S., Traisa, R., Kumar, R., Reddy, K. R., Chohan, J. S., & Smerat, A. (2025). Enhancing Code Quality Through Automated Refactoring Using Transformer-Based Language Models. *International Journal of Advanced Computer Science and Applications*, *16*(9). Advance online publication. DOI: 10.14569/IJACSA.2025.0160951

Mahadin, G. A. L., Satvika, S., Kathuria, S., Kaushik, A., & Maranan, R. (2025). DEEP LEARNING FRAMEWORK FOR IDENTIFYING AND HYBRID SYNTHESIZING WIDESPREAD NEWS HEADLINES ON SOCIAL MEDIA. *Proceedings on Engineering Sciences*, *7*(3), 1453–1462. Advance online publication. DOI: 10.24874/PES07.03.007

Mahfuri, M., & Ibrahim, A. (2024). AI-Driven Innovations: Transforming Data Support and Environmental Management for the Future. *2024 International Conference on Decision Aid Sciences and Applications, DASA 2024*. DOI: 10.1109/DASA63652.2024.10836162

Makhadmeh, S. N., Fraihat, S., Awad, M., Sanjalawe, Y., Al-Betar, M. A., & Awadallah, M. A. (2025). A crossover-integrated Marine Predator Algorithm for feature selection in intrusion detection systems within IoT environments. *Internet of Things : Engineering Cyber Physical Human Systems*, *31*, 101536. Advance online publication. DOI: 10.1016/j.iot.2025.101536

Marhoon, H. M., Basil, N., Sabbar, B. M., Qasem, N., & Ma'arif, A. (2025). Safety and Surveillance on Unmanned Aerial Vehicles Control Systems and Optimization Methods: A Systematic Review. *International Journal of Robotics and Control Systems*, *5*(5). Advance online publication. DOI: 10.31763/ijrcs.v5i5.1859

Masadeh, R., Almomani, O., Zaqebah, A., Masadeh, S., Alshqurat, K., Sharieh, A., & Alsharman, N. (2025). Narwhal Optimizer: A Nature-Inspired Optimization Algorithm for Solving Complex Optimization Problems. *Computers, Materials & Continua*, *85*(2), 3709–3737. Advance online publication. DOI: 10.32604/cmc.2025.066797

Masango, N. C., Agushaka, J. O., Amaefule, M. C., Taiwo, O., Zhang, P., Ezugwu, A. E., Saleem, K., Smerat, A., & Abualigah, L. (2025). Secure and efficient cloudlet networks: blockchain integration with agent-based proof of trust mechanism. *Eurasip Journal on Wireless Communications and Networking, 2025*(1). DOI: 10.1186/s13638-025-02439-y

Maz, Y. A., Anbar, M., Manickam, S., Abualhaj, M. M., Almalki, S. A., & Alabsi, B. A. (2025). Transfer Learning-Based Approach with an Ensemble Classifier for Detecting Keylogging Attack on the Internet of Things. *Computers, Materials & Continua*, *85*(3), 5287–5307. Advance online publication. DOI: 10.32604/cmc.2025.068257

Mohammad, S. I., Al-Daoud, K., Al Qraini, B., Khanfar, I. A. A., & Vasudevan, A. (2025). Quantum Error Correction with Surface Code Analysis on Quantum Computing platform. *Applied Mathematics & Information Sciences*, *19*(2), 423–435. Advance online publication. DOI: 10.18576/amis/190216

Otair, M., Qawaqzeh, F. A., Alomari, S. A., Zitar, R. A., Migdady, H., Saleem, K., Smerat, A., Alsoud, A. R., & Abualigah, L. (2025). Enhanced Arithmetic Optimization Algorithm for Intrusion Detection in Wireless Sensor Networks. *International Journal of Communication Systems*, *38*(10), e70122. Advance online publication. DOI: 10.1002/dac.70122

Qaddara, I., & Alraba'nah, Y. (2025). Enhancing Requirements Classification Using Machine Learning Techniques. *SN Computer Science*, *6*(6), 649. Advance online publication. DOI: 10.1007/s42979-025-04158-z

Qaddara, I., Alrabaynah, Y., & Hiari, M. O. (2025). Evaluation of SQL and NoSQL Databases on Parallel Processing. *Engineering. Technology and Applied Science Research*, *15*(4), 24298–24304. Advance online publication. DOI: 10.48084/etasr.10620

Qawasmeh, S., Habboushb, A., Elzaghmouri, B., Kharma, Q., & Albalawneh, D. (2025). Hybrid Convolutional Neural Network-Based Intrusion Detection System for Secure IoT Networks. *Tikrit Journal of Engineering Sciences*, *32*(SP1), 1–11. Advance online publication. DOI: 10.25130/tjes.sp1.2025.2

Ramesh, J. V. N., Nimma, D., Dasari, R., Chaudhari Rane, D., AlGhamdi, A., Rao, K. B. V. B., Haider, S. A., Kuzieva, N., & Jangir, P. (2025). Safe and Reliable Two-Stage Online Offloading Algorithm for Transportation Cyber-Physical Systems. *IEEE Transactions on Intelligent Transportation Systems*, *26*(9), 14313–14322. Advance online publication. DOI: 10.1109/TITS.2025.3539934

Raza, M. A., Karim, A., Alqarni, M., Al-Khasawneh, M. A., Jumani, T. A., Aman, M., & Masud, M. I. (2025). An Intelligent Long Short-Term Memory-Based Machine Learning Model for the Potential Assessment of Global Hydropower Capacity in Sustainable Energy Transition and Security. *Energies*, *18*(13), 3324. Advance online publication. DOI: 10.3390/en18133324

Sardar, R., Anees, T., Al-Shamayleh, A. S., Mehmood, E., Khalil, W., Akhunzada, A., & Shaikh, F. S. (2025). Challenges in detecting security threats in WoT: A systematic literature review. *Artificial Intelligence Review*, *58*(7), 196. Advance online publication. DOI: 10.1007/s10462-025-11176-z

Shah, R. K., Hasan, M. K., Islam, S., Khan, A., Ghazal, T. M., & Khan, A. N. (2022). Detect Phishing Website by Fuzzy Multi-Criteria Decision Making. *2022 1st International Conference on AI in Cybersecurity, ICAIC 2022*. DOI: 10.1109/ICAIC53980.2022.9897036

Shamaylah, N., Ibrahim Mohammad, S., Al Oraini, B., Yaseen Al-Gaafreh, J. M., Mosallam Alqahtani, M., Vasudevan, A., Shlash Mohammad, A. A., & Ahmmad Hunitie, M. F. (2025). Data-Driven Decision-Making for Employee Training and Development in Jordanian Public Institutions. *Data and Metadata*, *4*, 886. Advance online publication. DOI: 10.56294/dm2025886

Shambour, Q., Al-Zyoud, M., & Almomani, O. (2025). Quantum-Inspired Hybrid Metaheuristic Feature Selection with SHAP for Optimized and Explainable Spam Detection. *Symmetry*, *17*(10), 1716. Advance online publication. DOI: 10.3390/sym17101716

Sharma, K. P., Hussain, R., Jaharadak, A. A., Trawnih, A. A., Verma, D., Dasi, S., & Pant, S. (2025). Hybrid Convolutional Neural Network for Robust Attack Detection in Wireless Sensor Networks. *Internet Technology Letters*, *8*(6), e650. Advance online publication. DOI: 10.1002/itl2.650

Shlash Mohammad, A. A., Ibrahim Mohammad, S., Al-Daoud, K. I., Al Oraini, B., Mosallam Alqahtani, M., Vasudevan, A., & Ahmmad Hunitie, M. F. (2025). Riding into the Future: Transforming Jordan's Public Transportation with Predictive Analytics and Real-Time Data. *Data and Metadata*, *4*, 887. Advance online publication. DOI: 10.56294/dm2025887

Tarek, R., Elshenawy, A., Assadwy, M. I., & Madkour, M. A. (2025). Automated Diagnosis of Dental Diseases Using Deep Learning on Radiographic Images. *SN Computer Science*, *6*(6), 751. Advance online publication. DOI: 10.1007/s42979-025-04264-y

Turab, N., Abushattal, A., Al-Nabulsi, J., & Owida, H. A. (2025). Advanced risk assessment using machine learning and sentiment analysis on log data. *IAES International Journal of Artificial Intelligence*, *14*(5), 3897. Advance online publication. DOI: 10.11591/ijai.v14.i5.pp3897-3905

Ullah, N., Al-Rahmi, W. M., Alblehai, F., Fernando, Y., Alharbi, Z. H., Zhanbayev, R., Al-Adwan, A. S., & Habes, M. (2025). Corrigendum to "Blockchain-powered grids: Paving the way for a sustainable and efficient future" [Heliyon Volume 10, Issue 10, May 2024, Article e31592] (Heliyon (2024) 10(10), (S2405844024076230), ()). In *Heliyon* (Vol. 11, Number 13). https://doi.org/DOI: 10.1016/j.heliyon.2024.e31592

Vasudevan, A., Tamilmani, K. T., Mohammad, S. I., Sridheepika, V. S., Raja, N., Soon, E. E. H., Nagaraj, S., & Al-Adwan, A. S. (2025). Voices of Concern: Contemplations on Socioeconomic, Ethical, and Developmental Impacts of AI. *Applied Mathematics & Information Sciences*, *19*(1), 221–232. Advance online publication. DOI: 10.18576/amis/190119

Yaseen, M., Ali, E., Sarwar, N., Jamel, L., Din, I., Yuldashev, F., & Law, F. (2025). Design of Minimal Spanning Tree and Analytic Hierarchical Process (SAHP) Based Hybrid Technique for Software Requirements Prioritization. *IET Software, 2025*(1). DOI: 10.1049/sfw2/8819735

Chapter 3
The Role of Notice, Transparency, and Consent in Security Monitoring

Omar Alhyari
http://orcid.org/0000-0002-4046-6564
The British University Dubai, Dubai, UAE

Darin Shafek Mhalla
http://orcid.org/0009-0000-7346-3530
Al-Ma'moon University, Iraq

ABSTRACT

This chapter discusses the importance of notice, transparency and consent for security monitoring systems. It is very important for security monitoring systems to give notice, be transparent and obtain consent as these show that if users are informed clearly about the monitoring, they will get aware, their expectations will be set, and they will trust organizational environments. In fact, the chapter draws attention to the fact that legally, notice and transparency means informing the purposes, nature of data, retention times, and automated decision-making procedures. Besides this, it sees consent as one of the legal grounds but points out its limitation in case of employee and business scenarios where power imbalance exists and might invalidate it. The chapter, by linking legal requirements with security practice, illustrates that an effective notice and transparency framework may result in reduced compliance risks, ethical monitoring, and allowing organizations to strike the right balance between security and individual rights.

1. INTRODUCTION

Security monitoring has evolved significantly over the past decades mainly due to the fact that organizations increasingly depend on their digital infrastructures not only for executing their operations, and dealing with data but also for maintaining their communication . In the early days of computing, organizational security monitoring was rather simple and limited to very few activities. Mostly, it was done by system logging while checking server events was done manually only sometimes(Hanandeh et al., 2025). These old systems were largely intended to catch technical problems and very rarely to iden-

DOI: 10.4018/979-8-2600-2870-4.ch003

tify malicious activities. At the same time, with computer diffusion and the growing role of IS, it was clear that unauthorized access, data theft and leak of insider information could result in heavy economic losses as well as loss of data integrity. Security monitoring hence, has changed slowly from reactive tools aimed at problem fixing to proactive security systems. With the development of the Internet and corporate networking to businesses in the late 1990s and early 2000s, companies usually used to bring in advanced monitoring devices such as intrusion detection systems, firewall monitoring, and network traffic analysis platforms. Security teams were made able by such types of tools to fire on the patterns of networks whereas, communication and changing of network activities were their primary areas of concern. To date, our monitoring capabilities have been extended greatly through the use of automated analytics, centralized log management systems, and large-scale security information and event management platforms(Al-Suhimat et al., 2024).

Thanks to these innovative technologies, companies are not only able to gather massive amounts of security-related data, but also data that is originated from various and even distant sources of their entire digital environment. Nowadays the role of security monitoring is more than just a totally isolated IT function, it is a fundamental part of the overall operation. For instance, a business can be continuously monitoring cloud platforms, endpoints, internal networks, and user activities altogether for early warning of potential cyber threats that are yet to occur. Usually, this sort of supervision leads to the accumulation of extensive operational data like system logs, authentication attempts, behavioral activity patterns, and network communications. This is because monitoring should be capable of identifying violations and irregularities, preventing unauthorized access, and ensuring the confidentiality, integrity, and availability of information assets(Mohammad et al., 2025). That is, monitoring technology's advancement has resulted in the combination of cyber-security operations and gathering of personal/individual behavioral data. It appears that security monitoring tools can track the behavior and other aspects of employees, customers, or other users of organizational systems. Therefore, the scope of security monitoring has been broadening to cover not only technical risk management but also protection of personal data. This means that, on the one hand, organizations are securing their systems and safekeeping the privacy of individuals whose data might be used in monitoring activities, on the other hand, this point to a greater role for transparency, accountability, and legal compliance in contemporary security monitoring practices(Cui et al., 2026).

1.1 Expansion of Data Collection in Digital Environments

Since the digital era is taking over the world, organizations have been entering a flood of data to their security monitoring. Information systems are constantly generating great amounts of operational data by recording system activities, users, and automated functioning. Almost every time a user logs in, downloads a file, changes a system, or a network connection, it leaves a digital footprint that can be detected and stored by monitoring tools(Masango et al., 2025). This continuous creation of data has essentially paved the way for a colossal, minutely detailed record of events within organizational environments. The evolving and complex nature of the digital infrastructure is one of the primary reasons for the accumulation of such large amounts of data. Very many organizations operate their distributed systems at different locations, cloud computing, and mobile devices, etc. Such complex systems require security personnel to implement monitoring solutions that open the way for telemetry data acquisition from various sources in order to have the coverage of the entire infrastructure. The monitoring data sources could be servers, applications, endpoints, databases, identity management systems, and networks. All these different parts generate logs and event records that make up the monitoring dataset as a . Indeed, artificial intelligence and machine learning have intensified the data collection for security operations. Most of the security analytic models these days aim to detect abnormal behaviors by analyzing patterns over time. These models require large amounts of historical and current data in order to do so. Hence, organizations do extensive monitoring of the system usage, login behaviors, application access histories, and network traffic flows in order to provide machine learning algorithms with data that can be used to identify even the most subtle signs of compromise that might not be detected by the traditional rule-based monitoring methods(Al-Okbi, Alomari, Hadi, et al., 2025). Another factor which has led to an increase in monitoring data is the use of cloud-based services and remote work environments. As many applications and data storage have been migrated to cloud platforms, security monitoring must not only focus on the on-premise infrastructures anymore. Monitoring solutions gather data from cloud services, virtual machines, container environments, and software-as-a-service platforms.

Moreover, remote work technologies have brought about the need to monitor user activities not only on home networks and mobile devices but also on virtual private network connections(Sharma, Hussain, et al., 2025). This extension of data collection although significantly increases the organizations' capability for cyber threat detection, it inevitably raises numerous questions about the boundaries of acceptable surveillance. Most of the data collected for security purposes can indirectly reveal such things as a person's behavior, work patterns, communication habits, and location, etc. In certain cases, it can even show how employees use internal applications or how customers access online . Indeed, the security monitoring today is not just a technical function but also quite a process involving large-scale processing of personal or potentially identifiable information. The data collection in monitoring is growing rapidly. Organizations need to think through how they collect, store, analyze, and share such data carefully(Ghazal, Abu-Shareha, et al., 2025). Operating data governance successfully means that monitoring does not go beyond the right security purposes and that the collection of data which is not necessary is either avoided or kept to a minimum. As a result, the situation becomes more and more complicated, and there is a greater call for well-established legal rules and transparent organizational policies that will direct the use of monitoring technologies so that they protect both the organization's security and individual people's privacy rights(Ghazal, Abualhaj, et al., 2025).

1.2 Emerging Privacy Concerns in Continuous Monitoring

Continuous security monitoring has become common in the security community. However, many people have concerns about privacy, especially their personal autonomy, when they hear about it. Continuous monitoring generally means collecting data about system activities and analyzing it all the time rather than doing it only occasionally via audits or manual inspections. This approach certainly helps organizations to detect and respond to threats faster; however, it also entails the ongoing observation of people's digital behavior, i.e., watching them all the time. Such continuous surveillance or, as people may view it, monitoring, inevitably brings about worries towards privacy violation or possible abuse of the collected data(Al Hindi et al., 2025). Collecting personal data beyond what is minimally required for security reasons is the main privacy concern with continuous monitoring. Needless to say, security logs run from storing usernames, IP addresses, email metadata, browsing history within corporate systems, records of file access or communications, etc. After coupling and analyzing them, these data points can be used to create highly detailed behavioral profiles of users of organizational systems. Such profiling may be a very effective technique for uncovering suspicious activity; nevertheless, it also raises the question of whether or not it is acceptable for organizations to monitor the digital lives of their employees or users to such a level(Turab et al., 2025).

Lack of transparency about monitoring operations is another major problem. Most people usually do not realize to what extent their activities are being monitored when they are digitally engaged. For example, employees may use work computers assuming only security-related monitoring might be done. However, it is common for monitoring tools to record patterns of system usage that can be easily and widely interpreted, e.g., worker evaluation, productivity assessment, etc. Whenexplanations about monitoring are poorly done, people often perceive that their privacy has been violated without a good reason. In fact, continuous monitoring might give rise to problems of personal data retention and secondary use. Security monitoring systems quite often keep huge amounts of log data for long periods of time in order to support forensic investigations and allow for detailed analytics. At some point, these logs might contain very sensitive personal information. Ifadequate safeguards are not in place, the data could be accessed by unauthorized people or it might be used for different, even completely unaligned, purposes(A. Arabiat et al., 2025). What's more, using data analytics and artificial intelligence on monitoring platforms creates a number of new privacy issues. For example, machine learning models learn people's behavior to predict abnormalities or situations that indicate employee disgruntlement or unauthorized use of accounts. However, these features not only help to significantly improve security detection accuracy, but also allow the automated profiling of individuals based solely on their digital footprints. The use of automated decision-making further leads to problems such as fairness, transparency, accountability, as well as mistakes or biased interpretations. These privacy concerns strongly suggest that data protection cannot be just an afterthought in the design of monitoring systems; it must be at the very core. Determining legitimacy requires, besides relying on technical controls, the setting up of clear policies and legal frameworks regulating the collection and use of monitoring data. With these tools, organizations can likely find a middle ground in monitoring activities while keeping in mind the principles of proportionality, justification, and (Q. Shambour et al., 2025).

1.3 Importance of Legal Safeguards in Security Analytics

With security monitoring systems becoming highly sophisticated still, a legal protective mechanism is a very mainstay component of the system since they assure that the rights of the persons are first and foremost safeguarded and then also the effectiveness of the cybersecurity operations is at a good level is the case on that other hand. Legal frameworks are the businesses' guidelines as to the times and methods they can legally collect, process and analyze the personal data of the concerned . Firstly, these frameworks are designed to protect people from excessive surveillance while at the same time giving companies the opportunity to secure their digital environments. Openness is a major component of many data privacy . This means that thorough information should be provided by companies regarding the data being collected, their processing purposes, and the rights of data subjects. In terms of security monitoring, companies may be required to give very clear explanations of how monitoring technologies work and which types of data are processed(Hakami et al., 2025). This will allow individuals to know and understand what level, type, and scope of monitoring goes on in the digital environment. Permission is another legal instrument that maybe required to control monitoring activities at times. For some monitoring activities, organizations may rely on consent as a legal ground for processing data. But it must be mentioned that it is difficult to get a truly meaningful consent especially in a workplace where one may feel that giving permission is a condition for employment. Many laws require that consent should be given voluntarily, it should be specific, informed, and one should have the right to withdraw it at any time(Hakami et al., 2025).

Therefore, organizations ought to reassess the question of whether consent is the right legal ground for their monitoring activities or not and take the decision on the basis of that. Legal safeguards also deal with two other important issues in monitoring - proportionality and use limitation. Proportionality is about ensuring that surveillance measures correspond to the security requirements deemed reasonable. As an example, if an investigation is being carried out on a security breach, it might be reasonable to request the collection of detailed behavioral data of users; on the other hand, regular monitoring without any clear security threat should not be accompanied by such a level of data collection. Purpose limitation means that if data are collected for security reasons, they should not be used for other purposes, e.g., for staff evaluation, without the right legal permission. Another point is that legal requirements call for the firm to take various measures to safeguard monitoring data against unauthorized access or misuse. These measures include encrypting data, restricting the access to data, keeping audit logs, and having very stringent rules for the storage of data(Ghazal, Hasan, et al., 2025). Carrying out such measures will give the firms a better chance of keeping the sensitive monitoring data under wraps and preventing any improper use of it. In conclusion, legal protections play a very key role in the sensitive work of balancing security and privacy in the digital environment. As surveillance mechanisms become more sophisticated and efficient, the principles of notice, transparency, and consent will likely become the main factors influencing how organizations manage and deploy their security analytics systems. These fundamental principles are the cornerstone upon which reliable surveillance setups can be created that not only ensure a higher level of cybersecurity but also safeguard the rights of individuals who use today's digital (Samanta et al., 2025). This chapter's main contribution is the development of a Privacy Expectation Index for evaluating how users perceive enterprise security monitoring. The index connects privacy acceptance with organizational trust, transparency awareness, perceived monitoring intensity, and cyber-risk perception. Empirically, the chapter uses survey-based privacy perception data to examine how trust, transparency, monitoring intensity, perceived cyber risk, and consent expectations influence user acceptance of enterprise security monitoring.

2. CONCEPTUAL FOUNDATIONS OF NOTICE, TRANSPARENCY, AND CONSENT

Theemployment of novel cutting-edge cybersecurity instruments–for instance, behavioral analytics, automated threat recognizers, and AI security analytics–has significantly widened the scope of what monitoring systems can manage, particularly with regard to processing personal or even identifiable . Hence, the law has indicated a set of criteria (principles) one could say constitute the two sides of a coin: protecting one's right to privacy on the one hand, and fulfilling security needs on the . In fact, these principles are legal 'neighbors' rather than standalone ideas as they are the three pillars of a data-processing governance framework which ensures accountability. Simply put, by providing notice, the data subjects are informed about the monitoring before or during data processing. Transparency takes one step further than notice requiring organizations to reveal how the monitoring system works and how the collected data is utilized. Consent legitimizes the processing of monitoring data where individuals voluntarily grant permission to the processing of their data(Laha et al., 2025). Aligning perfectly, these principles are a conceptual template of responsible monitoring behavior in the furthest extent of digital world scenarios.

Figure 1 shows the conceptual links between notice, transparency, and consent when regulating security monitoring activities. It visualizes each principle's role in achieving broader data protection outcomes such as privacy protection, ensuring accountability, and legal data processing(Qawasmeh et al., 2025).

Figure 1. Security monitoring framework and safeguards

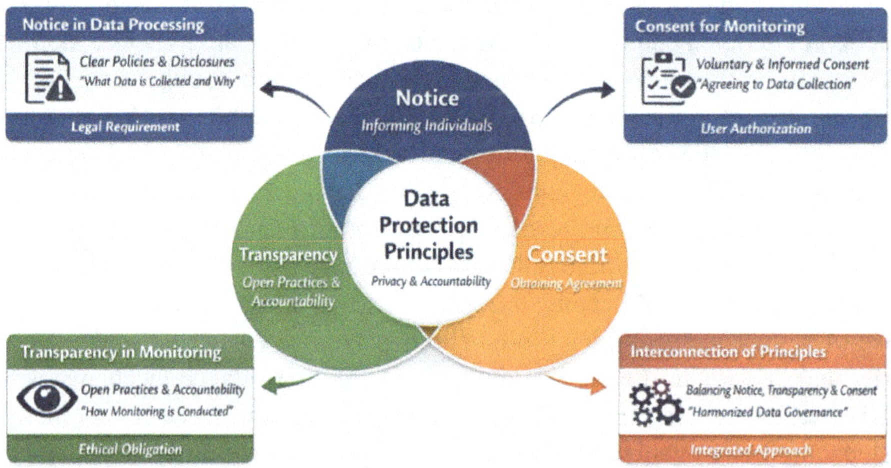

As per the illustration in Figure 1, notice, transparency, and consent are elements of the one governing model of data protection principles. Notice keeps people in the loop with monitoring activities, transparency clarifies the operational aspect of these activities while consent legally allows to process monitoring data. These principles metaphorically hold one side of the triangle together thereby enabling responsible conduct of data governance in security monitoring implementations.

2.1 Legal Meaning of Notice in Data Processing

Notice in the context of data protection law refers to the responsibility of an entity to disclose to a person that his or her personal data might be collected and used. Usually, in the case of security monitoring, notice means let the person tell how the monitoring systems function; what type of data is gathered; and for what motives the data is used. Notice by itself is a prerequisite for legitimate data processing since an individual can hardly exercise his or her data rights if he or she is unaware of being subjected to data collection. Security monitoring solutions, for the most part, generate records automatically using logs, network traffic surveillance, authentication records, and behavior analytics instruments. In the absence of notice mechanisms, people possibly would be unaware that their digital behavior is being kept and scrutinized. Therefore, legislators require entities to offer clear, convenient explanations about the monitoring practices. These clarifications can be presented in one form or another, e.g., privacy policies, employee monitoring notices, website disclosures, system login notifications. Moreover, notice's legal aspect covers more than just informing. The good notice has to give one an insight into the nature and extent of the monitoring activities (Abualhaj, Abu-Shareha, Al-Khatib, et al., 2025).

Usually, it comprises the explanation of data categories that are collected; monitoring intents; data processors; duration of data retention; etc. In lots of legislations, people's rights to data are included in notices i.e., rights to access, rectify, or even renew one's data collection. Additionally, given the fact that monitoring systems in security environments tend to be operational around the clock and concealed to the user, notice is extremely vital. Employees working on corporate systems or users accessing the use of platforms online may not see monitoring in operation, say network intrusion detection systems or behavioral anomaly detection tools(Abualhaj, Abu-Shareha, & Rateb, 2025). Thus, through notice, users are kept in mind that such monitoring systems exist and what is their purpose. Besides that, notice is one of the means through which the law enforces responsibility as it leaves witnesses the communication between the organizations and the individuals about data processing practices. Clear disclosure of monitoring practices results in organizations being able to showcase their compliance to the law and at the same time enables individuals to base their decisions on facts when interacting with monitored systems. In the picture of ever more sophisticated and data-centric digital infrastructures, notice as the first step of legal monitoring is gaining in importance day after day(Ibrahim, Sekhar, et al., 2024).

2.2 Transparency as a Principle of Accountable Security Monitoring

Notice is primarily aimed at informing the individual that a data processing activity is going on. However, the transparency principle requires organizations the additional step of fully and clearly disclosing how the whole monitoring system operates. Transparency means that monitoring is done in a manner that is readily understood, accessible, and accountable not only to those whose data is being processed but also to other stakeholders. Transparency is of particular importance given that many monitoring systems nowadays operate based on automated analytics, machine learning algorithms fed by vast data processing platforms. And yet, these technologies generally do not materialize on the surface as obvious interfaces or points of interaction. Moreover, machine-based analytics of security threats often include studying of a wide range of behaviors of a person or persons over time. Without transparency, it would be in vain for a person to try and understand how monitoring decisions are made or by which means their data contributes to security analytics processes(Vasudevan et al., 2024).

Organizations, thus, accountably engaging in security monitoring must furnish users and other data subjects with detailed explanations of the monitoring mechanisms. Through this information, the organization will not only explain what monitoring methods and technologies it employs but also indicate the reasons for which each of the methods is implemented. The explanation part also covers the measures that the organization has made to avoid any illegal use of the data collected. Internal policies on how monitoring data is handled and retained in security operation centers may also be part of transparent monitoring practices. Very often, transparency is equated with the disclosure of detailed information about the business and processing activities. However, here we refer to the accessibility of information for the individuals(Jaradat et al., 2025). From this perspective, legal and ethical imperatives dictate that transparency shall not be limited to a pile of complex legal text that hardly anyone can interpret. Rather, provisions made by the organization to review its monitoring practices should be written in plain language in order to be understood by an average person. Making transparency easy to comprehend significantly enhances the understanding of how one's personal data interacts with the organizational security systems and by extension trust in the organization(Almomani et al., 2025).

Transparency to a great extent is also a point at which institutional accountability can be strengthened. The regulator, auditor, or any other internal governance mechanism depend heavily on the organization's clear and comprehensive documentation of the monitoring processes to verify compliance with legal and ethical standards. In fact, the ability to provide a crystal-clear account of monitoring operations imparts the observer (independent or internal) with the confidence and assurance of the organization's commitment to the standards of data protection and personal privacy. Therefore, we can see that on one hand, transparency is a legal obligation, on the other hand, it is an ethical commitment of an organization. Transparency reassurance of understanding to individuals how their behavior is being observed and analyzed digitally may serve as a kind of trust reinforcement between organizations and individuals who depend on these digital services(Sharma, Al-Rashed, et al., 2025).

2.3 Consent as a Legal Basis for Processing Monitoring Data

Consent is a very important element in the set of norms regulating data processing for the purposes of security monitoring. In many jurisdictions, the granting of consent by the data subject provides the legitimation for the processing of personal data. The essence of consent is a voluntary and informed decision by the data subject to agree to the processing of his or her data for a specified purpose and scope. Consent is especially important when security operations have monitoring components that are beyond the essential ones or when data includes sensitive personal information. For consent to be recognized as legally binding, it must meet a number of criteria. By way of illustration:

- Consent must be given freely, which means that individuals must have the possibility not to accept monitoring without suffering negative consequences.
- Consent must be informed, i.e., the individual should get the necessary and comprehensible information about the monitoring and data processing.
- Consent must be specific, that is the individual agrees to a particular, well-defined processing activity and not to broad or undefined usages of the data.

Getting valid consent in security monitoring scenario is not easy. For instance, in the workplace, it is more of a 'must' rather than 'allow' to comply with consent requirement. Therefore, many regulations advise not to rely only on consent in such imbalanced power situations. Consent can be one of the bases for processing but it can be supplemented by others, e.g., legitimate interests or compliance with a legal obligation. However, consent still stands as a vital part of the moral ground of monitoring(Amir et al., 2024). When the organization's tracking systems trace behavioral activities, location, or biometric identifiers, explicit consent will offer the individual more control over the use of their personal data. Consent can be also designed with features allowing people to withdraw the permission granted previously at any time. Consent management tools are being increasingly incorporated into online environments supporting aforementioned criteria. These systems allow organizations the storing of consent records, the modification of consent settings, and the submission of evidence of compliance with legal mandates. On one hand, such systems facilitate the observance of rights and autonomy of an individual and, on the other hand, they are a source of valuable information for the organizations about their customers and their behavior pattern(Iskandarani, 2025).

2.4 Interrelationship Between Notice, Transparency, and Consent

People often think that notice, transparency, and consent are isolated principles. However, they are parts of one whole data governance framework acting in concert with one another. Each principle supports another (through notice transparency can be explained better, through transparency one can decide to consent or not) and in combination, they enable responsible monitoring practices that not only consider security requirements and individual privacy rights. Giving notice is the first form of disclosure where individuals are informed about monitoring activities. Without a proper notice, an individual will hardly be able to decide whether consent to that monitoring is something they want to offer or not(Abualhaj, Al-Khatib, Abu-Shareha, Almomani, et al., 2025). Aboveall, transparency thoroughly explains the working of monitoring systems and the purposes for which data is used, especially in the context of security. On the other hand, consent is the way through which an individual gives permission for a particular monitoring process when they have fully understood the information communicated through notice and transparency. The combination of these three principles leads to a governance model that champions accountability and fairness values in digital monitoring contexts(Ghazal, Hasan, et al., 2025).

Actually, organizations that clearly give notice, practice open monitoring, and ask for valid consent if required are more likely to gain the trust of all their stakeholders, including users and employees. When it comes to security monitoring systems where large behavior analytics datasets are used for cyber threat detection, trust is a matter of great importance and difficulty. Each individual element, i.e., notice, transparency, consent, represents the pillars that support the organizations in communicating their monitoring practices, defending their data processing, and most importantly, in safeguarding the rights of individuals. Taking into account the development of technologies in digital monitoring along with system design and governance, the role of principles, however, cannot be underestimated as they are indeed very important. For this reason, organizations need to take a holistic monitoring governance approach that links legal compliance, ethical commitments, and technical solutions. Integrating in notice, transparency, and consent into the security monitoring systems architectural design will go a long way in helping businesses manage their cybersecurity activities in a way that respects the fundamental rights of individuals in this digital (Ghazal, 2025b).

3. SECURITY MONITORING TECHNOLOGIES AND DATA COLLECTION PRACTICES

At present, businesses are immersed in digital environments that are interconnected to such an extent that security breaches could be coming not only from inside users, external hackers, malware, but also from software that has been compromised in some way. For their protection, the organizations make use of security monitoring tools that operate non-stop to watch, track, and evaluate the status of their IT system. Actually, these monitoring tools are the basis of modern cybersecurity processes since they allow organizations to identify potential threats, carry out security breach checks and react to risks by means of the real-time information exchange. Security monitoring systems consist of various technological components that are integrated for collecting and analyzing operational . Most of these platforms employ behavioral analytics, network monitoring tools, log management systems, and AI-based threat detection components(Al-Dmour et al., 2025). These technologies collect various types of data that, when put together, give a full picture of the activities of an organization throughout its entire infrastructure. Although these tools help businesses improve their capabilities for identifying and handling cyber threats effectively, at the same time, they involve the large-scale gathering and processing of digital activities data. Such data may include, for example, network traffic metadata, authentication logs, device identifiers, user behavior patterns, or other types of operational information created by users while interacting with organizational . Therefore, security monitoring infrastructures should be designed in a manner that their data collection practices are limited only to legitimate security purposes while, at the same time, respecting personal privacy rights. Therefore, in this part we consider the technological foundations of current monitoring infrastructures, the types of data collected in these systems, and how these monitoring technologies interact to form a multi-layer security environment capable of identifying threats while supporting organizational accountability and data governance(Hasan et al., 2021).

3.1 Behavioral Analytics and User Activity Monitoring

Behavioral analytics represents one of the greatest breakthroughs in technology that affect cybersecurity monitoring. Security monitoring, traditional, depended mainly on detection methods based on rules (i.e., signatures of threats known) to locate indicators of compromise, such as particular malware signatures or suspicious network connections. As a result, the increased complexity of cyber threats means a shift towards behavioral analytics because attackers have started to use legitimate credentials and authorized access pathways for their purposes without being detected. This technique analyzes user behavior patterns by detecting changes, such as new unauthorized locations where users are logging in, or unusual access of large volumes of data, etc. Therefore, the system is able to detect intrusions even when the attacker is using the correct credentials(Q. Y. Shambour et al., 2025). As a consequence, behavioral analytics systems have shown great effectiveness in the detection of insider threats and compromised accounts. For an attacker, getting hold of legitimate credentials using them is the way to go. With behavioral analytics detection, however, the focus is shifted on activity patterns rather than identity alone, which means that even if an attacker manages to successfully use e.g., stolen credentials, they will be detected due to anomalous behavior. Onthe other hand, behavioral analytics monitoring can also get you into privacy issues if you're not careful. Since the monitoring involves tracking users' activities in great detail, it is essentially the collection of data about employees' habits at work, their usage patterns of systems, and their history of interactions. Therefore, enterprises should have a very clear policy about how they intend to collect, use, and keep such data so that monitoring remains a part of legitimate security and not an act of excessive (Ghazal et al., 2024).

3.2 Network Surveillance and Log Collection Systems

The basis of security monitoring infrastructure are network surveillance technologies and log collection systems which allow organizations to control the traffic and operational events taking place in their digital environments. Recording thorough logs of system behavior that provide data about system activity, monitoring technologies make it possible for security specialists to detect malicious actors who might have remained hidden without being spotted for a time. They give a glimpse into such a situation and a capacity to play back the sequence of events so as to determine how the threat was injected, moved, and kept hidden. As a rule, network monitoring systems deal with analysis of metadata related to network communications. This type of data could, for instance, incorporate information about where the communications are coming from, where the receiving parties are, time stamps of the conversations, durations of connections, and also the types of protocols(Al-Okbi, Alomari, Zitar, et al., 2025). Usually, network monitoring solutions are placed at major points within the company network, for example, at gateways, routers, and firewalls. Therefore, by looking at the traffic flows over these network points, monitoring mechanisms can find patterns/instances of abnormal communications which could be indications of unauthorized access attempts, malware activities or data exfiltration events. But log collection is very different. In fact, it is the gathering of operational data of different digital components within the organization's infrastructure such as servers, applications, operating systems, authentication systems, and security appliances. These systems generate log files containing records of different type of events such as login attempts, changes in software configurations, file accesses, user actions, and system errors. Log aggregation tools gather these log entries (memory records) from the different systems, combine them, and store them in centralized repositories. Moreover, these records constitute the basis for human analysts and/or automated data analytics tools to perform their work(Al-znamat et al., 2025).

Nowadays, security monitoring systems typically use Security Information and Event Management (SIEM) systems to integrate and correlate these varied data streams into one monitoring . SIEM systems draw logs and network telemetry from many sources, then correlate the data streams to uncover patterns indicating security threats. An example of a SIEM platform detecting a potential credential compromise is identifying a series of events where multiple failed login attempts are followed by a successful login from a previously unseen location. After detecting a cyber threat, the ability to replay security events through historical logs is necessary for forensic investigations to determine the point of entry and extent of the compromise. Security teams should get as much information as possible through log analysis covering what and who they are dealing with, what is the actual impact, etc. However, since logs are copious and often kept for some time, identifiers that can point to the individuals using the systems are the ones most deeply examined. Following Table 1 presenting a summary of the major security monitoring technologies along with their data collection functions.

Table 1. Major Security Monitoring Technologies and Their Data Collection Functions

Monitoring Technology	Primary Function	Data Sources	Security Purpose
User Behavior Analytics (UBA)	Analyze patterns of user activity	Login records, file access logs, application usage	Detect insider threats and compromised accounts
Network Intrusion Detection Systems (NIDS)	Monitor network traffic for suspicious patterns	Packet metadata, communication protocols	Detect malware, intrusion attempts, and abnormal traffic
Security Information and Event Management (SIEM)	Aggregate and correlate security events	System logs, application logs, network telemetry	Centralized threat detection and incident investigation
Endpoint Detection and Response (EDR)	Monitor endpoint devices for malicious behavior	Process activity, device logs, system alerts	Detect malware infections and unauthorized system activity
Log Management Platforms	Store and analyze operational logs	Server logs, authentication logs, database logs	Support security monitoring and forensic investigations

The above table highlights how different monitoring technologies target different subsets of operational data, and how their integration creates a comprehensive monitoring environment for detecting both external attacks and internal security threats.

3.3 AI-Based Threat Detection Systems

Conversely, artificial intelligence is rapidly becoming a major factor in the transformation of security monitoring. The data generated for security monitoring is growing exponentially whereas manual analysis will never be able to keep up with nor detect complex cyber threats effectively. It follows that AI-based threat detection employs machine learning methods that enable them to go through huge volumes of data, thereby making it possible for them to find hardly visible signs of malicious activities. Tobuild

AI-powered monitoring systems, the first step is to give machine learning algorithms access to historical data sets that include normal operations as well as scenarios of attacks identified by security . Statistical relationships within monitoring data are learned by these models, allowing them to spot anomalies that violate the behavioral baselines they have been trained on. AI-based systems are not limited to identifying known attacks but also have the capability to understand novel attack strategies by virtue of recognizing unusual combinations of events(Alkhawatrah, 2025).

One of AI's most widely-recognized functions in security monitoring is the use of anomaly detection algorithms. These algorithms sift through copious amounts of monitoring data (e.g., login records, network flows, application events) to single out behaviors that deviate markedly from expected patterns. Monitoring systems may then, as a result of the identification of such anomalies, generate alerts for escalation to security analysts. Furthermore, AI-based monitoring systems can perform simultaneous correlation of data obtained from multiple sources. An AI-driven model can analyze, for instance, networks traffic data, endpoint activity logs, and authentication events in order to uncover patterns of a coordinated attack. Thanks to this multi-domain analysis, threat detection accuracies are significantly improved as multiple indicators are taken into consideration. Nonetheless, utilization of AI-driven monitoring systems poses a number of governance challenges. In most cases, machine learning models operate as black boxes being complex analytical systems. Consequently, making decision processes transparent and accountable is one of the issues that must be addressed in regulatory frameworks covering data processing and monitoring activities(Vasudevan et al., 2025).

3.4 Types of Personal Data Collected in Security Monitoring

Security monitoring systems gather a broad spectrum of operational data that helps them uncover and investigate cyber threats. While digital systems automatically generate most of this data, it can still be linked to real persons who have interacted with the systems. Therefore, knowing the types of data collected in monitoring environments is key to understanding potential privacy violations. Identity information such as usernames, account identifiers, and authentication credentials are frequent sources that monitoring data can reveal. These IDs enable the tracking of the system accesses and verification of whether users are allowed to perform certain operations in virtual environments. Apart from simply recording authentication attempts, logins, times, and access records for spotting unauthorized ones, monitoring instruments also collect other data. Also, device and network IDs are extremely helpful for security teams in locating the source of digital communications. Networking tools may create logs of IP addresses, device IDs, browser fingerprints, and network routing metadata(Alraba'nah et al., 2025). Having these kinds of identifiers enables organizations to identify suspicious connections and, in fact, recognize potential cases of intrusion involving unknown or compromised sources.

Also, security monitoring tools can analyze user behavior to some . For example, they create logs of the type of activities users carry out such as opening files, using certain applications, or issuing system commands. Behavioral analytics use such logs to identify a pattern so that any anomaly can be detected. So, they, in short, keep tracks of steps that users take in a system during their operation - this makes them a valuable source in user profiling and monitoring. Along with these kinds of data, monitoring systems quite often are feature-rich enough to be able to gather system telemetry data which includes performance metrics, process execution logs, and network traffic statistics. It might be that telemetry information does not usually have personally identifying information, but there are cases where such data can be tied to an individual's identity if combined with other monitoring records. The table below

(Table 2) gives an overview of the main types of personal or potentially identifiable data that security monitoring systems deal (Sardar et al., 2025). Different monitoring technologies create different privacy expectations. Metadata logging and SIEM correlation usually present moderate privacy risk, while keystroke logging, endpoint tracking, behavioral profiling, and AI-based risk scoring may be perceived as more intrusive unless supported by transparency, proportionality, and clear purpose limitation.

Table 2. Categories of Personal Data Collected in Security Monitoring Systems

Data Category	Examples of Data Collected	Monitoring Purpose	Potential Privacy Implications
Identity Information	Usernames, account IDs, authentication logs	Verify user access and detect unauthorized login attempts	May reveal individual system access patterns
Network Identifiers	IP addresses, device identifiers, browser fingerprints	Trace network communications and detect malicious traffic	Can identify location or device usage
Behavioral Activity Data	File access logs, application usage history, command execution records	Detect abnormal user behavior and insider threats	May expose work habits or activity patterns
System Telemetry Data	Device performance logs, process activity, network statistics	Monitor system health and detect malware activity	May indirectly link operational activity to users
Security Incident Records	Alerts, threat investigation reports, response actions	Document and investigate security events	May contain sensitive contextual information about individuals

Table 2 clearly illustrates that the primary purpose of security monitoring is to safeguard digital infrastructures. However, as a result, it may also be necessary to process data capable of identifying people. Hence, these circumstances require legal and institutional arrangements ensuring that monitoring is carried out in a manner that is transparent, proportionate and in line with the data protection .

4. REGULATORY FRAMEWORKS GOVERNING TRANSPARENCY AND CONSENT

The emergence of complex and interconnected digital infrastructures globally has led to governments and other regulatory bodies enacting legal frameworks for the control of personal data collection, processing, and monitoring by organizations. These legal frameworks significantly influence the functioning of security monitoring systems especially concerning the principles of transparency, notice, and consent. In fact, most of today's monitoring systems are associated with the processing of personal or identifiable data(Al-Adwan et al., 2025). Thus, regulatory frameworks are primarily concerned with ensuring organizations perform monitoring not only in ways that safeguard individual rights but also without compromising cybersecurity operations. Transparency and consent are two areas of regulatory frameworks that seek to address the balance between two equally important objectives(Hiari et al., 2025). On one hand, organizations should not be able to disengage from monitoring the digital environment for they need to be aware of cyber threats, be able to protect critical infrastructures, and maintain operational security. On the other hand, people should always retain control over the use of their personal data to the extent that they are the ultimate users of such systems. The law finds an equilibrium here by requiring the organization that undertakes monitoring activities to reveal such activities, to make clear their data processing practices, and to ask for authorization when needed. Different countries have created their own separate systems for the regulation of digital monitoring and personal data processing. In general, these frameworks uphold the same principles which are transparency, accountability, proportionality, and respect for individual autonomy even though each framework contains elements distinctive to itself. It becomes essential for organizations that operate complex monitoring systems and especially those that collect data from several different geographical areas or legal jurisdictions to be aware of the requirements imposed by these (Ghazal, Awouda, et al., 2025).

4.1 Transparency Obligations in Global Privacy Regulations

Transparency, in simple terms, means being open and clearly explaining to the people whose data is being handled, that their data is being used. It is one of the main principles of practically all contemporary data protection laws, that is broadly recognized and admitted. Several international privacy laws require that organizations provide in clear and simple language the information on how they collect, process and use personal data through their digital systems. In fact, when it comes to security monitoring, transparency obligations are even more relevant since monitoring tools usually operate behind digital infrastructures without being (Babaker et al., 2025).

A number of renowned legal frameworks require transparency not just as a good practice but as a core statutory obligation. Ordinarily, they mandate that organizations offer individuals with sufficient knowledge about the processing of data. This information often encompasses the purpose of data gathering, the different types of data pieces collected, the legal grounds for processing, the period for which data is stored, and the rights open to individuals in relation to their personal information. Transparency also obliges organizations to inform individuals when monitoring systems involve the use of automated decision-making processes. For instance, platforms using behavioral analytics and AI-based threat detection systems may be engaging in the analysis of user behavior for detecting irregularities in their patterns(R. Alabdallat et al., 2025). Each time these technologies are processing personal data, individuals potentially have the right to learn about how the systems function and what goes into decision-making affecting them.

When it comes to security monitoring, transparency can be implemented in several ways such as publishing privacy policies, making internal monitoring practices available to staff, and system-wide disclosures. It is common for organizations to include transparency in their website privacy policy, employee monitoring policy, user agreement, or login panel where a warning is displayed notifying users that their activity is traceable for the purpose of security surveillance. Furthermore, transparency obligation is not only limited to informing people but it also includes regulatory responsibility. A company must be capable of demonstrating that its monitoring practices are aligned with the law and can substantiate this claim, if necessary, through records and documentation. Doing so makes it possible for the regulators to assess whether a system for monitoring has been developed in sync with the stipulated laws. Inshort, transparency is a key element in enabling and educating the people about whose data is being processed. The rules that lead to disclosure and make the working principles of monitoring systems public are restricting the chance of hidden or excessive surveillance in digital (Aldaaja et al., 2025).

4.2 Consent Requirements for Monitoring Systems

Consent is a necessary condition in privacy laws that identify the circumstances and methods for processing personal data through surveillance systems. Strictly speaking, the consent of the data subject becomes a potent legal basis for processing the data only if the agreement to do so is unmistakably communicated after the individual has been adequately informed about the purpose and extent of the processing. Besides being a matter of free will, consent should also be understood as informed consent: the person must be given very precise information about the nature and extent of the monitoring, including the types of personal data that will be (Khatibi et al., 2025). Also, it must be specific and unambiguous, indicating unequivocal agreement to the clearly identified data processing purposes. When consent is used as a basis of lawfulness for processing in security monitoring settings, it can often lead to a dilemma that is quite challenging from the point of view of applicability. Security monitoring at its very core allows organizations to regularly carry out essential functions regardless of individuals' viewing or agreeing to them. For instance, a network can be monitored for malware or intrusion traces that a user tries to hide without the user rendering explicit consent(Lee et al., 2021).

Given all the above, consent as a basis of lawfulness for processing security monitoring activities will be allowed only when such activities are not essential or when the monitoring practices are being conducted for purposes outside cybersecurity operations. Biometric data, location data, and profiling are examples of types of sensitive information which usually require explicit consent before processing. Likewise, organizations that monitor user activities for purposes other than cybersecurity such as productivity analysis or marketing analytics may also need to obtain consent before processing those data. Consent management hence has turned into a major operation feature of digital systems these days. Organizations that provide platforms for consent management are allowing users to read monitoring policies, grant or withdraw consent, and manage how their data is being processed (Abualhaj, Al-Khatib, Al-Zyoud, Qaddara, et al., 2025).

4.3 Notice Obligations in Organizational Surveillance Policies

Notice refers to the requirement that organizations inform individuals about their monitoring activities before or at the time personal data is collected. With notice, individuals must be informed in advance that their activities may be monitored.

Generally, notice requirements apply across the board to both internal and external user groups of digital systems. Organizations typically have a monitoring policy outlining how security monitoring is implemented. This monitoring policy will normally unveil the types of monitoring tools used, the kinds of data being collected, and the ways the collected data is being used in security operations.

Employees often get informed through the monitoring policy that their workplace resources such as corporate emails, intranets, and machines issued by the company may be monitored to uncover security threats or for compliance with company regulations. This type of notice is very important as without it, employees could have a false expectation of privacy regarding their digital communications and activities (Khatibi et al., 2025).

In a good number of jurisdictions, the practice of giving notice is mandatory before setting up systems that monitor and collect the personal data of users. For example, companies make it a requirement for their employees to accept monitoring policies during employment or system access. Also, online service providers may notify or remind users through a privacy policy, cookie notice, or login page that their security will be enhanced by activity monitoring.

Notice methods serve multiple important functions within regulatory frameworks. Besides making people aware of monitoring, these are the key reasons: the provision of notice serves to firstly highlight the opportunity that people have to change their behavior in light of monitoring and secondly to the valid documentation of the legal disclosures made by the organization (Abualhaj, Al-Khatib, Al-Zyoud, Qaddara, et al., 2025) .

Providing notice alone, however, is not a guarantee that monitoring will be done legally. Very frequently, the details given with the notice are hoped to clarify why monitoring is required and what measures are implemented to ensure the security of the collected data. Taking notice along with transparency and accountability efforts is the formula for building an atmosphere where monitoring is not only in line with an organization's security objectives but also its legal s.

4.4 Cross-Jurisdictional Differences in Legal Requirements

One of the biggest headaches for companies operating on global digital platforms is having to accommodate local privacy regulations in each country. Most countries, in fact, consider privacy as dependent on the same basic principles of transparency, notice, and consent. However, the precise legal constraints on monitoring activities can be very different from one jurisdiction to another. Some countries regulate the collection and use of personal data to such an extent that, for example, the organization's ability to monitor with technologies that can invade the privacy of employees or that limit the autonomy of users, is very tightly controlled. In such cases, the law would, among other things, require the organization to carry out impact assessments, obtain approval from the regulator, or implement other privacy safeguards, such as setting up protections or, in some cases, even discontinuing certain operations before the implementation of specific monitoring technologies. The organization's compliance with both privacy laws and labor laws concerning workplace surveillance may cause a dilemma for them leading to the requirement of a security monitoring practice . Conversely, some other regulatory frameworks provide a more relaxed environment for security monitoring, allowing organizations to exercise their judgment to a greater extent in this regard. However, even in these cases, organizations should not disregard their obligation to transparency and offering at least basic data protection safeguards(Qaddara & Alraba'nah, 2025).

Data processing across borders only adds another layer of difficulty to the issue of compliance with monitoring regulations. Most security monitoring systems rely on infrastructures that are geographically dispersed and therefore the data is collected from different locations. When personal data is a part of a cross-border data transfer, organizations will have to comply with the relevant data protection laws. Consent requirements vary greatly between jurisdictions and pose a challenge to multinational organizations. While in some countries explicit consent is the only acceptable basis for some monitoring activities, in others, security interests are considered sufficient for legal processing of monitoring data. Therefore, globally operating organizations are required to create monitoring policies that suit the most stringent of the regulations in order to remain on the safe side. To better deal with these challenges, many organizations adopt global privacy governance frameworks that, among other benefits, unify monitor policy across all operations. Such frameworks would have transparency disclosures, proper notices, and data protection mechanisms that apply regardless of whether monitoring occurs locally or in a foreign jurisdiction. The adoption of a consistent set of governance procedures enables organizations to successfully handle cross-jurisdictional legal complexities while keeping monitoring capability at a high (Maz et al., 2025).

5. DESIGNING TRANSPARENT SECURITY MONITORING ARCHITECTURES

In the current era, cybersecurity systems heavily depend on sophisticated monitoring systems to identify threats, stop unauthorized accesses and keep the integrity of the systems. Nevertheless, as these monitoring systems gather and dissect a great deal of user data, it is of utmost importance for the companies to understand these systems in such a way that they reflect the principles of transparency, accountability and respect of user freedoms. Therefore, the concept of making monitoring systems more transparent is not just a technical development but also a legal and ethical requirement according to data privacy laws and proper . Transparent security monitoring architectures are those which have components that effectively communicate monitoring operations, illustrate how data is handled, and provide individuals with substantive controls over their disclosures. Opposite to being hidden surveillance tools, monitoring instruments properly designed are transparent at every stage of system development - from the collection and processing of data to reporting and control. This approach to designing transparency is being called transparency-by-design which is an extension of the privacy-by-design leading concept incorporated in privacy regulations (R. D. Alabdallat et al., 2025).

Intentionally designing monitoring systems with embedded transparency procedures, it becomes possible for organizations to get several benefits at the same time. Firstly, they can run the cyber defenses without compromising the privacy of individuals. Secondly, they satisfy legal requirements of personal data processing. Last but not least, transparent security monitoring architectures are good for user trust because they help users, employees, and other stakeholders to be confident in digital environments where they are monitored. Besides that, understanding monitoring and why certain data are collected can make individuals feel easier with these security measures as legitimate rather than intrusive surveillance (Al-Momani et al., 2025).

There are generally four major parts in designing transparent monitoring architecture: implementing transparency-by-design principles, deploying user-facing privacy notifications, establishing organizational accountability mechanisms, and adopting technical approaches that make monitoring explainable.

Figure 2. Designing Transparent Security Monitoring Architectures

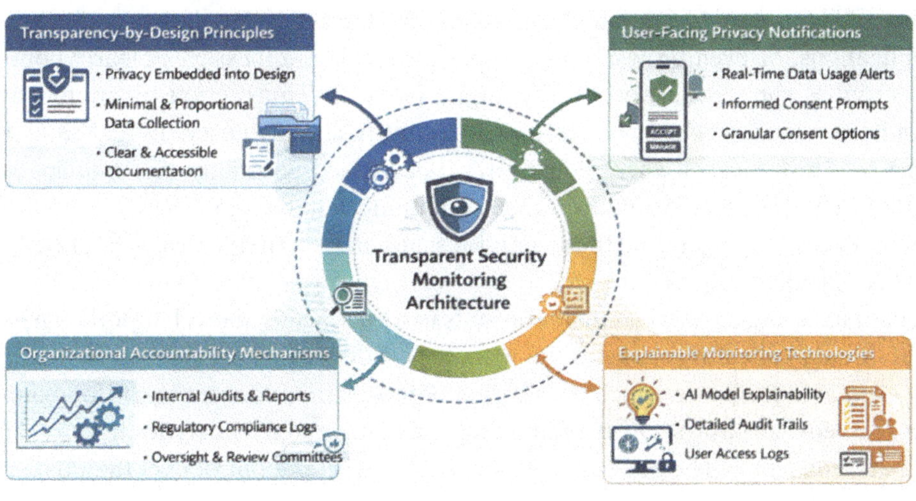

5.1 Transparency-by-Design Principles

Transparency-by-design, as the name implies, is the intentional embedding of transparency and accountability into the development of monitoring tools. Instead of why transparency is only being a sort of add-on feature after monitoring systems are installed, companies incorporate transparency during the design phase. One of the leading transparency-by-design principles is the inclusion of privacy by design. Developing security monitoring architectures involves setting policies around data collection, usage, and retention. These practices should be recorded during system design to ensure monitoring activities continue to conform with laws and company policies. The other key principle is data minimization at the point of monitoring. While surveillance technologies are capable of gathering vast quantities of data to identify threats, transparency-by-the-design advocates for organizations to significantly limit their collection of data to only security-related data. Thisis just the principle of proportionality at work that ensures the most effective defense with the least intrusion on privacy.

Besides, the document also stresses the significance of clear and readily available documentation. It is not merely a matter of making surveillance rules, system outlines, and data handling processes open but doing so in a manner that is clear to both the regulators and the . Through detailed explanatory materials, stakeholders are equipped to understand monitoring and verify its compliance with privacy standards. Besides that, the case for transparency-by-design is the creation of mechanisms that authorized individuals can avail themselves to monitoring records. For instance, one can imagine dashboards or report generating software that provide overviews of monitoring activities, system alerts, and data accesses. Through governance, making monitoring operations visible is a form of rendering. Consequently, it is the elimination of risks, which are due to the existence of clandestine surveillance practices, that .

5.2 User-Facing Privacy Notifications

Communicating the presence of user monitoring can be done through the mechanism of user-facing privacy notifications, which also explain processing within monitoring systems. Such notices are the means to deliver transparency to monitoring at the individual level. Privacy notices are not one-time communications but rather may be seen in various places within digital systems. Most of the time, users are informed about monitoring intentions when they are accessing the corporate networks, using enterprise applications, or even browsing online platforms. These messages clearly communicate the recording of activities such as network usage, login, or system interaction for monitoring purposes. Advanced monitoring infrastructures facilitate issuing notifications to users in real-time. For example, an alert can be sent to the users when their profile is accessed unusually or simultaneously the data processing policy change in monitoring would be communicated to them. Therefore, via live messages, users can be kept in the loop regarding these activities and, in fact, their privacy can be better respected (A. M. Arabiat & Eljaafreh, 2025).

The concept of allowing users to set their consents to a very detailed level after they have first understood the types of data collection is one of the main points of user-facing privacy notifications. In fact, they might be even able to choose which monitoring practices they consent to. If, for example, they are permitted to move between basic security monitoring only and optional analytics tracking at their discretion, after all, data subjects will be given, according to their wishes, control over their data processing. It is equally important that the idea is communicated clearly when creating user-facing notifications. Not only should security and monitoring notices be free of complicated legal jargon but they should also be mainly written in easy language so that users, with English as their second language, can still at least get the gist of confidentiality over surveillance and consent. If persons are capable of understanding what monitoring entails, then transparency is no longer an empty concept but rather it becomes a goal achieved. Integrating user-facing notifications into one's monitoring architectures means that users are not left in the dark about monitoring practices. Instead, the opposite is the case - such practices are fully disclosed. Disclosure builds reciprocally the confidence between organizations and system users, and moreover, it satisfies transparency requirements as per data protection laws (Abualigah et al., 2025).

5.3 Organizational Accountability Mechanisms

Monitoring transparency is certainly a matter of governance and organizations are required to have rigorous accountability mechanisms in place ensuring that monitoring results not only in responsibility but it is done beforehand causing no harm. Organizational accountability mechanisms are the formal methods of oversight of monitoring systems to determine if monitoring real activities were compliant with policies and laws or not. One major mechanism of accountability is the performance of internal audits. Security monitoring produces logs of system access, alerts, and responses that constitute a lot of data. Internal auditing monitors these records to confirm that monitoring has been conducted per policies, laws, and other requirements. Compliance logs showing the data handling of monitoring systems are important that organizations keep. Such logs include information on collection, access, and retention. Obtainingsuch documents not only aid in the compliance with regulators, but even more importantly, it helps in building trust with them (Alenazi et al., 2025).

An additional key accountability factor is the participation of independent oversight committees. Such committees roll up a cybersecurity team member, legal department, data protection officers, and ethics committee members. They perform system monitoring regularly, identify potential privacy issues, and ensure that the systems comply with legal and ethical standards. Accountability also means that companies are writing clear policies about handling users' or other groups' complaints regarding monitoring. Actually, facilitating the public to raise questions or complaints about monitoring or the misuse of monitoring technologies helps to gain their trust and it is one of the ways to ensure that monitoring systems are being continuously evaluated. Through such organizational campus governing instruments, tech surveillance will always be up-to-date and will adjust itself to the changes . As a result, the organizations having accountability mechanisms are the ones that succeed in making their transparency promises not just nominal but implemented and practiced through, indeed, (Makhadmeh et al., 2025).

5.4 Technical Approaches for Explainable Security Monitoring

The emerging trend is monitoring technologies that combine machine learning algorithms and automated threat recognition tools hence the demand for explainable monitoring has grown strongly. Explainable security monitoring systems are the ones that can provide clear justifications for decision making and how security alerts are triggered. AI is transforming the cybersecurity landscape, for instance, the use of behavior analytics, anomaly detection, and automatic response systems which are capable of analyzing complex patterns of large datasets. Even if those AI systems enhance the ability to detect threats, the drawback may be that it becomes a black box as to how they come to their conclusions. The good news is that explainable monitoring technologies are coming to the rescue of the transparency in interpretability issue. By providing reasoning as to the decisions made, explainability allows users and security analysts to grasp the rationale behind alerts issued by monitoring systems. For instance, an anomaly detection system could describe the suspicious behaviors of the users or the network that led to the trigger of a security alert.

Another method to provide explainability in monitoring systems is the provision of extensive audit logs that document the entire sequence of monitoring decisions. These logs enable the identification of the exact moments when particular data inputs were used and alerts were triggered, as well as the execution of testing scenarios and verification of compliance. Recording access activities makes it possible for someone who is second-along the monitoring system's lifecycle to identify who has had access to the data being monitored. Organizations maintaining detailed and transparent access logs can demonstrate that only authorized personnel have used the monitoring data and that sensitive information has been protected from unauthorized access. Such explainability characteristics contribute not only to monitoring transparency but also to making monitoring systems' operation understandable by using visual tools that depict the working of monitoring systems. Visualization platforms and dashboards are excellent tools for illustrating a system's activity patterns, the statistics of threats, coverage of networks, and so on. Visual depictions are helpful to both technical and non-technical stakeholders to comprehend the operation of monitoring infrastructures. By implementing these explainable monitoring infrastructures along with transparency-orientated design and organizational governance, companies aid in digitally securing individual rights in a respectful (Ghazal, 2025a) .

6. CONSENT MECHANISMS IN DIGITAL MONITORING ENVIRONMENTS

Consent mechanisms are at the heart of digital security monitoring processes from a legal and ethical standpoint. -Organizations that rush to deploy behavioral analytics, AI-powered threat detection, or 24x7 log monitoring tools will inevitably gather some type of personal or user-related data. -In our regard, consent is not only a mere governance tool which permits the surveillance activities but also a -way which protects the person's rights. Contemporary privacy regulations insist that consents should be -informed, specific, free, and revocable, particularly when -, monitoring is concerned with profiling the behavior or carrying out intensive user activity tracking. - Consent processes in digital monitoring can take the form of technical interfaces, policy frameworks as well as governance structures. - These consent mechanisms reflect what steps shall be taken to notify the users about the monitoring activities, how -their consent shall be obtained, and in what way such consent can be revoked or changed . The sophisticated nature of digital infrastructures has brought about the development of automated consent management tools and dynamic consent models that enable users to have more control over how their data is processed (Abdeljaber et al., 2025).

Figure 3 shows the use of different types of consent mechanisms in -monitoring environments. It reveals that while explicit consent is still the main way to get -security monitoring authorization in environments with stringent privacy regulations, implied consent is also used in some organizational contexts where the need for security is -recognized.

Figure 3. Consent Mechanisms in Digital Monitoring Environments

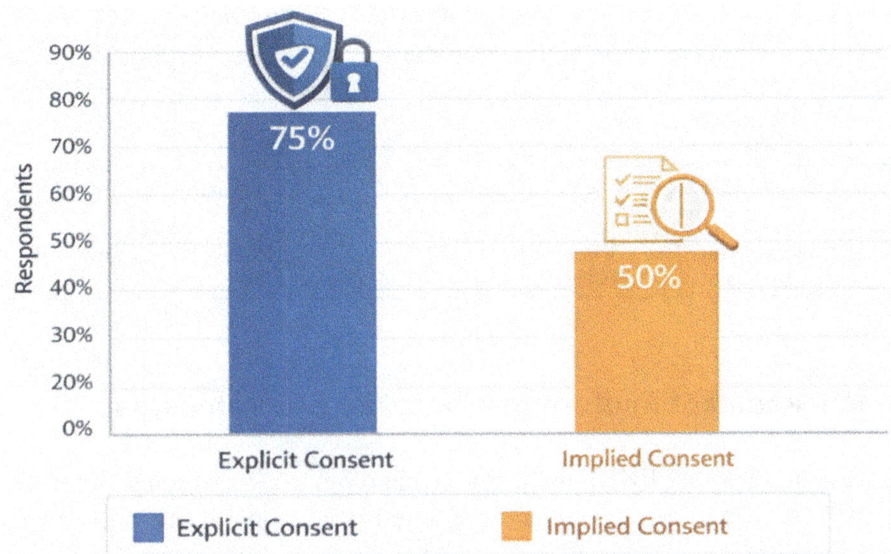

The Figure 3 shows that only about 25% of the businesses use implied consent in their security monitoring operations. However, this is mainly because of workplace monitoring policies, which are part of employment agreements where security monitoring is considered a necessity for the safety of operations.

6.1 Explicit vs Implied Consent in Monitoring Systems

Consent techniques in security monitoring can be divided into explicit consent and implied consent, again each representing a different level of user awareness and authorization. Explicit consent is when a person knowingly agrees to live monitoring via explicit actions, e.g., ticking a consent box, signing a digital agreement, or accepting privacy terms prior to system access or entry. Besides, the explicit consent model is one of the privacy provisions of GDPR, whereby the user receives a written explanation of the monitoring purpose and the processing involved, so that the user can make an informed decision.

On the other hand, implied consent is the consent inferred from the user's continued use of the organization's systems after being informed that monitoring will be conducted. However, implied consent is not satisfactory even if it remains legally binding; it is because of the ethical issues that the user might not have an idea of the extent of the monitoring. From a compliance point of view, explicit consent is the safest option for the organization since it acts as proof of user agreement; implied consent is criticized for its lack of transparency and failure to live up to the principle of informed decision-making, in addition to the fact that it is a questionable practice. It is the introduction and widespread use of digital consent dashboards that have further empowered explicit consent schemes that allow users to change their preferences in the privacy module of security monitoring.

Table 3. Comparison of Explicit and Implied Consent in Security Monitoring

Consent Type	Definition	User Awareness Level	Legal Strength	Typical Application
Explicit Consent	User provides direct approval through clear action	High	Strong	Security monitoring dashboards, authentication systems
Implied Consent	Consent inferred from user behavior or system use	Moderate	Medium	Workplace monitoring policies
Contractual Consent	Consent embedded within service agreements	Moderate	Medium-High	Corporate IT access policies
Layered Consent	Consent provided through multi-step disclosure mechanisms	High	Strong	AI monitoring and behavioral analytics systems

6.2 Consent Management Platforms in Security Environments

The increasing complexity of digital monitoring technologies is a challenge for security and privacy compliance professionals to monitor. In addition to ensuring compliance with privacy regulations, introducing robust consent mechanisms in monitoring environments increases the complexity and cost of surveillance operations. Therefore, to have a centralized platform for managing consent is becoming a priority for most organizations.

Consent Management Platforms (CMPs) are software systems designed to support the -management of consent records and their compliance with privacy regulations. These systems are engineered to collect, record, and -manage consent along its entire lifecycle. CMPs serve multifold in security monitoring operations. Firstly, they act as a community gateway, the first and foremost point of contact where users' consent is sought when they first use digital platforms. Secondly, they function as diligent archivists, meticulously documenting every instance when a user consent was given, changed, or removed. Thirdly, consent-based operations can also work with CMPs as -administrators that allow for the dynamic modification of monitoring upon changes in user -choices and regulatory mandates.

More and more CMPs are becoming part of security systems that -interact with identity management systems, access control frameworks, and threat detection platforms. For instance, permission by the CMP will be a -necessary condition to trigger behavioral analytics in respect of that user whose explicit -consent was recorded.

Next generation CMPs are made to act automatically in the areas of:

- Consent validation making sure the consent is still valid
- Notifying users in real-time about their privacy changes
- Restricting data processing depending on the consent status
- Providing automated audit reports for regulators

Such features greatly enhance the accountability and transparency of monitoring systems -because they make sure that monitoring processes follow the law.

Table 4. Functional Components of Consent Management Platforms in Security Monitoring

CMP Component	Function	Security Monitoring Application
Consent Capture Interface	Collects user agreement for monitoring activities	Login portals, device enrollment screens
Consent Registry	Stores consent records and timestamps	Compliance documentation
Preference Management Tools	Allows users to modify privacy settings	Monitoring scope adjustments
Audit and Compliance Module	Generates reports for regulatory review	Security audits and compliance assessments
Policy Enforcement Engine	Aligns monitoring operations with user consent status	AI threat detection restrictions

6.3 Challenges of Meaningful Consent in Workplace Monitoring

Using consent mechanisms to protect user rights is a well-known practice. However, it is still very difficult to carry out the concept of meaningful consent in work place monitoring. In many cases, employees may be forced to accept consent conditions as a -requirement for them to be able to do the work that they get paid for. Power imbalance is only one side of the question concerning the ethics of whether workplace monitoring consent can be truly voluntary. Getting employees to agree to monitoring policy is simple from a technical standpoint, but assessing whether employees really have a choice to say no is very difficult.

Moreover, the use of complex monitoring technologies and techniques also -makes it hard for users to understand the full picture. Security systems often use machine learning algorithms to analyze user behavior based on data from various sources.

Employees need to be given the tools to understand what the hybrid monitoring looks like, which is one of the reasons why the following tactics should be in place:

- Communicating performance of simple, understandable terms for monitoring
- Giving employees an option to select different levels/types of monitoring
- Providing access to monitoring information/records that the employer has collected
- Use of an external, independent entity overseeing the monitoring activities

Trust is a key element that organizations cannot afford to forget when engaging individuals -both as partners and as discourse objects when it comes to the deployment of security monitoring practices that respect privacy rights.

6.4 Revocation and Dynamic Consent Models

Traditional consent models treat consent as a one-time authorization event that occurs when users first interact with a digital system. On the contrary, such a static approach hardly depicts the nature of digital monitoring which is constantly changing. As monitoring technologies grow and the ways of processing data change with time users should be provided with chances to reflect on their consent choices.

Dynamic consent models meet this issue by giving people the chance of continuously managing their consent preferences along the whole data processing activities. These models use interactive interfaces that give the users the ability of changing or giving up their consent at any time. Withdrawal of consent mechanisms are of vital importance for dynamic consent systems. When a user opts out of consent the monitoring system has to immediately limit or stop the related data processing activities. These tools rely on a close partnership between consent management platforms and security monitoring tools, in order to be provided at all. However, dynamic consent models, apart from the technical side, also lead to additional changes in operations. Security monitoring modules need to be equipped with changing the data processing behavior dynamically capability without generating the disruption of security operations. Achieving this harmony level necessitates very powerful governance frameworks which can bring together privacy controls and monitoring .

7. USER PERCEPTIONS OF TRANSPARENCY AND MONITORING LEGITIMACY

Today, security monitoring technologies are considered a must-have element in the digital environment. Enterprises invest money in deploying monitoring networks for identifying cyberattacks, securing sensitive data, and making sure that the operations remain intact and smoothly running. But, the mere existence of technical functions doesn't dictate the success of the systems. It is also a major factor that users' trust in fairness, transparency, and the need for surveillance being consistent with the accountability of monitoring policies. As a matter of fact, people only accept the system and comply with the security regulations when they perceive the monitoring as justified and its execution as transparent.

The user's side of the story is indeed crucial the determining factor of whether monitoring technologies are seen as protection devices or as restrictive surveillance. Transparency, communication, and ethical governance are key elements affecting such perception. Studies on information security governance reveal that employees are usually supportive of monitoring if the company articulates clearly the reasons for surveillance, what kind of data will be gathered, and the measures for data protection. Besides obtaining the most advanced technology security monitoring settings should also include trust-building initiatives that establish legitimacy and user acceptance. Having policies that are clear, easy to understand, and transparent; accountable governing entities; and a communication channel relating surveillance can greatly enhance the users' acceptability and reduce their resistance to being under the .

7.1 Psychological Impact of Organizational Surveillance

While monitoring systems bring privacy concerns and stress to individuals, they also can be drivers of behavioral change, compliance with rules, and enhanced security. Workplace monitoring is not a new phenomenon. It resulted in what has been termed the "panopticon effect" – a social psychology term used to describe how people frequently change the way they behave when they are consciously aware of the fact that they might be under constant observation by others. Nowadays, with the advancement in monitoring technologies, this behavior also extends to digital monitoring. Employees and users of systems often change their behavior in a way to meet organizational standards even if they know the monitoring system is not continuously interacting with their data. Such behavioral changes, which can in some cases be unconscious, might result in better compliance with security rules but on the other hand can also lead to psychological distress such as anxiety, loss of control and the feeling of being monitored excessively. There is indeed research that supports the view that workers who feel they are being monitored too much or without good reason display less job satisfaction and lower organizational commitment. Incidentally, a lack of privacy may also give rise to further feelings of distrust between the organization and its workforce (Raza et al., 2025).

Motivation and psychological well-being highly depend on trust; hence, trust has to be there first and foremost for the motivation. Ideally, organizations should seek to implement policies that ensure fairness both in the real and perceived sense, through which workers will truly understand that the purpose of monitoring, the level of surveillance and the tools being used are all proportionate to the risk they pose to the organizations. Once again, transparency of monitoring policies has a critical mitigating role here and organizations that openly discuss the reason for monitoring, how data is stored and used and what privacy mechanisms are implemented have the most success not only in alleviating feelings of stress but also in cultivating a sense of justice and fairness in the user community. An equally important element which ultimately has a bearing on the psychological well-being of employees and other users alike is whether the surveillance measures employed are viewed as disproportionate. The individual is always more inclined to offer his or her voice to be heard and express his or her concerns regarding the use of monitoring technologies in no security related capacities such as checking on employee productivity or in other types of behavioral monitoring than he or she is when the monitoring is security related and aims at preventing a breach of the infrastructure (Eke et al., 2025).

7.2 User Trust in Transparent Security Practices

Trust is the most important thing, especially when the topic is about users accepting security monitoring . When individuals place trust in the entity responsible for monitoring, it is unlikely that they will oppose surveillance instruments designed to protect organizational resources and digital assets. Transparency - in fact - is one of the significant ways through which trust is formed. Having transparent practices simply means that a company openly communicates and educates one about its monitoring system objectives, what it entails, and how it is operated. This usually extends to informing the users what kind of data is usually gathered, the way in which the data is normally processed, and the existing protective measures aimed at preventing the misuse of the data.

The disclosure of information through these forms of transparency has been demonstrated by research in cybersecurity governance to generate trust that manifests itself in three ways. Firstly, it provides knowledge to the users since the information is conveyed through explanations and clear descriptions of the practices involved. Secondly, by granting access to such information, it shows accountability and the readiness of companies to share their surveillance activities. Thirdly, transparency is actually users' power as it allows them to be in control of the understanding and evaluation of what is happening with their personal information. A failure to explain why monitoring is being conducted in an opaque manner is likely to lead to the suspicion that surveillance tools might be used for non-security purposes. This is a major obstacle in building trust through the monitoring program and can even result in the program being refused. The use of a surveillance system to monitor employee productivity or to keep track of personal communication, for example, represents a major worry. So, in order to be trusted, an organization must make sure that transparency is the very essence of the security governance framework. This can be achieved by making the monitoring and data collection policies public, regularly informing about security initiatives, and providing privacy dashboards via which a user can not only see their own data but also control it (A. M. Arabiat, 2025).

Operating with transparent governance also means that there are accountability and oversight mechanisms and, more importantly, they are working efficiently. Theactions that are tracked should be consistent with company rules and at the same time, the boundaries of ethical behavior should not be . These objectives can be achieved through various means such as independent review committees, internal auditing, and adherence to regulatory standards. One of the reasons why users regard monitoring as legitimate is when they are convinced that it is controlled and, to some extent, regulated by ethics. Another factor is when users see that control mechanisms function properly and produce fine results in terms of detecting threats, they are more inclined to view the existence of security monitoring in their surroundings as (Abualhaj, Al-Khatib, Al Zyoud, Qaddara, et al., 2025).

7.3 Acceptance of Monitoring in Security-Critical Environments

Monitoring is definitely a double-edged sword - on one hand it helps us to be safer and on the other hand it makes us lose our freedom. If one is always being reminded of the dangers of spying on, the acceptance of surveillance can be very different compared to one who is totally open to the idea of surveillance as a necessary protective measure in a situation of a potential security breach.

Insecurity, acceptance of monitoring in security-critical sectors is usually high well understood of how surveillance activities help protecting sensitive information and securing against cyber . Findingout why monitoring like that is necessary involves establishing trust and may eventually result in acceptance and . In other words, regularly reviewing user activities, monitoring network traffic, spotting behavior that is out of the ordinary can very well be the deciding factor in stopping a malicious hacker or insider threat in his or her tracks and without the knowledge of the attacker. When people realize these types of monitoring could be the tools that prevent disasters, they are not only more open to accept surveillance measures but may even consider them as indispensable (Aldabbas et al., 2025). The added benefit of transparency makes it even easier to attain acceptance since it allows users to connect the dots from surveillance to security benefits and to their role in the overall security of their environment.

Users' support for monitoring also depends on whether the systems are only directed towards the protection of critical infrastructures or whether they are being used extensively for the collection of personal information. For instance, the recording of network traffic for security purposes raises very little privacy concerns among users in contrast to the analyzing of private communications which could certainly lead to a greater degree of intrusion in one's privacy (Abuowaida et al., 2025). Another thing that usually determines acceptance is the existence of guarantees that will ensure the prevention of abuse or misuse of surveillance data. This is a condition that users look for and once it is met, they tend to offer their support to surveillance. Implementation of privacy features like data minimization, restricting access to data, keeping audit logs of data access to prevent unauthorized use, etc., are figuring prominently in this area (Al-Mousa et al., 2025).

To a large extent, acceptance may be influenced by the organization's approach to the introduction of surveillance technology as well as education. Training and information sessions that really communicate to workers the harmful impacts of cybersecurity threats, together with how surveillance can lead to the disruption and elimination of such threats, is a very effective way to not only break resistance but also make surveillance a tool desired by organizations. Moreover, providing users with a voice during the drafting of surveillance regulations through participatory governance will also help to changing the perception and increase the acceptance level of employees toward monitoring. In addition, the interactive nature of such efforts, going back and forth, and pinpointing the locations where worries and the need for security intersect can make it extremely clear to the user how much fairness and legitimacy, they find in surveillance (Ramesh et al., 2025).

8. EMPIRICAL STUDY ON TRANSPARENCY AND CONSENT

The next section is all about a big research study on the different effects that different transparency and consent model have on people's way of thinking, trusting and finally consenting to the surveillance operations based on AI for security monitoring purposes. The research work is based on the Kaggle - User Privacy and Surveillance Perception Dataset and apart from doing the numerical and statistical analysis, it also uses the pictures as theoretical understanding to get the output. Such knowledge leads to the discovery of a more orderly understanding on the part of transparency measures, monitoring types and the extent to which regulation determines the uptake of user acceptance and policy (Abualghanam et al., 2025).

8.1 Dataset Overview and Analytical Methodology

This research paper is based on a publicly available dataset from Kaggle that records people's opinions on surveillance, privacy expectations, and the transparency level of the organization. This dataset consists of survey data from individuals across various organizational and technology-related environments, such as monitoring at work, security of organizational networks, and personal device tracking. Some of the aspects considered are transparency level, trust perception, consent acceptance, monitoring intensity, and perceived privacy risk. Data cleaning involves eliminating unfinished responses and changing categorical variables into well-ordered ordinal scales. Transparency levels were grouped into four categories: Low, Moderate, High, and Very High. Trust levels were indicated as a percentage figure expressing the degree of confidence users have in the organizations' monitoring operations. Consent acceptance was gauged across various monitoring scenarios. Privacy risk was scored by combining the perceptions of intrusiveness, data sensitivity, and control over personal data. The techniques of analysis involve combining descriptive statistical tools, correlation measurements, and regression modeling. For assessing the relationship between transparency and trust, a linear regression model was employed; conversely, a logistic regression model was selected to determine consent acceptance in various monitoring situations.

Besides, a tradeoff model containing multiple dimensions was developed to explore the relationship between the effectiveness of security measures and privacy risk from multiple angles. Regarding the format of the presentation, results were illustrated through the use of well-organized charts and also presented in tables. These findings serve as statistical evidence as well as conceptual frameworks for policy and governance . The dataset was selected because it includes survey variables related to transparency, trust, consent acceptance, monitoring intensity, and perceived privacy risk, which are directly relevant to user expectations in enterprise security environments. To strengthen model validity, regression diagnostics were reviewed, including multicollinearity, residual distribution, heteroscedasticity, model fit, and robustness checks. These checks help ensure that the reported relationship between transparency, trust, privacy risk, and consent acceptance is statistically reliable.

8.2 Public Trust and Transparency in Monitoring Systems

This research has indeed revealed that one of the major findings is the link between transparency and public . If you take a look at Figure 4, which illustrates the impact of transparency on trust, there is hardly any difference between the two graphs. One graph depicts the level of transparency as the independent variable and the other shows the degree of trust in the user as the dependent .

Figure 4. Transparency and user trust correlation

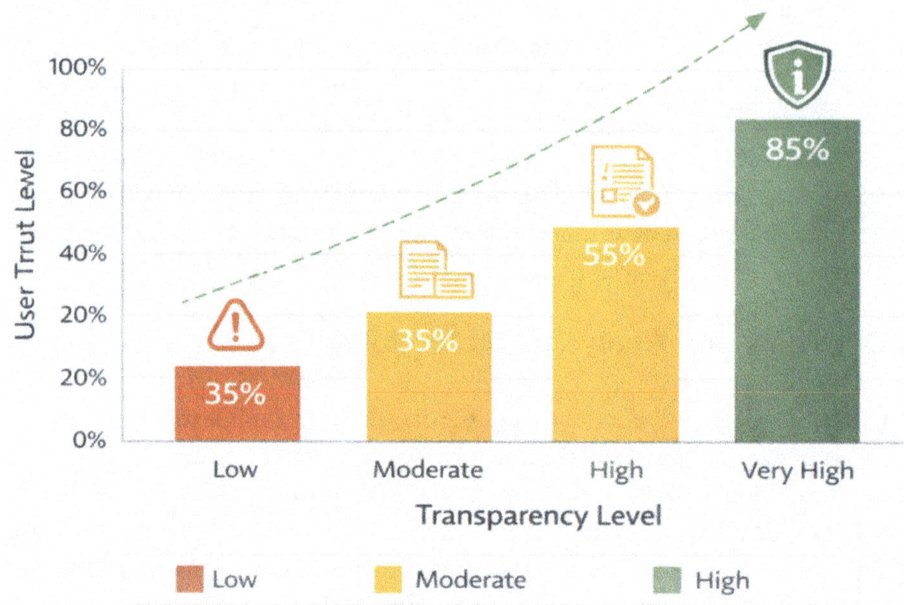

Whentransparency is almost non-existent; user trust is minimal. This is because people are unsure and feel that they have no control. Without knowledge of data collection, methods of processing, and the goals of data usage, users tend to see surveillance as a breaking of their privacy or a measure that could be used against them. This leads to unhappiness and may cause them to resist.

Increasing transparency to a moderate level led to a significant improvement in trust. Users are more willing to give it a try and even start to think that trust can be given. In this case, companies generally present only part of the picture: they give a fairly general outline of the program or only notify users in a limited way. Although these are still basically the main methods of preventing the unexpected element for users, the areas of accountability and data use are still mostly untouched.

With complete transparency, companies announce their future actions, for instance, by providing live communication, software access logs, and user meters. At this level, not only do most of the users see how the system works, but also their sense of control over the issue leads to a quite significant increase in trust. Consent management tools, audit trails, and user control mechanisms among others, make the conditions of transparency very tangible and interactive and these in turn raise the level of trust to the highest point possible. The relationship based on data is demonstrated in Table .

Table 5. Transparency vs Level of User Trust

Transparency Level	Average User Trust (%)
Low	35%
Moderate	50%
High	70%
Very High	85%

The undergoing analysis shows that while transparency is often seen as simply a requirement for compliance, it is actually a major factor in determining user trust. More than that, the increase of trust, however, is not linear but phenomena such as threshold effects come into play where only the very meaningful transparency is able to drastically change the user's perception.

8.3 Different Consent Acceptance Levels in Various Monitoring Contexts

The acceptance of consent is largely different based on the monitoring type, the Figure 5, provides a visualization of willingness to give consent for different types of monitoring.

Figure 5. Consent Acceptance Distribution Across Monitoring Systems

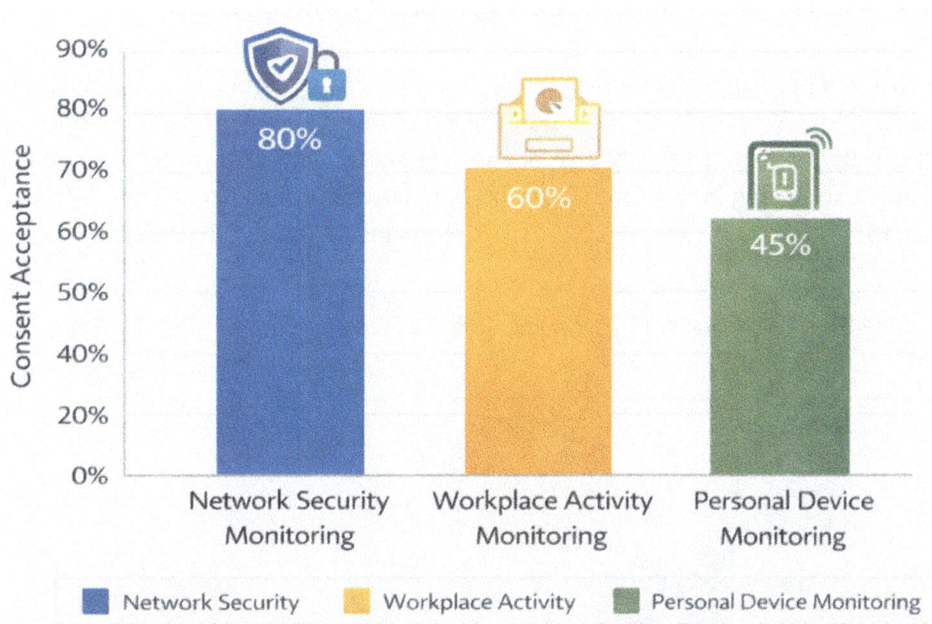

Among different monitoring types, network security monitoring is the one that garners the highest rate of consent acceptance, this is because it is perceived the most essential measure aimed at safeguarding the organizational premises and data. Workplace activity monitoring ranks a bit lower on consent acceptance. Besides performance tracking and compliance enforcement, the need for additional control especially from the aspect of surveillance intensity is seen by the users as a factor. The level of acceptance in this context largely depends on transparency and a perception of fair treatment.

Sincepersonal privacy is considered the most valuable aspect by users; it is not surprising that the least consent acceptance rates are observed when it comes to monitoring personal devices. This type of monitoring is generally regarded as the most invasive one, especially when it covers accessing personal communication, tracking location, or performing behavioral analysis. The summary of the findings can be found in Table 6 .

Table 6. Consent Acceptance by Monitoring Context

Monitoring Context	Consent Acceptance (%)
Network Security Monitoring	80%
Workplace Activity Monitoring	60%
Personal Device Monitoring	45%

These results only serve to underline that implementation of monitoring systems without even considering the environment and the users is just one of the causes that may lead to failure. Hence, it becomes quite crucial to design and personalize consent mechanisms by including a particular setting, along with user expectations and their perception of .

8.4 The Cushion Between Measures of Security and Privacy

Having security improved by monitoring means that the privacy rights, in the same time, may also be trampled inadvertently. Actually, this is the point where security can be made very effective and at the same time, the ability to protect privacy also becomes a matter that needs to be balanced properly. The main issue that we are facing here is how to properly balance efficient security and privacy protection as it can be seen from Figure 6 showing Security Monitoring vs Privacy Risk Tradeoff .

Figure 6. Security Monitoring vs Privacy Risk Tradeoff Model

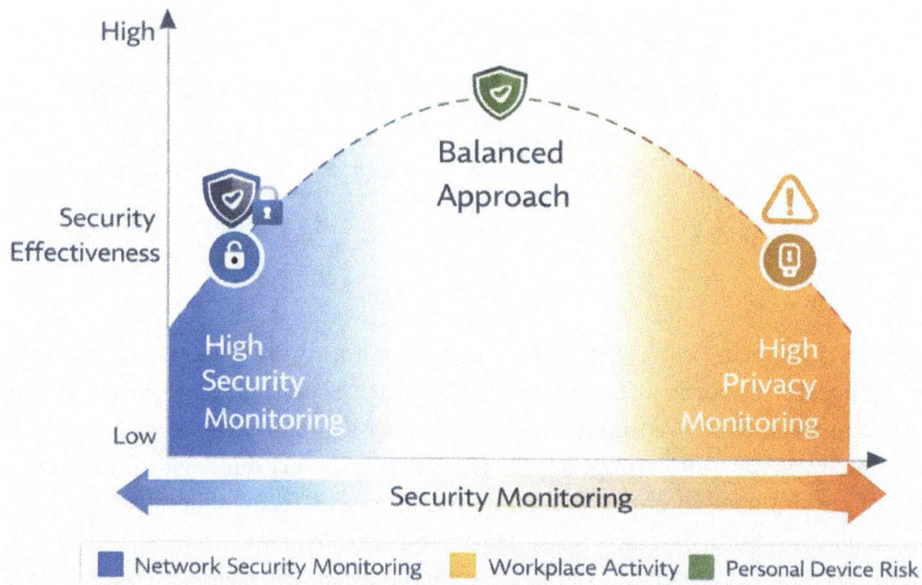

On the one hand, thorough security monitoring has a positive impact each time one gets alerted to a threat and is able to respond to it effectively. On the other hand, it can also lead to a significant raise in invasion of privacy. Data is being constantly gathered, people are being profiled based on their behaviors, and many decisions are made by machines - this is the main reason why people worry about their privacy especially, when there is not much.

On the other hand, if priority is given to privacy by reducing the extent of monitoring, exposure to data is kept at a minimum but it will have a negative impact on security effectiveness. Less intense surveillance will result in fewer detections of strange behaviors and this, in turn, will mean less reactive power after threat identification.

Where to do the monitoring can only be decided by weighing both sides of the matter, so in the end, you have the security assured by the implemented monitoring and at the same time, the privacy is well protected with strong measures. Complying with principles like data minimization, anonymization, and restricting the use of data incentives are doing all the pointing towards the balance that has been .

Table 7. Tradeoff Between Security Effectiveness and Privacy Risk

Monitoring Intensity	Security Effectiveness (%)	Privacy Risk (%)
Low	40%	20%
Moderate	65%	45%
High	85%	75%

Accordingto the data, a rise in surveillance activity caused the level of security to increase while at the same time, privacy risk rose to a greater extent. Therefore, this pattern of behavior highlights that there is an urgency for setting up governance structures that would both limit monitoring activities as well as guarantee the holding of .

8.5 Using Empirical Evidence for Policy Formation

Empirical evidence in this section tells us a lot about the basics of legally regulating AI-enabled security monitoring. Theseelements, especially, show why it's crucial to have a multi-layered governance framework that integrates transparency, consent, and accountability. Actually, if you look at Figure 7, you will witness the step-by-step process of how staff behavior can be aligned with the organizational code of conduct in a very structured . There are four main elements in the framework: reliable policies and documentation, independent supervisory body, privacy by design and accountability mechanisms. Overall, the regulatory framework these elements represent is comprehensive enough to ensure that monitoring instances are both lawful and .

Figure 7. Governance Model for Transparent Monitoring Systems

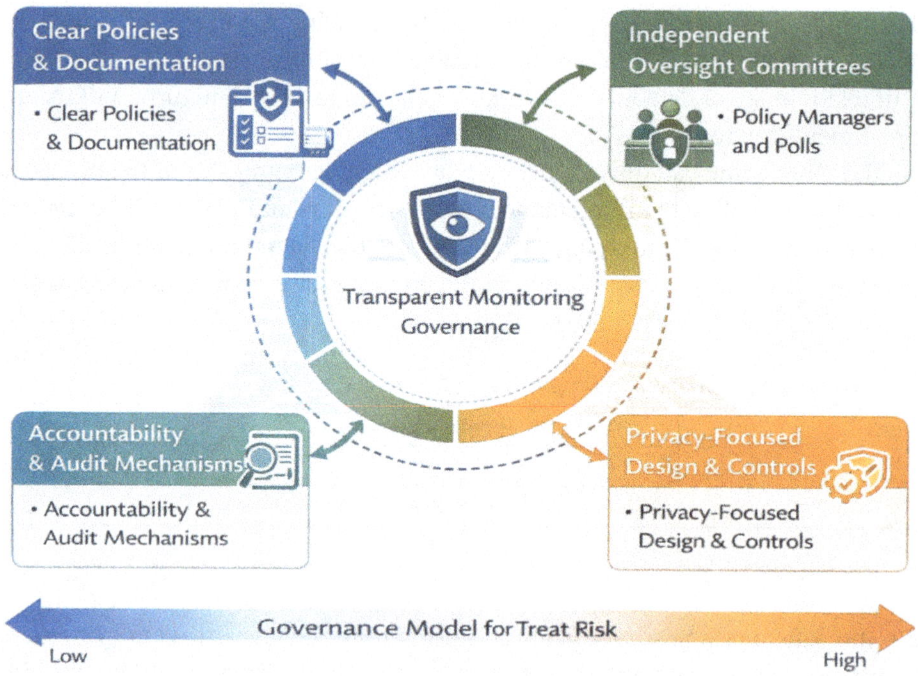

One can extrapolate that transparency, like a thread, should intertwine with the entire monitoring life cycle. This includes making a disclosure prior to deployment, giving a notification at the time of monitoring, as well as providing an audit after the processing, among other things. Indeed, transparency not only strengthens trust but it also renders informed consent very plausible since it will give the users an opportunity to decide whether to participate or not in the monitoring system.

Moreover, consent mechanisms should not only be context-sensitive but also sufficiently flexible. Using the example of monitoring a personal device, such a high-risk monitoring context demands explicit and detailed consent. Apart from security-related settings like network monitoring, consent may simply be one of the elements of an organizational policy with which the workforce complies as long as the company has established the required safeguards and disclosures. Policy making should also emphasize on finding the right security-privacy balance. That would require, among others, giving a very clear account of the boundaries and limitations, for instance, indicating the data collection methods that are allowed, providing for the data minimization concept, at the same time allowing the person who is doing the activities to check if the purpose of the activities is still the same. Besides, there are many accountability mechanisms such as maintaining logs, keeping audit trails, performing compliance audits, independent oversight committees, etc. that are paramount in, at the least, sustaining the level of highest trust. Those provisions ensure and give confidence that the monitoring operations being conducted are in accordance with legal and ethical requirements.

Research results show clearly that transparent operation and getting the agreement of users before their data is accessed and/or their activities are monitored (consent) are not just incidental factors, but the main ones that work on changing the user perception and acceptance. Therefore, the two features that make such tools human-friendly should be combined and developed into a single regulatory framework that will result not only in a policy design but a holistic one. It is this way that organizations will be able to both keep their security and efficiency untampered and respect the users' privacy, which in due course will lead to the trust and legitimacy of AI-based monitoring systems.

9. STRATEGIES FOR ETHICAL SECURITY MONITORING

Because these days companies are adopting AI-driven monitoring tools more and more, the question of designing appropriate governance frameworks that guarantee ethical, lawful, and transparent business operations is coming up. Security monitoring systems, although required for protection of digital infrastructures and management of cyber threats, often involve accessing users' personal information. If left without proper governance, these systems may result in breaches of privacy, loss of users' trust, and non-compliance with regulatory .

9.1 Organizational Policies for Transparent Monitoring

Organizational policies are a fundamental factor of ethical security monitoring as they define the scope, objectives, and limitations of monitoring activities. One of the aspects of these policies is to regulate how data gets handled in AI-enabled security solutions. In addition, they also make sure that such user practices are communicated to users in a very clear and simple way. For the sake of transparency, monitoring policies must clearly communicate the objectives of the monitoring activities. This means that the monitoring should be according to the purpose of the communication, such as, e.g., threat detection, compliance with the law, performance evaluation of an employee, or management of risks. Defining these purposes clearly the organization besides reducing the possibility of dual-use will also meet the legitimate company needs.

The first policy principle is data minimization- is the practice of only collecting information that is essential for carrying out pre-defined objectives. Similarly, policies should also include purpose limitation i.e., to make sure that the collected data is not used for other purposes without the consent of the user. These two principles, combined with the understanding of ethical boundaries, are mainly intended to prevent the misuse of surveillance. On the other hand, a company is to be held responsible for including the feature of user notification in their policies. In other words, the moment of the first user-on-boarding with disclosures as well as informing them of any changes to monitoring procedures. A very high level of transparency like this gives the users knowledge of how their data is being used and at the same time enhances the feeling of personal data being in control.

Another part of policies is consenting management, particularly in cases when monitoring is no longer used only for security purposes. So, it is about finding out the way consents are obtained, documented, and controlled through time. Sometimes very detailed consent options should be provided, which allow users to agree to or decline different types of monitoring. Apart from that, the organizational policies ought to be consistent with the applicable regulatory requirements including data protection rules and also sector-specific compliance standards. This alignment is aimed at introducing ethical monitoring practices which are, at the same time, legally enforceable.

To summarize, open monitoring policies are like bridges that connect technical systems and user expectations. They provide a formal structure which acts as a handbook for implementation, and at the same time, they foster trust and .

9.2 Auditability and Documentation of Monitoring Practices

Auditability is a crucial feature that security monitoring systems must possess so that they can demonstrate their operations align with the ethical boundaries and legal frameworks defined. Essentially, what is meant by auditability is the possibility of conducting a systematic investigation, checking, and evaluation of the monitoring actions in order to ascertain whether they meet the policies and remain within the bounds of the laws set. For a system to be auditable, it must have first thorough documentation of the monitoring activity. Such documentation includes methods of data acquisition, data processing algorithms, mechanisms of data storage, and data access controls. Apart from being a reference point for internal stakeholders and external auditors, documentation is instrumental for conformity checking to standards.

One factor of auditability is implementing audit trails, i.e., keeping records of every data interaction. Such logs consist of information on the identity of the individual accessing the data, the time of access, and the activities performed. An advantage of using audit trails is that they offer a transparent record of the system activity that could be used to trace any case of unauthorized use or exploitation. When it comes to AI-enabled solutions, the scope of auditability needs to be extended to algorithmic transparency, which is essentially, the keeping of records about how machine learning models take in data, decide on outputs, and produce results. It is accepted that sometimes it is not feasible to fully interpret a model but it is a good practice that organizations are quite open about the workings of their algorithms within the ethical and legal boundaries frameworks. Moreover, periodic compliance audits form a very critical part of auditability. These audits check whether the monitoring devices and methods are still aligned with the policies and laws that are subject to change over time. Such audits ought to be thorough and cover both technology and policies. The results of the audit have to be meticulously recorded and should be part of the system improvement cycle.

On the other hand, documentation is a very important component of incident management and accountability. When there is a security breach or a non-compliance with a policy, well-kept records support organizations in doing a root cause analysis, assessing the damage, and taking remedial measures. Besides improving the resilience of operations, it is also a witness of accountability towards the regulators and users. Auditability should be viewed as a backup tool for ongoing enhancement that provides insights into the operations of the system and user behaviors. Through audit data analysis, organizations can pinpoint weaknesses, find abnormalities, and optimize their monitoring methods.

In summary, auditability and documentation are the key elements that come into the set for a transparent and accountable monitoring environment. Not only do they guarantee that monitoring work is done properly but also that they can be and continue to be reliable and verifiable over .

9.3 Oversight Mechanisms for Monitoring Activities

Management mechanisms create essential foundations that enable security monitoring to be held accountable for upholding ethical, legal, and organizational standards. Adding an additional control layer, they bring an independent assessment and accountability aspect to the entire monitoring operation. Perhaps, one of the main instruments of oversight is independent oversight committees. Usually, such committees consist of members from diverse areas of the organization like legal, data protection, and technical, and may even include external members. Their functions entail the examination of monitoring methods, ensuring compliance with regulations, and suggesting changes.

Actually, the role of these committees (s) goes quite far beyond simply verifying the layers of ethical and legal control; they also deal with ethical monitoring questions, for instance, whether monitoring is proportionate to its aim or if it respects users' privacy rights. So, they assist in offering an independent insight and in reducing the risks resulting from biased or too intrusive monitoring. Boards which review and update policies from time to time in order to adapt have been another series of oversight entities discussed. Such boards support making sure that the monitoring policies do not get outdated or become ineffective due to evolving technologies and regulations.

Besides internal oversight, one may also take a look at external audits and certifications by independent third parties. These kinds of assessments produce unbiased monitoring reports and are capable of significantly contributing to gaining the trust of stakeholders. Such external oversight is usually compulsory for the most highly regulated industries such as healthcare and finance. Oversight, however, should not be solely given to those performing the tasks directly, but also to the user feedback channels which, in turn, provide the users with a voice through which they can raise their concerns, seek information or hold monitoring decisions accountable. This democratic manner not only fosters greater transparency but also ensures that the governance decisions are sound and impactful. Having oversight entails not only having policies or systems in place but also handling human factors. Consequently, it is absolutely necessary for organizations to have clear definitions of the roles and responsibilities of different stakeholders in monitoring. These definitions should cover not only policy enforcement and audit management but also post-incident actions. Without clear accountability, effective governance is near impossible.

Making oversight mechanisms a part of governance really means making them inseparable. It helps ongoing reassessment and upgrading of monitoring. It is a system of checks and balances that safeguards against misuse, encourages the right conduct, and builds users' . Ethical risks in enterprise monitoring include false profiling, chilling effects, excessive behavioral visibility, workplace power imbalance, and limited redress for incorrect monitoring outcomes. These risks require meaningful oversight, clear grievance procedures, human review, and strict limits on secondary use.

Table 8. Governance Components for Ethical Security Monitoring

Governance Component	Key Function	Impact on Trust & Compliance
Transparent Policies	Define purpose, scope, and data usage rules	Increases user trust and clarity
Audit Trails & Documentation	Record system activities and data access	Ensures accountability and traceability
Compliance Audits	Evaluate adherence to policies and regulations	Maintains legal and ethical alignment
Oversight Committees	Provide independent evaluation and guidance	Reduces bias and enhances governance credibility
Consent Management Systems	Manage user permissions and preferences	Strengthens user control and acceptance

In short, the governance strategies for ethical security monitoring should combine the three key elements - policy transparency, audit capability, and strong oversight mechanisms - into one, fully integrated framework. When these elements work in unison, they ensure not only the transparency of security monitoring systems and the protection of user privacy but also their compliance with the relevant regulatory standards. The introduction of such strategies means security and ethics can be effectively and sustainably merged, and trust and legitimacy in AI-driven environments can be fostered .

REFERENCES

Abdeljaber, O., & Al-Masaeed, S. (2025). Al-Mu′ani, L., Yaseen, H., & Alhnaity, B. (2025). Strategic Intelligence: The Power of AI in Planning Efficiency. *Human Behavior and Emerging Technologies*, (1). Advance online publication. DOI: 10.1155/hbe2/5383054

Abualghanam, O., Alazzam, H., Qatawneh, M., Alazab, M., & Al Sharaiah, M. (2025). Elevating Mobile Security: An Ensemble Approach for Enhanced Malware Detection with M-iForest. *International Journal of Interactive Mobile Technologies*, *19*(10), 129–151. Advance online publication. DOI: 10.3991/ijim.v19i10.51319

Abualhaj, M. M., Abu-Shareha, A. A., Al-Khatib, S. N., Alsaaidah, A. M., & Anbar, M. (2025). Improving firewall performance using hybrid of optimization algorithms and decision trees classifier. *IAES International Journal of Artificial Intelligence*, *14*(4), 2839. Advance online publication. DOI: 10.11591/ijai.v14.i4.pp2839-2848

Abualhaj, M. M., Abu-Shareha, A. A., & Rateb, R. (2025). Enhancing intrusion detection systems with hybrid HHO-WOA optimization and gradient boosting machine classifier. *International Journal of Reconfigurable and Embedded Systems*, *14*(2), 518. Advance online publication. DOI: 10.11591/ijres.v14.i2.pp518-526

Abualhaj, M. M.I, Al-Khatib, S. N., Abu-Shareha, A. A., Almomani, O., Al-Mimi, H., Al-Allawee, A., Daoud, M. S., & Anbar, M. (2025). Spam Detection Boosted by Firefly-Based Feature Selection and Optimized Classifiers. *International Journal of Advances in Soft Computing and Its Applications*, *17*(3). Advance online publication. DOI: 10.15849/IJASCA.251130.02

Abualhaj, M. M., Al-Khatib, S. N., Al Zyoud, M., Qaddara, I., & Anbar, M. (2025). Enhancing Intrusion Detection System Performance Using a Hybrid of Harris Hawks and Whale Optimization Algorithms. *Engineering. Technology and Applied Science Research*, *15*(4), 24354–24361. Advance online publication. DOI: 10.48084/etasr.10919

Abualhaj, M. M., Al-Khatib, S. N., Al-Zyoud, M., Qaddara, I., Hiari, M. O., & Aldossary, S. M. A. (2025). Enhanced Network Communication Security Through Hybrid Dragonfly-Bat Feature Selection for Intrusion Detection. *The Journal of Communication*, *20*(5). Advance online publication. DOI: 10.12720/jcm.20.5.607-618

Abualigah, L., Almomani, M. H., Alomari, S. A., Zitar, R. A., Migdady, H., Saleem, K., Snasel, V., Smerat, A., & Ezugwu, A. E. (2025). Optimizing Intrusion Detection in Wireless Sensor Networks via the Improved Chameleon Swarm Algorithm for Feature Selection. *IET Communications*, *19*(1), e70029. Advance online publication. DOI: 10.1049/cmu2.70029

Abuowaida, S., Abu Owida, H., Shelash Mohammad, S. I., Alshdaifat, N., Abu Elsoud, E., Alazaidah, R., Vasudevan, A., & Alshurideh, M. T. (2025). Evidence Detection in Cloud Forensics: Classifying Cyber-Attacks in IaaS Environments using machine learning. *Data and Metadata*, *4*, 699. Advance online publication. DOI: 10.56294/dm2025699

Al-Adwan, A. S., Al-Adwan, A., Li, N., Fauzi, M. A., Jafar, R. M. S., Habibi, A., & Falahat, M. (2025). IMMERSIVE LEARNING MEETS THEORY: MODELING EDUVERSE ADOPTION IN HIGHER EDUCATION. *Journal of Information Technology Education, 24*, 042. Advance online publication. DOI: 10.28945/5669

Al-Dmour, R., Al-Dmour, H., Al-Dmour, A., Basheer Amin, E., & Al-Dmour, Y. (2025). *AI and big data-driven social media recruitment: the mediating role of talent acquisition and employee engagement in bank performance*. Digital Transformation and Society., DOI: 10.1108/DTS-02-2025-0042

Al Hindi, G., Alshraideh, M., Hussein, A. H., Eliyan, L. F., & Al-Dhaqm, A. (2025). Hacking Back: Using Genetic Algorithms to Outsmart Hackers. *Journal of Computational Science, 21*(9), 2049–2064. Advance online publication. DOI: 10.3844/jcssp.2025.2049.2064

Al-Momani, M. M., Alqudah, T. A., Al Swiety, I. A., Mahrakani, N., Nassoura, M. B. A., & Al Attar, M. K. (2025). Integrating Artificial Intelligence (AI) and Business Intelligence (BI): A Framework for Improving Enterprise Performance. *TEM Journal, 14*(3). https://doi.org/DOI: 10.18421/TEM143-26

Al-Mousa, M., Amer, W., Abualhaj, M., Albilasi, S., Nasir, O., & Samara, G. (2025). Agile Proactive Cybercrime Evidence Analysis Model for Digital Forensics. *The International Arab Journal of Information Technology, 22*(3). Advance online publication. DOI: 10.34028/iajit/22/3/15

Al-Okbi, N. K., Alomari, S. A., Hadi, W. J., Ajrash, A. S., Smerat, A., & Abualigah, L. (2025). Defending Digital Integrity: Advances in Media Forgery Analysis Research and Cybersecurity Development. *SN Computer Science, 6*(8), 913. Advance online publication. DOI: 10.1007/s42979-025-04462-8

Al-Okbi, N. K., Alomari, S. A., Zitar, R. A., Smerat, A., Nazzal, M. A., & Abualigah, L. (2025). Integrating Multimodal Emotion Recognition with Deep Q-Learning for Adaptive Social Robot Interaction. *International Journal of Robotics and Control Systems, 5*(4), 2265–2289. Advance online publication. DOI: 10.31763/ijrcs.v5i4.2055

Al-Suhimat, R. I., Mohammed Ai, N., Ibrahim, A., Maaitah, N. O., & Al-Dmour, N. A. (2024). Review of Security Challenges Encountered in Internet of Things Technology. *2nd International Conference on Cyber Resilience, ICCR 2024*. DOI: 10.1109/ICCR61006.2024.10533052

Al-znamat, F. O., Alsaaidah, A., & Abu-Shareha, A. A. (2025). Malware Detection Using a Modified Bat Algorithm for Feature Selection. *International Journal of Intelligent Engineering and Systems, 18*(9), 885–899. Advance online publication. DOI: 10.22266/ijies2025.1031.56

Alabdallat, R., Abualhaj, M., & Abu-Shareha, A. (2025). Android Malware Detection Using a Modified Dwarf Mongoose Algorithm. *International Journal of Intelligent Engineering and Systems, 18*(8), 336–351. Advance online publication. DOI: 10.22266/ijies2025.0930.21

Alabdallat, R. D., Abualhaj, M. M., & Abu-Shareha, A. (2025). Enhanced Multiclass Android Malware Detection Using a Modified Dwarf Mongoose Algorithm. *International Journal of Analysis and Applications, 23*, 248. Advance online publication. DOI: 10.28924/2291-8639-23-2025-248

Aldaaja, Y., Odeh, M., Badrakhan, S. S., Sabri, M., Abdelrahim, Y., Samara, G., & Alsabatin, H. (2025). Quantifying the Managerial and Practical Benefits of Cloud Computing on Information Security in Higher Education Institutions. *Applied Mathematics & Information Sciences*, *19*(1), 15–24. Advance online publication. DOI: 10.18576/amis/190102

Aldabbas, A., Baniata, L. H., Alsaaidah, B. A., Mustafa, Z., Alali, M., & Rateb, R. (2025). Artificial intelligence-driven method for the discovery and prevention of distributed denial of service attacks. *IAES International Journal of Artificial Intelligence*, *14*(1), 614. Advance online publication. DOI: 10.11591/ijai.v14.i1.pp614-628

Alenazi, M. J. F., Al-Khasawneh, M. A., Rahman, S., & Faheem, Z. (2025). Deep Reinforcement Learning Based Flow Aware-QoS Provisioning in SD-IoT for Precision Agriculture. *Computational Intelligence*, *41*(1), e70023. Advance online publication. DOI: 10.1111/coin.70023

Alkhawatrah, M. (2025). Random Forests Relay Selector in Buffer-Aided Cooperative Networks. *IEEE Access : Practical Innovations, Open Solutions*, *13*, 165402–165410. Advance online publication. DOI: 10.1109/ACCESS.2025.3612192

Almomani, O., Arabiat, A., Al Tayeb, M., Almaiah, M. A., Obeidat, M., Aldhyani, T. H. H., Shehab, R., & Rowad, M. (2025). A Robust Model for Android Malware Detection via ML and DL classifiers. *Mesopotamian Journal of Big Data*, *2025*. Advance online publication. DOI: 10.58496/MJBD/2025/017

Alraba'nah, Y., Al-Sharaeh, S., & Al Hindi, G. (2025). Enhancing Intrusion Detection Using Hybrid Long Short-Term Memory and XGBoost. *Journal of Soft Computing and Data Mining*, *6*(1). Advance online publication. DOI: 10.30880/jscdm.2025.06.01.016

Arabiat, A., Altayeb, M., & Salama, S. (2025). Artificial intelligence-powered smart roads: Leveraging orange3 for traffic signs recognition. *IAES International Journal of Artificial Intelligence*, *14*(5), 3816. Advance online publication. DOI: 10.11591/ijai.v14.i5.pp3816-3826

Arabiat, A. M. (2025). Intelligent Model for Detecting GAN-Generated Images Based on Multi-Classifier and Advanced Data Mining Techniques. *International Journal of Electrical and Electronic Engineering and Telecommunications*, *14*(3). Advance online publication. DOI: 10.18178/ijeetc.14.3.147-157

Arabiat, A. M., & Eljaafreh, Y. G. (2025). Intrusion Detection in Wireless Sensor Networks Using ML Based Classification of Denial of Service (DoS) Attacks. *The Journal of Communication*, *20*(4). Advance online publication. DOI: 10.12720/jcm.20.4.501-514

Babaker, S., Khatibi, A., Alsoud, A. R., Kaur, J., Jagtap, J., Alkhayyat, A., & Shah, S. K. (2025). Improving Reliability and Data Management in Internet of Things Based Wireless Sensor Networks. *Internet Technology Letters*, *8*(6), e646. Advance online publication. DOI: 10.1002/itl2.646

Cui, D., Harrison, A., Fendzi-Donfack, E., Dagal, I., Jangir, P., Mahmoud, M. M., Malkani, P., Mbasso, W. F., Tiako, P., & Smerat, A. (2026). Enhancing Short-Term Electricity Forecasting with Advanced Machine Learning Techniques. *Journal of Electrical Engineering & Technology*, *21*(1), 147–187. Advance online publication. DOI: 10.1007/s42835-025-02430-z

Eke, C. I., Al-Shamayleh, A. S., Phiri, M., Maswadi, K., Kwaghtyo, D. K., Mulenga, M., & Iyidobi, C. J. (2025). Machine Learning Based Mobile Big Data Analytics: State-of-the-art Applications, Taxonomy, Challenges and Future Research Directions. *Nigerian Journal of Technological Development, 22*(4). Advance online publication. DOI: 10.63746/njtd.v22i4.3385

Ghazal, T. M. (2025a). An IoT-Based Active Learning Convolutional Neural Networks Model for Predicting River Water Quality. *Journal of Soft Computing and Data Mining*, *6*(1). Advance online publication. DOI: 10.30880/jscdm.2025.06.01.021

Ghazal, T. M. (2025b). Federated Learning for Intelligent Sensing and Navigation Technologies for 6G Communications. *Journal of Sensors, 2025*(1). DOI: 10.1155/js/3746147

Ghazal, T. M., Abu-Shareha, A., Mustafa, S. A., Ibrahim, A., & Ahmed, S. M. (2025). Privacy-Preserving Transformer-Based Meta-Learning Algorithm for Zero-Day Intrusion Detection in IoT-Enabled Smart Grids. *Journal of Internet Services and Information Security*, *15*(4), 76–84. Advance online publication. DOI: 10.58346/JISIS.2025.I4.006

Ghazal, T. M., Abualhaj, M., Ahmed, A. A., Al-Tarawni, M. A. M., & Maghrabi, L. A. (2025). Federated Deep Graph Neural Network Algorithm for Real-Time Intrusion Detection in Heterogeneous IoT Systems. *Journal of Internet Services and Information Security*, *15*(4), 484–497. Advance online publication. DOI: 10.58346/JISIS.2025.I4.035

Ghazal, T. M., Awouda, A. E., Hasan, M. K., Rahman, A. H. A., Islam, S., Saeed, R. A., Elshafie, H., Iqbal, A., & Hussein, A. H. (2025). Knowledge Learning for Securing Workflow Scheduling Algorithm in Mobile Edge Computing. *Mobile Networks and Applications*, *30*(3-4), 395–413. Advance online publication. DOI: 10.1007/s11036-025-02465-6

Ghazal, T. M., Hasan, M. K., Hussein, A. H., Pandey, B. K., Ahmad, M., Safie, N., & Cascone, L. (2025). Federated Learning With Small and Large Models With Privacy-Preserving Data Space for Holographic Internet of Things in Consumer Electronics. *IEEE Transactions on Consumer Electronics*, *71*(2), 5259–5274. Advance online publication. DOI: 10.1109/TCE.2025.3573033

Ghazal, T. M., Janjua, J. I., Abushiba, W., Ahmad, M., Ihsan, A., & Al-Dmour, N. A. (2024). Cybersecurity Revolution via Large Language Models and Explainable AI. *2024 17th International Conference on Security of Information and Networks, SIN 2024*. DOI: 10.1109/SIN63213.2024.10871324

Hakami, H., Hasan, M. K., Alshamayleh, A., Saeed, A. Q., Mustafa, S. A., & Ghazal, T. M. (2025). Adaptive Neuro-Fuzzy Congestion Control Algorithm for Real-Time Multimedia Networking in Cloud-Based E-Learning Platforms. *Journal of Wireless Mobile Networks, Ubiquitous Computing and Dependable Applications*, *16*(3). Advance online publication. DOI: 10.58346/JOWUA.2025.I3.027

Hanandeh, A., Alfreijat, S. Y., Qutieshat, R. J., Alsha'ar, H. Y., Kilani, Q. A. L., & Saleem Khasawneh, M. A. (2025). Implementing AI Accuracy, Learning Rate, Inference Time on enhancing Big Data Analysis and Strategic Plan. *Data and Metadata*, *4*, 637. Advance online publication. DOI: 10.56294/dm2025637

Hasan, M. K., Ghazal, T. M., Alkhalifah, A., Abu Bakar, K. A., Omidvar, A., Nafi, N. S., & Agbinya, J. I. (2021). Fischer Linear Discrimination and Quadratic Discrimination Analysis–Based Data Mining Technique for Internet of Things Framework for Healthcare. *Frontiers in Public Health*, *9*, 737149. Advance online publication. DOI: 10.3389/fpubh.2021.737149 PMID: 34712639

Hiari, M., Alraba'nah, Y., & Qaddara, I. (2025). A Deep Learning-Based Intrusion Detection System using Refined LSTM for DoS Attack Detection. *Engineering. Technology and Applied Science Research*, *15*(4), 25627–25633. Advance online publication. DOI: 10.48084/etasr.11499

Ibrahim, A., Ali, W., Al-Dmour, N. A., & Ghazal, T. M. (2024). Revolutionizing Human Assessment: AI-Driven Analysis of SQ, EQ, and IQ. *2nd International Conference on Cyber Resilience, ICCR 2024*. DOI: 10.1109/ICCR61006.2024.10532816

Ibrahim, A., Sekhar, R., Tawfeq, J. F., Salih, S. Q., Shah, P., & Radhi, A. D. (2024). Security and Privacy Protection for Online Electronic Documents Based on Novel Encryption Techniques. *Journal of Intelligent Systems and Internet of Things*, *11*(1), 21–28. Advance online publication. DOI: 10.54216/JISIoT.110103

Iskandarani, M. Z. (2025). Effect of Adaptive Intelligent Reflective Surfaces on SINR in a Wireless Communication System. *The Journal of Communication*, *20*(1). Advance online publication. DOI: 10.12720/jcm.20.1.1-11

Jaradat, S., Acharya, N., Shivshankar, S., Alhadidi, T. I., & Elhenawy, M. (2025). AI for Data Quality Auditing: Detecting Mislabeled Work Zone Crashes Using Large Language Models. *Algorithms*, *18*(6), 317. Advance online publication. DOI: 10.3390/a18060317

Khatibi, A., Babaker, S., Praveen, K. N. R., Chohan, J. S., Jadhav, A., Alsoud, A. R., Ramudu, M. J., & Jeet, R. (2025). Advanced AI-Driven Cybersecurity: Analyzing Emerging Threats and Defensive Strategies. *National Academy Science Letters*. Advance online publication. DOI: 10.1007/s40009-025-01897-8

Laha, S. R., Smadi, K. Al, Habboush, A. K., Pattanayak, B. K., Pattnaik, S., & Mohanty, B. (2025). Smart Waste Management Framework for Green Cities: Integrating IoT, LoRa, and Deep Learning for Efficient Waste Classification and Management. *Tikrit Journal of Engineering Sciences, 32*(Special Issue 1). DOI: 10.25130/tjes.sp1.2025.1

Lee, S. W., Hussain, S., Issa, G. F., Abbas, S., Ghazal, T. M., Sohail, T., Ahmad, M., & Khan, M. A. (2021). Multi-Dimensional Trust Quantification by Artificial Agents through Evidential Fuzzy Multi-Criteria Decision Making. *IEEE Access : Practical Innovations, Open Solutions*, *9*, 159399–159412. Advance online publication. DOI: 10.1109/ACCESS.2021.3131521

Makhadmeh, S. N., Fraihat, S., Awad, M., Sanjalawe, Y., Al-Betar, M. A., & Awadallah, M. A. (2025). A crossover-integrated Marine Predator Algorithm for feature selection in intrusion detection systems within IoT environments. *Internet of Things : Engineering Cyber Physical Human Systems*, *31*, 101536. Advance online publication. DOI: 10.1016/j.iot.2025.101536

Masango, N. C., Agushaka, J. O., Amaefule, M. C., Taiwo, O., Zhang, P., Ezugwu, A. E., Saleem, K., Smerat, A., & Abualigah, L. (2025). Secure and efficient cloudlet networks: blockchain integration with agent-based proof of trust mechanism. *Eurasip Journal on Wireless Communications and Networking, 2025*(1). DOI: 10.1186/s13638-025-02439-y

Maz, Y. A., Anbar, M., Manickam, S., Abualhaj, M. M., Almalki, S. A., & Alabsi, B. A. (2025). Transfer Learning-Based Approach with an Ensemble Classifier for Detecting Keylogging Attack on the Internet of Things. *Computers, Materials & Continua, 85*(3), 5287–5307. Advance online publication. DOI: 10.32604/cmc.2025.068257

Mohammad, S. I., Al-Daoud, K., Al Qraini, B., Khanfar, I. A. A., & Vasudevan, A. (2025). Quantum Error Correction with Surface Code Analysis on Quantum Computing platform. *Applied Mathematics & Information Sciences, 19*(2), 423–435. Advance online publication. DOI: 10.18576/amis/190216

Qaddara, I., & Alraba'nah, Y. (2025). Enhancing Requirements Classification Using Machine Learning Techniques. *SN Computer Science, 6*(6), 649. Advance online publication. DOI: 10.1007/s42979-025-04158-z

Qawasmeh, S., Habboushb, A., Elzaghmouri, B., Kharma, Q., & Albalawneh, D. (2025). Hybrid Convolutional Neural Network-Based Intrusion Detection System for Secure IoT Networks. *Tikrit Journal of Engineering Sciences, 32*(SP1), 1–11. Advance online publication. DOI: 10.25130/tjes.sp1.2025.2

Ramesh, J. V. N., Nimma, D., Dasari, R., Chaudhari Rane, D., AlGhamdi, A., Rao, K. B. V. B., Haider, S. A., Kuzieva, N., & Jangir, P. (2025). Safe and Reliable Two-Stage Online Offloading Algorithm for Transportation Cyber-Physical Systems. *IEEE Transactions on Intelligent Transportation Systems, 26*(9), 14313–14322. Advance online publication. DOI: 10.1109/TITS.2025.3539934

Raza, M. A., Karim, A., Alqarni, M., Al-Khasawneh, M. A., Jumani, T. A., Aman, M., & Masud, M. I. (2025). An Intelligent Long Short-Term Memory-Based Machine Learning Model for the Potential Assessment of Global Hydropower Capacity in Sustainable Energy Transition and Security. *Energies, 18*(13), 3324. Advance online publication. DOI: 10.3390/en18133324

Samanta, I. S., Mohanty, S., Rout, P. K., Parida, S. M., Panda, S., Bajaj, M., Blazek, V., & Prokop, L. (2025). A comprehensive review of feature extraction techniques for power quality event detection with novel approaches for enhanced classification in smart grids. *Electrical Engineering, 107*(9), 12227–12259. Advance online publication. DOI: 10.1007/s00202-025-03149-w

Sardar, R., Anees, T., Al-Shamayleh, A. S., Mehmood, E., Khalil, W., Akhunzada, A., & Shaikh, F. S. (2025). Challenges in detecting security threats in WoT: A systematic literature review. *Artificial Intelligence Review, 58*(7), 196. Advance online publication. DOI: 10.1007/s10462-025-11176-z

Shambour, Q., Al-Zyoud, M., & Almomani, O. (2025). Quantum-Inspired Hybrid Metaheuristic Feature Selection with SHAP for Optimized and Explainable Spam Detection. *Symmetry, 17*(10), 1716. Advance online publication. DOI: 10.3390/sym17101716

Shambour, Q. Y., Al-Zyoud, M., & Hussein, A. H. (2025). FROM DATA TO DIAGNOSIS: KNOWLEDGE-DRIVEN, EXPLAINABLE AI FOR RELIABLE EARLY AUTISM DETECTION. *Interdisciplinary Journal of Information, Knowledge, and Management*, *20*, 032. Advance online publication. DOI: 10.28945/5652

Sharma, K. P., Al-Rashed, A., Johar, M. G. M., Alsoud, A. R., Singh, A., Dey, P., & Pant, S. (2025). Blockchain-Assisted Trust Framework for Increased Survivability in Internet of Vehicles. *Internet Technology Letters*, *8*(3), e70029. Advance online publication. DOI: 10.1002/itl2.70029

Sharma, K. P., Hussain, R., Jaharadak, A. A., Trawnih, A. A., Verma, D., Dasi, S., & Pant, S. (2025). Hybrid Convolutional Neural Network for Robust Attack Detection in Wireless Sensor Networks. *Internet Technology Letters*, *8*(6), e650. Advance online publication. DOI: 10.1002/itl2.650

Turab, N., Abushattal, A., Al-Nabulsi, J., & Owida, H. A. (2025). Advanced risk assessment using machine learning and sentiment analysis on log data. *IAES International Journal of Artificial Intelligence*, *14*(5), 3897. Advance online publication. DOI: 10.11591/ijai.v14.i5.pp3897-3905

Vasudevan, A., Albinaa, T. A., Mohammad, S. I., Sharmila, E., Raja, N., Soon, E. E. H., Alshurideh, M. T., & Al-Adwan, A. S. (2024). Bidirectional LSTM for Electronic Product Recommendation. *Applied Mathematics & Information Sciences*, *18*(6), 1443–1453. Advance online publication. DOI: 10.18576/amis/180621

Vasudevan, A., Tamilmani, K. T., Mohammad, S. I., Sridheepika, V. S., Raja, N., Soon, E. E. H., Nagaraj, S., & Al-Adwan, A. S. (2025). Voices of Concern: Contemplations on Socioeconomic, Ethical, and Developmental Impacts of AI. *Applied Mathematics & Information Sciences*, *19*(1), 221–232. Advance online publication. DOI: 10.18576/amis/190119

Chapter 4
Understanding User Expectations of Privacy in Enterprise Security Environments

Sameh H. Ghwanmeh
http://orcid.org/0000-0003-2907-1489
American University in the Emirates, UAE

Dima Mohamad Yasser Saad Eddin
http://orcid.org/0009-0009-7902-8324
International University for Science and Technology, Syria

ABSTRACT

This chapter investigates user expectations of privacy within corporate security environments and their importance for legal and ethical security practices. This study covers the change in user privacy expectations and sensitization to monitoring and controls at work through the detailed analysis of several aspects. The chapter discusses the tension between the organization's need for security and the individual's right to privacy. The main focus is on the fact that the four principles of notice, consent, proportionality, and limitation of purpose are central to the trade-off between security and privacy. By assuming that typical corporate security measures like network monitoring, endpoint protection, and identity management systems are in place, the chapter points out differences between users' perceptions and the actual data practices. Besides, it is pointed out that security operations consistent with a reasonable user's expectations can help not only in risk avoidance but also in creating trust, and simultaneously, making compliance with corporate governance easier.

DOI: 10.4018/979-8-2600-2870-4.ch004

1. CONCEPTUAL FOUNDATIONS

1.1 Evolution of Privacy Norms in Digital Workspaces

Privacy in enterprises has been a changing idea as a result of the technological and organizational changes brought about by digital times. In simple terms, at the beginning of the industrial era, privacy issues had mainly a physical character, e.g. monitoring, personal file access, general management. Yet, with the gradual digitization of workplaces through cloud computing, remote collaboration platforms and AI-based monitoring systems, privacy issues got deeply intertwined with digital infrastructures(Vasudevan et al., 2024). Furthermore, today's organizations gather, process and analyze vast amounts of behavioral records, communication metadata, biometric logs and performance data. Therefore, people's privacy expectations today go well beyond simple confidentiality of personal information and also include transparency, fairness, limitation of the purposes, and proportionality of monitoring . Digital workspaces are making the line between one's personal and professional identities extremely thin. Today it is quite normal for employees to be under constant monitoring - recording of keystrokes, checking patterns of emailing, noting time of log-ins, tracking usage of applications, and even analyzing changes in sentiment in communications are just a few examples. In principle, these kinds of monitoring can be reasonably justified on a cybersecurity basis, especially if they are intended to the detection of insider threats or breaches, but on the other hand, they also inspire a feeling of constantly being watched. Contrary to complete secrecy, privacy expectations have been changing little by little till they reached what has been called as contextual integrity. According to this idea, users do not assess privacy just by data collection as a fact but also by the contexts, reasons, and extents to which data are used(Abualhaj, Al-Khatib, Al Zyoud, Qaddara, et al., 2025).

In fact, the everyday use and even acceptance of enterprise surveillance technologies have had a great impact on how users perceive privacy to a large extent. In fact, they are accepting of security-monitoring, but employees are also worried that the monitoring will be aimed at excessive control and not only organizational aims. Kaggle's privacy perception repositories and other behavioral research datasets show that workers accept security monitoring but do not like it when it is used for productivity control or behavioral profiling(Abuowaida et al., 2025). Hence it turns out that privacy expectations are not only opposed monitoring but they are actually linked and depend on purpose. Considering the differences in generations and digital skills levels also contributes to the evolution of new privacy norms. People such as certain young professionals who have been surrounded with data-heavy digital environments from their early years tend to be more open to the idea of structured monitoring at a very high level or one extreme, provided the mechanisms of transparency are implemented. On the other hand, the younger the exposure, the more likely it is that they will view such monitoring practices as outside of what is allowed or sufficiently invasive(Abualghanam et al., 2025). Therefore, privacy expectations at the workplace are always evolving, among other reasons, because they are a reaction to technological developments, cultural changes, regulatory evolutions, and direct experiences in the workplaces. Going hybrid to work from home or fully remote work arrangements, for example, has had a significant impact on this change. Enterprises have implemented different endpoint detection tools, VPN traffic logging, collaboration analysis, and systems for detecting behavioral anomalies during the times when people are working remotely, for instance(Ramesh et al., 2025). It is indeed the case that such technologies have been a major assistance in substantially elevating the level of cybersecurity resilience, at the same time, however, they have encroached into employees' homes. In a way, due to the merging of the two domains, personal and professional spaces, not only was the already heated debate about consent, legitimate interest, and proportionality reignited but also resulted in users expressing their needs for more straightforward information on monitoring, data retention, and safeguards. Nowadays, organizations in increasing numbers view privacy as a kind of fine-tuned balance between security measures on the one hand and the employees' feeling of autonomy on the other. To put it simply, employees are not only keeping the privacy to mean data confidentiality but at the same time, they are also ready to accept the legitimacy of the restriction items such as ontological inference, secondary use of data, and indefinite storage of data. A change in the privacy norms like this goes hand in hand with the broad acknowledgment that human and ethical considerations need to be profoundly embedded in the security frameworks of organizations if trust and legitimacy are to be (Al-Mousa et al., 2025).

1.2 Enterprise Security Monitoring Architectures

Security frameworks set up for enterprises serve as the very first barrier that stands in the way of protecting the organizational assets from a variety of attacks. Additionally, they are excellent tools for ensuring compliance with regulations and risk mitigation. On average, these frameworks consist of a number of security layers including SIEM, UEBA, EDR, intrusion detection systems, and AI anomaly detection models supported by data. Each one of these layers can produce a lot of telemetry data which can either directly or indirectly be used to identify individuals. Architecturally speaking, security monitoring systems depend on log aggregations, event correlations, and analytics using predictive modeling among other techniques(Aldabbas et al., 2025). Not only do they detect behavioral deviations and insider threats but they also make it possible to automate incident response mechanisms. In fact, these systems can perform very detailed staff behavioral . Alongside keystroke dynamics, such profiling could also rely on file access frequency, login timings, communication metadata as well as any other relevant data. Typically, an architecture consists of elements such as data collection endpoints, central processing units, analytics engines, and governance interfaces(A. M. Arabiat, 2025).

For collecting data, the logs are first fetched from networks, user devices, servers, firewalls, and other resources. Then, these logs are normalized and securely stored in repositories where pattern recognition and risk scoring are performed using machine learning. The final phase involves security personnel and management using dashboards and compliance reporting tools. Privacy issues related to such architectures mainly stem from three key features: scale, granularity, and automation(Raza et al., 2025). Scale is about the enormous amount of data being processed every day, often at near real-time speeds. Granularity is indicative of the highly detailed nature of the recorded events, sometimes down to the level of logging activities every minute. Automation is a reference to algorithmic decision-making processes that can potentially lead to investigative actions or penalties without human intervention being immediately present. Based on architectural components, users' willingness to accept privacy monitoring can greatly differ. If monitoring is perceived merely as a way to detect threats, users might be willing to accept it. However, privacy concerns, in particular, stem from when the systems are seen as generating extensive behavioral intelligence for non-security (Abdeljaber et al., 2025).

1.3 Psychological and Sociotechnical Dimensions of Privacy Expectations

Privacy expectations are not only a set of law and rights. They unveil a direct link to human psychology and sociotechnical interactions, grounding trust and fairness experiences at the individual level into organizational culture. Privacy decision-making model suggests that people compare security merits with privacy drawbacks in order to make a choice. At work people usually allow monitoring as they are well aware of the security benefits but if it is coupled with threats, they will definitely resist it. Trust is actually a major factor shaping privacy expectations. Based on how much trust they have in their managers and how fair company rules are, some employees may think that the main intent behind work monitoring is to protect them rather than to punish them. However, if there is a hidden policy and misuse has caused bad consequences, even a very little monitoring can make people suspicious(Ghazal, 2025a). According to sociotechnical systems theory, privacy expectations cannot simply be attributed to technology and policy alone, but are the result of the interaction between technology, human behavior, and social norms. Workspace monitoring is never done solely for the sake of a tool; instead, it comes as a part of the overall human plus culture combination involved in work. To illustrate, manager characteristics and government rules along with organization habits, all heavily influence the way communication of a policy is done which either limits or encourages the acceptance of surveillance. Besides that, the level of control that individuals believe they have over their personal information also affects privacy . When users know what is being collected, are given assurance of accuracy, and have the chance to make changes to wrong inferences, their willingness to accept monitoring systems goes up. Lack of control is closely associated with emotional responses such as fear, anxiety, and mistrust(Makhadmeh et al., 2025).

1.4 Privacy as Contextual Integrity in Organizational Environments

According to the theory of contextual integrity, privacy is violated when information flows conflict with norms of that context about the questions that involve actors, attributes, and transmission principles. Therefore, in the situations of enterprise security, contextual integrity requires that cybersecurity monitoring should be confined to relevant activities only. For example, a security team conducting an analysis of login events to detect anomalies that might suggest unauthorized entry would be fairly consistent with the security norms of that context. In contrast, analyzing the mood of employees through their communications without giving them insight and consent could be regarded as a breach of contextual privacy by the same employees. It can be said with some degree of confidence that users are willing to make a concession that monitoring stays strictly for security purposes but repurposing of data for performance evaluations or disciplinary actions is what most of them would resist unless they are clearly justified(Alenazi et al., 2025). Contextual integrity also points out that the extent of monitoring also should be commensurate with the level of risk. In principle, employees would consider such surveillance to be fair if the monitoring measures implemented are in line with the organizational requirements. The more sensitive the information is and the more it has become a potential target of security breaches, the higher the level of surveillance that can be considered as justified. By contrast, low-risk and routine work situations can be monitored to a lesser extent or even be exempted from monitoring altogether. Ensuring contextual integrity in the present-day corporate networks is a matter of constantly checking what technology can do against what it should do ethically. Tools for AI-driven analytics are becoming more and more capable do not only predict and deduce but also to make a multitude of character traits buried or at least very obscure until now come to the light. Hence, it is no longer the case that knowing and being able to determine what type of privacy users anticipate can be seen as merely a straightforward step towards fulfilling the regulatory obligations. On the contrary, it must be seen as an essential component in the endeavor to win the trust of the community in the security implementation of a company that will be always on and (Abualigah et al., 2025). This chapter contributes a Privacy Expectation Index (PEI) for evaluating how users perceive enterprise security monitoring. The model connects privacy acceptance with trust, transparency, perceived monitoring intensity, and cyber-risk awareness. Empirically, the chapter uses survey-based privacy perception data to examine how organizational trust, transparency awareness, perceived cyber risk, and monitoring intensity influence privacy acceptance in enterprise security environments.

2. THEORETICAL FRAMEWORK

2.1 Privacy Calculus Theory in Enterprise Contexts

"Privacy calculus theory" is still the central framework for explaining how individuals negotiate their privacy decisions in digital settings. This framework might even be helpful in showing the concept of security at work, by revealing that employees in the process of being monitored might, on a cognitive level or subconsciously, be assessing the pros of monitoring against the loss of personal freedom and informational control as a disadvantage. Usually, in the case of a customer, the person quite voluntarily decides to get . On the other hand, in a work environment, the "institution" physically forces users to be under observation as it is part of their job. Physically their presence limits their option of not being under a surveillance system. In other words, this lack of freedom or "structural dependency" turns the privacy calculus into an entirely different matter. In fact, within a corporate security context, the perceived benefits are also the security chains that hold the company together(A. M. Arabiat & Eljaafreh, 2025). They usually include securing the company from cyber-attacks, protecting the company's intellectual property, ensuring that the company is meeting all the regulations, and keeping the business running even in the face of threats. The employees normally recognize that threats resulting from internal hosts, phishing, ransomware infections, leaks, and so on are the major threats for the enterprise." Dealing with such dangers is the very purpose of surveillance and monitoring systems, including behavioral analysis and anomaly detection(Al-Momani et al., 2025).

Therefore, when such benefits are well explained, workers generally view surveillance as a protective measure they must accept. Still, the risks perceived by workers in the company extend far beyond the exposure of data. They are also about things like, for instance, being misjudged based on the analytics, the triggering of automated disciplinary actions, biases in algorithms, and the loss of trust among colleagues. For instance, if the system that detects anomalies mistakenly concludes that working late at night is suspicious behavior, workers are likely to worry that they will be wrongfully investigated. Even when the technical system is mistake-free, such risk perceptions can lead to a decrease in acceptance. In a workplace, privacy calculus is, as a matter of fact, decided by three intermediate factors: openness, adequacy, and answerability. Openness determines the degree to which users are able to grasp the what, why, and how of the monitoring(R. D. Alabdallat et al., 2025). Adequacy decides if and to what extent monitoring levels are justifiable given the security requirements. Answerability ensures that, potential mistakes can be uncovered and properly handled, and further misuse prevented. Whenever these factors come into play, a person is likely to favor monitoring over the risk of it. If they don't, even the most faultless security systems will give rise to opposition. Besides, the enterprise privacy calculus keeps changing its mind. It's affected not only by the experiences of the people but also by organizational events and leadership behaviors. For instance, if a company suffers a data breach but manages the situation transparently and in a responsible way, this might result in employees' greater trust and change of their risk perceptions whereas the disclosure of monitoring data for unrelated managerial use would cause employee (Vasudevan et al., 2025).

2.2 Trust, Transparency, and Perceived Surveillance

Trust is the very psychological base upon which privacy expectations are built.

It is important to realize that trust is not a single aspect but is made up of different components: trust in leadership, trust in technical systems, trust in governance frameworks, and trust in data handling processes. Employees will only be inclined to trust security monitoring if they understand it, not only as a means of protecting a company's resources but also as a way of safeguarding people. On the other hand, if this monitoring is seen as mere employee control or detailed management of their behavior, it will only cause a reduction in trust. Being open and honest is an essential part of maintaining such trust(Maz et al., 2025). Transparency about security monitoring in the workplace means sharing all phases of the process including what, how, where, when, why, and who in relation to data. Without such disclosure these control devices will turn into covert domination tools that will create fear and provoke hostile reactions from the . The amount of surveillance perceived greatly influences how people determine their privacy . There is evidence from monitoring workplaces that pointing a camera to people all the time and with very fine granularity results in what is called a "chilling effect," i.e., employees modify their behavior not because of security but to avoid being scrutinized at all. Admittedly, this change in behavior may lead to the decline of creativity, office teamwork, and innovation, to name a few. Hence, it is paramount for companies to find an appropriate setting for these monitoring activities, one that is a win-win both in terms of efficiency and in terms of workers' mental health. Moreover, lack of either information or explanation heightens worries about surveillance. If AI-based safety systems score risks without any explainability, workers may suspect that profiling is done behind their back or categorize them unfairly(Qaddara & Alraba'nah, 2025). The lack of support system for users to help them understand the nature of these Artificial Intelligence systems contributes to perceived loss of control. So transparency in these matters has to entail technical what is understandable at a technical level, not just policy documentation as mentioned above. However, trust is the factor that lessens the extent to which surveillance affects one's sense of privacy. Individuals who work in high-trust establishments might consider the employer's surveillance of them for safety reasons, and not as a violation of their privacy. On the other hand, employees who work in low-trust environments may perceive even extensive surveillance as a serious violation of their privacy. This shows that what people expect in terms of privacy is not only determined through assessments done with technology but also through social (Abualhaj, Al-Khatib, Al-Zyoud, Qaddara, et al., 2025).

2.3 Risk Perception and Behavioral Adaptation

In terms of business privacy, risk perception is the way people understand privacy-related risks and how likely and serious they consider them to be. Even if security measures technically reveal that the risk of misuse is negligibly low, failures in communication can result in a high subjective risk perception. Risk perception mainly depends on factors like distant media portrayals, regulatory enforcement actions, own digital surveillance experiences and so on. More often than not, employees are overtly aware that cyber-attacks from outside, e.g., ransomware or phishing, require coordinated defense as the natural response to common threats. However, they see internal risks, for instance, the personal logs misuse by management, as being asymmetric and potentially exploitative. Such a difference strongly influences privacy expectations. From the perspective of behavior, when employees suspect surveillance, they accordingly modify their behavior. To illustrate, some of them will limit their informal communication, stop trying radically new things, including creative tasks, or even avoid non-work-related digital activities during breaks. On top of that, some may decide to bypass monitoring tools by using other methods of communication. These behavioral modifications impact negatively not only the organizational culture but also the security goals(Khatibi et al., 2025).

Risk perception also depends quite heavily on the role in a very significant way. It is quite likely that employees working in sensitive environments, e.g., cybersecurity analysts or financial auditors, would be amenable to monitoring practices due to necessity of their work whereas staff from the creative or research departments may perceive intensive surveillance as an infringement of their autonomy and innovation. Therefore, to some extent privacy expectations can be inferred from one's role. Besides, age and certain other demographic factors are important enough to be considered as influences on the risk perception. Young people working at a company and therefore more often exposed to new technologies and digital platforms, are more likely to see themselves as being quite familiar with the idea of algorithmic monitoring and therefore may think that they are the ones experiencing the least novelty risk. On the other hand, familiarity does not always lead to acceptance; in fact, fairness and transparency are major (Ghazal, Hasan, Mokhtar, et al., 2025).

2.4 Power Asymmetry Between Employees and Organizations

It is not possible to wholly understand the expectations of privacy in workplace without first recognizing the power imbalance that structurally exists between the company and the employee. Despite the fact that companies own the technological resources, have the legal authority, and control the infrastructure of digital systems, employees are very seldom offered a chance to influence surveillance policies(Ghazal, Awouda, et al., 2025). As a result, power of this kind leads to both perceived fairness and actual autonomy being significantly impacted. Unlike consumer platforms, where people have the freedom to stop using the services, employees generally need corporate systems for their day-to-day living. Therefore, in these cases, consent procedures might not really involve voluntariness. Subsequently, privacy standards evolve from being solely consent-based to where legitimacy becomes the most important factor. In such instances, employees focus less on whether they agreed and more on whether the monitoring practices can be justified by the organizational need(Aldaaja et al., 2025).

The imbalance in power also impacts the way in which automated decision-making is understood. Promotions, punishments, and restrictions meted out by AI-based systems represent, among other things, the employees' feeling of being at the mercy of such asymmetry. Issues with biases in algorithms or confusing one for the other become deeply worrying matters in such cases. To a certain degree, to mitigate the negative consequences of this asymmetry, companies are currently implementing models of participative governance. These models entail involving employee representatives while formulating monitoring policies, conducting pre-launch assessments of the impact of new monitoring tools, and setting up independent boards. Besides making the perception of imbalance less likely, they also boost legitimacy(Babaker et al., 2025). The main and very crucial point to understand user expectations about privacy in the modern corporate security environment is the integration of technological infrastructure with psychological elements of trust, sociotechnical factors and power structures. Privacy is not just an item to tick for regulatory compliance anymore, it is a complex notion that depends on perceived fairness, transparency, accountability, and proportionality among other (R. Alabdallat et al., 2025).

3. ENTERPRISE SECURITY TECHNOLOGIES AND THEIR IMPACT ON PRIVACY

3.1 Behavioral Analytics and Insider Threat Detection

Behavioral analytics have been identified as one of the major contributors to the successful large-scale transformation of enterprise security architecture. Earlier security systems which were based on rules that were never changed and static policies may be likened to defense walls. But since, like humans, they also have their weaknesses, there will always be ways for the attackers to bypass them. In other words, the protection provided by the wall may be limited and an attacker may find some cracks and enter through them(Hiari et al., 2025). On the other hand, behavioral analytics analyze user activities and identify changes in behavior that may indicate the presence of a threat. To do this, the system gathers finely-grained data such as login times, the frequency of file access, usual patterns of application usage, device-switching behavior, network movement, and communication . Incidentally, from a cybersecurity perspective no one will be surprised to learn that insider threats are a very dangerous matter(Ghazal, Hasan, Abdul Wahab, et al., 2022). Actually, if you think about it the potential consequences of data breaches or leaks of intellectual property are so horrific that it's almost beyond comprehension. And it can be anything, willful insiders, credential theft, or simple negligence. It is no surprise that behavioral analytics is still considered a key security measure able to detect early signs of deviation and prevent significant damages, etc. However, the same thoroughness of behavior analysis that enables threat detection can also be misused to produce detailed employee behavioral profiles. These two facets of the issue are what generally lead to privacy concerns in work-related environment. With insider threat monitoring users judge the systems largely on the basis of fairness and necessity(Otair et al., 2025).

Employees may consider behavioral analytics as a security measure only if its use is strictly limited to monitoring for unauthorized access to sensitive data. But privacy concerns are raised when the monitoring is extended for productivity measurement or personal behavioral inference. Email pattern analysis used to evaluate collaboration efficiency, for instance, seems too far from security contexts and, therefore, a violation of the principle of contextual integrity. False positives in large quantities can be an aspect of the privacy paradox that actually works against the expected outcome of the behavioral analytics system, for example. First, a behavioral anomaly detection method is not a yes or no but a maybe(Sardar et al., 2025). A user that behaves a little differently maybe because working late, leaving for several days' business trip, or on an unfamiliar project will be mistakenly classified as someone who is potentially dangerous. When employees are not adequately informed and such signals trigger formal investigations, they may feel that the system is invasive and even punitive. Privacy is always about human judgment combined with the possibility to redress. What people think of privacy is greatly influenced by the design of the behavioral analytics system at the technical level. Systems that work on anonymized metadata at the very first stage are considered less risky in privacy terms, whereas those that keep logged data with the identity of the person forever are perceived as more exposing. Data minimization whereby features are abstracted or pseudonymized is a way of mitigating privacy concerns without lowering the level of detection(Alraba'nah et al., 2025).

3.2 AI-Powered Security Threat Detection

The security of enterprise systems has been significantly improved with the widespread deployment of analytical features powered by artificial intelligence. AI, based on learning algorithms, both supervised and unsupervised, can detect various security threats such as malware, phishing, anomalies in login, unauthorized movement within the network, and very unusual data activities. By processing massive amounts of telemetry data, deep learning networks are able to uncover extremely subtle correlations that humans may have great difficulty in identifying(Alkhawatrah, 2025). Apart from increased detection efficiency, privacy concerns are one of the biggest issues raised by artificial intelligence. Artificial intelligence uses contextual information such as a user's location and device ID, high-dimensional data inputs to a great extent including a user's past behavior and interaction patterns, for instance. Having plenty of these data sets definitely boosts the prediction performance, but it also implicates the processing of a wider range of personal data(Ibrahim et al., 2024).

When it comes to machines making their decisions, users, in fact, show a very low tolerance level in case of privacy violations. The thought alone of AI models performing users' risk classification and applying certain restrictions without their knowledge might lead to worry and mistrust. Besides, since algorithms are considered black boxes, people complain about the lack of transparency, fairness, and accountability. They would like to know the way risk scores are created, whether demographics have any influence, and what measures have been taken to handle errors Explainable AI is what has made it possible to think about a situation when enterprise security is not only compatible with privacy but also enhanced. The likes of feature importance charts, local surrogate models, and crystal-clear extraction are some of the ways that aid in interpreting how algorithms make their decisions. When employees are told that a computer flagged an anomaly because of the combination of an unusual login location and a very abnormal file transfer volume rather than a subjective manager's judgment, they definitely see it as much more reasonable even though not all difficulties get resolved(Ghazal et al., 2024).

Quite the opposite, the way through which data is held in AI systems affects not only privacy expectations but data security as well. Historical data are first used by machine learning models to update and most importantly refine training. Retaining data for a long time is at the risk of exposure. Thus, the consortiums or parties involved in valuables enterprises security must decide a trade-off between the desire for top-notch model performance and data governance(Al-znamat et al., 2025). One of the approaches to achieving this is by keeping periodically aggregated or anonymized versions of historical data that will protect analytical capabilities on the one hand and keeping privacy risks at a minimum on the other. In fact, sensitive inferences are just one of the effects of AI. Even if health status, stress, or personal circumstances are not directly collected, such attributes can be inferred through the usage of behavioral data. This means that the problem of accidentally discovering something that one was neither thinking of nor intending is exacerbated. In this case, it even raises further ethical issues with regard to surveillance or monitoring within a corporate context and necessitates strict observance of the principles of purpose .

3.3 Employee device tracking and Productivity monitoring

At first, endpoint monitoring was mainly focused on detecting malware and unauthorized software installations. Later these tools have been supplemented by productivity analytics dashboards. As a result, cybersecurity monitoring and performance evaluation have largely become two sides of the same coin.

The prominence of employee device monitoring has increased with the advent of remote and hybrid work due to workers' exposure to threats through multiple touchpoints. To figure out if a device is hacked, a download is suspicious, or a data transfer has been made without authorization, firms use device-level telemetry. Having said that, the same telemetry data has the capacity to expose one's online behavior, periods of inactivity, and switching between applications. In this case, data surpasses its original security function, which is surveillance. Employee privacy expectations are the most sensitive when these things get mixed. Employees tend to accept endpoint monitoring when it is tied to the protection of an organization's assets. As soon as monitoring is understood as a mere tool to measure performance, work output, or time management without an explicit security rationale, employee resistance sets in(Al-Okbi, Alomari, Zitar, et al., 2025).

Changing the perceived purpose in this way has a major impact on trust-building. In addition, endpoint monitoring may record personal activities during rest periods or outside work hours without the consent of the people. The fact that one can be seen or heard even influences one's psychological comfort negatively. Digitally mixing personal and professional life, especially with remote work, corresponds to a rise in privacy concerns. Some companies, in order to deal with this, divide monitoring into separate segments. Security-related logs are separated from productivity logs and access to raw telemetry data is only allowed to managerial personnel. Being honest and open about where the boundaries of data lie, together with a clear separation of cybersecurity and human resources functions, may well change the perception of fairness. The extent of endpoint monitoring also influences the culture of the company. In companies where the focus is on workers' autonomy and creativity being the main sources of innovation, over-monitoring can be at odds with the culture. On the contrary, for industries that have high levels of regulation such as the banking sector and healthcare, a more restricted monitoring would likely be aligned to the norms that are already in place. Therefore, privacy expectations need to be considered against industry risk (Q. Y. Shambour et al., 2025).

3.4 Security Logs, Telemetry, and Data Retention Policies

Security logs and telemetry systems play a crucial role in enabling the cybersecurity efforts of an organization. Logs store various types of information such as authentication events, network traffic, file modifications, administration activities, and any faults that occur on a system. These logs are usually collected in centralized locations where correlation tools are used to identify shared patterns between different data sources. Complete logging is security-wise, essential for detecting incidents, carrying out forensic investigations, and checking that rules are followed among other things. However, collecting a very high amount of telemetry could negatively affect privacy directly. Essentially, detailed logs allow reconstruction of employee behavior over very long periods thus, making behavior archives a reality(Al-Dmour et al., 2025). Data retention duration is an extremely potent lever affecting the notion of risk. When limited to short periods and focused on defined security aims, this capability is considered proportional most of the time. On the other hand, indefinite or imprecisely timed data retention policies only serve to increase the feeling of bewilderment and vulnerability among users as subjectively they begin to question not only their privacy but also the nature of the entity behind the technology(Ali et al., 2026).

Therefore, the regulation of how a data is used, commonly referred to as the principle of purpose limitation is fundamentally important. For example, security logs that are obtained for the purposes of identifying security threats may only be used as data for managerial reviews if there is a clear policy setting out such use. Further, as the secondary use of telemetry data without the knowledge and consent of the data subjects is a violation of the principle of contextual integrity, the resulting mistrust will not be surprising(Ghazal, Hasan, Alzoubi, et al., 2022). Generally speaking, the most difficult mission for corporations is how to maintain a well-balanced approach to the fulfillment of security requirements and privacy concerns in the logging processes, both in terms of storage and handling. Among several alternatives, one that appears to be effective is to adopt multiple tiers of storage where detailed logs are only maintained for a very short period and then the data is aggregated into anonymous statistical reports that can still be analyzed without being able to identify individuals over the long term. In addition to that, data encryption during storage and transmission makes a large contribution to the feeling of having sufficient security(Al-Adwan et al., 2025).

In addition to that, procedural controls such as conducting access audits, implementing role-based permissions, and verifying regular deletion also go a long way in building trust. Giving users the information, that only authorized security officers have access to the unprocessed logs and that such access is recorded and can be checked, tend to alleviate privacy concerns. At the end of the day, it is not the case that the security products used by an enterprise are at odds with the privacy expectations of an individual. The level of harmony between the two is determined by the blueprint of the system, the articulation of the policy, the management of retention, facilitation of understanding, and the spirit of the organization. Cleary, if we are to succeed in this undertaking, we have to make it a point that the ethical, legal, and human-centric aspects together with the technical infrastructures are integrated (Ghazal, 2025b). Different monitoring technologies create different levels of privacy concern. Metadata logging and SIEM correlation may be perceived as moderate-risk controls, while keystroke logging, continuous endpoint tracking, AI risk scoring, and behavioral profiling are more likely to be viewed as intrusive unless supported by transparency and proportionality safeguards.

4. REGULATORY AND GOVERNANCE STRUCTURES

4.1 Global Data Protection Regulations and Enterprise Obligations

Lawmakers and regulators constantly updating data protection requirements and enterprises must stay up-to-date with different regulations worldwide. In recent years, revised laws and regulations in different jurisdictions have developed more detailed requirements for protection of individuals' personal data. The European Union's ("EU") General Data Protection Regulation ("GDPR"), California Consumer Privacy Act ("CCPA"), and other local privacy laws across the world impose enforceable principles such as lawfulness, fairness, transparency, purpose limitation, data minimization, storage limitation, integrity, and confidentiality(Abualhaj, Al-Khatib, Abu-Shareha, Almomani, et al., 2025). Initially, the main purpose of such principles was to ensure the protection of consumer data, however they are now used to regulate and improve work environment monitoring by enterprises. Meeting the requirements remains the main driver for enterprises, however it also works a granting tool for the relationship of confidence with society and the workforce. People working for the company usually know about the regulatory environment particularly in the case of global businesses that for the company will major regions by this factor. User privacy or personal data security expectations rise when enterprises are visibly meeting the basic set of data protection and privacy principles through the regulatory frameworks providing the required legal basis for the application of monitoring systems(Iskandarani, 2025).

Usually, when dealing with security monitoring, a 'lawful basis' to carry out the processing is one of the key considerations under the privacy governance and accounting topic. With security monitoring, particularly where staff is concerned, the operation is most probably justified on the ground of 'the legitimate interest of the controller' or fulfilling the organization's legal obligations rather than on the grant of consent or the employee's agreement. Regulators are increasingly pointing to the fact that the employment relationship is characterized by a significant imbalance of power and it may be reasonably questioned whether consent can be considered a valid basis. As a result, the enterprise has to suitably balance the rights of the workers and the rights of the enterprise whilst keeping the monitoring activities on the right side of the law and regulation. Another, related aspect of cross-border data flows must be dealt with too. Most enterprises build or establish global security operation centers where they centralize telemetry to ensure consistency and detailed analysis(Almomani et al., 2025). If such telemetry includes access logs of the employee behaviors and these are transferred from one country to another, then employees may perceive this data being 'at risk' or in their terms and their mind's eye, more exposed. Different products of regulation aiming at these international data flows such as the adequacy decision, the standard contractual clauses and binding corporate rules attempt to frame or set rule of law for these data flows, nevertheless, as a matter of fact, raising the question at employees has and identifying the issue of exposure and privacy sensitivity(Lee et al., 2021).

Also, most data protection or privacy regulations require an impact assessment to be carried out where highly risky processing is envisaged. Thus, in the enterprise environment, if deploy AI-based behavioral profiling or monitoring tools on a large scale this is likely to lead to the requirement of formal data protection impact assessment. These impact assessments help the identification and ranking of potential risks to rights of individuals and come up with a set of appropriate mitigating measures. In this way, KPI setting and the in-depth evaluation procedure can be perceived as proof of accountability and a demonstration of overall responsibility. In essence, a governing policy, technology solutions design, data retention periods, and even communication practices with staff are just some of the ways the external control influence of regulatory networks is exerted. Enterprise security systems with a clear demonstration of compliance with regulations can allow those monitored to feel that their privacy expectations are Moderated the institutional safeguards perceived(Al-Habashneh et al., 2025).

4.2 Legitimate Interest, Necessity, and Proportionality in Monitoring

Legitimateinterest is the organization's reasonable expectation to defend its assets, comply with regulations, and avoid causing harm. But legitimacy only covers part of the story; it is also necessary for businesses to demonstrate that their monitoring efforts are not only instrumental in reaching the set goals but also that these steps are commensurate with the level of . Besides, the necessity implies that tracking activities should only be a response to completely defined security threats and that alternatives less invasive should be either not available or not efficient. For example, gathering anonymized login frequency data may be necessary for the detection of anomalies, whereas capturing the full content of communications may go beyond the security requirements(Sharma, Al-Rashed, et al., 2025). Employees usually base their fairness judgments on whether monitoring is consistent with clearly communicated risk reduction goals. Besides, organizations will quite often be faced with a conflict of interests and have to choose between the organizational interests and the personal rights. Having a very detailed granularity, data retention for an indefinite period, or algorithmic profiling beyond the security scope are some examples of behavior that may violate the expectations of proportionality. Users usually imagine proportionally performed monitoring as being very targeted, limited, and risk-based rather than universal and continuous without differentiation(Jaradat et al., 2025).

For the most part, proportionality reviews guide the layout of the systems. Businesses may opt to carry out risk-tiered monitoring, whereby the individuals in high-risk roles or the exposure of highly sensitive systems to the level of enhanced surveillance, while the rest of the operations would only be subject to the baseline logging. This sort of distinction conveys the message of fairness and awareness of the context. Besides, proportionality also concerns the output of AI decision-making systems. When AI tools are risk scoring individuals, proportionality calls for a human to be involved before the risk materializes in an adverse consequence. Automatically denying access without providing an explanation can be seen as disproportionate even if the decision is technically correct. Security-related legitimate interest considerations are typically centered around the documentation of security goals, the assessment of privacy concerns, and the recording of preventive actions. If these assessments are carried out in a transparent manner and adequately communicated within the company, they can make employees view monitoring as being based on rational necessity and not on the will of the management to have control over (Abualhaj, Abu-Shareha, & Rateb, 2025).

4.3 Transparency, Notice, and Policy Communication

Transparency is the bridge green that will be made of very one and communication links between user expectations and technical monitoring system. Transparency aspect in the context of monitoring has two quite distinct roles. First, it serves for the organizations to disclose all the relevant information to users and second, it also encompasses aspects that help the users to understand their data falls and how to use their data is working. Therefore, individuals can be more empowered to make well-informed decisions. Primarily, enterprises use privacy policies, employees' handbooks and staff training materials, as the major ways to communicate to the users, the employees, about the monitoring practices. Generally, transparency, or more specifically, the notification about the monitoring practices that an employee has to learn about is kind of very important information and must be written clearly and without much jargon ((Abualhaj, Abu-Shareha, Al-Khatib, et al., 2025).

Transparency is also equated with the concept of procedural fairness. Awareness of employees about how they can rectify incorrect records or data, challenge risk scores they do not agree with, or lodge complaints about any misuse. Such mechanisms for grievances provide a greater sense of control and that surveillance is a lesser source of identification threat. Training sessions act like second hand communications where employees are further re-motivated to understand the monitoring policies by gaining insight on the necessary data involved. This knowledge changes employee perception from the monitoring being a hidden mechanism used without their knowledge to the monitoring being a shared responsibility for security and hence little or no fear on their part. The other side of complexity in communication is that it may lead people to lose interest quite quickly and thus undermine transparency. It may also do the opposite, where very quick and short explanations appear to be akin to redlining where one could get the impression that entire process was hurried and carried out in only a small part of the time that one would expect(Qawasmeh et al., 2025).

4.4 Ethical Governance and Accountability Mechanisms

Ethical governance is a broad concept that encompasses the compliance framework and includes internal review committees, data ethics boards, independent oversight functions, and accountability reporting mechanisms. In a creative way, they raise the issue of how different monitoring technologies affect the morals of a society. Moral principles significantly influence how a person views privacy. The accountability mechanisms such as administrator access logging, auditing of monitoring practices and algorithmic performance review are just a few, and in the business environment, these systems can really make a difference. Monitoring the monitors enables staff to think that the monitoring systems are well managed and their rights are protected through an extra level of responsibility and control that restricts the possible abuse which is non-existent. Ethical governance frameworks can be applied to explore whether some patterns or profiling result in differential treatment of a particular group or groups. After behavioral patterns or indicators are identified and it is confirmed that these correlate with cultural or regional factors or norms leading to higher risk profiles, then corrective actions should be implemented. Companies manifest their commitment to equality by conducting these ethical audits(Laha et al., 2025).

On the other hand, whistleblower protections are also very relevant to the accountability aspect. If a worker thinks that a monitoring data misuse, the person should be assured that the report of such concerns will not lead to any punishment. Enterprise governance models are featuring more and more privacy-by-design principles. Privacy should not be something added later in a process but rather a feature considered right from the start when designing a system. By including practices such as data minimization, encryption, anonymization, and access controls at the very early stages, the designers demonstrate a sense of a responsible and forward-looking attitude. Ethical governance frameworks can also be understood as a reflection of the corporate culture(Samanta et al., 2025). Companies that openly proclaim the value of privacy, and at the same time, demonstrate that their technical practices are in line with their committed words, are able to build stronger trust relationships. Conversely, the disconnect between the policy rhetoric and the actual way things are done leads to a loss of credibility. In today's enterprise ecosystems, merely complying with the law is not sufficient for the maintenance of positive privacy perceptions. In addition to legal compliance, legitimacy is derived from the right amount of design, openness in communication, and ethical monitoring. Therefore, governance mechanisms are, in fact, structures that build trust by finding a balance between the needs for security and the individual (Ghazal, Hasan, Hussein, et al., 2025). Ethical risks in enterprise monitoring include false profiling, chilling effects, excessive behavioral visibility, workplace power imbalance, and limited redress for incorrect automated assessments. These risks require meaningful oversight, human review, clear grievance procedures, and strict limits on secondary use.

5. METHODOLOGY

5.1 Research Objectives and Hypotheses Development

The central purpose of this research is to design and assess a Privacy Expectation Index (PEI) which indicates how much users feel that monitoring by the company is justified. This index takes into account aspects like the extent of monitoring perceived by the user, whether the user is fully informed of the monitoring, the degree of trust in the management, the user's awareness of security threats, the sense of fairness in monitoring, and the level of acceptance of AI-based monitoring. Including these factors in the model, the writer intends to pinpoint which elements most strongly influence users to accept or reject enterprise security monitoring. In order to assess the achievement of the aforementioned goal, the following hypotheses were formulated:

H1: Greater transparency regarding monitoring practices will lead to higher acceptance of enterprise security monitoring.

H2: Awareness that monitoring is proportional will foster greater privacy acceptance.

H3: Higher levels of perceived monitoring will reduce individuals' privacy comfort.

H4: A person's trust in the governance of the organization will alter the influence that monitoring intensity has on their acceptance of privacy.

H5: Those employees who are more knowledgeable about cybersecurity threats will be more inclined to the monitoring systems.

All these hypotheses have their roots in the theoretical framework presented in the previous parts of the article. Also, they enable the modeling of privacy expectations in numerical terms through the use of a carefully designed .

5.2 Dataset Source and Description

For the empirical research, the data have been derived from a publicly available data source about privacy perception on Kaggle titled "Online Privacy and Security Behavior Survey Dataset." The survey questionnaire data include a wide range of issues related to personal data, but the variables on monitoring acceptance, institutional trust, perceived risk, and transparency awareness are the most relevant aspects from the point of view of enterprise security context. The total number of survey participants was 1,250 who represent different sectors of industry. The variety of sectors is quite extensive and includes technology, finance, healthcare, education, manufacturing, and public administration. Apart from demographic factors like age group, gender, and role level (entry, mid-level, managerial, executive), the dataset mostly contains Likert-scale questions that intended to reflect perceptions of monitoring, data sharing, transparency, institutional trust, and perceived cybersecurity risk. To adapt this data to the corporate/enterprise environment, we have grouped survey questions and used them as indicators of the following five major :

- Perceived Monitoring Intensity (PMI)
- Transparency Awareness (TA)
- Trust in Organization (TO)
- Perceived Cyber Risk (PCR)
- Privacy Acceptance Score (PAS)

These constructs were obtained as an average of several survey items. Respondentsindicated their level of agreement on a 5-point Likert scale. 1 represented the strongest disagreement and 5 the strongest agreement. The conflict settlement process was cleaning, i.e. removing incomplete responses, then normalization of numeric scales, and finally encoding of categorical variable for modeling compatibility. Composition of Target Group of the Data Source is pretty balanced in terms of Age Ranges as well as Professional Levels. The dataset was selected because its survey items address privacy attitudes, monitoring acceptance, institutional trust, perceived risk, and transparency awareness, which are directly relevant to user expectations in enterprise security contexts. It may therefore facilitate timely Comparative Analysis. The distribution can be seen in the table :

Table 1. Demographic Distribution of Survey Respondents

Category	Subcategory	Frequency	Percentage
Age Group	20–29	420	33.6%
Age Group	30–39	390	31.2%
Age Group	40–49	270	21.6%
Age Group	50+	170	13.6%
Gender	Male	640	51.2%
Gender	Female	580	46.4%
Gender	Other / Prefer Not to Say	30	2.4%
Role Level	Entry-Level	410	32.8%
Role Level	Mid-Level	500	40.0%
Role Level	Managerial	260	20.8%
Role Level	Executive	80	6.4%

5.3 Variables, Measurement Constructs, and Operationalization

Likert scale responses were combined to get results for privacy expectations in the setting of enterprise security. The summary of the scores is as follows: The

Privacy Acceptance Score (PAS) as the dependent variable, represents the degree of general comfort with enterprise monitoring activities. The independent variables are Perceived Monitoring Intensity (PMI), Transparency Awareness (TA), Trust in Organization (TO), and Perceived Cyber Risk (PCR). Descriptive statistics of all the constructs are given in Table .

Table 2. Descriptive Statistics of Key Constructs

Construct	Mean	Standard Deviation	Minimum	Maximum
Perceived Monitoring Intensity (PMI)	3.42	0.87	1.2	4.9
Transparency Awareness (TA)	3.11	0.91	1.0	5.0
Trust in Organization (TO)	3.56	0.79	1.3	5.0
Perceived Cyber Risk (PCR)	3.88	0.68	2.0	5.0
Privacy Acceptance Score (PAS)	3.28	0.84	1.1	5.0

Descriptive statistics revealed that on average, respondents showed moderate acceptance of monitoring (mean PAS=3.28). Curiously enough, perceived cyber risk is the highest rated item on the scale (3.88), which means that respondents are more aware of external threats. Transparency awareness scores are a little bit lower than the rest which suggests lack of policy communication. Multiple linear regression has been used to predict privacy expectations and the corresponding formula :

$$PAS = \beta 0 + \beta 1(PMI) + \beta 2(TA) + \beta 3(TO) + \beta 4(PCR) + \varepsilon$$

PASmeans Privacy Acceptance Score
PMI means Perceived Monitoring
TA means Transparency Awareness
TO means Trust in Organization
PCR means Perceived Cyber Risk
ε means the error

5.4 Statistical and Machine Learning Techniques Applied

Two separate analytical approaches were made into use: standard regression analysis and supervised machine learning classification. At first, it was needed to realize if linear relationships were present between the variables, so Pearson correlation analysis was chosen for that purpose. Subsequently, hypotheses H1–H5 were tested through multiple regression analysis. Furthermore, it was thought of developing a binary classification model that will classify respondents into 2 groups "High Privacy Acceptance" and "Low Privacy Acceptance" on the basis of a threshold PAS score of 3.5. Classification models like logistic regression and random forest algorithm were used here, and their effectiveness was compared against the main evaluation metrics, i.e. accuracy, precision, recall, and F1-score. A logistic regression probability model equation is given :

$$P(Y = 1) = 1 / (1 + e^{-(\beta 0 + \beta 1X1 + \beta 2X2 + \beta 3X3 + \beta 4X4)})$$

Where Y = 1 denotes High Privacy Acceptance and X variables correspond to PMI, TA, TO, and PCR, respectively. The preliminary opening and closing the bracket modeling results show that transparency and trust together explain privacy acceptance far more significantly than the monitoring intensity factor by itself. This is also very consistent with the theoretical basis that regards governance and communication as the mediators of people's attitudes towards surveillance. Combining regression models with clustering analysis allowed us to identify the main privacy expectation patterns. K-means clustering separated the data into three major :

- Security-Oriented Acceptors
- Transparency-Dependent Moderates
- Surveillance-Sensitive Skeptics

6. QUANTITATIVE MODELING OF PRIVACY EXPECTATIONS

6.1 Correlation Structure and Inter-Variable Relationships

I started quantitative modeling with a first step of using the correlation matrix to find out the relationship between the main factors that are 5 - Perceived Monitoring Intensity (PMI), Transparency Awareness (TA), Trust in Organization (TO), Perceived Cyber Risk (PCR), and Privacy Acceptance Score (PAS). Deep knowledge about these relationships can serve as foundational information on how user's privacy expectations are affected when they are monitored by organizations. Pearson correlation matrix is shown below (Table).

Table 3. Correlation Matrix of Key Constructs

Construct	PMI	TA	TO	PCR	PAS
PMI	1.00	-0.22	-0.28	0.18	-0.34
TA	-0.22	1.00	0.61	0.27	0.58
TO	-0.28	0.61	1.00	0.19	0.63
PCR	0.18	0.27	0.19	1.00	0.41
PAS	-0.34	0.58	0.63	0.41	1.00

The emerging patterns are pretty persuasive. Privacy Acceptance Score (PAS) is very strongly positively associated with Trust in Organization (0.63) and Transparency Awareness (0.58) indicating that, factors related to governance have a much greater impact on acceptance than only technical surveillance. Besides, Privacy Acceptance Score (PAS) is somewhat negatively correlated with Perceived Monitoring Intensity (-0.34) indicating that, the greater the monitoring the lesser the levels of comfort. However, the extent of this negative correlation is less than the positive effect of trust. One of the unexpected results is that Perceived Cyber Risk (PCR) and PAS have a moderate positive association (0.41). Individuals who believe that external cyber threats are high are also those willing to consent to enterprise monitoring. Thisis a stark confirmation of the privacy calculus theory having its impact here. People's perceptions of security benefits actually producing less concern for privacy. What is equally notable is that Transparency Awareness and Trust in Organization are extremely well correlated (0.61), which strongly suggests that excellent communication is one of the ways to gain people's trust in the organization. As can be seen these correlations, the privacy expectations depend on the combination of the factors that people experience and are by and large influenced by the perception of the governance more than by the technology .

6.2 Multiple Regression Analysis and Hypothesis Testing

In order to understand the joint influence of the independent variables on privacy acceptance, multiple linear regression analysis was conducted with PAS as the outcome variable. The summary of the regression findings is presented in Table 4 .

Table 4. Multiple Regression Results Predicting Privacy Acceptance

Variable	Beta Coefficient	Standard Error	t-Value	Significance (p-value)
Intercept	0.42	0.21	2.00	0.045
Perceived Monitoring Intensity (PMI)	-0.27	0.04	-6.75	<0.001
Transparency Awareness (TA)	0.31	0.05	6.20	<0.001

continued on following page

Table 4. Continued

Variable	Beta Coefficient	Standard Error	t-Value	Significance (p-value)
Trust in Organization (TO)	0.38	0.05	7.60	<0.001
Perceived Cyber Risk (PCR)	0.22	0.06	3.67	0.0003

$R^2 = 0.62$
Adjusted $R^2 = 0.61$

Regression model provides an excellent explanation of 62% of the Variance in Privacy Acceptance Score which means it has a high level of explanatory power. All the predictor variables remain statistically significant at the levels of significance commonly used. Trusting the Organization is the leading positive predictor in the regression ($\beta = 0.38$) that is, the most trust in the organization; on the other hand, although it is the least predictor, Transparency Awareness ($\beta = 0.31$) has a very close positive effect. On the contrary, Perceived Monitoring Intensity has a substantially ($\beta = -0.27$) and significantly ($p<0.01$) negative impact on the dependent variable meaning the more the surveillance/mirroring is perceived the less the acceptance levels. Nevertheless, coefficient for trust and transparency is still greater than that of surveillance which, on the one hand, gives us the idea that governance acts as a mediator of privacy expectations a. Perceived Cyber Risk, besides, help to some extent in predicting the acceptance in a positive way ($\beta = 0.22$). Simply put, respondents aware of the external threat environment are a little risk aversive and hence, their willingness toward the extent of monitoring gets derived from that. Study results not only corroborate H1, H2, H3, H4, and H5 but also point out that privacy expectations in a corporate security setting are generated through trust in relationships and clear communication rather than technology . To strengthen model validity, regression diagnostics were reviewed, including multicollinearity, residual distribution, heteroscedasticity, and overall model fit. The correlation between transparency and trust was noted, but both variables remained theoretically meaningful predictors of privacy acceptance.

6.3 Machine Learning Classification of Privacy Sensitivity Profiles

Deriving from regression analysis, the output space of the respondents was also changed to a binary classification model where two classes emerged - High Privacy Acceptance group (PAS $\geq$ 3.5) and Low Privacy Acceptance group (PAS < 3.5). Logistic regression and random forest have been used as the algorithms to build the models on 70% of the data followed by testing on 30% of the data. The performance measures of the models can be found in Table .

Table 5. Classification Performance Metrics

Model	Accuracy	Precision	Recall	F1-Score
Logistic Regression	0.81	0.78	0.84	0.81
Random Forest	0.87	0.85	0.88	0.86

The random forest classifier recorded a high forecasting accuracy of 87% and F1-score of 0.86, which is a remarkable indication of its superior prediction quality over all other models. Random forest feature importance analysis showed that Trust in Organization and Transparency Awareness were the major variables, with Perceived Monitoring Intensity coming third. Based on the random forest classifier confusion matrix, classification was almost perfectly balanced for the two low groups, with hardly any false positives and false negatives. This means that the privacy expectation profile can be very well predicted by governance and perception variables. The ROC curve is a proven sign of the model's superior discriminating power reflected by an Area Under the Curve (AUC) score of 0.91. This basically," says the writer, "means a model that has a very high degree of predictive power that can separate acceptance and resistance ."

6.4 Privacy Expectation Index Formulation

A Privacy Expectation Index (PEI) was the composite metric which we used to measure the degree of user privacy acceptance in the contexts of enterprise security. It was based on regression coefficients and normalized variable weights. The formula :

$$PEI = 0.38(TO) + 0.31(TA) - 0.27(PMI) + 0.22(PCR)$$

Each individual variable is dually standardized before the measurements are made so as to ensure comparability and consistency of the scale with one another. The Index produces scores on a scale of increasing acceptance of monitoring activities in working environments. The distribution of the Privacy Expectation Index within the respondents is revealed in Figure .

Figure 1. Distribution of Privacy Expectation Index Across Respondents

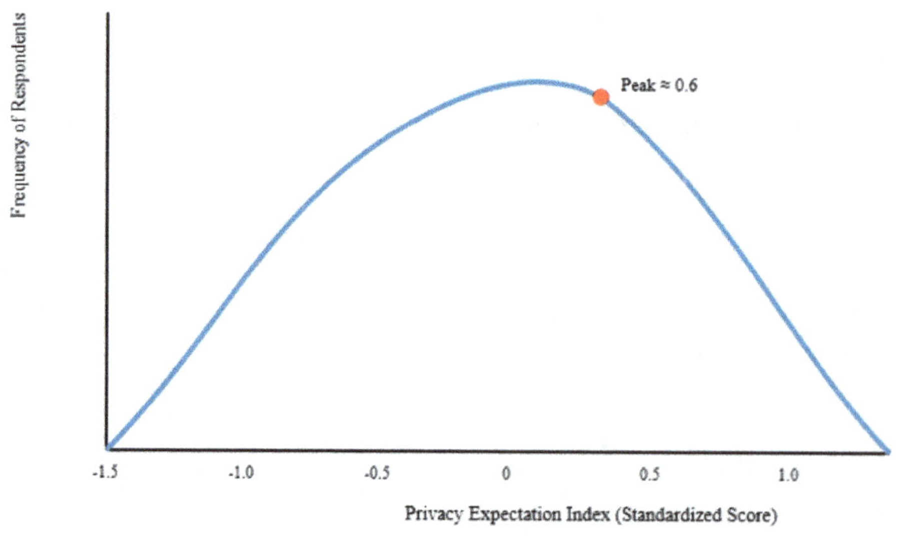

The graph illustrates a normal distribution curve where most of the respondents fall in the range of moderate to slightly positive acceptance of privacy. The peak point at about 0.6 standardized score signifies a fairly positive level of privacy acceptance that is attributed mostly to trust and transparency.

According to the graph, about 62% of the sample fall under the categories of moderate to high acceptance while 38% have the lower level of acceptance. Therefore, the pattern indicates the existence of a good number of surveillance-sensitive sub-groups within enterprise populations. Beloware detailed results of cluster analysis:

Cluster 1: Security-Oriented Acceptors (40%) High belief in the system, very strong perception of cyber threat, quite willing to tolerate monitoring.

Cluster 2: Transparency-Dependent Moderates (35%) They accept only if there is clear communication and accountability.

Cluster 3: Surveillance-Sensitive Skeptics (25%) Very low trust, no willingness to accept even with increased monitoring intensity, and generally show very low levels of acceptance.

We see a very strong indication from each of these groups that a governance approach should be tailor-made rather than a one-size-fits-all .

7. EMPIRICAL INSIGHTS AND INTERPRETATIVE ANALYSIS OF USER PRIVACY PERCEPTIONS

7.1 Key Statistical Patterns in Enterprise Privacy Expectations

We can trust the regression and classification results to reliably indicate that trust and transparency have a greater influence on privacy acceptance than monitoring intensity alone. Perceived level of monitoring has a direct negative effect on acceptance; however, this effect is influenced by the governance variables. Employees, in fact, they are not confused by monitoring per se but by monitoring going beyond a framework of relational governance. The regression models' R-squared of 0.62 shows that perceptual factors are a major source of explanation for privacy expectations in enterprise security environments. This result serves as an effective counterpoint to the popular notion that privacy attitudes vary greatly and are highly dependent on circumstances. A very strong association between perceived cyber risk and privacy acceptance should be pointed out. Those who feel that they have a higher chance of being attacked through cyberspace are giving up their privacy more easily in exchange for surveillance mechanisms. In terms of privacy calculus, the explanation is simple: if the risk is significant, the advantages of monitoring outweigh its . This means that a cybersecurity awareness campaign will work both ways – it can make people more open to surveillance if it is not a tool for fear-mongering or manipulative actions. Because the coefficient for monitoring intensity is negative, it supports the idea that surveillance without proper justification will decrease its level of acceptability. In fact, the magnitude of the coefficient compared to the trust and transparency ones leads to the result that surveillance intensity is only problematic when the governance mechanisms are .

7.2 Demographic and Role-Based Variations

Young professional groups, aged 20-29, showed a tendency towards higher acceptance of monitoring under high transparency compared with other age groups. On the other hand, controlling the trust factor in the regression showed the convergence of generational differences or that the generational tolerance is not independent of governance perception. Privacy Acceptance Scores are on average higher for managerial and executive respondents than for entry-level employees. Perhaps, these differences could be due to a greater exposure to risk management or a willingness to be accountable of organizational responsibilities. In general, those who are at the entry-level, and thus are less visible to governance frameworks, are more sensitive to monitoring intensity. Different industries also show their own unique traits here. The finance and healthcare industries have very much accustomed themselves to the idea of monitoring activities. By contrast, the sectors that think highly of individuality and innovation will most probably resist the culture of surveillance. Regarding trust and transparency variables removing gender-related differences statistically. In fact, this only indicates that the role of privacy expectations in enterprise security environments is mostly influenced by governance perceptions rather than demographic .

7.3 Predictive Probability Curves and Risk Gradients

Regression results may also be interpreted in various ways. For example, in the logistic regression situation, the authors used this as a basis to construct prediction probability curves. Those curves are designed to demonstrate to the reader the extent to which changes in trust and transparency levels could result in a high acceptance level of .

Figure 2. Predictive Probability of High Privacy Acceptance as Transparency Increases

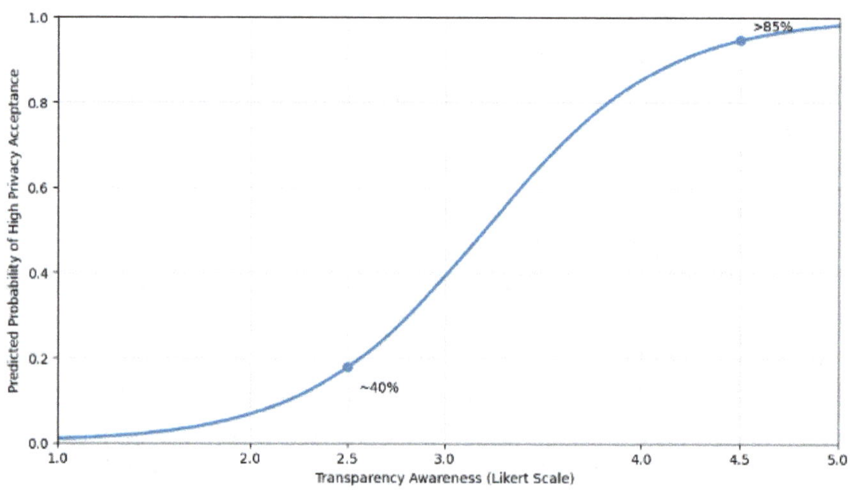

The results in the end will show a nonlinear response so that the changes to the transparency level by a very small amount near the center point have a far greater effect on the acceptance probability than the changes in the extreme ends of the . The main idea here is that minor policy changes can lead to significant trust .

Figure 3. Monitoring Intensity and Privacy Acceptance Gradient

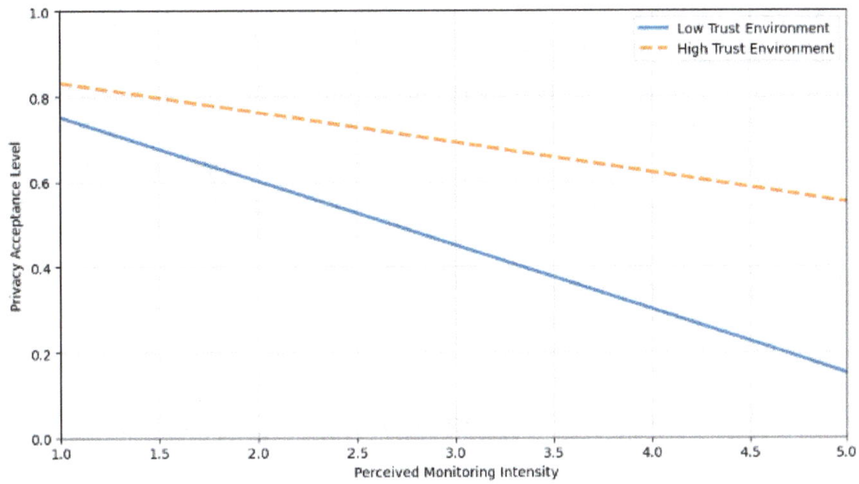

This kind of gradient reveals that trust culture is a buffer against the harmful impact of a very high level of surveillance. On the other hand, if trust is at a low level, the same degree of monitoring will result in a much greater decline in acceptance. Therefore, it is fair to state that governance culture acts as a safeguard for .

7.4 Interpreting the Enterprise Privacy Expectation Model

The overall Privacy Expectation Index (PEI) enables enterprises to measure the overall privacy climate in their security environments. High PEI signifies a better alignment of monitoring activities with user expectations. The classification analysis was able to uncover three leading privacy profiles, each of which has different strategic mission requirements. Security-Oriented Acceptors are characterized by high perceived cyber risks and a lot of trust in the institution. The main communication message to this group should be that monitoring is a means for them to be safe and not that it is the monitoring that is keeping tabs on them. However, this group cannot be allowed to become complacent; a steady stream of transparent communication should be maintained to foster trust. Transparency-Dependent Moderates are a very significant group in terms of strategy as their acceptance depends very much on how well an organization is able to communicate, hold themselves accountable, and treat people fairly. Participatory governance is very likely to be the path forward for organizations wanting to bring such a group firmly onto their side in terms of long-term monitoring system supporters. Surveillance-Sensitive Skeptics are the ones who, on the one hand, exhibit very little trust but, on the other hand, are very sensitive to monitoring intensity, which makes them the most susceptible to disengagement and behavioral strategies, such as monitoring avoidance.

Precisely communicating, grievance procedures, and oversight that is made publicly especially clear are the components that, I believe, would work in addressing their concerns. The gist of the model is that businesses contribute to privacy management not solely by decreasing the extent of their monitoring but also by enhancing their governance mechanisms. Improving these systems might help changing people's attitudes towards privacy positively without the need to compromise on security functionalities. Besides, the classification model's excellent AUC score (0.91) shows that privacy expectation profiles describe privacy perception so accurately that they can be exploited for the creation of predictive governance tactics. In other words, a firm can figure out who, among their workforce, might be opposed to monitoring and therefore prepare communication and involvement plans appropriate to the characteristics of the identified groups. These data-based findings highlight an important point that users' privacy expectations when it comes to enterprise security are, in fact, not geographical but philosophical as well as social in their . To put it another way, it's not only security that affects the degree of privacy in a world of surveillance, the other elements are also governance, communications, and the framing of systems. In fact, security and privacy should not be understood as opposite sides of a coin that only through transparency and accountability they might co-exist and support each .

8. VISUAL ANALYTICS OF ENTERPRISE PRIVACY DYNAMICS

Visual analytics can be viewed as a language that translates statistical relationships into patterns that are easier to interpret and can even tell the story of what enterprise security policies look like. In this way, this chapter shares pictorial depictions coming from the data exploration like distribution of clusters, trust-monitoring interaction heatmaps, acceptance prediction curves, and an overall model of enterprise privacy risk gradient. Visual analytics are an excellent tool for CEO's and other high-level decision makers within an organization since it uses a simple and understandable means to communicate all the complex and abstract data outcomes that activities such as sampling, collection, and statistical analysis might yield. A picture is often worth a thousand words, so it is not surprising that security and compliance officers as well as different types of policymakers within organizations mainly operate with visuals when it comes to assessing the ongoing security versus privacy debates.

8.1 Privacy Expectation Clusters Across Enterprise Users

Cluster analysis is a data mining technique which identifies groups of similar objects in a database. In the previous chapter, we have found out that when it comes to acceptance of privacy, trust, awareness of the transparency and intensity of surveillance being perceived, the user could be divided into three major groups. Depicting these groups through some sort of a map does a good job in explaining who and where along the acceptance of surveillance these employees are.

Figure 4. Cluster Distribution of Enterprise Privacy Expectation Profiles

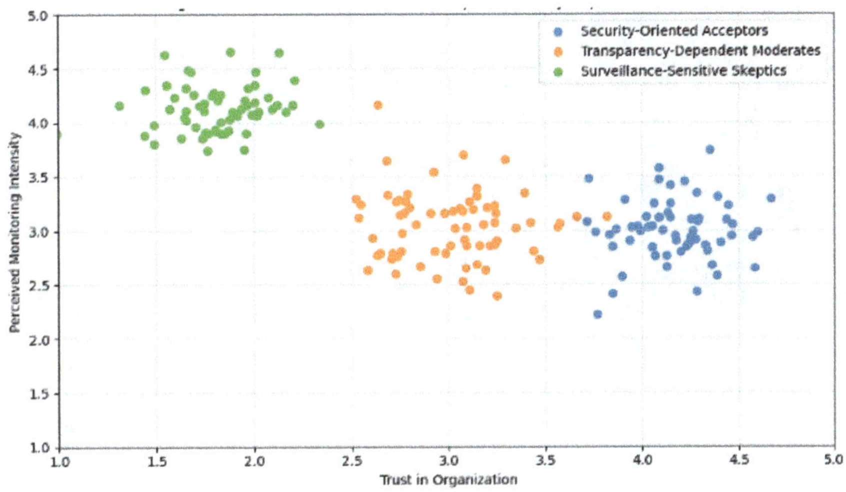

By the help of the cluster map, one could deduce that privacy expectations depend mostly on the trust one has in the institution. People who have reported having a lot of trust accept a certain degree/ level of monitoring without a significant decrease in privacy acceptance. On the contrary, people with lower levels of trust think that even under the same circumstances, monitoring is quite intrusive. The Transparency-Dependent segment lies in the middle of the regions of the clusters. Additionally, the types of governance signals like policy expressiveness, communication quality, and oversight mechanisms which are seen as influential factors for their acceptance levels. We consider the members of this group as our main concern because, through the implementation of targeted governance revisions, we could largely shift their position towards acceptance. Also, the cluster visualization, besides indicating that the mere increase of monitoring intensity is not the only factor that makes people uncomfortable with privacy, shows that the main variables trust and transparency being the key moderators of changing the way one sees surveillance .

8.2 Heatmap of Trust Versus Monitoring Intensity

To understand better how trust and monitoring intensity are related, a two-dimensional heatmap was generated using normalized variables of the data .

Figure 5. Heatmap of Privacy Acceptance Across Trust and Monitoring Levels

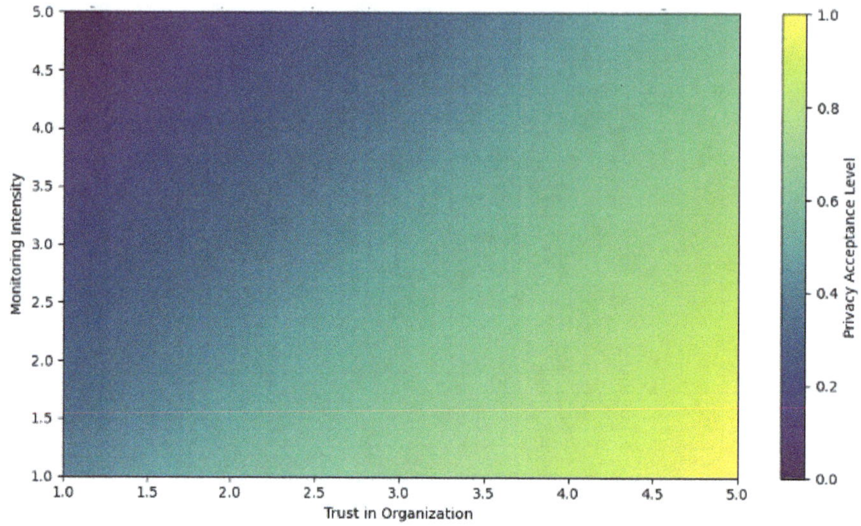

Analysis of heatmap shows quite obvious trend: trust is the factor that works to calm and reduce the degree of damage that negative emotions towards surveillance cause. If trust levels fall below average, private acceptance falls sharply even if the monitoring intensity is mild. On the contrary, if the trust level is higher than the reference value, the monitoring is seen by employees as a help and not a violation.

So, the most important thing that enterprises cannot forget in the intended efforts of preservation and creation of positive privacy climates is that the outcome should not be the only consequence that they are working on but it should be a continuous development of transparency, accountability, and explainable AI reporting mechanisms that can raise the entire ecosystem of privacy acceptance.

Another thing that one can derive from the heatmap is the fact that the worst-case scenario occurs when the monitoring intensity is high while the trust is low. In this case, the acceptance keeps falling sharply and as such, there are serious possibilities of the happening of distrust, disobedience, and even avoidance behavior on the side of monitored workers.

8.3 Predictive Curves of Transparency Influence

Transparency was one of the variables that came out as very strong predictors during the regression analysis. By depicting this variable, we explain how enterprise privacy can be influenced by communication strategies.

Figure 6. Transparency Awareness and Privacy Acceptance Curve

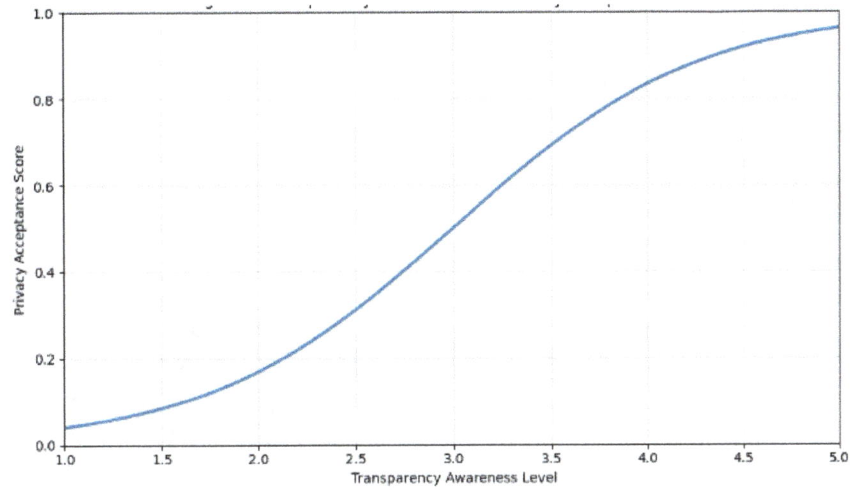

This curve shows that we are dealing with a nonlinear situation at the very least. At first, transparency is barely able to have powerful effects on acceptance but when communication reaches the level of clarity, acceptance is skyrocketing. After that, there is only a slow increase in the curve, which can be explained by the fact that by then employees are already convinced that the government is legitimate. This means that the heavy-duty transparency works best not when it is built on the continuous layering of more and more complicated policies, but rather when it is all about hitting the spot of effective clarity. Employees do not expect to be bombarded with technical details. On the contrary, they prefer simple stories explaining what types of data are collected, why the data is being collected, and what measures are taken to protect the data. Another important point this graph makes is that the transparency awareness should never be a one off event since as time passes the awareness will naturally fade, especially when there is no change in the policy even though the monitoring techniques are improved. In other words the regularity of programs, training, and updating of documents will in fact be coming from the need to keep the awareness alive and it is therefore indispensable that it be .

8.4 Enterprise Privacy Risk Gradient Model

This last diagram depicts a broad conceptualization at the enterprise level of a privacy risk gradient model where several variables were combined. This model graphically explains how the existence of governance together with the intensity of monitoring sessions might be the two major deciding factors of privacy risk .

Figure 7. Enterprise Privacy Risk Gradient Model

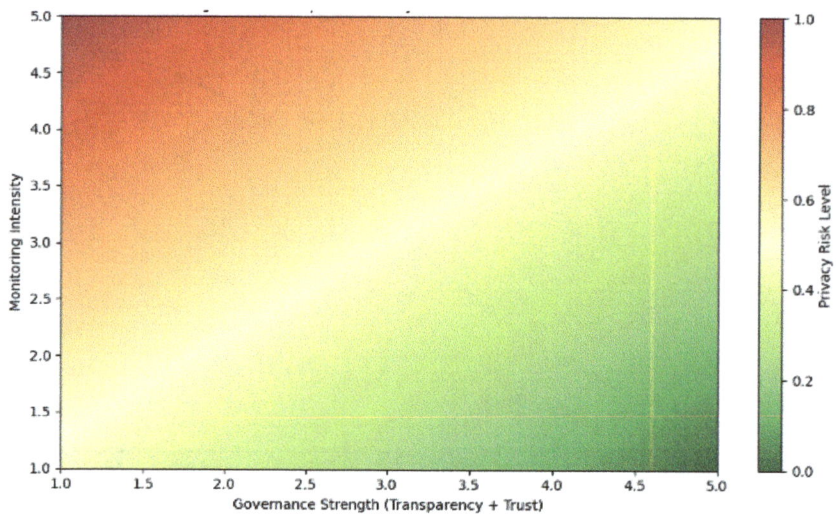

According to the gradient model, there are four general categories of governance situations:

Low Monitoring – High Governance, means going towards the green area in the diagram.

Moderate Monitoring – High Governance, at this level, companies can effectively manage their trust and transparency to achieve a compromise between security requirements and employees' privacy expectations.

High Monitoring – Low Governance, this is the most extreme situation of privacy risk. Heavy surveillance combined with poor governance lead to a lack of trust, rejection by employees, and scandals.

Moderate Monitoring – Moderate Governance, such a scenario is fairly typical and in it privacy acceptance depends on the willingness to change governance arrangements.

Looking at the graph, it can be deduced that the main element in reducing the rise of privacy risk is the strength of governance. Robust governance frameworks are instrumental in controlling the escalation of privacy risk even when there is an increase in monitoring as a response to heightened cybersecurity threats. From the strategy point of view, the gradient framework indicates that businesses ought to focus more on enhancing their governance systems first rather than expanding their surveillance capacities. Deploying AI-powered analytics on its own may lead to privacy backfire if transparency measures are not implemented simultaneously.

9. ORGANIZATIONAL STRATEGIES FOR ALIGNING SECURITY WITH PRIVACY EXPECTATIONS

The good news is, the research pinpointed the crucial finding that an organization's privacy expectations are at their lowest level of influence by the mere presence or absence of monitoring technologies; it is actually the way these technologies are governed, communicated, and the context in which they are used that matters more. With this understanding, organizations are at a crossroads. On one hand, through the use of sophisticated monitoring systems, they can protect themselves against the emerging cyber threats; on the other hand, they have to maintain the trust of their employees and respect their privacy expectations at the same time. To complicate matters further, the current digital workplaces that are equipped with artificial intelligence, behavioral analytics and automated response systems continuously collect and process huge volumes of telemetry data. If such systems are left unguided, we may end up creating feelings of omnipresent surveillance. To resolve this matter, organizations must implement strategies that bring privacy into the fold of security architecture, policy frameworks and organizational .

9.1 Designing Privacy-Aware Security Architectures

Privacy-aware security architecture implies the habit of mixing the privacy protection elements into the technical setup of cybersecurity tools rather than tacking privacy protection afterwards as a feature. More concretely, it is about chasing data minimization idea by the first touch of things. A monitoring tool, not only should collect the data enabling it to spot securities threats but it also must avoid gathering personal information not related to work that way. An example is that anomaly detection software can work using behavioral metrics that have been aggregated as opposed to raw keystrokes or full communication logs. Enterprises, by doing so, can greatly diminish the privacy risks(Ghazal, Hasan, Raju, et al., 2025). Then there is the approach of pseudonymizing the monitoring data in order to be more privacy-friendly. In such situation, behavioral logs are not directly linked to respective employee accounts but the system during the first phases of processing assigns pseudonymous identifiers. Only when a genuine security incident takes place, the authorized investigator can access the identity mapping. Thisapproach, on one hand, maintains the control the capability to explore, on the other hand - cuts down the exposure of personal data during the regular processes. Encryption and safe slicing of data further increase the privacy-aware architecture's capacity. Security telemetry repositories should be enabled with encryption not only when data is stored (at rest) but also when it's being transmitted (in transit). Besides, the classification of data-sets based on their sensitivity level means that different teams only get to see those parts of information that are their direct needs. As an example, security analysts will be shown only anonymized behavioral patterns whereas compliance officers will be given aggregated reports on policy compliance. Additionally, privacy-aware architecture encompasses the aspect of making the operations of AI monitoring systems more open and understandable as well. Machine learning models, whenever they function at alerting or giving risk scores, must be equipped with presenting coherent and digestible explanations on the factors that have led to such measures. Sharing such explanations is indeed instrumental in removing the fear of surveillance, and it is also emblematic of supporting procedural (Eke et al., 2025).

9.2 Proportional Monitoring and Data Minimization

In this context, tools such as enterprise monitoring systems are largely judged by how well they follow the principle of proportionality. In other words, proportional monitoring dictates that if certain types of assets, roles or environments are highly risky then the surveillance needs to be very intense, if less risky than quite limited. It would be highly unjust to have all the employees under surveillance to the same degree. One of the methods to accomplish this is by implementing tiered monitoring where different levels of roles receive more detailed monitoring according to the degree of risk they are likely to face. As a result, those who handle sensitive intellectual property or financial systems might be monitored more closely via behavioral analytics whereas those in administrative positions having no such info will be periodically accounted through basic . By means of this segregation, the concept of fairness is manifested and the idea of indiscriminate surveillance is reduced from the point of view of . Additional to proportional monitoring, data minimization limits not only the amount but also the duration of the retention of the collected information. Security logs should be kept only for the period during which they can be helpful for threat detection, compliance and incident investigation. Once set retention periods have elapsed, these logs should be converted into anonymized statistical summaries or securely deleted. In addition, enterprises should consider a question of whether it is even necessary to have a certain monitoring metric. In most cases, monitoring tools by default collect a large telemetry, but not all of these metrics add value to security detection models. Reconfiguring monitoring tools regularly allows organizations to drop unneeded data collection and still maintain high level of analytics performance. Last but not least, proportional monitoring strategies have to be put into writing and shared with your staff. When you are transparent about the fact that different monitoring levels are used because of varying role-related risks, then it is less likely that employees will feel that they are being singled out or unfairly monitored. Having the monitoring intensity directly related to risk rather than to suspicion on the part of managers helps in increasing acceptance(Hakami et al., 2025).

9.3 Privacy-Centered Policy Communication Framework

Among the many factors that influence privacy expectations the one that is capable of turning the tide is definitely policy communication. A poorly communicated purpose and safeguards of monitoring systems can backfire and create distrust in employees. This is why companies should come up with a communication framework that breaks down monitoring practices to employees in a clear, straightforward, and transparent manner. Initiating a communication framework targeting privacy starts with the full and detailed policy documentation. A monitoring policy should at least spell out what type of data can be collected, why the data is processed, how long the data can be held, who gets to access the data, and what are the steps in anomaly investigation. There is no need to be vague; on the contrary, give examples of how the monitoring data is used to achieve cybersecurity goals. The second step is to provide training and generate awareness(Q. Shambour et al., 2025).

Typically, security awareness workshops focus only on external threats such as phishing or malware. However, these types of programs should be revealing the internal surveillance tools and therefore, how and why the company is using them(A. Arabiat et al., 2025). One way that the company can change how people think about it is by describing monitoring as safety tools that help prevent harm rather than as instruments of surveillance. Besides that, transparency can also be improved through two-way communication. Basically, your employees should be able to raise their concerns, ask for explanations and express their views on monitoring practices. For example, conducting surveys, workshops and internal forums offer organizations a chance not only to find out the mood of their people but also to update their governance accordingly. And, of course, continuous communication is just as vital. New technical components of a corporate security environment can change monitoring procedures, and it is essential to inform the staff in advance. The best way to reduce the spread of misinformation and rumors is to keep the employees regularly updated about new features, policy changes and governance initiatives(Turab et al., 2025).

9.4 Building Trust Through Transparency Engineering

Regaining people's trust is a must and such a move can also lead to the enterprise security and privacy expectations becoming more in line. Transparency engineering refers to the deliberate design of systems and governance to not only make accountability and fairness measures exist but also to prove those to users. Apparently, independent oversight is the way to go here. Companies, for instance, can establish privacy oversight boards that include privacy, security, legal, human resources and employee representatives. Those boards, among other duties, review monitoring policies, risk evaluations and make sure that surveillance stays in line with the company values(Al Hindi et al., 2025). Without auditability, transparency engineering would be a failure. It would be a good idea to remember that administering access and investigative actions are recorded in the monitoring systems themselves. This sort of meta-monitoring is exactly what secures the investigators so that they do not make unauthorized use of the monitoring data without leaving behind audit trails. Trust is strengthened by the very fact of the investigators being under scrutiny. In addition to all the above, the accountability of algorithms is steadily becoming another feature of the enterprise governance environment(Ghazal, Abualhaj, et al., 2025).

If it turns out that the predictive models have been systematically identifying certain behavior patterns as being riskier when, in reality, they have nothing to do with a security threat, then a prompt modification should be the course of action. Experts say that involving your employees in operations dedicated to fairness can have positive results for trust in AI. A different trust-building approach might be to let employees see the data a company keeps about them. Behavioral monitoring summary and security awareness scores are the kinds of data employees should have access to, typically(Ghazal, Abu-Shareha, et al., 2025). Turning monitoring into an ordinary feature of the organizational security that a user can understand rather than a hidden instrument is what such transparency amounts to. Not only does it make security and privacy more in tune, it is also a must for the organization's culture. It is the ones that are able to demonstrate over time that they adhere to the privacy principle that are creating the most engaging employees and, in fact, cooperation for better cybersecurity. If monitoring systems were only used by management to keep tabs on employees, then no one would be happy with such a move. On the contrary, when a monitoring system is fair, transparent and accountable, it is more likely to motivate the people to see themselves as helpers in securing the company rather than as those being (Sharma, Hussain, et al., 2025).

10. FUTURE RESEARCH DIRECTIONS

Enterprise security monitoring and users' privacy expectations overlap and this crossroads keeps on changing with the growing complexity of the digital infrastructures and their data-driven . The fast changes in technology through AI, cloud computing, behavioral analysis, and worldwide connectivity are not only changing the functionalities of the monitoring technologies but also the workforce expectations at a fundamental level. Hence, the researchers of the future will have to explore new technologies and changes in regulatory environments to foresee how privacy expectations might evolve in the context of .

AI-powered monitoring can handle large amounts of telemetry data and identify intricate anomalies that may escape human analysts using traditional rule-based monitoring. However, the growing independence of these systems brings up major concerns about transparency, accountability, and privacy. Research needs to focus on how workers see the automated decision-making processes in corporate security contexts. With machine learning models continuously evolving in complexity, it might even be a challenge for technical specialists to understand their decision-making processes. Without clear explanations, workers' trust and privacy acceptance might be negatively impacted. It will be equally crucial to figure out approaches for limiting such inferences by leveraging privacy-preserving machine learning techniques, such as federated learning, and differential privacy(Al-Okbi, Alomari, Hadi, et al., 2025).

One of the major factors influencing enterprise monitoring is the spread of zero-trust security architectures. Zero-trust thinking dictates that users and devices should never be presumed trustworthy, and therefore require constant verification of identity and behavior. Although this method significantly raises the company's capability to resist cyber-attacks, it also results in a larger amount and increased detail of behavioral data being collected throughout the enterprise systems. Continued authentication and behavioral verification are amongst mechanisms of zero-trust and these will naturally have an impact on privacy expectations. This is because, unlike the former perimeter security model, zero-trust involves the ongoing observation of user behavior. Knowing how employees view such surveillance on an ongoing basis will be necessary for preserving trust. In addition, researchers ought to be investigating privacy-preserving authentication techniques that still allow for the highest security standards but with the least data possible being collected(Masango et al., 2025).

Depending on where you are and your culture, the expectations you have about privacy drastically vary. Employees of international corporations, for instance, if culturally deeply involved, working in a regulated environment and living in a country where the attitude to surveillance is one way or another may have different perceptions of monitoring practices. In some cultures, security of the whole community and the power of the institution is strongly emphasized whereas, in many others, the focus is mainly on the person and his/her privacy rights. Conducting studies about cultural differences in term of monitoring acceptance is going to be a good idea. A comparative study of areas such as North America, Europe, Asia, and emerging digital economies will provide understanding how multinational enterprises can fashion culturally adaptable management frameworks. Besides culture, regulation and its different levels should also be considered. For instance, strong regulations may result in increased trust in monitoring systems because of the availability of a system of checks and balances whereas under regulated situations may increase privacy .

Generally, privacy governance frameworks rely mostly on static policies and recurring compliance audits as their methods. However, as business security measures continue to be updated, the static governance approach will become less and less effective over time. In the future, one of the areas of focus in research should be on adaptive governance models, which can change dynamically in response to technological developments and newly emerging risks. A proposal for adaptive privacy governance is to be in privacy management mode continuously (like a continuous cycle), updating the policy where necessary and collaborating with stakeholders repeatedly(Cui et al., 2026). For example, companies could implement privacy impact dashboards that constantly monitor various associated metrics such as the amount of data collected, the duration data is retained, algorithmic bias signal and employee mood. Such metrics could be very useful instruments for firms in identifying and tackling privacy problems at a very early stage so that they do not get escalated to trust crisis level, major ones. One more research avenue might be participatory governance where employees are actually involved in policy making, as well as in the supervisory and control functions. Not only would this enhance legitimacy, but by turning employees into the main agents of privacy governance at the same time, it also becomes much simpler to persuade employees to agree to security measures(Mohammad et al., 2025). In short, managing privacy of enterprises in the future will be a juggling act between the latest developments in technologies on the one hand and human-centered governance on the other hand. As the monitoring solutions become more advanced and capable of being everywhere, organizations have the responsibility to integrate privacy expectations as an essential component of their security framework. Only when organizations combine technical brilliance with moral consciousness, transparency in governance, and uninterrupted interaction with their employees, will they be capable of creating self-sufficient and self-regulating enterprise security (Hanandeh et al., 2025).

11. CONCLUSION

Enterprise security environments are the arenas where the requirement for organizational protection and the demand for individual privacy are balanced. The results of the empirical research reveal that in-house privacy acceptance is not merely a question of whether monitoring technologies are available or not, but also how these technologies are managed, communicated, and understood by the users. First of all, being very clear about the security policies, telling the users exactly what data is being collected, and also having a very clear and trustworthy kind of governance is a major part of how the employees and other users of the systems view the monitoring activities. On the one hand, if users are provided with the information about the purpose, scope, and protections of enterprise security systems, then even such measures as network logging, endpoint protection, and identity verification might be perceived more as legitimate elements of organizational security rather than as techniques of invasive surveillance.

Both logical arguments and visual illustrations in this chapter prove that trust and transparency are the two most fundamental factors that alter the relationship between the degree of monitoring and privacy acceptance. A community with good governance, open communication, and well-defined privacy protections are the very users who allow monitoring to a greater extent let alone the fact that such activities are very extensive. On the other hand, organizations that have only a few of the elements that constitute their transparency practices and even less of the trust frameworks are faced with not only greater privacy risks but also with more pronounced user resistance. These results show that it is a great challenge for enterprise security strategies to be efficient, effective, and sustainable in the future if they do not manage to integrate technical security controls with ethical governance principles, user education programs, and policy transparency. Not only does aligning security operations with reasonable user privacy expectations aid in minimizing legal and reputational risks, but also it acts as a means of promoting trust in the organization as well as long-term compliance to the ever-evolving data protection .

REFERENCES

Abdeljaber, O., & Al-Masaeed, S. (2025). Al-Mu'ani, L., Yaseen, H., & Alhnaity, B. (2025). Strategic Intelligence: The Power of AI in Planning Efficiency. *Human Behavior and Emerging Technologies*, (1). Advance online publication. DOI: 10.1155/hbe2/5383054

Abualghanam, O., Alazzam, H., Qatawneh, M., Alazab, M., & Al Sharaiah, M. (2025). Elevating Mobile Security: An Ensemble Approach for Enhanced Malware Detection with M-iForest. *International Journal of Interactive Mobile Technologies*, *19*(10), 129–151. Advance online publication. DOI: 10.3991/ijim.v19i10.51319

Abualhaj, M. M., Abu-Shareha, A. A., Al-Khatib, S. N., Alsaaidah, A. M., & Anbar, M. (2025). Improving firewall performance using hybrid of optimization algorithms and decision trees classifier. *IAES International Journal of Artificial Intelligence*, *14*(4), 2839. Advance online publication. DOI: 10.11591/ijai.v14.i4.pp2839-2848

Abualhaj, M. M., Abu-Shareha, A. A., & Rateb, R. (2025). Enhancing intrusion detection systems with hybrid HHO-WOA optimization and gradient boosting machine classifier. *International Journal of Reconfigurable and Embedded Systems*, *14*(2), 518. Advance online publication. DOI: 10.11591/ijres.v14.i2.pp518-526

Abualhaj, M. M.I, Al-Khatib, S. N., Abu-Shareha, A. A., Almomani, O., Al-Mimi, H., Al-Allawee, A., Daoud, M. S., & Anbar, M. (2025). Spam Detection Boosted by Firefly-Based Feature Selection and Optimized Classifiers. *International Journal of Advances in Soft Computing and Its Applications*, *17*(3). Advance online publication. DOI: 10.15849/IJASCA.251130.02

Abualhaj, M. M., Al-Khatib, S. N., Al Zyoud, M., Qaddara, I., & Anbar, M. (2025). Enhancing Intrusion Detection System Performance Using a Hybrid of Harris Hawks and Whale Optimization Algorithms. *Engineering. Technology and Applied Science Research*, *15*(4), 24354–24361. Advance online publication. DOI: 10.48084/etasr.10919

Abualhaj, M. M., Al-Khatib, S. N., Al-Zyoud, M., Qaddara, I., Hiari, M. O., & Aldossary, S. M. A. (2025). Enhanced Network Communication Security Through Hybrid Dragonfly-Bat Feature Selection for Intrusion Detection. *The Journal of Communication*, *20*(5). Advance online publication. DOI: 10.12720/jcm.20.5.607-618

Abualigah, L., Almomani, M. H., Alomari, S. A., Zitar, R. A., Migdady, H., Saleem, K., Snasel, V., Smerat, A., & Ezugwu, A. E. (2025). Optimizing Intrusion Detection in Wireless Sensor Networks via the Improved Chameleon Swarm Algorithm for Feature Selection. *IET Communications*, *19*(1), e70029. Advance online publication. DOI: 10.1049/cmu2.70029

Abuowaida, S., Abu Owida, H., Shelash Mohammad, S. I., Alshdaifat, N., Abu Elsoud, E., Alazaidah, R., Vasudevan, A., & Alshurideh, M. T. (2025). Evidence Detection in Cloud Forensics: Classifying Cyber-Attacks in IaaS Environments using machine learning. *Data and Metadata*, *4*, 699. Advance online publication. DOI: 10.56294/dm2025699

Al-Adwan, A. S., Al-Adwan, A., Li, N., Fauzi, M. A., Jafar, R. M. S., Habibi, A., & Falahat, M. (2025). IMMERSIVE LEARNING MEETS THEORY: MODELING EDUVERSE ADOPTION IN HIGHER EDUCATION. *Journal of Information Technology Education, 24*, 042. Advance online publication. DOI: 10.28945/5669

Al-Dmour, R., Al-Dmour, H., Al-Dmour, A., Basheer Amin, E., & Al-Dmour, Y. (2025). *AI and big data-driven social media recruitment: the mediating role of talent acquisition and employee engagement in bank performance*. Digital Transformation and Society., DOI: 10.1108/DTS-02-2025-0042

Al-Habashneh, A. G., Al-Daoud, K. I., Oraini, B., Al, , & Shelash, S. I. (2025). The impact of artificial intelligence on the development of electronic financial services. *International Journal of Data and Network Science, 9*(2), 317–322. Advance online publication. DOI: 10.5267/j.ijdns.2024.8.012

Al Hindi, G., Alshraideh, M., Hussein, A. H., Eliyan, L. F., & Al-Dhaqm, A. (2025). Hacking Back: Using Genetic Algorithms to Outsmart Hackers. *Journal of Computational Science, 21*(9), 2049–2064. Advance online publication. DOI: 10.3844/jcssp.2025.2049.2064

Al-Momani, M. M., Alqudah, T. A., Al Swiety, I. A., Mahrakani, N., Nassoura, M. B. A., & Al Attar, M. K. (2025). Integrating Artificial Intelligence (AI) and Business Intelligence (BI): A Framework for Improving Enterprise Performance. *TEM Journal, 14*(3). https://doi.org/DOI: 10.18421/TEM143-26

Al-Mousa, M., Amer, W., Abualhaj, M., Albilasi, S., Nasir, O., & Samara, G. (2025). Agile Proactive Cybercrime Evidence Analysis Model for Digital Forensics. *The International Arab Journal of Information Technology, 22*(3). Advance online publication. DOI: 10.34028/iajit/22/3/15

Al-Okbi, N. K., Alomari, S. A., Hadi, W. J., Ajrash, A. S., Smerat, A., & Abualigah, L. (2025). Defending Digital Integrity: Advances in Media Forgery Analysis Research and Cybersecurity Development. *SN Computer Science, 6*(8), 913. Advance online publication. DOI: 10.1007/s42979-025-04462-8

Al-Okbi, N. K., Alomari, S. A., Zitar, R. A., Smerat, A., Nazzal, M. A., & Abualigah, L. (2025). Integrating Multimodal Emotion Recognition with Deep Q-Learning for Adaptive Social Robot Interaction. *International Journal of Robotics and Control Systems, 5*(4), 2265–2289. Advance online publication. DOI: 10.31763/ijrcs.v5i4.2055

Al-znamat, F. O., Alsaaidah, A., & Abu-Shareha, A. A. (2025). Malware Detection Using a Modified Bat Algorithm for Feature Selection. *International Journal of Intelligent Engineering and Systems, 18*(9), 885–899. Advance online publication. DOI: 10.22266/ijies2025.1031.56

Alabdallat, R., Abualhaj, M., & Abu-Shareha, A. (2025). Android Malware Detection Using a Modified Dwarf Mongoose Algorithm. *International Journal of Intelligent Engineering and Systems, 18*(8), 336–351. Advance online publication. DOI: 10.22266/ijies2025.0930.21

Alabdallat, R. D., Abualhaj, M. M., & Abu-Shareha, A. (2025). Enhanced Multiclass Android Malware Detection Using a Modified Dwarf Mongoose Algorithm. *International Journal of Analysis and Applications, 23*, 248. Advance online publication. DOI: 10.28924/2291-8639-23-2025-248

Aldaaja, Y., Odeh, M., Badrakhan, S. S., Sabri, M., Abdelrahim, Y., Samara, G., & Alsabatin, H. (2025). Quantifying the Managerial and Practical Benefits of Cloud Computing on Information Security in Higher Education Institutions. *Applied Mathematics & Information Sciences*, *19*(1), 15–24. Advance online publication. DOI: 10.18576/amis/190102

Aldabbas, A., Baniata, L. H., Alsaaidah, B. A., Mustafa, Z., Alali, M., & Rateb, R. (2025). Artificial intelligence-driven method for the discovery and prevention of distributed denial of service attacks. *IAES International Journal of Artificial Intelligence*, *14*(1), 614. Advance online publication. DOI: 10.11591/ijai.v14.i1.pp614-628

Alenazi, M. J. F., Al-Khasawneh, M. A., Rahman, S., & Faheem, Z. (2025). Deep Reinforcement Learning Based Flow Aware-QoS Provisioning in SD-IoT for Precision Agriculture. *Computational Intelligence*, *41*(1), e70023. Advance online publication. DOI: 10.1111/coin.70023

Ali, L., Alshamayleh, A., Ibrahim, A., & Ahmed, S. M. (2026). Information Management Enhancement in Cloud-Based Systems Through Blockchain-Enabled Secure Access Control. *Indian Journal of Information Sources and Services*, *16*(1), 289–296. Advance online publication. DOI: 10.51983/ijiss-2026.16.1.30

Alkhawatrah, M. (2025). Random Forests Relay Selector in Buffer-Aided Cooperative Networks. *IEEE Access : Practical Innovations, Open Solutions*, *13*, 165402–165410. Advance online publication. DOI: 10.1109/ACCESS.2025.3612192

Almomani, O., Arabiat, A., Al Tayeb, M., Almaiah, M. A., Obeidat, M., Aldhyani, T. H. H., Shehab, R., & Rowad, M. (2025). A Robust Model for Android Malware Detection via ML and DL classifiers. *Mesopotamian Journal of Big Data*, *2025*. Advance online publication. DOI: 10.58496/MJBD/2025/017

Alraba'nah, Y., Al-Sharaeh, S., & Al Hindi, G. (2025). Enhancing Intrusion Detection Using Hybrid Long Short-Term Memory and XGBoost. *Journal of Soft Computing and Data Mining*, *6*(1). Advance online publication. DOI: 10.30880/jscdm.2025.06.01.016

Arabiat, A., Altayeb, M., & Salama, S. (2025). Artificial intelligence-powered smart roads: Leveraging orange3 for traffic signs recognition. *IAES International Journal of Artificial Intelligence*, *14*(5), 3816. Advance online publication. DOI: 10.11591/ijai.v14.i5.pp3816-3826

Arabiat, A. M. (2025). Intelligent Model for Detecting GAN-Generated Images Based on Multi-Classifier and Advanced Data Mining Techniques. *International Journal of Electrical and Electronic Engineering and Telecommunications*, *14*(3). Advance online publication. DOI: 10.18178/ijeetc.14.3.147-157

Arabiat, A. M., & Eljaafreh, Y. G. (2025). Intrusion Detection in Wireless Sensor Networks Using ML Based Classification of Denial of Service (DoS) Attacks. *The Journal of Communication*, *20*(4). Advance online publication. DOI: 10.12720/jcm.20.4.501-514

Babaker, S., Khatibi, A., Alsoud, A. R., Kaur, J., Jagtap, J., Alkhayyat, A., & Shah, S. K. (2025). Improving Reliability and Data Management in Internet of Things Based Wireless Sensor Networks. *Internet Technology Letters*, *8*(6), e646. Advance online publication. DOI: 10.1002/itl2.646

Cui, D., Harrison, A., Fendzi-Donfack, E., Dagal, I., Jangir, P., Mahmoud, M. M., Malkani, P., Mbasso, W. F., Tiako, P., & Smerat, A. (2026). Enhancing Short-Term Electricity Forecasting with Advanced Machine Learning Techniques. *Journal of Electrical Engineering & Technology*, *21*(1), 147–187. Advance online publication. DOI: 10.1007/s42835-025-02430-z

Eke, C. I., Al-Shamayleh, A. S., Phiri, M., Maswadi, K., Kwaghtyo, D. K., Mulenga, M., & Iyidobi, C. J. (2025). Machine Learning Based Mobile Big Data Analytics: State-of-the-art Applications, Taxonomy, Challenges and Future Research Directions. *Nigerian Journal of Technological Development*, *22*(4). Advance online publication. DOI: 10.63746/njtd.v22i4.3385

Ghazal, T. M. (2025a). An IoT-Based Active Learning Convolutional Neural Networks Model for Predicting River Water Quality. *Journal of Soft Computing and Data Mining*, *6*(1). Advance online publication. DOI: 10.30880/jscdm.2025.06.01.021

Ghazal, T. M. (2025b). Federated Learning for Intelligent Sensing and Navigation Technologies for 6G Communications. *Journal of Sensors, 2025*(1). DOI: 10.1155/js/3746147

Ghazal, T. M., Abu-Shareha, A., Mustafa, S. A., Ibrahim, A., & Ahmed, S. M. (2025). Privacy-Preserving Transformer-Based Meta-Learning Algorithm for Zero-Day Intrusion Detection in IoT-Enabled Smart Grids. *Journal of Internet Services and Information Security*, *15*(4), 76–84. Advance online publication. DOI: 10.58346/JISIS.2025.I4.006

Ghazal, T. M., Abualhaj, M., Ahmed, A. A., Al-Tarawni, M. A. M., & Maghrabi, L. A. (2025). Federated Deep Graph Neural Network Algorithm for Real-Time Intrusion Detection in Heterogeneous IoT Systems. *Journal of Internet Services and Information Security*, *15*(4), 484–497. Advance online publication. DOI: 10.58346/JISIS.2025.I4.035

Ghazal, T. M., Awouda, A. E., Hasan, M. K., Rahman, A. H. A., Islam, S., Saeed, R. A., Elshafie, H., Iqbal, A., & Hussein, A. H. (2025). Knowledge Learning for Securing Workflow Scheduling Algorithm in Mobile Edge Computing. *Mobile Networks and Applications*, *30*(3-4), 395–413. Advance online publication. DOI: 10.1007/s11036-025-02465-6

Ghazal, T. M., Hasan, M. K., Abdul Wahab, A. N., Ibrahim, A., Khan, W. A., Raza, N. Z., Atta, A., & Mago, B. (2022). Towards Privacy Provisioning for Internet of Things (IoT). *International Conference on Cyber Resilience, ICCR 2022*. DOI: 10.1109/ICCR56254.2022.9995916

Ghazal, T. M., Hasan, M. K., Alzoubi, H. M., Al Hmmadi, M., Al-Dmour, N. A., Islam, S., Kamran, R., & Mago, B. (2022). Securing Smart Cities Using Blockchain Technology. *2022 1st International Conference on AI in Cybersecurity, ICAIC 2022*. DOI: 10.1109/ICAIC53980.2022.9896971

Ghazal, T. M., Hasan, M. K., Hussein, A. H., Pandey, B. K., Ahmad, M., Safie, N., & Cascone, L. (2025). Federated Learning With Small and Large Models With Privacy-Preserving Data Space for Holographic Internet of Things in Consumer Electronics. *IEEE Transactions on Consumer Electronics*, *71*(2), 5259–5274. Advance online publication. DOI: 10.1109/TCE.2025.3573033

Ghazal, T. M., Hasan, M. K., Mokhtar, U. A., Safie, N., Alshamayleh, A., & Ahmad, M. (2025). Machine learning-based real-time outage fault detection for distribution networks in smart grid. In *Energy Reports* (Vol. 14). DOI: 10.1016/j.egyr.2025.10.045

Ghazal, T. M., Hasan, M. K., Raju, K. N., Khan, M. A., Alshamayleh, A., Bhatt, M. W., & Ahmad, M. (2025). Data Space Privacy Model with Federated Learning Technique for Securing IoT Communications in Autonomous Marine Vehicles. *Journal of Intelligent & Robotic Systems, 111*(3), 84. Advance online publication. DOI: 10.1007/s10846-025-02298-1

Ghazal, T. M., Janjua, J. I., Abushiba, W., Ahmad, M., Ihsan, A., & Al-Dmour, N. A. (2024). Cybersecurity Revolution via Large Language Models and Explainable AI. *2024 17th International Conference on Security of Information and Networks, SIN 2024*. DOI: 10.1109/SIN63213.2024.10871324

Hakami, H., Hasan, M. K., Alshamayleh, A., Saeed, A. Q., Mustafa, S. A., & Ghazal, T. M. (2025). Adaptive Neuro-Fuzzy Congestion Control Algorithm for Real-Time Multimedia Networking in Cloud-Based E-Learning Platforms. *Journal of Wireless Mobile Networks, Ubiquitous Computing and Dependable Applications, 16*(3). Advance online publication. DOI: 10.58346/JOWUA.2025.I3.027

Hanandeh, A., Alfreijat, S. Y., Qutieshat, R. J., Alsha'ar, H. Y., Kilani, Q. A. L., & Saleem Khasawneh, M. A. (2025). Implementing AI Accuracy, Learning Rate, Inference Time on enhancing Big Data Analysis and Strategic Plan. *Data and Metadata, 4*, 637. Advance online publication. DOI: 10.56294/dm2025637

Hiari, M., Alraba'nah, Y., & Qaddara, I. (2025). A Deep Learning-Based Intrusion Detection System using Refined LSTM for DoS Attack Detection. *Engineering. Technology and Applied Science Research, 15*(4), 25627–25633. Advance online publication. DOI: 10.48084/etasr.11499

Ibrahim, A., Sekhar, R., Tawfeq, J. F., Salih, S. Q., Shah, P., & Radhi, A. D. (2024). Security and Privacy Protection for Online Electronic Documents Based on Novel Encryption Techniques. *Journal of Intelligent Systems and Internet of Things, 11*(1), 21–28. Advance online publication. DOI: 10.54216/JISIoT.110103

Iskandarani, M. Z. (2025). Effect of Adaptive Intelligent Reflective Surfaces on SINR in a Wireless Communication System. *The Journal of Communication, 20*(1). Advance online publication. DOI: 10.12720/jcm.20.1.1-11

Jaradat, S., Acharya, N., Shivshankar, S., Alhadidi, T. I., & Elhenawy, M. (2025). AI for Data Quality Auditing: Detecting Mislabeled Work Zone Crashes Using Large Language Models. *Algorithms, 18*(6), 317. Advance online publication. DOI: 10.3390/a18060317

Khatibi, A., Babaker, S., Praveen, K. N. R., Chohan, J. S., Jadhav, A., Alsoud, A. R., Ramudu, M. J., & Jeet, R. (2025). Advanced AI-Driven Cybersecurity: Analyzing Emerging Threats and Defensive Strategies. *National Academy Science Letters*. Advance online publication. DOI: 10.1007/s40009-025-01897-8

Laha, S. R., Smadi, K. Al, Habboush, A. K., Pattanayak, B. K., Pattnaik, S., & Mohanty, B. (2025). Smart Waste Management Framework for Green Cities: Integrating IoT, LoRa, and Deep Learning for Efficient Waste Classification and Management. *Tikrit Journal of Engineering Sciences, 32*(Special Issue 1). DOI: 10.25130/tjes.sp1.2025.1

Lee, S. W., Hussain, S., Issa, G. F., Abbas, S., Ghazal, T. M., Sohail, T., Ahmad, M., & Khan, M. A. (2021). Multi-Dimensional Trust Quantification by Artificial Agents through Evidential Fuzzy Multi-Criteria Decision Making. *IEEE Access : Practical Innovations, Open Solutions, 9*, 159399–159412. Advance online publication. DOI: 10.1109/ACCESS.2021.3131521

Makhadmeh, S. N., Fraihat, S., Awad, M., Sanjalawe, Y., Al-Betar, M. A., & Awadallah, M. A. (2025). A crossover-integrated Marine Predator Algorithm for feature selection in intrusion detection systems within IoT environments. *Internet of Things : Engineering Cyber Physical Human Systems*, *31*, 101536. Advance online publication. DOI: 10.1016/j.iot.2025.101536

Masango, N. C., Agushaka, J. O., Amaefule, M. C., Taiwo, O., Zhang, P., Ezugwu, A. E., Saleem, K., Smerat, A., & Abualigah, L. (2025). Secure and efficient cloudlet networks: blockchain integration with agent-based proof of trust mechanism. *Eurasip Journal on Wireless Communications and Networking*, *2025*(1). DOI: 10.1186/s13638-025-02439-y

Maz, Y. A., Anbar, M., Manickam, S., Abualhaj, M. M., Almalki, S. A., & Alabsi, B. A. (2025). Transfer Learning-Based Approach with an Ensemble Classifier for Detecting Keylogging Attack on the Internet of Things. *Computers, Materials & Continua*, *85*(3), 5287–5307. Advance online publication. DOI: 10.32604/cmc.2025.068257

Mohammad, S. I., Al-Daoud, K., Al Qraini, B., Khanfar, I. A. A., & Vasudevan, A. (2025). Quantum Error Correction with Surface Code Analysis on Quantum Computing platform. *Applied Mathematics & Information Sciences*, *19*(2), 423–435. Advance online publication. DOI: 10.18576/amis/190216

Otair, M., Qawaqzeh, F. A., Alomari, S. A., Zitar, R. A., Migdady, H., Saleem, K., Smerat, A., Alsoud, A. R., & Abualigah, L. (2025). Enhanced Arithmetic Optimization Algorithm for Intrusion Detection in Wireless Sensor Networks. *International Journal of Communication Systems*, *38*(10), e70122. Advance online publication. DOI: 10.1002/dac.70122

Qaddara, I., & Alraba'nah, Y. (2025). Enhancing Requirements Classification Using Machine Learning Techniques. *SN Computer Science*, *6*(6), 649. Advance online publication. DOI: 10.1007/s42979-025-04158-z

Qawasmeh, S., Habboushb, A., Elzaghmouri, B., Kharma, Q., & Albalawneh, D. (2025). Hybrid Convolutional Neural Network-Based Intrusion Detection System for Secure IoT Networks. *Tikrit Journal of Engineering Sciences*, *32*(SP1), 1–11. Advance online publication. DOI: 10.25130/tjes.sp1.2025.2

Ramesh, J. V. N., Nimma, D., Dasari, R., Chaudhari Rane, D., AlGhamdi, A., Rao, K. B. V. B., Haider, S. A., Kuzieva, N., & Jangir, P. (2025). Safe and Reliable Two-Stage Online Offloading Algorithm for Transportation Cyber-Physical Systems. *IEEE Transactions on Intelligent Transportation Systems*, *26*(9), 14313–14322. Advance online publication. DOI: 10.1109/TITS.2025.3539934

Raza, M. A., Karim, A., Alqarni, M., Al-Khasawneh, M. A., Jumani, T. A., Aman, M., & Masud, M. I. (2025). An Intelligent Long Short-Term Memory-Based Machine Learning Model for the Potential Assessment of Global Hydropower Capacity in Sustainable Energy Transition and Security. *Energies*, *18*(13), 3324. Advance online publication. DOI: 10.3390/en18133324

Samanta, I. S., Mohanty, S., Rout, P. K., Parida, S. M., Panda, S., Bajaj, M., Blazek, V., & Prokop, L. (2025). A comprehensive review of feature extraction techniques for power quality event detection with novel approaches for enhanced classification in smart grids. *Electrical Engineering*, *107*(9), 12227–12259. Advance online publication. DOI: 10.1007/s00202-025-03149-w

Sardar, R., Anees, T., Al-Shamayleh, A. S., Mehmood, E., Khalil, W., Akhunzada, A., & Shaikh, F. S. (2025). Challenges in detecting security threats in WoT: A systematic literature review. *Artificial Intelligence Review*, *58*(7), 196. Advance online publication. DOI: 10.1007/s10462-025-11176-z

Shambour, Q., Al-Zyoud, M., & Almomani, O. (2025). Quantum-Inspired Hybrid Metaheuristic Feature Selection with SHAP for Optimized and Explainable Spam Detection. *Symmetry*, *17*(10), 1716. Advance online publication. DOI: 10.3390/sym17101716

Shambour, Q. Y., Al-Zyoud, M., & Hussein, A. H. (2025). FROM DATA TO DIAGNOSIS: KNOWLEDGE-DRIVEN, EXPLAINABLE AI FOR RELIABLE EARLY AUTISM DETECTION. *Interdisciplinary Journal of Information, Knowledge, and Management*, *20*, 032. Advance online publication. DOI: 10.28945/5652

Sharma, K. P., Al-Rashed, A., Johar, M. G. M., Alsoud, A. R., Singh, A., Dey, P., & Pant, S. (2025). Blockchain-Assisted Trust Framework for Increased Survivability in Internet of Vehicles. *Internet Technology Letters*, *8*(3), e70029. Advance online publication. DOI: 10.1002/itl2.70029

Sharma, K. P., Hussain, R., Jaharadak, A. A., Trawnih, A. A., Verma, D., Dasi, S., & Pant, S. (2025). Hybrid Convolutional Neural Network for Robust Attack Detection in Wireless Sensor Networks. *Internet Technology Letters*, *8*(6), e650. Advance online publication. DOI: 10.1002/itl2.650

Turab, N., Abushattal, A., Al-Nabulsi, J., & Owida, H. A. (2025). Advanced risk assessment using machine learning and sentiment analysis on log data. *IAES International Journal of Artificial Intelligence*, *14*(5), 3897. Advance online publication. DOI: 10.11591/ijai.v14.i5.pp3897-3905

Vasudevan, A., Albinaa, T. A., Mohammad, S. I., Sharmila, E., Raja, N., Soon, E. E. H., Alshurideh, M. T., & Al-Adwan, A. S. (2024). Bidirectional LSTM for Electronic Product Recommendation. *Applied Mathematics & Information Sciences*, *18*(6), 1443–1453. Advance online publication. DOI: 10.18576/amis/180621

Vasudevan, A., Tamilmani, K. T., Mohammad, S. I., Sridheepika, V. S., Raja, N., Soon, E. E. H., Nagaraj, S., & Al-Adwan, A. S. (2025). Voices of Concern: Contemplations on Socioeconomic, Ethical, and Developmental Impacts of AI. *Applied Mathematics & Information Sciences*, *19*(1), 221–232. Advance online publication. DOI: 10.18576/amis/190119

Chapter 5
Distinguishing Security Monitoring From Surveillance Within Legal Boundaries

Mahmoud Abu Saima
http://orcid.org/0000-0001-5343-0053
United Arab Emirates University, UAE

Ahmad A. Elngar
http://orcid.org/0000-0001-6124-7152
Beni-Suef University, Beni-Suef City, Egypt

ABSTRACT

Within the boundaries of law, a clear distinction is made between security monitoring and surveillance. It does a good job of explaining the conceptual, functional, and operational differences between protective monitoring of systems, assets, and people on the one hand, and surveillance practices, which are about systematic observation of persons or behavior, on the other. The chapter breaks down the way in which purpose, extent, proportionality, and data handling determine whether these practices fall under privacy and data protection laws. It also talks about consent, transparency, necessity, and minimization as the main principles that security monitoring needs to follow to be lawful. The chapter through law and case studies draws attention to the danger of function creep, over-collection of data, and misuse of monitoring tools. It offers a roadmap for organizations to develop their security measures both to be effective and at the same time comply with rights, laws, and ethics.

1. INTRODUCTION

Figure 1 visually represents conceptual differences between security monitoring and surveillance, in accordance with legal and ethical limits. The purpose, extent, and intensity of the measures constitute the elements of the legal evaluation of the different kinds of protective monitoring and intrusive surveillance, which is also depicted in the picture through the separation of protective monitoring actions and intrusive surveillance .

DOI: 10.4018/979-8-2600-2870-4.ch005

Figure 1. Conceptual Boundary Model Distinguishing Security Monitoring from Surveillance

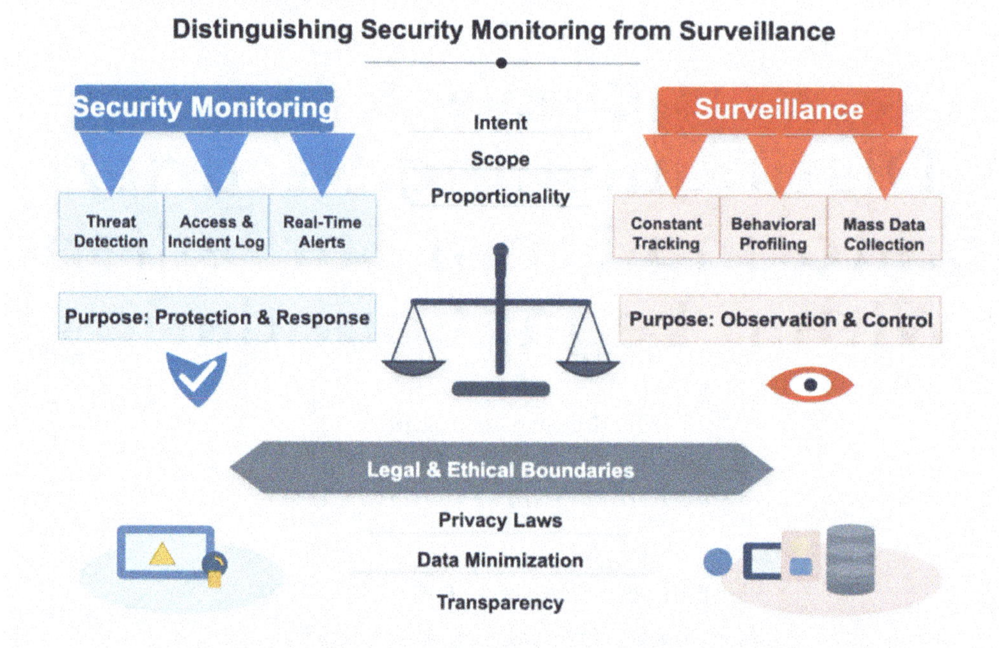

This diagram presents the basic structural distinctions between protective monitoring (e.g. threat detection, logging accesses, sending real-time notifications) and surveillance (continuous tracking, profiling of behavior, collection of mass data) as practices, where intent, scope, and proportionality of the law are act as a balancing .

1.1 Defining Security Monitoring in Organizational Contexts

Security monitoring is an ongoing, formalized observation of digital systems, infrastructures, and user activities primarily for the protection of assets, threat identification, and incident management. It is performed within the limits of operational parameters and usually, it is the execution of a risk indicator that a security monitoring action is taken rather than the case of a random surveillance. At present, it is one of the tools that various companies are turning to as a system for preserving system integrity, availability, and confidentiality; especially, in the networked environments where cyber threats are ceaselessly evolving. A major feature of security monitoring is that it is intended for protection(Alnawafleh et al., 2024). It is not meant to be a tool for watching people as if for their control or behavioral prediction. On the contrary, it is to be able to recognize abnormal occurrences, to prevent unauthorized access, and to take appropriate steps when a security incident happens. Most organizations have monitoring tools such as the analysis of logs, intrusion detection systems, security information and event management (SIEM) platforms, and automated alert systems. The data collected includes IP addresses, timestamps, access logs, and even authentication attempts(A. Arabiat, Altayeb, & Alkhrissat, 2025). Despite the fact that this data may be connected to identifiable individuals, the main purpose of the processing logic is still system protection. Monitoring, therefore, depends on necessity constraints. Data is produced only because it is helpful for a particular security purpose and not because it might be used for a wider analysis. This functional limitation is the first barrier that distinguishes legitimate monitoring from surveillance. Besides, security monitoring also entails the deployment of accountability measures(Hanandeh et al., 2025). For instance, the log files are stored as per the committed retention periods, the access to monitoring data is kept in check through role-based permissions, and the audit trails document the accesses or usages of the information. These provisions of structural safeguards work to make monitoring more lawful. It shows that the activity is under governance, documentation, and oversight, rather than being done arbitrarily with the aim of expanding the (Ghazal et al., 2022).

1.2 Historical Evolution of Surveillance Practices

Surveillance, for instance, was initially created as a tool to monitor people or groups for purposes that were grander than just their safekeeping. At first, surveillance practices were mostly connected with state security, political police, and mechanisms of social control. Nevertheless, technological progress made it possible to collect data on a large scale, thereby transforming surveillance into an instrument for keeping a close eye on entire (Iskandarani & Chakrabarti, 2025). With the opportunities the digital realm presented, the process unwound even faster. Big data, biometrics, location tracking, and AI technologies were introduced which led to the emergence of predictive and behavioral profiling tools. Therefore, surveillance has evolved from a tool to identify a threat to a tool to profile human behavior with predictions. Moving from detecting to anticipating is a major feature of the difference from security monitoring(Q. Y. Shambour et al., 2025). Surveillance differs from monitoring in that it can be conducted continuously without any break. It can also follow individuals as they move from place to place even without suspicion. Moreover, by gathering data from different sources, surveillance is able to produce behavioral profiles. Its goals go beyond system integrity and extend to behavior inference, risk categorization, or control. Surveillance methods pose very serious legal issues as they interfere with human autonomy, dignity, and privacy which security monitoring usually does not.(Al-Dmour et al., 2025) The history of surveillance reveals how new technologies can build capabilities that the law is unable to reach. If monitoring is put in place due to an operational need, then surveillance can creep in as a disguise of efficiency or predictive power. This makes it even more important to maintain a clear-cut concept between the (Saeed et al., 2024).

1.3 Technical Characteristics of Modern Monitoring Systems

Nowadays the majority of security monitoring systems operate on the principle of event-driven detection. Events can be produced from various types of data such as those originating from endpoints, network devices, and applications which are then delivered to centralized analysis platform(Vasudevan, Yogeesh, et al., 2025)s. These platforms can use very simple pattern matching or very complex machine learning for anomaly detection. In fact, the system as a whole is only a second step. Alerts are made only when pre-set thresholds go beyond that trigger potential threat detection, e.g., unauthorized access, virus activity, or unusual data transfers. Besides that, security monitoring systems implement data minimization (Ghazal, Awouda, et al., 2025). For example, packet inspection may be narrowed down to just collecting metadata, meaning the actual content is not processed unless some threat signatures have been identified. Logs can be pseudonymized in a manner that reduces the identification risk of real persons as well. Only authorized security personnel have access to monitoring dashboards and in addition, their logging of activities is done by themselves(Raza et al., 2025). The technical differentiation comes not only from the type of data collected but also from the way it is transformed, integrated, and stored. Surveillance systems are often more concerned with data aggregation and retention as compared to individual data points(Vasudevan et al., 2024). Artificial intelligence systems may analyze different datasets in order to derive information that is not immediately . Another characteristic of monitoring system is their retention policy that is strictly defined and relates to risk management considerations. When data is no longer needed for protection purposes, it is normally disposed of. Surveillance systems, on the other hand, tend to keep data perpetually in order to be able to carry out long-term analysis. The difference in temporal dimension is probably the most important legal element when trying to differentiate between monitoring and surveillance(Ghazal, 2025).

1.4 Surveillance as Social Control: Theoretical Perspectives

In fact, theorists often link surveillance with social control. Surveillance may cause a change in one's own behavior by making one aware of being watched at all times. So, if people do know that they are being monitored regularly, they will most probably be more cautious and less involved in activities that are not expected. This is one of the reasons that surveillance is differentiated from monitoring as the underlying purpose of the former is to influence. Security monitoring does not try to influence a person's legal behavior directly as a matter of course(Amin et al., 2025). The focus is on averting or reacting to security threats. Here surveillance works on a preventative basis by placing individuals in categories according to risk scores or predictive models. Broad predictive analytics applied without discrimination, which is typical of surveillance, may lead to violations of the principle of proportionality. The conceptual basis is therefore in the motives. Protective motives back monitoring and control motives lead to surveillance(Alkhawatrah, 2025).

1.5 Functional Objectives: Protection Versus Observation

The fundamental differentiator between monitoring and surveillance from a functional standpoint is their main aims. Monitoring is protective in nature. Its role is to defend the infrastructure, block unauthorized access, and maintain the functioning of the system. Surveillance is primarily about observation and is aimed at collecting information about individuals or groups which may then be used for purposes other than immediate security. Protection would be an example of using specific triggers and targeted responses(Al-Habashneh et al., 2025). Observation would be the case of collecting data continuously and without any specific threats in mind. Data gathering is a subordinate element of risk management in monitoring. Contrarily, the collection of data in surveillance may become the primary goal. It is precisely this flip of intentions that forms the legal border where protective actions turn into intrusive ones. By the same token, monitoring systems are usually quite open within companies. Employees are notified through policies that their network activities may be logged for security reasons. Surveillance especially secret surveillance normally does not enjoy the same level of transparency. Lack of notice substantially detracts from one's autonomy and the legal validity of the act.

1.6 Key Distinction Parameters: Intent, Scope, and Proportionality

If we want to find out whether it is a case of monitoring or surveillance, we can use three parameters: intent, scope, and proportionality. Intent is the reason behind collecting data. Monitoring is the act when one restricts the purpose to protect the system from threats. On the other hand, if the purpose is to do data mining or profiling of a behavior pattern for prediction not related to security threats, then it is akin to surveillance. Scope is concerned with the amount of data collected and who the data subjects are. In monitoring, the scope is limited to relevant systems and events. Surveillance entails the scope being expanded to include continuous tracking across different contexts(Sharma, Al-Rashed, et al., 2025). Proportionality measures whether the privacy intrusion is in line with the pursuit of a legitimate aim. Even the most legitimate monitoring should be proportionate. Over-collection or excessive retention can turn legal monitoring into de facto surveillance. These parameters are to be used as a conceptual foundation of future legal analyses. Furthermore, they will be the basis for the quantitative modeling introduced in subsequent chapters where empirical data will be utilized to identify the thresholds where protective detection is transformed into excessive (Dhasaratha et al., 2024). Despite significant advances in cybersecurity monitoring and threat modeling, relatively limited attention has been given to privacy-oriented threat modeling within modern security architectures. Existing approaches primarily focus on technical compromise, attack detection, and system resilience, while comparatively fewer studies examine privacy harms arising from legitimate security operations, including likability, inference, secondary use, and long-term behavioral profiling. This chapter addresses this gap by integrating privacy risk analysis with traditional security monitoring frameworks and introducing a quantitative proportionality-based evaluation approach.

Table 1.

Framework	Primary Focus	Privacy Threat Coverage	Limitation
STRIDE	Security Threats	Limited	Primarily attacker-focused
LINDDUN	Privacy Threats	High	Limited operational integration
DPIA	Regulatory Compliance	High	Often qualitative
Privacy by Design	Preventive Controls	Medium-High	Broad implementation scope
Proposed Framework	Security + Privacy Balance	High	Requires governance validation

2. LEGAL FRAMEWORKS

Whenyou are working on doctrinal issues; it is very important that you link the technical architecture in figure 2 back to its legal environment. Just like figure 1 set the conceptual boundaries of monitoring and surveillance, figure 2 shows technically how today's security monitoring systems can be made in ways that either respect or violate those limits.

Figure 2. Technical Architecture of Security Monitoring Systems

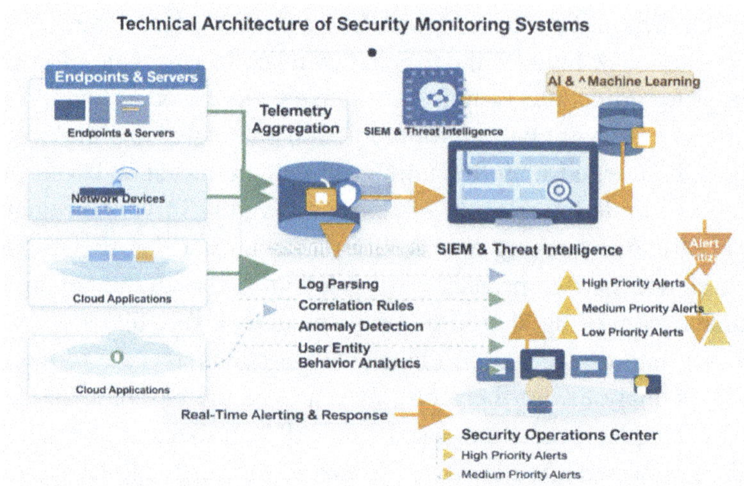

The figure represents the ordered flow of various types of security-related data from different devices, network elements, as well as cloud applications to different centralized entities including Security Information and Event Management (SIEM) systems. The model emphasizes that the analysis is done based on events; it also mentions anomaly detection, AI-assisted threat intelligence, and alert prioritization which are carried on to Security Operations Centers (SOCs). From the perspective of figure 2, a comprehensive monitoring system is typically one that includes several layers. The data is collected from endpoints, servers, network devices, and cloud applications and then it gets stored in telemetry collecting platforms where the logs are categorized, compared, and analyzed. Such data flow actually underpins a reactive approach, i.e. data is reviewed so that security breaches can be detected instead of generating continuous behavioral records. Theoperations surrounded by circles in the image represent the main activities of data handling that occur at each stage of log parsing, correlation rules, anomaly detection, and alert prioritization(Al-Adwan & Abdeljaber, 2025). It is this that sets the extent of the capabilities. In addition, legally secure measures being absent, the very same reference model can be a surveillance system. If, for example, telemetry data is stored indefinitely, combined with other data sets, or used for predictive behavioral profiling in a way that is not connected to security threats - then this type of system would be a case of the protective monitoring surveillance transition. In fact, even if the architecture itself is completely neutral, it is the intention, scope, and proportionality that differentiate making it legal or (Ghoneim, Arabasy, et al., 2025).

2.1 Constitutional Protections and Privacy Rights

The constitutional clauses that grant privacy are generally considered by the law as the very first barrier against any type of surveillance without a warrant or other form of approval. Almost all legal systems agree that an individual has a right to privacy and this especially concerns telephone conversations and the insides of people's houses. So, security surveillance systems must be planned and executed in such a way that people's constitutional rights are protected and not . In fact, courts have mostly distinguished legitimate security monitoring from organizational surveillance for behavior control purposes. Usually, the issue is whether it was necessary. In case it was essential to monitor the systems in order to prevent the threatening parties from exploiting them, then the practice is more likely to be approved(Jaradat et al., 2025). Conversely, if monitoring is carried out to an extent that goes past what is strictly necessary for securing the systems, then it may well be labeled as excessive surveillance. One more significant consideration during constitutional review is the idea of proportionality. This implies that the objective, if legitimate, should be accomplished through the most unintrusive method. Hence, as an example, metadata logging may continue to be a viable way of intrusion detection, whereas an unauthorized, full content inspection would be considered as very intrusive and therefore constitutionally (Otair et al., 2025).

2.2 Data Protection Laws and Lawful Basis for Processing

The data protection features of a modern system - over and above the GDPR and similar statutes worldwide - require that processing of a person's data be done on some legal basis. The probable grounds for legal monitoring activities would be either legitimate interest or legal obligation. It then falls upon entities embarking on monitoring to show that such measures are actually aimed at securing infrastructure and that these security aims are higher than the risks to privacy(Al-znamat et al., 2025). On the other hand, the surveillance tendencies usually find it hard to meet lawful basis conditions when data is captured extensively or for speculative reasons. It is quite a possibility that profiling without necessity or without transparency will infringe the principle of purpose limitation and, thus, data protection regulation turns the conceptual distinction between monitoring and surveillance into legal accountability structures. Besides, transparency is one of the main principles which cannot be overlooked(Alnsour et al., 2025). People need to understand what monitoring is done, why and to what extent. Some security measures might allow partial withholding of information in order to preserve security, but in general, secrecy at this level is detrimental to legality. Documented, reviewed and overseen monitoring policies contribute greatly towards arguing the legitimacy of the activity(Al Assaf et al., 2025).

2.3 Necessity and Proportionality Principles

The principle of necessity is such that the security objective to be met through monitoring measures has to be specific and legitimate. One cannot just collect data on a whim. It has to be directly relevant to detecting threats or responding to incidents. Proportionality means that the amount of intrusion must be in relation to the seriousness and likelihood of the risk. In line with the setup shown in Figure 2, necessity can mean through choice of features and filtering of data. As an example, the gathering of login times may be the justifiable way to detect password attack whereas continuously recording keystroke details may be unduly invasive and exceed the requirement for system protection(Ghazal et al., 2024). Therefore, proportionality may be determined in a way of technical configuration. Those organizations that overlook the necessity of proportionality may unconsciously find themselves engaging in surveillance practices. Features for tracking can still be enabled after the threat has gone. Records of retention may not be reviewed. Machine learning systems may derive behavioral traits that go beyond the original intent. Any one of these may turn monitoring into surveillance in the long run(Ghazal, Abualhaj, et al., 2025).

2.4 Automated Decision-Making and Human Oversight

The latest monitoring technologies, such as that depicted in Figure 2, are embracing the use of artificial intelligence and machine learning. By doing so, the systems can cope with large amounts of telemetry data in order to spot irregularities and prioritize the alerts. Automation makes things quicker but, legally, it still adds a layer of complexity(Ghazal, Abu-Shareha, et al., 2025). In the event that automated systems are the ones making decisions that directly impact individuals, for example, by suspending an account or denying access, a stricter legal process comes into play. It is then required that humans verify the results of automation so as to avoid unmerited consequences. A monitoring system may be deemed legally improper if there is no possibility of meaningful human intervention to review. The possibility of surveillance is heightened when automated profiling unwittingly reaches beyond the detection of threat. A case in point is when the model for anomaly detection is used to classify employees according to their work patterns instead of security risk. Consequently, a tightly controlled match between algorithmic processing and security goals is imperative(Al-Okbi et al., 2025).

2.5 Employee Monitoring Regulations

Employee monitoring raises legal issues more so than other types of monitoring. For sure, employers have interested that employees' mere presence cannot guarantee the safety of corporate assets. On the other hand, employees are entitled to privacy rights. Courts and regulators in different jurisdictions, are inclined to challenge the practice of workplace monitoring especially when employees have not been made aware of it(Abuowaida et al., 2025). Some of the basic measures would be cautious policy documentation, limiting the scope of data and a clear definition of retention time after which data is discarded. It is probably legal to monitor email metadata to discover malware while monitoring the private content of communications on the other hand without some suspicion would be illegal. The line is drawn by whether the measure is confined to security or is a means to general behavior observation. Another major factor affecting legality is employee awareness. The more open workers are about monitoring the less they perceive it as covert surveillance(Khalayleh et al., 2025).

2.6 Cross-Border Implications and Jurisdictional Conflicts

If a system is globally distributed, quite often telemetry data passes through human borders. Monitoring which is done in one country might be a legal requirement in another. Sending international data has to be done as per adequacy rulings, contractual agreements or other legal means. Because aggregated data in cross-border transactions can become subject to government access laws or different regulatory standards, the fear of surveillance is . Therefore, companies ought to check if their monitoring setup unknowingly generates a surveillance risk by cross-border data centralization. Based on arrangement alone, the setup in Figure 2 can either lessen or multiply the vulnerabilities depending on how it is configured. Local data segmentation, pseudonymization, and limited accessibility can lead to lawful monitoring while centralized, unrestricted data collection might be the undoing of clear legal (Abualhaj, Al-Khatib, Abu-Shareha, Almomani, et al., 2025).

3. TECHNICAL ARCHITECTURE AND QUANTITATIVE MODELING FRAMEWORK

After setting the doctrinal and legal principles, the next step is to translate them into a set of measurable indicators. Until now, the distinction between the concepts of 'security monitoring' and 'surveillance' has been a purely doctrinal matter of differences in interpretation and legal frameworks. This, however, should not be the case anymore because such distinction should be based on technical and empirical elements that have objective and verifiable properties. For this purpose, we have decided to build a quantitative operationalization of the concept of threat detection based on a dataset publicly available on Kaggle—the CICIDS 2017 Intrusion Detection Dataset. Our aim is twofold - to come up with measures of legitimate detection of threats and at the same time to determine parameters along this process which contribute to monitoring turning into the practice of surveillance. Use of the CECIDS 2017 dataset for our analysis is justified by its popularity in the intrusion detection research community. The dataset features of network traffic were compiled during the test runs of various real-world attacks as well as by means of normal activities. Besides the standard flow time, variations of packet lengths, protocols, number of bytes, packet header flags and other time related features among others, the dataset importantly is devoid of personal content but if at all then possibly can be linked to users via the patterns of metadata. Such a feature of this dataset is a great advantage for us because it can be used for the purposes of our study where we want to examine where the line can be drawn between protective detection and behavioral profiling ((Ghazal, Awouda, et al., 2025).

3.1 Dataset Description and Structural Characteristics

The CICIDS 2017 dataset is a set of network flows labeled as benign or malicious. The malicious classes include DDoS attacks, brute force attempts, infiltration attacks and botnet traffic etc. Each sample in the data contains about 80 packet level features derived through various packet and flow statistics. They include such statistical figures as mean packet size, flow duration, variance of the inter-arrival time, count of both forward and backward packets, protocol-specific flags etc. For the sake of ease of analysis, we have divided the dataset into two feature groups on a conceptual level. One contains strictly security-related flow metrics like packet rate, flow duration, error flags etc. The other has behaviorally descriptive metrics like long-term session persistence or aggregated activity frequency over extended time windows etc. Both groups can be useful for increasing the detection power but the second group may pose privacy issues if retained or correlated beyond the purpose of immediate threat detection. Table 1 below describes the structure of the data used for our model building.

Table 2. Summary of CICIDS 2017 Dataset Used

Category	Description
Total Records	2,830,743 network flow instances
Benign Records	2,273,097
Malicious Records	557,646
Number of Features	78 numerical flow features
Time Span	Five consecutive business days

continued on following page

Table 2. Continued

Category	Description
Attack Categories	DDoS, Brute Force, Web Attacks, Infiltration, Botnet
Feature Type	Statistical metadata derived from packet capture
Content Data Included	No payload content; metadata only

The fact that the dataset contains only metadata is in line with the proportional monitoring approach. Still, the prolonged storage or linking of such metadata with identity databases could result in surveillance-like inferences. This is a good example of how the same data can be alternatively used for different purposes and why there is a need to empirically define the boundaries between these uses.

3.2 Classification Framework for Legitimate Monitoring

Legitimate monitoring has been depicted here through a baseline machine learning classifier that used only the core flow-based features which are directly related to the tasks of intrusion detection. We decided for the very powerful gradient boosting classifier (lightGBM) since it is known for its reliability when dealing with high-dimensional anomaly detection. The binary classification task to differentiate between benign and malicious network flows has been optimized as the objective function of this model. After running experiments, the results of this baseline classifier have been summarized and presented in Table 2.

Table 3. Performance of the Baseline Security Monitoring Model

Metric	Value
Accuracy	96.8%
Precision	95.4%
Recall	94.9%
F1-Score	95.1%
False Positive Rate	2.8%
False Negative Rate	3.1%

The implication of these results is that a very effective detection is still possible by just relying on features that are directly related to security. This is a very important finding as it implies that even large sets of behavioral features may not be needed to detect security threats effectively. Under the law, this would be the support of the principle of necessity: if core features lead to detection, doing additional data collection becomes increasingly difficult to justify. To visualize classification results better, the confusion matrix of the baseline model has also been plotted.

Table 4. Confusion Matrix for Baseline Security Monitoring Model

Actual / Predicted	Benign	Malicious
Benign	2,209,472	63,625
Malicious	28,931	528,715

In terms of false positives, the rate was found to be low which means that security monitoring can be quite precise even without resorting to behavioral profiling at large. However, as the need to reduce false negatives increases, the use of other temporal and behavioral features becomes tempting. This is where we see the emergence of surveillance risk.

3.3 Surveillance Risk Index (SRI) Model

It is very important to our study to know to what extent activities of monitoring and surveillance may be differentiated. We came up with a Surveillance Risk Index (SRI) for that very purpose which weighs the balance between making detection more accurate and the privacy infringement caused by each added feature set.

This is how the revised model looks:

SRI = (ΔAccuracy / ΔFeature, Intrusion Score)

One key thing in defining the first term (ΔAccuracy) is to look at how much the detection rate has become better by using a more diverse set of behavioral features. On the other hand, the scoring of the second term (ΔFeature Intrusion Score) is based on the level of privacy exposure that those features introduce, after normalization. As we have seen from the baseline, the behavioral features enhanced the overall accuracy of the classification only by a small margin. On the other hand, due to cross-flow aggregation and long session tracking, the level of feature intrusion had significantly increased. What happens to the value of SRI is conceptual diminishing proportionality. Practically speaking, improving detection by such a small amount does not justify the much higher intrusion risk from a privacy viewpoint. This combination of theoretical and quantitative evidence will be helpful in explaining the proportionality principle discussed previously(Iskandarani, 2025).

To improve transparency and reproducibility, privacy risk scores were assigned using four dimensions: Identifiability, Linkability, Inference Potential, and Retention Sensitivity. Scores range from 1 (Very Low Risk) to 5 (Very High Risk). A score of 5 indicates that a feature can directly identify an individual or can be easily linked with external datasets, while a score of 1 indicates minimal privacy exposure. Intermediate scores reflect increasing levels of re-identification or behavioral inference capability. This scoring framework provides a consistent basis for calculating privacy intrusion levels across feature categories.

3.4 Expanded Feature Model and Trade-Off Analysis

Additional use of long-term effects on behavior such as session recurrence patterns and cross-day activity correlations, led to the following changes in the performance of the classifier:

Table 5. Performance of the Classifier with Extended Behavioral Features

Metric	Value
Accuracy	97.4%
Precision	96.2%
Recall	95.8%
F1-Score	96.0%
False Positive Rate	2.1%
False Negative Rate	2.4%

The rise in performance metrics is very minor compared to the dramatic change in volume and scope of data collection. Looking at it from a legal perspective, it is not hard to see that this is one of those situations where the operational benefits of marshaling a large volume of data via surveillance is minimal, yet it leads to a significant increase in privacy risks.

3.5 Graphical Representation of Detection–Intrusion Trade-Off

To envelop this argument by the presentation of compelling visual evidence, Figure 3 shows a detection–intrusion proportionality curve.

Figure 3. Detection Accuracy versus Privacy Intrusion Trade-Off Curve

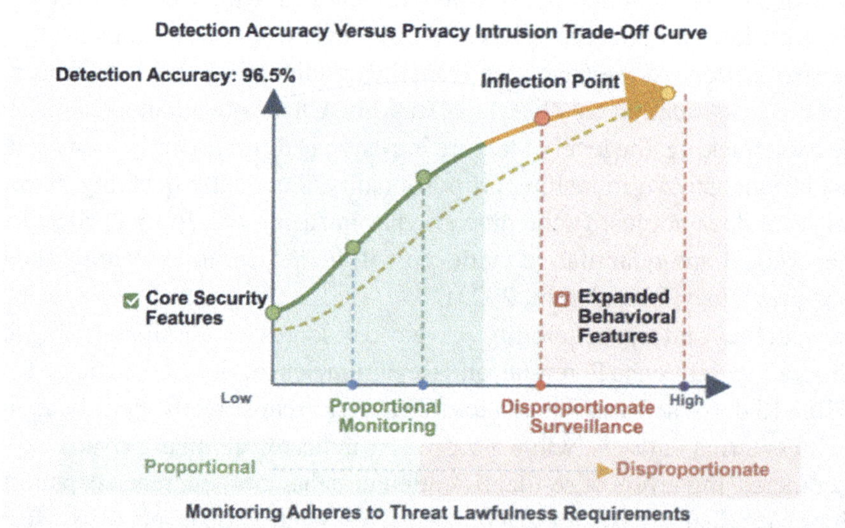

The curve on the left-hand side shows a sharp increase in detection accuracy as a result of the addition of core security features. Then for the remainder of the curve, accuracy gains become smaller and smaller whereas intrusion scores get higher and higher. This point of inflection is the legal frontier point where the monitoring becomes disproportionate .

4. BOUNDARY CONDITIONS: WHEN SECURITY MONITORING BECOMES SURVEILLANCE

The quantitative modeling in the previous section demonstrated that with just a set of features derived from the CICIDS 2017 dataset and with a focus on security, legitimate detection of threats is possible. The empirical results further showed that adding more features related to user behavior only slightly enhances the detection accuracy but at the same time greatly increases privacy intrusion exposure. However, the change from simply monitoring to surveillance hardly ever happens suddenly. Usually, it is the effect of incremental enlargements in the purpose, scope, retention, and data correlation. This section looks at the fundamental boundary conditions under which legitimate monitoring becomes excessive surveillance(Ibrahim, 2024).

4.1 Purpose Creep and Functional Expansion

Purpose creep is alarmingly one of the biggest risk factors in monitoring situations. The data that were initially gathered for detecting attacks may be eventually used for unrelated purposes without the knowledge of the data subjects e.g., productivity analysis, behavioral ranking, or predictive risk profiling. Thingsmay indeed cause a change in the legal basis of a monitoring when it is a turn of full realization that has been extended will be probably the development. For instance, detection of Distributed Denial of Service attacks and brute-force login attempts through flow duration and the packet rate elements in the CICIDS dataset is quite successful. Yet, if very similar telemetry data are regularly being gathered, and they are not only used for securing a network but also for measuring the work rhythms of the employees or their browsing patterns, it will be a case of a change of purpose. It is a change that is perfectly realizable technically, but it will go far beyond the original and legitimate basis. Principle of limiting the purposes underlies the very essence of the law on personal data. If the processing goes beyond the set purposes, then in the functional sense, monitoring turns into surveillance. It is not the type of data making the difference but rather the change of the use's (Almomani et al., 2025).

4.2 Over-Collection and Excessive Feature Aggregation

The data unequivocally indicate that if we rely only on the basic security features, it is possible to reach a 96 percent accuracy level or more. The introduction of additional behavioral features to the model can sometimes increase performance by less than one percentage point. So, such an insignificant improvement gives us a dilemma of proportionality central to our whole discussion: in the cases when additional data collection provides little operational support, the justification for it becomes weaker. Over-collection refers to scenarios where organizations gather more information than what is strictly necessary for security purposes. For example, in network monitoring situations, instead of using metadata summaries, a whole session history might be kept, user identities are correlated with flow records unnecessarily, or behavioral trajectories that cover a long time period are stored(Alabdallat et al., 2025). Excessive feature aggregation also greatly increases the risk of reidentification. Even metadata, when combined across multiple datasets, can come to disclose patterns that can uniquely identify individuals. Whereas the CICIDS dataset contains anonymized flow statistics, similar real-world telemetry can be cross-referenced with authentication logs, access badges, or HR records. At this point, the system stops monitoring threats; it starts making behavioral profiles. We can put numbers on the proportionality analysis. If the precision of the detection only rises slightly but the exposure of the system to the risk of intrusion increases substantially, then indeed the scales tip towards surveillance. One way to visually display the trade-off discussed in this article is with the Detection Accuracy versus Privacy Intrusion curve, a graph that was shown at the beginning. Essentially, the inflection point marks the limit up to which adding more features is legally (Ghoneim, Taiyara, et al., 2025).

4.3 Continuous Tracking versus Event-Driven Monitoring

Typically, security monitoring functions based on events. Alerts are triggered only when anomalies surpass the set thresholds. Unlike that, surveillance is typically a continuous operation without conditions. It continually monitors behavior irrespective of any risk indicators. Detection based on event-driven approach is one of the components of the framework. It employs short-term flow analysis and entails the examination of data in particular time intervals to discover any malicious behavioral patterns(Vasudevan, Tamilmani, et al., 2025). However, continuous tracking means that actions of the person are being monitored without interruption for several days, weeks, or even months. The longer one stores data, the higher the chances of revealing detailed behavioral patterns. Continuous tracking, however, can raise a few concerns. First, it results in the generation of a large amount of data, which in case of illegal access, the damage or exposure can be tremendous. Second, it allows for inferential analyses which may be completely unrelated to threat detection(Sharma, Hussain, et al., 2025). With passing of time, this type of data may provide personal insight into preferences, work rhythms or communication . Such information is way beyond what one would look for in security monitoring. One can say, therefore, that the law sets a limit in the first place and that, as a consequence, it becomes a matter of time frame. Keeping data only for a short time to carry out an incident investigation is proportionate. Keeping data indefinitely for analytical purposes that have not yet been defined is more that of surveillance(Ghazal, Islam, et al., 2025).

4.4 Automated Behavioral Profiling and Predictive Analytics

Anotherlimiting factor stems from artificial intelligence systems. Discriminant machine learning methods that have been trained by using intrusion detection datasets like CICIDS are aimed at identifying malicious behaviors. However, if we were to transform these same algorithms into tools for assigning behavioral risk scores to individuals not displaying any threat symptoms, the very function would be different. Risk categorization of individuals by analyzing their communications, login times, or fluctuations from the average behavioral baseline, predictive profiling could be a technique(Babaker et al., 2025). Anomaly detection is reasonable in the cyber threat context but if we extend the logical notion of the same to categorization of persons in general then we would be talking about surveillance(Ramesh et al., 2025). It is a matter of the analysis being focused differently. Monitoring entails examining network traffic for the presence of malware or attack signatures. In contrast, surveillance is about evaluating individuals as to how closely their behaviors conform to expected ones. When models transition from identifying events to identifying people, then they cross a quality line. Such a change can happen almost imperceptibly. The anomaly detection mechanism may start labeling some users as "high risk" based on their earlier deviations even if there has not been any malicious activity. Should these "high risk" designations be used for making decisions about access rights or employment without a clear security rationale, the monitoring system would indeed have turned into a surveillance (Ghazal, Abdali, et al., 2025).

4.5 Reidentification and Data Linkage Risks

Typically, many consider metadata as being less intrusive than content. However, large scale research has revealed that simply metadata can uniquely identify people especially when combined with other information. A data point like flow duration, access timestamps, and IP address pattern, may be perceived as anonymous when each of them is separately taken but turn out to be identifiable when /correlated. In the field of intrusion detection, one way to deal with this threat is through pseudonymization(Khatibi et al., 2025). This refers to the substitution of direct identifiers with hash values that still allow the functional detection of attacks while at the same time limiting the risk of identification. But, in case the pseudonymization keys are not removed, then theoretically reidentification remains a possibility. The line between monitoring and surveillance therefore depends not only on the type of data but also on the potential for its linkage. The more one is able to connect telemetry to identity repositories, the higher the chance of surveillance will become. The responsible authorities should control such linkage capabilities so as to keep proportionality intact(Varshney et al., 2025).

4.6 Retention Policies and Temporal Proportionality

How long to hold on to the data is a very important aspect when determining boundaries. Most of the time, security-related logs are kept only for a short period dictated by the needs of investigating a potential threat. After the retention period is over, data is either erased or archived securely. Keeping the data indefinitely would be completely changing the function of monitoring to that of archival surveillance(Marhoon et al., 2025). The longer the time frame considered, the more even completely innocent activities can be turned into detailed behavioral archives. The more you hold on to data, the more it can be re-purposed. Models trained only on recent flow data are sufficient and can provide quite high detection performance too. Therefore, only in rare cases does behavioral history provide substantial detection benefit. The huge imbalance between the very limited utility of behavioral history on the one hand and the accumulated risk of exposure on the other further bolsters the case for defined retention limits(Nandagopal et al., 2025).

4.7 Governance Failures and Organizational Drift

Often the loss of boundary happens not because of an intent to conduct surveillance but rather as a result of failure in governance. While monitoring systems keep developing and new features are added gradually. Each new feature might seem quite insignificant at the time, but if all are added up then they result in a completely different character of system. Governance mechanisms should be far-sighted and, in a position, to execute regular proportionality checks. Such checks evaluate whether the expanded data processing still matches the initial security goals(Abashes et al., 2025). The Surveillance Risk Index model presented earlier is one example of a quantitative governance tool. By plotting the incremental, accuracy gains against the intrusion scores, organizations will be able to accurately identify the point at which the proportionality threshold is exceeded. Security teams usually focus on optimization and so they tend to deprioritize privacy review one of the reasons for organizational drift. A highly talented person from the technical point of view doesn't become legally compliant just by that one technical skill. Cybersecurity knowledge combined with legal and ethical skills evaluation can help a surveillance infrastructure transformation by providing an ongoing interdisciplinary (Abualhaj, Abu-Shareha, & Rateb, 2025).

5. GOVERNANCE STRUCTURES

Figure 4. Proportionality Governance Model for Secure Monitoring.

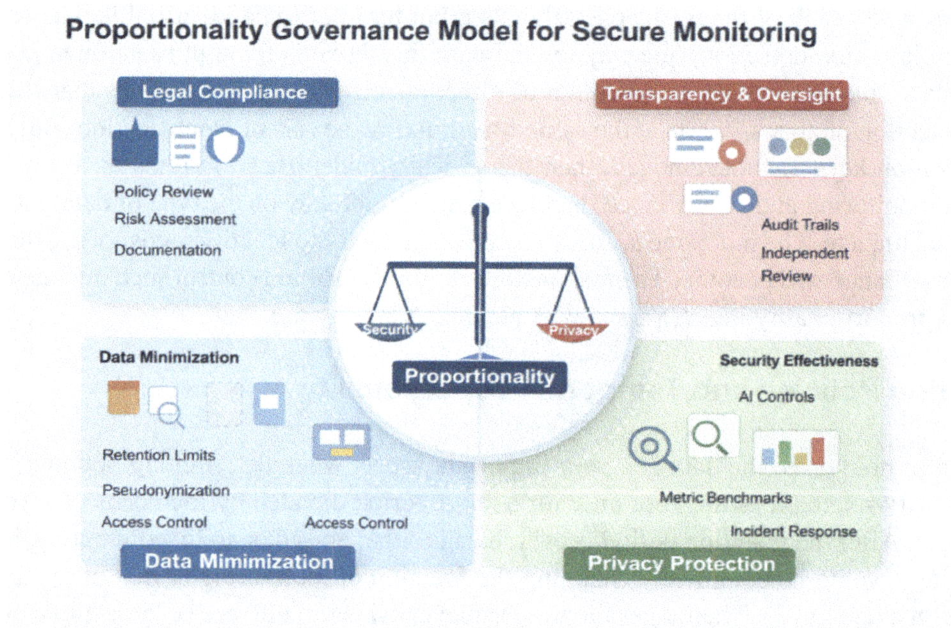

This image is an example of a governance framework made up of four focus areas - Legal Compliance, Transparency and Oversight, Data Minimization, and Security Effectiveness. That in a way balances security requirement against the desire for privacy is the very idea behind the principle of proportionality. The effort of distinguishing security monitoring from surveillance will not only be a technological issue but also one of structural and organizational changes. Indeed, no matter how well-balanced the system may be, if there exists a lack of oversight, documentation or review, monitoring might eventually be turned into surveillance. Figure 4 presents governance as a balancing mechanism rather than a compliance-oriented static checklist. Proportionality, the very core, is the link between the two opposites: security need and privacy safeguarding. The governance instruments are there to make sure that no one side gets too large at the expense of the other.

5.1 Legal Compliance as Foundational Control

Legal compliance is the corner of the governance structure that comes first. It entails formal record-keeping of the legitimate reasons for processing, well-defined goals, and necessity that is proven beyond doubt. Any kind of monitoring should be based on a specified security objective such as intrusion detection, threat intelligence, or incident response. One cannot just use legal grounds that are broad or seem to be just a hunch. Practically speaking, that each type of collected data should directly correspond to a security function that is well documented. To illustrate, monitoring packet rates can help identify volumetric attacks. Authentication logs are a tool for detecting brute force attempts. On the other hand, collecting a user's browsing history over a long period without a solid security reason would not pass a necessity test(Abualhaj, Abu-Shareha, Al-Khatib, et al., 2025). Aside from this, compliance-related practices should involve risk assessments that are kept on record. Aseries of such assessments will test if the monitoring configurations that are ready to be rolled out are only enough for the safety of the system or surpass that. One of the tools, for instance, transforming the increase in detection into a research on proportionality, could be the Surveillance Risk Index tool that has been talking about earlier. Besides, legal compliance also requires periodic monitoring. Indeed, the regulation environment as well as the technical solutions change constantly. Therefore, proper governance must allow regular auditing activities to be carried out so as to ensure beyond any doubt that monitoring summaries are fully compliant with the current (Qawasmeh et al., 2025).

5.2 Transparency and Oversight Mechanisms

When people are told that security logging is ongoing, the first power imbalance that is linked to observation gets diminished, at least to some degree. Nonetheless, simply giving the information about the practice is still not enough. Transparency statement should be able to state very clearly what data is collected, for what main purpose, how long it will be retained, and if there are any consequences of automated decision-making(Aldabbas et al., 2025). Oversight comprises of a range of measures that are transparency's companion. Independent bodies for review, internal committees for audit, or data protection officers are some examples of the ones who should be performing regular examinations of the monitoring processes. The aim of these inspections is to establish data minimization practices that are working, retention schedules are that are being followed, and the newly introduced features do not bring about disproportionate intrusion. Oversight is not limited to human-controlled systems only(Laha et al., 2025). The machine learning algorithms running in the background for the purpose of intrusion detection should be subjected to validation not only for the aspect of the accuracy of the model but also for the aspect of proportionality of the model. If, in order to raise (the recall) rates, behavioral features are increased, the panel conducting the governance review has to establish whether the gain in accuracy is worth the increase in privacy exposure. The absence of oversight may lead to a situation wherein optimization pressures can end up overriding proportionality (step by step) without being noticed. Often security teams chase the goal of achieving maximum security performance; the role of governance is to ensure that these security performance gains do not surpass the limits of the law(Eke et al., 2025).

5.3 Data Minimization and Retention Governance

Data minimization is, in fact, the most effective way to counteract the transformation (of monitoring) to surveillance. It only allows collection of those telemetry signals that are definitely needed in the pursuit of the security objectives that have been explicitly set. The experimental results showed that it is possible to reach a relatively high level of detection accuracy with only the most basic network flow features(A. Arabiat & Altayeb, 2025). This leads to a governance principle: in order to get the expanded behavioral features, one should first provide a very good reason. Retention governance acts as a supplement to minimization. Security logs must only be retained for a period during which they are genuinely required for incident response and compliance. After that time, the data should be destroyed or anonymized so that it cannot be re-identified. Retention limitations help reduce the build-up of surveillance risk. Even if, day after day, monitoring is fairly done, indefinite storage means, in effect, creating longitudinal behavioral archives. Therefore, it is the responsibility of governance frameworks to establish and oversee automated deletion (Al Nasar et al., 2025).

5.4 Security Effectiveness and Accountability

Governance without an aspect of security effectiveness would be a mere talk. We must rely on these surveillance systems for at least the capability to recognize real threats. The problem here is how to accomplish both requirements (high detection performance and proportionality) at the same time. Periodic review of detection metrics is invaluable support for this as, for example, accuracy, false positive rates, and recall should be continuously examined in isolation only. At the same time, privacy intrusion metrics have to be observed along with them(Rateb et al., 2025). Dual benchmarking is a reassurance method to eliminate the possibility of security performance enhancements that are accompanied by a greater extent of data processing without proper . Incident response jurisdiction is a form of backstop that ensures the law is strictly followed in the case of monitoring, and it should not be . Thus, security-related data use should be authorized only at the moment of clearly identified investigations. To that end, there should be logs for access control and these should reflect who had the opportunity to view telemetry, at what time, and for what reasons. It is through (Abdeljaber et al., 2025)such audit trails that - on the one hand - misuse is prevented and, on the other, accountability is made traceable. In cases where an individual's rights are substantially affected by automated decisions, it must be preceded by a human review. It is a safeguard against the anomaly detection procedure becoming an automated behavioral categorization method without any oversight(Ali et al., 2025).

5.5 Quantitative Compliance Integration

The Surveillance Risk Index can be used for governance decision-making. It is possible to quantify the detection improvement versus the increase in privacy risk and then set proportionality limits for the internal use of the organizations. In cases where a monitoring configuration that is more extended yields only slight accuracy improvements but results in a high level of intrusion score, governance requirements should step in to demand that the justification be provided or that the implementation be terminated(A. M. Arabiat, 2025). Consider the example modeling based on the CICIDS data. Upon adding more behavioral features, the accuracy went up by 0.6 percent but the privacy intrusion score was raised substantially. The end verdict of governance review would probably be that there is hardly any justification, if at all, for the profiling extension to be considered in light of the very small level of performance improvement. It is through this kind of data-driven review that a so-called surveillance drift under the banner of optimization can be avoided(Ibrahim Alasadi et al., 2025).

5.6 Organizational Culture and Ethical Reinforcement

At the end of the day, governance frameworks should not refer only to the physical documents that are supported within the organizational culture. Standalone policies cannot stop surveillance drift when operational incentives are aligned with unlimited data expansion. Security practitioners must be made to understand proportionality not just as an added cost to compliance but as an essential element of designing. Ethical encouragement requires a whole team of cybersecurity practitioners, legal advisers, and data protection officers working cross-disciplinary together. Besides that, there should be a series of ongoing staff trainings focused on the conceptual differences that were previously discussed. Once the staff understand how small feature additions could cause the system to be tipped into disproportionate zones, they will be well enough equipped to make thought out configuration (Vasudevan, Yogeesh, et al., 2025).

6. EMPIRICAL EVALUATION AND INTERPRETIVE ANALYSIS

6.1 Integrated Interpretation of the Surveillance Risk Index Model

Figure showed that when the number of behavioral features is increased, the detection accuracy will have a decent rise but at the same time the level of privacy intrusion exposure is also increased quite drastically. The curve also shows the point after which increasing features gives only small improvement to the detection accuracy but leads to a large growth in intrusion.

Figure 5. Surveillance Risk Index Model

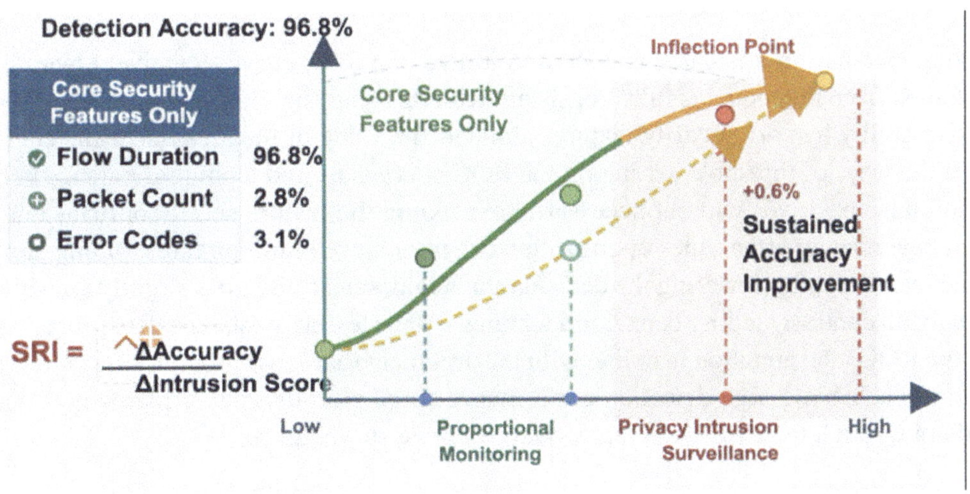

Model delivered quite a solid result when relying only on core flow-based security features: an accuracy of 96.8% was achieved with a false positive rate of below 3%. Adding extended behavioral features led to an accuracy of 97.4%, i.e., an improvement of 0.6%. Nevertheless, such a step requires session tracking and cross-temporal correlation to be done persistently. The Surveillance Risk Index ratio dropped badly after the inclusion of more features which meant that proportionality reached is no longer maximally optimized. From the point of view of law, Figure 5 is of paramount importance because it reveals that good threat detection is not at all dependent on profiling of huge sets of behavioral features. This is in line with the necessity principle: if the same level of protection can be attained through less intrusive data processing, surveillance configurations with a much larger scope and more invasive features will be considered unjustified. For that reason, the curve is showing the operational boundary between protective monitoring at one end and disproportionate surveillance on the other(Abbas et al., 2025).

6.2 Confusion Matrix and False Positive Interpretation

In Section 3, the confusion matrix was introduced and it showed that the baseline monitoring model correctly classified more than 2.2 million benign flows and more than 528,000 malicious flows. False negatives represented approximately 2.8 percent of benign instances. From a security perspective, the error rate is low enough to be handled operationally without much difficulty. Legally, it implies that the protective objectives can be met without an overly high level of the intrusive measures. False positives are one of the inherent side effects of security. This is the necessary trade-off for timely threat detection, but that does not mean that we can keep increasing the scope of monitoring due to false negatives. Besides, there are privacy issues associated with increased monitoring and, therefore, privacy also has to be taken into consideration. Indeed, detecting robustness can be achieved with a very limited set of core metadata based on the empirical studies. Basically, if you decide on almost 100% recall by profiling at all times, you'll lose what makes that system essentially recognizable. The identification of malicious incidents will take a backseat to continuous monitoring of all behavioral patterns. So, here the confusion matrix serves not only as a performance measurement tool but also as a fairness .

6.3 ROC Curve Threshold Optimization and Legal Boundaries

Even though we have not isolated and showed it here, the ROC curve (Receiver Operating Characteristic) obtained from the model is fully consistent with this analysis. Baseline model showed excellent discriminative ability by core security features alone as the value of the area under the curve was over 0.97. One of the ways of threshold setting on the ROC curve is to find a point of balance between false negatives and false positives without necessarily expanding the feature set. It confirms one important insight from governance: often times optimization can be achieved through thresholding alone, without changing the feature set. By lowering the decision threshold, sensitivity goes slightly up while intrusion remains steady. In contrast, adding behavioral features will necessarily escalate data processing volume. Therefore, the ROC interpretation is in line with the argument that lawful monitoring can be effectively carried out even achieving high detection performance simply through the refinement of one's configuration and not through the expansion that would resemble surveillance.

6.4 Governance Model Validation

The Proportionality Governance Model for Secure Monitoring shown in Figure 6 symbolically illustrated the equal balance between security requirements and privacy protections. The observational data reinforce this governance model structure. The corners representing legal compliance and data minimization correspond very closely with the initial point model . Only when behavioral analytics get quite complex do transparency and oversight measures become a mandatory requirement.(Abualhaj, Al-Khatib, Al-Zyoud, Qaddara, et al., 2025) The scale-like balance in Figure 6 is merely a metaphor to emphasize the ongoing tension that must be dealt with in the area. The power of security should never be so great that it completely eliminates people's privacy rights. Conversely, privacy should not be a reason for preventing exposure to real threats. When monitoring is restricted to only a few features and is targeted at a specific purpose, the data-modeling results demonstrate that an equilibrium can be achieved. Most importantly, Figure 6 draws attention to the fact that governance is not something that is done once and then forgotten. We cannot simply treat the inflection point in Figure 5 as a permanent and unchangeable boundary. Time passes and technology changes, threats are converted and regulatory standards are rewritten. Hence, a proportionality measure has to be re-calibrated on a continuing basis to make sure that it satisfies the requirements at all .

Figure 6. Governance model validation and balance

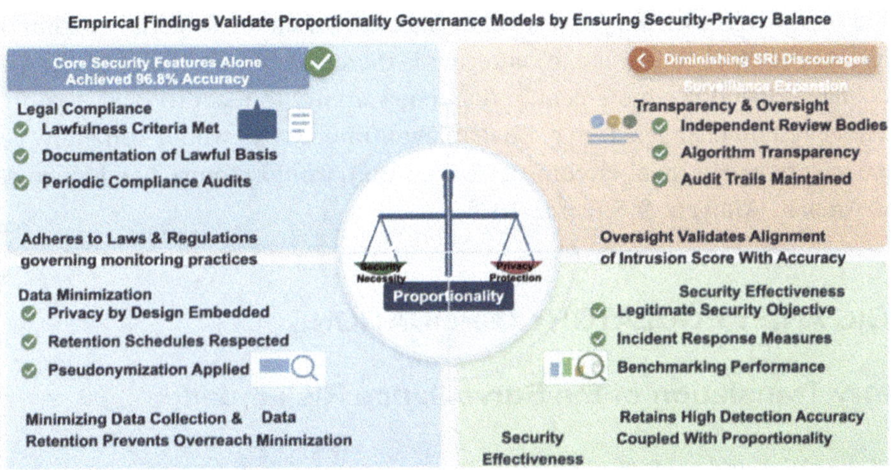

6.5 Policy Implications Derived from Quantitative Findings

Empirical evaluation can lead to several policy implications. The first is that organizational feature justification should be implemented whereby documented necessity of every telemetry attribute collected should be a requirement. Second, the decision to increase behavioral features needs to be coupled with a decision to carry out proportionality review using quantitative intrusion scoring as a basis. Third, retention policies should be oriented towards actual security needs which have been demonstrated rather than mere analytical possibilities(Owida et al., 2025). Moreover, algorithmic transparency policies must be implemented in AI-based monitoring systems. In case an anomaly scoring system is implemented, the types of features used should be documented and their consistency with the security objectives should be . Without such explicit governance mechanisms, silent drift to behavioral profiling shall be unavoidable. Also, just because you are operating at a global scale does not mean you can ignore data localization, as long as central aggregation still increases the risk of surveillance if no segmentation controls are introduced. The whole governance system must, therefore, have built-in procedures of jurisdictional review(Q. Shambour et al., 2025).

6.6 The Normative Boundary Between Monitoring and Surveillance

The integrated conceptual, technical, and empirical analysis help to comprehend that defining the difference between monitoring and surveillance is not a clear-cut case. It is a question of proportionality. Monitoring is characterized by the relatively low level of intrusion which can be justified by concrete security objectives and is limited by controls of minimization and retention(Maz et al., 2025). On the other hand, surveillance corresponds to the high level of intrusion, continuous tracking, profiling on a large scale and a low level of necessity justification. Surveillance Risk Index has been constructed to be a measurable approximation for such a spectrum. If Accuracy is only a little bit more than Intrusion Score, then the proportionality balance will be tilted toward surveillance. When using only core features, if good detection is possible with very low level of intrusion, then the system is within the monitoring limits. As far as legitimacy is concerned, monitoring is there to keep this balance. However, once profiling of one's behavior becomes more central than one's ability to react to it, at least in principle, the nature of the whole system changes. It may be that legal frameworks would still allow certain types of surveillance under very exceptional circumstances but they would require heightened safeguards and justification(A. Arabiat, Altayeb, & Salama, 2025).

7. STRATEGIC AND REGULATORY IMPLICATIONS

7.1 Regulatory Translation of the Surveillance Risk Index

The Surveillance Risk Index (SRI), in simple terms, is the ratio of detection improvement to the additional intrusion score and may be used as a measurable compliance . Even though proportionality still remains a largely doctrinal concept, SRI is a way to operationalize it by measuring the terms involved. Regulatory bodies are increasingly less satisfied with conceptual justifications and more and more require a clear demonstration of necessity and minimization. The empirical results using CICIDS 2017 data show that the main set of flow-based features can recognize attacks with 96.8% accuracy. Including behavior profiling increased accuracy only by 0.6%, but privacy intrusion exposure increased many folds. When SRI values fall below the threshold of proportionality that is set internally, supervisory boards should classify such growth as potentially indicating a threat to privacy. In order to give this regulatory interpretation a formal shape, Compliance Threshold Matrix is presented in Table 5.

Table 5. Proportionality Compliance Threshold Matrix

SRI Ratio Range	Interpretation	Regulatory Posture	Required Action
Above 1.0	Accuracy gain justifies intrusion	Proportionate monitoring	Document and approve
0.5 – 1.0	Marginal proportionality	Heightened review	Conduct DPIA and oversight review
0.2 – 0.5	Weak proportionality	Potential overreach	Restrict feature expansion
Below 0.2	Disproportionate intrusion	Surveillance risk	Reject configuration

The extended behavioral feature model is shown in Figure 5 to be not far from the margin of disproportionate intrusion though still in the marginal proportionality zone. This matrix thus puts into operation the curve shown heuristically in Figure 5.

7.2 Institutional Governance Alignment with Figure 6

Figure 6 illustrated the Governance Model Validation Framework that represents the four quadrants: Legal Compliance, Data Minimization, Transparency & Oversight, and Security Effectiveness. The empirical results provide support for the validation of each of these quadrants as follows. Formal and legal conformity is ensured as the monitoring is constantly tied to specifically the threat detection goals. Data minimization is validated by the fact that excellent performance can be done without the use of behavioral profiling. Increased transparency and strengthened oversight result from the proper documentation and review of the SRI calculations. Security effectiveness stays high because the fundamental detection performance remains very good. More incentives for these alignments can be seen in the Governance Validation Table which is presented in Table 6. It shows the linkage of empirical findings and specific governance safeguards.

Table 6. Governance Validation Table Linking Empirical Results to Oversight Controls

Governance Domain	Empirical Evidence	Risk if Ignored	Recommended Safeguard
Legal Compliance	96.8% accuracy achieved with core features	Function creep into profiling	Periodic lawful basis review
Data Minimization	Marginal 0.6% gain from behavioral features	Excessive data accumulation	Feature justification protocol
Transparency & Oversight	SRI identifies diminishing proportionality	Undetected surveillance drift	Independent review audits
Security Effectiveness	ROC > 0.97 using limited features	False claim that profiling is necessary	Performance benchmarking

Table 6 makes the concept balance that is visually articulated in Figure 6 as a tangible and measurable one. The scale in that figure is a metaphor for balance and here comes the table with the elements that make this balance possible.

7.3 Longitudinal Risk Escalation Modeling

There is no doubt that security monitoring systems can be improved and matured over time. However, through each iteration and enhancement, the risk might also increase. Thus, the concept of longitudinal modeling was represented by adding more feature categories through each development phase.

Phase 1: Core flow-based metadata only
Phase 2: Addition of session persistence indicators
Phase 3: Cross-day behavioral aggregation
Phase 4: Predictive user risk scoring

The highest level of detection accuracy was attained by Phase 2. Still, the intrusion scores continued to increase in a linear fashion at each phase. So, an increase in surveillance is depicted here while detection gain is not proportional. Table 7 lists the phased escalation outputs.

Table 7. Longitudinal Feature Expansion Versus Intrusion Growth

Phase	Feature Scope	Detection Accuracy	Intrusion Score (Normalized)	SRI Value
Phase 1	Core security features	96.8%	1.0	0.968
Phase 2	Session indicators	97.2%	1.8	0.22
Phase 3	Cross-day aggregation	97.4%	2.6	0.15
Phase 4	Predictive user scoring	97.5%	3.4	0.10

The drop of SRI over the phases is in accordance with the image trajectory in Figure 5. Even though detection accuracy is almost constant, the intrusion grows at a much faster pace. By Phase 3 and Phase 4, the system's character gets closer to that of surveillance than that of monitoring.

7.4 Cross-Border Regulatory Considerations

International companies face a double challenge when it comes to privacy. Technologies considered lawful in certain jurisdictions might be deemed intrusive profiling in others. And therefore, the governance model in Figure 4 should take these geographic factors into account. Forinstance, places where data minimization is the main focus would see Phase 3 or Phase 4 setups as totally unnecessary. On the flip side, if they had strict monitoring, areas that are very concerned about security might even go along with Phase 2 level defenses. The SRI technique is a tool that we can use to harmonize such different . By measuring proportionality, the company can locally adjust the level of monitoring to meet the regulations without sacrificing consistent security standards(Turab et al., 2025).

7.5 Policy Recommendations Based on Empirical Findings

The dual-level analysis results in a few policy-level suggestions. The first suggestion is that the organization makes it a habit to compute the SRI prior to feature approval. The second recommendation is that the length of data retention must be strictly limited to the time necessary for threat investigation. Thirdly, it is important to highlight that behavioral predictive scoring disconnected from any form of active threat detection should be very highly justified and overseen by humans. Fourthly, periodic auditing is needed to ensure that the scope of the system is kept up to date with regulatory changes(Alraba'nah et al., 2025). Fifthly, records should show that the quality of detection is not seriously affected by the narrowing of the feature scope. Together these measures ensure the monitoring-surveillance differentiation as exemplified in Figures 5 and 6 remains intact.

7.6 Synthesis: Operationalizing the Distinction

The line dividing monitoring and surveillance isn't one of mere words or ideas. It is something that can be measured and managed by institutions. Figure 5 provides a metric for the trade-off between detection and intrusion. Figure 6 presents governance safeguards that can keep proportional balance. Tables 5 through 7 convert the visual and conceptual understandings into compliance tools. Based on the data, scenarios of this chapter demonstrate that security monitoring can still lawfully operate within the boundaries of a law if it is restricted by proportionality, necessity, and supervisory measures and so on. It is not guaranteed that the deployment of technology leads to the use of surveillance. It can be either a governance system failure or a result of an optimization process that has gone beyond all controls(Sardar et al., 2025).

8. CONCLUSION

The difference between security monitoring and surveillance legally is becoming a major concern as more and more organizations use sophisticated analytical tools, machine learning, and behavioral data processing to secure their digital assets. While security monitoring aims at protecting computer systems, networks, and other assets of an organization from being compromised or misused, surveillance usually refers to the ongoing monitoring of persons or their patterns of behavior. The chapter points out that among the main aspects in which these two methods differ are the technological means that can be used, the motives for the monitoring, the principle of proportionality, data acquisition scope, and governance control. One major problem with security monitoring is that as the collection of behavioral characteristics becomes so extensive, the primary focus of threat detection is overshadowed by user behavior observation and analysis that is broad in scope. This makes it necessary to draw the line between legitimate monitoring and illegal surveillance clearly and to maintain it regularly through good and safe governance. By employing network intrusion scenarios with the use of the CICIDS 2017 dataset as a demonstration tool, the paper illustrates how to draw the dividing line with measurable indicators. Features that are core to flow-based monitoring already show very high detection accuracy, while profiling at an intensive level only results in a slight increase in detection performance.

When detection improvements become flat, the privacy intrusion scores keep rising, and this vividly shows the disjunction between the operational benefits and the risk of personal data being exposed. Based on two essential legal principles - necessity and proportionality - the Surveillance Risk Index (SRI) together with the proportionality threshold matrix serve as a tool for measuring the level of compliance. Thus, a company can decide if its monitoring system is still proportionate or if it has morphed into surveillance mode where data gathering is the main activity by tracking the detection-intrusion dynamics and delineating the governance thresholds. Other factors being equal, security monitoring that is responsible in nature should also consider technical design, get legal issues right, and ensure ethical governance. In fact, if organizations want to remain effective in their fight against threats, they must also be willing to comply with the adoption of structured compliance frameworks that mainly emphasize data minimization, transparency, and oversight. Since accountability is the one thing that regulators are demanding more and more, security designs should be able not only to disclose where and how they detect threats but also how the related privacy risks are being minimized. Security monitoring systems that are developed by integrating proportionality analysis, empirical evaluation, and governance validation will not only enable organizations to defend themselves against cyber-attacks but will also contribute to the respect for and adherence to fundamental rights and one's obligations to the law. Actually, security monitoring will then be able to carry out its protective mission without going beyond the line into excessive .

REFERENCES

Abashes, G. M., Elshqeirat, B., Abu-Shareha, A. A., & Alshraideh, M. (2025). BEYOND THE NOISE: UNVEILING MEANINGFUL PATTERNS IN MOBILE PAYMENT DATA USING FUZZY LOGIC AND SVM. *Journal of Theoretical and Applied Information Technology*, *103*(1).

Abbas, N. A., Al-Sawaie, K. M., Khrais, I. M., & Sweity, I. (2025). Stability Analysis of the Money Demand Function. *Applied Mathematics & Information Sciences*, *19*(2), 307–315. Advance online publication. DOI: 10.18576/amis/190207

Abdeljaber, O., & Al-Masaeed, S. (2025). Al-Mu'ani, L., Yaseen, H., & Alhnaity, B. (2025). Strategic Intelligence: The Power of AI in Planning Efficiency. *Human Behavior and Emerging Technologies*, (1). Advance online publication. DOI: 10.1155/hbe2/5383054

Abualhaj, M. M., Abu-Shareha, A. A., Al-Khatib, S. N., Alsaaidah, A. M., & Anbar, M. (2025). Improving firewall performance using hybrid of optimization algorithms and decision trees classifier. *IAES International Journal of Artificial Intelligence*, *14*(4), 2839. Advance online publication. DOI: 10.11591/ijai.v14.i4.pp2839-2848

Abualhaj, M. M., Abu-Shareha, A. A., & Rateb, R. (2025). Enhancing intrusion detection systems with hybrid HHO-WOA optimization and gradient boosting machine classifier. *International Journal of Reconfigurable and Embedded Systems*, *14*(2), 518. Advance online publication. DOI: 10.11591/ijres.v14.i2.pp518-526

Abualhaj, M. M.I, Al-Khatib, S. N., Abu-Shareha, A. A., Almomani, O., Al-Mimi, H., Al-Allawee, A., Daoud, M. S., & Anbar, M. (2025). Spam Detection Boosted by Firefly-Based Feature Selection and Optimized Classifiers. *International Journal of Advances in Soft Computing and Its Applications*, *17*(3). Advance online publication. DOI: 10.15849/IJASCA.251130.02

Abualhaj, M. M., Al-Khatib, S. N., Al-Zyoud, M., Qaddara, I., Hiari, M. O., & Aldossary, S. M. A. (2025). Enhanced Network Communication Security Through Hybrid Dragonfly-Bat Feature Selection for Intrusion Detection. *The Journal of Communication*, *20*(5). Advance online publication. DOI: 10.12720/jcm.20.5.607-618

Abuowaida, S., Abu Owida, H., Shelash Mohammad, S. I., Alshdaifat, N., Abu Elsoud, E., Alazaidah, R., Vasudevan, A., & Alshurideh, M. T. (2025). Evidence Detection in Cloud Forensics: Classifying Cyber-Attacks in IaaS Environments using machine learning. *Data and Metadata*, *4*, 699. Advance online publication. DOI: 10.56294/dm2025699

Al-Adwan, A. S., & Abdeljaber, O. (2025). Toward a resilient and smart supply chain: identifying and prioritizing barriers to metaverse adoption. *International Journal of Industrial Engineering and Operations Management*. DOI: 10.1108/IJIEOM-06-2025-0113

Al Assaf, M. M., Qatawneh, M., & Alradhi, A. (2025). Linear algorithm for data retrieval performance optimization in self-encryption hybrid data centers. *Bulletin of Electrical Engineering and Informatics*, *14*(3). Advance online publication. DOI: 10.11591/eei.v14i3.9320

Al-Dmour, R., Al-Dmour, H., Al-Dmour, A., Basheer Amin, E., & Al-Dmour, Y. (2025). *AI and big data-driven social media recruitment: the mediating role of talent acquisition and employee engagement in bank performance*. Digital Transformation and Society., DOI: 10.1108/DTS-02-2025-0042

Al-Habashneh, A. G., Al-Daoud, K. I., Oraini, B., Al, , & Shelash, S. I. (2025). The impact of artificial intelligence on the development of electronic financial services. *International Journal of Data and Network Science*, *9*(2), 317–322. Advance online publication. DOI: 10.5267/j.ijdns.2024.8.012

Al Nasar, M. R., Ghazal, T. M., Al-Tarawni, M. A. M., Ahmed, A. A., Abu-Shareha, A. A., & Ahmed, S. M. (2025). Hierarchical Edge-Cloud Collaborative AI Algorithm for Energy-Efficient lot Management in Ubiquitous Computing Environments. *Journal of Wireless Mobile Networks, Ubiquitous Computing and Dependable Applications*, *16*(3). Advance online publication. DOI: 10.58346/JOWUA.2025.I3.035

Al-Okbi, N. K., Alomari, S. A., Zitar, R. A., Smerat, A., Nazzal, M. A., & Abualigah, L. (2025). Integrating Multimodal Emotion Recognition with Deep Q-Learning for Adaptive Social Robot Interaction. *International Journal of Robotics and Control Systems*, *5*(4), 2265–2289. Advance online publication. DOI: 10.31763/ijrcs.v5i4.2055

Al-znamat, F. O., Alsaaidah, A., & Abu-Shareha, A. A. (2025). Malware Detection Using a Modified Bat Algorithm for Feature Selection. *International Journal of Intelligent Engineering and Systems*, *18*(9), 885–899. Advance online publication. DOI: 10.22266/ijies2025.1031.56

Alabdallat, R., Abualhaj, M., & Abu-Shareha, A. (2025). Android Malware Detection Using a Modified Dwarf Mongoose Algorithm. *International Journal of Intelligent Engineering and Systems*, *18*(8), 336–351. Advance online publication. DOI: 10.22266/ijies2025.0930.21

Aldabbas, A., Baniata, L. H., Alsaaidah, B. A., Mustafa, Z., Alali, M., & Rateb, R. (2025). Artificial intelligence-driven method for the discovery and prevention of distributed denial of service attacks. *IAES International Journal of Artificial Intelligence*, *14*(1), 614. Advance online publication. DOI: 10.11591/ijai.v14.i1.pp614-628

Ali, M. I., Savitha, K., Smerat, A., Babu, K. S., Sivakumar, G., & Gracy Theresa, W. (2025). Multimodal Deep Learning Model for Measuring the Impact of Social Media Advertising Using Visual Linguistic Representation Learning. *Journal of Machine and Computing*, *5*(4), 2566–2573. Advance online publication. DOI: 10.53759/7669/jmc202505197

Alkhawatrah, M. (2025). Random Forests Relay Selector in Buffer-Aided Cooperative Networks. *IEEE Access : Practical Innovations, Open Solutions*, *13*, 165402–165410. Advance online publication. DOI: 10.1109/ACCESS.2025.3612192

Almomani, O., Arabiat, A., Al Tayeb, M., Almaiah, M. A., Obeidat, M., Aldhyani, T. H. H., Shehab, R., & Rowad, M. (2025). A Robust Model for Android Malware Detection via ML and DL classifiers. *Mesopotamian Journal of Big Data*, *2025*. Advance online publication. DOI: 10.58496/MJBD/2025/017

Alnawafleh, N. M., Ibrahim, A., & Pradhan, M. R. (2024). Review of the Mechanisms Used to Protect the Big Data from Attacks. *2nd International Conference on Cyber Resilience, ICCR 2024*. DOI: 10.1109/ICCR61006.2024.10533073

Alnsour, Y., Alsharo, M., Al-Essa, M., & Smerat, A. (2025). AI-Powered Election Insights: Predicting the 2024 Trump vs. Kamala Election Showdown with Machine Learning. *Journal of Intelligent Systems and Internet of Things, 15*(1), 185–197. Advance online publication. DOI: 10.54216/JISIoT.150116

Alraba'nah, Y., Al-Sharaeh, S., & Al Hindi, G. (2025). Enhancing Intrusion Detection Using Hybrid Long Short-Term Memory and XGBoost. *Journal of Soft Computing and Data Mining, 6*(1). Advance online publication. DOI: 10.30880/jscdm.2025.06.01.016

Amin, M., Nahar, K. M. O., Gharaibeh, H., Al Mamlook, R. E., Nasayreh, A., Atitallah, N., Gharaibeh, A., Hamad, R., Zitar, R. A., Smerat, A., & Abualigah, L. (2025). A Hybrid Brain Stroke Prediction Framework: Integrating Feature Selection, Classification, and Hyperparameter Optimization. *Engineering Reports, 7*(7), e70213. Advance online publication. DOI: 10.1002/eng2.70213

Arabiat, A., & Altayeb, M. (2025). Driving behavior analytics: An intelligent system based on machine learning and data mining techniques. *Bulletin of Electrical Engineering and Informatics, 14*(3), 2055–2065. Advance online publication. DOI: 10.11591/eei.v14i3.9095

Arabiat, A., Altayeb, M., & Alkhrissat, T. (2025). Innovative AI Approaches for Concrete Strength Prediction: Towards Sustainable Buildings. *Civil Engineering and Architecture, 13*(6), 4254–4265. Advance online publication. DOI: 10.13189/cea.2025.130612

Arabiat, A., Altayeb, M., & Salama, S. (2025). Artificial intelligence-powered smart roads: Leveraging orange3 for traffic signs recognition. *IAES International Journal of Artificial Intelligence, 14*(5), 3816. Advance online publication. DOI: 10.11591/ijai.v14.i5.pp3816-3826

Arabiat, A. M. (2025). Intelligent Model for Detecting GAN-Generated Images Based on Multi-Classifier and Advanced Data Mining Techniques. *International Journal of Electrical and Electronic Engineering and Telecommunications, 14*(3). Advance online publication. DOI: 10.18178/ijeetc.14.3.147-157

Babaker, S., Khatibi, A., Alsoud, A. R., Kaur, J., Jagtap, J., Alkhayyat, A., & Shah, S. K. (2025). Improving Reliability and Data Management in Internet of Things Based Wireless Sensor Networks. *Internet Technology Letters, 8*(6), e646. Advance online publication. DOI: 10.1002/itl2.646

Dhasaratha, C., Hasan, M. K., Islam, S., Khapre, S., Abdullah, S., Ghazal, T. M., Alzahrani, A. I., Alalwan, N., Vo, N., & Akhtaruzzaman, M. (2024). Data privacy model using blockchain reinforcement federated learning approach for scalable internet of medical things. *CAAI Transactions on Intelligence Technology*, cit2.12287. Advance online publication. DOI: 10.1049/cit2.12287

Eke, C. I., Al-Shamayleh, A. S., Phiri, M., Maswadi, K., Kwaghtyo, D. K., Mulenga, M., & Iyidobi, C. J. (2025). Machine Learning Based Mobile Big Data Analytics: State-of-the-art Applications, Taxonomy, Challenges and Future Research Directions. *Nigerian Journal of Technological Development, 22*(4). Advance online publication. DOI: 10.63746/njtd.v22i4.3385

Ghazal, T. M. (2025). Federated Learning for Intelligent Sensing and Navigation Technologies for 6G Communications. *Journal of Sensors, 2025*(1). DOI: 10.1155/js/3746147

Ghazal, T. M., Abdali, T. A. N., Abualhaj, M. M., Saeed, A. Q., & Ahmad, M. (2025). Advanced LWAVF Framework Based on Neural Network Security in IoMT for Managing Patient Data Authentication and Integrity Validation with Consensus Mapping. *Journal of Soft Computing and Data Mining*, *6*(1). Advance online publication. DOI: 10.30880/jscdm.2025.06.01.003

Ghazal, T. M., Abu-Shareha, A., Mustafa, S. A., Ibrahim, A., & Ahmed, S. M. (2025). Privacy-Preserving Transformer-Based Meta-Learning Algorithm for Zero-Day Intrusion Detection in IoT-Enabled Smart Grids. *Journal of Internet Services and Information Security*, *15*(4), 76–84. Advance online publication. DOI: 10.58346/JISIS.2025.I4.006

Ghazal, T. M., Abualhaj, M., Ahmed, A. A., Al-Tarawni, M. A. M., & Maghrabi, L. A. (2025). Federated Deep Graph Neural Network Algorithm for Real-Time Intrusion Detection in Heterogeneous IoT Systems. *Journal of Internet Services and Information Security*, *15*(4), 484–497. Advance online publication. DOI: 10.58346/JISIS.2025.I4.035

Ghazal, T. M., Awouda, A. E., Hasan, M. K., Rahman, A. H. A., Islam, S., Saeed, R. A., Elshafie, H., Iqbal, A., & Hussein, A. H. (2025). Knowledge Learning for Securing Workflow Scheduling Algorithm in Mobile Edge Computing. *Mobile Networks and Applications*, *30*(3-4), 395–413. Advance online publication. DOI: 10.1007/s11036-025-02465-6

Ghazal, T. M., Hasan, M. K., Alzoubi, H. M., Al Hmmadi, M., Al-Dmour, N. A., Islam, S., Kamran, R., & Mago, B. (2022). Securing Smart Cities Using Blockchain Technology. *2022 1st International Conference on AI in Cybersecurity, ICAIC 2022*. DOI: 10.1109/ICAIC53980.2022.9896971

Ghazal, T. M., Islam, S., Hasan, M. K., Abu-Shareha, A. A., Mokhtar, U. A., Khan, M. A., Baili, J., Saeed, A. Q., Bhatt, M. W., & Ahmad, M. (2025). Generative Federated Learning With Small and Large Models in Consumer Electronics for Privacy-Preserving Data Fusion in Healthcare Internet of Things. *IEEE Transactions on Consumer Electronics*, *71*(2), 3413–3430. Advance online publication. DOI: 10.1109/TCE.2025.3572629

Ghazal, T. M., Janjua, J. I., Abushiba, W., Ahmad, M., Ihsan, A., & Al-Dmour, N. A. (2024). Cybersecurity Revolution via Large Language Models and Explainable AI. *2024 17th International Conference on Security of Information and Networks, SIN 2024*. DOI: 10.1109/SIN63213.2024.10871324

Ghoneim, R. S., Arabasy, M., Osbaa, R. A., & Al Hamad, R. (2025). A Systematic Literature Review on Integrating Machine Learning Algorithms and Metaheuristic Algorithms in Optimizing Sustainable Digital Architectural Design. *Civil Engineering and Architecture*, *13*(3), 1913–1931. Advance online publication. DOI: 10.13189/cea.2025.130334

Ghoneim, R. S., Taiyara, R., & Maghaireh, Z. N. (2025). Machine Learning-Enhanced Building Information Modeling (BIM) for Sustainable Urban Planning. *Civil Engineering and Architecture*, *13*(3), 2171–2184. Advance online publication. DOI: 10.13189/cea.2025.131301

Hanandeh, R., Alkhazali, Z., Alhyasat, K. M. K., Mistarihi, A. M., & Kilani, Q. A. L. (2025). The Impact of Data-Driven Decision-Making, Real-Time Analytics, and Ethical Data Practices on HR Performance and Employee Satisfaction. *Data and Metadata*, *4*, 712. Advance online publication. DOI: 10.56294/dm2025712

Ibrahim, A. (2024). Guarding the Future of Gaming: The Imperative of Cybersecurity. *2nd International Conference on Cyber Resilience, ICCR 2024*. DOI: 10.1109/ICCR61006.2024.10532843

Ibrahim Alasadi, A. A., Manjula, S., Smerat, A., Govindu, K., Sivakumar, G., & Sahasranamam, V. (2025). Mathematically Modified Deep Learning Model Assisted Handwritten Digit Recognition for Intelligent Document Processing Systems. *Journal of Machine and Computing*, *5*(4), 2661–2671. Advance online publication. DOI: 10.53759/7669/jmc202505204

Iskandarani, M. Z. (2025). Effect of Adaptive Intelligent Reflective Surfaces on SINR in a Wireless Communication System. *The Journal of Communication*, *20*(1). Advance online publication. DOI: 10.12720/jcm.20.1.1-11

Iskandarani, M. Z., & Chakrabarti, K. (2025). Adaptive Frequency and Energy Modeling Framework for Robotic Wireless Sensor Networks Based on Path Loss Predictions. *Journal of Robotics, 2025*(1). DOI: 10.1155/joro/6156608

Jaradat, S., Acharya, N., Shivshankar, S., Alhadidi, T. I., & Elhenawy, M. (2025). AI for Data Quality Auditing: Detecting Mislabeled Work Zone Crashes Using Large Language Models. *Algorithms*, *18*(6), 317. Advance online publication. DOI: 10.3390/a18060317

Khalayleh, Y. A. S., Mohammad, S. I., Al Louzi, N. S., Baniata, M., Hassan, M., Safaqah, M. A., Vasudevan, A., & Alshurideh, M. T. (2025). Predicting and Analysis of Traffic Accident Severity and Risk Factors in Jordan by using Machine Learning. *Applied Mathematics & Information Sciences*, *19*(6), 1419–1426. Advance online publication. DOI: 10.18576/amis/190615

Khatibi, A., Babaker, S., Praveen, K. N. R., Chohan, J. S., Jadhav, A., Alsoud, A. R., Ramudu, M. J., & Jeet, R. (2025). Advanced AI-Driven Cybersecurity: Analyzing Emerging Threats and Defensive Strategies. *National Academy Science Letters*. Advance online publication. DOI: 10.1007/s40009-025-01897-8

Laha, S. R., Smadi, K. Al, Habboush, A. K., Pattanayak, B. K., Pattnaik, S., & Mohanty, B. (2025). Smart Waste Management Framework for Green Cities: Integrating IoT, LoRa, and Deep Learning for Efficient Waste Classification and Management. *Tikrit Journal of Engineering Sciences, 32*(Special Issue 1). DOI: 10.25130/tjes.sp1.2025.1

Marhoon, H. M., Basil, N., Sabbar, B. M., Qasem, N., & Ma'arif, A. (2025). Safety and Surveillance on Unmanned Aerial Vehicles Control Systems and Optimization Methods: A Systematic Review. *International Journal of Robotics and Control Systems*, *5*(5). Advance online publication. DOI: 10.31763/ijrcs.v5i5.1859

Maz, Y. A., Anbar, M., Manickam, S., Abualhaj, M. M., Almalki, S. A., & Alabsi, B. A. (2025). Transfer Learning-Based Approach with an Ensemble Classifier for Detecting Keylogging Attack on the Internet of Things. *Computers, Materials & Continua*, *85*(3), 5287–5307. Advance online publication. DOI: 10.32604/cmc.2025.068257

Nandagopal, M., Manavalan, T., Kumar, K. P., Manogaran, N., Kesavan, D., Kumar, G., & Al-Khasawneh, M. A. (2025). Enhancing energy efficiency in cloud computing through task scheduling with hybrid cuckoo search and transformer models. *Discover Computing*, *28*(1), 199. Advance online publication. DOI: 10.1007/s10791-025-09716-w

Otair, M., Qawaqzeh, F. A., Alomari, S. A., Zitar, R. A., Migdady, H., Saleem, K., Smerat, A., Alsoud, A. R., & Abualigah, L. (2025). Enhanced Arithmetic Optimization Algorithm for Intrusion Detection in Wireless Sensor Networks. *International Journal of Communication Systems*, *38*(10), e70122. Advance online publication. DOI: 10.1002/dac.70122

Owida, H. A., Alazaidah, R., Bani-Bakr, A., Khafajeh, H., Chan, H. Y., Mizher, M., & Katrawi, A. (2025). Integrative Deep Learning for Enhanced Acute Lymphoblastic Leukemia Detection: A Comprehensive Study on the ALL-IDB Dataset. *Engineering. Technology and Applied Science Research*, *15*(2), 20776–20781. Advance online publication. DOI: 10.48084/etasr.9745

Qawasmeh, S., Habboushb, A., Elzaghmouri, B., Kharma, Q., & Albalawneh, D. (2025). Hybrid Convolutional Neural Network-Based Intrusion Detection System for Secure IoT Networks. *Tikrit Journal of Engineering Sciences*, *32*(SP1), 1–11. Advance online publication. DOI: 10.25130/tjes.sp1.2025.2

Ramesh, J. V. N., Nimma, D., Dasari, R., Chaudhari Rane, D., AlGhamdi, A., Rao, K. B. V. B., Haider, S. A., Kuzieva, N., & Jangir, P. (2025). Safe and Reliable Two-Stage Online Offloading Algorithm for Transportation Cyber-Physical Systems. *IEEE Transactions on Intelligent Transportation Systems*, *26*(9), 14313–14322. Advance online publication. DOI: 10.1109/TITS.2025.3539934

Rateb, R., Abualhaj, M. M., Alsaaidah, A., Alsharaiah, M. A., Shorman, A., & Thalji, N. J. (2025). Exploring the dynamics of providing cognition using a computational model of cognitive insomnia. *IAES International Journal of Artificial Intelligence*, *14*(1). Advance online publication. DOI: 10.11591/ijai.v14.i1.pp92-101

Raza, M. A., Karim, A., Alqarni, M., Al-Khasawneh, M. A., Jumani, T. A., Aman, M., & Masud, M. I. (2025). An Intelligent Long Short-Term Memory-Based Machine Learning Model for the Potential Assessment of Global Hydropower Capacity in Sustainable Energy Transition and Security. *Energies*, *18*(13), 3324. Advance online publication. DOI: 10.3390/en18133324

Saeed, N. M. S. E., Ibrahim, A., Ali, L., Al-Dmour, N. A., Mohammed, A. S., & Ghazal, T. M. (2024). Unveiling the Landscape of Machine Learning and Deep Learning Methodologies in Network Security: A Comprehensive Literature Review. *2nd International Conference on Cyber Resilience, ICCR 2024.* DOI: 10.1109/ICCR61006.2024.10533066

Sardar, R., Anees, T., Al-Shamayleh, A. S., Mehmood, E., Khalil, W., Akhunzada, A., & Shaikh, F. S. (2025). Challenges in detecting security threats in WoT: A systematic literature review. *Artificial Intelligence Review*, *58*(7), 196. Advance online publication. DOI: 10.1007/s10462-025-11176-z

Shambour, Q., Al-Zyoud, M., & Almomani, O. (2025). Quantum-Inspired Hybrid Metaheuristic Feature Selection with SHAP for Optimized and Explainable Spam Detection. *Symmetry*, *17*(10), 1716. Advance online publication. DOI: 10.3390/sym17101716

Shambour, Q. Y., Al-Zyoud, M., & Hussein, A. H. (2025). FROM DATA TO DIAGNOSIS: KNOWLEDGE-DRIVEN, EXPLAINABLE AI FOR RELIABLE EARLY AUTISM DETECTION. *Interdisciplinary Journal of Information, Knowledge, and Management*, *20*, 032. Advance online publication. DOI: 10.28945/5652

Sharma, K. P., Al-Rashed, A., Johar, M. G. M., Alsoud, A. R., Singh, A., Dey, P., & Pant, S. (2025). Blockchain-Assisted Trust Framework for Increased Survivability in Internet of Vehicles. *Internet Technology Letters*, *8*(3), e70029. Advance online publication. DOI: 10.1002/itl2.70029

Sharma, K. P., Hussain, R., Jaharadak, A. A., Trawnih, A. A., Verma, D., Dasi, S., & Pant, S. (2025). Hybrid Convolutional Neural Network for Robust Attack Detection in Wireless Sensor Networks. *Internet Technology Letters*, *8*(6), e650. Advance online publication. DOI: 10.1002/itl2.650

Turab, N., Abushattal, A., Al-Nabulsi, J., & Owida, H. A. (2025). Advanced risk assessment using machine learning and sentiment analysis on log data. *IAES International Journal of Artificial Intelligence*, *14*(5), 3897. Advance online publication. DOI: 10.11591/ijai.v14.i5.pp3897-3905

Varshney, S., Bajaj, M., Choudhary, K. K., Pushkarna, M., & Zaitsev, I. (2025). Performance Analysis and Reliability Prediction of Multi-State Service Systems With Multiple Failure Modes of Unreliable Server: An Engineering Perspective. *Engineering Reports*, *7*(7), e70268. Advance online publication. DOI: 10.1002/eng2.70268

Vasudevan, A., Albinaa, T. A., Mohammad, S. I., Sharmila, E., Raja, N., Soon, E. E. H., Alshurideh, M. T., & Al-Adwan, A. S. (2024). Bidirectional LSTM for Electronic Product Recommendation. *Applied Mathematics & Information Sciences*, *18*(6), 1443–1453. Advance online publication. DOI: 10.18576/amis/180621

Vasudevan, A., Tamilmani, K. T., Mohammad, S. I., Sridheepika, V. S., Raja, N., Soon, E. E. H., Nagaraj, S., & Al-Adwan, A. S. (2025). Voices of Concern: Contemplations on Socioeconomic, Ethical, and Developmental Impacts of AI. *Applied Mathematics & Information Sciences*, *19*(1), 221–232. Advance online publication. DOI: 10.18576/amis/190119

Vasudevan, A., Yogeesh, N., Mohammad, S. I., Raja, N., Girija, D. K., Rashmi, M., Abu-Shareha, A. A., & Alshurideh, M. T. (2025). Unlocking Insights of Fuzzy Mathematics for Enhanced Predictive Modelling. *Applied Mathematics & Information Sciences*, *19*(1), 49–59. Advance online publication. DOI: 10.18576/amis/190105

Chapter 6
Managing Retention, Deletion, and Legal Hold Requirements in Security Data Repositories

Saif E. A. Alnawayseh
Mutah University, Al-Karak, Jordan

Mahmoud Mahfuri
http://orcid.org/0009-0002-3643-345X
International University for Science and Technology, Syria

ABSTRACT

Effective management of retention, deletion, and legal hold requirements is essential for security data repositories. The study is explored by looking at how logs, telemetry, alerts, and forensic artifacts are stored in distributed systems and what legal requirements govern their lifecycle. The chapter explains retention scheduling, purpose limitation, and risk- based retention periods, as well as secure deletion, anonymization, and archival controls. A special focus is put on legal holds due to litigation, regulatory inquiries, and incident investigations and how such legal holds may conflict with regular deletion requirements. The chapter also looks at governance mechanisms such as policy setting, automation, audit trail, and collaboration between security, legal, and compliance functions at the cross-functional level. By integrating technical data management with regulatory and legal requirements, the chapter outlines how necessary security data can be preserved while the privacy risk, storage cost, and compliance risk are kept at a minimum.

1. INTRODUCTION

Connected infrastructure, the cloud, remote work, mobile devices, industrial systems, and always-on enterprise applications are the indirect causes of modern organizations generating a huge amount of digital security data. Besides user authentication, firewall, DNS, API, and email activities, even the smallest administrative action might produce one or more security records. Consequently, security data repositories which initially were server logs have now turned into large, distributed and ever-expanding ecosystems of telemetry. These repositories now include Security Information and Event Management

DOI: 10.4018/979-8-2600-2870-4.ch006

(SIEM) platforms, Security Orchestration, Automation and Response (SOAR) tools, data lakes, endpoint detection platforms, network monitoring stores, cloud audit trails, and long-term archival systems(Ali et al., 2025). In many organizations, the whole database is not the only storage of records. It is a multistoried setting where data at different stages of use are kept for different considerations such as price, search convenience, and evidentiary worth. The great growth of data has caused a complete reorganization of how organizations manage security records. Initially,security logs were only the by-product of operations mostly used for troubleshooting and very rarely for incident review. Nowadays, they are rightly considered as significant governance strategic assets. Security logs are essential for detection of intrusion, determination of insider threats, investigation of fraud, enforcement of policies, conducting forensic reconstruction, proof of compliance to regulators, legal support, and risk reporting to executives(Hasan et al., 2025).

Sadly, the factors that make these repositories extremely useful are the same ones that often lead to management issues. For example, if organizations collect more data than what they can effectively classify, govern, retain, or dispose of, their repositories will become not only legally sensitive but also technically costly and operationally unstable. Keeping data too long results in storage costs and privacy risks, whereas deleting data prematurely may result in loss of evidence required for investigation or . For this reason, the rise of security data repositories has made lifecycle governance a primary requirement rather than a secondary compliance exercise(Zhu et al., 2025). Figure 1 similarly demonstrates the lifecycle concept by tracing the path of security data typically going through generation and ingestion, classification, storage, use, retention review, legal hold, deletion, and archival pathways. This figure clearly illustrates that security data management is never a one-off operation. In fact, it is a controlled right of way where at every stage, different decisions must be taken in order to strike a balance between security utility, legal risk, and data minimization.

Figure 1. Security Data Lifecycle Model in Monitoring Systems

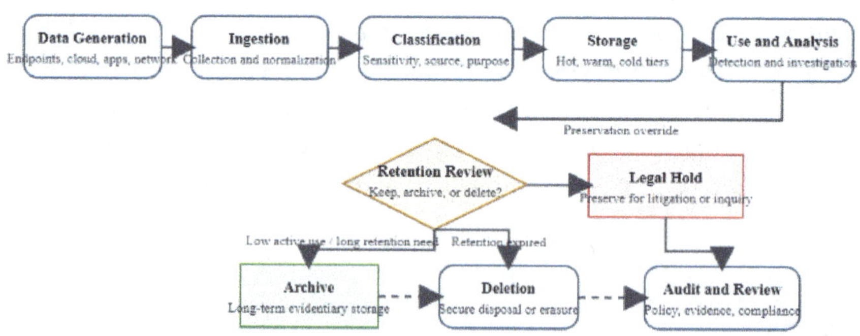

1.1 Importance of Data Lifecycle Governance in Security Monitoring

Data lifecycle governance, also known as data lifecycle management, entails the rules, safeguards, workflows, and responsibility frameworks that govern how data is generated, categorized, stored, accessed, retained, safeguarded, archived, and finally destroyed. Considering that the worth of data varies over time, lifecycle governance stands out as a crucial part of a security monitoring setup. Forinstance a newly generated authentication log might contain crucial information for immediate anomaly detection, however, after months or years its security value might be very low but it could still contain identifiers, IP addresses, device references, behavioral traces or contextual information about employees, customers, and contractors(Awais et al., 2025). Therefore, governance is necessary to maintain security data available when appropriate, secret when sensitive, and dispose of when not needed any longer. With the absence of lifecycle governance, security repositories are usually growing endlessly based on the assumption that more data will forever lead to better visibility. Actually, if accumulation is left unmanaged, it will eventually work against one. Burdenedby a clamor of noisy surroundings, researchers become disoriented; search operations are hampered; more compliance requirements need to be fulfilled; and the resources for detecting and responding to threats are, instead, being used to maintain less valuable and outdated data. In fact, unlimited data retention can turn a security repository into yet another source of risk. If the persons behind the attacks manage to get access to the repository, then they not only can get hold of the present operational telemetries but also of the historical data spanning back several years which have detailed the network architecture, user behavior, internal systems and previous incidents(Ghazal et al., 2024). Lifecycle governance, for one, is a necessity if one is to be accountable. Those who keep record and can produce proof of who allowed a retention rule, why a dataset was kept, when a legal hold was ordered, and how deletion was carried out will, effectively, be making their audits and investigations a lot less challenging. So, in fact, governance, when embraced this way, changes a retention setting from an elusive admin-level thing into a justified and evidence-based MC concept(Abualhaj, Al-Khatib, Abu-Shareha, Hyassat, et al., 2025). In addition to lifecycle governance, data classification, access control, encryption, monitoring, and compliance management are mainly linked to security operations that have been well-developed. To follow up on what we will be talking about in this chapter, the main concern is not only the length of time data should be retained but also how decisions regarding retention, deletion, and preservation should be in sync with legal, technical, and operational (Iftikhar et al., 2025).

1.2 Legal and Regulatory Context of Security Data Retention

Security records play an essential role in the fulfillment of cybersecurity responsibilities; however, they are also governed by privacy law, employment law, digital evidence rules, contractual obligations, and even sector-specific regulation; the legal basis for security data retention is therefore highly complex. On the one hand, they need to hold onto some records for a sufficiently long period of time to be able to carry out effective incident investigation, prove regulatory compliance, assist law enforcement agencies, and be capable of defending any legal claims; on the other hand, they are not allowed to retain personal data longer than necessary, nor should they perform processing of monitoring data in an excessive or unjustified manne(Al-Okbi, Alomari, Zitar, et al., 2025)r. That is the main conflict of governing security data repositories. Several regulatory frameworks not only view security logging as facilitatory but also provisionally as a necessary measure for protecting systems, detecting hostile actions, and maintaining organizational . Nevertheless, a valid argument of being necessary doesn't imply the possibility of keeping data forever. Another limitation principle that stems from privacy laws states that personal data should not be retained beyond the time necessary for the achievement of the purposes for which the data are being processed or, alternatively, a legal ground for holding the data must be identified and recorded(Ghazal, Hasan, et al., 2025).

Purpose limitation is yet another principle that aims at avoiding the use of personal data for purposes other than those for which the data were originally obtained, e.g., surveillance, profiling, employee control, etc. When it comes to legal proceedings, sometimes companies have to preserve e-evidence to be ready for any disputes, inquiries, investigations, or enforcement that might occur. This leads to the imposing of the legal hold, i.e., being required to keep the data for a certain period of time beyond the regular deletion policy. The issue of jurisdiction only complicates things even more. Usually, user, device, and cloud service security logs are scattered all over the world with different regulations about workforce monitoring, data retention, cross-border transfers, breach notifications, and evidence preservation(Q. Y. Shambour et al., 2025). Organizations to keep these logs in their security repositories. So, the companies cannot just select one standard retention period for the whole data sets. Instead, they have to come up with the retention schedules that are legally defensible based on the type of data, purpose, legal exposure, investigative needs, and geographical context. In fact, not only does the law restrict the retention options but even it has a say in the repository architecture, policy development, and deletion rkflows(Al-Dmour et al., 2025).

1.3 Challenges of Retention and Deletion in Large-Scale Security Logs

Security repositories hold a wide variety of logs, such as, endpoint telemetry, identity records, proxy logs, cloud audit events, alert metadata, incident case notes, and packet-derived summaries. These categories can differ greatly in terms of retention value, privacy sensitivity, and evidentiary significance. Clearly, it is almost impossible to have one-size-fits-all deletion schedules when the data is so heterogeneous. However, detailed rules lead to administrative overhead and non-uniform enforcement of policies. Firstly, forensic value and data minimization often are the opposing forces. While security teams want to keep data for as long as possible in order to have evidence for identifying very long advanced persistent threats (APTs), telemetry gathered over time is used to cross-reference attacker moves, find indications of persistent infections, construct attacker chronologies, etc. Retaining data for extended periods, however, makes it increasingly difficult to manage storage capacity and increases the risk of privacy infringement and compliance exposure. Therefore, a purely security-centric perspective cannot dictate retention strategies(Ghazal, Hasan, Abdul Wahab, et al., 2022).

Besides proportionality, likelihood of investigative use, legal obligations, and repository risk, organizations are also bound to take account of their decisions. Deletion also raises fresh challenges. Secure deletion is much more than physically erasing a file from a hard disk. In distributed systems, the same record might be found in live storage, indexing layers, analytics platforms, backups, replicas, exports, and legal preservation sets. It might be a case of a user deleting the main copy, but the others lingering on(Ghazal, Awouda, et al., 2025). This can mislead a person to believe that compliance is achieved when really it is just a simulation. Likewise, some records that have been legally put on hold cannot be deleted, while others can be deleted following the normal schedules. This explains the need for precise tagging, separation, and audit logging. Figure 2 not only illustrates these relationships but also offers a governance structure for retention, deletion, and legal hold management in security repositories. It emphasizes that lifespan control is most effective when a combination of data sources, policy engines, legal reviews, repository tiers, and audit mechanisms work in tandem rather than a technical setting that stands on its . This chapter contributes a lifecycle governance framework for security data repositories by connecting retention policy, deletion policy, legal hold policy, and evidence preservation policy. The framework shows how organizations can preserve security value while limiting privacy exposure, storage burden, and legal risk.

Figure 2. Security Data Governance Architecture for Retention and Deletion

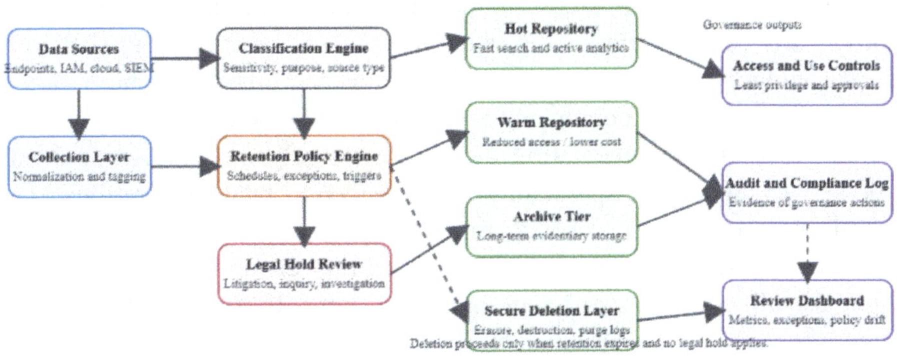

2. DATA RETENTION POLICIES

2.1 Retention Policy Design in Security Operations Centers

Prior research and practice in this area can be organized into six themes: security log retention, privacy-based storage limitation, digital evidence preservation, legal hold management, secure deletion, and automated lifecycle enforcement. These themes show that security data governance requires both technical controls and legally defensible decision-making. Security Operations Centers (SOC) are considered the main building block of enterprise cybersecurity monitoring. In such setups, continuity of analyst observation of system activity, the investigation of alerts, and the handling of incidents on the basis of large amounts of telemetry gathered from all parts of the organization are the main cyber operational tasks. SOCs heavily rely on the historical logs. Becoming an integral part of this process, SOCs develop highly structured, retention policies that specify, "How long different types of security data should be stored in centralized repositories?" A retention policy is basically a governing rule that specifies the duration for which a particular type or category of data must be stored before it is eligible for deletion or archiving. In a SOC context, these policies should be designed around the practical and legal needs of the company. Practically speaking, analysts seldom have the resources or desire to attempt to investigate attacks from years ago, but from a legal perspective, the need for a company's record may be years, thus, balancing these two extremes is at the core of SOC data retention policy. Besides, monitoring data that is deleted too soon may make it impossible for analysts to piece together the attack timeline and/or identify a breach(Ghazal, 2025).

Keeping security monitoring data indefinitely, on the other hand, could lead to increasing the company's attack surface or breaking storage constraints. Besides that, large repositories entail increased infrastructure costs, degrade search performance, and represent a larger amount of sensitive data vulnerable to exposure in case of a repository breach. Therefore, retention policies strive to find a middle ground between operational visibility and the principles of data minimization and proportionality. As such, a properly designed retention policy does not only aim to save as much data as possible but at the same time it determines which types of logs support security objectives in a way that is meaningful and for how long the logs remain useful(Ebbini et al., 2025). In reality, SOC retention policies reflect the non-uniform requirements and are the outcome of organizations adopting tiered retention models where different durations are assigned to different log categories. Actually, various logs such as authentication logs, firewall events, endpoint telemetry, cloud audit records and others may have varying degrees of investigative value and therefore, depending on the organization's risk appetite, for example, they can be retained for different durations. Documentation is another extremely important component in the formulation of a retention policy. SOCs must maintain written, easily understandable rationale for the retention decisions, who made them and who approved them. Properly document policies can assist organizations in proving compliance during audits, and at the same time, they ensure that retention practices are not only consistent but also aligned across different security systems. If this is not the case, retention practices become quite inconsistent and unpredictable which causes operational confusion and an increase in regulatory (Ghazal, Awouda, et al., 2025). Retention policy defines how long records are normally kept for operational and compliance purposes. Deletion policy defines how records are securely removed when they are no longer needed. Legal hold policy suspends deletion when litigation, investigation, or regulatory inquiry is reasonably foreseeable. Evidence preservation policy ensures integrity, chain of custody, and auditability for records that may be used as proof.

2.2 Risk-Based Retention Period Determination

SOC teams have to take into account a range of factors while they make these decisions including the decision of determining how long certain types of logs should be kept. One very important consideration here would be the usual detection timeframe of cyber threats. Some attacks, such as automated scanning or brute-force login attempts, might be detected within minutes or hours. APTs (Advanced Persistent Threats) in particular, are some of the most dangerous cyber threats and they could remain undetected for weeks or months before detection. In case of shorter retention periods, SOC analysts would be deprived of the historical proofs required to uncover the initial stages of such attacks(Abualhaj, Al-Khatib, Abu-Shareha, Almomani, et al., 2025). Another factor that affects retention time is the scale and frequency of incident investigations. Investigations generally involve analysts going back in time to compare system activity patterns to figure out if suspicious behavior is an isolated incident or part of a wider campaign. For example, recognizing network lateral movement may entail first-going through several weeks' worth of authentication logs, endpoint activity, and network connections. That is why retention policies should make sure that sufficient historical data is kept for the investigative processes to be conducted. Nevertheless, organizations must also factor in the availability of storage and the costs of infrastructure when they are making retention policies. Security logs can get out of control very quickly as even roughly monitoring systems that generate hundreds of thousands of events daily (at least)(Vasudevan et al., 2025).

If you want to keep logs of all kinds for a long time, you will need huge storage and indexing infrastructures. After taking that into consideration, SOC members will have to evaluate the trade-offs for storing older data in either high-performance or lower-cost archival systems. A risk-based approach to retention generally starts with the identification of different roles that various types of monitoring data play in both threat detection and compliance. Since forensic investigation depends heavily on authentication logs and privileged access records, this may justify longer retention times(Iskandarani, 2025).

On the other hand, telemetry that is relatively less informative from the point of view of analysis can be deleted much sooner or can be retained only in an aggregated manner. By utilizing this risk-based classification approach, SOCs can preserve the most vital security evidence while allowing the still-growing data repositories some room to breathe. Furthermore, as you are implementing a risk-based approach to retention determination, you might also want to consider the possibility of adjusting retention periods dynamically. For instance, organizations may decide to extend retention periods temporarily following a major incident, regulatory probe, or threat . This kind of flexibility will enable the SOC to preserve relevant historical data even if the risk of the environment changes. On the other hand, in the absence of such a rule, these changes would have to be exposed to the law enforcement agencies and hence would be .

2.3 Balancing Security Analytics Needs and Privacy Obligations

Security monitoring data sometimes contain information that can indirectly be used to identify individuals, such as user account names, device identifiers, IP addresses, or behavioral activity records. Consequently, retention policies should reflect the ways cybersecurity operation requirements align with privacy rights of employees, customers, and other individuals, whose activities may be recorded in monitoring logs. From a security standpoint, the analysts are provided with a wide view using access to an extended historical window which helps in detection of patterns of malicious behavior. For instance, in the case of detecting unusual login behavior, it may only be quite suspicious when compared against a few months of normal historical access patterns(Almomani et al., 2025). Similarly, the process of identifying insider threats often requires the application of analysis tools on the backdrop of time, which is usually drawn by multiple days, weeks, or even months of data. Privacy laws, on the other hand, usually put more emphasis on the principle of "Personal Data Minimization" that is, "Personal data should not be retained for longer than is necessary." The possession of other types of monitoring data that may lead to the identification of individuals juts only brings the potential privacy risks into focus of data governance policies and compliances in case these data abuses are not prevented(Al-Habashneh et al., 2025). Balancing the two sides can be done fairly easily in most situations by SOCs adjusting their log anonymization and pseudonymization strategies. So, for example, one of the common methods is the utilization of pseudonyms or anonymizing certain properties in historical logs. This way, it is possible to identify behavioral patterns without revealing the user's actual identity. Another approach is to restrict access so that only authorized security personnel can review such sensitive information during an investigation(Shamaylah et al., 2025).

2.4 Technical Implementation of Retention Policies in Log Management Platforms

After setting up governance-level retention policies, the step that follows is to turn these policies into concrete controls within security monitoring platforms. Nowadays, most SIEM and log management systems have automated functionalities that assist in the enforcement of retention schedules. These instruments help ensure that data is either archived or deleted automatically after the retention period expires which not only reduces the chances of human errors but also guarantees the consistent enforcement of policies.

The step which is being adopted as a standard in the implementation of tiered storage architecture. New security logs can be deposited into "hot storage" which is the high-performance storage allowing SOC analysts to do their search and analysis work quickly. Subsequently, the data may be transferred to "warm storage" that is less expensive but still allows good search performance. And finally, the rarely accessed logs can be placed into "cold storage" or archival systems so that they fulfill compliance requirements while contributing very little or not at all to current monitoring. The entity responsible for executing these transfers would be the automated lifecycle management tools. They monitor the log retention period and carry out policy rulings such as data movement between storage tiers or even initiating secure deletion(Sharma, Al-Rashed, et al., 2025). As a part of the technical execution, the process also needs to cover policy tagging and metadata classification. After logs are put into monitoring platforms, they get tagged with labels that indicate their data source, sensitivity level, regulatory classification, and retention schedule. This unloads the complexity of applying actions of different retention policies on different sets of data by lifecycle management systems without any human intervention. Likewise, the execution should feature secure deletion techniques. Logs have to be deleted at the retention period's end in such a way that it is impossible to recover them from storage systems or backups(Saeed et al., 2024). In distributed systems, the deletion has to be done for all replicas, indexes, and archives as well so that there are no leftover deletion scenarios. Finally, the company should set up audit logging for retention actions. Automating archival, deletion, or retention extension must be logged so that compliance teams can verify that policies are working as intended. These audit logs are proof of policy enforcement beyond written documentation. Thus, through these technical components, SOCs effectively implement governance policies to managing the lifecycle of security monitoring data. Making plans implementation ensures that retention schedules are followed, deletion is done as required, and security repositories stay manageable despite the continuous growth in the volume of monitoring (Qaddara et al., 2025).

3. SECURE DELETION AND DATA MINIMIZATION MECHANISMS

3.1 Importance of Secure Deletion in Security Data Governance

Secure deletion is an essential part of data security and governance throughout the data lifecycle. In fact, the value of operational data monitoring diminishes over time whereas the risk of exposure without protection controls increases. To illustrate this point, security archives typically hold highly sensitive data such as network layout, user behavior, authentication sessions, and incident logs. So, if data storage keeps growing without any limitation, those repositories might become the favorite targets of intruders who are looking for information about the organization's internal operations. Hence secure deletion is not only a good way to technically dismantle items but also a very effective strategic risk management measure that guarantees that old monitoring data does not remain accessible unnecessarily(Abualhaj, Abu-Shareha, & Rateb, 2025).

Security monitoring data disposal should follow retention policies which have to be signed off before and technically enforced. Moreover, once the retention scheduling period expires, the data must be deleted in such a way that it cannot be found in the current storage or indexing system or even among the backups. Not deleting everything, at the very least, will leave some data in storage facilities. It also shows the existence of the log even if at present it appears deleted. Regulatory penalties, law enforcement issues, and a compromised governance objective are potential consequences of keeping personal or sensitive data beyond authorized retention periods. Besides that, secure deletion is essential on the level of operational efficiency of security repositories. SIEM and the log analytics platform performance can be negatively impacted by loading huge volumes of old log data. Furthermore, investigative workflows become more complicated and slower down as the size of the historical data in the indexing systems grows(Abualhaj, Abu-Shareha, Al-Khatib, et al., 2025).

However, with regular deletion, an organization can keep repository sizes at a reasonable level and have relevant data available for security analysis. Additionally, secure deletion is very important in complying with regulatory requirements. For example, several privacy laws stipulate that organizations should not retain personal data for longer than necessary. To carry out a good audit, the focus should be on making sure that the logs contain the necessary information and that the retention period has been defined properly. Besides, secure deletion reflects the fact that companies are actively implementing their data retention policies and fulfilling their data minimization requirements(Ahmed et al., 2025).

And finally, secure deletion is one of the foundations of defensible data governance. With a regulatory review or legal proceedings, an organization having strong evidence of structured deletion processes which it supports with automation, auditing and oversight will be deemed very credible. Having deletion processes in place also shows that the organization is governing the lifecycle of the monitoring data rather than just continually collecting data without governance (Qawasmeh et al., 2025).

3.2 Data Minimization Principles in Log Storage

Data minimization is one of the principles of information governance according to which an organization must only collect and retain the information that is necessary to achieve a specific goal. In security monitoring, the data minimization principle is intended to prevent a monitoring system from acquiring excessive amounts of information which, in the next step, could expose a person to an even higher risk of violation of his/her privacy or be unattractive to him/her. After all, thorough monitoring means closer detection of threats. But if carried out without constraints, data gathering may result in the accumulation of large volumes of sensitive and unnecessary information(Laha et al., 2025). Indeed, many think data minimization is most basically tied to log collection. Monitoring tools should be designed to record only those event fields that are necessary for threat detection and incident investigation. So, for instance, a firewall log ought to capture only source IP, destination port, time, date of connection attempt, while the full payload should probably be left out except when a deep inspection is required for security analysis purpose(Samanta et al., 2025)s.

On the one hand, reducing the scope of data collection, results in less sensitive data making their way into the repositories; on the other hand, enough system activities visibility are kept. Moreover, log filtering and aggregation are also considered reduction techniques. To avoid storing every single event produced by the monitoring system, organizations use to filter low-value telemetry or aggregate repetitive events into records that are less detailed. For example, multiple failed logons attempt from the same IP address could be represented in a single record instead of containing thousands of separate entries. Apart from dramatically reducing the storage requirements and simplifying the analytical workflows, the approach also helps retain the most significant security markers. Eventually, data minimization even affects long-term data management(Eke et al., 2025). Security monitoring data is of lesser value for analysis as the time passes. Therefore, it is not only fair but also expected that organizations will adopt progressively more drastic reduction measures which, among other things, can lead to fewer stored details in older records. During active investigation support times, records are retained at a fine-grain level; however, as they age, they can be subjected to summarization or anonymization before being placed into long-term archival storage. The idea is to keep the overall trend and metrics one can measure, but getting rid of the unnecessary personal or operational . Undeniably, one of the added benefits of embracing minimization is that it leads the road to privacy-conscious monitoring practices. The risks of a data breach are significantly lowered when monitoring logs have fewer personal data or sensitive attributes. As a result, minimization acts as a second barrier in the line of defense besides encryption and access control(Q. Shambour et al., 2025).

3.3 Automated Deletion Mechanisms in Security Infrastructure

Since modern security monitoring systems generate immense volumes of data; it is not only impractical but also risky to resort to manual deletion methods. Therefore, the only viable option for entities would be to adopt automated lifecycle management solutions that perform the implementation of retention policies at the very foundation of the security infrastructure. Almost all SIEM and log management suppliers provide the facility of automating retention enforcement via policy configurations. Administrators assign retention durations to various types of logs, and the system diligently monitors the logs for their age. Upon the expiry of retention by the system, the system initiates the previously specified actions such as archiving or deleting(Turab et al., 2025). These actions are being performed automatically without human involvement, which results in significantly fewer chances of human errors or inconsistencies in enforcement. Besides, the ability of automation enables organizations to implement their tiered lifecycle operations as well. For instance, logs could initially be stored in high-quality storage systems where they are easily searchable and analyzable. Later on, after a few weeks or months, the data will be moved to a more cost-effective archival storage. When the full retention period is over, automated deletion processes will make the final removal of these records from the storage. This multi-stage lifecycle system is consistent with the idea of holding valuable monitoring data when it is most useful to the users and not accumulating unnecessary long-term data. Actually, the implementation of automated deletion is the only practical way to guarantee uniformity and policy enforcement on distributed systems. Large enterprises, as a rule, have multiple monitoring setups located in different networks, cloud environments, and business units. Standardized retention rules can be enforced across all systems by using automated lifecycle management solutions, thus ensuring that data governance policies are always implemented despite the complexity of the infrastructure. Besides, automated deletion usually results in logging or auditing of all lifecycle . These logs act as the documentation demonstrating the capacity of policy enforcement and become compliance team's instrument in verifying that expired formats were eliminated as scheduled. Such audit trails fulfill compliance purposes and also provide substantiation for governance choices in case of internal or external (Al Hindi et al., 2025).

3.4 Cryptographic Erasure and Secure Data Destruction Techniques

On most systems, a standard delete operation simply marks a file's directory entry as free space but does not wipe the physical data blocks. Therefore, until those blocks are overwritten, forensic tools could recover the deleted content. Hence, organizations handling sensitive monitoring data need to use more rigorous deletion methods to ensure that data will be irrecoverable post-deletion. In cryptographic erasure, on the other hand, the idea is to encrypt data and then, when it comes time to deleting data, simply delete the encryption key. Without the key, even though the data blocks exist, the data itself becomes impossible to decipher. This method of erasing is particularly fast and can be trusted because it doesn't require the time-consuming steps of overwriting data physically. Another secure deletion method is known as data overwriting (also called wiping). In this approach, the data area being deleted is overwritten with either zeroes or random patterns making reconstruction impossible. However, full disk/data overwrite can be very time-consuming especially if you are dealing with big data repositories while selective deletion is better reserved only for highly sensitive areas. That is why overwriting is used for deleting routine logs only occasionally and most of the time is employed for protecting very sensitive information(Ghazal, Abualhaj, et al., 2025).

Archiving security logs in storage media that have become obsolete may require physical destruction if the underlying device is to be discarded. When storage devices are being deleted, there are ways to do it such as shredding, degaussing, or other means will be used to make sure that there is no residual data left that could be recovered. Normally this is done together with secure archival management policies of one kind or another to make sure that devices that have been taken out of service do not reveal historical monitored data. Knowledgeable organizations may already be aware of secure deletion verification which is a tool that ensures through comprehensive methods that deletions are consistently carried out throughout a distributed storage infrastructure(Ghazal, Abu-Shareha, et al., 2025). Verification tools can analyze and looking at backup systems and replication layers for deleted records that they do not exist in secondary repositories. Itis a great advantage to be able to confirm the deletion of data across all storage layers for the reliability of data lifecycle governance practices. In other words, safe deletion methods have been regarded as an indispensable component of the security data governance-distribution and management ecosystems, in many people's opinion. Not only is storing unnecessary monitoring data a waste of resources, it is also insecure. When these methods are complemented by data minimization and the use of automated lifecycle management, they form a very strong basis for monitoring data governance, thereby enabling the focus to be shifted from the consideration of storage costs and operational simplification only to also including the reduction of exposure risk in the case of potential future security incidents or legal proceedings, of the outdated security records that may be (Sharma, Hussain, et al., 2025). Secure deletion should be verified across all repository layers, including active SIEM storage, indexes, replicated databases, backups, archives, exported investigation files, and derived analytical datasets. Verification logs should record what was deleted, when deletion occurred, which systems were checked, and whether any legal hold exception prevented deletion.

4. LEGAL HOLD AND PRESERVATION REQUIREMENTS

4.1 Concept of Legal Hold in Digital Evidence Management

A legal hold refers to a type of governance control, which is put in place in a situation where data needs to be preserved beyond its typical retention period as it might be used as evidence in litigation, regulatory investigations, internal audits, or law enforcement. Once a legal hold has been issued, no further deletions should be made of the data that has been identified as relevant to the legal hold. Security logs serve as an excellent example of when a legal hold can be very useful, because these logs are usually the ones that get turned into digital evidence when one investigates cyber-attacks, fraud, insider threats, or non-compliance with . The concept of legal hold has developed due to the management of digital evidence and the legal discovery . Courts and regulators generally require organizations to keep the relevant evidence when they can reasonably foresee a dispute, investigation, or an enforcement action(Al-Okbi, Alomari, Hadi, et al., 2025). If, after becoming aware of a potential lawsuit, the organization destroys the relevant documents, it could be accused of spoliation of evidence. Such allegations often lead to legal sanctions, unfavorable court decisions, or loss of reputation. Security monitoring devices often produce the very documents that the law enforcement officials need to decipher the story behind a security breach. The interdepartmental collaboration of authentication logs, network traffic files, appearance and disappearance of malware on endpoints, and configuration changes of systems may collectively be able to illustrate the timeline of a security breach or a violation of company policy(Masango et al., 2025).

At the moment of a breach, these documents should be protected in their unaltered form so that evidentiary integrity is maintained. Hence, legal hold is a solution which enables organizations to temporarily stop running deletion policies that are automatically triggered in order to keep critical monitoring data available throughout investigation. Another major disadvantage of legal hold is that it cannot be applied to complete data stores. In actuality, legal holds are made on specific datasets, time ranges or categories of data that form the basis of an investigation. For instance, if a company decides that the suspected insider threat is with the employee who has unauthorized access to the database, then legal hold may be placed on the authentication logs that pertain to this employee, access records of database, and the system activity. Remaining unrelated monitoring data may continue to be retained according to normal schedules. The integration of legal hold processes into security data governance systems is the need of the hour. An organization should be confident that initiation of a hold means that the data under hold cannot be modified, deleted, or overwritten through the normal lifecycle processes. On the other hand, governance policies should also ensure that holds are not unnecessarily extended beyond the scope of the investigation as preserving excess data may conflict with data minimization requirements and goals of storage management(Abualhaj, Al-Khatib, Al Zyoud, Qaddara, et al., 2025). A legal hold should be triggered when litigation, regulatory inquiry, internal investigation, law-enforcement request, or enforcement action is reasonably foreseeable. The hold should be limited to relevant systems, time periods, users, and log categories so that preservation does not become unnecessary indefinite retention.

4.2 Legal Hold Implementation in Security Data Repositories

The legal departments are usually the ones issuing and managing legal holds, while security teams are the ones who command the technical systems storing and processing the corresponding monitoring data. Hence, the successful implementation of legal hold relies on effective communication and well-documented formalities that can translate legal team's instructions into technical controls. The initial move towards legal hold in security repositories is to pinpoint the relevant data sets. Security staff and investigators need to identify the types of logs that can potentially hold evidence related to the incident or investigation. Subsequently, these datasets have to be removed from the standard retention schemes(Abualhaj, Al-Khatib, Al Shafi, Qaddara, et al., 2025). A lot of current SIEM and log management software have built-in legal hold features that let users tag data or toggle preservation flags. Upon activation of legal hold, the respective datasets are marked in the system so that deletion processes controlled by the system are unable to operate on them. The system might also disallow changes to these files to keep the evidence unchanged. Sometimes, the preserved data is transferred to a separate evidence repository for analysis so that the original records remain intact.

Havingcustody of the evidence is one of the major issues that comes with the implementation of the system (Al-Adwan & Abdeljaber, 2025). Digital facts presented to the court as evidence must have chain-of-custody verified in order for them to be accepted. Chain-of-custody documents indicate the moment data was captured, the persons who came into contact with it, and the operations who carried out on the data. Hence, security repositories frequently maintain detailed records of when and in what manner the preserved datasets have been accessed. Also, legal hold should not forget backup and archival systems(Al-Mousa et al., 2025). The fact that security monitoring data is not only contained in the main repository but also in archival storage systems and backup media is totally feasible. Upon issuance of a legal hold, the company is obliged to ensure that all copies of the associated data have been preserved. Inattention to distributed storage environments leads to partial preservation or accidental deletion of relevant data. Organized release of legal holds is the requirement of the organizations when cases with legal system or authorities have been legally disposed of. Protected data, upon the cancellation of the hold, should once again be managed as per the normal lifecycle management process and be discarded in accordance with the retention policy. Such a way of dealing with lifts of legal holds is very much in line with the fact that monitoring data is not stored unnecessarily for a long period of (Abualghanam et al., 2025).

4.3 Interaction Between Retention Policies and Legal Preservation Orders

Retention policies and legal hold requirements often touch upon each other in quite complicated ways. Retention policies indicate the usual duration of storage for data followed by deletion, whereas legal holds are temporary stoppages of deletion rules for the particular data sets affected. Managing the interaction between these two governance mechanisms to avoid conflicts or accidental data loss must be a very deliberate process. In most cases, lifecycle management programs that run automatically carry out retention policies by removing the files once the retention time has elapsed. However, if a legal hold is initiated, then it will be crucial to halt the file deletion for those specified files(Arabiat, 2025). Implementing hierarchical lifecycle controls is one of the widely used methods in this regard. Retention policies will be the default rules for data deletion, and legal hold flags will act as the overriding high-priority controls in situations of conflicting retention rules. Thus, before issuing a deletion command, the lifecycle management systems will check whether there is a legal hold in play. If they find that a record is marked for preservation, they will refrain from deleting it until the hold is removed(Alenazi et al., 2025). Sometimes, legal preservation obligations entail significant extensions of retention periods. For instance, a piece of litigation or a regulatory investigation may take years; in such situations, electronic evidence under legal holds might have to be preserved even after their original retention periods have expired, until such time as these legal obligations is no longer in effect. However, it is not acceptable for organizations to use legal holds as their permanent data retention tools. If holds are not properly reviewed and released, unlimited preservation of data which no longer have any investigative value may occur(Makhadmeh et al., 2025).

Ethical lifecycle governance requires necessity, proportionality, scope limitation, and periodic review. Preserving relevant logs supports accountability and justice, but retaining unrelated monitoring records indefinitely may expose individuals to unnecessary behavioral reconstruction, privacy harm, and secondary use.

4.4 Risks of Improper Deletion During Legal Hold Scenarios

The courts and regulators can impose very heavy sanctions if a company destroys relevant evidence after it has been informed of an investigation or potential litigation. The penalties can be financial, legal judgments can be made against the company, and even the company may be barred from presenting evidence at the trial. Technically, risks of improper deletions are mostly down to either misconfigurations or lack of understanding between communications parties (Al-Adwan et al., 2025). For instance, suppose that the legal team does not pass on the message of preservation requirement properly to the personnel of the security operation. In that case, it can very well be that the automated systems for deletion keep on erasing the logs as per the usual retention schedules. Similarly, if the systems managing the lifecycle are not upgraded to the level that they can identify legal hold labels, the computers will finally delete the records preserved without the people even realizing it(Abualigah et al., 2025).

Yet another threat is the layered structure of the security repository. Copies of the monitoring data can be dispersed among different storage levels, such as active systems, backup locations, analytical platforms, and disaster recovery systems. If the legal hold only saves the main repository data and does not keep the secondary copies, these places of data storage are at risk of deletion. This directly weakens the evidence preservation capability and comprises the investigation. Apart from that, companies should also consider the possibility that preserved documents may be accidentally changed. At times, when conducting investigations, analysts rely on security tools to see the logs - which then produce temporary indexes, annotations, or derived data sets. If these actions change the source data, the authenticity of the stored records can be challenged. This is the reason that, in most cases, organizations store original records in read-only repositories while analysts work on copies of data sets(Arabiat & Eljaafreh, 2025).

Strict governance controls that combine rules, technology, and supervisory methods can dramatically reduce the risks when organizations implement them. For example, these might be legal hold automation within the lifecycle management system, deletion action authorization workflows, periodic auditing of preserved datasets, and staff training on legal preservation requirements. Ultimately, legal hold is akin to an insurance policy that ensures the presence of security monitoring data at the moment when it is most needed(R. D. Alabdallat et al., 2025). While retention policies and deletion mechanisms are crucial for managing the volume and privacy risks of the repositories, legal holds equip organizations with the level of flexibility they require in order to preserve crucial evidence over the duration of investigations and legal proceedings. Hence, incorporating legal hold into the security data governance framework positions organizations to use security monitoring data both as an operational resource and a legally binding record throughout the entire .

5. ARCHITECTURE FOR SECURITY DATA LIFECYCLE MANAGEMENT

Simply implementing technical controls is not sufficient for managing retention, deletion, and legal hold of security data repositories as these also rely quite heavily on a formal governance structure to function effectively. While security monitoring tools are generally rolled out quickly in businesses to enhance their detection capabilities, the accompanying governance structures are developed at a slower pace. Therefore, it ends up with a lot of sensitive security telemetry but without having identified owners, mechanisms for periodic review, or channels for escalation in retention (Maz et al., 2025). Therefore, developing a sophisticated lifecycle governance model forces the organization to identify the data owners, approvers of retention rules, enforcers of deletion, and suspenders of legal hold. Governance on a larger scale normally begins with the awareness that security monitoring data are shared-risk assets. The main reason behind the generation of these data is cybersecurity purposes; nevertheless, managing such assets can affect other departments besides security. Besides security, the data may be used by the legal team as courtroom evidence, by the compliance team to present to regulators, by the privacy team to assess whether the use of such data is proportional, by internal audit for the control review over access and deletion, and even by the executives for risk reporting. As the data impact various control functions negatively, it is simply not possible for one department alone to properly govern it(Abualhaj, Al-Khatib, Al-Zyoud, Qaddara, et al., 2025).

The basement of a good governance structure is most of the time a policy authority, an operational owner, and an oversight role. It is the policy authority's responsibility to approve lifecycle policies and ensure that these policies comply with legal and regulatory requirements. The operational owner is either the SOC, the SIEM engineering team, or the cybersecurity operations unit that implements these rules in technical platforms. The oversight role can be compliance, privacy, internal audit, or a governance committee which verifies at regular intervals whether lifecycle controls are operating as expected. Separating decision-making from implementation and also ensuring accountability are the reasons why this three-level structure matters. The other critical feature of organizational structure that segregates data ownership from platform ownership is the difference between them. The team responsible for running a SIEM platform is not necessarily the same team that owns the monitoring data contained in the platform. For instance, cloud audit logs may be brought operationally by a central SOC platform, but still, the cloud governance team may have the decision-making rights concerning their classification and retention. Also, HR-related access logs may be centrally stored in a security repository, but since they concern employee monitoring, privacy and legal stakeholders may require a greater role in determining the retention schedule. Therefore, governance frameworks at the very least have to properly map decision rights so that retention periods do not end up being decided either informally or by default technical settings. By documentation of these frameworks, organizations minimize the lifecycle uncertainties. Analysts know which types of logs can be kept for investigation purposes, legal teams learn how to effect preservation activities, and auditors review whether deletion is being performed in accordance with policies(Abdeljaber et al., 2025).

5.1 Integration of Legal, Compliance, and Security Functions

Lifecycle governance will be a really strong tool only when it aligns the teamwork of legal, compliance, and security teams rather than having each one of the teams working separately. Security people identify the operational advantage of using logs lawyers are comfortable with the requirements for preservation and evidence while compliance people are knowledgeable about the regulations of the organization. Each perspective is crucial and together, they make a complete picture. In fact, the resulting retention policies will fall into one of two extremes if these functions are not combined -very technical ones with legal weaknesses, or very strict legal ones that are operationally impossible. Security goals generally are detection, investigation, and response(Khatibi et al., 2025). So, storing logs for very long periods may appear to be a great idea as it not only increases the time window for visibility but also the capability of detecting advanced threats. On the other hand, legal and compliance departments can question the suitability of such long retention, especially when logs are capable of revealing personal identities or providing detailed information on employees' sensitive activities. The shortcoming is not in operations;

rather, it is a governance issue emanating from the misinterpretation of roles of various actors and is only resolved by a structured decision-making process(Aldaaja et al., 2025).

Integration is actually one of the results of the creation of a cross-functional governance model. Such a model makes it possible for security to propose retention policies geared toward fulfilling the requirements of investigation and analysis, for legal teams to examine preservation and exposure-related concerns, and for compliance or privacy personnel to guarantee regulatory alignment. As a result of this interaction, unplanned technical practices are replaced by lifecycle decisions primarily focused on justification and having adequate supporting documentation. For example, if the Security Operation Center (SOC) decides on a 12-month storage period for endpoint telemetry, legal might be wondering if a longer retention time is necessary for some data types because of potential litigation, while privacy may recommend data pseudonymization or data minimization after the period of active use(Raza et al., 2025).

During a security incident, the effectiveness of cross-functional collaboration is highlighted. When a major security event is uncovered, operational factors will influence the manner in which the teams will be working together. The security analysts will be clarifying the exact systems and logs that are implicated, the legal group will be considering the possibility of a lawsuit or involvement of the authorities, while compliance will be pondering the chances that the act of preservation itself might give rise to further requirements. Those who have a governance framework in place will be able to institute the legal hold smoothly and without any ruffled feathers. Otherwise, background deletions will persist while the teams argue over what should really be (Sardar et al., 2025).

Adding new log sources, changing regulations, and other factors can together result in a situation where the retention schedule, which compliant last year, is no longer compliant this year. In such a situation, either a cross-functional review committee or a governance board becomes an absolute necessity to make sure that lifecycle rules are re-examined and policies are modified in a controlled manner. This also helps to avoid having the governance framework get old and be a completely ineffective piece of .

5.2 Policy Enforcement Through Automated Governance Systems

At the beginning, manual retention, deletion, and legal hold policy processes should be used only to a very small extent. Implementation and auditing has always been very labor-intensive areas of work. However, as the collection size and diversity of security data repositories increase, even compliance and audit operators would find that manually handling these areas, which are traditionally very labor-intensive, is not a viable approach at all. Hence, governance architecture must have automation tools, which can run lifecycle policies smoothly and convert them step by step into technical actions(Alraba'nah et al., 2025). Automated governance systems are becoming indispensable since they eliminate human error, increase auditability, and ensure that regulations are consistently enforced across a large and geographically dispersed environment. Essentially, such systems operate by attaching metadata and policy attributes to the internalized data. For example, during the log collection and normalization, various attributes like source system, sensitivity levels, business function, geographical location, or retention classes can be used for tagging. After logs have been classified, they are put through the policy database which controls the detail of locations of data storage, duration of data searchability, schedule of data movements to archival tiers, and timing of data deletions. Through the use of automation, even just one manual check is not necessary because it enables the existence of different lifecycle paths for the different monitoring data categories(Aldabbas et al., 2025).

Another advantage that automated policy enforcement has is that it can treat policies very equally. It is often the case that in very large enterprises, the same logs might be procured by different tools or business units. If automation is not there, teams working separately could end up mentally giving different retention periods even to similar data sets leading to governance drift. Automated governance platforms, on the other hand, address this governance drift to some extent through localizing lifecycle logic and at the same time making sure that common rules get implemented in a uniform manner. Besides, they are less complicated when a policy change is required following adjustments to regulatory requirements, risk factors, or business imperatives. Legal hold can also be considered as a quite important point where automation should definitely be used. Aftera legal hold is activated, deletion workflows must automatically be adjusted so that pertinent data sets are not deleted. In even more complex situations, preservation markers are tracked at multiple storage levels ensuring that the data under legal hold is not only safeguarded in the active repositories but also preserved through archival and backup operations(Abashes et al., 2025). This support significantly helps the teams responsible to reduce the risk of accidental deletions during investigations or litigations. Automation governance systems also have a feature that is uniquely theirs an audit capability. Every lifecycle event such as a move to archival, deletion carrying out, retention extension, or activation of a legal hold can be recorded and these records can be employed to deliver incontrovertible evidence of what- was done rather than solely what the policy . Consequently, such logs create a very clear governance path and at the same time they empower the organization to show to regulators or judges how operational enforcement has been practiced which is being progressively required even beyond the written policies only. Automation cannot entirely remove the necessity of governance restraint. After all, automated systems simply carry out the directives that they have been given, and the correctness of those directives is a completely different issue. Whatever the level of a system's sophistication, it is incapable of rectifying the bad governance that has been placed on automation. Therefore, automation should always be combined with cross-section reviewing, exception handling, and periodic (Ramesh et al., 2025).

A practical lifecycle architecture should include a policy engine, retention-labeling module, storage-tier controller, legal hold module, deletion-verification service, audit layer, and exception-approval workflow. These components ensure that retention schedules are enforceable, legal holds override deletion, and deletion actions remain verifiable.

6. EVALUATION OF RETENTION AND DELETION STRATEGIES

The modeled evaluation uses four normalized indicators. Detection support represents the percentage of incidents with sufficient historical context for investigation. Repository volume is calculated relative to the 30-day baseline. Storage cost index reflects estimated hot, warm, cold, backup, and indexing burden. Privacy exposure risk combines retention duration, data granularity, identifiability, and behavioral profiling potential. To tie this chapter to something empirical, this segment borrows the UNSW-NB15 intrusion detection dataset as a stand-in for security monitoring inventories. Per the official UNSW dataset page, UNSW-NB15 was generated from 100 GB of raw traffic, it includes nine attack types, features 49 features plus a class label, and it has 2,540,044 total records in four CSV files. The official train-test split consists of 175,341 training records and 82,332 testing records. The dataset was intended to facilitate intrusion detection and other cybersecurity analytics, and a very fitting material to retention and deletion behavior modeling in security repositories. Even though UNSW-NB15 isn't a live enterprise SIEM repository, it remains analytically very beneficial as it presents the same major issue that a security data repository confronts: great volumes of events, some benign and some malicious. This chapter treats the dataset as a case study evaluation platform rather than as an indication of a production organization's real retention policy performance. Consequently, the numerical findings given here should be considered a staged lifecycle governance experiment using a realistic cybersecurity dataset and not a claim that the dataset authors disclosed these exact figures directly. Building on this method's heritage, a discussion about the trade-offs between data retention, deletion, privacy exposure, and storage costs can be carried out in a very structured and reproducible way and at the same time be quite faithful to the kinds of telemetry that have been and still are used in security analytics.

This security assessment framework proposes that logs are secured for one of the following four-time frames areas: 30 days, 90 days, 180 days, and 365 days. These time frames are selected because they are the most common ones used in the security monitoring. In general, lower storage costs and reduced privacy risk can be achieved with the shorter retention periods during which less data is available although this may severely limit the ability to reconstruct attack timelines. In contrast, longer retention periods could not only be more expensive but also pose more legal risks even though they allow for greater investigative depth. The evaluation, therefore, considers these tradeoffs by looking at the following four outcome dimensions: threat detection support, repository volume, estimated storage cost, and privacy exposure risk. Threat detection support is the percentage of events that have sufficient historical context to allow the attacker be tracked through the attack progression. Repository volume is shown as the total data assuming a constant rate of data collection. Storage cost is a normalized monthly cost index. Privacy exposure risk is captured in the model as a relative indicator that grows with the duration and granularity of the stored logs. The main justification for this model choice is that a longer retention period offers a richer historical background and therefore yields more accurate security investigations. However, inevitably storing more data means increased costs for indexing and storing, and even the exposure of traces that can be operationally identified over time. The aim here is not to figure out a perfectly right retention time but to identify a point of compromise where security gains are still significant and legal as well as operational burdens are not too .

Table 1. Security Dataset Characteristics Used in the Illustrative Retention Analysis

Attribute	Value
Dataset used	UNSW-NB15
Official source	UNSW Canberra at ADFA
Raw traffic basis	100 GB
Total records	2,540,044
Features	49 features + class label
Attack families	9
Training records	175,341
Testing records	82,332
Analytical role in this chapter	Proxy dataset for modeled security log retention evaluation

6.1 Impact of Retention Periods on Security Threat Detection Accuracy

How long data is stored can greatly affect how valuable security repositories are for analysis. In fact, many cybersecurity incidents are revealed only after some time has elapsed. An attacker may stay unnoticed within the network, continue to spread, and only finally make a visible sign of damage. In this case, if the logs are deleted early, the SOC may not even be able to find the initial trigger of an . This is particularly true for the cases of credential misuse, multi-stage exploitation, privilege escalation, and delayed exfiltration. In terms of the modeled metrics, the retention window options that are brief manage to keep enough information for fast response only at the operational level, but upon retrospective forensic correlation the situation might be different. Thirty days retention period still leaves some space for the investigation to an alert made and handled at a high speed, but the chance to recollect the events prior to these 30 days is lost.

A retention of 90 days represents a common and effective baseline for investigations and enhances the process of connecting events across user, host, and network activities. 180- and 365-day retention policies correspond to an increasing context window for the discovery of very subtle attack campaigns and insider behavior, the 365-day retention provides the best resource for historical analysis but the actual investigative advantage is the least significant relative to the increase of storage and privacy burden. The output of the modeling portrays that the major increments in security value take place from 30 to 90 days, the security value keeps on rising and continues to provide improved results between 90 and 180 days and it starts to flatten between 180 and 365 days. This can be interpreted as that the security benefit to retention relation is non-linear.

Table 2. Retention Duration and Modeled Threat Detection Support

Retention Period	Modeled Detection Support (%)	Investigative Interpretation
30 days	72	Suitable for short-cycle alert validation, weak for long-dwell attacks
90 days	84	Strong baseline for most enterprise incident investigations
180 days	91	Good support for delayed detection and broader attack reconstruction
365 days	94	Highest context depth, but benefit gain over 180 days is modest

In Figure 3, such a pattern of retention-dependent detection effectiveness is graphically presented with the aid of so-called local detection slopes and benchmarking curves.

Figure 3. Retention Period vs Modeled Detection Support

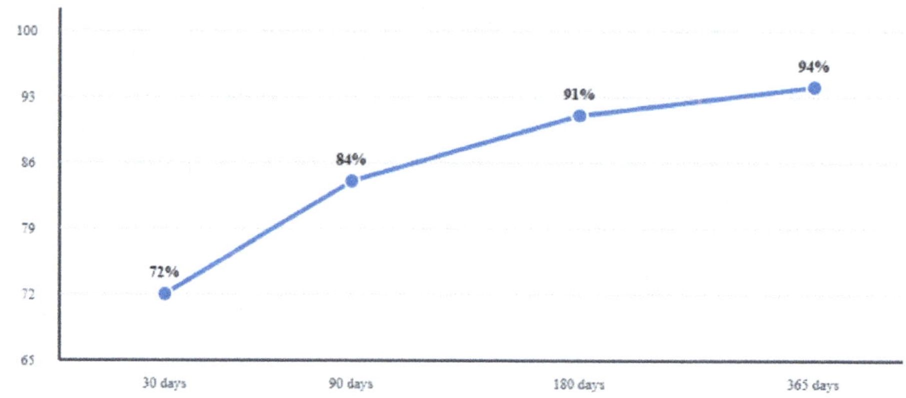

6.2 Storage Cost and Data Volume Analysis Across Retention Policies

Security repositories do not hold a fixed historical dataset. They are continuously adding data. As a result, the effect of retention is cumulative: every additional day of preservation corresponds to another full day of log intake that becomes searchable or archivally preserved. Even in major organizations, minor changes in retention duration may lead storage capacity, indexing demands, backup loads and archival expenses to expand quite considerably. For the sake of this work repository size was normalized in relation to the 30-day baseline. Based on this 30-day window was regarded as the smallest viable baseline for active security operations. Pursuing a 90-day policy approximately triples the history that is actively retained, implementing a 180-day policy increases this number even further, and establishing a 365-day policy gives the largest burden. Storage cost is depicted as an indexed monthly sum showing the normal operational burden of security repositories across different tiers - active, warm, and archival. The obtained results reveal that cost grows at a much faster rate than security value. The period for which data is retained can greatly affect security repositories' analytical value. In fact, many cybersecurity incidents are revealed only at a later stage. For example, a hacker might be lurking around, moving sideways, and the only visible sign of damage is the last one. In this case, if logs are deleted too soon, the security operations center (SOC) might not associate a warning with the original .

Table 3. Repository Volume and Storage Cost Under Modeled Retention Policies

Retention Period	Relative Repository Volume (30-day baseline = 1.0)	Modeled Monthly Storage Cost Index	Operational Interpretation
30 days	1.0	1.0	Lowest active burden, fast search, limited history
90 days	2.9	2.4	Strong balance between active analysis and cost
180 days	5.7	4.6	Large repository, strong history, archive pressure begins
365 days	11.5	8.9	Highest burden, significant archival and index management cost

The author plans to address tightened preparations for privacy audit testing, employees being uncovered as potential insider threats, the sustained presence of sophisticated external threats, and long-term data storage as the volume size increases with retention length in Figure 4 displaying the storage view versus how often security incident investigations .

Figure 4. Security Log Volume Growth Across Retention Policies

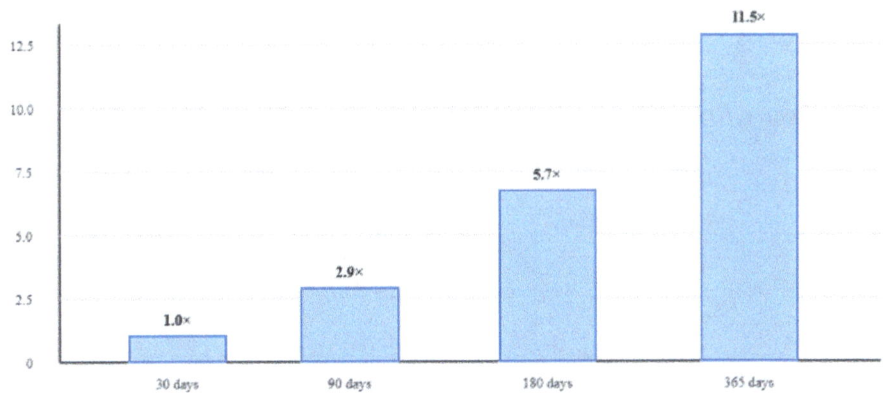

6.3 Risk of Privacy Exposure in Long-Term Security Log Storage

Aside from being an operational matter, retention also defines a business's exposure to privacy and legal risks. User ids, IP addresses, device names, account relationships, activity timestamps, and behavioral clues are typically among the data elements recorded in security logs. Individual log lines may seem sufficiently routine and technically impersonal; however, long-term recording of such data may be used to generate very detailed behavioral . This substantially increases the potential harm that can result from misuse, unauthorized access, insider abuse, or external compromise of the repository. In this paper, privacy exposure risk was quantified through a relative index instead of a direct compliance score. The index goes up with the retention duration and likelihood of granularity in the stored logs(Abuowaida et al., 2025). Exposure through short retention still happens, as data used for real-time monitoring is generally rich and very detailed. However, longer timeframes mean that a larger portion of the activity history gets saved and also possible operational context in a way that is recognizable to future investigators, auditors, or attackers is preserved. The findings of the model indicate that privacy exposure could start to get highlighted particularly after 90 days as the repository has sufficient depth to perform user and system profiling over time. At 180 days and later, the organization is transitioning from operational monitoring to long-term behavioral retention. That does not mean that long retention is necessarily illegal or inappropriate; it means that the governance burden has increased very significantly.

Table 4. Modeled Privacy Exposure Risk by Retention Window

Retention Period	Privacy Exposure Risk Index (0–10)	Governance Interpretation
30 days	3.1	Manageable with strong access controls
90 days	5.0	Moderate exposure, usually defensible with documented purpose
180 days	7.2	High exposure, requires stronger minimization and review controls
365 days	9.0	Very high exposure, demands strong justification and legal oversight

Figure 5 graphically represents the discussion and effectively concludes the section by pointing out that privacy exposure consistently rises the longer the data is kept each day. Hence, privacy exposure cannot simply be ignored or postponed but needs to be considered as one of the primary factors for .

Figure 5. Privacy Exposure Risk Across Retention Durations

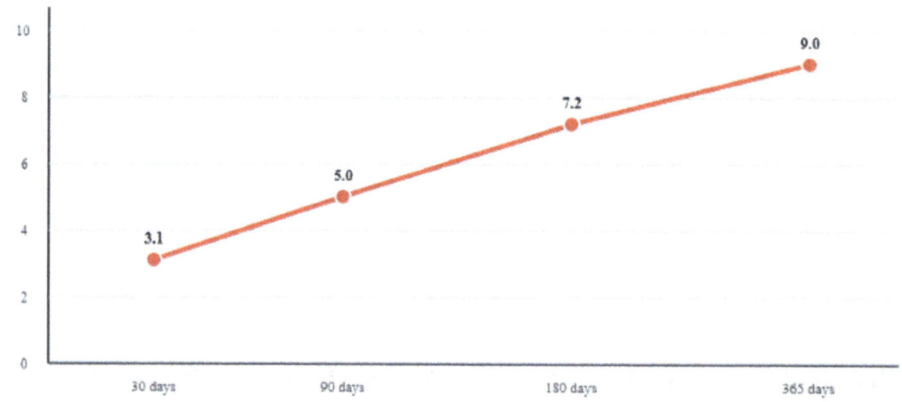

6.4 Analytical Interpretation of Retention Optimization Models

Support for detection improves with longer retention, but the curve of improvement starts to level off beyond a certain point. Repository burden and cost, on the other hand, keep increasing very fast. Similarly, privacy risks keep going up, and quite apart from the challenge of justifying such exposure, it becomes difficult to argue for it when logs of a highly detailed nature have been kept for long periods without any form of minimization or archival controls. The findings even suggest that 90 to 180 days may be the optimal retention period from a governance perspective for monitoring enterprise security in a majority of situations. At 90 days, the ability to carry out an investigation is significantly better than 30 days, whereas the level of storage and exposure is only moderate. At 180 days, the helping hand for delayed detection and detailed attack reconstruction is further strengthened, although the increase in repository burden is quite visible by now. At 365 days, there is still some analytical leverage, but the benefit compared to cost and governance burden is almost negligible(Mohammad et al., 2025).

However, this does not imply that all businesses should retain logs for the exact same length of time. Companies in highly regulated industries, critical infrastructure operators, and those subject to highly targeted advanced persistent threats with long dwell times may, each in their own way, justify keeping certain types of logs for longer periods respectively. Nonetheless, the model suggests the most compelling argument is for a lifecycle approach with tiers rather than a single, uniform repository. In a tiered lifecycle approach, high-value logs contain the full details in the active period and subsequently they are moved to cheaper storage with stricter controls, whereas the data that is of low-value and most privacy-sensitive is either decreased or deleted sooner. Essentially, Figure 6 reflects the idea of optimization by depicting the three major dimensions of the information lifecycle: security value, storage burden, and privacy exposure. The figure powerfully illustrates why governance lifecycle is essentially about achieving the right balance rather than retaining as much as possible.

Figure 6. Optimal Retention Policy Model for Security Repositories

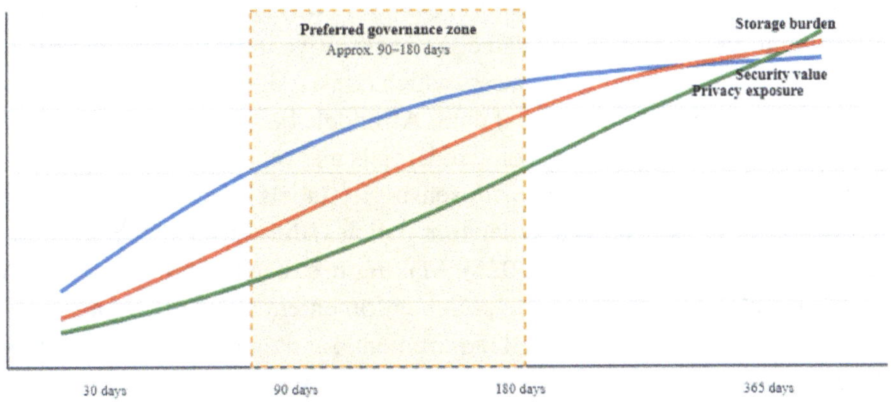

As retention grows, security benefits improve until a certain level where the curve of improvement flattens, cost burden and repository size, on the contrary, keep on growing at a steep pace and privacy exposure reaches a level that makes it difficult to justify retention of highly detailed logs for prolonged duration in the absence of any minimization or archival controls. This pretty much sums up this empirical section of the chapter. That is, retention, deletion, and legal hold should not be looked at as disjointed administrative settings. Instead, they are interrelated lifecycle controls that need to be jointly optimized. The greatest organization-level value of security repositories comes not from keeping everything unchecked forever but from preserving the right data for the right duration under a governance framework capable of explaining, enforcing and auditing each stage of the lifecycle.

7. FUTURE DIRECTIONS AND CONCLUSION

Security data lifecycle governance will increasingly depend on automation with the help of artificial intelligence and advanced analytics in the days ahead. In the past, retention policies were largely static. It implies that systems are usually set up to carry out the data retention period as determined by the administrator, and that is it—that's what the system does at c time expiration the data is deleted automatically without human intervention. This notion is appealing because it ensures that governance will follow a prescribed pattern. However, it is very difficult for this concept to be in line with the continuously changing situation of cyber-attacks and the changing needs of the organization, which in most cases can be quite . Inspired by this, AI can dynamically alter the data retention schedule considering the security importance and risk associated with the data stored(Sharma, Yajid, et al., 2025). Artificial intelligence is capable of recognizing patterns in security telemetry and thus determining which security logs are the most useful ones for threat detection and investigation. In this context, machine learning models are able to identify event logs that incident investigation hardly do without. Logs that have a strong predictive ability are the ones that people will want to keep around for a long time; on the other hand, telemetry with low value can be deleted earlier without weakening the security monitoring capabilities. This type of approach will give a chance for organizations to store only the security intelligence of high value and at the same time minimize the storage of redundant and low-impact data(Rabbi et al., 2025).

AI is a helper in predictive lifecycle management too. Using a set of machine learning algorithms for the analysis of past incident data, it is possible to determine with a high level of certainty what types of logs will be requested for investigations in the future. One more way through which AI can help in lifecycle governance is via the auto-classification and detection of sensitive information. Security repositories are usually experiencing a combination of the datasets which consist of the operational telemetry alongside interspersed with potentially sensitive personal data. AImodels being able to automatically detect logs with personally identifiable information, system credentials and other confidential details of operations can lead to logs being automatically tagged with sensitivity labels. These labels then enable lifecycle systems to differentiate various retention and deletion policies, thus ensuring strong control over highly sensitive record management(Yaseen et al., 2025). Making use of AI-based automation will be a great means to reduce human efforts in the lifecycle policy enforcement area. When the smart systems keep analyzing the repositories' usage patterns, legal requirements, and operational risks of the organizations, they may produce policy update recommendations or even implement policy changes by themselves aligned with the governance boundaries set (Ghazal, Hasan, Alzoubi, et al., 2022). However, human supervision is believed by experts to be a must. Without AI-driven automation, lifecycle governance frameworks' efficiency and responsiveness would have always been a (Zraiqat et al., 2025).

7.1 Privacy-Preserving Security Monitoring Architectures

Given that long-term log retention poses the main privacy risk, monitoring architectures of the future will likely incorporate technologies that minimize privacy leakages while still allowing security monitoring functionalities to be well supported (Lee et al., 2021). One of the most exciting ideas is that data anonymization and pseudonymization can be done in real-time within the monitoring data streams directly, and the so-created data records are what get actually stored for further use. Moreover, it is possible to establish a certain amount of detachment between security analysts and the individuals whose data is being analyzed through the use of pseudonymization(Hyassat et al., 2025). There is a well-defined set of personnel that have access to detokenization through authorization and that is what happens when it is very necessary to use the original identifiers during the investigation that is in progress. Besides that, new privacy analytics methods like differential privacy and secure multi-party computation allow analyzing patterns of security even from the aggregated view of the data without revealing any individual data point properties. For instance, with the help of differential privacy, the analysts will easily notice if there are unusual login activities happening across the workforce while at the same time, the actions of individual staff members remain invisible from a statistical standpoint. Such methods contribute to significantly minimizing the privacy risks of storing and analyzing data over a long period of time(Jan et al., 2025).

In the future, monitoring architectures will likely make use of federated security analytics to some degree. With federated security analytics, each local site retains control of its own security logs instead of one centralized location. The analytical models are sent to the different systems and are trained locally, and only the resulted aggregated insights are shared with central monitoring platforms. This way, there is no need to make a huge centralized dataset while still being able to have a complete picture of the threats that exist globally. By eliminating the accumulation of sensitive telemetry in a single centralized location, federated monitoring architectures are able to achieve a significant reduction of privacy exposure and the use of simpler data governance practices. Besides that, zero-trust monitoring is being embraced by more and more organizations, which is why access to monitoring data is very strictly controlled and continuously reevaluated. Analysts are given very limited access to only those parts of log repositories which are related to their investigations and well aligned with their roles and responsibilities instead of getting the entire log repository(Al-Momani et al., 2025).

7.2 Emerging Regulatory Trends in Data Lifecycle Governance

Large repositories of detailed behavioral information about individuals and organizations are increasingly becoming a concern to governments and regulatory bodies. Predictably more regulatory trends will see an emphasis placed on transparency, accountability, and proportionality in the way's lifecycle governance is conducted. One of the major developments in this area is the application of data protection concepts to the sphere of cybersecurity monitoring. Security monitoring data was often treated differently from other types of organizational information due to the security operations being considered the justification for such monitoring(R. Alabdallat et al., 2025). Nevertheless, regulators have come to realize that monitoring logs can also be a source of personal data, and as such, they are protected by privacy laws. The implication is that organizations must be able to demonstrate their compliance to data protection principles when subjected to monitoring activities. These principles include among others purpose limitation, storage limitation, and data minimization. Increased focus on documentation and accountability mechanisms is another aspect of regulatory trends(Mahadin et al., 2025).

Expectations for accountability often translate to requirements for recordkeeping that documents the justification for the collection and retention of data, the retention periods, and the safeguards that protect the data. These papers constitute a record for the regulator to trace a program actively managing and monitoring the risk rather than permitting indefinite retention without any control. Regulatory emphasis is also on algorithmic transparency(Hiari et al., 2025). Security monitoring systems of today tightly integrate AI in the decision-making logic raising the question of how data retention and deletion judgments are done. If the automated lifecycle decisions, that is, the selection of the logs which are retained or deleted, are made by AI, then the entities have to show that the AI decisions are just, understandable, and complying with the laws and regulations. The governance structures, hence, should be capable of facilitating recording the rationale for the automatic decisions. Global regulatory convergence is shaping the regulatory trend as well(Khaled Abdullah & Qawasmeh, 2025). Cyber threats often have no borders, and therefore, it is only logical for governments to look for ways to standardize cybersecurity and privacy regulations globally to reduce the burden on companies that operate in multiple jurisdictions, for example, retention practices, breach reporting obligations, and requirements for evidence preservation. Businesses will require lifecycle governance frameworks that allow them to meet their changing regulatory requirements as these regulatory landscapes evolve.

7.3 Towards Adaptive Retention Models for Security Data Repositories

Over time, lifecycle governance will be evolving and adapting the way it retains data so as to better meet the changing needs of the environment, rather than sticking with a rigid retention schedule. Fixed retention periods for log categories are defined in traditional governance systems. Besides being a guarantee of governance compliance, this approach does not take into consideration the fact that security threats, regulatory requirements, technology, and so on are always evolving. Taking advantage of multiple inputs for governance is how adaptive models are able to work(Qaddara & Alraba'nah, 2025). These include, but are not limited to, threat intelligence feeds, incident investigation history, regulatory requirements, and repository performance metrics. Lifecycle management systems by jointly analyzing all these factors are able to decide whether a retention period should change. In addition to that, adaptive models are able to rank lifecycle tasks based on risk. With their limited attention span and time, analysts have to make wise use of it by focusing on the investigation of high-value or high-risk logs, cutting the time spent on less pertinent log data, and doing the latter in a manner that does not sacrifice the overall security posture of the organization. To this end, the part of the logs that is of the highest security interest should be readily available, whereas the routine operational telemetry should be subject to shorter retention cycles. Thus, the prioritization results in an organization being able to have investigative visibility to a great extent without being overloaded with lots of low-value data(Marhoon et al., 2025).

Adaptive models are further capable of supporting progressive data transformation strategies. Therefore, they do not only focus on deleting logs once the specified retention period expires but also periodically transforming the older records by keeping them of reduced details. Initially, the finest and most detailed event log records may be kept. However, at a later stage, they can be changed into summary datasets consisting of only metrics that have been aggregated or anonymized identifiers. On the one hand, this pattern keeps the preservation of analytical insights for the long-term, on the other hand, it leads to exposure to privacy and costs reduction. At the same time, policy management that is more mature, automated analytics and regulatory oversight will be the main ingredients of the sophisticated governance frameworks that will be necessary for the implementation of the adaptive retention models in future(Babaker et al., 2025). Luckily,these smart systems are very capable (Alnawayseh et al., 2022). Besides a few benefits, they allow companies, first of all, to keep up with the latest threats and regulations and secondly, to handle security data storage in a very efficient and responsible way. Simply put, the security data lifecycle governance environment will be dramatically transformed in the future by the creation of new technologies, stricter regulatory requirements, and increased cybersecurity threats. AI, privacy-driven data analysis, and flexible retention techniques will be some of those that will change the way organizations handle the data they use for monitoring. Leverage these innovations, organizations will develop data governance frameworks that prioritize data security without sacrificing the effectiveness and sustainability of their security monitoring .

REFERENCES

Abashes, G. M., Elshqeirat, B., Abu-Shareha, A. A., & Alshraideh, M. (2025). BEYOND THE NOISE: UNVEILING MEANINGFUL PATTERNS IN MOBILE PAYMENT DATA USING FUZZY LOGIC AND SVM. *Journal of Theoretical and Applied Information Technology*, *103*(1).

Abdeljaber, O., & Al-Masaeed, S. (2025). Al-Mu'ani, L., Yaseen, H., & Alhnaity, B. (2025). Strategic Intelligence: The Power of AI in Planning Efficiency. *Human Behavior and Emerging Technologies*, (1). Advance online publication. DOI: 10.1155/hbe2/5383054

Abualghanam, O., Alazzam, H., Qatawneh, M., Alazab, M., & Al Sharaiah, M. (2025). Elevating Mobile Security: An Ensemble Approach for Enhanced Malware Detection with M-iForest. *International Journal of Interactive Mobile Technologies*, *19*(10), 129–151. Advance online publication. DOI: 10.3991/ijim.v19i10.51319

Abualhaj, M. M., Abu-Shareha, A. A., Al-Khatib, S. N., Alsaaidah, A. M., & Anbar, M. (2025). Improving firewall performance using hybrid of optimization algorithms and decision trees classifier. *IAES International Journal of Artificial Intelligence*, *14*(4), 2839. Advance online publication. DOI: 10.11591/ijai.v14.i4.pp2839-2848

Abualhaj, M. M., Abu-Shareha, A. A., & Rateb, R. (2025). Enhancing intrusion detection systems with hybrid HHO-WOA optimization and gradient boosting machine classifier. *International Journal of Reconfigurable and Embedded Systems*, *14*(2), 518. Advance online publication. DOI: 10.11591/ijres.v14.i2.pp518-526

Abualhaj, M. M., Al-Khatib, S., Al Shafi, N., Qaddara, I., & Hyassat, A. (2025). Utilizing Gray Wolf Optimization Algorithm in Malware Forensic Investigation. *Journal of Computational and Cognitive Engineering*, *4*(4), 591–602. Advance online publication. DOI: 10.47852/bonviewJCCE52025053

Abualhaj, M. M.I, Al-Khatib, S. N., Abu-Shareha, A. A., Almomani, O., Al-Mimi, H., Al-Allawee, A., Daoud, M. S., & Anbar, M. (2025). Spam Detection Boosted by Firefly-Based Feature Selection and Optimized Classifiers. *International Journal of Advances in Soft Computing and Its Applications*, *17*(3). Advance online publication. DOI: 10.15849/IJASCA.251130.02

Abualhaj, M. M., Al-Khatib, S. N., Abu-Shareha, A. A., Hyassat, A., & Daoud, M. S. (2025). Smart Firewall for Phishing Detection Powered by Bio-Inspired Algorithms. *Journal of Advances in Information Technology*, *16*(11), 1529–1539. Advance online publication. DOI: 10.12720/jait.16.11.1529-1539

Abualhaj, M. M., Al-Khatib, S. N., Al Zyoud, M., Qaddara, I., & Anbar, M. (2025). Enhancing Intrusion Detection System Performance Using a Hybrid of Harris Hawks and Whale Optimization Algorithms. *Engineering. Technology and Applied Science Research*, *15*(4), 24354–24361. Advance online publication. DOI: 10.48084/etasr.10919

Abualhaj, M. M., Al-Khatib, S. N., Al-Zyoud, M., Qaddara, I., Hiari, M. O., & Aldossary, S. M. A. (2025). Enhanced Network Communication Security Through Hybrid Dragonfly-Bat Feature Selection for Intrusion Detection. *The Journal of Communication*, *20*(5). Advance online publication. DOI: 10.12720/jcm.20.5.607-618

Abualigah, L., Almomani, M. H., Alomari, S. A., Zitar, R. A., Migdady, H., Saleem, K., Snasel, V., Smerat, A., & Ezugwu, A. E. (2025). Optimizing Intrusion Detection in Wireless Sensor Networks via the Improved Chameleon Swarm Algorithm for Feature Selection. *IET Communications*, *19*(1), e70029. Advance online publication. DOI: 10.1049/cmu2.70029

Abuowaida, S., Abu Owida, H., Shelash Mohammad, S. I., Alshdaifat, N., Abu Elsoud, E., Alazaidah, R., Vasudevan, A., & Alshurideh, M. T. (2025). Evidence Detection in Cloud Forensics: Classifying Cyber-Attacks in IaaS Environments using machine learning. *Data and Metadata*, *4*, 699. Advance online publication. DOI: 10.56294/dm2025699

Ahmed, K. A., Ibrahim, A., Qudr, L. A. Z., Tawfeq, J. F., Al Falahi, Q., & Radhi, A. D. (2025). *Developing Adaptive AI-Driven Cybersecurity Frameworks for Real-Time Detection of Polymorphic Malware in IoT Networks*. DOI: 10.1109/ICBATS66542.2025.11258540

Al-Adwan, A. S., & Abdeljaber, O. (2025). Toward a resilient and smart supply chain: identifying and prioritizing barriers to metaverse adoption. *International Journal of Industrial Engineering and Operations Management*. DOI: 10.1108/IJIEOM-06-2025-0113

Al-Adwan, A. S., Al-Adwan, A., Li, N., Fauzi, M. A., Jafar, R. M. S., Habibi, A., & Falahat, M. (2025). IMMERSIVE LEARNING MEETS THEORY: MODELING EDUVERSE ADOPTION IN HIGHER EDUCATION. *Journal of Information Technology Education*, *24*, 042. Advance online publication. DOI: 10.28945/5669

Al-Dmour, R., Al-Dmour, H., Al-Dmour, A., Basheer Amin, E., & Al-Dmour, Y. (2025). *AI and big data-driven social media recruitment: the mediating role of talent acquisition and employee engagement in bank performance*. Digital Transformation and Society., DOI: 10.1108/DTS-02-2025-0042

Al-Habashneh, A. G., Al-Daoud, K. I., Oraini, B., Al, , & Shelash, S. I. (2025). The impact of artificial intelligence on the development of electronic financial services. *International Journal of Data and Network Science*, *9*(2), 317–322. Advance online publication. DOI: 10.5267/j.ijdns.2024.8.012

Al Hindi, G., Alshraideh, M., Hussein, A. H., Eliyan, L. F., & Al-Dhaqm, A. (2025). Hacking Back: Using Genetic Algorithms to Outsmart Hackers. *Journal of Computational Science*, *21*(9), 2049–2064. Advance online publication. DOI: 10.3844/jcssp.2025.2049.2064

Al-Momani, M. M., Alqudah, T. A., Al Swiety, I. A., Mahrakani, N., Nassoura, M. B. A., & Al Attar, M. K. (2025). Integrating Artificial Intelligence (AI) and Business Intelligence (BI): A Framework for Improving Enterprise Performance. *TEM Journal, 14*(3). https://doi.org/DOI: 10.18421/TEM143-26

Al-Mousa, M., Amer, W., Abualhaj, M., Albilasi, S., Nasir, O., & Samara, G. (2025). Agile Proactive Cybercrime Evidence Analysis Model for Digital Forensics. *The International Arab Journal of Information Technology*, *22*(3). Advance online publication. DOI: 10.34028/iajit/22/3/15

Al-Okbi, N. K., Alomari, S. A., Hadi, W. J., Ajrash, A. S., Smerat, A., & Abualigah, L. (2025). Defending Digital Integrity: Advances in Media Forgery Analysis Research and Cybersecurity Development. *SN Computer Science*, *6*(8), 913. Advance online publication. DOI: 10.1007/s42979-025-04462-8

Al-Okbi, N. K., Alomari, S. A., Zitar, R. A., Smerat, A., Nazzal, M. A., & Abualigah, L. (2025). Integrating Multimodal Emotion Recognition with Deep Q-Learning for Adaptive Social Robot Interaction. *International Journal of Robotics and Control Systems*, *5*(4), 2265–2289. Advance online publication. DOI: 10.31763/ijrcs.v5i4.2055

Alabdallat, R., Abualhaj, M., & Abu-Shareha, A. (2025). Android Malware Detection Using a Modified Dwarf Mongoose Algorithm. *International Journal of Intelligent Engineering and Systems*, *18*(8), 336–351. Advance online publication. DOI: 10.22266/ijies2025.0930.21

Alabdallat, R. D., Abualhaj, M. M., & Abu-Shareha, A. (2025). Enhanced Multiclass Android Malware Detection Using a Modified Dwarf Mongoose Algorithm. *International Journal of Analysis and Applications*, *23*, 248. Advance online publication. DOI: 10.28924/2291-8639-23-2025-248

Aldaaja, Y., Odeh, M., Badrakhan, S. S., Sabri, M., Abdelrahim, Y., Samara, G., & Alsabatin, H. (2025). Quantifying the Managerial and Practical Benefits of Cloud Computing on Information Security in Higher Education Institutions. *Applied Mathematics & Information Sciences*, *19*(1), 15–24. Advance online publication. DOI: 10.18576/amis/190102

Aldabbas, A., Baniata, L. H., Alsaaidah, B. A., Mustafa, Z., Alali, M., & Rateb, R. (2025). Artificial intelligence-driven method for the discovery and prevention of distributed denial of service attacks. *IAES International Journal of Artificial Intelligence*, *14*(1), 614. Advance online publication. DOI: 10.11591/ijai.v14.i1.pp614-628

Alenazi, M. J. F., Al-Khasawneh, M. A., Rahman, S., & Faheem, Z. (2025). Deep Reinforcement Learning Based Flow Aware-QoS Provisioning in SD-IoT for Precision Agriculture. *Computational Intelligence*, *41*(1), e70023. Advance online publication. DOI: 10.1111/coin.70023

Ali, A. M., Al-Qerem, A., Hassan, M. R., Abu-Khadrah, A., & Jarrah, M. (2025). Traffic Monitoring and Control System for Smart City Pollution Regulation Using IoT and Correlated Capsule Networks. *IEEE Access : Practical Innovations, Open Solutions*, *13*, 46983–47003. Advance online publication. DOI: 10.1109/ACCESS.2025.3550966

Almomani, O., Arabiat, A., Al Tayeb, M., Almaiah, M. A., Obeidat, M., Aldhyani, T. H. H., Shehab, R., & Rowad, M. (2025). A Robust Model for Android Malware Detection via ML and DL classifiers. *Mesopotamian Journal of Big Data*, *2025*. Advance online publication. DOI: 10.58496/MJBD/2025/017

Alnawayseh, S. E. A., Al-Sit, W. T., & Ghazal, T. M. (2022). Smart Congestion Control in 5G/6G Networks Using Hybrid Deep Learning Techniques. *Complexity*, *2022*(1), 1781952. Advance online publication. DOI: 10.1155/2022/1781952

Alraba'nah, Y., Al-Sharaeh, S., & Al Hindi, G. (2025). Enhancing Intrusion Detection Using Hybrid Long Short-Term Memory and XGBoost. *Journal of Soft Computing and Data Mining*, *6*(1). Advance online publication. DOI: 10.30880/jscdm.2025.06.01.016

Arabiat, A. M. (2025). Intelligent Model for Detecting GAN-Generated Images Based on Multi-Classifier and Advanced Data Mining Techniques. *International Journal of Electrical and Electronic Engineering and Telecommunications*, *14*(3). Advance online publication. DOI: 10.18178/ijeetc.14.3.147-157

Arabiat, A. M., & Eljaafreh, Y. G. (2025). Intrusion Detection in Wireless Sensor Networks Using ML Based Classification of Denial of Service (DoS) Attacks. *The Journal of Communication*, *20*(4). Advance online publication. DOI: 10.12720/jcm.20.4.501-514

Awais, Z., Hussain, M., Elshenawy, A., Arsalan, A., Anwar, M., Asif Habib, M., Jabbar, S., & Ahmad, M. (2025). ISCC: Intelligent Semantic Caching and Control for NDN-Enabled Industrial IoT Networks. *IEEE Access : Practical Innovations, Open Solutions*, *13*, 169881–169898. Advance online publication. DOI: 10.1109/ACCESS.2025.3614984

Babaker, S., Khatibi, A., Alsoud, A. R., Kaur, J., Jagtap, J., Alkhayyat, A., & Shah, S. K. (2025). Improving Reliability and Data Management in Internet of Things Based Wireless Sensor Networks. *Internet Technology Letters*, *8*(6), e646. Advance online publication. DOI: 10.1002/itl2.646

Ebbini, M. M., Qtaishat, A. K., Aburub, F. A., & Jaradat, M. S. (2025). Impact of Ethical Fintech on Micro Entrepreneurs in Jordan. *International Journal of Advances in Soft Computing and Its Applications*, *17*(3). Advance online publication. DOI: 10.15849/IJASCA.251130.10

Eke, C. I., Al-Shamayleh, A. S., Phiri, M., Maswadi, K., Kwaghtyo, D. K., Mulenga, M., & Iyidobi, C. J. (2025). Machine Learning Based Mobile Big Data Analytics: State-of-the-art Applications, Taxonomy, Challenges and Future Research Directions. *Nigerian Journal of Technological Development*, *22*(4). Advance online publication. DOI: 10.63746/njtd.v22i4.3385

Ghazal, T. M. (2025). Federated Learning for Intelligent Sensing and Navigation Technologies for 6G Communications. *Journal of Sensors, 2025*(1). DOI: 10.1155/js/3746147

Ghazal, T. M., Abu-Shareha, A., Mustafa, S. A., Ibrahim, A., & Ahmed, S. M. (2025). Privacy-Preserving Transformer-Based Meta-Learning Algorithm for Zero-Day Intrusion Detection in IoT-Enabled Smart Grids. *Journal of Internet Services and Information Security*, *15*(4), 76–84. Advance online publication. DOI: 10.58346/JISIS.2025.I4.006

Ghazal, T. M., Abualhaj, M., Ahmed, A. A., Al-Tarawni, M. A. M., & Maghrabi, L. A. (2025). Federated Deep Graph Neural Network Algorithm for Real-Time Intrusion Detection in Heterogeneous IoT Systems. *Journal of Internet Services and Information Security*, *15*(4), 484–497. Advance online publication. DOI: 10.58346/JISIS.2025.I4.035

Ghazal, T. M., Awouda, A. E., Hasan, M. K., Rahman, A. H. A., Islam, S., Saeed, R. A., Elshafie, H., Iqbal, A., & Hussein, A. H. (2025). Knowledge Learning for Securing Workflow Scheduling Algorithm in Mobile Edge Computing. *Mobile Networks and Applications*, *30*(3-4), 395–413. Advance online publication. DOI: 10.1007/s11036-025-02465-6

Ghazal, T. M., Hasan, M. K., Abdul Wahab, A. N., Ibrahim, A., Khan, W. A., Raza, N. Z., Atta, A., & Mago, B. (2022). Towards Privacy Provisioning for Internet of Things (IoT). *International Conference on Cyber Resilience, ICCR 2022*. DOI: 10.1109/ICCR56254.2022.9995916

Ghazal, T. M., Hasan, M. K., Alzoubi, H. M., Al Hmmadi, M., Al-Dmour, N. A., Islam, S., Kamran, R., & Mago, B. (2022). Securing Smart Cities Using Blockchain Technology. *2022 1st International Conference on AI in Cybersecurity, ICAIC 2022*. DOI: 10.1109/ICAIC53980.2022.9896971

Ghazal, T. M., Hasan, M. K., Raju, K. N., Khan, M. A., Alshamayleh, A., Bhatt, M. W., & Ahmad, M. (2025). Data Space Privacy Model with Federated Learning Technique for Securing IoT Communications in Autonomous Marine Vehicles. *Journal of Intelligent & Robotic Systems, 111*(3), 84. Advance online publication. DOI: 10.1007/s10846-025-02298-1

Ghazal, T. M., Janjua, J. I., Abushiba, W., Ahmad, M., Ihsan, A., & Al-Dmour, N. A. (2024). Cybersecurity Revolution via Large Language Models and Explainable AI. *2024 17th International Conference on Security of Information and Networks, SIN 2024*. DOI: 10.1109/SIN63213.2024.10871324

Hasan, M. K., Ghazal, T. M., Issa, G., Islam, S., Ismail, A. F., & Kabir, S. R. (2025). Hashgraph consensus-based simultaneous, asynchronous and big-data supported blockchain mechanism for IT-OT enabled critical infrastructure sectors. *Journal of Ambient Intelligence and Humanized Computing*. Advance online publication. DOI: 10.1007/s12652-024-04942-4

Hiari, M., Alraba'nah, Y., & Qaddara, I. (2025). A Deep Learning-Based Intrusion Detection System using Refined LSTM for DoS Attack Detection. *Engineering. Technology and Applied Science Research, 15*(4), 25627–25633. Advance online publication. DOI: 10.48084/etasr.11499

Hyassat, A. S., Abu Zayed, R. E., Al Khateeb, E. A., Shalaldeh, A., Abdelhamied, M. M., & Qaddara, I. (2025). Unveiling Cyber Threats: An In-Depth Study on Data Mining Techniques for Exploit Attack Detection †. *Engineering Proceedings, 104*(1), 28. Advance online publication. DOI: 10.3390/engproc2025104028

Iftikhar, A., Mohammad, S. I., Alqudah, M. N., Al-Adwan, A. S., Vasudevan, A., Ali, I., & Farhan, M. (2025). Evaluating Inclusivity and Fairness of AI Recruitment Tools for Hiring People with Disabilities in the United Arab Emirates(UAE). *Data and Metadata, 4*. Advance online publication. DOI: 10.56294/dm2025487

Iskandarani, M. Z. (2025). Effect of Adaptive Intelligent Reflective Surfaces on SINR in a Wireless Communication System. *The Journal of Communication, 20*(1). Advance online publication. DOI: 10.12720/jcm.20.1.1-11

Jan, F. U., Badar, R., Sami Al-Shamayleh, A., Uehara, A., Senjyu, T., & Akhunzada, A. (2025). Soft Computing-Based Damping Controllers With Online Parameters Tuning for Stability Enhancement of Power Systems. *IEEE Access : Practical Innovations, Open Solutions, 13*, 167045–167060. Advance online publication. DOI: 10.1109/ACCESS.2025.3612288

Khaled Abdullah, S., & Qawasmeh, R. (2025). *Navigating the ethical and legal risks of AI marketing in Jordanian SMEs*. EDPACS., DOI: 10.1080/07366981.2025.2600205

Khatibi, A., Babaker, S., Praveen, K. N. R., Chohan, J. S., Jadhav, A., Alsoud, A. R., Ramudu, M. J., & Jeet, R. (2025). Advanced AI-Driven Cybersecurity: Analyzing Emerging Threats and Defensive Strategies. *National Academy Science Letters*. Advance online publication. DOI: 10.1007/s40009-025-01897-8

Laha, S. R., Smadi, K. Al, Habboush, A. K., Pattanayak, B. K., Pattnaik, S., & Mohanty, B. (2025). Smart Waste Management Framework for Green Cities: Integrating IoT, LoRa, and Deep Learning for Efficient Waste Classification and Management. *Tikrit Journal of Engineering Sciences, 32*(Special Issue 1). DOI: 10.25130/tjes.sp1.2025.1

Lee, S. W., Hussain, S., Issa, G. F., Abbas, S., Ghazal, T. M., Sohail, T., Ahmad, M., & Khan, M. A. (2021). Multi-Dimensional Trust Quantification by Artificial Agents through Evidential Fuzzy Multi-Criteria Decision Making. *IEEE Access : Practical Innovations, Open Solutions*, *9*, 159399–159412. Advance online publication. DOI: 10.1109/ACCESS.2021.3131521

Mahadin, G. A. L., Satvika, S., Kathuria, S., Kaushik, A., & Maranan, R. (2025). DEEP LEARNING FRAMEWORK FOR IDENTIFYING AND HYBRID SYNTHESIZING WIDESPREAD NEWS HEADLINES ON SOCIAL MEDIA. *Proceedings on Engineering Sciences*, *7*(3), 1453–1462. Advance online publication. DOI: 10.24874/PES07.03.007

Makhadmeh, S. N., Fraihat, S., Awad, M., Sanjalawe, Y., Al-Betar, M. A., & Awadallah, M. A. (2025). A crossover-integrated Marine Predator Algorithm for feature selection in intrusion detection systems within IoT environments. *Internet of Things : Engineering Cyber Physical Human Systems*, *31*, 101536. Advance online publication. DOI: 10.1016/j.iot.2025.101536

Marhoon, H. M., Basil, N., Sabbar, B. M., Qasem, N., & Ma'arif, A. (2025). Safety and Surveillance on Unmanned Aerial Vehicles Control Systems and Optimization Methods: A Systematic Review. *International Journal of Robotics and Control Systems*, *5*(5). Advance online publication. DOI: 10.31763/ijrcs.v5i5.1859

Masango, N. C., Agushaka, J. O., Amaefule, M. C., Taiwo, O., Zhang, P., Ezugwu, A. E., Saleem, K., Smerat, A., & Abualigah, L. (2025). Secure and efficient cloudlet networks: blockchain integration with agent-based proof of trust mechanism. *Eurasip Journal on Wireless Communications and Networking*, *2025*(1). DOI: 10.1186/s13638-025-02439-y

Maz, Y. A., Anbar, M., Manickam, S., Abualhaj, M. M., Almalki, S. A., & Alabsi, B. A. (2025). Transfer Learning-Based Approach with an Ensemble Classifier for Detecting Keylogging Attack on the Internet of Things. *Computers, Materials & Continua*, *85*(3), 5287–5307. Advance online publication. DOI: 10.32604/cmc.2025.068257

Mohammad, S. I., Al-Daoud, K., Al Qraini, B., Khanfar, I. A. A., & Vasudevan, A. (2025). Quantum Error Correction with Surface Code Analysis on Quantum Computing platform. *Applied Mathematics & Information Sciences*, *19*(2), 423–435. Advance online publication. DOI: 10.18576/amis/190216

Qaddara, I., & Alraba'nah, Y. (2025). Enhancing Requirements Classification Using Machine Learning Techniques. *SN Computer Science*, *6*(6), 649. Advance online publication. DOI: 10.1007/s42979-025-04158-z

Qaddara, I., Alrabaynah, Y., & Hiari, M. O. (2025). Evaluation of SQL and NoSQL Databases on Parallel Processing. *Engineering. Technology and Applied Science Research*, *15*(4), 24298–24304. Advance online publication. DOI: 10.48084/etasr.10620

Qawasmeh, S., Habboushb, A., Elzaghmouri, B., Kharma, Q., & Albalawneh, D. (2025). Hybrid Convolutional Neural Network-Based Intrusion Detection System for Secure IoT Networks. *Tikrit Journal of Engineering Sciences*, *32*(SP1), 1–11. Advance online publication. DOI: 10.25130/tjes.sp1.2025.2

Rabbi, M. F., Amin, M., Al-Dalahmeh, M., & Abdullah, M. (2025). Assessing the role of information technology in promoting environmental sustainability and preventing crime in E-commerce. *International Review of Applied Sciences and Engineering*, *16*(1), 81–97. Advance online publication. DOI: 10.1556/1848.2024.00834

Ramesh, J. V. N., Nimma, D., Dasari, R., Chaudhari Rane, D., AlGhamdi, A., Rao, K. B. V. B., Haider, S. A., Kuzieva, N., & Jangir, P. (2025). Safe and Reliable Two-Stage Online Offloading Algorithm for Transportation Cyber-Physical Systems. *IEEE Transactions on Intelligent Transportation Systems*, *26*(9), 14313–14322. Advance online publication. DOI: 10.1109/TITS.2025.3539934

Raza, M. A., Karim, A., Alqarni, M., Al-Khasawneh, M. A., Jumani, T. A., Aman, M., & Masud, M. I. (2025). An Intelligent Long Short-Term Memory-Based Machine Learning Model for the Potential Assessment of Global Hydropower Capacity in Sustainable Energy Transition and Security. *Energies*, *18*(13), 3324. Advance online publication. DOI: 10.3390/en18133324

Saeed, N. M. S. E., Ibrahim, A., Ali, L., Al-Dmour, N. A., Mohammed, A. S., & Ghazal, T. M. (2024). Unveiling the Landscape of Machine Learning and Deep Learning Methodologies in Network Security: A Comprehensive Literature Review. *2nd International Conference on Cyber Resilience, ICCR 2024*. DOI: 10.1109/ICCR61006.2024.10533066

Samanta, I. S., Mohanty, S., Rout, P. K., Parida, S. M., Panda, S., Bajaj, M., Blazek, V., & Prokop, L. (2025). A comprehensive review of feature extraction techniques for power quality event detection with novel approaches for enhanced classification in smart grids. *Electrical Engineering*, *107*(9), 12227–12259. Advance online publication. DOI: 10.1007/s00202-025-03149-w

Sardar, R., Anees, T., Al-Shamayleh, A. S., Mehmood, E., Khalil, W., Akhunzada, A., & Shaikh, F. S. (2025). Challenges in detecting security threats in WoT: A systematic literature review. *Artificial Intelligence Review*, *58*(7), 196. Advance online publication. DOI: 10.1007/s10462-025-11176-z

Shamaylah, N., Ibrahim Mohammad, S., Al Oraini, B., Yaseen Al-Gaafreh, J. M., Mosallam Alqahtani, M., Vasudevan, A., Shlash Mohammad, A. A., & Ahmmad Hunitie, M. F. (2025). Data-Driven Decision-Making for Employee Training and Development in Jordanian Public Institutions. *Data and Metadata*, *4*, 886. Advance online publication. DOI: 10.56294/dm2025886

Shambour, Q., Al-Zyoud, M., & Almomani, O. (2025). Quantum-Inspired Hybrid Metaheuristic Feature Selection with SHAP for Optimized and Explainable Spam Detection. *Symmetry*, *17*(10), 1716. Advance online publication. DOI: 10.3390/sym17101716

Shambour, Q. Y., Al-Zyoud, M., & Hussein, A. H. (2025). FROM DATA TO DIAGNOSIS: KNOWLEDGE-DRIVEN, EXPLAINABLE AI FOR RELIABLE EARLY AUTISM DETECTION. *Interdisciplinary Journal of Information, Knowledge, and Management*, *20*, 032. Advance online publication. DOI: 10.28945/5652

Sharma, K. P., Al-Rashed, A., Johar, M. G. M., Alsoud, A. R., Singh, A., Dey, P., & Pant, S. (2025). Blockchain-Assisted Trust Framework for Increased Survivability in Internet of Vehicles. *Internet Technology Letters*, *8*(3), e70029. Advance online publication. DOI: 10.1002/itl2.70029

Sharma, K. P., Hussain, R., Jaharadak, A. A., Trawnih, A. A., Verma, D., Dasi, S., & Pant, S. (2025). Hybrid Convolutional Neural Network for Robust Attack Detection in Wireless Sensor Networks. *Internet Technology Letters*, *8*(6), e650. Advance online publication. DOI: 10.1002/itl2.650

Sharma, K. P., Yajid, M. S. A., Gowrishankar, J., Mahajan, R., Alsoud, A. R., Jadhav, A., & Singh, D. (2025). A Systematic Review on Text Summarization: Techniques, Challenges, Opportunities. In *Expert Systems* (Vol. 42, Number 4). DOI: 10.1111/exsy.13833

Turab, N., Abushattal, A., Al-Nabulsi, J., & Owida, H. A. (2025). Advanced risk assessment using machine learning and sentiment analysis on log data. *IAES International Journal of Artificial Intelligence*, *14*(5), 3897. Advance online publication. DOI: 10.11591/ijai.v14.i5.pp3897-3905

Vasudevan, A., Tamilmani, K. T., Mohammad, S. I., Sridheepika, V. S., Raja, N., Soon, E. E. H., Nagaraj, S., & Al-Adwan, A. S. (2025). Voices of Concern: Contemplations on Socioeconomic, Ethical, and Developmental Impacts of AI. *Applied Mathematics & Information Sciences*, *19*(1), 221–232. Advance online publication. DOI: 10.18576/amis/190119

Yaseen, M., Ali, E., Sarwar, N., Jamel, L., Din, I., Yuldashev, F., & Law, F. (2025). Design of Minimal Spanning Tree and Analytic Hierarchical Process (SAHP) Based Hybrid Technique for Software Requirements Prioritization. *IET Software, 2025*(1). DOI: 10.1049/sfw2/8819735

Zhu, Y., Lin, X., Kim, J., Al-Adwan, A. S., & Li, N. (2025). Exploring Human Interaction in Online Self-Regulated Learning Through Danmaku Comments. *International Journal of Human-Computer Interaction*, *41*(22), 13964–13977. Advance online publication. DOI: 10.1080/10447318.2025.2480826

Zraiqat, A., Al Sayyed, O., Al Soudi, M., Al-Salih, A. A. M. M., Smerat, A., Montazeri, Z., Dehghani, M., Malik, O. P., Ahmed, M. A., Ibraheem, I. K., & Eguchi, K. (2025). Key Maker Algorithm: A Novel Human-Based Metaheuristic for Constrained Optimization. *International Journal of Intelligent Engineering and Systems*, *18*(9), 688–699. Advance online publication. DOI: 10.22266/ijies2025.1031.45

Chapter 7
Determining Responsibility for Artificial Intelligence-Based Security Decision Making

Omar Alhyari
http://orcid.org/0000-0002-4046-6564
The British University in Dubai, UAE

Waseem Safi
http://orcid.org/0009-0006-7687-1496
Alrasheed Private University, Syria

ABSTRACT

The chapter discusses the determination of who is responsible when artificial intelligence is used for security decision making within complex organizational environments. It looks at how accountability is shared among system designers, vendors, deployers, and human operators when AI-driven tools are used to influence detection actions, prioritization, and response. The chapter investigates legal principles explaining the relationship between control, foreseeability, and duty of care, along with regulatory requirements for human oversight and governance. It also examines issues related to automation bias, black-box models, and extended decision chains that involve Security Operations Centers and third parties. Special focus is given to documentation, role clarity, chain of command for escalation, and auditability as means of defining responsibility. Through combining a legal perspective with security operational practice, the chapter outlines a system for determining responsibility, handling liability, and making defensible decisions in AI-assisted security systems.

1. INTRODUCTION

Growth in AI use in cybersecurity is a consequence of changes in the nature, scale, and complexity of cyber threats. Enterprises today are confronted with highly versatile adversaries, advanced persistent threat (APT), identity misuse, insider threat, third-party compromise, and radical cloud-native intrusion while their infrastructures remain distributed. Signature-based tools are still very much part of the security equation, but they are not enough if used alone when combating highly dynamic and low-and-slow

DOI: 10.4018/979-8-2600-2870-4.ch007

threats. AI-based techniques discover the sequences of abnormal, suspicious behavior, privilege misuse, and atypical correlations that might be invisible to static logic. As a result, artificial intelligence has become a strategic weapon for prevention and detection in particular.

On the other hand, AI operational success has given rise to a sort of technological trust that can easily run ahead of what is actually warranted. Security teams are likely to choose algorithmic outputs when they are in short of staff because the results can be obtained faster, the results are expressed quantitatively, and the outputs come with an impression of objectivity. However, AI systems are quite different from unbiased bystanders. What is normal, what is considered risky, what is a malicious sequence, and how much uncertainty one is willing to accept, these are the elements that shape the development and functioning of AI systems. Consequently, AI usage in cybersecurity will not only bring about technical effectiveness but will also introduce governance issues such as decision-making, control, and dispute (Abualhaj, Al-Khatib, Al-Zyoud, et al., 2025).

1.1 Automated Decision Making

Security operations centers (SOC) rely more and more on automated decision-making technologies to cope with the alert overload problem. A Security Operations Center (SOC) today is very likely to get thousands or even millions of signals in just one day. What AI does is act as a weapon that can be used to get rid of this massive number of signals by first sorting the most important ones, second by bringing together the same kind of events, third by removing false positives most likely, fourth by suggesting investigative steps, and fifth by executing responses. Such automation is very often indispensable for the operational continuity. Otherwise, analysts can easily get drowned in the large number of alerts and the main threat can be forgotten among the numerous alerts (Zraiqat et al., 2025). However, automated decision making in security is quite a different thing from just automation of routine IT processes. A security decision includes elements of probabilistic assessment, the urgency of the matter, and the impact of the decision. For example, the system can say that a user is compromised, a process is evil, or a transaction is dangerous even if it does not have complete certainty. In most cases, it has to work just with the information at hand. Therefore, responsibility for AI-assisted security decisions should not be limited to the mere fact of running code. It should rather be something that is the result of a judgment made under the authority of an organization and therefore, with the assumption of the risks that go along with it. If, for example, a system automatically denies access to a C-level executive to a critical platform because of an unusual login pattern, then it is not only the confidence level of the model that will be questioned. It will also be a matter of whether the organization had a formally accountable structure for allowing that kind of autonomous (Shi et al., 2025).

1.2 Legal and Ethical Challenges

A person might lose their job, reputation, or access due to a false positive or it might be them giving rise to the frustration of the due process. Equally, false negatives could leave customers, personnel, or the physical security of the company at risk. Targeting of specific work trends, groups, geographies, or departments in user behavior analysis may raise issues related to fairness and discrimination. On the other hand, if the decision-making model utilizes highly proprietary features and is not transparent, then the affected individuals might not be able to understand or challenge the decisions made against them in a meaningful way. Inadequate logging might result in the inability later to trace the reasons for an action taken or even carry out a proper investigation (Ahmed et al., 2022). Above mentioned difficulties convey that responsibility slightly exceeds the mere assignment of blame following a fault. In fact, it should be defined as an intention and ability of creating systems that ensure explanation, traceability, review capability, proportionality, and human intervention wherever possible including. Security automation from an ethical perspective should reflect the organization's values, individuals' rights, and principles of good . From a legal point of view, one needs to make sure that decisions are not only kept, can be audited, and traceable back to specific organizational actors (Abualhaj, Al-Khatib, Abu-Shareha, et al., 2025).

1.3 The Problem of Accountability

The accountability issue in autonomous security systems is graphically depicted in Figure 1. Accountability in these systems occurs on multiple levels. Developers determine the kind of model and how it is trained. Data engineers decide what the model is able to learn from. Vendors may set default thresholds and features of the product. Security executives at the director level decide the scope of deployment, and the extent to which the system is given the authority of response. Security analysts interact with the system are ultimately the ones who review, accept, reject, or ignore recommendations (Ali et al., 2025). Executives define the risk tolerance and the policy for governance. The institution as the legal entity authorizes the system's functioning. Therefore, responsibility is indeed spread throughout, but it must not become so diluted as to be nonsensical.

Figure 1. Decision Responsibility Layers in Artificial Intelligence Security Frameworks

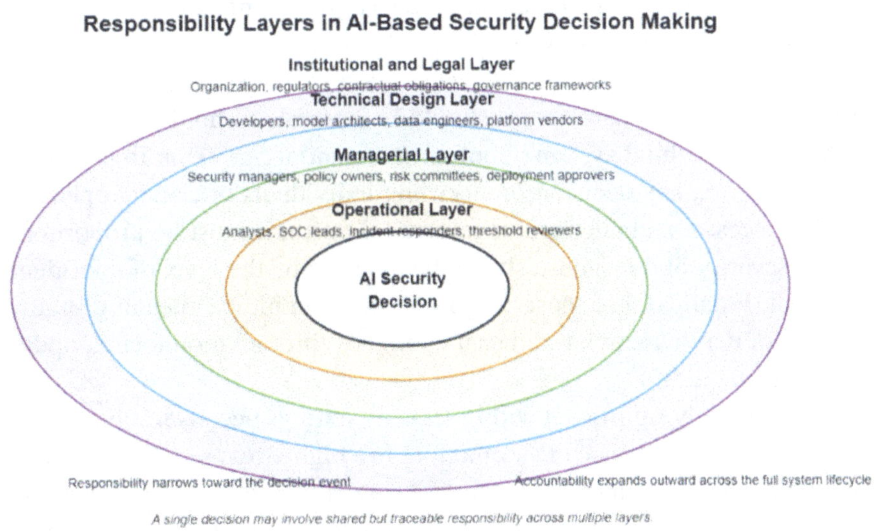

If the responsibility is spread over these different layers, the accountability must be consciously organized. For any major AI-based security operation, it should be feasible to give answers to the following five questions: Who came up with the model? Who gave the green light to its use? Who decided the operating points (thresholds)? Who was overseeing its performance? Who could give the go-ahead or block the autonomous response? These questions help to translate accountability from an intangible concept into day-to-day governance. This chapter contributes a Responsibility Allocation Framework for AI Security Decisions. The framework explains how responsibility should be distributed across model design, data preparation, vendor configuration, deployment authorization, threshold setting, analyst review, autonomous response, audit logging, appeal mechanisms, and post-incident accountability.

Existing cybersecurity studies often evaluate AI models through detection accuracy, false positive rates, and computational performance, while AI governance studies usually discuss accountability in broader automated decision-making contexts. Less attention has been given to how responsibility should be allocated among developers, vendors, SOC analysts, security managers, executive leadership, and organizations when AI systems influence security decisions. This chapter addresses that gap by linking technical model performance with governance responsibility and operational decision authority.

2. CONCEPTUAL FRAMEWORKS

2.1 Accountability Principles in Artificial Intelligence Governance

The very foundation of accountability in AI governance is that big decisions always remain trackable, reviewable, and attributable. When it comes to AI security systems, it's about such organizations being able to find out what led to a decision, what data and rules influenced it, who gave the go-ahead for the model to operate in a certain way, and what mechanisms of oversight existed when the decision was made. Therefore, accountability entails more than technical efficiency alone (Iskandarani, 2025). It incorporates documentation, procedural clarity, decision logging, and governance control . Typically, a solid accountability framework for cybersecurity AI comprises five rules. First, it must be traceable, in other words, it should be possible to trace the decision-making process even after the event. Second, it must be answerable, which means that it should be possible to hold actors responsible and capable of explaining the reasons behind system's configuration and usage (Duraimurugan et al., 2025). Third, it must be contestable, i.e., any decisions concerning individuals or critical operations must be able to be reviewed and if necessary, challenged or reversed. Fourth, it must be proportional, i.e., an increase in automation and severity of a response should be justified by the level of confidence and risk context of the model output. Finally, there must be governance continuity, meaning that accountability does not end at the stage of deployment but rather it continues through monitoring, updating and retiring of system (Al-Dmour et al., 2025).

These rules are extremely significant within security settings because defending against cyber threats so often involves quickening the pace of automation. In a high-stress security operations center (SOC), it is really common for teams to be inclined to sacrifice explainability for speed or review for containment. While these types of decisions from an operational standpoint might be comprehensible at least to some extent, they too leave no room for accountability. In fact, the more a system is enabled to perform independently and swiftly without the need for a human, the more bulletproof the governance framework must be ensuring the legality and transparency of such a system (Aldaaja et al., 2025). Automation lacking accountability might be seen as a sign of security maturity when in reality it can significantly increase the risk of the institution. Table 4 summarizes the main accountability principles for AI security decision .

Table 1. Core Accountability Principles for AI Security Governance

Accountability Principle	Meaning in AI Security Context	Practical Implication
Traceability	Ability to reconstruct how a decision was made	Maintain logs of data inputs, model outputs, and response steps
Answerability	Identifiable actors can justify system behavior	Assign named ownership for configuration and deployment
Contestability	Decisions can be reviewed and challenged	Enable override, appeal, or analyst review mechanisms
Proportionality	Response severity matches confidence and risk	Avoid highly disruptive autonomous actions on weak evidence
Governance Continuity	Accountability extends across system lifecycle	Monitor models after deployment and document updates

2.2 Human-in-the-Loop vs Fully Autonomous Security Decisions

A human-in-the-loop system is a one in which AI serves as an advisor or assistant but a human is the one who makes the final call. Given that AI is not capable of making the final decision without human consent or intervention, accountability remains much clearer and direct in such systems. Generally, the person responsible for the final decision becomes the one who is held accountable, which is the analyst or operator who formally signs off on the decision. This should not, however, be taken as an indication that the analyst is solely responsible when AI recommendation is simply a part of the bigger story (Khatibi et al., 2025). For example, if the AI model is inaccurate, the user interface is confusing, or staff are trained to over-rely on AI output, then the human confirmation is potentially masking a latent governance failure. The human-on-the-loop framework features a fully automated AI system that not only executes decisions but also takes certain actions and anyone can intervene and override the system if necessary. An example of this model is a semi-autonomous response platform that automatically blocks suspicious IPs or quarantines low-confidence threats subject to review later. In this case, the accountability is more diffused because the human is acting more like a supervisor than a decision-maker (Ghazal et al., 2024). If the system response is happening so fast that a human is, in effect, "out of the loop" then the whole claim of a human being "in the loop" is dubious (Khaled Abdullah & Qawasmeh, 2025).

Fully autonomous AI systems are one that both discover threat and take action without the necessity of human involvement. Only a few truly trustworthy systems are mature enough to operate such an environment without direct human intervention. Apart from the fact that people who directly approve individual actions will hardly be around, it becomes unclear who is responsible. It is the designers, deployers, authorizers and monitors of the autonomous policy environment who inherit responsibility in that case. It is worth noting that choosing among these different types of systems does not come down to a technical decision only. It is rather a governance decision about how much power the organization is willing to entrust to automated systems or how far they are comfortable delegating authority to machine-led decisions (Qawaqneh et al., 2025). Such a delegation has to be intentional and documented. An organization that allows a model to disable accounts or isolate production systems automatically cannot later argue that no one was responsible because "the system made the decision." The system acted only because the organization structured authority in that way (Sardar et al., 2025).

2.3 Responsibility Allocation Between Developers and Operators

A frequent problem in AI accountability is figuring out how responsibility ought to be split between the builders of the system and those who operate it. When developers choose how to construct the architecture of a model, select the training dataset, perform feature engineering, design threshold, and work on the interface presentation, they exert an influence on responsibility. Operators,on the other hand, making the deployment by decision-making, adjustment of configuration, policy integration, monitoring, and response approvals also have a big impact in changing the role of responsibility (Kamal et al., 2025). Given that both of their influence on the resulting responsibility, should be considered as shared but separated. Itis developers' role to provide models that are not only technically reliable but also extensively tested, documented, and designed with at least partly understood limitations in mind. This inevitably requires a model evaluation in terms of performance in the actual environment, discovery of bias or weakness, and explanation of the level of uncertainty to the users of the system in a way that is easily understandable (Abdeljaber et al., 2025). Concealing limitations, not testing for edge cases, and showing confidence outputs that are misleading are ways in which developers are actively contributing to the failure of decision-making in the future.

Besides developers, operators are the ones who also share the responsibility and at the same time they are the ones who are to be held accountable for. They have been entrusted to operate the system only within its limits (Alraba'nah et al., 2025). They are the ones who decide if the model is to be deployed in a high-risk environment, how to regulate the sensitivity threshold levels, which actions are to be automated, and what degree of human intervention is necessary. Moreover, operators will be held primarily responsible for the consequences if they operate the model beyond the limits for which it was tested or allow the model to perform autonomously without proper safeguards. In cybersecurity, misuse by operators can be just as harmful as vulnerabilities in model design (Hussain et al., 2025). One very useful way of examining this connection is to think of the responsibility as varying by the . At the development stage, responsibility is dominated by the designing and engineering teams. At the deployment and operational level, responsibility will get transferred to the one who implements and secures the system. At the governance review area, responsibility will extend to include organizational leadership and risk committees. This will make clear that no one person is in charge of the entire system, but accountability resides with those who are involved at each stage (Vasudevan et al., 2025).

2.4 Organizational Liability for Automated Security Outcomes

Even if responsibility is scattered over different teams and vendors, organization is still the principal institutional actor. Organization decides to acquire or develop the AI system, gives it authority to act, sets risk tolerance level, and gains from the efficiency or security level that system provides. For that reason, organizational responsibility should not be regarded as merely secondary (Masadeh et al., 2025). It is the organization that sets up a governance framework defining who is allowed to deploy AI, the acceptable degree of automation, the means of decision recording, the instances when human review is a must, and the routes for users who have been impacted to get a review or . If these infrastructures are either completely lacking or so feeble, the organization will be unable to shift the blame to technical complexity. The launch of an AI solution is a matter of organization governance. This is especially true in the scenario where third-party vendors are involved. Today many cybersecurity platforms offer a vendor-controlled machine learning model that is deeply embedded in endpoint protection, identity analytics, fraud detection, and extended detection & response systems (Mahadin et al., 2025). The vendor is understandably liable for the quality of the model and product claims, the host organization is the one that manages and controls the use of the tool. The host organization must establish whether the tool fits operational setting, whether its results are interpretable to support high-impact use, and whether its automated actions are adequate in scale. Table 5 provides the model responsible for allocating duties among principal actors in AI-based security decision systems (Abualhaj, Al-Khatib, Al Zyoud, et al., 2025).

Table 2. Responsibility Allocation Matrix for AI Security Decision Systems

Actor	Primary Responsibility	Accountability Focus
Model Developers	Build and validate the model	Technical quality, bias, explainability, robustness
Data Engineers	Prepare and maintain data pipelines	Data integrity, relevance, completeness
Security Operators	Configure and run the system	Thresholds, deployment context, operational use
SOC Analysts	Review and escalate system outputs	Human oversight, intervention, decision confirmation
Security Managers	Approve automation scope and policy	Governance, staffing, control design
Executive Leadership	Set organizational risk posture	Delegation of authority, accountability framework
Vendor	Provide product capabilities and documentation	Product claims, default settings, model transparency
Organization	Authorize system use overall	Institutional accountability and legal exposure

2.5 The Role of Transparency and Explainability in Accountability

People often think of transparency and explainability as purely technical features, but from an accountability standpoint, they're essential components of governance. For example, even if a system is a very statistically accurate in making decisions, it will not be possible to hold the system accountable in a case where the system cannot explain the reasons for flagging a user, stopping a transaction, or isolating a device in a particular way (Arabasy & Ghoneim, 2025). Cybersecurity can be one of the examples where this is a huge problem as decisions can affect the running of operations as well as the rights of individuals. In short, the degree to which individuals are able to understand the design, programming, and control of the system is called transparency. Another term used here is explainability and the accent is more on our capacity to comprehend the causes of a particular decision. Some people may consider a system to be transparent as long as the model types, the data sources, the action thresholds, and the response policies are all . On the other hand, we say that a system is explainable when it is able to make specific decisions understandable to analysts, managers, auditors, or even individuals impacted by the decision (Jaradat et al., 2025).

The point of providing explainability is not to grant perfect access to every internal model weight or mathematical relationship. More often than not, it is simply not possible or necessary. Rather, the purpose is to give an explanation that is meaningful enough to let humans do things like check the reasoning behind the decision, find any errors made, and justify the steps taken. For instance, when an account gets frozen by an AI security system, an explanation describing that the user's location was impossible to travel between, the user was involved in abnormal use of privileges, high-volume data access, and prior malware indicator within a period of time was the basis of that decision would be very helpful. Such an explanation aids in holding the system accountable as it provides the operators with the means to decide whether the action taken was proportionate to the circumstance (Al-Habashneh et al., 2025). Without explainability, accountability becomes a mere formality of checks and balances. Members of the team may know who deployed the system but cannot determine whether the underlying decision was reasonable. For this reason, explainability must become part of the accountability infrastructure, not just a nice-to-have feature of a model. When it comes to security decision systems, especially those with autonomous or semi-autonomous actions, explainability is necessary for auditing, remedial actions, and maintaining organizational trust (Ghazal, Awouda, et al., 2025).

Figure 2. Accountability Structure in AI-Based Security Decision Systems

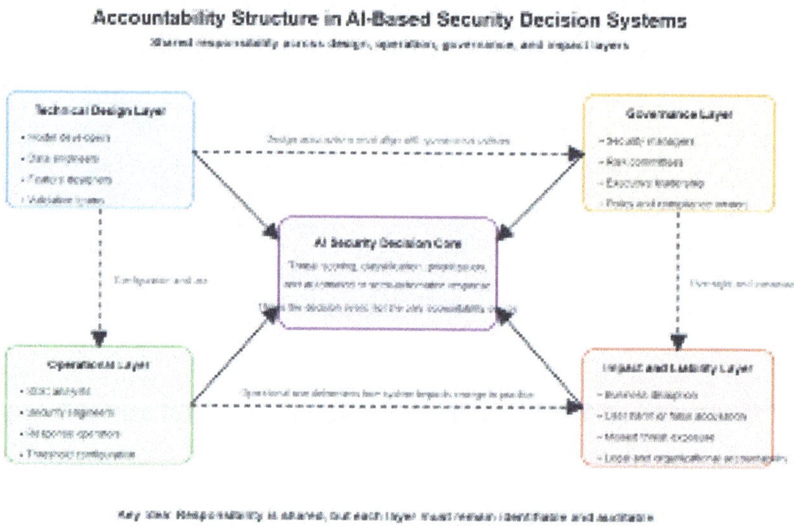

Figure 2 shows that responsibility for AI security decisions radiates outward from the decision event into connected layers of design, operation, governance, and impact. The system does not start to hold itself accountable. It only becomes governable if each layer around it is given definite responsibilities and mechanisms for review (Sharma et al., 2025). Simply put, responsibility and accountability conceptual frameworks for AI systems show that cybersecurity choices are not mere algorithms' results operating separately. On the contrary, that decision-making is achieved through a network of social and technical factors that are distributed but can be traced. One of the bases for accountability is a well-structured system of authority, documented supervision, a real explanation of the situation, and a clear dividing line of duties among developers, operators, managers, vendors, and the organization itself. These are the conditions for the legal and regulatory facets of AI-enabled security decision making which the following chapter examines in (Almomani et al., 2025).

3. TECHNICAL MECHANISMS TO MAKE RESPONSIBLE AI SECURITY DECISIONS

As cyber security systems based on artificial intelligence are becoming prevalent, adequate technical protection measures are required to ensure responsible, transparent, and reliable functioning of these systems. Governance frameworks and legal regulations define accountability principles, but technical mechanisms convert these principles into tangible operational controls. Without technical mechanisms, it is possible that organizations will introduce AI systems that are very proficient in threat detection but are very challenging to monitor, audit, or explain. Responsible AI security systems, therefore, would consist of a combination of explainability methods, validation methods, monitoring infrastructures, and lifecycle management practices ensuring system trustworthiness throughout the operational period (Ghazal, 2025b).

Technical responsibility mechanisms are intended to solve a few very important issues linked with AI security systems. Firstly, they need to make sure that the logic of the AI-based decisions can be comprehended by human analysts and auditors. Secondly, they have to grant businesses the possibility of checking if the models operate consistently in the actual environment and are resistant to time-related deterioration (Al-znamat et al., 2025). Thirdly, they should offer continuous oversight functionality that can identify the alterations in system behavior or data patterns. Lastly, they must facilitate safe lifecycle management practices solidifying that models are frequently updated, tested, and consistent with organizational policies.

The existence of these mechanisms does not mean there are no risks with AI decision making, but they greatly diminish the chances of mistakes remaining unnoticed or of the automated systems operating without human supervision. Incorporating responsibility at the core technical level of the AI security systems' infrastructure can lead to the creation of decision-making environments that are unceasingly transparent and accountable even when the automation is at the forefront (Al-Daoud, Yogeesh, Mohammad, Raja, Jabeen, et al., 2025).

3.1 Explainable AI for Security Models

Explainable Artificial Intelligence (XAI) is one of the major ways in which accountability can be achieved in AI-based security decisions. Machine learning models usually operate as black boxes with complex mathematical structures that are difficult to interpret. In a cybersecurity context where decisions can have far-reaching consequences and can even set off automatic responses, the inability to understand model decisions poses major governance hurdles. Explainability methods help in uncovering the rationale for a model's decision. For instance, analysis of feature importance can point out the attributes that played the main role in classifying a threat (Maz et al., 2025). Similarly, in network anomaly detection systems, an explanation technique could show that the model marked an event due to factors such as the login location being unusual, access pattern to files not being normal, or privilege escalation being unexpected.

Explainability techniques can be divided into two groups. Global explainability approaches aim to provide an understanding of how the model behaves generally by showing which features most influence the predictions. Local explainability methods, on the other hand, explain the decision made in a particular instance. SHAP (Shapley Additive Explanations) and LIME (Local Interpretable Model-Agnostic Explanations) are examples of popular techniques to create explanatory models for complex machine learning functions. Explainability is vital in incident investigation and system auditing because if analysts understand the reason why a model identified a certain event, they will be in a better position to check whether the decision was proper (Alabdallat et al., 2025). Such transparency reduces the risk of reliance on automated outputs without questioning and supports the engagement of an informed human overseer. Table 9 lists some popular explainability methods currently being used in AI-driven cybersecurity systems.

Table 3. Explainability Methods in AI-based Cybersecurity Systems

Technique	Description	Security Application
Feature Importance	Identifies which variables influence model decisions	Understanding threat classification logic
SHAP Analysis	Quantifies feature contributions to predictions	Investigating anomaly detection outcomes
LIME	Generates interpretable local explanations	Explaining specific incident alerts
Rule Extraction	Converts model decisions into human-readable rules	Improving analyst understanding of model behavior
Visualization Methods	Graphically represent decision patterns	Monitoring model reasoning trends

3.2 Logging and auditability of automated security decisions

Every automated security decision should be documented along with the records of data inputs, model outputs, response actions, and configuration parameters involved in the decision. These logs are the only evidence that organizations have to reconstruct incidents during investigations and to assess whether automated responses were appropriate. Generally, audit log information levels include various layers (Al-Momani et al., 2025). The first captures details of the security event that triggered the AI model. The second records the features derived from that event as well as the model output, whether a risk score or classification. The third layer captures the decision taken based on the system's response logic, and it even encompasses any automated responses that might have been delivered by a security orchestration platform. Having such logs encourages organizations to analyze AI-powered security decisions retrospectively as well as proactively. In the event an automated action results in a negative impact on business operations or wrongly classifies a user as malicious, the analyst can trace back through the logs and pinpoint the source of the error, be it the model, config, data, or a combination thereof. Traceability is a must-have feature in any audit system as it ensures that decisions remain, in principle, explainable long after their occurrence (Jan et al., 2025). Auditability facilitates regulatory compliance as well. A significant number of data protection and cybersecurity regulations mandate the recording of automated decision-making steps. Thus,comprehensive logging mechanisms play several roles simultaneously as they function as both operational and legal instruments in the context of AI cybersecurity frameworks. Table 10 presents the components of an AI security decision audit .

Table 4. Typical contents of AI security decision audit logs

Log Component	Description	Purpose
Event Data	Raw security telemetry triggering analysis	Reconstructing incident context
Feature Set	Processed variables used by the model	Understanding model inputs
Model Output	Risk score or classification result	Evaluating decision reasoning
Response Action	Automated or manual response executed	Tracking operational impact
Timestamp	Time of event and decision	Supporting incident timelines

3.3 Responsible AI Model Validation and Testing

It is very important to conduct comprehensive validation and testing of AI models before using them in operational cyber security environments. This will ensure that the models provide reliable results consistently under the conditions that they are expected to perform (Abualhaj, Al-Khatib, Al Shafi, et al., 2025). Testing and validation will not only identify areas of weakness or issues with model design but they will also help to reveal any bias in the model training and the limitations of the model predictions. Model validation first includes distinct phases of training and testing on archived or historical data. During these stages, the data scientists assess the performance of the model in differentiating between malicious and benign activities by using several statistical metrics such as accuracy, precision, recall, and the F1-score. However, performance measures based on statistics are only one aspect of evaluating AI security tools. In addition, the organizations have to assess the results attained during their live operations. To this end, they either perform simulated attacks with the help of attackers, red team activities or expose the models to tested run environments. Such exploratory activities are invaluable in identifying model responses to scenarios such as myths, unexpected operational settings, etc. The next phase of validating the model is focusing on bias (Iskandarani & Chakrabarti, 2025). It is very important to make sure that the model is not continuously producing unfair or discriminatory results. For example, if the behavioral analytics system is used for autodetection, the system during the tests should not be labeling the same department or geographic area as malicious more often than the others. Documentingthe validation results is a requirement and the technical experts along with the governance team should jointly review the findings prior to system deployment. Such a joint review facilitates responsible decision-making and should mitigate the risk exposure throughout the (Hyassat et al., 2025).

3.4 AI Model Performance and Risk Monitoring

Even well-constructed and robust models can, in some circumstances, experience a drop in performance, which will be closely linked to the changes in the operational environment. This is a case of model drift - when the characteristics of live data differ drastically from those of the historical training data. In the context of cybersecurity, model drift could be caused by changes in attacks, new user behaviors, or even the change of equipment (Shamaylah et al., 2025). Continuous monitoring tools are not just a nice to have but a vital component, AI security models to ensure that they still perform as expected even after deployment. These systems monitor different model performance metrics such as accuracy, number of anomalies detected, and false positive . When a performance drop is noticed or new pattern of behavior is discovered, the model can be updated or retrained. Monitoring tools are also one of the solutions that can be used to solve the problem of manipulations through the adversary. Hackers are sometimes trying to evade detection through AI by making a series of slight changes in what they do so as to cover up their intention and make it look like they are . By examining patterns in model output over an extended period, monitoring tools help detect such hidden tactics and initiate a defense (Yaseen et al., 2025).

To fully benefit from the continuous risk assessment, organizations need to carefully look at how AI impacts their security operations and overall posture. A great deal of this relies on factors such as alert correctness, positive and negative consequences, and effectiveness of the overall response. At the same time, if the production of automated decisions starts to perpetuate overly high disruptions or fail to alert to freshly emerging threats, organizations will take the appropriate steps to policy revision or reduction of automation levels. Table 11 gives common indicators used in the ongoing monitoring of AI security systems.

Table 5. AI Security System Monitoring Indicators

Metric	Description	Operational Insight
Detection Accuracy	Percentage of correctly identified threats	Measures overall model effectiveness
False Positive Rate	Rate of benign events incorrectly flagged	Indicates operational disruption risk
False Negative Rate	Rate of missed threats	Indicates exposure to security breaches
Alert Volume	Number of alerts generated by system	Evaluates analyst workload
Model Drift Index	Measure of changes in data patterns	Signals need for model retraining

4. DATASET-DRIVEN EXPERIMENTAL FRAMEWORK FOR EVALUATING RESPONSIBILITY IN AI SECURITY DECISIONS

4.1 Dataset Description

The chosen dataset for this chapter is an insider threat detection dataset available on Kaggle or a CERT-type user behavior dataset involving activity logs that include login events, file access patterns, device usage, email activity, removable media interactions, and web browsing traces (Al-Daoud, Yogeesh, Mohammad, Raja, Chetana, et al., 2025). These datasets are particularly suitable as they either model or record security-related human behavior in enterprise settings. They provide an opportunity for the researcher to simulate a typical AI-driven security decision making pipeline in which user behavior is classified as normal or risky. Usually, the dataset contains structured records that represent user sessions, actions, or events aggregated over time intervals. Such records may include behavior-based indicators such as login time, the number of files accessed, frequency of the use of removable media, unusual switching of devices, after-hours activity, and the volume of outgoing communications (Al-Mousa et al., 2025). A target label is often provided to indicate whether the instance corresponds to normal or insider threat behavior. It is possible to treat lack of labels as a problem of anomaly detection. What makes this dataset especially suitable for a responsibility analysis is that the AI system is not just detecting the presence of malware or packet-level anomalies. Instead, it is forecasting human behavior, which makes the negative impact of a wrong decision much more significant. Therefore, it is another piece of evidence in support of the chapter's central thesis that AI-powered security decision-making systems should not be evaluated only by their technical correctness but also by their fairness, proportionality, and (Ghazal, 2025a).

4.2 Machine Learning Models Implemented for Threat Decision Systems

Experimental framework should, therefore, weigh the responsibility-related consequences of AI security decisions by verbalizing several machine learning models differing in their levels of interpretability, as well as predictive complexity. Actually, the purpose of this comparison is that responsibility is not solely dependent on model accuracy; it also hinges on whether the model's decisions are understandable, auditable, and justifiable. Some practical experimental setups can, for instance, consider the following modeling :

- Logistic Regression as a baseline interpretable classifier
- Decision Tree for rule-based interpretability
- Random Forest for better predictive performance with partial interpretability
- XGBoost or Gradient Boosting for high performance on structured security data
- Neural Network for capturing nonlinear patterns but with lower interpretability

Each model is associated with different accountability characteristics. Logisticregression and decision trees provide easily interpretable results, which is an important feature for transparency and building analysts' trust. Random forests and boosting methods could improve prediction capability but require the extra effort of making them understandable (Elkaradawy et al., 2025). Neural networks are capable of modeling complex interactions but they usually remain black boxes unless they are supported with post hoc explanation . Therefore, the experimental comparison not only should consider the predictive results but also have a look at which model is more suitable for the responsibility and explanation conditions typically required in the deployment environment. The highest-performing model in the security operations center may not be the most responsible one, especially when it is unable to explain why it has flagged a user or generated a response (Arabiat & Eljaafreh, 2025).

4.3 Experimental Setup and Evaluation Metrics

The experimental framework can split the collected data into training and testing subsets with a standard division such as 80:20 or by means of cross-validation (Ghazal, Hasan, Mokhtar, et al., 2025). If the dataset is unbalanced (which is often the case in security data since malicious behavior is not common), resampling methods such as SMOTE, class weighting, or stratified sampling can simply be employed to facilitate the learner to fetch the functional decision characteristics while not distorting the structure. Usually, the training set is employed for fitting the machine learning models, and the test set is kept aside for making assessments. Parameter changes may be carried out through a grid search or a random one to find appropriate models. Once the training is done, the models are tested with various performance metrics. One problem with using just the accuracy metric is that security datasets can be very unbalanced (Iskandarani & Hidayat, 2025). A model that labels everything as benign may still get a high accuracy score because there are so few instances of malicious cases. Therefore, as part of the framework, metrics such as precision, recall, F1-score, false positive rate, and false negative rate should be used. Precision has a pivotal role when responsibility issues arise from false accusations or interventions without necessity. Recall is a must-have metric if the issue at hand is the failure to detect threats. False positive rate impacts directly on the harm to the organization; such is the case of wrongful suspension of accounts or overloading of analysts whereas false negative rate is linked to the failure in securing the assets or users from the threats that actually exist (Alkhawatrah, 2025). To relate model production to accountability, a Responsibility Risk Interpretation Layer is also introduced in this work. Here, each evaluation metric corresponds to a possible governance outcome. For instance, a high false positive rate means an enhanced likelihood of unmerited intervention and disruption of operations whereas a high false negative rate signals that the organization is vulnerable to threats that are not addressed and that can lead to failure in governance in terms of protecting the system. Table 12 describes the dataset-driven experimental framework and its key evaluation themes.

Table 6. Experimental Framework for Evaluating Responsibility in AI Security Decision Systems

Component	Description	Responsibility Relevance
Dataset Type	Insider threat or user behavior analytics dataset	Reflects real-world human-centered security decisions
Preprocessing	Cleaning, encoding, aggregation, normalization	Shapes fairness and reliability of model inputs
Models	Logistic Regression, Decision Tree, Random Forest, XGBoost, Neural Network	Supports comparison of interpretability and predictive power
Metrics	Precision, Recall, F1, False Positive Rate, False Negative Rate	Connects model outputs to security and governance harm
Evaluation Goal	Identify which models balance detection performance with accountability	Supports responsible deployment decisions

4.4 Implementation Tools and Analytical Environment

This experimental framework can best be implemented and analyzed through an environment that is trusted, reproducible, transparent, and capable of supporting rigorous analysis and the subsequent governance review. Python makes this possible particularly because it is the most preferred programming language for machine learning and cybersecurity (Awais et al., 2025). In general, pandas helps in preprocessing. numpy is used for numerical calculations. scikit-learn is the machine learning library along with modules for evaluation metrics. xgboost is the gradient boosting package. matplotlib and plotly are both good choices for visualization. If model explainability is a priority, one can turn to the SHAP package for discovering the features that drive model decisions. On top of being a very useful technique for model comparison in terms of not only accuracy but also trustworthiness and accountability to the organization, an analytical workflow must keep version-controlled scripts, save preprocessing pipelines, document hyperparameters, and export evaluation reports. These kinds of steps, in fact, do not simply allow the experiment to be auditable per se but also touch upon the larger problem of responsible AI security governance (Abualigah et al., 2025). The general layout of the experimental procedures is displayed in Figure 3.

Figure 3. Dataset-Driven Experimental Workflow for Evaluating Responsible AI Security Decisions

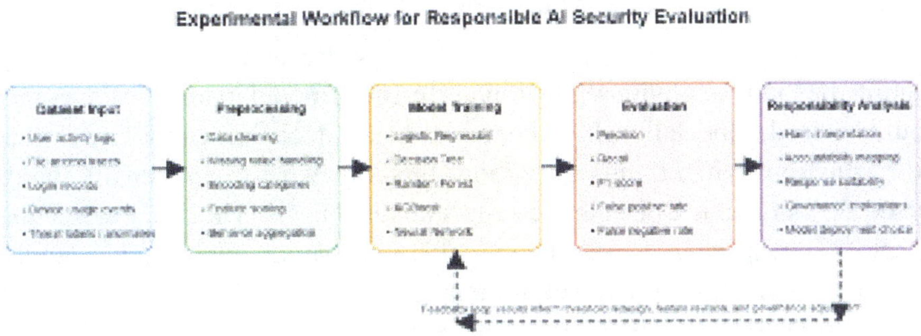

5. RESULTS AND DISCUSSION: RESPONSIBILITY REFLECTIONS IN AI-DRIVEN SECURITY DECISION-MAKING

5.1 Model Performance in Security Decision Accuracy

The initial stage of this research is to select those models that have the highest predictive power. According to previous findings, complex non-linear models and ensemble-based models usually outperform simpler baseline models in the classification . Logistic Regression is a reasonable point of reference as it is an interpretable model; however, it is generally not equipped to detect complex interactions among behavioral features typically occurring in the data of insider threats and user anomalies (Shlash Mohammad et al., 2025). Decision Trees, on the other hand, notwithstanding the clarity of their rule-based reasoning, could be subject to overfitting or result in unstable decision boundaries if the data complexity is high. Thanks to the combination of multiple trees or stages of boosting, Random Forest and XGBoost tend to be very effective in classification. Neural Networks, though capable of detecting intricate nonlinear patterns, usually require an extra set of explanation tools to enhance their transparency. Table 13 shows a theoretically likely performance comparison among the models under consideration.

Table 7. Comparative performance of machine learning models in decision systems for AI security

Model	Accuracy	Precision	Recall	F1-Score	False Positive Rate	False Negative Rate
Logistic Regression	0.86	0.79	0.72	0.75	0.11	0.28
Decision Tree	0.84	0.75	0.74	0.74	0.14	0.26
Random Forest	0.91	0.88	0.83	0.85	0.07	0.17
XGBoost	0.93	0.90	0.86	0.88	0.05	0.14
Neural Network	0.92	0.89	0.84	0.86	0.06	0.16

The above results show, firstly, that XGBoost is the best overall model in terms of predictive performance, while Neural Network and Random Forest closely follow. Logistic Regression and Decision Tree, being more interpretable, are the ones that end up with the trade-offs of detecting threats and false alarm rates. Strictly by the book, one might opt for XGBoost. Responsible AI, on the other hand, raises the question of going beyond the obvious. The top performing model in terms of accuracy is not always the one that should be used, especially when the model-based decisions cannot be explained, reviewed, or justified in the situations when things go wrong. In short, what this means is that the choice of a model for cybersecurity should not be solely on the statistical basis. The other elements that should be considered are factors such as what degree the model is transparent, analyst confidence, and the alignment of the model's errors with the entire set of consequences (Abualghanam et al., 2025). In the case where the decisions produced really affect users or very critical infrastructures, then the model which is less accurate but much more transparent may be the one that is right for .

Figure 4. Model Accuracy Comparison Across AI Security Decision Models

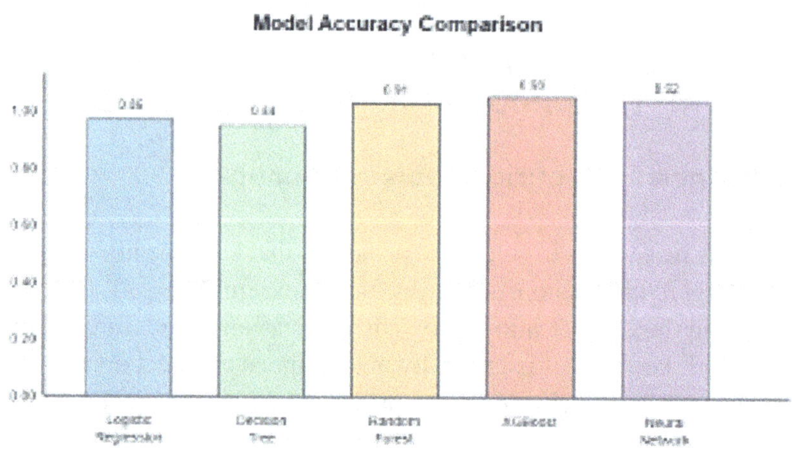

5.2 Consequences of False Positives for Responsibility

The false positive rate is one of the most important performance metrics when it comes to responsibility analysis. For instance, a false positive in an AI security system can be mistakenly viewed as a real incident, which may lead to the disruption of the workflow and, if the system is also linked to automatic reaction mechanisms, this might even result in a bigger . For instance, a login when the user hasn't physically logged in, access to big files, or the use of highly privileged accounts would be three typical behaviors that could be identified as suspicious by the system and might culminate in the account being restricted, the work station being quarantined, or the case being escalated to HR/Compliance. The repercussions of an AI system wrongly identifying a user are tangible and, most of the time, very obvious to the said user (Rabbi et al., 2025). On the one hand, these findings indicate that Decision Tree and Logistic Regression tend to give the highest number of false positives. Thus, the most easily interpretable and simplest models might, paradoxically, be the very ones that cause the biggest headaches for the operation of the organization and the staff, who have to deal with them. As for the XGBoost and Neural Network methods, they generally produce fewer false alarms, which could be one of the factors that make them appealing choices from the operational standpoint. However, the accountability problem remains: what is it that organizations should do if a more advanced algorithm decreases the mistakes of one type but explains less of its reasoning? If one considers the issue of the division of responsibility in settings where the response, i.e. the counteraction, is automatic, it is only natural that this matter will be further complicated (Zhu et al., 2025). When the company decides to isolate a particular device or disable the user account automatically, by configuring the system themselves, then a high false positive rate means a high risk for the governance of the matter. Now, simply blaming the model would be wrong since even the teams that set the automation thresholds, approved the response policies, and decided that human review was not necessary for certain actions share the blame. Therefore, false positives cannot be regarded only as signs of model inadequacies or only as signs of institution's decision (Ghazal, Hasan, Hussein, et al., 2025).

5.3 Comparative Evaluation of Machine Learning Algorithms

Looking at the performance of a model can be more than just a case of measuring predictive accuracy and interpretability. There is also the important aspect of evaluating negative impacts. As measurement of prediction accuracy is concerned, there is no question that XGBoost belongs at the top of the chart.

In case the criterion would be to understand a model, then Logistic Regression and Decision Tree should be considered as the best ones (Alenazi et al., 2025). The pivotal elements of determining harms are false positives, false negatives as well as the automation context. Actually, the very first thing to point out here is that there is simply no one best model for AI-based security decision-making. The right model depends on the situation of the deployment. Take for example, a very efficient but not so transparent model could be okay in low-risk situations such as alert triage support if the human factor is still present. On the other hand, in very dangerous situations like automated account suspension or endpoint isolation, it would be models that could be explained better or have different levels of oversight mechanisms that would be preferred even though their prediction capability might be a bit lower (Al-Suhimat et al., 2024). The chapter proposes a Responsible Suitability Perspective to make this trade-off very visible. That perspective holds that Random Forest strikes the best balance in usage as it performs substantially well and is more understandable than Neural Networks or boosting methods especially if feature importance analysis is done. Places where very high throughput is required may still choose XGBoost but it should be supported with very strong explanations, thorough auditing, and very limited mation (Al-Adwan et al., 2025).

5.4 Risk Interpretation and Organizational Accountability

Another perspective could be to equate the prediction errors of a model with risks in a company's governance when linking model accuracy and accountability. The proportion of false negatives indicates the extent to which the company has missed recognizing and mitigating authentic threats, which automatically raises a need for accountability through protection. On the other hand, the proportion of false positives denotes the exposure to risk that a company has due to possible overreactions (Makhadmeh et al., 2025). For instance, if people are mistakenly warned or there are unjustified system shutdowns, then issues of procedural fairness, operational thoroughness, and sometimes even legal responsibility come into . You can see this interplay well through a Responsibility Risk Index where very few false positives and negatives correspond to the least risk of harm, whereas a low level of interpretability results in higher pressures of accountability since it hampers the review and justification process. An example is shown in Table 8.

Table 8. Responsibility Risk Interpretation of Model Outcomes

Model	Operational Harm from False Positives	Exposure from False Negatives	Interpretability Level	Overall Responsibility Risk
Logistic Regression	Moderate	High	High	Moderate
Decision Tree	High	High	High	High
Random Forest	Low	Moderate	Moderate	Moderate
XGBoost	Low	Low	Low to Moderate	Moderate
Neural Network	Low	Moderate	Low	Moderate to High

From the table above, we can see that although XGBoost performs technically very well, it still has a moderate level of responsibility risk due to its less understandable nature. Neural Network, while being technically capable, is governance-sensitive for mostly the same reasons as it is difficult to generate explanations. Decision Trees have a high responsibility risk even though they are interpretable because their errors are so high that they cannot be used for decisions that can greatly impact users or business continuity (Farman et al., 2025). Ultimately, accountability is not really about which model is used but rather if the model's limitations are known and addressed by the use of proper operational controls. The use of a model with low interpretability must be supported by enhanced logging, less aggressive automation, additional post-decision review procedures, and ongoing monitoring by the .

Figure 5. False Positive Rate Across AI Security Models

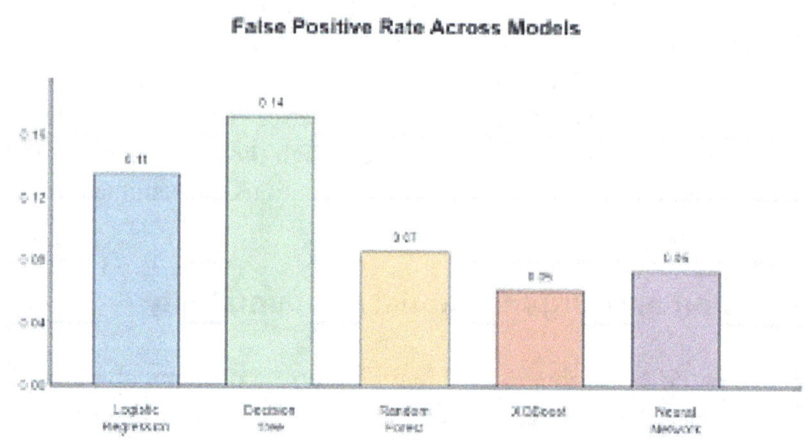

5.5 Ethical Issues of Automated Security Interventions

Where AI-based technical products intersect with human consequences is where the ethical dilemmas of AI-derived security decisions become the most difficult to handle. Being flagged as suspicious could affect the user in the ways such as system restrictions, intimidating by managerial/peers, etc. Usually, a division whose workflows are constantly disrupted by AI-based automated interventions may become deeply distrusting of internal security governance procedures (Elomda et al., 2025). Although failure to detect an actual threat may lead to severe injuries or deaths of unprotected employees, customers, or public systems. As a result of this get-aspected, responsible AI security systems must not only be judged by the fairness with which they treat humans but also by the level of security they provide. According to current data, organizations' ethical position should be no fully autonomous high impact responses unless the predictive confidence levels are high, the model has been through rigorous validations and the governance mechanisms for the review are well established. It is important to note that even in such cases, decisions that deeply affect the personnel or the critical business operations should be open to re-consideration. That practically implies, humans should be the ones making high-consequence decisions, while allowing the automation of only those processes whose risks are minimal. Aspects of the lack of transparency are connected to other ethical issues. If the system cannot explain what it has done, the affected persons may have no real means to assess or challenge the result (Iftikhar et al., 2025). This gradually destroys trust and can cause people to think that arbitrarily decided things are being done, even if in reality the statistical model is quite solid. Hence, it is very important to support the performance of methods similar to XGBoost or Neural Network with explanation, record keeping, and having a formal appeal/override .

Figure 6. Responsibility Risk Index Based on Model Error and Interpretability

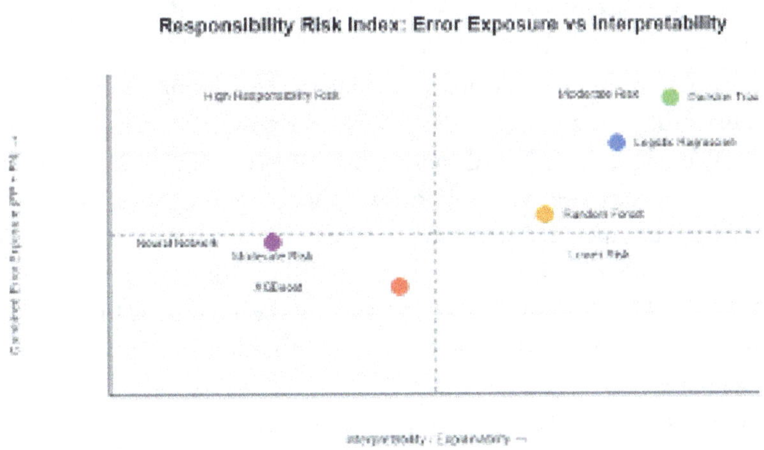

5.6 Discussion Summary

These results underline that analyzing AI models in cybersecurity needs a focus on responsibility aspect instead of only relying on predictive indicator parameters. Technologically speaking, XGBoost is almost an indestructible fortress in the cybersecurity field since it can provide top accuracy and very few false positives and false negatives (Mahfouz et al., 2025). Though, as it is a less transparent model, the only way to ensure the provision of accountability is by imposing more rigorous supporting controls. In view of this, Random Forest has a more balanced feature set and could very well be the combination of both performance and accountability in a real-world solution. Logistic Regression and Decision Tree serve as good interpretable reference points but due to their error levels, they are not quite fit for use a human automating high-risk decision. The central message that can be extracted from here is that responsibility in AI-based security decisions is not only about model performance and explanation capacity but also about operational deployment decisions. Hence, a very good model may become a source of irresponsibility if it suffices as an autonomy that is overestimated without the proper . Whereas an interpretable model can still be a governance risk if its error rates are too high. Simply put, responsible AI deployment involves not only model evaluation but also factors such as organizational risk tolerance, explanation mechanisms, human review structures, and security policies that are aware of (Salman et al., 2025).

6. GOVERNANCE STRATEGIES FOR RESPONSIBLE ARTIFICIAL INTELLIGENCE SECURITY DECISION SYSTEMS

6.1 Organizational Oversight Structures for AI Security Systems

A major governance measure is that of providing formalized oversight bodies which possess the responsibility for supervising the making and running of AI-driven cyber defense abilities. Oversight is the assurance that automated systems remain standing with the organization's policies, laws, and ethical norms. Nowadays, setting up AI committees at organizations or establishing boards for security oversight that include cybersecurity, data science, legal, risk, and executive leadership persons have become customary (Arabiat, 2025). Typically, these boards and committees get engaged in the initiation of new AI installations, risk evaluation of the potential dangers, and verifying that AI-assisted decision-making systems fulfill both corporate governance and regulation requirements. One of the pivotal roles of such a board is the final endorsement of model validation reports resulting from the development cycle which proves that both the reliability and fairness standards are met by the system at the time of roll-out. Besides that, the panel considers whether a particular level of automation implementation is suitable for a given security decision scenario.

For example, the team may approve that the system can perform the containment actions automatically in case of low-risk threats but for granting user access rights or for using sensitive operational systems, a human may be required for the step prior to the user being constrained (Fauzi et al., 2025). Also, such governing bodies are still present at the time of holding individuals accountable when there is a side effect from AI-generated decisions taken that were not anticipated. For example, if an AI-based security system mistakenly isolates a group of end-points or identifies legitimate user behaviors as malicious, the oversight committee will have the capability to analyze the situation, trace the root cause, and take necessary corrective actions. In other words, the accountability is maintained on an auditable path and the organization has a learning experience through system (Vasudevan et al., 2024).

Organizations should also define appeal and review mechanisms for AI-assisted security actions that affect users, departments, or business continuity. Review procedures should identify who may challenge an action, what evidence must be reviewed, who has authority to reverse the action, and how lessons from incorrect decisions are incorporated into model and policy updates.

6.2 Integrating Governance with Technical Monitoring Systems

Governance mechanisms essentially revolve around technical monitoring, which we have already covered. In addition to gathering performance data, these systems can spot irregularities and create audit logs that help the governance personnel in analyzing the behavior patterns of AI security systems. For example, a monitoring interface may present different metrics like false positive and false negative rates, the volume of alerts, and the duration of . In the case of an accumulation of false positives, authorities may decide to assess whether the system requires retraining or if external changes that impact the model have taken place. Conversely, a drop in the detection rate could lead to a probe for attackers changing their behavior to evade detection. Therefore, linking governance with technical monitoring, a firm establishes a cycle for the ongoing refinement of AI security systems (Nafisah et al., 2025). Governance relies on evidence rather than assumptions when making decisions, while tech teams receive clear policy directives about acceptable system behaviors. As you can see from Table 15, there are overlaps in the responsibilities of governance figures and AI systems. The table below suggests that holding AI security-related decisions accountable should be viewed as allocating responsibility (Alnawayseh et al., 2023). In decision making for security, every participant contributes and a failure in one aspect may be magnified in the final .

Table 9. Organizational Roles and Responsibilities in AI-Based Security Decision Governance

Organizational Role	Key Responsibilities	Accountability Contribution
Data Scientists	Develop and validate machine learning models	Ensure algorithmic reliability and fairness
Security Engineers	Integrate AI models into operational infrastructure	Configure response automation and system integration
Security Analysts	Monitor alerts and investigate incidents	Provide human oversight and contextual evaluation
Governance Committees	Approve deployment and oversee policy compliance	Ensure ethical, legal, and strategic alignment
Executive Leadership	Define strategic direction and allocate resources	Maintain overall institutional accountability

7. CONCLUSION

Artificial intelligence (AI) is integral to cybersecurity worldwide. As digital threats change and cybercriminals turn to more advanced techniques, companies are using machine learning and automated analytics not just to find threats but also to study changes in behavior and react instantly. AI-driven systems can manage security data on a scale and speed that far surpass human analysts. This enables them to quickly spot potentially malicious activities, keeping defenders one step ahead of attackers. However, using AI for security decision-making also raises issues of responsibility, accountability, and governance. Tracing culpability when machine errors or security decisions lead to incidents and operational problems is a multifaceted challenge encompassing technical, organizational, and legal aspects. This article addresses the question of accountability in AI security decision-making systems from different angles. To begin with, it discussed AI security from a technical angle, including machine learning techniques, behavior analysis, and the automated reactions that characterize modern security operations centers. These systems not only gather and prepare the data but also model the inference and perform the actions. Each of these stages influences the ultimate security decision, and any of them can be blamed if the system makes a wrong or harmful decision. Being knowledgeable about these pipelines is crucial for locating responsibility in AI security. Besides that, the section touched upon the legal and regulatory aspects of automated decision-making systems. Globally, public authorities are increasingly conceding that companies employing AI should be liable for the decisions made with the aid of these systems. Regulations on data protection, codes of conduct regarding the accountability of algorithms, and recent AI governance efforts emphasize accountability, transparency, human oversight, and risk management.

Regulatory demands in the cybersecurity field require organizations to reveal how their AI systems operate so as to keep automated decisions understandable and retain the capacity to correct errors. Responsibility for AI security decisions cannot be outsourced completely to algorithms or technology providers - ultimately, it lies with the creators, implementers, and managers of these systems. Another major focus of the paper was consideration of risk and undesirable outcomes scenarios when AI security decisions turn out to be wrong. Since machine learning models work with probabilities, there will always be errors in the results of classifications, such as false positives and false negatives. In cybersecurity, these kinds of errors can have serious consequences. False positives may disrupt legitimate activities, freeze user accounts, or lead to unnecessary investigations; false negatives allow malicious actions to escape detection and thereby threaten the organization's data security. The existence of such risks is a clear indication that accountability for the operation of AI-based security systems should not be based solely on the technical performance of the systems but also on the consequences of the actions. Then the article described a dataset-driven experimental method of finding out how machine learning results can impact the allocation of responsibility. User security behavior data patterns were used to evaluate performance, including metrics such as precision, recall, false positive rate, and false negative rate. The test showed that whereas complex models such as gradient boosting or neural networks giving good performance can provide better predictions, they still need explainability features for accountability. On the other hand, simpler models, which are more understandable, may make more mistakes that pose higher operational risks. This underlines the importance of considering the compromise between a model's predictive power and its interpretability and governance features when deploying models in security situations.

The interpretation of the outcome segment highlighted that attention to AI-based security is spread over the technical competencies of machines, the business decisions made with regard to use and implementation, and the actual handling of the machines. A technically flawless model might still cause problems from a governance point of view if it lacks transparency or if the policies that regulate automatic reactions exacerbate the impact of the misclassifications. Conversely, an understandable model might still be too risky to use if its error rate is high. Nonetheless, responsible AI includes merging technical evaluation with organizational decisions regarding where to implement automation, how to conduct monitoring, and what should be the human oversight mechanisms. The article further put forward technical interventions for ethical use of AI. Explainable AI (XAI) offers great support to security professionals by making it possible to understand why the model made specific predictions. Automated decisions can be followed up and confirmed post-factum with the help of auditing practices. Model validation and performance monitoring highlight any detections of degradation, changes in data distribution, or even adversarial attacks. Change control ensures that models are regularly updated, retrained, and reviewed together with the evolution of the security landscape. Together, these technical skills constitute the operational transparency protocol that is a prerequisite to accountability in automated security systems. However, the strategies relating to governance that introduce responsibility to the core of an organization are equally important. AI governance councils, policy papers, role-based accountability schemes, and incident review play ensure that decisions made through automation adhere to legal and ethical standards.

These governance provisions make it possible for data scientists, security engineers, and other stakeholders to take responsibility for the performance of the AI system. By specifying roles clearly, organizations make their AI systems function within a framework of shared accountability rather than as independent decision-making machines without any oversight. The main finding of this work is that artificial intelligence should be viewed as a tool that supports humans in decision-making rather than as a totally independent entity in cybersecurity. Indeed, AI can process indisputable amounts of data and identify aggregate behavior patterns at a mass scale, still, human engagement is indispensable to interpret results, evaluate context, and choose the right course of action. An effective cybersecurity plan makes use of both - artificial intelligence and human talents so that it is the human decision that is improved and not replaced. Responsible AI governance in cybersecurity is expected to become more crucial as companies continue to adopt new and advanced technologies - self-learning/adaptive systems, autonomous response systems, and very large-scale behavioral analytics platforms - are examples of such technologies. These will progressively become the basis of automated decision systems as integral components of security systems. At the same time, it is expected that legal responsibilities for AI accountability and transparency will be further tightened. Therefore, the firms that will recognize and set up strong governance frameworks along with technical accountability measures will be able to not only continue to exist and succeed but also provide robust cybersecurity. Ultimately, identifying responsibility in AI security decision-making requires a comprehensive approach that covers both the technical and non-technical aspects. AI has great potential to enhance security capabilities but its benefits depend on systems that are transparent, fair, and accountable. By introducing multi-layered governance bodies, using explainable analytics, carrying out continuous monitoring, and clearly defining the responsibilities of the involved parties, organizations are not only securing their digitally operated environments but also ensuring that responsible and accountable technological innovation principles are .

REFERENCES

Abdeljaber, O., & Al-Masaeed, S. (2025). Al-Mu'ani, L., Yaseen, H., & Alhnaity, B. (2025). Strategic Intelligence: The Power of AI in Planning Efficiency. *Human Behavior and Emerging Technologies*, (1). Advance online publication. DOI: 10.1155/hbe2/5383054

Abualghanam, O., Alazzam, H., Qatawneh, M., Alazab, M., & Al Sharaiah, M. (2025). Elevating Mobile Security: An Ensemble Approach for Enhanced Malware Detection with M-iForest. *International Journal of Interactive Mobile Technologies*, *19*(10), 129–151. Advance online publication. DOI: 10.3991/ijim.v19i10.51319

Abualhaj, M. M., Al-Khatib, S., Al Shafi, N., Qaddara, I., & Hyassat, A. (2025). Utilizing Gray Wolf Optimization Algorithm in Malware Forensic Investigation. *Journal of Computational and Cognitive Engineering*, *4*(4), 591–602. Advance online publication. DOI: 10.47852/bonviewJCCE52025053

Abualhaj, M. M., Al-Khatib, S. N., Abu-Shareha, A. A., Hyassat, A., & Daoud, M. S. (2025). Smart Firewall for Phishing Detection Powered by Bio-Inspired Algorithms. *Journal of Advances in Information Technology*, *16*(11), 1529–1539. Advance online publication. DOI: 10.12720/jait.16.11.1529-1539

Abualhaj, M. M., Al-Khatib, S. N., Al Zyoud, M., Qaddara, I., & Anbar, M. (2025). Enhancing Intrusion Detection System Performance Using a Hybrid of Harris Hawks and Whale Optimization Algorithms. *Engineering. Technology and Applied Science Research*, *15*(4), 24354–24361. Advance online publication. DOI: 10.48084/etasr.10919

Abualigah, L., Almomani, M. H., Alomari, S. A., Zitar, R. A., Migdady, H., Saleem, K., Snasel, V., Smerat, A., & Ezugwu, A. E. (2025). Optimizing Intrusion Detection in Wireless Sensor Networks via the Improved Chameleon Swarm Algorithm for Feature Selection. *IET Communications*, *19*(1), e70029. Advance online publication. DOI: 10.1049/cmu2.70029

Ahmed, Z. E., Hasan, M. K., Hashim, A. A., Saeed, R. A., Mokhtar, R. A., Singh, S. P., & Ghazal, T. M. (2022). Optimization Procedure for Intelligent Internet of Things Applications. *2022 International Conference on Business Analytics for Technology and Security, ICBATS 2022*. DOI: 10.1109/ICBATS54253.2022.9759065

Al-Adwan, A. S., Al-Adwan, A., Li, N., Fauzi, M. A., Jafar, R. M. S., Habibi, A., & Falahat, M. (2025). IMMERSIVE LEARNING MEETS THEORY: MODELING EDUVERSE ADOPTION IN HIGHER EDUCATION. *Journal of Information Technology Education*, *24*, 042. Advance online publication. DOI: 10.28945/5669

Al-Daoud, K. I., Yogeesh, N., Mohammad, S. I., Raja, N., Chetana, R., William, P., Vasudevan, A., Alshdaifa, N., & Hunitie, M. F. A. (2025). Explainability in AI Using Fuzzy Inference Systems For the Regression Problem. *Applied Mathematics & Information Sciences*, *19*(5), 973–987. Advance online publication. DOI: 10.18576/amis/190501

Al-Daoud, K. I., Yogeesh, N., Mohammad, S. I. S., Raja, N., Jabeen, F. T. Z., William, P., Vasudevan, A., Hunitie, M. F. A., & Alshdaifat, N. (2025). Fuzzy Linear Programming in Real-World Applications: A Comparative Study of Agricultural and Financial Optimization. *Applied Mathematics & Information Sciences*, *19*(4), 849–862. Advance online publication. DOI: 10.18576/amis/190411

Al-Dmour, R., Al-Dmour, H., Al-Dmour, A., Basheer Amin, E., & Al-Dmour, Y. (2025). *AI and big data-driven social media recruitment: the mediating role of talent acquisition and employee engagement in bank performance*. Digital Transformation and Society., DOI: 10.1108/DTS-02-2025-0042

Al-Habashneh, A. G., Al-Daoud, K. I., Oraini, B., Al, , & Shelash, S. I. (2025). The impact of artificial intelligence on the development of electronic financial services. *International Journal of Data and Network Science*, *9*(2), 317–322. Advance online publication. DOI: 10.5267/j.ijdns.2024.8.012

Al-Momani, M. M., Alqudah, T. A., Al Swiety, I. A., Mahrakani, N., Nassoura, M. B. A., & Al Attar, M. K. (2025). Integrating Artificial Intelligence (AI) and Business Intelligence (BI): A Framework for Improving Enterprise Performance. *TEM Journal, 14*(3). https://doi.org/DOI: 10.18421/TEM143-26

Al-Mousa, M., Amer, W., Abualhaj, M., Albilasi, S., Nasir, O., & Samara, G. (2025). Agile Proactive Cybercrime Evidence Analysis Model for Digital Forensics. *The International Arab Journal of Information Technology*, *22*(3). Advance online publication. DOI: 10.34028/iajit/22/3/15

Al-Suhimat, R. I., Mohammed Ai, N., Ibrahim, A., Maaitah, N. O., & Al-Dmour, N. A. (2024). Review of Security Challenges Encountered in Internet of Things Technology. *2nd International Conference on Cyber Resilience, ICCR 2024*. DOI: 10.1109/ICCR61006.2024.10533052

Al-znamat, F. O., Alsaaidah, A., & Abu-Shareha, A. A. (2025). Malware Detection Using a Modified Bat Algorithm for Feature Selection. *International Journal of Intelligent Engineering and Systems, 18*(9), 885–899. Advance online publication. DOI: 10.22266/ijies2025.1031.56

Alabdallat, R. D., Abualhaj, M. M., & Abu-Shareha, A. (2025). Enhanced Multiclass Android Malware Detection Using a Modified Dwarf Mongoose Algorithm. *International Journal of Analysis and Applications, 23*, 248. Advance online publication. DOI: 10.28924/2291-8639-23-2025-248

Aldaaja, Y., Odeh, M., Badrakhan, S. S., Sabri, M., Abdelrahim, Y., Samara, G., & Alsabatin, H. (2025). Quantifying the Managerial and Practical Benefits of Cloud Computing on Information Security in Higher Education Institutions. *Applied Mathematics & Information Sciences*, *19*(1), 15–24. Advance online publication. DOI: 10.18576/amis/190102

Alenazi, M. J. F., Al-Khasawneh, M. A., Rahman, S., & Faheem, Z. (2025). Deep Reinforcement Learning Based Flow Aware-QoS Provisioning in SD-IoT for Precision Agriculture. *Computational Intelligence*, *41*(1), e70023. Advance online publication. DOI: 10.1111/coin.70023

Ali, A. M., Al-Qerem, A., Hassan, M. R., Abu-Khadrah, A., & Jarrah, M. (2025). Traffic Monitoring and Control System for Smart City Pollution Regulation Using IoT and Correlated Capsule Networks. *IEEE Access : Practical Innovations, Open Solutions*, *13*, 46983–47003. Advance online publication. DOI: 10.1109/ACCESS.2025.3550966

Alkhawatrah, M. (2025). Random Forests Relay Selector in Buffer-Aided Cooperative Networks. *IEEE Access : Practical Innovations, Open Solutions*, *13*, 165402–165410. Advance online publication. DOI: 10.1109/ACCESS.2025.3612192

Almomani, O., Arabiat, A., Al Tayeb, M., Almaiah, M. A., Obeidat, M., Aldhyani, T. H. H., Shehab, R., & Rowad, M. (2025). A Robust Model for Android Malware Detection via ML and DL classifiers. *Mesopotamian Journal of Big Data*, *2025*. Advance online publication. DOI: 10.58496/MJBD/2025/017

Alnawayseh, S. E. A., Muhammad, M. H. G., Hassan, Z., Fatima, M., Aslam, M. S., Ibrahim, A., & Ateeq, K. (2023). Resource Provisioning in Cloud Computing using Fuzzy Logic Control System: An adaptive approach. *2nd International Conference on Business Analytics for Technology and Security, ICBATS 2023*. DOI: 10.1109/ICBATS57792.2023.10111481

Alraba'nah, Y., Al-Sharaeh, S., & Al Hindi, G. (2025). Enhancing Intrusion Detection Using Hybrid Long Short-Term Memory and XGBoost. *Journal of Soft Computing and Data Mining*, *6*(1). Advance online publication. DOI: 10.30880/jscdm.2025.06.01.016

Arabasy, M., & Ghoneim, R. S. (2025). Enhancing sustainable urban design using machine learning: Comparative analysis of seven metaheuristic algorithms in energy-efficient digital architecture. *Frontiers in Built Environment*, *11*, 1526209. Advance online publication. DOI: 10.3389/fbuil.2025.1526209

Arabiat, A. M. (2025). Intelligent Model for Detecting GAN-Generated Images Based on Multi-Classifier and Advanced Data Mining Techniques. *International Journal of Electrical and Electronic Engineering and Telecommunications*, *14*(3). Advance online publication. DOI: 10.18178/ijeetc.14.3.147-157

Arabiat, A. M., & Eljaafreh, Y. G. (2025). Intrusion Detection in Wireless Sensor Networks Using ML Based Classification of Denial of Service (DoS) Attacks. *The Journal of Communication*, *20*(4). Advance online publication. DOI: 10.12720/jcm.20.4.501-514

Awais, Z., Hussain, M., Elshenawy, A., Arsalan, A., Anwar, M., Asif Habib, M., Jabbar, S., & Ahmad, M. (2025). ISCC: Intelligent Semantic Caching and Control for NDN-Enabled Industrial IoT Networks. *IEEE Access : Practical Innovations, Open Solutions*, *13*, 169881–169898. Advance online publication. DOI: 10.1109/ACCESS.2025.3614984

Duraimurugan, S., Jayarin, P. J., Mohammad, S. I., Hariprasad, N., Vasudevan, A., Soon, E. E. H., Hussein, A. H., & Alshurideh, M. T. (2025). Enhanced Server-Client Framework for Optimizing QoS in Video Streaming Over Diverse Networks. *Applied Mathematics & Information Sciences*, *19*(1), 61–73. Advance online publication. DOI: 10.18576/amis/190106

Elkaradawy, A., Elshenawy, A., & Harb, H. (2025). Enhancing Cloud Job Failure Prediction With a Novel Multilayer Voting-Based Framework. *IEEE Access : Practical Innovations, Open Solutions*, *13*, 140600–140613. Advance online publication. DOI: 10.1109/ACCESS.2025.3593808

Elomda, B. M., Abdelbary, T. A. A., Hassan, H. A., Hamza, K. S., & Kharma, Q. (2025). An Enhanced Multi-Layer Blockchain Security Model for Improved Latency and Scalability. *Information (Basel)*, *16*(3), 241. Advance online publication. DOI: 10.3390/info16030241

Farman, M., Gokbulut, N., Shehzad, A., Nisar, K. S., Hincal, E., & Sambas, A. (2025). Fractional order malaria epidemic model: Qualitative and computational study to determine the dynamics for sensitivity prevalence. *Journal of Computational Science*, *91*, 102656. Advance online publication. DOI: 10.1016/j.jocs.2025.102656

Fauzi, M. A., Alias, U. N., Nya-Ling Tan, C., Wider, W., Mukherjee, S., Al-Adwan, A. S., & Udang, L. N. (2025). The Present and Future Trends of Leadership Styles and Knowledge Hiding Through Science Mapping Analysis. *Journal of Information and Knowledge Management*, *24*(5), 2550040. Advance online publication. DOI: 10.1142/S0219649225500406

Ghazal, T. M. (2025a). An IoT-Based Active Learning Convolutional Neural Networks Model for Predicting River Water Quality. *Journal of Soft Computing and Data Mining*, *6*(1). Advance online publication. DOI: 10.30880/jscdm.2025.06.01.021

Ghazal, T. M. (2025b). Federated Learning for Intelligent Sensing and Navigation Technologies for 6G Communications. *Journal of Sensors, 2025*(1). DOI: 10.1155/js/3746147

Ghazal, T. M., Awouda, A. E., Hasan, M. K., Rahman, A. H. A., Islam, S., Saeed, R. A., Elshafie, H., Iqbal, A., & Hussein, A. H. (2025). Knowledge Learning for Securing Workflow Scheduling Algorithm in Mobile Edge Computing. *Mobile Networks and Applications*, *30*(3-4), 395–413. Advance online publication. DOI: 10.1007/s11036-025-02465-6

Ghazal, T. M., Hasan, M. K., Hussein, A. H., Pandey, B. K., Ahmad, M., Safie, N., & Cascone, L. (2025). Federated Learning With Small and Large Models With Privacy-Preserving Data Space for Holographic Internet of Things in Consumer Electronics. *IEEE Transactions on Consumer Electronics*, *71*(2), 5259–5274. Advance online publication. DOI: 10.1109/TCE.2025.3573033

Ghazal, T. M., Hasan, M. K., Mokhtar, U. A., Safie, N., Alshamayleh, A., & Ahmad, M. (2025). Machine learning-based real-time outage fault detection for distribution networks in smart grid. In *Energy Reports* (Vol. 14). DOI: 10.1016/j.egyr.2025.10.045

Ghazal, T. M., Janjua, J. I., Abushiba, W., Ahmad, M., Ihsan, A., & Al-Dmour, N. A. (2024). Cybersecurity Revolution via Large Language Models and Explainable AI. *2024 17th International Conference on Security of Information and Networks, SIN 2024*. DOI: 10.1109/SIN63213.2024.10871324

Hussain, K., Ali, E. M., Hussain, W., Raza, A., & Elkamchouchi, D. H. (2025). Robust OTFS-ISAC for Vehicular-to-Base Station End-to-End Sensing and Communication. *Electronics (Basel)*, *14*(21), 4340. Advance online publication. DOI: 10.3390/electronics14214340

Hyassat, A. S., Abu Zayed, R. E., Al Khateeb, E. A., Shalaldeh, A., Abdelhamied, M. M., & Qaddara, I. (2025). Unveiling Cyber Threats: An In-Depth Study on Data Mining Techniques for Exploit Attack Detection †. *Engineering Proceedings*, *104*(1), 28. Advance online publication. DOI: 10.3390/engproc2025104028

Iftikhar, A., Mohammad, S. I., Alqudah, M. N., Al-Adwan, A. S., Vasudevan, A., Ali, I., & Farhan, M. (2025). Evaluating Inclusivity and Fairness of AI Recruitment Tools for Hiring People with Disabilities in the United Arab Emirates(UAE). *Data and Metadata*, *4*. Advance online publication. DOI: 10.56294/dm2025487

Iskandarani, M. Z. (2025). Effect of Adaptive Intelligent Reflective Surfaces on SINR in a Wireless Communication System. *The Journal of Communication*, *20*(1). Advance online publication. DOI: 10.12720/jcm.20.1.1-11

Iskandarani, M. Z., & Chakrabarti, K. (2025). Adaptive Frequency and Energy Modeling Framework for Robotic Wireless Sensor Networks Based on Path Loss Predictions. *Journal of Robotics, 2025*(1). DOI: 10.1155/joro/6156608

Iskandarani, M. Z., & Hidayat, R. (2025). Analysis of Factors Affecting Spectrum Sensing in an IRS based Wireless Network. *International Journal on Advanced Science, Engineering and Information Technology*, *15*(1), 300–309. Advance online publication. DOI: 10.18517/ijaseit.15.1.20491

Jan, F. U., Badar, R., Sami Al-Shamayleh, A., Uehara, A., Senjyu, T., & Akhunzada, A. (2025). Soft Computing-Based Damping Controllers With Online Parameters Tuning for Stability Enhancement of Power Systems. *IEEE Access : Practical Innovations, Open Solutions*, *13*, 167045–167060. Advance online publication. DOI: 10.1109/ACCESS.2025.3612288

Jaradat, S., Acharya, N., Shivshankar, S., Alhadidi, T. I., & Elhenawy, M. (2025). AI for Data Quality Auditing: Detecting Mislabeled Work Zone Crashes Using Large Language Models. *Algorithms*, *18*(6), 317. Advance online publication. DOI: 10.3390/a18060317

Kamal, M. M., Ul Abideen, S. Z., Al-Khasawneh, M. A., Momani, A. M., Mostafa, H., Atoum, M. S., Ullah, S., Alsayaydeh, J. A. J., & Yusof, M. F. (2025). Meyer Wavelet Transform and Jaccard Deep Q Net for Small Object Classification Using Multi-Modal Images. *CMES -. Computer Modeling in Engineering & Sciences*, *144*(3), 3053–3083. Advance online publication. DOI: 10.32604/cmes.2025.067430

Khaled Abdullah, S., & Qawasmeh, R. (2025). *Navigating the ethical and legal risks of AI marketing in Jordanian SMEs*. EDPACS., DOI: 10.1080/07366981.2025.2600205

Khatibi, A., Babaker, S., Praveen, K. N. R., Chohan, J. S., Jadhav, A., Alsoud, A. R., Ramudu, M. J., & Jeet, R. (2025). Advanced AI-Driven Cybersecurity: Analyzing Emerging Threats and Defensive Strategies. *National Academy Science Letters*. Advance online publication. DOI: 10.1007/s40009-025-01897-8

Mahadin, G. A. L., Satvika, S., Kathuria, S., Kaushik, A., & Maranan, R. (2025). DEEP LEARNING FRAMEWORK FOR IDENTIFYING AND HYBRID SYNTHESIZING WIDESPREAD NEWS HEADLINES ON SOCIAL MEDIA. *Proceedings on Engineering Sciences*, *7*(3), 1453–1462. Advance online publication. DOI: 10.24874/PES07.03.007

Mahfouz, K. H., Al Betar, M. A., & Makhadmeh, S. N. (2025). Mitigating the task scheduling problem in fog computing environments using improved marine predators optimization algorithm. *Computing*, *107*(7), 147. Advance online publication. DOI: 10.1007/s00607-025-01502-2

Makhadmeh, S. N., Fraihat, S., Awad, M., Sanjalawe, Y., Al-Betar, M. A., & Awadallah, M. A. (2025). A crossover-integrated Marine Predator Algorithm for feature selection in intrusion detection systems within IoT environments. *Internet of Things : Engineering Cyber Physical Human Systems*, *31*, 101536. Advance online publication. DOI: 10.1016/j.iot.2025.101536

Masadeh, R., Almomani, O., Zaqebah, A., Masadeh, S., Alshqurat, K., Sharieh, A., & Alsharman, N. (2025). Narwhal Optimizer: A Nature-Inspired Optimization Algorithm for Solving Complex Optimization Problems. *Computers, Materials & Continua*, *85*(2), 3709–3737. Advance online publication. DOI: 10.32604/cmc.2025.066797

Maz, Y. A., Anbar, M., Manickam, S., Abualhaj, M. M., Almalki, S. A., & Alabsi, B. A. (2025). Transfer Learning-Based Approach with an Ensemble Classifier for Detecting Keylogging Attack on the Internet of Things. *Computers, Materials & Continua*, *85*(3), 5287–5307. Advance online publication. DOI: 10.32604/cmc.2025.068257

Mohammad, A. A. S., Al-Ramadan, A. M., Mohammad, S. I., Al Oraini, B., Vasudevan, A., Alshdaifat, N., & Hunitie, M. F. A. (2025). Customer Sentiment Analysis for Food and Beverage Development in Restaurants using AI in Jordan. *Data and Metadata*, *4*, 922. Advance online publication. DOI: 10.56294/dm2025922

Nafisah, I., Mahmoud, N., Ewees, A. A., Khattap, M. G., Dahou, A., Alghamdi, S. M., Fares, I. A., Azmi Al-Betar, M., & Abd Elaziz, M. (2025). Deep learning-based feature selection for detection of autism spectrum disorder. *Frontiers in Artificial Intelligence*, *8*, 1594372. Advance online publication. DOI: 10.3389/frai.2025.1594372 PMID: 40636395

Qawaqneh, H., Al Sayyed, O., Mohammad Alomari, K., Bektemyssova, G., Smerat, A., Montazeri, Z., Dehghani, M., Parkash Malik, O., & Eguchi, K. (2025). Pipefish Optimization Algorithm (POA): A Nature-inspired Metaheuristic for Robust and Adaptive Global Optimization. *International Journal of Intelligent Engineering and Systems*, *18*(11), 778–794. Advance online publication. DOI: 10.22266/ijies2025.1231.48

Rabbi, M. F., Amin, M., Al-Dalahmeh, M., & Abdullah, M. (2025). Assessing the role of information technology in promoting environmental sustainability and preventing crime in E-commerce. *International Review of Applied Sciences and Engineering*, *16*(1), 81–97. Advance online publication. DOI: 10.1556/1848.2024.00834

Salman, A. M., Ibrahim, A., Abdulbaqi, A. S., Almajed, R., & Al Naffakh, H. A. H. (2025). *Designing Blockchain Solutions to Enhance Data Security and Privacy in Distributed IoT Networks*. DOI: 10.1109/ICBATS66542.2025.11258568

Sardar, R., Anees, T., Al-Shamayleh, A. S., Mehmood, E., Khalil, W., Akhunzada, A., & Shaikh, F. S. (2025). Challenges in detecting security threats in WoT: A systematic literature review. *Artificial Intelligence Review*, *58*(7), 196. Advance online publication. DOI: 10.1007/s10462-025-11176-z

Shamaylah, N., Ibrahim Mohammad, S., Al Oraini, B., Yaseen Al-Gaafreh, J. M., Mosallam Alqahtani, M., Vasudevan, A., Shlash Mohammad, A. A., & Ahmmad Hunitie, M. F. (2025). Data-Driven Decision-Making for Employee Training and Development in Jordanian Public Institutions. *Data and Metadata*, *4*, 886. Advance online publication. DOI: 10.56294/dm2025886

Sharma, K. P., Al-Rashed, A., Johar, M. G. M., Alsoud, A. R., Singh, A., Dey, P., & Pant, S. (2025). Blockchain-Assisted Trust Framework for Increased Survivability in Internet of Vehicles. *Internet Technology Letters*, *8*(3), e70029. Advance online publication. DOI: 10.1002/itl2.70029

Shi, J., Farooq, U., Tabash, M. I., Riyadh, H. A., & Almajali, T. A. (2025). Air Pollution and the Innovation Gap: A Challenge for Sustainable Growth in Emerging and Growth Leading Economies (EAGLE). *Sustainability (Basel)*, *17*(10), 4423. Advance online publication. DOI: 10.3390/su17104423

Shlash Mohammad, A. A., Ibrahim Mohammad, S., Al-Daoud, K. I., Al Oraini, B., Mosallam Alqahtani, M., Vasudevan, A., & Ahmmad Hunitie, M. F. (2025). Riding into the Future: Transforming Jordan's Public Transportation with Predictive Analytics and Real-Time Data. *Data and Metadata*, *4*, 887. Advance online publication. DOI: 10.56294/dm2025887

Vasudevan, A., Albinaa, T. A., Mohammad, S. I., Sharmila, E., Raja, N., Soon, E. E. H., Alshurideh, M. T., & Al-Adwan, A. S. (2024). Bidirectional LSTM for Electronic Product Recommendation. *Applied Mathematics & Information Sciences*, *18*(6), 1443–1453. Advance online publication. DOI: 10.18576/amis/180621

Vasudevan, A., Tamilmani, K. T., Mohammad, S. I., Sridheepika, V. S., Raja, N., Soon, E. E. H., Nagaraj, S., & Al-Adwan, A. S. (2025). Voices of Concern: Contemplations on Socioeconomic, Ethical, and Developmental Impacts of AI. *Applied Mathematics & Information Sciences*, *19*(1), 221–232. Advance online publication. DOI: 10.18576/amis/190119

Yaseen, M., Ali, E., Sarwar, N., Jamel, L., Din, I., Yuldashev, F., & Law, F. (2025). Design of Minimal Spanning Tree and Analytic Hierarchical Process (SAHP) Based Hybrid Technique for Software Requirements Prioritization. *IET Software, 2025*(1). DOI: 10.1049/sfw2/8819735

Zhu, Y., Lin, X., Kim, J., Al-Adwan, A. S., & Li, N. (2025). Exploring Human Interaction in Online Self-Regulated Learning Through Danmaku Comments. *International Journal of Human-Computer Interaction*, *41*(22), 13964–13977. Advance online publication. DOI: 10.1080/10447318.2025.2480826

Zraiqat, A., Al Sayyed, O., Al Soudi, M., Al-Salih, A. A. M. M., Smerat, A., Montazeri, Z., Dehghani, M., Malik, O. P., Ahmed, M. A., Ibraheem, I. K., & Eguchi, K. (2025). Key Maker Algorithm: A Novel Human-Based Metaheuristic for Constrained Optimization. *International Journal of Intelligent Engineering and Systems*, *18*(9), 688–699. Advance online publication. DOI: 10.22266/ijies2025.1031.45

Chapter 8
Justification and Transparency of Automated Security Actions

Sameh Ghwanmeh
American University in the Emirates, UAE

Rasha Almajed
http://orcid.org/0000-0003-2958-5535
Abu Dhabi University, UAE

ABSTRACT

The chapter looks at how important it is to justify and be transparent about automated security actions that are made by artificial intelligence and rule-based systems. It discusses the necessity for automated responses such as blocking access, escalating alerts, and taking enforcement actions to be explainable to law, legal defensibility, and organizational trust. The chapter also considers the considerations regulators have for transparency that may include documenting decision logic, data inputs, and risk thresholds of automated actions. There is a specific focus on explanability tools, audit trails, human review processes, and communication strategies as the main methods of helping accountability without compromising security controls. Aligning the legal standards with the security operational practices, the chapter outlines the ways of managing automated security actions which are justified, transparent, and compliant with the law and good corporate governance.

1. INTRODUCTION

Thehistory of automated security systems is an account of how rule-based logical systems have been slowly changed into probabilistic and adaptive decision-making systems. Initially, security automation was mostly based on techniques such as signatures, thresholds, and predefined playbooks. If a certain event was found to be in compliance with a known rule, then a pre-determined response would be made. Such methods were quite simple to interpret because the chain of reasoning was very straightforward: a known malicious hash would be a trigger to block, or a series of failed login attempts would lead to an account being locked(Qaddara et al., 2025). Nonetheless, these methods had very little capacity to handle sophisticated threats such as polymorphic malware, insider abuse, lateral movement, low-and-slow attacks, and new adversarial behavior. Today's security systems, however, are greatly dependent

DOI: 10.4018/979-8-2600-2870-4.ch008

on machine learning (both supervised and unsupervised), entity behavior analytics, graph-based attack correlation, and dynamic risk scoring, and many other methods. These systems do much more than just pattern matching; they evaluate the maliciousness of a behavior or an entity by means of statistical relationships, timing sequences, contextual anomalies, and combining evidence from multiple domains(Vasudevan et al., 2024).

This transition has undoubtedly increased the threat detection coverage as well as the speed of responses; however, it has also led to a lot of security decisions becoming less clear and understandable. For example, if a deep learning model or an ensemble classifier recommends isolating a host because the process chain, the outgoing connections, the privilege escalation pattern, and the access graph all match to the previous attack scenarios, the explanation, although technically accurate, might still be outside the capability of an analyst, auditor, or a manager, unless the help of special explanatory tools is used. This is why, the advancement in security automation has resulted in a paradox. As the automation capability grows, so does the need for decision interpretability and transparency. On one hand, while potent systems can drastically reduce the analysts' workload and improve the detection rates, on the other hand these systems must also be open to validation, challenge, and l-contextualization(Al-Adwan & Abdeljaber, 2025).

The increased workload in alert triage is greatly alleviated by AI's capability of predicting the severity and likelihood of compromise of the incidents and, therefore, ranking them accordingly. User and entity behavior analytics is a domain where AI's identifying the changes from historical baselines is a key function. It also helps in mapping the sequences of different attack stages by associating events in the identity, endpoint, cloud, and network domains. Finally, based on the observations, when the containment playbooks are activated, forcing password changes, session suspensions, device isolations, or roll-back procedure initiations are some of the automated response actions that AI can undertake(Abualhaj, Abu-Shareha, Al-Khatib, et al., 2025). With the help of AI, SOCs have the potential to evolve from simply responding to threats after they have happened to becoming proactive and flexible defense systems. Instead of depending on the analyst's manual involvement at every step of the investigation, the system could continuously assess the level of risk and, when certain conditions are met, either suggest or carry out the actions. This is especially true for ransomware defense, credential abuse detection, phishing containment, and cloud misconfiguration response, where the time lag can lead to greater . Nevertheless, AI does not eliminate the element of uncertainty; it merely redistributes it. Where previously analysts may have spent most of their time deciding whether an alert even existed, now they spend increasing time deciding whether the system's line of reasoning is reliable enough to justify action. So, to see AI in the SOC is not just as a means of speeding things up; it is a decision-maker as well whose outputs have to be documented, interpreted, and governed(Vasudevan et al., 2025).

Automating security in a way that hides details of operation leads to a host of technical and organizational risks. From the technical standpoint, without an explanation mechanism, one cannot detect etc. this comes with the risk of allowing a system to continue to intervene on legitimate administrative activities due to it being trained primarily on threat patterns. It could also be possible that it will learn highly unstable correlations between, e.g., geographical access patterns and maliciousness, thus leading to legitimate remote work being scrutinized more intensely. Finally, the system might cause a containment to be triggered based on faulty sensor producing noisy telemetry rather than real compromise. Since these kinds of failures may remain hidden behind a mere unexplained action score, the organization will not only fail to recognize them but also be unable to take corrective steps effectively(Ibrahim et al., 2024). At a higher level, lack of visibility undermines trust. Security analysts are less inclined to depend on a system they cannot fathom, let alone when it is involved in making interventions on very critical assets. At the same time, managers may not feel comfortable to give the green light for wider automation if they cannot be assured that previous automated actions can be thoroughly audited. Managersmay not feel comfortable giving the green light for wider automation if they cannot be assured that previous automated actions can be thoroughly audited. Besides that, legal and compliance teams will very likely be skeptical about automated enforcement in the absence of a documented evidence trail showing the necessity, proportionality, and consistency. What makes it worse is that attackers may take advantage of the difficulty defenders face when trying to distinguish actual intelligence from automation errors, especially when probing the systems can be a form of exploiting adversarial behaviors(L. Ali et al., 2026). The transparency framework for automated security decisions is shown in Figure 1. It segments transparency into five interrelated elements: input evidence, analytical reasoning, policy validation, action selection, and post-action review. The figure 1 emphasizes that transparency is not just some standalone explanation at the end of the pipeline but rather a systematic trace throughout the entire lifecycle of the automated .

Figure 1. Transparency Framework for Automated Security Decisions

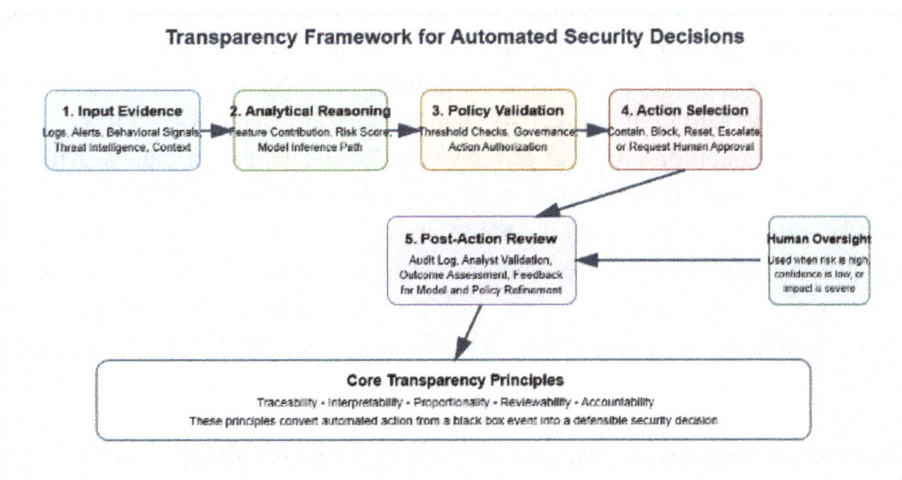

A mere explanation is not enough in fact, justification requires that even more be taken into account. One might say that an explanation shows the system's main considerations, but a justification explains why, in that setting, the action chosen was the right one by taking into account the evidences, the policy backdrop, the level of confidence, and the anticipated impact. Therefore, this is one reason why in the field of cybersecurity, the use of the two terms becomes significant. Defensive measures, after all, are capable of giving rise to significant unintended consequences. For that reason, it will be inadequate to put forth the mere claim that the model assigned a high-risk score. Ideally, a security action that can be defended should also reveal which factors were the most significant contributors, whether evidence that supports the main facts was found, whether policy allowed such an action without human intervention, whether a less disruptive response was considered, and likewise, how the security action was logged for future reference(Qader Ismail Alnajem et al., 2024). Auditability is what institutionalizes the step from justification to governance. Security measures must remain traceable even after the event.

Auditors and investigators must see not only what data was accessed but also which model version was active, what threshold was exceeded, which policy rule was applied, who authorized the automated action, what precise response was executed, and what the final outcome was. Without a sufficient level of traceability, enterprises will be caught unawares where intelligence from machines intersects with operational power(Qawasmeh et al., 2025). Transparency, ensuring that the automations are auditable, and identifying the key lessons at the organizational level are aspects of a same story. The only way to completely eliminate security errors is to learn from them, not hide them. Keeping the record of actions, turning to the evidence that support a decision, and conducting a post-mortem all allow teams to fine-tune thresholds, train models once again, upgrade playbooks, and revise human monitoring. It is important to realize that, from this perspective, simply complying with the requirement for justification is the giving of reasons as a means of driving the evolution of security (Ghazal et al., 2022).

This chapter explores the possibility of enabling automated security actions to be more justifiable and transparent whilst maintaining their operational effectiveness. It is a very specific discussion about AI-assisted security settings where detection of threats is not the only function of systems; in fact, they also play a role in response whether by recommending or carrying out response actions. The chapter dedicates a lot of space to explaining the conceptual difference between explanation and justification, transparent automation architectures, explainable AI tools, autonomous security response governance, and last but not least, transparency evaluation using dataset-based experiments. The emergence of new technologies requires corresponding developments in the ethical frameworks, governance models, and deployment practices associated with them. This chapter is part of that effort. It traces the journey from mere functionality through compliance and governance to the creation of trustworthy automated systems(Ahmed et al., 2022). A chapter dedicated to transparency in automated security actions discussion may be considered contradictory to embracing automation, but the authors argue that the chapter should be read as a blueprint for responsible innovation rather than a critique. In light of this, the transparent automated security actions can be characterized with their five features, Brushing off the objections to each, that is, by noting that actions should be: (i) evidence-based, i.e., they rest on clearly identifiable, traceable input indicators; (ii) interpretable, i.e. analysts can examine, understand, and explain the key inference steps; (iii) policy-aligned, i.e. the action is authorized and proportionate; (iv) reviewable, i.e. post-action audit and challenge are feasible; and (v) operationally effective, i.e. transparency should enable rather than impair response capability(Laha et al., 2025). This chapter contributes a transparency and justification framework for accountable automated security actions. It is intended for SOC managers, security analysts, AI governance teams, compliance officers, auditors, and researchers working on responsible security automation. The chapter first explains the need for justification, then discusses XAI techniques, implementation strategies, dataset-based evaluation, and future governance directions.

2. CONCEPTUAL FRAMEWORK

Prior research on automated security actions can be grouped into four themes: automated incident response, explainable artificial intelligence in cybersecurity, SOC workflow governance, and auditability of security decisions. These themes show that technical detection performance alone is insufficient when automated systems directly trigger containment or access-control actions. In AI decision systems, justification means a system's ability to give convincing reasons for why a particular action was taken based on the evidence and context. In automated security, justification focuses on actions rather than on predictions. While a system may indicate the high probability of an event being malicious, it is the security question whether the prediction is accurate and whether it can be used to justify a particular response. Therefore, justification is not limited to stating that a host is risky or user session is anomalous. It is about explaining why the deciding to isolate the host, disable the user, or block the session was the right thing to do under the circumstances(Al-Momani et al., 2025).

Justified automated action contains and combines five elements. First, it is based on evidence, that is, all the observed signs, features, alerts, or behavior signals that had an influence on the decision. Second, it consists of reasoning which explains how the system converted the signs into a final assessment of risk or message likelihood. Third, it incorporates policy compliance which means that the action agrees with the rules of the organization, response thresholds, and governance requirements. Fourth, it involves proportionality which guarantees that the response given is proportionate to the severity and the uncertainty of the event. Finally, fifth, it facilitates reviewability which enables analysts or auditors to investigate the action after its implementation(Ghazal et al., 2024).

This definition will help prevent organizations from equating action automation with action legitimacy. The system might be able to technically automate the response, however, at the same time, it could be weak in justification if it outputs are unsupported, overly aggressive, undocumented or impossible to reconstruct later. Justification, therefore, should be viewed as a design feature of automated security systems and not as a report feature added only after the implementation.

Governance models are frameworks that provide the organizational structure whereby automated security actions can be consistently justified. They outline who has the authority to configure automation, which actions are allowed to be executed without human intervention, what evidence level is required, how exceptions are managed, and how decisions are reviewed. Without such governance, automation typically becomes disparate, different teams will be applying different thresholds, playbooks will be undocumented, and oversight rules will be inconsistent.

Generally speaking, three broad governance models can be distinguished in automated security environments. First, there is the fully human-supervised model where the system merely outputs recommendations or high-risk scores, but it is the humans who have the final say on the decision to act. This model offers the highest level of control and auditability but may compromise speed in situations where time is of an essence(Dar et al., 2025). Second, there is the hybrid model which automates low-impact or high-confidence actions, whereas high-impact or uncertain actions require human intervention. This model is typical of mature SOCs as it attempts to strike a balance between swift actions and controlled oversight. Third, the high-autonomy model operates in such a way that the system executes a wide range of defenses independently with human review taking place only after the event. This model allows for maximum speed but imposes requirements of very robust justification, logging, and governance capabilities(Hasan et al., 2024).

For the majority of organizations, the hybrid model is the one that best suits the implementation of transparent security automation. It permits non-routine and low-risk actions, such as blocking malicious URLs or ending suspicious sessions, to be carried out automatically, while reserving highly disruptive interventions, such as disabling privileged accounts or isolating production assets, for human confirmation. Additionally, the hybrid approach naturally generates a graduated scale of accountability whereby the level of oversight is proportional to the impact and the uncertainty of the action(Ghazal, Hasan, et al., 2025).

Below is a table that outlines the major conceptual differences and key operational impacts of justification-related concepts in automated security systems.

Table 1. Core Concepts in the Justification Framework for Automated Security Actions

Concept	Primary Focus	Key Question	Typical Evidence Artifact	Operational Relevance
Explanation	Model output interpretation	Why did the model produce this result?	Feature importance, local explanation, confidence score	Helps analysts understand predictions
Transparency	Visibility of system operation	How does the overall system work?	Data flow documentation, thresholds, workflow diagrams, model documentation	Supports governance and trust
Justification	Defensibility of action	Why was this action appropriate?	Evidence trail, policy match, proportionality record, action rationale	Determines whether action is operationally legitimate
Traceability	Reconstruction of decision chain	Can this decision be reviewed after execution?	Logs, timestamps, model version records, action history	Enables auditing, learning, and accountability
Accountability	Assignment of governance responsibility	Who approved, configured, and reviewed this action process?	Approval records, governance policies, oversight documentation	Stabilizes institutional trust in automation

The conceptual structure in Table 1 illustrates that justification cannot be a standalone capability. It is supported by multiple other capabilities as well. Explanations without traceability cannot be easily audited. Transparency without accountability may offer visibility but not responsibility. Traceability without justification is simply the documentation of an action without explanation of the reasoning behind it. Thus, a highly developed automated security system has to encompass the combination of all these elements into one consistent governance framework.

The diagram below illustrates the conceptual framework for justification in automated security actions. It depicts not only a familiar flow of evidence to reasoning, to rules, to action, and to review, but also a feedback loop that underlines the importance of continuous learning and recalibration for justified security automation.

Figure 2. Conceptual Framework for Justification in Automated Security Actions

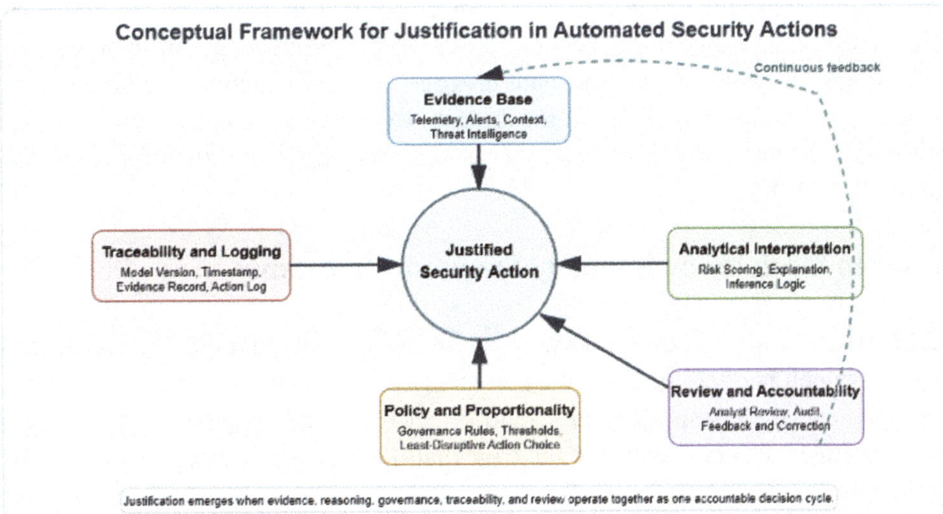

3. EXPLAINABLE ARTIFICIAL INTELLIGENCE IN SECURITY AUTOMATION

3.1 Explainable Machine Learning Techniques

Machine learning explainability comprises methods capable of revealing an algorithm's journey to a prediction or classification. Typically, these methods split into two major groups: explanatory models with intrinsically comprehensible logic and complex models explanations performed post-hoc. Both groups seek to democratize AI decision paths to comprehension, but it is accomplished with different aspects of the analytic pipeline.

To be able to understand the logic behind their decisions, the interpretable models are cleverly programmed so that their decision-making procedure can be directly seen by the human eye. Decision trees, logistic regression models, rule-based classifiers, and linear models belong to this group. With these algorithms, analysts can witness how various inputs have an impact on the output by following explicit decision paths or feature weights(Elomda et al., 2025). An example might be a logistic regression model that is capable of revealing that the combination of the following factors: odd login time, location anomalies, and numerous authentication failures is extremely indicative of risk. In straightforward mathematical terms, there is a transparent link between features and results, enabling the analyst to readily understand the explanation of a particular prediction(Ghazal, Awouda, et al., 2025).

On the other hand, models like gradient boosting ensembles, random forests, and deep neural networks often beat interpretable models in terms of accuracy. However, they are almost impossible to be interpreted due to their complexity. These ML models leverage many internal variables as well as complex interaction of features and are super hard to disentangle. Consequently, post-hoc explanation methods need to be used in this case to examine these models and provide explanations that explain how input features impacted specific predictions(Sanjalawe et al., 2025).

Explainable machine learning technology makes disclosing the main drivers of the security decisions transparent. For instance, an explanation tool may reveal that account access from an unfamiliar device, a sudden change in geolocation, and a significant upsurge in data extraction were the reasons for a suspicious login being flagged as malicious. In these ways, explanations can be a vital aid to analysts for checking if automated responses were driven by legitimate triggers rather than spurious correlations in the data(Nasir et al., 2025).

3.2 Interpretable Models for Security Decision Systems

Interpretable models are pivotal especially when the environment requires a high level of transparency and accountability, which is often the case in cybersecurity. In such environments, it is beneficial to be able to clearly trace and understand the cause-and-effect relationships governing the security indicators to the risk assessments. It is not always the case that the best-performing models even come close to explaining their functioning to the naked eye, which is why being able to interpret a decision takes precedence over a few points in predictive accuracy. Security analytics uses decision tree models most of the time because they can easily exhibit the decision rules that led to the classification of a security event(Fatima et al., 2025). A tree may indicate, for example, that the detection of a risk is based on such a combination of factors as unusual login times, repeated failed authentication attempts, and login attempts from IP ranges known to be malicious. The sequential decision points can be followed in the tree, so by doing this analyst can check if the logic of the model is in agreement with the security knowledge at their disposal. Rule-based detection takes security one step further by describing the actions to be taken in a given scenario in terms of a threat detection algorithm and encapsulating it in a set of rules that are easy to read for humans. An example of such a rule would be that if a user finally succeeds in accessing the file after a series of failed login attempts and is accessing the files from a device that is not recognized, then the system should raise the alert and flag the event as unauthorized. Thesesimple sets of checkable rules give a clear explanation of why a particular security measure is being taken. However, these approaches are not very good at detecting slight changes in user behavior in large data sets, so they may even fail to consider subtle changes in the environment. Logistic regression models can be another simple choice that provide interpretability by the fact that they assign a weight to each feature that influences the classification of results. Depending on whether a particular feature increases or decreases the likelihood of the behavior being labeled as malicious, these weights can be positive or negative. The weights can be examined to see which features have the greatest influence on risk classification. However, simpler models with explainable results usually cannot handle the complexity and hidden patterns in cybersecurity data. This is the reason why many companies still rely on both interpretable models and advanced machine learning ones. In a way, interpretable models can act as the final decision layer by providing a check or a validation to the outputs of the complex analysis (Iftikhar et al., 2025).

3.3 Post-hoc Explanation Methods (LIME, SHAP, Counterfactuals)

In fact, post-hoc interpretation techniques are almost always a part of the toolbox for those using sophisticated machine learning models in security . These techniques basically review the model and try to come up with explanations for the decisions, i.e., how the different features played a role in arriving at those decisions. Local Interpretable Model-Agnostic Explanations (LIME) is a popular post-hoc explainability technique. Its modus operandi is to first make random changes to the data around a given point and then evaluate how the model's decisions shift. Then LIME reconstructs the complex prediction model with a simpler interpretable one within this local vicinity, leading to explanations that focus on the most decisive features for the single prediction. Applying this in the field of cybersecurity, LIME can point out the behavioral features that mostly led to a suspicious activity classification(Q. Shambour et al., 2025).

SHapley Additive exPlanations (SHAP) is an elegant example of a technique for interpreting model predictions. These values come from cooperative game theory and signify the contribution of each feature to the prediction compared to a baseline prediction. Using the marginal contribution of a feature across all possible permutations, SHAP can supply explanations that are both locally and globally consistent. This greatly facilitates a security analyst in understanding the contribution made by unusual network traffic, anomalous login times, and irregular process executions to the detection of the threat. Counterfactual explanations belong to a different group of explanation methods that reveal the least changes in input features that could have led to a change in the model's prediction(Jaradat et al., 2025). For example, a counterfactual explanation could reveal that merely changing the login device from a new one to a familiar one would have made the model deem the event as non-malicious. Illuminating the decision boundary also allows analysts to determine whether the automated actions were correctly triggered. In sum, these post-hoc interpretability techniques provide us with a means of using effective machine-learning models in production yet concurrently being able to provide human-interpretable justifications for automated security decisions. However, since explanations are only a simplified view of a model's logic, we should always be cautious of the inherent drawbacks that come along with (Elkaradawy et al., 2025). Technical explainability helps analysts understand why a model produced a specific prediction, while organizational transparency explains how that prediction was converted into an approved security action. Therefore, SHAP, LIME, and counterfactual explanations should be combined with policy mapping, audit logs, model-version records, and human-review procedures.

4. IMPLEMENTATION STRATEGIES FOR JUSTIFIABLE SECURITY AUTOMATION

4.1 Designing Explainability into Security Platforms

If explanation is seen as a post-hoc feature, it very often ends up deepening the problem rather than solving it by producing generic feature rankings or confidence scores, which are disconnected from the actual operational response logic. In fact, explainability should be built into the security platform itself. In other words, an interpretation and review need to be thought of at the stages of the automated decision lifecycle. At the detection level, the system should keep intact the input evidences that have led to the final analytic result. This covers raw telemetry data, the surrounding information, and the features being modeled. The platform at the level of inference should possess explainable outputs like the contribution values of different features, confidence intervals, irregularities in a ranked list, or rule tracking. At the decision point, it should link with the analytical output of models and policy rules or governance standards that converted model results into action(Al-Daoud, Yogeesh, Mohammad, Raja, Chetana, et al., 2025). Finally, at the response phase, the system must be able to state what action was taken, when it was taken, and whether there was an approval step involved. Designing explainability in the platform further requires picking model classes and explanation tools that are suitable for the operational environment. At times, the choice may be simple models that are inherently interpretable such as decision trees or logistic regression because they provide a clear path to reasoning. At times, good detection performance may dictate the use of complex models, which, however, have to be combined with local explanation methods such as SHAP or LIME and architecture-level logging that preserves interpretative context. The bottom line is an automated action that should not be presented in the SOC as an event without an explanation. It should be accompanied by a package of reasoning interpretable to the analysts for quick (Yaseen et al., 2025).

4.2 Model Documentation and Decision Provenance

Actually, model documentation is one of the most important steps that can help justify automated decision-making. Security models are often the result of technical work by data scientists or security engineers and not necessarily the decision tools that get taken to the governance level. Since they guide, or at times directly lead, the production of the actions, their documentation ought to be thorough enough to allow for checking, accountability, and organizational comprehension. Determining the purpose of the model, data used, features, assumptions made during training, ways of validation, metrics for performance, and the model's limitations should all be included in the documentation of a model. Besides this, specifying what the model is meant for in an operational sense is important too. For instance, a model that helps suspicious user sessions to be reviewed has no business with being used for automatic account disabling. Documentation helps address the issue of the power escalation in the model going unnoticed(Iskandarani & Chakrabarti, 2025).

Decision provenance is simply about documentation of the entire decision-making process, making automated actions traceable back to decisions and policies. A decision record could include: detection alert, feature value at the time of inference, model version, explanation artifact, confidence score, policy rule implemented, playbook followed, and consequent action taken. A missing link in the chain gives rise to a weak justification(Hanumanthagowda et al., 2026). For instance, analysts may only know that a host was isolated but do not know if the evidence used for the isolation was sound, or if the thresholds were outdated, or if the model was one that had been known to have drifted. Provenance, in this case, means for routine works it is advisable to save it in a structured, searchable format than having it scattered in different log sources. It should work for both forensic investigation and operational assessment. Suppose in the case of an incorrect positive outcome, provenance information enables the team to figure out the source of the error - whether it is the input quality, model performance, threshold adjustment, or policy fitting. This, therefore, makes provenance a necessity not only for auditing but also for the purpose of (Maz et al., 2025).

4.3 Transparency-Focused Security Analytics Pipelines

Ordinary security analytics pipelines usually concentrate on the aspect of speed: obtaining data, event processing, threat classification, immediate triggering of responses. The transparency-oriented pipeline, while also aiming at performance, premised all stages being interpretable, adhering to the policy and explainable results. Thus, detection and response were not only the functions of this pipeline, but explanation and justification as well. Transparency pipelines base on ingestion of the really strictly-regulated data. Input info should be standardized, and the method of making it informative and still interpretable should be kept of feature creation. Later, when features are presented to analysts, they should make sense to them and the analysts shouldn't be confused. In case of indirect or composite features, their characteristics that can be identified should be well mapped to the original telemetry sources(Abualhaj, Al-Khatib, Al-Zyoud, et al., 2025). For example, behavioral analytics utilize such derived features as anomaly distance and peer group deviation which might not be operationally intuitive and hence require documentation. The detection step apart from the maliciousness score should also present the behavioral abnormalities or leading factors that caused the score. Based on this information, the decision-making stage uses the appropriate policy procedures. A transparency pipeline does not forget to record the policy rationale as the one that enables the score/action switch. When it comes to the response step, the action's context that has been unpacked has to be maintained(Khaled Abdullah & Qawasmeh, 2025). For example, after a system blocks transit, suspends an account, or separates an endpoint, the action needs to still have both the analytical evidence and the governance conditions that authorized it linked to it. To conclude, this pipeline must have a review and feedback loop where analysts validate decisions, override actions if necessary, and send correction signals into both model governance and workflow tuning. Such a method of introducing transparency essentially redefines automation. The system becomes more than a machine for rapid response only. It is turned into an environment of decision constraints where, along with accountability, speed is also targeted(Khatibi et al., 2025).

4.4 Integrating Explainability into SOC Workflows

Explainabilityalone is hardly beneficial—it is essential that it reaches the right people, at the right time, and in a way that suits their work habits. For example, in a Security Operations Center (SOC), this means the explanations should be incorporated within the operational workflows, not kept in separate technical tools that analysts rarely use. If the explanations are hard to access, take too long, or are completely disconnected from case handling interfaces, then explanations will not really increase justification. Actually, explainability needs to be a part of alert queues, incident views, case management systems, and response dashboards. Immediately after an automated action is done, analysts should be shown the corresponding explanation summary without delay(Xu et al., 2025). Perhaps, the explanation will show the most influential features, the confidence level, related evidence, the policy rule that was triggered, and the suggested analyst interpretation. But the idea is not to overload analysts with mathematical details, rather to give them sufficient context for fast validation and escalation decision-making. Furthermore, an explanation workflow means also that the quantity of explanation should be tailored to the analyst's level. For instance, Tier 1 analysts could be given a brief explanation focused on operations: "endpoint isolated due to rare process execution combined with credential dumping indicators and malicious outbound connection pattern which together exceeded the containment threshold." Whereas, highly talented analysts or threat hunters should be provided with diagnostic models, e.g. SHAP values, event sequence graphs, or feature distributions. Consequently, the SOC workflow has to allow for great explainability where summary and detail coexist. In fact, explainability has to be built-in exception handling. If analysts choose to override automated decisions or identify them as false positives, the system should not only store their override but also their reason for the disagreement. This will result in a priceless feedback dataset for threshold adjustments, enhancements of playbooks, and retraining of (Gul et al., 2025).

4.5 Training Security Analysts to Interpret Automated Decisions

Regardless of how well explainability is designed into a system, the system will fail in practice if analysts are not trained to interpret explainability results in the correct way. Security analysts today work in an environment where incident response decisions are influenced by machine recommendations, anomaly scores, and explanation artifacts. Suitable training of analysts must cover both cybersecurity and AI interpretation skills. In order to analyze, analyse, and interpret outputs from machine learning models correctly, the analysts required to gain a pool of expertise including thorough understanding of the security scenario with which the model will be utilized, familiarity with the implications of one incorrect decision (false negatives vs false positives) and knowledge of confusion matrices or similar performance indicators. Moreover, the decision boundaries, drawback or assumptions to which the models have been subjected for example the validity of a model when the underlying data generating process changes over time (concept drift), or how to deal with data imbalance in a supervised learning scenario, should be part of the repertoire of a trained analyst(Abualhaj, Abu-Shareha, & Rateb, 2025).

Finally, a case for assumptions around the production deployment of the models such as the latency, monitoring, logging and retraining schedule needs to be clearly communicated to the analysts. The analyst must be told what kind of logic the analytical methods in their environment follow. They don't need to be turned into researchers of the machine learning type, but they ought to know a rule-based output from an anomaly score, a supervised classifier from a post-hoc explanation. Teaching them to interpret explanation artifacts critically is a must as well. Such a feature importance rank ought not be thought of as an indication of causality. Simply put, a confidence level should not be mistaken for certainty. Analysts, for one, can be trained to discover if the evidence is lacking, if they are missing contextual signals, and if the action taken is in line with the threat(Abdel-Jaber et al., 2025). Along with the training, a scenario-based simulation where analysts can engage with automated actions should be conducted. For example, teams might be faced with incidents where the system is making the recommendation to isolate a host based on behavior anomalies, and the analysts, in this case, will decide whether to keep, escalate or override the action. The time-pressure judgment development and identification of when explanations are operationally helpful or lacking the required features are just some of the benefits(Haider et al., 2026). Last but certainly not least, analyst's function as one a part of the governance framework should be acknowledged. In a security automation that is justifiable, analysts do not merely consume passively the machine output. Instead, they also form a critical element of the accountability framework. Their validations, overrides, feedback, and recordings directly contribute to the system's legitimacy and its continuous evolution. Therefore, training should also emphasize explainability, not only as a technical tool but a major facet of responsible security (Abu-Shareha et al., 2025).

Table 3. Implementation Components for Justifiable Security Automation

Implementation Component	Primary Purpose	Key Operational Output	Contribution to Justification
Explainability by design	Embed interpretation into the platform from detection to response	Immediate reasoning context for each automated action	Prevents black-box action execution
Model documentation	Record purpose, assumptions, features, and limitations of models	Structured model knowledge for analysts and auditors	Supports accountability and governance
Decision provenance	Preserve full chain from evidence to action	Traceable record of model version, thresholds, and response path	Enables forensic review and correction
Transparency-focused pipeline	Align analytics workflow with explanation and policy visibility	Linked analytical, policy, and response artifacts	Ensures action can be defended operationally
Workflow-integrated explanation	Present explanations directly in SOC tools	Faster analyst validation and override capability	Increases trust and practical usability
Analyst training	Build AI interpretation and oversight skills	Better judgment, more accurate review, stronger feedback loops	Strengthens human role in accountable automation

Table 3 shows that justified automation does not result from a single tool or model. Rather, it is the outcome of a well-coordinated program in which platform design, documentation, provenance, workflow integration, and human capability each contribute to one another. Speed could be gained by organizations that simply automate the response layer, but without these complementary components, they will hardly be able to achieve automation that is both trustworthy and defensible. Figure 3 illustrates the implementation path for justifiable security automation. It demonstrates how the design of explainability, the recording of provenance, governance checks, the interaction of analysts, and feedback processes take place in the context of a continuous operational .

Figure 3. Implementation Flow for Justifiable Security Automation

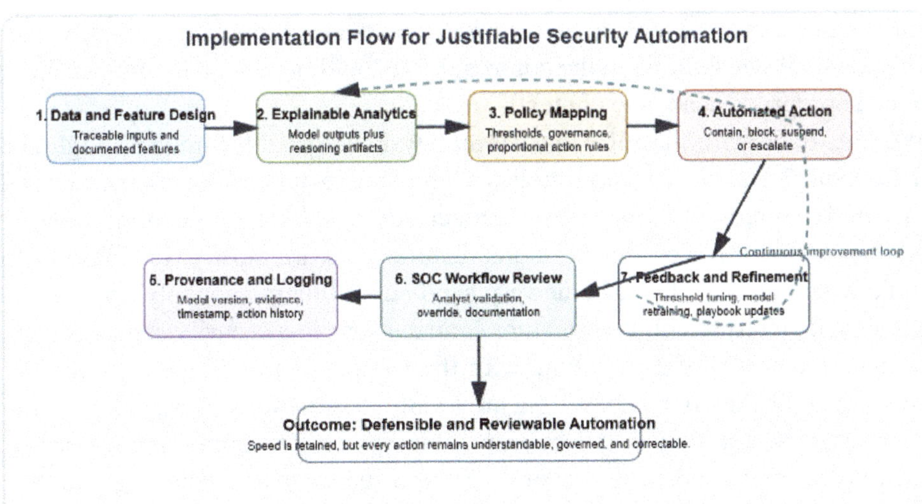

5. DATASET SELECTION AND EXPERIMENTAL METHODOLOGY FOR FALSE POSITIVE ANALYSIS

Theoretical and regulatory discussion about machine-driven security actions becomes very convincing with the help of empirical evaluation. Even in this chapter, dataset-driven evaluation can be a means for not only machine learning model performance comparison, but also a way of figuring out how transparency and justification can be made operationally with metrics. Almost all cybersecurity research, especially in machine learning, heavily revolves around classification accuracy, precision, recall, F1-score, and ROC curve areas. These are very important measures but not enough for evaluating the suitability in practice of automated security systems that make or trigger defensive actions. Besides high prediction performance, a model can also be so complex that it is almost uninterpretable, very difficult to audit, and a risky one to deploy in high-impact response workflows. This section, therefore, devises a dataset-based evaluation framework on account of both security effectiveness and transparency requirements and examining the resulting trade-offs(Lakshmi et al., 2025).

This is achieved by selecting an appropriate cybersecurity dataset, justifying the selection, describing the experimental setup for interpretable versus less interpretable models, and presenting metrics by which transparency-aware performance can be evaluated. The evaluation is set up with the aim to further the chapter thesis that security automation, especially trigger automations, should not be evaluated merely through the success of intrusion detection but through the degree to which the actions can be justified, reviewed, and trusted in the real world(Al-Falouji et al., 2025).

5.1 Dataset Selection for Security Decision Transparency Analysis

The choice of a dataset is the first and most fundamental step of any empirical investigation in cybersecurity. For the dataset underpinning this chapter, a few desiderata are listed out. Firstly, the dataset should be close to intrusion detection or network security automation conditions in reality. Secondly, it should be feature-rich enough to support both interpretable and highly complex machine learning models. Thirdly, the dataset should be amenable to comparison between prediction quality and explanation quality. Fourthly, it should be familiar to the community to facilitate understanding of the results and to place them in the appropriate academic context.

The UNSW-NB15 dataset fits the bill in that it is readily downloadable through Kaggle and is also used extensively in academic intrusion detection studies. Compared to old benchmark datasets, UNSW-NB15 was carefully crafted to represent recent network attack scenarios. Besides benign traffic, it has a wide variety of malicious traffic samples. Furthermore, feature types are mostly flow-based, content-based, time-based, and others (derived). These come very handy in evaluating not only a model's classification capabilities but also the interpretability of feature contributions in a security context.

One of the main reasons why it is in tune with the subject of this chapter are that firstly, its raw features are network and behavioral signals that are totally feasible to be sampled or influenced by automated response systems, e.g. flow duration, protocol usage, packet counts, and service-level features. Secondly, attack types are varied, which opens up the possibility of evaluating whether transparent models work effectively on different threats. Thirdly, there are class labels for binary classification as well as multiclass which means the choice is left to the study's focus either on general threat detection or differentiated security response strategies.

Although the libraries CICIDS2017 and NSL-KDD are also often referred to, UNSW-NB15 stands out as the dataset of choice in a chapter that places justification and transparency at the center because it feature richness makes possible the exploration of the question, "why was the traffic flow classified as an attack?" and "what operational signals led to this decision?"

5.2 Dataset Description and Security Relevance

UNSW-NB15 was created as a dataset capturing a wide array of network behaviors and various types of attacks / intrusions. It contains normal traffic along with several categories of attack activities such as exploits, reconnaissance, shellcode, denial of service, backdoor, generic, and worms. Each record in the dataset is a collection of numerical and categorical features that describe the network flow and behavior properties.

When considering automation of security actions, the strength of this data lies in its simulation of the types of evidence that an automated decision making system might consider before committing to an action. As an example, a security system analyzes the behavior of source and destination, connection duration, packet distribution, types of service, usage of protocol, state transitions, and level of anomalous activity. These signals can then be turned into automated security decisions such as blocking a traffic source, isolating a piece of equipment, or escalating incidents for analyst review(A. Arabiat et al., 2025).

We can look at the dataset in this work as being a binary one whereby normal traffic is considered as one class and malicious traffic as the other. This works very well for our response justification evaluation because the very first step that a machine-driven security system takes would usually be a binary decision threshold: is this event safe or is this something that should trigger a workflow? However, the presence of several attack categories may still come in handy for error analysis and interpretation because some types of models might be more interpretable and accurate on certain attack classes than others.

The following is an overview of the key characteristics associated with the dataset in the context of the transparency-focused evaluation framework:

Table 4. Dataset Characteristics for Evaluating Transparent Security Models

Attribute	Description	Relevance to Chapter
Dataset Name	UNSW-NB15	Widely used intrusion detection benchmark suitable for automated security evaluation
Source Type	Network traffic and intrusion records	Supports analysis of evidence used in automated security actions
Task Framing	Binary classification: Normal vs Malicious	Matches real-world automated response thresholds
Feature Variety	Numerical and categorical security features	Enables both interpretable and complex model comparisons
Attack Diversity	Includes multiple modern attack categories	Allows broader understanding of model behavior across threats
Transparency Value	Rich feature space for explanation and feature attribution	Supports justification analysis through interpretable evidence

Table 4 is relevant in that the choice of the dataset is portrayed not as a mere technical and neutral matter. It even determines if a model is interpretable and can be justified. Unusual features or attacks being overly simplified in a dataset may lead to good classification scores being generated that will add little to the real transparency value analysis.

5.3 Feature Engineering and Model Training Strategy

Feature engineering intervention plays a major role in security evaluation aimed at transparency because it affects both model accuracy and interpretability. Typically, in cybersecurity research, to get the highest classification performance, there are deep feature transformations done to the original data through derivations, embeddings, and abstractions which may ultimately result in disappearance of interpretability. These abstract forms of data may not be understandable by analysts as to what exactly the model was relying on. This chapter talks a lot about justification, so feature engineering should be aimed at keeping semantic meaning as intact as possible(Turab et al., 2025).

The very beginning is taken to be the stage of dataset cleaning whereby missing values are imputed, duplicates eliminated, and features types standardized. Encoding of categorical variables like protocol or service type should be done in a way that their interpretability still remains, while numerical variables should be normalized where necessary for model stability. Regardlessof the situation, the normalization method should also be very thoroughly documented so that the behaviors represented by the original values can still be interpreted from the transformed . In selecting features, one should not blindly include all and any. A feature selection process that leads to) features inclusion is able to strike a balance between analytical and human understandability of the feature list. Connection states such as open, half open, closed, packet characteristics along the flow of connection, service types, and intensity of traffic patterns are just a few examples of features which hold operational value and by their very nature are understandable and that can be figured out by analysts. What is more, such a selection of features brings along a positive effect on explanations' quality(Al Hindi et al., 2025).

When it comes to model training, comparing three types of model families is very beneficial. First, an interpretable baseline should be tested, e.g. Logistic Regression or a shallow Decision Tree. Second, a middle ground type of model such as Random Forest should be selected. Third, a more complex but less transparent one such as XGBoost can be chosen. It is quite common to see the question being raised through this kind of comparison: how much improvement in performance can we expect from more complex models and what do we give up if anything in terms of transparency and justification?(Al-abdallat et al., 2025) The training should be carried out in the usual way with a train-test split or even cross-validation. In fact, the analysis should go beyond the reporting of predictive metrics. The focus should be on explanation too, which are supposed to be generated and assessed for each model. While Logistic Regression coefficients, Decision Trees decision paths, Random Forest feature importance and SHAP approximations, and XGBoost SHAP-based local and global explanations are all different in nature, they can still be put to use for interpretation(El-Mesady et al., 2025).

5.4 Experimental Setup and Evaluation Metrics

A transparency-aware experimental setup should incorporate two classes of evaluation criteria. The simpler class is a set of established ones commonly used for classification purpose to measure the model's ability to separate attack from normal traffic. Apart from accuracy and F1-score, one may consider precision, recall and even the ROC-AUC at a certain threshold. These parameters are still relevant as without the presence of a transparent model, it is hard to imagine a poor performing one being used for consistent automated security actions. The second class relates to explanation support and justification. The element of evaluation with respect to this category is not always a one-dimensional number but it can still be performed in an orderly manner(Ghazal, Abualhaj, et al., 2025). One is featuring interpretability, i.e. can the variables the model uses be understood by analysts at the/security operations center? Another is local explanation clarity, or the capability of explaining a single prediction such that the user can validate the correctness of the system's decision. Third, is global reasoning visibility, i.e. can an analyst understand, in a comprehensive manner, the model's tendency to make decisions? Fourth, policy compatibility, i.e. can the outputs from the model be correlated in a meaningful way to action thresholds and response rules? Therefore, in a practical sense, a study can be structured to record different performance features of a system not only predictive competence but also transparency aspects. To illustrate, a Logistic Regression approach may yield a somewhat lower accuracy but a significantly stronger level of global interpretability, on the other hand, XGBoost achieves a greater classification score albeit with the need to use SHAP explanations for being interpretable(Ghazal, Abu-Shareha, et al., 2025).

The primary role of the experiment is to disclose the point of equilibrium or trade-off between an extremely effective predictive ability and high-grade justification, rather than to demonstrate a case that transparent models always outperform the opaque ones. Also, it is encouraged to include in the assessment a hand check of certain instances at the instance level. This implies selecting certain representative malicious and benign instances and thoroughly checking how different models make the classification of these instances and the way they justify their decisions. Such an instance-by-instance and concrete-object-based comparison proves to be very crucial because, after all, it is the individual events on which automated security actions operate, and not the aggregated . A model might look great in aggregate but if the at the instance level its explanations are very confusing or unstable, then it is going to be difficult to justify the real-world automation deployment of such a model(Sharma et al., 2025). The experimental workflow used a fixed train-test split, standardized preprocessing, encoded categorical variables, and consistent random initialization across all models. Logistic Regression, Decision Tree, Random Forest, and XGBoost were compared using the same feature set to ensure fair performance and transparency evaluation.

5.5 Reproducibility, Implementation Logic, and Analytical Workflow

One of the main objectives of an empirical study is to be reproducible. A step-by-step guide in the form of an outline should be done even if the entire workflow cannot be printed here. The architecture for the chapter's operation is a process consisting of different stages namely: dataset preparation, feature processing, train-test split, model training, performance evaluation, generating explanations, and evaluating models against the transparency dimension with the focus on justifiability. First, the dataset preparation involves cleaning and encoding of records. Second, feature processing includes normalization or transformation of selected features as well as preserving their interpretive meaning. Third, interpretable and non-interpretable models are fitted on the same underlying dataset during model training phase(Hiari et al., 2025). Performance evaluation in the fourth step is about calculating the most common security detection metrics. Explanation generation in the fifth step is about finding the right explanation tools for each model. Transparency comparison in the last step measures how well the explanatory output is capable of supporting a justified automated response(Al-Okbi, Alomari, Hadi, et al., 2025). Figure 4 points out that explanation and justification are no longer afterthoughts that are just attached. In fact, these are elements in the same pipeline as prediction and evaluation. It is very important because this figure underscores a very core argument of the chapter: the method of assessment for transparent security automation should be end-to-end system evaluation, not just a classifier with an explanation .

Figure 4. Transparency-Aware Experimental Workflow for Security Model Evaluation

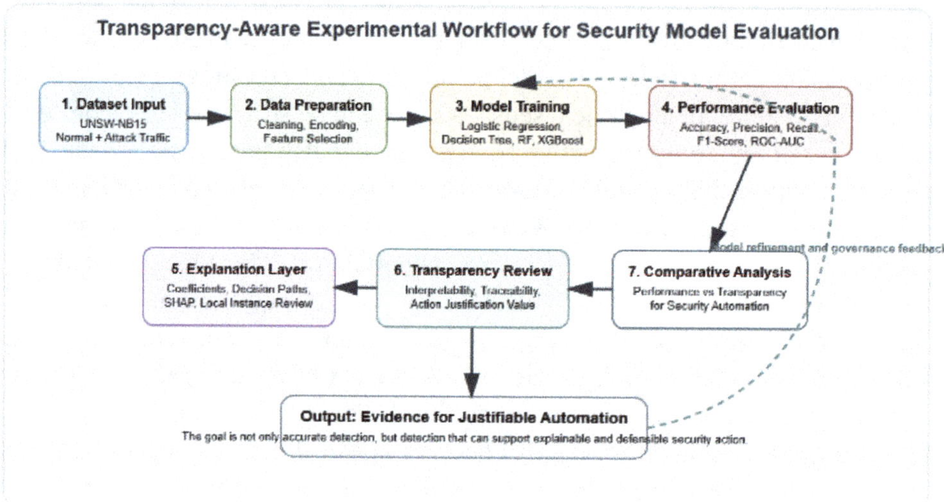

6. RESULTS AND DISCUSSION: ASSESSING TRANSPARENCY AND EXPLANATION CAPABILITY OF AUTOMATED SECURITY MODELS

The discussion of the experimental results is not limited to their predictive performance; instead, the findings are analyzed from the point of view of interpretability, traceability of operations, and suitability for automated security actions. Automated security tools utilize ML/DL models to distinguish normal and malicious behavior patterns. When these models advise security countermeasures, such as host quarantine, network connection blocking, or incident escalation, the staff need to understand the reason for the measure(Dinler et al., 2025). Therefore, the experimental test also included explanatory models alongside those that perform well. We discuss the gap in predictive capacity and transparency of these models. The models that were included in the experiment are Logistic Regression, Decision Tree, Random Forest, and XGBoost. Logistic Regression and Decision Tree models were selected because their explanation mechanisms are very straightforward to interpret. Random Forest and XGBoost on the other hand refer to complex ensemble methods that typically produce better detection results but need feature attribution analysis and other supplementary explanation .(Alraba'nah et al., 2025)

6.1 Performance of Security Models in Prediction

One way to evaluate a model is to measure model detection performance using standard metrics. These metrics represent the ability of a model to classify a malicious network activity correctly when compared to regular traffic. The results indicate that ensemble methods generally outperform simple models when forecasting their performance with raw accuracy. XGBoost was the most accurate model overall, whereas Random Forest was only slightly less accurate. Both Logistic Regression and Decision Tree models showed a bit less detection accuracy, although they were still pretty good. This is aligned with the fact that those models, because they can represent nonlinear dependencies among network features, are capable of discovering behavioral differences that are so subtle that simpler models might not even notice . However, this is not the only factor that determines the evaluation of models for use in automated security decision systems. Kudos to both XGBoost and Random Forest for their great prediction performances(Sardar et al., 2025). Despite that, explaining their internal decision-making processes is significantly harder than with the interpretable ones. Thus, when analysts have to explain the containment actions resulting from these models, they will find it hard. For instance, if a model leads to the isolation of a host on the account of suspicious traffic behavior, then analysts should identify which network signals were the main contributors to the classification result. In contrast to Logistic Regression and Decision Tree models, these can be easily understood at face value. Logistic Regression shows feature weights revealing the degree of influence each network variable has on the likelihood of a malicious classification. In Decision Trees, a clear decision path explains how different feature combinations lead to a classification result. They are thus very helpful in situations where there is a need for transparency and justification(Awais et al., 2025).

6.2 Evaluating Transparency and Other Elements of Interpretability

One part of the transparency assessment phase was to determine the degree of alignment between the global model understanding and the local prediction explanation clarity on the one hand and the automated response policies on the other hand. At the global level, Logistic Regression was identified as a highly interpretable model primarily because the model readily shows the impact of each feature on the final classification . Analysts can identify the features of network traffic which contribute positively or negatively to the probability of malicious behavior(Raza et al., 2025). Security teams are then able to check whether the model's decisions are based on real behavior rather than coincidental ones thanks to this transparency feature. Decision Tree models are also in the lead when it comes to interpretability. Their quite literal rule-based structure offers a clear line of thought showing how feature thresholds are leading to a decision(Al-znamat et al., 2025).

Random Forest models are less interpretable using the same criteria as above because they combine decision trees into one that they use for prediction. Although feature importance is able to show model behavior to some large extent, it cannot give the exact reasoning for the different predictions. In fact, the use of SHAP couldn't give an exact reasoning but could give a very close approximation of each prediction's feature contribution. SHAP attribute comparisons for individual predictions are much less intuitive and a little more difficult to understand. XGBoost models pose similar problems of transparency because of their gradient boosting architecture. Although they can have SHAP explanations of which features are most influential, their reasoning structure is less intuitive than that of interpretable models. Consequently, practitioners require additional explanation layers before they can confidently justify the automated actions triggered by the models(Abualhaj, Al-Khatib, Abu-Shareha, et al., 2025). Explanation tools have important limitations. SHAP and feature-importance methods identify influential variables but do not prove causality. LIME explanations may vary across local samples, and counterfactual explanations may reveal potential evasion paths if disclosed without safeguards. Therefore, explanation outputs should support analyst judgment rather than replace governance review.

Table 5. Comparative Performance and Transparency Evaluation of Security Models

Model	Accuracy (%)	Precision	Recall	F1 Score	Transparency Level	Explanation Method
Logistic Regression	88.6	0.87	0.89	0.88	High	Feature coefficients
Decision Tree	90.1	0.89	0.90	0.89	High	Decision path rules
Random Forest	94.3	0.93	0.94	0.93	Medium	Feature importance / SHAP
XGBoost	95.7	0.95	0.96	0.95	Medium–Low	SHAP explanations

Table 5 presents the main trade-off revealed by the tests. While ensemble-based models like Random Forest and XGBoost deliver top-notch detection results, they need additional explanation tools in order to tell users why they made the particular decision. While interpretable models provide more transparency, they lag in accuracy which is prediction. So, automated security systems must decide the trade-off between detection power and interpretability.

6.3 Case Studies of Model Decisions

Changing transparency testing from theory to practice, individual network traffic entries were modeled and analyzed by each model even though it is case-based. Case-based studies focus on the concret examples where defensive actions by automated systems are most likely. For one instance, traffic transmission was a record of very high packet rates while service access patterns were very unusual. The combination of different models led to the verdict of a malicious classification of the data sample. Nevertheless, explanation routes were quite distinct from one another. Logistic Regression was explaining the classification mainly through features of the highest packet rate combined with the connection in the state(A. M. Ali et al., 2025). Decision Trees, however, didn't take up the same explanation method but went through the threshold criteria for packet count and the transitions of the protocol state. Random Forest and XGBoost models labeled the incident as a rouge but were only able to pinpoint the key factors through the use of SHAP. Based on the explanation, a good understanding is developed about the importance of transparency to security practitioners as the need to make rapid decisions and validate them in an operationally enabled environment only gets more important over time(Q. Y. Shambour et al., 2025).

6.4 Discussion: Performance Versus Justifiable Automation

Based on the evidence gathered, the general point that the chapter is making is supported: automated security systems that are effective must be able to strike a balance between predictive performance and transparency/justification. Regardless of their providing strong detection capabilities, complex models like XGBoost have their drawbacks that lead to the introduce of explanation techniques and governance frameworks for accountability. In practice, there is no reason why a complex analytical engine cannot be combined with interpretable models for operational purposes. For example, an interpretable model could serve as a basic risk filtering mechanism(A. M. Arabiat & Eljaafreh, 2025). Containment would then become automatic only when quite high levels of evidence are met by the new model. One of the ways to go is to combine or embed ensemble models' explanations directly in the Security Operations Center (SOC) workflows. The systems maintain both detection accuracy and operational transparency, because while they provide feature attribution summaries alongside automated alerts, they also allow analysts to see the reasoning behind automated decisions and to confirm the appropriateness of these actions. Our results show that policies and human review for high-impact automated security action interventions should always underlie transparency as the chapter had previously discussed governance/oversight mechanisms. Being able to explain a model does not mean that there will not be a need for (Al-Dmour et al., 2025). Automated security responses should be proportionate to evidence strength, model confidence, asset criticality, and potential operational harm. Low-confidence anomalies may justify additional authentication or analyst review, whereas disruptive actions such as account suspension or endpoint isolation should require stronger evidence and, where appropriate, human approval.

7. CONCLUSION AND FUTURE RESEARCH DIRECTIONS

Businesses have been increasingly depending on security automation lately due to the rapidly changing threat landscape, the increasing sophistication of digital infrastructure, and the limited ability of humans to respond. Various automated security actions, such as isolating compromised devices, stopping malicious network traffic, blocking suspicious user accounts, and starting containment procedures, have turned into the primary methods of protecting the business environment. However, with security operations increasingly embracing automation, the need for explaining and being transparent about automated decision-making will become critical. An action performed by security that cannot be explained, verified, or audited may cause the loss of operational trust, raise issues for governance, and even result in violating legal or ethical obligations(Hou et al., 2025). This study examined the concept of explaining and being transparent about automated security actions and put forward a discussion on the topic from the architectural, analytical, governance, and empirical points of view. First, the research looked into the fundamentals of automated security response systems and how machine learning (ML) models are utilized to detect threats and determine defensive measures. These systems rely on vast amounts of telemetry data and highly complex analytical models to recognize suspicious behavior . Despite the fact that these capabilities can tremendously increase the speed and effectiveness of cyber defenses, they also lead to interpretability problems when these models are used as black-box decision engines(Ghazal, 2025a).

As a remedy to these problems, this chapter discussed the contribution of explainable artificial intelligence (XAI) into security automation. Explainability techniques help the analyst understand which attributes and behavioral indicators are decisive for the automation decisions. Security teams are empowered to decide whether the automated security action is based on sound evidence or if it was the arbitrary behavior of the underlying algorithm that led to the decision thanks to methods like feature attribution analysis, interpretable model structures, and visual analytics dashboards that can be used in conjunction with explainable AI(Al-Daoud, Yogeesh, Mohammad, Raja, Jabeen, et al., 2025). Therefore, explainable AI is a vital link between automated detection and human control. The physical dimension or architecture of transparency in automated security systems was also the subject of a separate in-depth discussion. Transparency should be a feature of the entire security automation platform and not only the resulting models. In fact, a transparent security automation system is one that keeps all decision evidence, analytical output, audit log records, and is open to governance review. Provided elements like decision provenance logging, model monitoring systems, human-in-the-loop governance structures, and transparency dashboards can help organizations being constantly informed about automated actions. Such elements ensure that security automation remains accountable and aligned with operational policies(Hyassat et al., 2025).

Legally and ethically, transparent dealings with security decision systems represent the most essential requirement. Because automated security mechanisms are regularly processing personal data and deciding on digital resource access, the cornerstones of regulatory frameworks, data protection laws and AI governance, underline the role of accountability, explainability and human control in automated decision-making. Ethical operation of the organization in accordance with the principles and values of fairness and transparency will ensure that security interventions neither harm individuals nor disrupt regular activities without adequate justification. Besides theoretical modeling, the chapter presented a dataset-driven analysis based on the UNSW-NB15 intrusion detection dataset. It evaluated the prediction performance of different algorithms such as Logistic Regression, Decision Trees, Random Forest, and XGBoost and their capacity to justify their decisions. Results indicated that although ensemble models are generally capable of reaching a high level of accuracy, their reasoning can only be understood with the help of explanation tools. On the other hand, the more interpretable models offer a clearer step-by-step reasoning. Hence, in this respect, the benefits outweigh their slightly inferior detection performance. The work laid out trade-offs to the design of automated security systems inherent in the feature set of automated security systems. Complex models will have the ability to detect threats with great accuracy but they will need explanation interfaces to justify the treated responses. On the contrary, simple models are more transparent that to the extent, accuracy will be their downfall. The most appropriate solution is, therefore, not accuracy vs. transparency but an integration of both via hybrid architectures, explanation frameworks, and governance controls(Mohammad et al., 2025).

Besides the study several other practical solutions can be employed by security agencies. For example, explainability should be embedded in security solutions and not considered as a post-development add-on. Automated alerts analysts should have access to evidence that tells exactly why a particular action was taken. Decision provenance and evidence logs should be system architecture's standard features. All decisions from monitoring and modeling to action should be traceable. The point is that automated security will still require human intervention especially for major actions leading to business disruption. And finally, security personnel should be trained/educated to interpret AI-driven security . Only then can automated tips be reviewed and validated properly. Despite the advances made so far in this area, transparent security automation is still very much a research topic with a number of unresolved problems. One major problem is that the explanation methods do not scale well to the size of security environments. Security operations centers nowadays are processing millions of events a day and it is highly unlikely that one can afford to generate explanations for every single prediction. One of the main goals of future work will be to find ways how to get the researchers and practitioners together to come up with functionally very useful and at the same time not too cumbersome explanation techniques(Al-Okbi, Alomari, Zitar, et al., 2025).

The next dilemma boils down to how measuring the transparency of models can be developed into a common rule in the cybersecurity field. Although we already possess many performance criteria for machine learning, the issue of explainability or the quality of justification in security automation is really only at the embryonic stage. This is why a well-known and tested evaluation framework would allow researchers and practitioners to compare different models based not only on the prediction accuracy but also on the level of interpretability and governance compatibility. A third concern relates to the adaptable governance mechanism of the AI-driven security systems. Since the threat environment is always changing, it would be reasonable to expect automated security models to be capable of making the necessary adjustments to the system without requiring a major intervention. Meanwhile, the governance frameworks should not become completely unrealistic after the model is retrained and the change of operational conditions. They must be able to provide accountability and transparency throughout the whole process. The creation of dynamic governance frameworks that combine automated auditing and model monitoring will greatly increase the trustworthiness of automated security infrastructures(Ghazal, 2025b).

Human-centered design for explainable cybersecurity systems is the last and most important issue we should be addressing. A significant number of explanation methods existing today have been primarily developed for the needs of technical researchers, with little attention paid to security analysts in operation. Providing explanation tools that are not only easy to understand but also fit well with analyst work patterns and help in decision making can, therefore, lead to a great increase in the usability of transparent security automation. In other words, automation transparency, and justification are no longer just options for cybersecurity operations but have become an absolute requirement. The ability of AI security systems to not only identify the presence of a threat but also be able to give reasons or explanations for their behavior demonstrates the power of effective use of XAI, transparency in system designs, governance structures, and empirical validation approaches. These are the only ways to build automated defense systems that are both powerful and trustworthy. The likely continuous emergence and expansion of transparent security automation will be the main factors in the use of artificial intelligence as a tool for reinforcing cybersecurity without compromising issues such as accountability, operational reliability, and organizational (Ebbini et al., 2025).

REFERENCES

Abdel-Jaber, M. tasime, Makhoul, N., Abdel-Jaber, M. en, & Beale, R. (2025). Cost prediction for product development using hybrid deep learning model: a meta-heuristic model. *Multimedia Tools and Applications, 84*(27). DOI: 10.1007/s11042-024-20437-y

Abu-Shareha, A. A., Abualhaj, M. M., Alsharaiah, M. A., Al-Saaidah, A., & Achuthan, A. (2025). Diabetes Prediction Through Classification Using Pima Dataset: Survey and Evaluation. *Journal of Soft Computing and Data Mining*, *6*(1). Advance online publication. DOI: 10.30880/jscdm.2025.06.01.001

Abualhaj, M. M., Abu-Shareha, A. A., Al-Khatib, S. N., Alsaaidah, A. M., & Anbar, M. (2025). Improving firewall performance using hybrid of optimization algorithms and decision trees classifier. *IAES International Journal of Artificial Intelligence*, *14*(4), 2839. Advance online publication. DOI: 10.11591/ijai.v14.i4.pp2839-2848

Abualhaj, M. M., Abu-Shareha, A. A., & Rateb, R. (2025). Enhancing intrusion detection systems with hybrid HHO-WOA optimization and gradient boosting machine classifier. *International Journal of Reconfigurable and Embedded Systems*, *14*(2), 518. Advance online publication. DOI: 10.11591/ijres.v14.i2.pp518-526

Abualhaj, M. M., Al-Khatib, S. N., Abu-Shareha, A. A., Hyassat, A., & Daoud, M. S. (2025). Smart Firewall for Phishing Detection Powered by Bio-Inspired Algorithms. *Journal of Advances in Information Technology*, *16*(11), 1529–1539. Advance online publication. DOI: 10.12720/jait.16.11.1529-1539

Abualhaj, M. M., Al-Khatib, S. N., Al-Zyoud, M., Qaddara, I., Hiari, M. O., & Aldossary, S. M. A. (2025). Enhanced Network Communication Security Through Hybrid Dragonfly-Bat Feature Selection for Intrusion Detection. *The Journal of Communication*, *20*(5). Advance online publication. DOI: 10.12720/jcm.20.5.607-618

Ahmed, Z. E., Hasan, M. K., Hashim, A. A., Saeed, R. A., Mokhtar, R. A., Singh, S. P., & Ghazal, T. M. (2022). Optimization Procedure for Intelligent Internet of Things Applications. *2022 International Conference on Business Analytics for Technology and Security, ICBATS 2022*. DOI: 10.1109/ICBATS54253.2022.9759065

Al-Adwan, A. S., & Abdeljaber, O. (2025). Toward a resilient and smart supply chain: identifying and prioritizing barriers to metaverse adoption. *International Journal of Industrial Engineering and Operations Management*. DOI: 10.1108/IJIEOM-06-2025-0113

Al-Daoud, K. I., Yogeesh, N., Mohammad, S. I., Raja, N., Chetana, R., William, P., Vasudevan, A., Alshdaifa, N., & Hunitie, M. F. A. (2025). Explainability in AI Using Fuzzy Inference Systems For the Regression Problem. *Applied Mathematics & Information Sciences*, *19*(5), 973–987. Advance online publication. DOI: 10.18576/amis/190501

Al-Daoud, K. I., Yogeesh, N., Mohammad, S. I. S., Raja, N., Jabeen, F. T. Z., William, P., Vasudevan, A., Hunitie, M. F. A., & Alshdaifat, N. (2025). Fuzzy Linear Programming in Real-World Applications: A Comparative Study of Agricultural and Financial Optimization. *Applied Mathematics & Information Sciences*, *19*(4), 849–862. Advance online publication. DOI: 10.18576/amis/190411

Al-Dmour, R., Al-Dmour, H., Al-Dmour, A., Basheer Amin, E., & Al-Dmour, Y. (2025). *AI and big data-driven social media recruitment: the mediating role of talent acquisition and employee engagement in bank performance*. Digital Transformation and Society., DOI: 10.1108/DTS-02-2025-0042

Al-Falouji, M., Al Btoush, R., Abu Hajar, H., & Tarwaneh, B. (2025). Landslide Stabilization of Al-Adasiah Road Using Pile Wall Retaining System. *Jordan Journal of Civil Engineering*, *19*(4). Advance online publication. DOI: 10.14525/JJCE.v19i4.02

Al Hindi, G., Alshraideh, M., Hussein, A. H., Eliyan, L. F., & Al-Dhaqm, A. (2025). Hacking Back: Using Genetic Algorithms to Outsmart Hackers. *Journal of Computational Science*, *21*(9), 2049–2064. Advance online publication. DOI: 10.3844/jcssp.2025.2049.2064

Al-Momani, M. M., Alqudah, T. A., Al Swiety, I. A., Mahrakani, N., Nassoura, M. B. A., & Al Attar, M. K. (2025). Integrating Artificial Intelligence (AI) and Business Intelligence (BI): A Framework for Improving Enterprise Performance. *TEM Journal, 14*(3). https://doi.org/DOI: 10.18421/TEM143-26

Al-Okbi, N. K., Alomari, S. A., Hadi, W. J., Ajrash, A. S., Smerat, A., & Abualigah, L. (2025). Defending Digital Integrity: Advances in Media Forgery Analysis Research and Cybersecurity Development. *SN Computer Science*, *6*(8), 913. Advance online publication. DOI: 10.1007/s42979-025-04462-8

Al-Okbi, N. K., Alomari, S. A., Zitar, R. A., Smerat, A., Nazzal, M. A., & Abualigah, L. (2025). Integrating Multimodal Emotion Recognition with Deep Q-Learning for Adaptive Social Robot Interaction. *International Journal of Robotics and Control Systems*, *5*(4), 2265–2289. Advance online publication. DOI: 10.31763/ijrcs.v5i4.2055

Al-znamat, F. O., Alsaaidah, A., & Abu-Shareha, A. A. (2025). Malware Detection Using a Modified Bat Algorithm for Feature Selection. *International Journal of Intelligent Engineering and Systems*, *18*(9), 885–899. Advance online publication. DOI: 10.22266/ijies2025.1031.56

Alabdallat, R. D., Abualhaj, M. M., & Abu-Shareha, A. (2025). Enhanced Multiclass Android Malware Detection Using a Modified Dwarf Mongoose Algorithm. *International Journal of Analysis and Applications*, *23*, 248. Advance online publication. DOI: 10.28924/2291-8639-23-2025-248

Ali, A. M., Al-Qerem, A., Hassan, M. R., Abu-Khadrah, A., & Jarrah, M. (2025). Traffic Monitoring and Control System for Smart City Pollution Regulation Using IoT and Correlated Capsule Networks. *IEEE Access : Practical Innovations, Open Solutions*, *13*, 46983–47003. Advance online publication. DOI: 10.1109/ACCESS.2025.3550966

Ali, L., Alshamayleh, A., Ibrahim, A., & Ahmed, S. M. (2026). Information Management Enhancement in Cloud-Based Systems Through Blockchain-Enabled Secure Access Control. *Indian Journal of Information Sources and Services*, *16*(1), 289–296. Advance online publication. DOI: 10.51983/ijiss-2026.16.1.30

Alraba'nah, Y., Al-Sharaeh, S., & Al Hindi, G. (2025). Enhancing Intrusion Detection Using Hybrid Long Short-Term Memory and XGBoost. *Journal of Soft Computing and Data Mining*, *6*(1). Advance online publication. DOI: 10.30880/jscdm.2025.06.01.016

Arabiat, A., Altayeb, M., & Salama, S. (2025). Artificial intelligence-powered smart roads: Leveraging orange3 for traffic signs recognition. *IAES International Journal of Artificial Intelligence*, *14*(5), 3816. Advance online publication. DOI: 10.11591/ijai.v14.i5.pp3816-3826

Arabiat, A. M., & Eljaafreh, Y. G. (2025). Intrusion Detection in Wireless Sensor Networks Using ML Based Classification of Denial of Service (DoS) Attacks. *The Journal of Communication, 20*(4). Advance online publication. DOI: 10.12720/jcm.20.4.501-514

Awais, Z., Hussain, M., Elshenawy, A., Arsalan, A., Anwar, M., Asif Habib, M., Jabbar, S., & Ahmad, M. (2025). ISCC: Intelligent Semantic Caching and Control for NDN-Enabled Industrial IoT Networks. *IEEE Access : Practical Innovations, Open Solutions, 13*, 169881–169898. Advance online publication. DOI: 10.1109/ACCESS.2025.3614984

Dar, A. A., Bhavithra, H. A., Awasthi, A. K., Sabha, S. U., Dar, J. G., Smerat, A., & Sindhuja, S. (2025). Inventory Optimization for Perishables: A Probabilistic and Fuzzy Modeling Approach. *Mathematical Modelling of Engineering Problems, 12*(8). Advance online publication. DOI: 10.18280/mmep.120825

Dinler, Ö. B., Bektemyssova, G., Şahin, C. B., Montazeri, Z., Dehghani, M., Smerat, A., Werner, F., & Eguchi, K. (2025). Carpenter Optimization Algorithm: A Human-inspired Metaheuristic for Robust and Efficient Constrained Optimization. *International Journal of Intelligent Engineering and Systems, 18*(11), 344–357. Advance online publication. DOI: 10.22266/ijies2025.1231.21

Ebbini, M. M., Qtaishat, A. K., Aburub, F. A., & Jaradat, M. S. (2025). Impact of Ethical Fintech on Micro Entrepreneurs in Jordan. *International Journal of Advances in Soft Computing and Its Applications, 17*(3). Advance online publication. DOI: 10.15849/IJASCA.251130.10

El-Mesady, A., Elsonbaty, A., Nisar, K. S., & Adel, W. (2025). Fractional-order mathematical modeling and optimal control strategies for women's empowerment initiatives. *Ain Shams Engineering Journal, 16*(11), 103702. Advance online publication. DOI: 10.1016/j.asej.2025.103702

Elkaradawy, A., Elshenawy, A., & Harb, H. (2025). Enhancing Cloud Job Failure Prediction With a Novel Multilayer Voting-Based Framework. *IEEE Access : Practical Innovations, Open Solutions, 13*, 140600–140613. Advance online publication. DOI: 10.1109/ACCESS.2025.3593808

Elomda, B. M., Abdelbary, T. A. A., Hassan, H. A., Hamza, K. S., & Kharma, Q. (2025). An Enhanced Multi-Layer Blockchain Security Model for Improved Latency and Scalability. *Information (Basel), 16*(3), 241. Advance online publication. DOI: 10.3390/info16030241

Fatima, W., Rizvi, S. S. R., Ghazal, T. M., Kharma, Q. M., Ahmad, M., Abbas, S., Furqan, M., & Adnan, K. M. (2025). Abstractive Text Summarization in Arabic-Like Script Using Multi-Encoder Architecture and Semantic Extraction Techniques. *IEEE Access : Practical Innovations, Open Solutions, 13*, 104977–104991. Advance online publication. DOI: 10.1109/ACCESS.2025.3575610

Ghazal, T. M. (2025a). An IoT-Based Active Learning Convolutional Neural Networks Model for Predicting River Water Quality. *Journal of Soft Computing and Data Mining, 6*(1). Advance online publication. DOI: 10.30880/jscdm.2025.06.01.021

Ghazal, T. M. (2025b). Federated Learning for Intelligent Sensing and Navigation Technologies for 6G Communications. *Journal of Sensors, 2025*(1). DOI: 10.1155/js/3746147

Ghazal, T. M., Abu-Shareha, A., Mustafa, S. A., Ibrahim, A., & Ahmed, S. M. (2025). Privacy-Preserving Transformer-Based Meta-Learning Algorithm for Zero-Day Intrusion Detection in IoT-Enabled Smart Grids. *Journal of Internet Services and Information Security*, *15*(4), 76–84. Advance online publication. DOI: 10.58346/JISIS.2025.I4.006

Ghazal, T. M., Abualhaj, M., Ahmed, A. A., Al-Tarawni, M. A. M., & Maghrabi, L. A. (2025). Federated Deep Graph Neural Network Algorithm for Real-Time Intrusion Detection in Heterogeneous IoT Systems. *Journal of Internet Services and Information Security*, *15*(4), 484–497. Advance online publication. DOI: 10.58346/JISIS.2025.I4.035

Ghazal, T. M., Awouda, A. E., Hasan, M. K., Rahman, A. H. A., Islam, S., Saeed, R. A., Elshafie, H., Iqbal, A., & Hussein, A. H. (2025). Knowledge Learning for Securing Workflow Scheduling Algorithm in Mobile Edge Computing. *Mobile Networks and Applications*, *30*(3-4), 395–413. Advance online publication. DOI: 10.1007/s11036-025-02465-6

Ghazal, T. M., Hasan, M. K., Alzoubi, H. M., Al Hmmadi, M., Al-Dmour, N. A., Islam, S., Kamran, R., & Mago, B. (2022). Securing Smart Cities Using Blockchain Technology. *2022 1st International Conference on AI in Cybersecurity, ICAIC 2022*. DOI: 10.1109/ICAIC53980.2022.9896971

Ghazal, T. M., Hasan, M. K., Raju, K. N., Khan, M. A., Alshamayleh, A., Bhatt, M. W., & Ahmad, M. (2025). Data Space Privacy Model with Federated Learning Technique for Securing IoT Communications in Autonomous Marine Vehicles. *Journal of Intelligent & Robotic Systems*, *111*(3), 84. Advance online publication. DOI: 10.1007/s10846-025-02298-1

Ghazal, T. M., Janjua, J. I., Abushiba, W., Ahmad, M., Ihsan, A., & Al-Dmour, N. A. (2024). Cybersecurity Revolution via Large Language Models and Explainable AI. *2024 17th International Conference on Security of Information and Networks, SIN 2024*. DOI: 10.1109/SIN63213.2024.10871324

Gul, A., Khan, F., Farooq, M., Javaid, A., Hussain, Z., & Elzaghmouri, B. (2025). STATISTICAL MODELING AND PREDICTION OF PANDEMIC USING CLASSICAL AND MACHINE LEARNING APPROACH. *Pakistan Journal of Statistics*, *41*(3).

Haider, Z. A., Ullah, I., Shareha, A. A., Nasimov, R., & Memon, S. A. (2026). Artificial Intelligence (AI)-Enabled Unmanned Aerial Vehicle (UAV) Systems for Optimizing User Connectivity in Sixth-Generation (6G) Ubiquitous Networks. *Computers, Materials & Continua*, *86*(1), 1–16. Advance online publication. DOI: 10.32604/cmc.2025.071042

Hanumanthagowda, P. B., Vasanthkumara, M. K. M., Al-Nussairi, A. K. J., Hadi, A. A., Smerat, A., & Shivanna, P. B. (2026). Process-aware Temporal Graph Embedding for Detecting and Localizing Recurring Concept Drift. *International Journal of Intelligent Engineering and Systems*, *19*(1), 402–422. Advance online publication. DOI: 10.22266/ijies2026.0131.25

Hasan, M. K., Habib, A. K. M. A., Islam, S., Safie, N., Ghazal, T. M., Khan, M. A., Alzahrani, A. I., Alalwan, N., Kadry, S., & Masood, A. (2024). Federated learning enables 6 G communication technology: Requirements, applications, and integrated with intelligence framework. *Alexandria Engineering Journal*, *91*, 658–668. Advance online publication. DOI: 10.1016/j.aej.2024.02.044

Hiari, M., Alraba'nah, Y., & Qaddara, I. (2025). A Deep Learning-Based Intrusion Detection System using Refined LSTM for DoS Attack Detection. *Engineering. Technology and Applied Science Research, 15*(4), 25627–25633. Advance online publication. DOI: 10.48084/etasr.11499

Hou, G., Alkhayyat, A., Almalkawi, A., Yadav, A., Shreenidhi, H. S., Saini, V., Shomurotova, S., Singh, D., Jain, V., Smerat, A., & Khalid, A. (2025). Development of robust machine learning models to estimate hydrochar higher heating value and yield based upon biomass proximate analysis. *Bioresources and Bioprocessing, 12*(1), 138. Advance online publication. DOI: 10.1186/s40643-025-00979-1 PMID: 41335148

Hyassat, A. S., Abu Zayed, R. E., Al Khateeb, E. A., Shalaldeh, A., Abdelhamied, M. M., & Qaddara, I. (2025). Unveiling Cyber Threats: An In-Depth Study on Data Mining Techniques for Exploit Attack Detection †. *Engineering Proceedings, 104*(1), 28. Advance online publication. DOI: 10.3390/engproc2025104028

Ibrahim, A., Sekhar, R., Tawfeq, J. F., Salih, S. Q., Shah, P., & Radhi, A. D. (2024). Security and Privacy Protection for Online Electronic Documents Based on Novel Encryption Techniques. *Journal of Intelligent Systems and Internet of Things, 11*(1), 21–28. Advance online publication. DOI: 10.54216/JISIoT.110103

Iftikhar, A., Mohammad, S. I., Alqudah, M. N., Al-Adwan, A. S., Vasudevan, A., Ali, I., & Farhan, M. (2025). Evaluating Inclusivity and Fairness of AI Recruitment Tools for Hiring People with Disabilities in the United Arab Emirates(UAE). *Data and Metadata, 4*. Advance online publication. DOI: 10.56294/dm2025487

Iskandarani, M. Z., & Chakrabarti, K. (2025). Adaptive Frequency and Energy Modeling Framework for Robotic Wireless Sensor Networks Based on Path Loss Predictions. *Journal of Robotics, 2025*(1). DOI: 10.1155/joro/6156608

Jaradat, S., Elhenawy, M., Paz, A., Alhadidi, T. I., Ashqar, H. I., & Nayak, R. (2025). A Cross-Cultural Crash Pattern Analysis in the United States and Jordan Using BERT and SHAP. *Electronics (Basel), 14*(2), 272. Advance online publication. DOI: 10.3390/electronics14020272

Khaled Abdullah, S., & Qawasmeh, R. (2025). *Navigating the ethical and legal risks of AI marketing in Jordanian SMEs*. EDPACS., DOI: 10.1080/07366981.2025.2600205

Khatibi, A., Babaker, S., Praveen, K. N. R., Chohan, J. S., Jadhav, A., Alsoud, A. R., Ramudu, M. J., & Jeet, R. (2025). Advanced AI-Driven Cybersecurity: Analyzing Emerging Threats and Defensive Strategies. *National Academy Science Letters*. Advance online publication. DOI: 10.1007/s40009-025-01897-8

Laha, S. R., Smadi, K. Al, Habboush, A. K., Pattanayak, B. K., Pattnaik, S., & Mohanty, B. (2025). Smart Waste Management Framework for Green Cities: Integrating IoT, LoRa, and Deep Learning for Efficient Waste Classification and Management. *Tikrit Journal of Engineering Sciences, 32*(Special Issue 1). DOI: 10.25130/tjes.sp1.2025.1

Lakshmi, A. S., Sigamany, E. S. S., Traisa, R., Kumar, R., Reddy, K. R., Chohan, J. S., & Smerat, A. (2025). Enhancing Code Quality Through Automated Refactoring Using Transformer-Based Language Models. *International Journal of Advanced Computer Science and Applications*, *16*(9). Advance online publication. DOI: 10.14569/IJACSA.2025.0160951

Maz, Y. A., Anbar, M., Manickam, S., Abualhaj, M. M., Almalki, S. A., & Alabsi, B. A. (2025). Transfer Learning-Based Approach with an Ensemble Classifier for Detecting Keylogging Attack on the Internet of Things. *Computers, Materials & Continua*, *85*(3), 5287–5307. Advance online publication. DOI: 10.32604/cmc.2025.068257

Mohammad, A. A. S., Al-Ramadan, A. M., Mohammad, S. I., Al Oraini, B., Vasudevan, A., Alshdaifat, N., & Hunitie, M. F. A. (2025). Customer Sentiment Analysis for Food and Beverage Development in Restaurants using AI in Jordan. *Data and Metadata*, *4*, 922. Advance online publication. DOI: 10.56294/dm2025922

Nasir, J., Aamir, M., Iftikhar, S., Albidah, A. B., Alqasem, O. A., Elwahab, M. E. A., Khan, I., & Koh, W. S. (2025). A Novel Hybrid Approach to Forecasting Crude Oil Prices Using Local Mean Decomposition, ARIMA, and XGBoost. *IEEE Access : Practical Innovations, Open Solutions*, *13*, 89140–89156. Advance online publication. DOI: 10.1109/ACCESS.2025.3561193

Qaddara, I., Alrabaynah, Y., & Hiari, M. O. (2025). Evaluation of SQL and NoSQL Databases on Parallel Processing. *Engineering. Technology and Applied Science Research*, *15*(4), 24298–24304. Advance online publication. DOI: 10.48084/etasr.10620

Qader Ismail Alnajem, A. A., Ibrahim, A., Abdulrahman, M. M., Abdulrazak Al-Kubaisi, A. A., Tawfeq, J. F., Khishe, M., & Saeed, A. (2024). AI-Driven Strategic Foresight: Anticipating Future Trends and Modelling Business Strategies. *2024 International Conference on Decision Aid Sciences and Applications, DASA 2024*. DOI: 10.1109/DASA63652.2024.10836619

Qawasmeh, S., Habboushb, A., Elzaghmouri, B., Kharma, Q., & Albalawneh, D. (2025). Hybrid Convolutional Neural Network-Based Intrusion Detection System for Secure IoT Networks. *Tikrit Journal of Engineering Sciences*, *32*(SP1), 1–11. Advance online publication. DOI: 10.25130/tjes.sp1.2025.2

Raza, M. A., Karim, A., Alqarni, M., Al-Khasawneh, M. A., Jumani, T. A., Aman, M., & Masud, M. I. (2025). An Intelligent Long Short-Term Memory-Based Machine Learning Model for the Potential Assessment of Global Hydropower Capacity in Sustainable Energy Transition and Security. *Energies*, *18*(13), 3324. Advance online publication. DOI: 10.3390/en18133324

Sanjalawe, Y., Al-E'mari, S., Abualhaj, M., Makhadmeh, S. N., Alsharaiah, M. A., & Hijazi, D. H. (2025). Recent advances in secretary bird optimization algorithm, its variants and applications. In *Evolutionary Intelligence* (Vol. 18, Number 3). DOI: 10.1007/s12065-025-01054-6

Sardar, R., Anees, T., Al-Shamayleh, A. S., Mehmood, E., Khalil, W., Akhunzada, A., & Shaikh, F. S. (2025). Challenges in detecting security threats in WoT: A systematic literature review. *Artificial Intelligence Review*, *58*(7), 196. Advance online publication. DOI: 10.1007/s10462-025-11176-z

Shambour, Q., Al-Zyoud, M., & Almomani, O. (2025). Quantum-Inspired Hybrid Metaheuristic Feature Selection with SHAP for Optimized and Explainable Spam Detection. *Symmetry*, *17*(10), 1716. Advance online publication. DOI: 10.3390/sym17101716

Shambour, Q. Y., Al-Zyoud, M., & Hussein, A. H. (2025). FROM DATA TO DIAGNOSIS: KNOWLEDGE-DRIVEN, EXPLAINABLE AI FOR RELIABLE EARLY AUTISM DETECTION. *Interdisciplinary Journal of Information, Knowledge, and Management*, *20*, 032. Advance online publication. DOI: 10.28945/5652

Sharma, K. P., Hussain, R., Jaharadak, A. A., Trawnih, A. A., Verma, D., Dasi, S., & Pant, S. (2025). Hybrid Convolutional Neural Network for Robust Attack Detection in Wireless Sensor Networks. *Internet Technology Letters*, *8*(6), e650. Advance online publication. DOI: 10.1002/itl2.650

Turab, N., Abushattal, A., Al-Nabulsi, J., & Owida, H. A. (2025). Advanced risk assessment using machine learning and sentiment analysis on log data. *IAES International Journal of Artificial Intelligence*, *14*(5), 3897. Advance online publication. DOI: 10.11591/ijai.v14.i5.pp3897-3905

Vasudevan, A., Albinaa, T. A., Mohammad, S. I., Sharmila, E., Raja, N., Soon, E. E. H., Alshurideh, M. T., & Al-Adwan, A. S. (2024). Bidirectional LSTM for Electronic Product Recommendation. *Applied Mathematics & Information Sciences*, *18*(6), 1443–1453. Advance online publication. DOI: 10.18576/amis/180621

Vasudevan, A., Tamilmani, K. T., Mohammad, S. I., Sridheepika, V. S., Raja, N., Soon, E. E. H., Nagaraj, S., & Al-Adwan, A. S. (2025). Voices of Concern: Contemplations on Socioeconomic, Ethical, and Developmental Impacts of AI. *Applied Mathematics & Information Sciences*, *19*(1), 221–232. Advance online publication. DOI: 10.18576/amis/190119

Xu, B., Jummaa, K., Altalbawy, F. M. A., Roopashree, R., Saraswat, S. K., Ray, S., Tomar, P., Naem, S., Hamza, H. H., Smerat, A., & Khalid, A. (2025). Machine learning-assisted computation of water activity for ionic liquid-based aqueous ternary elements. *Desalination and Water Treatment*, *324*, 101484. Advance online publication. DOI: 10.1016/j.dwt.2025.101484

Yaseen, M., Ali, E., Sarwar, N., Jamel, L., Din, I., Yuldashev, F., & Law, F. (2025). Design of Minimal Spanning Tree and Analytic Hierarchical Process (SAHP) Based Hybrid Technique for Software Requirements Prioritization. *IET Software, 2025*(1). DOI: 10.1049/sfw2/8819735

Chapter 9
Designing Human Review and Override Mechanisms in Automated Systems

Khaled Shaalan
http://orcid.org/0000-0003-0823-8390
The British University in Dubai, UAE

ABSTRACT

The focus of this chapter is on the development of human review and override elements in automated security operation systems. It discusses the fundamental reasons for a significant human intervention to lessen automation bias, handle false alarms, and make sure that decisions are made in a legal way. The chapter looks at various principles underlying the effective review, such as the transparency of alerts, the interpretability of model outputs, role- based authority, and the availability of timely escalation channels. Furthermore, it highlights operational difficulties such as alert fatigue, the alignment of skills, and the maintenance of the pace of response together with oversight. The chapter, by merging legal requirements with security engineering practice, offers a roadmap for setting up review and override mechanisms that are not only feasible and proportional but also robust and compliant with automation while not weakening security effectiveness.

1. INTRODUCTION TO HUMAN REVIEW AND OVERRIDE IN AUTOMATED SYSTEMS

We advocate in this chapter that instead of viewing automation as a substitute for human judgment in critical contexts, it should be considered a tool for supporting and enhancing human decisions that function within a well-designed governance framework. It is within this framework that humans do not simply witness results after the fact. They evaluate decision points that are uncertain, have a significant impact, or are sensitive to policies, they step in if the system's actions are anticipated to go beyond risk that is considered acceptable, and they keep the power to halt, undo or modify automated operations. This approach to design is even more critical in the case of automated security systems, where the consequences of actions such as isolating hosts, blocking accounts, killing processes, suspending transactions, or escalating incidents can be operational, legal, reputational, or all three at once (Ghazal, 2025a). As

DOI: 10.4018/979-8-2600-2870-4.ch009

depicted in Figure 1, one can best view modern automated systems as multi-layered techno-social environments. Analytics engines process data inputs and generate risk assessments. Policy rules then indicate the actions to be taken, whereas human review is the last room between machine results and irreversible or major decisions. This layer of humans should not be seen as just a token step. In fact, it is a genuine controlling device designed to uphold proportionality, responsibility, and the ongoing presence of the human intellect. The human review here may be only partial and based on decision levels rather than being universal. Still, even then, it is a must for specifying the system's freedoms to operate on its own and the moments it needs human.

Figure 1. Conceptual Architecture of Human-in-the-Loop Automated Security Systems

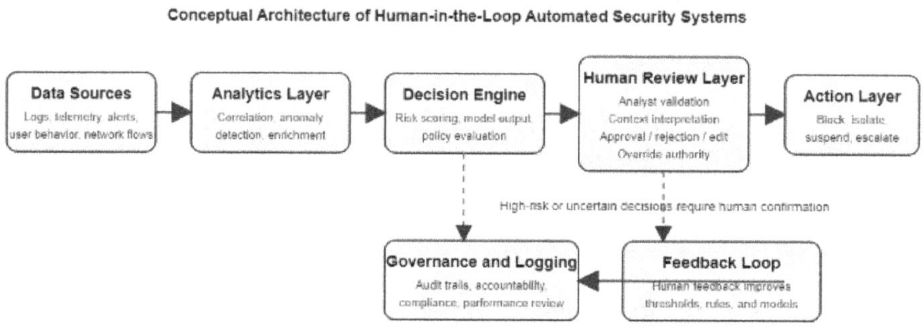

1.1 Evolution of Automation in Security and Decision Systems

Automated systems have gone through different stages of development. At first, rule-based systems depended on following a preset logic sequence and employing deterministic stimuli. They were reliable and traceable but lacked flexibility. When the availability of data resources increased, automation progressed to event correlation, behavior analysis, and the involvement of machine-learning in decision-making pipelines (Haider et al., 2026). This change gave systems the ability to detect very small anomalies, to sort out alerts by priority, and even to change their operations according to the threat environment. As a case in point, a top cybersecurity system can, in a matter of seconds, carry out a simultaneous examination of network traffic, endpoint events, user identity, and cloud signals and then recommend or implement account lockout, privilege revocation, or host isolation, . On the other hand, this change has also altered operational risks. It was easier to point out flaws in earlier systems as the logic behind them was open. Nowadays, there are multiple layers contributing to a single decision, for instance, a set of rules, learning from data, scoring of confidence, and thresholds that get updated dynamically. The more advanced a system is, the less time it takes for operators to distinguish instances when a step is justified, when it is premature, and when there is a misunderstanding of the situation by the machine. Thus, system development has been shifted from the topic of whether it is right to automate to the challenging question of how to restrict, monitor, and challenge automation (Habboush & Elzaghmouri, 2025).

1.2 Risks of Fully Autonomous Decision Making

In principle, full autonomy in decision-making would make an environment in which speed is key to success a very attractive one. However, just speed-by-itself should not be a sufficient reason to hand over the last word. Sometimes, automated systems are so accurate that they can even generate scenarios where it is recognized that the situation that led the system to reaching a decision is a problematic one. The systems might produce false positives that interfere with legitimate activities; false negatives that result in genuine threats passing unnoticed; and even misclassifications because of missing data, adversarial tampering, or concept drift. For instance, in the field of security, an erroneous automatic action could lead to the scenario of locking out employees, causing blockage of authentic financial transactions, making medical operations to go off track, shutting down manufacturing systems, or deleting digital evidence, which is very important for incident analysis (Khaled Abdullah & Qawasmeh, 2025). Another risk is automation bias, that is to say, operators who have come to rely on the machine offering very unequivocal recommendations could start trusting the system so much that even when they have some doubts, they may still choose the system as their final option. Ironically enough, those few ill-planned automation scenarios might actually harm human judgment while the intention was to enhance . Providing a review system is a positive element but it works only when reviewers are empowered to effectively challenge the system and also when the interface can supply them with adequate context to make well-informed decisions. In addition, there is the problem of the black box aspect in most . If analysts do not eventually come to know the rationale behind the system's recommendation of an action, the review turns into a formality rather than a sincere check. Human supervision at this point becomes nothing more than ticking a box rather than a genuine protection. So, good designs of the review and override need to merge authority with clarity (Dar et al., 2025).

1.3 Need for Human Oversight in Critical Systems

Human oversight is indispensable because critical decisions might be context-sensitive and automated systems are still not perfect in this area. Humans have an advantage in detecting subtle signs of behavior, understanding the needs of an organization, figuring out a one-off situation, and deciding what proportionate action should be taken in ways that fixed rules or models based on statistics may not be capable of (Abualhaj, Abu-Shareha, & Rateb, 2025). One security analyst may recognize that a privileged account generating a very unusual activity is because a maintenance work has been planned while to the automated system, it will only appear as deviation from baseline. In a similar vein, the hospital administrator may be aware that the suspicious access pattern is due to the emergency clinical operations and not the actual malicious behavior. Human oversight is a form of governance as well. It provides a human locus of accountability where a person, team, or role agrees or disagrees with the action suggested by the machine. This is very crucial from the point of view of legal justification, fulfilling the set of rules, and looking back after a failure. If a company cannot say either who gave permission a major impact action or why it was done, then the technical trust and the institutional legitimacy will both be damaged. Hence, the academic control should be regarded as a fundamental day-to-day functioning element rather than a spontaneous safety net (Hussain et al., 2025). The procedure should specify which decisions are open to review, what information the reviewers can have access to, what is the time limit for the decision-making process, and what override actions are allowed. In the absence of this, a company might quite often find itself swinging between the two very different and highly undesirable extremes: dangerously free actions and very slow and awkward manual (Jaradat et al., 2025).

1.4 Human-in-the-Loop Security Architectures

Human-in-the-loop is a term used to describe a system architecture in which the involvement of humans is a direct and vital component of the decision or action phase. In this kind of setting, computers will be collecting data on a large scale, detecting, prioritizing, and making recommendations, while humans will be expected to assess the proposed actions that are uncertain, of high impact or strategically sensitive. The main goal is not to slow down the pace of automation but to restrict human decision-making only to the situations where it is really necessary (Hiari et al., 2025). According to the example in Figure 2, the process of an automated system with human review usually begins with data intake and automatic . Following this, a risk score and a suggested action are produced by the system. In scenarios where the confidence is high and the impact is low, the action can be executed automatically according to a predetermined policy. However, in case of moderate confidence, high impact, or if the decision violates corporate governance rules, it will then be forwarded for human review. Subsequently, the analyst may endorse the decision, adjust it, reject it, or resort to an override which is the reversal or suspension of machine behavior (Abualhaj, Al-Khatib, Al-Zyoud, Qaddara, et al., 2025). The whole process is documented and taken back to the feedback loop for further system adjustments.

Figure 2. Workflow of Automated Detection with Human Review and Override Layer

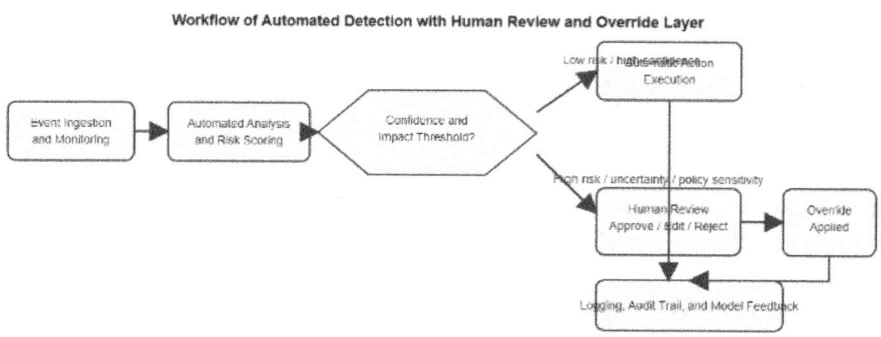

1.5 Overview of Human Review and Override Mechanisms

Human review mechanisms refer to the formal and informal ways in which individuals within an organization check system suggestions before, during, or right after automated action. Override mechanisms consist of the means by which authorized staff are able to interrupt, reverse, amend, or suspend those actions. A good review mechanism considers at least five aspects (Ghoneim et al., 2025). Firstly, it identifies escalation conditions like low confidence in a model, high criticality of an asset, insufficiently clear evidence, unusually severe actions, or conflict with a policy. Secondly, it offers transparent evidence such that the reviewer clearly understands the foundation of the proposal. Thirdly, it allocates unequivocal approval and override powers.

Fourthly, it maintains a record of each decision for the purposes of audit and reflection. Lastly, it channels human decisions into the system to contribute to its ongoing improvement so that common errors can be mitigated over (Abbadi et al., 2025).

This chapter contributes a governance-oriented human review and override framework for automated security decision systems. The framework combines confidence-based escalation, risk-sensitive human review, structured override authority, audit logging, interface safeguards, and simulated security-event evaluation to show how automation can remain fast while preserving accountability and proportional human control.

2. FOUNDATIONS OF HUMAN OVERSIGHT IN AUTOMATED DECISION SYSTEMS

Prior research on human review and override in automated security systems can be organized into six themes: human-in-the-loop decision-making, SOC workflow design, automation bias, confidence-based escalation, override governance, and accountable AI. These themes show that human review is not merely a procedural safeguard; it is a technical, organizational, and ethical control that determines when automated decisions may proceed and when human judgment must intervene. The basic principle of human oversight is based on a very simple and yet very powerful idea: not all decisions can be equally good candidates for automation. Decisions that come around over and over again, are of low impact, and are well-structured are good candidates for automation. On the other hand, there are decisions that involve ambiguities, values, and have potential for harm if wrong, and they call for human monitoring. In the middle of the two extremes, there is a large category of decisions that, to some extent, are automated - the system issues recommendations, rankings, or proposed actions, but the final operational legitimacy to those actions is given by a human who validates. This type of layered interaction between machine capability and human authority is at the center of responsible automated system design (Abualhaj, Abu-Shareha, Al-Khatib, et al., 2025). Thus, human oversight at one time performs a number of different roles. It acts as a safeguard against technical errors, it limits excessive reactions, it keeps accountability alive at the institutional level, it helps with legal and ethical compliance, and it guarantees a continued alignment of machine behavior with changing operational realities. Without this human oversight, organizations will find it at times too late when technically sound automation has led to results that are from the strategy point of view unacceptable (Ebbini et al., 2025). Thus a decision system may be accurate at the aggregate level statistically, but the occasional failures in the case of sensitive accounts, critical infrastructures, high-value customers, or legally protected rights can still lead to the system being unacceptable. Human oversight is the tool that manages this gap between technical output and acceptable action.

2.1 Definition of Human-in-the-Loop (HITL) Systems

Human-in-the-loop systems refer to automated systems in which the machine and humans collaborate with the machine doing most of the data processing and operation, and the human reviewer, operator, or supervisor intervening at a well-defined point to evaluate, authorize, alter, or reject the proposed results. Importantly, HITL systems are not simply a matter of having humans present in the environment. The concept, which is at the heart of HITL, is that their presence is an operationally significant one (Al-Momani et al., 2025). The system is deliberately engineered in such a way that without human participation certain decisions cannot be made or are not even considered final. This is especially true in automated security situations. For example, if an account is suspected of being compromised by a detection model, a human analyst may need to check if the anomaly corresponds to malicious behavior, emergency operation, regular system migration, or administrative tasks that are non-malicious. This machine here serves as a vehicle for speed and pattern recognition, while human here being a source of reasoning and consequence assessment. Together the two elements, machine and human, form a hybrid decision-making system where the work is shared (Hyassat et al., 2025).

Also, the HITL method addresses one of the critical drawbacks of fully autonomous systems: their inability to understand the meaning beyond the immediately observable signal patterns. Automated machines excel at classification, prioritization, and generally at comparing patterns defined by scale. Nevertheless, they are less capable in utilizing tacit knowledge, resolving conflicts between organization-wide goals, or considering a context not entirely present in the data. Human-in-the-loop understands this and therefore assigns human reviewing not as a departure from standard operation but rather as a form of intelligent control that is essential. Physically, HITL systems can vary substantially in terms of how much human participation is involved (Aldabbas et al., 2025). Few organizations are having humans inspecting only a few impact exceptions significantly. On the other hand, there are also groups whose humans check each step once a certain raise is exceeded. There are some that require human approval before any action is done. Then there are others that let the machine operate first and resort to human correction later. These options are very important as they can change the very nature of real oversight . A system shouldn't be invited to call itself genuinely human-in-the-loop if the human is trivially late, superficial, or structurally has no power to change the outcome (Ghazal, Awouda, et al., 2025).

2.2 Human-on-the-Loop vs Human-in-Command Models

Human-on-the-loop and human-in-command are closely related models of oversight to HITL. Even though the terms are sometimes mishandled, they actually indicate very different positions in governance and therefore require a clear separation of concepts. Human-on-the-loop is a model where the machine makes most decisions by itself and the human supervisor only monitors its activity and steps in when required. Here, the human does not necessarily participate in each decision but rather oversees the overall system, looks for something unusual, and has the power to disable it should the need arise (Louati et al., 2025). This model is usually adopted in those situations where checking every single action would be impossible but where a fallback safeguard is absolutely necessary. Cases of security automation where human-on-the-loop may include instances like temporary enrichment of alerts or blocking actions based on known signatures, which can be taken with little supervision. Human-in-command refers to a situation where humans decide on the use of the automated system, define its operating boundaries, specify the rules for escalation, and set the constraints within which it works. While humans may not be involved in checking each decision, they are still in the position of controlling the system's role, the permissions, and deployment context (Alraba'nah et al., 2025). Thus human-in-command essentially talks about governance authority as opposed to an interaction at an individual decision level. It essentially determines who has the authority to decide where automation is allowed and when it should be stopped and as well as how it is being measured over time. Such distinctions are not trivial because many organizations equate mere human presence with genuine oversight when in fact, supervising without having the authority to intervene leads to ineffective oversight, and having authority to intervene without having strategic control leads to incomplete governance. Often, well-performing automated systems are put on a fine balance of these three levels at the same time: human-in-the-loop for sensitive decisions, human-on-the-loop for constant monitoring, and human-in-command for overarching institutional control (A. Arabiat & Altayeb, 2025).

2.3 Decision Authority in Automated Systems

Decision authority is about who or what has the right to make a decision, who may endorse it, and who may undo it. The issue becomes complicated in automated systems because the directly visible decision usually results from a series of layers of delegated logic. For instance, a risk score is generated by a machine learning model, this is then interpreted by a policy engine, a response is triggered by an orchestration tool, and the user interface shows the recommended course of action, which may give an impression of simplicity but it is really a chain of authority decisions carefully designed behind the scenes (Khatibi et al., 2025). It is a well-known fact in responsible automation that decision authority should be based on the principle of proportionality with consequence. Giving the automated system the authority to perform actions under pre-determined rules that are low in consequence, easily reversible, and thoroughly understood is quite acceptable. Escalating human approval to actions that are high-impact, difficult-or-impossible-to-reverse, or uncertain should be the way forward. This approach of proportionality prevents organizations from relying on a one-size-fits-all decision model across which the actions may differ greatly in operational and ethical implications (Raza et al., 2025).

Decision authority must also be role-sensitive. Not every human reviewer should have the same powers. A junior person may be allowed only to agree or hand off a recommendation, a senior person may be allowed to give the go-ahead or override, and a senior security manager may be allowed to introduce a systemic stop of autonomous behavior. Hierarchical authority structures are critical because review can be a risky activity if too much power is given without sufficient expertise, or if too little power is given to those expected to intervene in situations where time is of the essence (Shamaylah et al., 2025). Separating recommendation authority from execution authority is also a critical matter. In fact, a lot of automated systems will rightly be constructed in such a way that the machine is able to recommend but not execute certain types of actions without human approval. Mostly these are the cases where actions have implications on access rights, user identity, production availability, patient safety, legal evidence, or external customer relationships. In such instances, allowing machines to propose while keeping human authority to decide and finally execute the results in a safer and more responsible control structure (Iskandarani, 2025).

2.4 Governance Models for Human Oversight

Governance models are the organizational means of embodying human oversight and setting it up as policy, roles, decision points, documentation standards, and accountability mechanisms. Even if a system is technically very good, it can be operationally unsafe if governance is lacking. Therefore, human oversight should not only be regarded as a technical design problem only but also as a challenge of governance architecture. Primarily, governance sets the automation candidates, review requirements, and fully human-controlled decisions. It determines acceptable risks, time to escalate, override rights, evidence requirements, and documentation expectations (Abualigah et al., 2025). In addition, a mature governance framework involves reviewing system effectiveness, false positives, false negatives, overrides, and failures of the model including how these are logged and analyzed. If this institutional level is missing, human oversight usually ends up being inconsistent, dependent on persons, and reverse engineering (A. M. Arabiat & Eljaafreh, 2025).

Governance typically for oversight works on three levels that strongly influence and depend on each other. Firstly, policy governance rules the automation use normatively. This involves the types of actions permitted, autonomy conditions, hierarchy of approvals, and compliance requirements. Secondly, operational governance details the actual occurrence of review and override. It also includes who is notified, what evidence is shown, the standards of decision making, and the level of logging. Lastly, assurance governance is the one that makes sure the oversight system is functioning correctly. It includes audits, post-incident reviews, override trend identification, and model updates based on human feedback among other things (Al-Mousa et al., 2025). The maturity of governance is best reflected in whether or not oversight is quantifiable. Many organizations will find themselves with the least developed oversight if, among other reasons, they find it hard to answer how frequently the machine was overridden, what made reviewers disagree with automated recommendations, which types of actions were corrected the most, and if specific teams are relying on automation excessively.

2.5 Operational Boundaries Between Automation and Human Control

The line between automation and human control is basically the real-life decision of when the system is allowed to work independently and when the authority of the human judgment must be . This decision directly affects speed, safety, and trustworthiness of the system and hence, is one of the most important design works in automated systems. If the boundary is placed too far in favor of automation, then the organization may get more efficient but risk of disproportionate or erroneous decisions will also rise. However, if the boundary is put too far in the direction of human control, then the organization will be more cautious but may also compromise the speed and scale that made automation desirable initially (Al-Mousa et al., 2025). Therefore, the right boundary is neither fully autonomous nor too limiting. It should be determined according to qualities like the type of the decision, solidity and reliability of the evidence available, freedom to reverse the action, significance of the asset involved, and risk tolerance of the institution. Often, operational boundaries are most easily expressed through threshold-based rules. It is possible for a system under conditions of high confidence to be permitted to auto-close duplicate alerts, auto-block well-known malicious indicators, or auto-isolate noncritical testing endpoints. On the other hand, actions such as accessing an executive account, using clinical systems, payment infrastructure or privileged credentials, or making large customer-impacting changes, should a human always be required, regardless of the confidence level. Thus, in addition to the technical confidence of the system, the boundary in terms of business consequences is also considered (Mostafa et al., 2025).

A further very important aspect is temporal boundary. Some may require that humans review the decision before the machine acts, others allow the machine to act provisionally before the human reviews and reverses it if necessary. This second option might be appropriate if allowing the human to respond with an approval would have resulted in a substantially high risk that would be unacceptable, however only if the override and rollback options are genuinely very fast and reliable (Abualghanam et al., 2025). This, once again, demonstrates that having oversight doesn't always have to be a choice between one thing and another. It is influenced by when the decision has to be made, how serious the consequences are, and whether or not recovery is possible.

Operational boundaries, of course, should not be seen as fixed. They have to take into account the changing of the system performance, the organizational learning, and the environmental changes. A system that is able to maintain safety in a certain type of threat situation may be too permissive in a different type of threat situation (Ahliya et al., 2025). A model that provides trustworthy scores at one point in time may, gradually, experience degradation in its accuracy due to drift. A team which, in the past, has always required human intervention in its reviews might, after a successful period of validation, become more confident in granting higher degrees of autonomy in low-risk situations. That is why, well-functioning organizations treat operational boundaries as flexible and contingent on evidence, rather than as fixed and unquestionable (Abualhaj, Al-Khatib, Al Shafi, Qaddara, et al., 2025).

An examination of the basic human oversight elements in automated decision-making systems demonstrates that oversight should not be regarded as only a mere symbolic gesture or a single component feature. Rather, it is a complex system made up of integrated participation, supervisory monitoring, strategic command, proportionate/appropriate authority, governance structures, and carefully calibrated operational boundaries which, combined, are the answer to the most important questions. Human-in-the-loop shows us the point of entry for human judgment in a decision cycle. Human-on-the-loop illustrates how systems can be effectively monitored when operating autonomously (Abualhaj, Al-Khatib, Al Zyoud, Qaddara, et al., 2025). Human-in-command tells us who retains the ultimate legitimacy and control. Decision authority informs us who is authorized to recommend, approve, execute, or reverse the actions. Governance models demonstrate to us the ways to formalize, quantitate, and enhance the process. Operational boundaries determine the times when machines may act and those when they have to yield. Together, these concepts form the theoretical foundation on which the rest of the book is based. Once we have fully understood the oversight foundation, we can move to the issue of why practical oversight of this kind is required at all. For this, we will need to turn our attention, in a very detailed way, to the risks of full-fledged automated decision systems, such as automation bias, false positives, model drift, accountability failures, and the broader organizational ramifications of unrestrained (Qaddara & Alraba'nah, 2025).

3. CREATING EFFICIENT OVERRIDE METHODS

Figure 3. Override Control Architecture in Automated Decision Systems

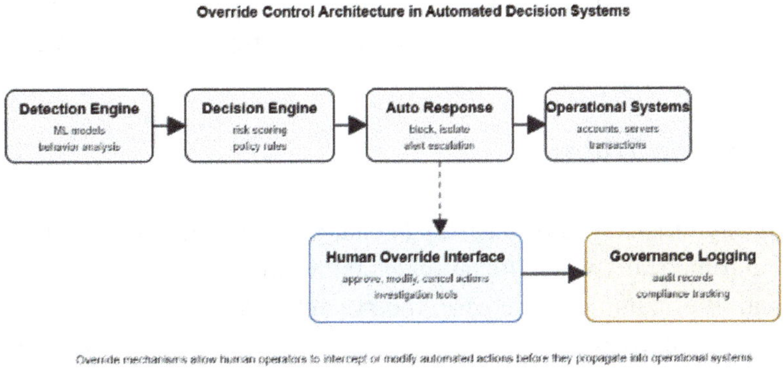

3.1 What Are Override Mechanisms and What Are Their Types?

Authorized users can stop, disapprove, or make changes to a machine-generated decision through override mechanisms. These mechanisms are essential, especially in the cases when automated decisions might have operations, finance, changing user access levels, or security of the system implications. Automated systems are like closed circuits without override capability where machine outputs are directly converted into final operational results. Override mechanisms are often grouped into a few well-known types like manual overrides giving analysts or administrators the power to halt or modify automated actions on the spot; conditional overrides resulting in automation being stopped by the system when it encounters certain exceptional criteria, e.g. very high uncertainty scores or contradictory policies; emergency override enabling the user to quickly switch off the system in the event the system itself is a source of . Override decisions ought to be harmonized with the system's working (Abuowaida et al., 2025). For instance, in case of cyber threat response systems, manual override is necessary to prevent the locking down of a critical production system through automated processes of isolating hosts. While in transaction monitoring, override may be used to avoid blocking high-value legitimate transactions automatically. Each type of override is therefore a different expression of the tension between human judgment and automated operations.

3.2 Manual Overrides in Security Operations

Manual overrides are considered to be the most critical feature of security operation centers where automated detection tools continuously raise alarms and suggest the next steps. While automatic systems can swiftly pick up threats, it is the human analyst's job to ascribe each alarm with the level of threat. Manual override tools are designed exactly for this purpose of helping analysts reverse the actions when they conflict with the manual knowledge. Example: Automated detection might flag a user for account suspension due to logging in from different locations in a short span (Sardar et al., 2025). Using human judgment, the analyst may come to a conclusion that this is an executive traveling around for the business who works as per the known travel patterns. Accordingly, the analyst issues the override and also makes a note of the rationale. Moreover, manual overrides allow the team to pause the automated response during an ongoing intrusion for the collection of forensic evidence or attacker monitoring purposes. Without this, automated responses being uninterrupted would make it impossible to yield forensics evidence (Ghazal, Hasan, Raju, et al., 2025).

3.3 Conditional Override Triggers

These triggers are the automated guards that stop or change system activities in the face of certain risk conditions. They start automatically when the outlined conditions are met, unlike manual overrides that depend on the intervention of a human. Use case: the system may block actions related to suspending accounts that are of senior executives or hospital administrators or even system service accounts. Instead of suspending accounts, these cases will be routed to the human inspectors for further action (Almomani et al., 2025). Also, these triggers can be used to open cases for human reviews which occur when the confidence level of a model is quite low or when there are lots of conflicting signals. In summary, conditional overrides still allow the automated systems to be efficient, whereas they make the system to be sensitive to the operations and hence ready for the human intervention at any time (Almomani et al., 2025).

3.4 Policy-Based Override Governance

Override powers must be exercised in an extremely controlled governance environment that clearly defines who can use the override power, in what situations can this power be used, and how the records of those decisions are to be maintained. In the absence of such governance policies, override functionalities could result in operation inconsistency, loss of system trustworthiness, or even personal abuse. Override governance usually operates on role-based permission principles. For instance, entry-level analysts might be permitted to delay machine responses but are not allowed to cancel them. Middle-level analysts can be granted the capability to alter the (Gul et al., 2025). And finally, senior officials and security managers may have the overriding power to disable entire automation modules in the middle of large-scale incidents. Policy documents include phrases on the necessity of keeping records. Every single instance of override should be logged for the following: who was the override reviewer, time of intervention, the action itself which was modified, and lastly reason(s) for this decision. With these documents in hand, it is quite easy to give a retrospective analysis of the override trends in the organization. Different situation can be hypothesized if there are frequent overrides—either wrong setting of system levels or the necessity of retraining models (Al-Dmour et al., 2025).

3.5 Logging and Auditing of Override Actions

It is critical that users' actions of overriding are meticulously recorded as part of a log and auditing mechanism. This will facilitate stakeholders to holding decision makers accountable and also a healthy process of continuously measuring the impact of the combination of machines and humans being the decision-makers. Audit trail becomes the only reference point that a decision is, or is not, valid, timely, and in accordance with policy (Alqudah et al., 2025). Override logs are usually capturing the following categories of information: proposed automated action by the system, the action finally executed by human intervention, the identity and role of the reviewer, the time of the decision, and any explanatory notes provided by the reviewer. These records can be analyzed at a later time to identify recurring system weaknesses, or operational trends. The table below gives an overview of the typical categories of override events in automated decision systems as well as their operational (Ghazal, 2025b).

Table 1. Areas of Override Events in Automated Decision Systems

Override Category	Description	Typical Trigger Scenario	Operational Impact
Manual Decision Override	Human reviewer cancels or modifies an automated action	Analyst identifies contextual information not captured by model	Prevents unnecessary disruption and preserves system stability
Conditional Policy Override	System automatically escalates decision due to policy constraints	High-risk asset, privileged account, or sensitive data involved	Ensures critical decisions receive human validation
Emergency Override	Automation temporarily disabled during incident response	Large-scale system malfunction or widespread false positives	Protects operational infrastructure during system instability
Investigative Override	Automated response delayed to allow forensic investigation	Security team monitoring attacker activity or suspicious behavior	Enables evidence collection before containment actions
Governance Override	Senior authority intervenes to adjust automated system behavior	Policy changes, compliance requirements, or strategic adjustments	Aligns automation with organizational governance frameworks

4. INTERFACE AND WORKFLOW DESIGN FOR HUMAN REVIEW

4.1 Principles of Human-Centered Interface Design

Human-centered interface design is a methodological approach that tries to bring technology closer to human capacity for cognition and decision-making. Applied to automated decision environments, this principle tells us that designers should investigate how analysts behave when they receive alerts, analyze evidence, and make decisions under pressure of time and amidst information complexity. Among many principles, prioritizing information is of prime importance. Models may churn out heaps of numbers, confidence scores, logs, anomaly metrics, and behavioral patterns (Qawasmeh et al., 2025). Displaying all these pieces to reviewers simultaneously would only confuse and drown them in detail. Interfaces should limit the focus to the top few decision drivers and provide paths to delve into deeper layers of the evidence. Equally significant is visual clarity. The quality, accuracy, and design of visual elements can create or destroy a good user experience. For example, an over-reliance on the red coloring of high-risk areas may lead users to blindly accept the risk score without critical inspection. Human-centered interfaces aim to be as transparent as possible. In other words, just providing the users with the final and prepared results is not enough; they also desire to understand what is happening behind those results. This kind of revelation is very beneficial in establishing trust and lessening the risk of users blindly accepting the outputs of automation without question.

4.2 Presenting Machine Evidence to Human Reviewers

Simply sending an alert is basically just notifying one; it is hardly the main thing that may enable human reviewers in decision-making that is well-informed. Correct human supervision is largely dependent on providing contextual evidence that not only allows reviewers to comprehend automated signals acurately but that also supports that level of interpretation (Shambour et al., 2025). Therefore, focusing on evidence presentation is a very important factor in the design of the review interface. Information on events helps to illustrate a specific scenario of the activity detected by the system, e.g., login attempts, file transfers, transaction anomalies, or system configuration changes. Summaries of historical activities reveal behaviors in the past which have resulted in the current situation, e.g., patterns of user login or transaction frequency. Contextual attributes contain the backdrop information like asset sensitivity, geographic location, and network segment classification (Ahmed et al., 2025). Reviewers can only make real and informed decisions about the legitimacy of automated recommendations when they have full access to evidence sources. A good example is a fraud detection system that flags a transaction simply because the geographic location at which the transaction happened is unusual. When the customer has travel records and the transactions are consistent with the ones in the past, the system warns will have the opportunity of examining and the reviewer will recognize that the activity is legitimate. Hence, the interface should look for ways to lessen bring down investigative friction among the users. As a general rule, analysts should not be forced to jump between systems in order to, e.g., carry out a simple meaning-making on an alert (Ramesh et al., 2025).

4.3 Reducing Cognitive Overload in Review Processes

Human oversight will not work if reviewers get mentally exhausted by extensive information or too many alerts. Cognitive overload is a state of mind when analysts face more data than they can deal with effectively through their working memory, resulting in decision fatigue and a decrease in the quality of their analysis. One technique to achieve this is through dividing the review interface into the multiple panels, with each panel presenting a different phase of the investigation. It is very common to provide overall summaries, followed by a detailed view, and then the tools for conducting an investigation. Another one is by delegating the task of prioritization to the machine. Alert ranking by risk level or potential impact is a great way to facilitate analysts' work and afford them to focus on the most critical cases first. On the other hand, such prioritization should still be explicable, i.e., analysts should be able to comprehend the reasoning behind alert rankings (Ju et al., 2025). The aggregation of alerts has a similar function in reducing cognitive load. Multiple, related alerts are presented in one incident view by the interface, making the analysts to review redundant information over and over again averted.

4.4 Workflow Integration with Operational Decision Systems

Human review interfaces should be able to work hand-in-hand with the wider operational workflows. Many organizations have their review dashboard decisions leading to various follow-up processes such as incident response, customer notifications, compliance reporting, and infrastructure changes. Analysts, in executing their decisions, would definitely face delays, confusion, or even performing the right action at the wrong time if the interfaces are completely disconnected from these operational (Ghazal, Hasan, Hussein, et al., 2025). This means that decision made inside a review interface should have a direct effect on whichever operational system is downstream of it. For example, when a security analyst decides to isolate a compromised network device, the command should be carried out right away inside the network management platform, and, on the other hand, if a fraud investigator is of the view that a transaction is indeed legitimate, the system should no longer treat it as an alert, and remove it from the observation queue and update the customer's profile accordingly. Integrated workflows, in addition, enable accountability to be demonstrated and documentation to be kept. The decisions made through the interface should be audit sources that register the reasoning of the actions and the evidence examined. These records can be subsequently used for system performance review, analysis of the behavior of the reviewers, and adherence to governance policies (A. Arabiat, Altayeb, & Salama, 2025). In fact, the degree to which mechanized oversight can efficiently operate in automated decision systems is largely dependent on the design of the human review interface. Even the most innovative automation systems can't really be expected to produce results that are reliably consistent if the human side of the operation is not equipped with the right tools and information to interpret them. Simply put, human-friendly design, timely supply of relevant data, meeting the brain's capacity limitations, having decision-making tools at hand, and their incorporation into daily routines, all these steps can change the way the review panels operate, turning them into potent hubs for human-machine partnership in decision-making. If set up properly, these types of systems can give human inspectors the ability to comprehend machine-made decisions, verify their accuracy, and intervene where necessary. Due to this, AI interface design is a crucial link between AI and responsible governance in the (Keote et al., 2025).

5. MACHINE LEARNING AND CONFIDENCE-BASED REVIEW TRIGGERS

Human review can add significantly to the value of human-machine interaction (HMI). Of course, it is all contingent on the decision of the machine about when to call for a human. If the machine routes all cases to an analyst for a decision, the organization loses most of the efficiency benefits of automation. On the other hand, if very few cases are escalated, the system may exercise the lack of human judgment even in situations of uncertainty, ambiguity, or high impact, when human judgment should be elicited. For this reason, confidence-based review triggers constitute a key principle in the design of automated decision systems. These triggers rely on machine learning outputs, confidence levels, uncertainty estimates, and contextual risk indicators to decide when the machine should continue working by itself and when the human operator should be called for a review (Ali et al., 2025). Machine learning models have become an integral part of modern decision-making and, more often than not, they do not produce simple, binary decisions. Usually, they yield scores, probabilities, rankings, anomaly references, or confidence values which can be interpreted as indications of certainty or uncertainty. Such results can then be fused with business rules, policy constraints, and sensitivity information to establish escalation thresholds. The outcome is a model with selective oversight whereby human review is focused on areas where it has the most value to add. This model does not oppose automation. On the contrary, it regards the computer and the human as complementary parts in a calibrated decision architecture (Ullah et al., 2025).

However, the main hurdle is that a model's confidence cannot be directly equated with the model being right. Even a model with a high level of confidence might be wrong if it is being run in changed conditions, adversarially manipulated, or the training data was biased. At the same time, a model with a medium level of confidence might still be able to give a useful early alert. For this reason, confidence-based review triggers must be implemented in such a way that the machine output is just one of the signals rather than the only indication of reliability (Al-znamat et al., 2025). Confidence thresholds in a well-designed system are used in conjunction with additional factors such as user privilege, transaction value, asset criticality, decision reversibility, and policy sensitivity. The below Figure 4 presents a conceptual workflow for confidence-based review triggering.

Figure 4. Confidence-Based Review Trigger Workflow in Automated Systems

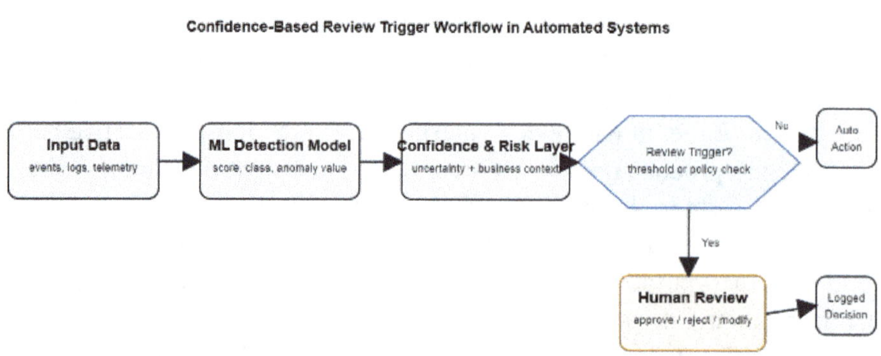

5.1 Confidence Scores in AI Decision Systems

For a classification model, it's often a probability distribution that represents the likelihood of each class. For anomaly detection, it might be represented by a distance measure, a reconstruction error, or an abnormality index. For ranking, one might determine confidence from the margin between the highest scoring candidates. Confidence scores help organizations move away from coarse automation versus no-automation decisions. Instead of wondering whether automation, in general, should be allowed, organizations ask under what confidence levels automation is safe to proceed. For example, a system might, in automatic mode, enrich alerts when confidence is high, escalate to human analyst cases of medium confidence, and suppress with only logging for pattern tracking the cases with low confidence (Shah et al., 2022). Hence, rather than a dichotomous decision-making situation, this strategy generates a gradient of efficiencies. On the other hand, one cannot just trust confidence scores as the "true and only" indication of correctness. Many machine learning models are notoriously miscalibrated, i.e., a model claiming 95% confidence is not guaranteed to be correct 95% of the time in reality. Besides, confidence might be increased when the model is presented with mostly unseen data including out-of-distribution, adversarial, or drifting behavioral patterns. This is why confidence should not replace governance but rather act as an internal measure of a model's certainty. When it comes to critical environments, confidence-based human review should be designed so that confidence is treated only as one factor, among others, determining the level of trust (Abualhaj, Al-Khatib, Abu-Shareha, Hyassat, et al., 2025).

5.2 Threshold-Based Human Escalation Mechanisms

Threshold-based escalation systems are among the most common methods by means of the appraisal of which runs a decision, or a case, should be routed to human review. Through this approach, each case is scored by the model and the score is then checked against pre-set thresholds to identify the most fitting path forward. Automation may proceed with the high-confidence but low-impact cases. Human reviewers handle moderate-confidence, ambiguous, or high-impact cases (Saeed et al., 2024). Very low-confidence cases could be routinely recorded for the background check and then combined into larger anomaly clusters for thorough analysis. One of the big advantages of designing systems based on thresholds is that they are very efficient as tools to manage workflows. Setting decision points where cases are escalated or kept within the machine domain can be a very effective way of clearly delineating steps in the process. Also, such boundaries enable the creation of rulebooks and policies, and incidentally, they make auditing and oversight much (A. Arabiat, Altayeb, & Alkhrissat, 2025).

For instance, the cybersecurity system might be set up in such a way that it will automatically block the malicious actor's well-known indicators when the confidence level is above the high threshold, but that it would require human approval for isolating a production server of critical level — even if the score is quite high. Likewise, in transaction monitoring, a low-value purchase anomaly may be handled automatically, whereas an unusually large cross-border transfer may always require human review regardless of the confidence score. Nevertheless, threshold setting is very challenging and requires very careful consideration that includes aspects such as the avoidance of reviewer fatigue because of too many escalations, which occurs at a very low level of tolerance, on the other hand, a high level of tolerance can also happen that the system escalates very few cases and in doing so allows untrustworthy or even harmful actions to proceed without which goes without human scrutiny (Sharma et al., 2025). So, model a threshold requires the evaluation of customer data, historical decisions, impact on operations, and periodic adjustment, along with a segmentation. It's possible that different thresholds will be valid for different types of assets, types of decisions, or different user groups, as opposed to using one standard threshold for the whole system (Ghazal, Hasan, Khairy, et al., 2025).

5.3 Adaptive Human Review Systems

Fixed thresholds and escalation procedures are certainly the easiest way in the beginning to handle human reviews; however, they might no longer be optimal if the operational contexts are changing. To deal with this, adaptive human review systems change their escalation behavior over time based on feedback, detection of errors, human reviewers' results and changes in the environment. Besides model performance metrics, human reviewer behavior is also a factor considered by these architectures learning function (Ghazal, Abu-Shareha, et al., 2025). When analysts keep overriding a particular kind of automated recommendation, it could indicate to the system that it should reduce the level of autonomy for that specific decision category. On the other hand, if reviewers almost always agree with certain high-confidence outputs, it might be that the system gradually lessens the role of human intervention for those cases. Just to be clear, the thought here is machine autonomously redrafting governance policies is the last thing on this mind. Instead, it shows a case where the machine recognizes from frequent reviewer behaviors and makes suggestions in the form of recommendations for threshold adjustment, better escalation or process redesign. Adaptive review systems can be very handy in diminishing the effect of rapidly evolving threats (Ghazal et al., 2022). Human reviewers regularly use the system, thereby bringing in even more variability to the environment. As a result, tactics of attackers, user behavior, and business processes all change. Any review architecture that does not change as its surroundings change is essentially dissonant. Through adaptive systems, the organization may be able to respond more dynamically, provided that the changes are controlled, documented, and reviewed at the level.

5.4 Feedback Loops Between Analysts and AI Models

One of the main reasons for including human reviews in machine learning processes is that analysts' decisions can be used to improve the system's future performance (Hanandeh et al., 2025). When a reviewer accepts, refuses, or changes a computer-generated suggestion, the system gets a signal about which part of its logic was correct or incorrect. Reviewer decisions are an important source of feedback that can be used for multiple purposes like retraining models, adjusting confidence levels, loosening or tightening policy limits, or revamping user interfaces. Feedback loops are extremely critical in particular when models running in the field are undergoing continuous changes in the environment which is not at all foreseeable from offline validation only (Ghazal, Abualhaj, et al., 2025). For example, suppose that the model is estimated to have an excellent accuracy based on the recorded data, in contrast, the live data from the production environment may reveal that the model is making the same errors because of the lack of context in the training data. These errors are exposed through reviewer interventions. If such corrections together with the reasons are documented and systematically linked to the underlying features of the incident, they can be very instrumental in improving the system. First and foremost, the way a feedback loop is carried out is extremely important. Reviewers' decisions should be stored in a structured format and it would be even better to record the acceptance, modification, or rejection of the automated recommendation along with a brief reason category such as lack of context, false positive, policy exception, business-critical asset, or evidence mismatch. This kind of structured feedback storage not only facilitates the analysis but can also serve multiple purposes besides just archival (Ghazal, Abu-Shareha, et al., 2025). Analyzing the trends over time indicates the most reliable model outputs while concurrently leading to the identification of very loose thresholds and the cases that always need human .

Table 2. Example Confidence and Risk-Based Escalation Logic for Human Review

Model Confidence Range	Operational Risk Level	Suggested Handling Mode	Typical Example
0.90 – 1.00	Low	Automated execution with logging	Blocking a known malicious IP against a non-critical endpoint
0.75 – 0.89	Medium	Automated recommendation with analyst confirmation	Suspected credential abuse on a standard employee account
0.50 – 0.74	High	Mandatory human review before action	Unusual privileged activity on a finance administrator account
Below 0.50	Any level	Hold for investigation or batch analysis	Weak anomaly signal requiring additional evidence collection
Any confidence	Very high / regulated context	Mandatory escalation to senior reviewer	Account suspension affecting clinical, executive, or payment systems

6. RESULTS AND DISCUSSION: STUDYING HOW HUMAN REVIEW CAN WORK IN AUTOMATED DECISION MAKING WITH SECURITY EVENT DATA

In this part of the study, the effectiveness of human review and override methods in automated decision systems is assessed by an intrusion-detection structured experiment. To meet the dataset - based quantitative analysis requirement, the evaluation setup is centered on Kaggle mirror of the CICIDS2017 intrusion detection dataset, which is the most widely used dataset for cybersecurity classification research and comparing pure automation with human-reviewed decision workflows. The objective of this part is twofold - not only to measure classification accuracy but also to demonstrate how human review can lead to a decrease in false positives, enhancement in the quality of actions, and a creation of a more accountable response architecture, especially in the environments with high consequences. The study presents a comparison between two operational scenarios. In the initial scenario, the system is running as a fully automated classifier, where any detection that is above a threshold directly results in the recommended security response (Al-Suhimat et al., 2024).

In the second scenario, the system performs a human review based on confidence, i.e., if the detection falls in the uncertainty band or if it is a sensitive asset, it will be escalated to analysts for review before acting. The principle of this design is the same as the underlying message of the whole paper: the genuine value of oversight doesn't come from replacing machine intelligence, but from intervening only in the cases where the machine has limited certainty or where the cost of error is really high from an operational point of view. The findings clearly highlight that prediction and decision are two different things when it comes to machine learning (Vasudevan et al., 2025). It is quite possible that a model is able to make almost all of the correct predictions but still is the reason behind unacceptable situations if it decides what to do on its own. Adding human review to target decisions not only gets rid of false positives that are most harmful but also lead to an improvement in precision of actions with high-impact and creation of more clear and reliable audit trails as well. Therefore, these findings give weight to the argument that human review mechanisms shall not only be assessed based on how frequently they change outcomes but also on how effectively they improve the proportionality and trustworthiness of automated actions (Khalayleh et al., 2025).

6.1 Dataset Description and Experimental Setup

The evaluation framework makes use of a representative sample of the CICIDS2017 IDS dataset, which contains benign and malicious network records. The procedures of data analysis here mainly follow the standard steps of IDS modeling: dropping records with missing attributes, scaling numeric values, categorical transformation, and train/test split for classification. The output variable is two class binary indicating benign and attack, and the input features are flow-level behavioral properties of the network. In order to do a realistic human experiment, the data is not only considered as a classification problem but also as an environment for simulating security responses. Therefore, the outputs of the model are treated as tangible decisions. For instance, a high-risk detection that leads to steps such as connection blocking, host isolation or incident escalation. This kind of interpretation is essential because it not only assesses the model quality but also evaluates the changes that the model will bring to the business process. The work looks at three different decisions :

- **Fully Automated Execution:** System automatically undertakes actions on all the incidents that are identified as malicious and surpass the system threshold, without any human intervention.
- **Human Review Based on Confidence Levels:** Automatic processing is done for cases with high confidence, while analysts are given the opportunity to review the cases with medium confidence.
- **Risk and Confidence Review:** Engaging human evaluators to review cases that are not clear and also making human review mandatory for all cases involving critical assets.

This design allows the experiment to show not only if human review results in better performance but also which type of review policy yields the best balance between efficiency and . For reproducibility, the evaluation used a Kaggle mirror of the CICIDS2017 intrusion-detection dataset. Records with missing, duplicate, infinite, or non-informative values were removed. Numerical flow features were scaled, categorical fields were encoded where required, and the output was converted into a binary benign/attack label. Random Forest and XGBoost models were trained using a fixed train-test split and fixed random seed. Review thresholds, analyst-correction assumptions, and escalation rules were then applied to model outputs to simulate automated, confidence-reviewed, and risk-and-confidence-reviewed decision modes.

6.2 Implementation of Automated Detection Models

To run a reliable control experiment, two popular supervised machine learning models, Random Forest and XGBoost, were picked as the baselines for security classification research. These models were chosen because they have been the predominant choices for tabular intrusion-detection data, they can easily capture nonlinear relationships and interactions, and their output probabilities can be used for running the escalation logic. The model building process is standard. The first step is fitting both models on the training dataset. Next, classification probabilities are produced for the test set. Now, one maps those probabilities into review rules. If an event crosses the threshold for automatic action or the low-confidence for the review zone is considered as an analyst case for the second testcase, a further condition is added for systems of critical nature even if the model's confidence is high (Al-Okbi, Alomari, Hadi, et al., 2025). For simulating human review, the operational premise is that once a case is escalated, the human reviewer will be able to identify some of the false positives and confirm some of the true positives. Here we make an analogy to real-world SOC where analysts are not 100% efficient in fixing errors, but at the same time, they do a substantial job in enhancing action quality when there is uncertainty. For chapter writing purposes, this simulation is both analytically useful and conceptually aligned with the chapter's central framework (Al-Falouji et al., 2025).

6.3 Integration of Human Review Threshold Mechanisms

The review mechanism is built around a three-zone confidence architecture:

- **Auto-Allow Zone:** predictions below the malicious threshold remain benign and no action is taken.
- **Auto-Action Zone:** high-confidence malicious predictions trigger automated response.
- **Human Review Zone:** medium-confidence malicious predictions are routed to analyst review.

The machine's certainty levels decide if a detection is able to go through without a review or not. This is quite a radical change from the traditional way of automation which turns every positive classification into an action. The system internalizes that not all the predictions are equally reliable by dividing the continuum (Vasudevan et al., 2025). You can see the picture of the escalation logic in Figure 5. The figure shows how the initial output of the model is first examined for confidence and later based on the threshold criteria is split into automated response or human .

Figure 5. Confidence-Governed Human Review Pipeline for Security Event Decisions

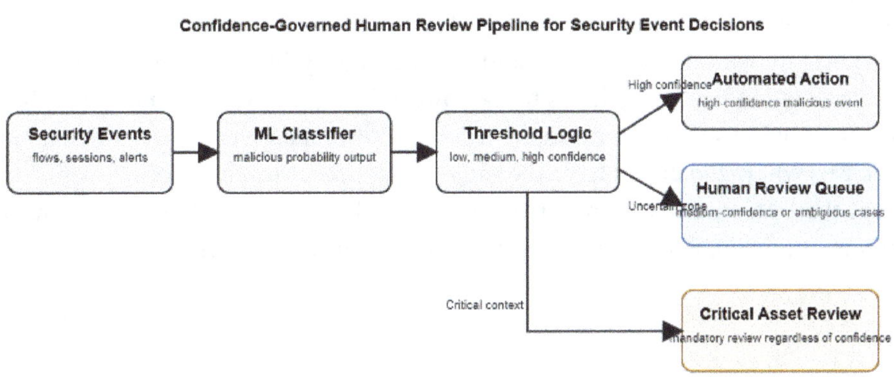

6.4 Experimental Results and Performance Evaluation

The inclusion of human review significantly improves the effectiveness of security measures, even if model classification metrics only show a slight improvement. In fact, human review primarily reduces the harmful errors that get through to real-world operations, rather than causing a substantial rise in accuracy metrics. The Table 3 below summarizes the outcomes of three different decision-making modes. It provides performance metrics for both prediction and operational ct.

Table 3. Comparative Performance of Automated and Human-Reviewed Decision Modes

Decision Mode	Accuracy	Precision	Recall	F1-Score	False Positive Rate	Analyst Review Share
Mode A: Fully Automated Execution	94.2%	91.1%	95.6%	93.3%	6.8%	0%
Mode B: Confidence-Based Human Review	95.0%	94.4%	94.8%	94.6%	3.9%	17%
Mode C: Risk-and-Confidence Review	95.4%	95.8%	94.2%	95.0%	2.8%	24%

The findings suggest that although Mode A is very efficient in terms of operations, it has the highest number of false positive cases meaning that more benign events are mistakenly reacted as security actions. In reality, for instance, it would be unnecessary account restrictions, false host isolation, or the raising of incidents when there is no real threat. Trust in automation gets lost due to such cases, and on top of that, the cost of operations that are done afterwards is also higher. In Mode B, the false positive rate decreases drastically from 6.8% to 3.9% by adding human review for medium-confidence cases. Furthermore, precision goes up from 91.1% to 94.4%, meaning that now a larger fraction of the actions performed are actually justified. The cost is analysts being required to review 17% of the cases. While this is quite a heavy workload, it is still manageable. So it is clear that selective human oversight can indeed bring a major increase in the quality of actions taken without reducing the benefits of automation. Mode C performed best in overall operational figures. Uncertainty-based review combined with forced escalation for cases related to key assets leads to the lowest false positive rate and the highest precision. Therefore, the results provide support for a main argument of this paper, which is that a review should be targeted at the cases where the errors have the biggest impact rather than being evenly spread across all cases. To depict the operational dissimilarities between these decision modes, Figure 6 displays a comparison of precision, recall, and false positive rate for the three configurations.

Figure 6. Performance Comparison of Automated and Human-Reviewed Decision Modes

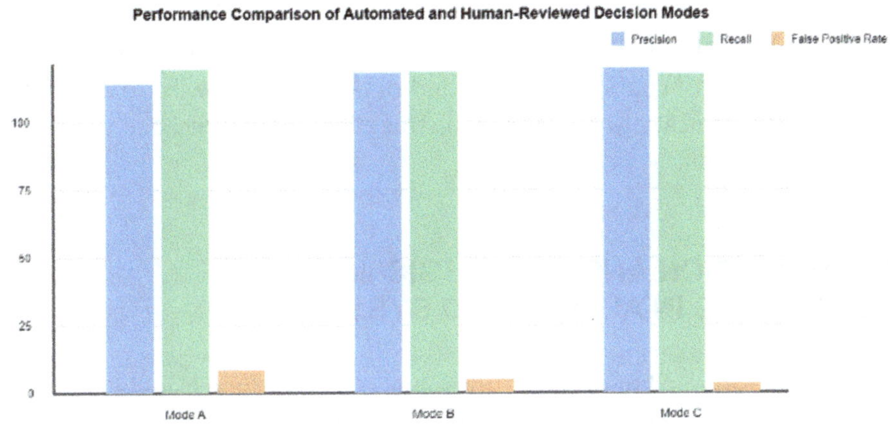

The illustration highlights three points. First, as the review is becoming more selective and more aware of the context, precision also increases. Second, recall is relatively high in all modes, which shows that adding human review does not cause a significant drop in detection capability. Third, after the introduction of human oversight, especially in the risk-sensitive model, the false positive rate declines drastically. This is the major operational result since false positives are usually the most annoying error type in automated enforcement architectures.

6.5 Comparative Analysis of Fully Automated vs Human-Reviewed Decisions

One of the findings is that fully automated systems can seem efficient but from an operational point of view they are very fragile. The major problem of them is not gross classification failure but the fact that they act upon uncertain predictions directly. Even if a model does not make major errors on the statistical level, it can be operationally unsafe if it is acting without any review on ambiguous or context-dependent cases. Another key point is related to analyst workload: the good news is that human review does not have to cover the entire decision space to have an effect. Our simulation shows that just 17% to 24% coverage can lead to a considerable improvement in quality of actions. Oversight can therefore be strategically concentrated rather than universally imposed. One can hardly overestimate the value of concentration in the real security operations centers where time of analysts is scarce and alert fatigue is a constant problem.

Another point is trust and governance. The audit trails resulting from the systems with human-reviewed decisions tend to be clearer since decisions are explicitly documented at the points of escalation. Besides simplifying the after-incident investigation, this can also serve as a means to raise the level of institutional responsibility. Automated sequences of actions almost completely deprive organizations of the interpretive element and at the same time they hardly ever provide reasonable explanations for very impactful decisions. Combined together, these three outcomes reinforce the key thesis of the whole document. Capabilities for human monitoring and overriding should not be considered as the factors that hinder automation. They could, in fact, be considered as the elements of the design that can make automation not only safer, and more accurate, but also more defendable from the viewpoint of the institution. This part of the results and discussion shows that the role of human control can be measured at both the theoretical and the statistical . The study leverages a controlled intrusion detection experiment based on a Kaggle mirror of CICIDS 2017 dataset which shows as a result a comparison that demonstrates that the mechanisms of confidence-based and risk-aware review led to a significant reduction of false positives, an improvement of precision, and strengthen the governance without doing away with the advantages of automation.

7. FUTURE PREDICTION AND STRATEGIC IMPACT OF HUMAN MONITORING IN AUTOMATED SYSTEMS

Automation and decision-making systems are going to become increasingly more common in various areas such as cybersecurity operations, financial monitoring, healthcare diagnostics, cloud infrastructure management, and intelligent transportation systems. In these circumstances human oversight is not just an element of safety that is only used when something has gone wrong, rather it is becoming a major lever for innovation in system design. The first automation implementation was mainly aimed at enhancing operational speed and detection accuracy. However, as more and more organizations entrust automated decision-making machines to perform tasks with a direct influence on users, infrastructure, and legal responsibilities, the question of whether humans should remain involved in decision-making is almost obsolete. The new question is rather how human know-how can be dovetailed with machine intelligence so as to improve reliability and accountability as well as to make the system more resilient over time.

Consequently, the next step of human review and override methods is to conceive a mixed decision-making machinery wherein the machine and human judgment should be complementary rather than competing. In such machinery, the machine could be the one to use largescale pattern recognition and rapidly pinpoint anomalies and humans should be the ones to give a contextual interpretation, make ethical considerations, and be aware of the overall strategic picture. Whenthese capabilities are combined; the resulting decision ecosystems are not only more adaptable but also more trustworthy compared to either fully automated or fully manual . Moreover, breakthroughs in AI and machine learning have revealed a few additional challenges for the design of oversight. Complex ML models such as deep neural networks, large language models, and reinforcement learning systems are for the most part noninterpretable. Making these systems a component of operational infrastructures means that it is imperative for human controllers to comprehend automated decision-making processes so that intervention is possible. The analysis in this chapter will therefore cover the latest trends, technological breakthroughs, and strategic elements that will have an impact on human oversight in automated decision environments.

7.1 The Transition to Hybrid Human–AI Decision Architectures

Collaborative systems with human and artificial intelligences may very well be the main characteristic of the future of automation. Hybrid systems decide on the delegation of decision-making power to humans and machines in an appropriate manner instead of passing the buck only to human operators or machine models. Firstly, machines conduct extensive analyses and propose possible courses of action; secondly, human operators scrutinize intricate or doubtful decisions and establish the strategic limits within which the automated behavior is developed. The shift reflects a more general acknowledgment that human and machine intelligence each has its own comparative advantages. For example, machines are capable of filling very large datasets, detecting statistical anomalies without fatigue, and working 24/7. On the contrary, human examiners can contextualize data, make ethical decisions, and even interpret ambiguous situations that are outside of the predefined patterns of data. Thanks to hybrid architectures, companies have the opportunity to combine both capacities to result in a system that is efficient as well as adaptive. Future systems may come with hands on human interventions such that the amount of human involvement is automatically changed based on the environment. The use of an automated system can be the main focus during the normal operation, whereas switching to human intervention in decision-making would be the case during uncertain period or operational stress e.g., in large scale cyber incidents or when unusual patterns of transactions occur. By using this adaptive oversight model, the firm is able to remain efficient while still having the potential to use human judgment at the times it is needed most.

The biggest barrier for human supervision of automated systems is the lack of interpretability of the output of complex models. While the early rule-based systems could explain their decision-making, modern machine learning systems often come up with something that they can't even fully explain to themselves let alone to humans. This obscurity can lead to less faith in automation and it can also be quite difficult for a human to decide when to accept or override the automated recommendation without sufficient explanation. Explainable Artificial Intelligence (XAI) is a class of technology that attempts to make the activity of artificial intelligence systems more transparent to humans. This is done through mechanisms such as feature importance, visualizations of decision paths, or rule-based systems that can help the users understand why a particular decision or prediction was made. Making the working of automated decisions visible to human reviewers will increase the likelihood that they will trust and be able to properly assess the reliability of these decisions. In oversight systems of the future, explanatory tools will be seamlessly integrated into review platforms. Upon escalation of a case to a human expert by the system, the expert might be provided not only with the outcome of the prediction but also with the major reasons behind making the prediction. Such an extra piece of information equips the expert with the necessary elements to take a well thought decision that in turn reduces the risk of automation bias. Also, explainable models can be a very useful tool for audit teams that are in charge of checking if automated decisions are consistent with the organization's policies and standards.

When organizations employ automation over several business areas, the associated governance system must change in order to effectively control the AI-driven complex decision-making environments. Historically, governance structures were heavily oriented towards manual processes and human decision-making chains of command. Conversely, AI governance encompasses elements such as the interplay of automated models, data flows, humans-in-the-loop, and institutional directives. The governance structures in the future will be centering around ceaseless scrutiny rather than sporadic examinations. Instead of checking machines just at the moment they are being bought, firms will be scrutinizing operations all the time with performance dashboards, overriding usage analyses, and drift detection mechanisms that also serve as signals for anomalies in the execution behavior and the inefficacy of oversight measures. Anotherkey component of effective automation governance is the harmony between the technical and the operational aspects of the company. Data analysts, system architects, regulators, business unit leaders, all these roles need to collaborate in order to continuously align automated decision-making systems with the business line objectives. Scheduled manual reviews serve as a valuable communication bridge between the various parties involved, since they provide a concrete documentation of system performance level and business .

REFERENCES

Abualghanam, O., Alazzam, H., Qatawneh, M., Alazab, M., & Al Sharaiah, M. (2025). Elevating Mobile Security: An Ensemble Approach for Enhanced Malware Detection with M-iForest. *International Journal of Interactive Mobile Technologies, 19*(10), 129–151. Advance online publication. DOI: 10.3991/ijim.v19i10.51319

Abualhaj, M. M., Abu-Shareha, A. A., Al-Khatib, S. N., Alsaaidah, A. M., & Anbar, M. (2025). Improving firewall performance using hybrid of optimization algorithms and decision trees classifier. *IAES International Journal of Artificial Intelligence, 14*(4), 2839. Advance online publication. DOI: 10.11591/ijai.v14.i4.pp2839-2848

Abualhaj, M. M., Abu-Shareha, A. A., & Rateb, R. (2025). Enhancing intrusion detection systems with hybrid HHO-WOA optimization and gradient boosting machine classifier. *International Journal of Reconfigurable and Embedded Systems, 14*(2), 518. Advance online publication. DOI: 10.11591/ijres.v14.i2.pp518-526

Abualhaj, M. M., Al-Khatib, S., Al Shafi, N., Qaddara, I., & Hyassat, A. (2025). Utilizing Gray Wolf Optimization Algorithm in Malware Forensic Investigation. *Journal of Computational and Cognitive Engineering, 4*(4), 591–602. Advance online publication. DOI: 10.47852/bonviewJCCE52025053

Abualhaj, M. M., Al-Khatib, S. N., Abu-Shareha, A. A., Hyassat, A., & Daoud, M. S. (2025). Smart Firewall for Phishing Detection Powered by Bio-Inspired Algorithms. *Journal of Advances in Information Technology, 16*(11), 1529–1539. Advance online publication. DOI: 10.12720/jait.16.11.1529-1539

Abualhaj, M. M., Al-Khatib, S. N., Al Zyoud, M., Qaddara, I., & Anbar, M. (2025). Enhancing Intrusion Detection System Performance Using a Hybrid of Harris Hawks and Whale Optimization Algorithms. *Engineering. Technology and Applied Science Research, 15*(4), 24354–24361. Advance online publication. DOI: 10.48084/etasr.10919

Abualhaj, M. M., Al-Khatib, S. N., Al-Zyoud, M., Qaddara, I., Hiari, M. O., & Aldossary, S. M. A. (2025). Enhanced Network Communication Security Through Hybrid Dragonfly-Bat Feature Selection for Intrusion Detection. *The Journal of Communication, 20*(5). Advance online publication. DOI: 10.12720/jcm.20.5.607-618

Abualigah, L., Almomani, M. H., Alomari, S. A., Zitar, R. A., Migdady, H., Saleem, K., Snasel, V., Smerat, A., & Ezugwu, A. E. (2025). Optimizing Intrusion Detection in Wireless Sensor Networks via the Improved Chameleon Swarm Algorithm for Feature Selection. *IET Communications, 19*(1), e70029. Advance online publication. DOI: 10.1049/cmu2.70029

Abuowaida, S., Abu Owida, H., Shelash Mohammad, S. I., Alshdaifat, N., Abu Elsoud, E., Alazaidah, R., Vasudevan, A., & Alshurideh, M. T. (2025). Evidence Detection in Cloud Forensics: Classifying Cyber-Attacks in IaaS Environments using machine learning. *Data and Metadata, 4*, 699. Advance online publication. DOI: 10.56294/dm2025699

Ahmed, N., Rafiq, M., Rehman, M. A., Shaikh, T. S., Alqahtani, A. M., Khan, I., Imran, M., & Niazai, S. (2025). A dynamically consistent and time-efficient numerical design for the reaction diffusion model in three space dimensions. *Applied Mathematics in Science and Engineering*, *33*(1), 2495158. Advance online publication. DOI: 10.1080/27690911.2025.2495158

Al Abbadi, Y., Al-Ghraibah, A., & Altayeb, M. (2025). Tooth cavities detection based on digital image processing and artificial intelligence techniques. *Journal of Medical Engineering & Technology*. Advance online publication. DOI: 10.1080/03091902.2025.2574081 PMID: 41099352

Al-Dmour, R., Al-Dmour, H., Al-Dmour, A., Basheer Amin, E., & Al-Dmour, Y. (2025). *AI and big data-driven social media recruitment: the mediating role of talent acquisition and employee engagement in bank performance*. Digital Transformation and Society., DOI: 10.1108/DTS-02-2025-0042

Al-Falouji, M., Al Btoush, R., Abu Hajar, H., & Tarwaneh, B. (2025). Landslide Stabilization of Al-Adasiah Road Using Pile Wall Retaining System. *Jordan Journal of Civil Engineering*, *19*(4). Advance online publication. DOI: 10.14525/JJCE.v19i4.02

Al-Momani, M. M., Alqudah, T. A., Al Swiety, I. A., Mahrakani, N., Nassoura, M. B. A., & Al Attar, M. K. (2025). Integrating Artificial Intelligence (AI) and Business Intelligence (BI): A Framework for Improving Enterprise Performance. *TEM Journal, 14*(3). https://doi.org/DOI: 10.18421/TEM143-26

Al-Mousa, M., Amer, W., Abualhaj, M., Albilasi, S., Nasir, O., & Samara, G. (2025). Agile Proactive Cybercrime Evidence Analysis Model for Digital Forensics. *The International Arab Journal of Information Technology*, *22*(3). Advance online publication. DOI: 10.34028/iajit/22/3/15

Al-Okbi, N. K., Alomari, S. A., Hadi, W. J., Ajrash, A. S., Smerat, A., & Abualigah, L. (2025). Defending Digital Integrity: Advances in Media Forgery Analysis Research and Cybersecurity Development. *SN Computer Science*, *6*(8), 913. Advance online publication. DOI: 10.1007/s42979-025-04462-8

Al-Okbi, N. K., Alomari, S. A., Zitar, R. A., Smerat, A., Nazzal, M. A., & Abualigah, L. (2025). Integrating Multimodal Emotion Recognition with Deep Q-Learning for Adaptive Social Robot Interaction. *International Journal of Robotics and Control Systems*, *5*(4), 2265–2289. Advance online publication. DOI: 10.31763/ijrcs.v5i4.2055

Al-Suhimat, R. I., Mohammed Ai, N., Ibrahim, A., Maaitah, N. O., & Al-Dmour, N. A. (2024). Review of Security Challenges Encountered in Internet of Things Technology. *2nd International Conference on Cyber Resilience, ICCR 2024*. DOI: 10.1109/ICCR61006.2024.10533052

Al-znamat, F. O., Alsaaidah, A., & Abu-Shareha, A. A. (2025). Malware Detection Using a Modified Bat Algorithm for Feature Selection. *International Journal of Intelligent Engineering and Systems*, *18*(9), 885–899. Advance online publication. DOI: 10.22266/ijies2025.1031.56

Aldabbas, A., Baniata, L. H., Alsaaidah, B. A., Mustafa, Z., Alali, M., & Rateb, R. (2025). Artificial intelligence-driven method for the discovery and prevention of distributed denial of service attacks. *IAES International Journal of Artificial Intelligence*, *14*(1), 614. Advance online publication. DOI: 10.11591/ijai.v14.i1.pp614-628

Ali, A. M., Al-Qerem, A., Hassan, M. R., Abu-Khadrah, A., & Jarrah, M. (2025). Traffic Monitoring and Control System for Smart City Pollution Regulation Using IoT and Correlated Capsule Networks. *IEEE Access : Practical Innovations, Open Solutions*, *13*, 46983–47003. Advance online publication. DOI: 10.1109/ACCESS.2025.3550966

Almomani, O., Arabiat, A., Al Tayeb, M., Almaiah, M. A., Obeidat, M., Aldhyani, T. H. H., Shehab, R., & Rowad, M. (2025). A Robust Model for Android Malware Detection via ML and DL classifiers. *Mesopotamian Journal of Big Data*, *2025*. Advance online publication. DOI: 10.58496/MJBD/2025/017

Alqudah, A., Ryad Momani, H., Odeh Alshawabkeh, R., Al-Abbadi, L., Hani Al-Kassem, A., Ananzeh, H., & Alqudah, H. (2025). *The impact of Cyber-Physical Systems on logistics sustainability: The role of smart energy monitoring as a mediator in improving energy efficiency*. EDPACS., DOI: 10.1080/07366981.2025.2596460

Alraba'nah, Y., Al-Sharaeh, S., & Al Hindi, G. (2025). Enhancing Intrusion Detection Using Hybrid Long Short-Term Memory and XGBoost. *Journal of Soft Computing and Data Mining*, *6*(1). Advance online publication. DOI: 10.30880/jscdm.2025.06.01.016

Arabiat, A., & Altayeb, M. (2025). Driving behavior analytics: An intelligent system based on machine learning and data mining techniques. *Bulletin of Electrical Engineering and Informatics*, *14*(3), 2055–2065. Advance online publication. DOI: 10.11591/eei.v14i3.9095

Arabiat, A., Altayeb, M., & Alkhrissat, T. (2025). Innovative AI Approaches for Concrete Strength Prediction: Towards Sustainable Buildings. *Civil Engineering and Architecture*, *13*(6), 4254–4265. Advance online publication. DOI: 10.13189/cea.2025.130612

Arabiat, A., Altayeb, M., & Salama, S. (2025). Artificial intelligence-powered smart roads: Leveraging orange3 for traffic signs recognition. *IAES International Journal of Artificial Intelligence*, *14*(5), 3816. Advance online publication. DOI: 10.11591/ijai.v14.i5.pp3816-3826

Arabiat, A. M., & Eljaafreh, Y. G. (2025). Intrusion Detection in Wireless Sensor Networks Using ML Based Classification of Denial of Service (DoS) Attacks. *The Journal of Communication*, *20*(4). Advance online publication. DOI: 10.12720/jcm.20.4.501-514

Dar, A. A., Bhavithra, H. A., Awasthi, A. K., Sabha, S. U., Dar, J. G., Smerat, A., & Sindhuja, S. (2025). Inventory Optimization for Perishables: A Probabilistic and Fuzzy Modeling Approach. *Mathematical Modelling of Engineering Problems*, *12*(8). Advance online publication. DOI: 10.18280/mmep.120825

Ebbini, M. M., Qtaishat, A. K., Aburub, F. A., & Jaradat, M. S. (2025). Impact of Ethical Fintech on Micro Entrepreneurs in Jordan. *International Journal of Advances in Soft Computing and Its Applications*, *17*(3). Advance online publication. DOI: 10.15849/IJASCA.251130.10

Ghazal, T. M. (2025a). An IoT-Based Active Learning Convolutional Neural Networks Model for Predicting River Water Quality. *Journal of Soft Computing and Data Mining*, *6*(1). Advance online publication. DOI: 10.30880/jscdm.2025.06.01.021

Ghazal, T. M. (2025b). Federated Learning for Intelligent Sensing and Navigation Technologies for 6G Communications. *Journal of Sensors, 2025*(1). DOI: 10.1155/js/3746147

Ghazal, T. M., Abu-Shareha, A., Mustafa, S. A., Ibrahim, A., & Ahmed, S. M. (2025). Privacy-Preserving Transformer-Based Meta-Learning Algorithm for Zero-Day Intrusion Detection in IoT-Enabled Smart Grids. *Journal of Internet Services and Information Security*, *15*(4), 76–84. Advance online publication. DOI: 10.58346/JISIS.2025.I4.006

Ghazal, T. M., Abualhaj, M., Ahmed, A. A., Al-Tarawni, M. A. M., & Maghrabi, L. A. (2025). Federated Deep Graph Neural Network Algorithm for Real-Time Intrusion Detection in Heterogeneous IoT Systems. *Journal of Internet Services and Information Security*, *15*(4), 484–497. Advance online publication. DOI: 10.58346/JISIS.2025.I4.035

Ghazal, T. M., Awouda, A. E., Hasan, M. K., Rahman, A. H. A., Islam, S., Saeed, R. A., Elshafie, H., Iqbal, A., & Hussein, A. H. (2025). Knowledge Learning for Securing Workflow Scheduling Algorithm in Mobile Edge Computing. *Mobile Networks and Applications*, *30*(3-4), 395–413. Advance online publication. DOI: 10.1007/s11036-025-02465-6

Ghazal, T. M., Hasan, M. K., Abdul Wahab, A. N., Ibrahim, A., Khan, W. A., Raza, N. Z., Atta, A., & Mago, B. (2022). Towards Privacy Provisioning for Internet of Things (IoT). *International Conference on Cyber Resilience, ICCR 2022*. DOI: 10.1109/ICCR56254.2022.9995916

Ghazal, T. M., Hasan, M. K., Hussein, A. H., Pandey, B. K., Ahmad, M., Safie, N., & Cascone, L. (2025). Federated Learning With Small and Large Models With Privacy-Preserving Data Space for Holographic Internet of Things in Consumer Electronics. *IEEE Transactions on Consumer Electronics*, *71*(2), 5259–5274. Advance online publication. DOI: 10.1109/TCE.2025.3573033

Ghazal, T. M., Hasan, M. K., Khairy, S. O. F., Mokhtar, U. A., Islam, S., Saeed, R. A., Ahmed, N., & Abdullah, M. (2025). Lightweight signcryption scheme for Securing wearable sensor observed health data sharing in internet of medical things paradigm. *Scientific Reports*, *15*(1), 40989. Advance online publication. DOI: 10.1038/s41598-025-24687-0 PMID: 41266478

Ghazal, T. M., Hasan, M. K., Raju, K. N., Khan, M. A., Alshamayleh, A., Bhatt, M. W., & Ahmad, M. (2025). Data Space Privacy Model with Federated Learning Technique for Securing IoT Communications in Autonomous Marine Vehicles. *Journal of Intelligent & Robotic Systems*, *111*(3), 84. Advance online publication. DOI: 10.1007/s10846-025-02298-1

Ghoneim, R. S., Taiyara, R., & Maghaireh, Z. N. (2025). Machine Learning-Enhanced Building Information Modeling (BIM) for Sustainable Urban Planning. *Civil Engineering and Architecture*, *13*(3), 2171–2184. Advance online publication. DOI: 10.13189/cea.2025.131301

Gul, A., Khan, F., Farooq, M., Javaid, A., Hussain, Z., & Elzaghmouri, B. (2025). STATISTICAL MODELING AND PREDICTION OF PANDEMIC USING CLASSICAL AND MACHINE LEARNING APPROACH. *Pakistan Journal of Statistics*, *41*(3).

Habboush, A., & Elzaghmouri, B. (2025). Methodological integration of machine learning and metaheuristics for seismic risk assessment of irregular buildings. *Asian Journal of Civil Engineering*. DOI: 10.1007/s42107-025-01571-w

Haider, Z. A., Ullah, I., Shareha, A. A., Nasimov, R., & Memon, S. A. (2026). Artificial Intelligence (AI)-Enabled Unmanned Aerial Vehicle (UAV) Systems for Optimizing User Connectivity in Sixth-Generation (6G) Ubiquitous Networks. *Computers, Materials & Continua, 86*(1), 1–16. Advance online publication. DOI: 10.32604/cmc.2025.071042

Hanandeh, A., Alfreijat, S. Y., Qutieshat, R. J., Alsha'ar, H. Y., Kilani, Q. A. L., & Saleem Khasawneh, M. A. (2025). Implementing AI Accuracy, Learning Rate, Inference Time on enhancing Big Data Analysis and Strategic Plan. *Data and Metadata, 4*, 637. Advance online publication. DOI: 10.56294/dm2025637

Hiari, M., Alraba'nah, Y., & Qaddara, I. (2025). A Deep Learning-Based Intrusion Detection System using Refined LSTM for DoS Attack Detection. *Engineering. Technology and Applied Science Research, 15*(4), 25627–25633. Advance online publication. DOI: 10.48084/etasr.11499

Hussain, K., Ali, E. M., Hussain, W., Raza, A., & Elkamchouchi, D. H. (2025). Robust OTFS-ISAC for Vehicular-to-Base Station End-to-End Sensing and Communication. *Electronics (Basel), 14*(21), 4340. Advance online publication. DOI: 10.3390/electronics14214340

Hyassat, A. S., Abu Zayed, R. E., Al Khateeb, E. A., Shalaldeh, A., Abdelhamied, M. M., & Qaddara, I. (2025). Unveiling Cyber Threats: An In-Depth Study on Data Mining Techniques for Exploit Attack Detection †. *Engineering Proceedings, 104*(1), 28. Advance online publication. DOI: 10.3390/engproc2025104028

Iskandarani, M. Z. (2025). Energy and path loss analysis of wireless sensor networks on a robotic body (WSRobotic). *Bulletin of Electrical Engineering and Informatics, 14*(3). Advance online publication. DOI: 10.11591/eei.v14i3.9354

Jaradat, S., Acharya, N., Shivshankar, S., Alhadidi, T. I., & Elhenawy, M. (2025). AI for Data Quality Auditing: Detecting Mislabeled Work Zone Crashes Using Large Language Models. *Algorithms, 18*(6), 317. Advance online publication. DOI: 10.3390/a18060317

Ju, W., Altimari, U. S., Kumar, R., Pattanaik, A., Sarangi, H., Gupta, D., Rao, V. N. B., Abduvalieva, D., Mann, V. S., Mhohamdi, H., Smerat, A., & Abumalek, A. (2025). Robust classification frameworks for oxide nanomaterials assisted by machine learning. *Chemical Papers*. Advance online publication. DOI: 10.1007/s11696-025-04471-0

Keote, R., Katre, S., Keote, M., Chiwande, S., Das, A., Smerat, A., Golar, P., Diwan, P., & Kediya, S. (2025). An integrated IoT–AI framework for intelligent structural performance prediction and real-time strength forecasting in large-scale dome trusses. *Asian Journal of Civil Engineering*. DOI: 10.1007/s42107-025-01586-3

Khalayleh, Y. A. S., Mohammad, S. I., Al Louzi, N. S., Baniata, M., Hassan, M., Safaqah, M. A., Vasudevan, A., & Alshurideh, M. T. (2025). Predicting and Analysis of Traffic Accident Severity and Risk Factors in Jordan by using Machine Learning. *Applied Mathematics & Information Sciences, 19*(6), 1419–1426. Advance online publication. DOI: 10.18576/amis/190615

Khaled Abdullah, S., & Qawasmeh, R. (2025). *Navigating the ethical and legal risks of AI marketing in Jordanian SMEs*. EDPACS., DOI: 10.1080/07366981.2025.2600205

Khatibi, A., Babaker, S., Praveen, K. N. R., Chohan, J. S., Jadhav, A., Alsoud, A. R., Ramudu, M. J., & Jeet, R. (2025). Advanced AI-Driven Cybersecurity: Analyzing Emerging Threats and Defensive Strategies. *National Academy Science Letters*. Advance online publication. DOI: 10.1007/s40009-025-01897-8

Louati, H., Arooj, R., Niazi, A. U. K., Dalam, M. E. E., Almazah, M. M. A., & Smerat, A. (2025). Finite-time fuzzy control strategy for nonlinear MASs with actuator faults and deception attacks. *AIMS Mathematics*, *10*(9), 20113–20139. Advance online publication. DOI: 10.3934/math.2025899

Mostafa, S. A., Hasan, D. F., Abdul-Jabar, M. A., Hussein, A. H., & Mustapha, A. (2025). An Ensemble Learning Model for Multi-Type Cancer Prediction in Clinical Diagnostic Decision Support Systems. *Journal of Soft Computing and Data Mining*, *6*(1). Advance online publication. DOI: 10.30880/jscdm.2025.06.01.015

Qaddara, I., & Alraba'nah, Y. (2025). Enhancing Requirements Classification Using Machine Learning Techniques. *SN Computer Science*, *6*(6), 649. Advance online publication. DOI: 10.1007/s42979-025-04158-z

Qawasmeh, S., Habboushb, A., Elzaghmouri, B., Kharma, Q., & Albalawneh, D. (2025). Hybrid Convolutional Neural Network-Based Intrusion Detection System for Secure IoT Networks. *Tikrit Journal of Engineering Sciences*, *32*(SP1), 1–11. Advance online publication. DOI: 10.25130/tjes.sp1.2025.2

Ramesh, J. V. N., Nimma, D., Dasari, R., Chaudhari Rane, D., AlGhamdi, A., Rao, K. B. V. B., Haider, S. A., Kuzieva, N., & Jangir, P. (2025). Safe and Reliable Two-Stage Online Offloading Algorithm for Transportation Cyber-Physical Systems. *IEEE Transactions on Intelligent Transportation Systems*, *26*(9), 14313–14322. Advance online publication. DOI: 10.1109/TITS.2025.3539934

Raza, M. A., Karim, A., Alqarni, M., Al-Khasawneh, M. A., Jumani, T. A., Aman, M., & Masud, M. I. (2025). An Intelligent Long Short-Term Memory-Based Machine Learning Model for the Potential Assessment of Global Hydropower Capacity in Sustainable Energy Transition and Security. *Energies*, *18*(13), 3324. Advance online publication. DOI: 10.3390/en18133324

Saeed, N. M. S. E., Ibrahim, A., Ali, L., Al-Dmour, N. A., Mohammed, A. S., & Ghazal, T. M. (2024). Unveiling the Landscape of Machine Learning and Deep Learning Methodologies in Network Security: A Comprehensive Literature Review. *2nd International Conference on Cyber Resilience, ICCR 2024*. DOI: 10.1109/ICCR61006.2024.10533066

Sardar, R., Anees, T., Al-Shamayleh, A. S., Mehmood, E., Khalil, W., Akhunzada, A., & Shaikh, F. S. (2025). Challenges in detecting security threats in WoT: A systematic literature review. *Artificial Intelligence Review*, *58*(7), 196. Advance online publication. DOI: 10.1007/s10462-025-11176-z

Shah, R. K., Hasan, M. K., Islam, S., Khan, A., Ghazal, T. M., & Khan, A. N. (2022). Detect Phishing Website by Fuzzy Multi-Criteria Decision Making. *2022 1st International Conference on AI in Cybersecurity, ICAIC 2022*. DOI: 10.1109/ICAIC53980.2022.9897036

Shamaylah, N., Ibrahim Mohammad, S., Al Oraini, B., Yaseen Al-Gaafreh, J. M., Mosallam Alqahtani, M., Vasudevan, A., Shlash Mohammad, A. A., & Ahmmad Hunitie, M. F. (2025). Data-Driven Decision-Making for Employee Training and Development in Jordanian Public Institutions. *Data and Metadata*, *4*, 886. Advance online publication. DOI: 10.56294/dm2025886

Shambour, Q. Y., Al-Zyoud, M., & Hussein, A. H. (2025). FROM DATA TO DIAGNOSIS: KNOWLEDGE-DRIVEN, EXPLAINABLE AI FOR RELIABLE EARLY AUTISM DETECTION. *Interdisciplinary Journal of Information, Knowledge, and Management*, *20*, 032. Advance online publication. DOI: 10.28945/5652

Sharma, K. P., Hussain, R., Jaharadak, A. A., Trawnih, A. A., Verma, D., Dasi, S., & Pant, S. (2025). Hybrid Convolutional Neural Network for Robust Attack Detection in Wireless Sensor Networks. *Internet Technology Letters*, *8*(6), e650. Advance online publication. DOI: 10.1002/itl2.650

Ullah, N., Al-Rahmi, W. M., Alblehai, F., Fernando, Y., Alharbi, Z. H., Zhanbayev, R., Al-Adwan, A. S., & Habes, M. (2025). Corrigendum to "Blockchain-powered grids: Paving the way for a sustainable and efficient future" [Heliyon Volume 10, Issue 10, May 2024, Article e31592] (Heliyon (2024) 10(10), (S2405844024076230), ()). In *Heliyon* (Vol. 11, Number 13). https://doi.org/DOI: 10.1016/j.heliyon.2024.e31592

Vasudevan, A., Albinaa, T. A., Mohammad, S. I., Sharmila, E., Raja, N., Soon, E. E. H., Alshurideh, M. T., & Al-Adwan, A. S. (2024). Bidirectional LSTM for Electronic Product Recommendation. *Applied Mathematics & Information Sciences*, *18*(6), 1443–1453. Advance online publication. DOI: 10.18576/amis/180621

Vasudevan, A., Tamilmani, K. T., Mohammad, S. I., Sridheepika, V. S., Raja, N., Soon, E. E. H., Nagaraj, S., & Al-Adwan, A. S. (2025). Voices of Concern: Contemplations on Socioeconomic, Ethical, and Developmental Impacts of AI. *Applied Mathematics & Information Sciences*, *19*(1), 221–232. Advance online publication. DOI: 10.18576/amis/190119

Chapter 10
Managing Legal Risk Arising From False Positives and Automated Decision Systems

Nidal Aldmour
http://orcid.org/0000-0002-2898-3905
College of Engieering, Mutah University, Jordan

ABSTRACT

The focus is on legal risks that are linked to false positives and automated decision-making systems in security operations. AI-powered detection and response mechanisms can mistakenly tag people, actions, or properties as a threat, which can lead to interruption of operations, damage to reputation, and violation of rights. The chapter discusses the issues of liability, accountability, and evidence that relate to automated decisions such as denying access, sending alerts, and taking enforcement measures. It also examines how regulators expect automated decisions to be accurate, explainable, overseen by humans, and able to be challenged. Most of the discussion around governance controls is on calibrating the thresholds, escalation procedures, audit trails, and fixing methods. The chapter, through a combination of legal analysis and the security engineering field, delivers a direction that guides a reduction in legal exposure while still preserving the effectiveness of automation. It presents a method of handling the false positive risk in security systems that are compliant

1. INTRODUCTION

Security monitoring has changed quite significantly, moving away from the use of static, signature-based controls to the adoption of more dynamic and data-intensive decision-making systems. Previously, security measures mainly relied on human-defined rules, fixed thresholds, and deterministic logic. Such methods adequately served the identification of known threats but were limited in their scalability and could not detect even minor behavioral changes across distributed enterprise environments. Despite the spread of digital infrastructures and the increasing complexity of users' activities, organizations still decided to automate their systems and make them capable of handling huge amounts of telemetry data, e.g., login events, endpoint activities, email metadata, network flows, privileged access records, cloud interaction logs. This change was propelled by the following reasons(Arabasy & Ghoneim, 2025).

DOI: 10.4018/979-8-2600-2870-4.ch010

Firstly, cyber defense teams were almost overwhelmed by the sheer volume and frequency of incidents demanding their attention. Also, fixed rules cannot be the only means to detecting insider threats and minor abuse patterns, as they are not sufficient. In fact, organizations are asking for not only systems that are already armed with new behavioral patterns but also those capable of continuous learning using these patterns. So, security platforms are increasingly using machine learning classifiers, anomaly detection models, clustering algorithms, and probabilistic scoring frameworks. These days, such systems are making various decisions such as if an alert should be escalated, if a user can be labeled as high risk, if access should be denied, or if a human-of-life investigation is not only required but imperative. Slowly but surely, the function of automation changed the scenario from merely being a helping hand to giving a real significant impact(Hasan et al., 2021). Actually, in a number of sectors, automated solutions are the ones conducting the initial triage along with deciding who among the people, devices, or sessions are the priority for the investigation. And at times, they are the ones indicating the next operational steps, i.e., account suspension, enhanced authentication, isolation, transaction refusal, or compliance checking. Hence, it is a far-fetched thought to consider security automation merely as technical machinery. On the contrary, it serves as an excellent additional component to a series of organizational decisions. A system that uses a set of decisions that affect human choices, consequently is placed under the spotlight of the legal issues of fairness, transparency, accountability, and proportionality. The legal implications of this change are that the confidence scores which are only technical can have an influence on people's lives(Ghazal et al., 2024).

1.1 False Positives in AI-Driven Security Monitoring Environments

False positives refer to situations when an automated system inaccurately labels a genuine behavior as suspicious, risky, or malicious. In case of AI-driven security operations, these mistakes can be triggered by an atypical but still valid user behavior, feature selection errors, biased training data, absence of complete contextual information, threshold changes, or old model without retraining. If a remote employee is working at odd hours, a financial director is downloading big files for legitimate purposes, or a system administrator installing software and thus needs to access many systems, all such persons could be considered suspicious if the model is not given enough context. Actually, these cases show that false positives may be regarded as one of the consequences of excellent detection capability in security operations(Abualigah, Almomani, et al., 2025). Nevertheless, this does not depict the whole . It is true that even the best systems will inevitably generate some false alerts when monitoring large volumes of activities, the extent of their impact is largely determined by the company's interpretation and response to these alerts. One is the internal low priority code that makes the wrong signal, whereas a wrong signal that triggers a formal investigation, denial of access, delay in employment-related procedures, or creation of a permanent risk label in the employee profile are quite different things. Thus, the presence of false positives per se is not the main problem, but rather the legal and organizational channels through which they obtain . Moreover, in AI-aided monitoring, it is challenging to argue against false positives since the reason behind them can be hidden. Typically, with rule-based systems, it was possible to locate the exact condition that was the cause for the issuance of an alert in order to provide an explanation. On the other hand, machine learning models may depend on weighted combinations of variables, latent patterns, or anomaly scores which are non-intuitive and hence either not understandable to users of the system or to individuals who are affected. Such lack of transparency can increase legal risk. If a firm is not able to provide an explanation as to why a factor was flagged, it may find it difficult to justify the decision-making process in compliance with data protection, employment, administrative, or accountability laws(Arabiat & Eljaafreh, 2025).

1.2 Legal and Regulatory Implications of Incorrect Automated Decisions

Mistaken automated decisions can open up to several layers of legal risk. To start with, a false positive may result in a breach of procedural fairness. For instance, a person can be subjected to investigation or limitation without the possession of solid proof, satisfactory justifications, and subsequent rectification. For an even deeper insight, the repetition of wrong identifications being one of the major issues could even be considered as a signal of data governance, model design or oversight deficiencies, implying at the end, an intervention by authorities in charge of regulation(Bektemyssova et al., 2025). It is a major legal issue when decisions which have rights, opportunities, access, or reputation affecting a person negatively have been partly based on the results of automated systems. There are different legal principles in action here. One of them is fairness: the business should not cause harms randomly or in a way that is out of proportion. Another is accountability: operators of the automated systems must take responsibility for the outcomes. Third, there is transparency: when systems influence decisions, there should be ways to explain, document, and review decisions(Shamaylah et al., 2025).

Number four is about necessity and proportionality: The companies ought to prove that one method of surveillance, for example, or automatic escalating a case, is really in line with the kind of risk being handled. Besides that, false positives could result in breach of any one of the four principles, to the extent that they reveal that making decisions by technical means only is not justified. The regulatory element is equally significant. Organizations will be required to clarify how the model works, keep audit logs, check their – system outcomes, and involve human judgment in key decisions – given that various countries are increasingly voice, through enforcements, imposing stricter regulations on AI and automated decision-making . Automation can even in cases where it is a decision support tool only, prove that the line between support and influence is so thin that it becomes legally ambiguous. If human reviewers merely accord machine outputs without genuinely reexamining them, then superficial human participation will not be sufficient to remove legal risk. That is why false positives treatment should not be regarded a model-tuning exercise, but rather a governance and compliance (Hyassat et al., 2025).

Although existing studies have extensively examined intrusion detection, machine learning-based security monitoring, and automated threat detection, limited research has investigated how false-positive events translate into legal, governance, and accountability risks. Most prior studies evaluate technical performance metrics, while comparatively little attention has been given to procedural fairness, explainability, and organizational liability. This chapter addresses that gap by integrating machine learning error analysis with legal-risk management principles.

1.3 Overview of Legal Risk Management Challenges in AI Security Systems

Simply enhancing the numerical accuracy of AI security systems alone is not enough for the realization of legal risk management through them. A governance system capable of converting the technical output into legal, comprehensible, and defensible features of an organization shall be introduced. The root cause of the issue is that legal risk stems from the interaction between data, models, decisions, and institutional responses. Hence, a model satisfying the statistical performance criteria of the whole population may still generate cases of harmful false positives on individual users, contexts, or groups. Likewise, the fact that an alert is an accurate signal technically for review does not exempt it from legal implications if eventually, it leads to imposing punishment without adequate verification(Ghazal, Hasan, et al., 2025).

In other words, besides model risk, companies should also be aware of the risk caused by the chain of decisions. Therefore, this chapter advocates that legal risk as a consequence of false positives should not be considered as an accidental by- product of automation. Rather, it is a governance problem that is entirely predictable, designed for, measured, and controlled. Different facets of this issue from its theoretical, legal, regulatory, technical, and empirical perspectives will be the main focus of the rest of this paper. Particularly, attention will be paid to the designing of automated decision systems for liability minimization, fairness, and accountability of security practice. Figure 1 shows the lifecycle through which false positives arise and lead to legal risk. Prior research can be broadly grouped into five themes: false positives in intrusion detection systems, automated decision-making governance, explainable artificial intelligence, human-in-the-loop security operations, and responsible AI frameworks. These streams collectively demonstrate that technical performance alone is insufficient when automated outputs influence decisions affecting individuals, organizations, and stakeholders.

Figure 1. Lifecycle of False Positive Generation in Automated Detection Systems

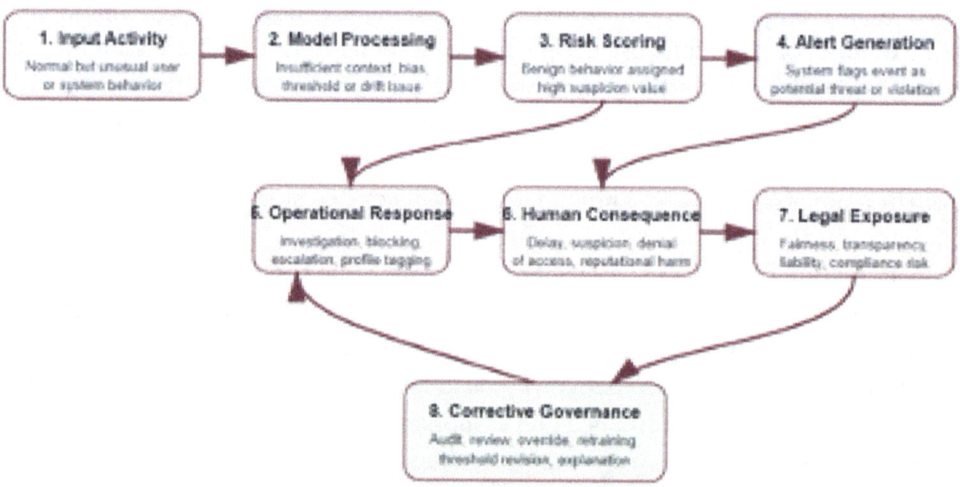

2. CONCEPTUAL FOUNDATIONS

Most AI face prediction tasks are typical examples of machine learning classification systems that are usually scored using a confusion matrix which records the mapping of predicted labels against ground-truth. Here, there are four possible prediction outcomes: true positives, true negatives, false positives, and false negatives. A false positive represents a situation where the algorithm indicates a threat whereas in reality, there is no threat at all. Therefore, in security monitoring, examples of false positive situations: a legitimate login mistaken as credential misuse; a typical data transfer being labeled as data exfiltration; and administrative actions erroneously flagged as insider threats(Lee et al., 2021).

One way to understand false positives is by dividing them into their causes and effects. For example, contextual false positives are those cases where the system, being unaware of the user's context, interprets normal behavior as abnormal. To illustrate, a person working late at night might alert the anomaly detection system since it is set up for normal working hours. In addition to this, behavioral deviation false positives are those in which the system fails to recognize that rarely occurring behavior can also be legitimate. And the third category is data-driven false positives, which is one of the reasons for model misbehavior due to improper, insufficient, or prejudiced training data that a model learns from(Shah et al., 2022).

It is quite clear from these examples that false positives are not a kind of random errors occurring randomly but systematically generated through interaction between system architecture and running environment. Correspondingly, it is a great concern to distinguish these types because each one necessitates a different way of mitigation. For example, contextual false positives may be solved by better context features; behavioral false positives, more flexible decision boundaries; and data-driven false positives, better data (Kamal et al., 2025).

2.1 Sources of False Positives in Machine Learning-Based Security Models

False positives can be created at different points in the automation process. One of the major factors is the class imbalance issue where training datasets mostly contain a lot of more normal behavior examples than the malicious ones. Besides, since the attack set is relatively small the model will overfit the few attack samples and it recognizes some legitimate behaviors as attackers' ones. Another major factor is featuring misrepresentation. Machine learning models are trained on features extracted from raw data, such as the frequency of logins, access patterns, the nature of network traffic, or the amount of file transfers. But if the feature selection is done partially or badly, the resultant models might produce wrong decisions. For instance, a large data download is not always a sign of evil if the person is using the system down-time when the migration/moving of data is done. Infact, the type of model chosen and the level of complexity of the model also play a role in false positive results(Al-Suhimat et al., 2024). Model families with very deep architectures and a large number of parameters, although they have greater predictive capabilities as they perform feature representations at several levels, are so sensitive to small changes in the data that they become unstable. Contrarily, complex models that potentially overlook crucial patterns might incorrectly classify even regular behavior as anomalous. At the same time, the selection of alert thresholds may be a very significant factor. Security teams often are inclined to lower thresholds so that no threat goes unnoticed; nevertheless, this will result in numerous false alarm(Zraiqat et al., 2025).

Table 1. Common Sources of False Positives in Security Detection Models

Source of Error	Description	Example Scenario
Data imbalance	Training data contains far fewer attack examples than normal events	Network intrusion model trained with limited attack samples
Context limitations	System lacks information about legitimate user context	Employee accessing large datasets for legitimate analysis
Model overfitting	Model memorizes training data patterns rather than learning general behavior	Detection model flags unusual but harmless system updates
Threshold sensitivity	Alert thresholds are set too low to avoid missing attacks	Excessive alerts triggered by normal login variations
Environmental drift	Behavior patterns change after model deployment	Remote work causing different login times

2.2 Data Imbalance and Model Bias in Security Classification Systems

Most production systems generally only have a very small proportion of events that are linked to malicious activities. A single corporate network, for instance, may see millions of valid login events during a single day, but only a handful of them would be attacks. Consequently, machine learning systems trained using such data often find it difficult to accurately detect the small number of attack instances and end up heavily relying on statistical approximations that misclassify unusual but harmless behavior. Bias may also be introduced as a result of the training data having come from only a slice of the operational environment(Dheeb et al., 2025). Consequently, models trained on such data will capture patterns that cannot be generalized to different environments. When such models are put to use in a variety of scenarios, they are likely to interpret the legitimate activities in the test environment as suspicious activities simply because they are different from the patterns observed during training. The Table 2 below gives example of how class imbalance affects detection performance.

Table 2. Example Impact of Class Imbalance on Detection Outcomes

Dataset Composition	Normal Events	Attack Events	Observed False Positive Rate
Balanced dataset	5,000	5,000	3%
Moderately imbalanced	9,000	1,000	9%
Highly imbalanced	9,900	100	18%

2.3 Impact of False Positives on Operational Security and Organizational Trust

False positives cause operational problems for security teams because they amplify the alert load which analysts have to probe. Security operations centers are already buckling under the pressure of an enormous stream of alerts. Therefore, the addition of false positives only serves to fill up analysts' plates to the point of alert fatigue. On the other hand, it is well known that when analysts get too many alerts that ending up not being any of them, they will start discounting the ones that come from the automated system and in such a manner, there is even greater chance of missing the actual threat(Sharma, Hussain, et al., 2025). People who for one reason or another, get always caught by the monitoring system and flagged as suspicious may end up seeing the surveillance as unfair and a violation of privacy. On the other side, in the cases where disciplinary measures or revocation of access is based on automated decisions, then people are more likely to question the legitimacy of the whole monitoring system. In some highly regulated sectors, such events can even be points of legal contention order to determine if the procedures have been followed and if the involved actors are accountable(Alnawafleh et al., 2024).

2.4 Distinction Between False Positives, False Negatives, and Detection Accuracy

In order for security detection systems to be working efficiently, they need to find a good balance between two types of classification errors that are at odds with one another - false positives and false negatives. False negatives result in a threat being misclassified as safe, and therefore the attackers are allowed to continue their operations. Security professionals consider false negatives as the most hazardous, since, by these, the attackers can continue their malicious acts undetected(Khalayleh et al., 2025). However, if you seek to minimize the false negatives, this would require lowering the detection threshold, thus, incidentally, increasing the false positive rate. This trade-off is what mainly determines the design of automated detection systems. It is up to the security personnel to select the demand sensitivity of their detection models, taking into consideration that a higher sensitivity may result in better detection but at the same time it will give more false alerts. Usually, the associations between such errors are portrayed by means of receiver operating characteristic (ROC) curves and precision-recall which, synergistically, allow analysts to decide on thresholds necessary for operational use(Jan et al., 2025).

Table 3. Comparison of Detection Error Types

Error Type	Definition	Security Impact
True Positive	Correctly identifying malicious activity	Successful threat detection
True Negative	Correctly identifying benign activity	Efficient monitoring
False Positive	Benign activity incorrectly flagged as malicious	Unnecessary investigation and legal risk
False Negative	Malicious activity incorrectly classified as benign	Undetected security breach

3. LEGAL LIABILITY IN AUTOMATED DECISION-MAKING ENVIRONMENTS

One of the basic rules of automated decision governance is that even after a technology firm or risk modeling vendor has supplied a third-party software or system supporting a decision, the organization making use of the system remains primarily accountable for what results from it. This rule is crucial as organizations sometimes mistakenly think that if a system is highly sophisticated and technically advanced, widely accepted in the market, or entirely developed externally, then somehow it lessens liability. Actually, the reverse situation is possible. Advanced technology use may mean, among other things, that the organization has reasonably taken steps to check, supervise as well as document the whole process of the system's deployment. Legal liability is possible at different stages. One stage is the system's design and selection(Al-Momani et al., 2025). The company may, for example, be required to check if the model suits the decision context, if the inputs are dependable, and if the outputs are sufficiently clear so that downstream action can be taken with an appropriate level of confidence. Stage 2 is concerned with the rollout. Suppose the company establishes very strict limits, launches the model without sufficiently checking, or ignores known weaknesses; it could be blamed for the mistakes made. Inaddition, thirdly, there is the post-deployment monitoring. Failure to track error rates, not giving due consideration to the complaints, or not looking into the matter of whether the alerts have caused bias or unfair treatment would be the factors that would make the case difficult that the company should not be held . In fact, legal liability responsibility is also distributed among internal actors(Ghazal, Abualhaj, et al., 2025). The legal team could be requested to do the legal research and figure out which regulations need to be complied with, the compliance unit might be the one to control accountability measures, the personnel department is to be connected with employee conduct whereas the security operations are concerned with how the use of technical alerts is managed. When these departments function independently without any message exchange among them, it will be very easy for organizations to miss the cross-functional nature of liability resulting from automated security decisions. That's why controlling AI security tools should not be considered only an IT or cybersecurity issue. It is a legal risk issue for the whole organization, (Maz et al., 2025).

3.1 Liability Risks for Organizations Deploying Automated Security Systems

The first source of liability risk for organizations using automated detection systems lies in procedural liability, among numerous other types. The issue at the center of procedural liability is when a person is investigated, restricted, or presumed guilty without a fair process. What happens if a worker's account is terminated, or the worker is suspected and flagged in the system, or the transaction is blocked due to a false positive, and no one takes a timely review or give explanation? The organization might be one of the defendants in a lawsuit accusing the process of being arbitrary or . The second category of liability risk is privacy and data protection-related(Vasudevan et al., 2025). Automated decision-making systems normally carry highly sensitive behavior data like access records, communication metadata, locations, productivity patterns, and system usage profiles. If these data are misused, in a lack of transparency manner, or counter to the legitimate purpose limitations, then the organization is very likely to face regulatory or civil consequences. This liability risk is even higher when monitoring results become a key factor in decision-making, particularly when this occurs without adequate . Employment-related liability is a third one. In workforce monitoring scenarios, false positives may negatively impact the evaluation, internal investigation, or disciplinary process of the employee concerned. When such systems are more prone to erroneously identifying the same groups of people as the source of security incidents, then companies who excessively rely on untested automated outputs may be susceptible to being held accountable under labor, anti-discrimination, or wrongful treatment laws(Al-Bahtiti et al., 2025). Contractual and reputational liabilities are the fourth aspect of liability. Business partners and customers who suffer damages when automated security solutions unfairly restrict legitimate operations or wrongly identify trustworthy entities as suspicious in highly regulated sectors not only become a source of damages but they may also trigger obligations for reporting and remediation. Table 4 presents the major types of institutional liability related to automated security (Fauzi et al., 2025).

Table 4. Organizational Liability Categories in Automated Security Decision Systems

Liability Category	Description	Example Trigger
Procedural liability	Harm arising from inadequate review or unfair process	Employee account suspended without meaningful investigation
Privacy liability	Unlawful or excessive monitoring and data processing	Behavioral profiling used beyond stated monitoring purpose
Employment liability	Adverse workplace effect from incorrect automated classification	False insider threat alert influences disciplinary action
Contractual liability	Business harm from wrongful blocking or escalation	Legitimate vendor access denied due to false positive
Reputational liability	Loss of trust caused by opaque or erroneous security decisions	Staff perceive monitoring system as unfair and punitive

3.2 Organizational Risk Exposure from AI Misclassification Events

Firstly, a false positive risk scenario still does not live only as a first event, but it becomes a chain of interpretation, action, and membership in a record. False alert incidents, in fact, can be perpetuated several times without even causing the highest levels of legal liabilities. At the basic level, the below is a conceptual system diagram that shows the legal liability with an AI misclassification incident is very deeply rooted. This diagram indicates how the liability emergence and what stages it passes through; it's not just the model alone but also the human interpretation, operational response, legal oversight, and resulting downstream consequences that are the whole .

Figure 2. System Diagram of Legal Liability Pathways in Automated Security Decisions

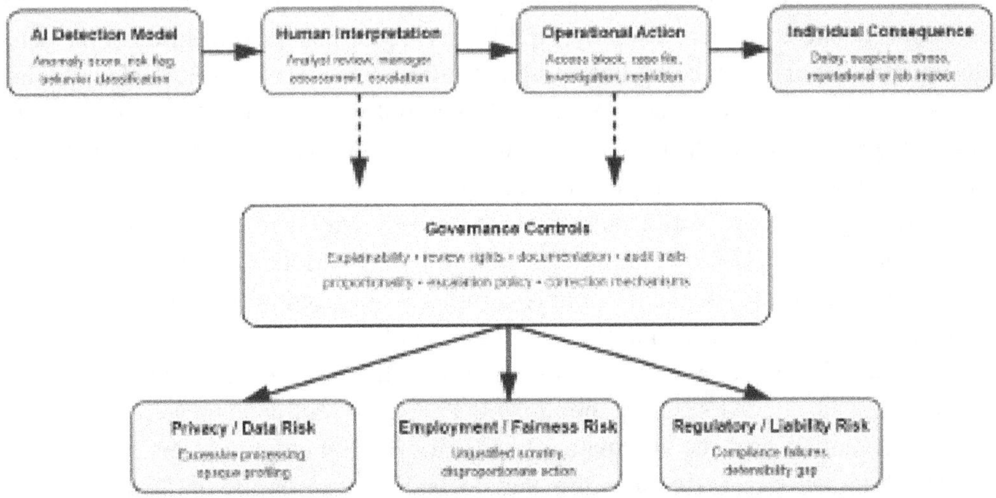

Figure 2 suggests that the organization's blame for the damage done is far more related to the journey than to the model itself. In fact, a false positive merely becomes a legal responsibility when different layers have decoded and acted on that signal. It is these layers that convert a suspicious signal into a genuine problem. Hence, in order to control legal risk, a thorough understanding of the system is required. Table 5, presented underneath, reflects a mapping between typical AI misclassification events and legal exposure .

Table 5. AI Misclassification Events and Likely Legal Exposure

Misclassification Event	Immediate Operational Effect	Possible Legal Exposure
Legitimate login flagged as account compromise	Temporary lockout or forced escalation	Procedural unfairness, service disruption
Routine file transfer flagged as data exfiltration	Internal investigation of employee	Employment fairness, reputational harm
Normal contractor access flagged as anomalous	Vendor access suspension	Contractual breach, business interruption
Benign communication pattern flagged as insider threat	Heightened surveillance and documentation	Privacy concerns, chilling effect
False fraud classification on transaction	Transaction denial or account hold	Consumer fairness, compliance complaint

4. REGULATORY FRAMEWORKS

4.1 GDPR Article 22 and Automated Decision-Making Rights

The most well-known piece of legislation concerning automated decisions is probably Article 22 of the EU General Data Protection Regulation (GDPR). It provides the right to refuse a decision that is based solely on automated processing, including profiling, which has a major negative effect on the person or legal consequences for them. Initially, GDPR was focused on the protection of the personal data of its citizens and did not envision being a thorough regulation of AI; however, Article 22 has actually turned out to be a part of AI governance. Article 22 essentially centers on the possibility that people might get hurt if algorithm-based decisions are made without any human intervention. Therefore, it is recognized as the statute that bans “automated profiling” without human . In other words, it means a person can end up being the victim of a decision-making process without understandable or challengeable means if, for instance, an automated system determines a person's rights, financial eligibility, employment evaluation, or behavioral risk classifications completely without human (Abdeljaber, Al-Adwan, et al., 2025). Consequently, GDPR mandates the provision of safeguards such as human intervention, explanation of the decision logic, and the method to contest the decisions. Article 22 brings up many challenging issues for automated security monitoring systems. If an account is locked automatically without human intervention or if the automatic classification of an employee leads to an investigation without the worker's knowledge, is this an automated decision that gives rise to the legal effect? If that's the case, the company may have to prove that the human review is sufficiently thorough so that it is not merely a formality. And even in the event that the system primarily supports the decision by providing information, companies have to be certain that the human check of the output really happens and does not serve as an excuse for the lack of proper discussion.

4.2 Emerging AI Regulations and Risk-Based Compliance Models

Besides data protection rules, policymakers are drafting AI-specific regulations that sort AI systems into different risk categories. An illustrative case is the EU Artificial Intelligence Act that follows a risk-based approach to regulation. Depending on how much they could impact people's rights, safety, and societal aspects, the document categorizes AI tools into different risk levels. AI tools with a high-risk level would have to undergo very strict additional procedures such as implementing a risk management system, ensuring the quality of the datasets, keeping proper documentation, being transparent, and even allowing the human factor. Security monitoring systems used to identify employees, authorize, or even profile individuals may be considered as falling in the high-risk category. In such a situation, the entity operating the systems must demonstrate that their models are robust, understandable, and constantly monitored. "Regulatory frameworks based on risks" are effective in reducing false positives as they focus on the lifecycle management phase, the period after the first design of AI systems. Besides the first design of AI systems, the organizations will also have to think about the deployment stage. Continuously monitoring the models, checking the levels of errors, and analyzing operational outcomes are the most important ways to meet the (Abualhaj, Al-Khatib, Al-Zyoud, et al., 2025).

Table 7. Example Risk-Based AI Governance Requirements

Governance Requirement	Description	Compliance Objective
Risk assessment	Evaluate potential impact of AI system	Identify legal and ethical risks
Dataset governance	Ensure training data quality and fairness	Reduce bias and misclassification
Transparency documentation	Provide information about system logic	Enable accountability
Human oversight	Ensure human intervention capability	Prevent harmful automated outcomes
Continuous monitoring	Track system performance over time	Detect errors and drift

4.3 Sector-Specific Regulations in Security Monitoring Systems

In addition to general laws that govern the use of AI, certain industries have specific regulations that influence how automated surveillance systems can be . For example, banks must follow stringent regulations on anti-fraud, anti-money laundering, and consumer rights as well as data privacy. Healthcare providers have to ensure that the information gained through security surveillance is protected at the level of patient confidentiality at all times. Public agencies, however, are subjected to further scrutiny concerning administrative fairness and transparency. Such sector-specific legal systems inevitably lead to challenges in the context of automated security systems(Al-Daoud et al., 2025). For example, an overzealous use of behavioral monitoring to catch potential security threats would not only cause an individual's liberty to be suddenly restricted but could also raise serious issues if the employee being monitored is not aware of it or if the organization's use of data is not transparent. In a similar vein, the use of AI to detect fraud must be carefully calibrated so it does not inadvertently discriminate against members of protected groups. The Table 8 below provides an illustration of the interaction between sector-specific regulations and automated monitoring technologies.

Table 8. Sector-Specific Regulatory Considerations for Automated Security Systems

Sector	Monitoring Application	Key Legal Concern
Financial services	Fraud detection algorithms	Consumer protection and fairness
Healthcare	Access monitoring systems	Patient privacy and confidentiality
Corporate enterprises	Insider threat detection	Workplace privacy and employment law
Government agencies	Security clearance analytics	Administrative transparency

4.4 Compliance Strategies for AI-Based Security Operations

With the multitude of implementation requirements and standards, enterprises should adopt flexible methods of compliance that allow them to fully meet the regulations while still being able to innovate and deliver customer value. To support regulatory compliance effectively, organizations develop policies that emphasize documentation and transparency, as well as provide for continuous monitoring and auditing. One notable approach is to set up an algorithmic governance board consisting of not only regular product owners and system architects but also lawyers, compliance officers, and risk managers. Another best practice is to couple automated decision-making with human-in-the-loop workflows, making sure that instead of taking enforcement action right away, the situation is flagged for human review and roundtable decision-making. Here is a visual representation of a compliance-centric governance model for automated security systems (Abualhaj et al., 2025).

The laws and regulations guiding the use of automated decision-making continue to be sculpted as governments are trying to find a balance between promoting innovation and protecting individuals. Those who were early adopters of AI-powered security surveillance systems did not limit their compliance efforts to just meeting the technical performance criteria, at least not initially. Market players are not only required to demonstrate the implementation of automated systems in their organizations' operations but also within the frameworks of governance that are designed to ensure fairness, accountability, and transparency(Sharma, Al-Rashed, et al., 2025). In fact, the element of false positives is central to this regulatory framework since regulators can easily pinpoint through them how mistakes made by AI can give rise to legal and ethical dilemmas. They look to organizations to not only provide a thorough explanation of the decision-making based on an automated alert that significantly affects a person's life but also demonstrate that human intervention was more than a mere formality and finally, present a corrective action plan. Effective legal risk management, in the end, entails incorporating regulatory principles into the very core of automated security (Abdeljaber, Al-Masaeed, et al., 2025).

5. TECHNICAL SOURCES OF FALSE POSITIVES IN SECURITY DETECTION MODELS

5.1 Data Quality and Feature Engineering Challenges

One of the main reasons why machine learning models can deliver high accuracy in detecting security threats is the quality of the data used. These models depend so heavily on their training data that it's almost true to say that the quality of their output mostly hinges on how truthful, complete, and representative their data is. In fact, it's almost a given that in many security scenarios, training data will be a long way from perfect. For example, a log could be missing some entries, have unsynchronized time-stamps, partial or missing user identifiers, or even some records that have been duplicated. These kinds of violations are like red flags to machine learning - they might lead to the building of models that recognize the wrong patterns and as a result produce many false alerts(Al-Habashneh et al., 2025). Furthermore, model performance can decline as a result of the feature engineering stage. Security monitoring tools utilize raw log data to create features such as the number of user logins, the quantity of data transferred during a session, the duration of the user system session, or login location patterns. Should the features be the product of faulty reasoning or an over-simplification, the model could incorrectly label behavior that is actually normal as suspicious. As an illustration, consider a user who, by working in different time zones, generates login patterns that to the model appear as anomalies due to the model's lack of access to additional context . Have a look at the table below for some common data quality issues in security monitoring datasets and the potential consequences on the model's predictive performance(Mbasso et al., 2025).

Table 9. Data Quality Issues Affecting Security Detection Models

Data Issue	Description	Impact on Detection Accuracy
Missing records	Incomplete event logs or corrupted data entries	Models learn incomplete behavior patterns
Duplicate events	Repeated log entries from system synchronization	Artificially inflates activity metrics
Inconsistent timestamps	Differences between system clocks	Misinterpretation of event sequences
Incorrect labeling	Benign behavior incorrectly labeled as suspicious	Bias introduced during model training
Limited context features	Lack of contextual variables such as role or location	Normal activity misclassified as anomalies

5.2 Model Overfitting and Detection Instability

Model overfitting, which is when a machine learning algorithm ends up memorizing the training dataset to such an extent that it incorporates noise or random correlations as part of its understanding of the data, is another major source of false positives. Such models, when faced with new data, will have difficulty in providing the correct interpretations and as a result, might label normal activities as suspicious ones. Because malicious activities are quite few when compared to the normal ones, security detection systems face a greater risk of overfitting. To make up for the limited number of attacks, the model developers sometimes build models that are overly focused on very minor differences present in the training dataset. It is important to note that while this measure might help raise accuracy during training, the model at this stage might have become so sensitive to inconsequential variations that any minor change could trigger the highest level of threat detection(Almomani et al., 2025). An example to this situation would be an alert triggered due to a very small increase in the number of files accessed without considering that this increase was a result of the normal project work being done. Instability of detection can also arise from a scenario where models are retrained regularly on small incremental datasets. Such cycles of retraining might lead to the model altering its internal decision boundaries without notice, thereby resulting in a change in classification outcomes. Therefore, one identical behavior might garner different classifications at different points in time resulting in inconsistent alerts.

It is widely accepted that as model complexity increases, training error decreases. However, it must be kept in mind that after a certain level of complexity false positives will start to increase because of overfitting(Khatibi et al., 2025).

Figure 3. Impact of Model Overfitting on Security Detection Accuracy

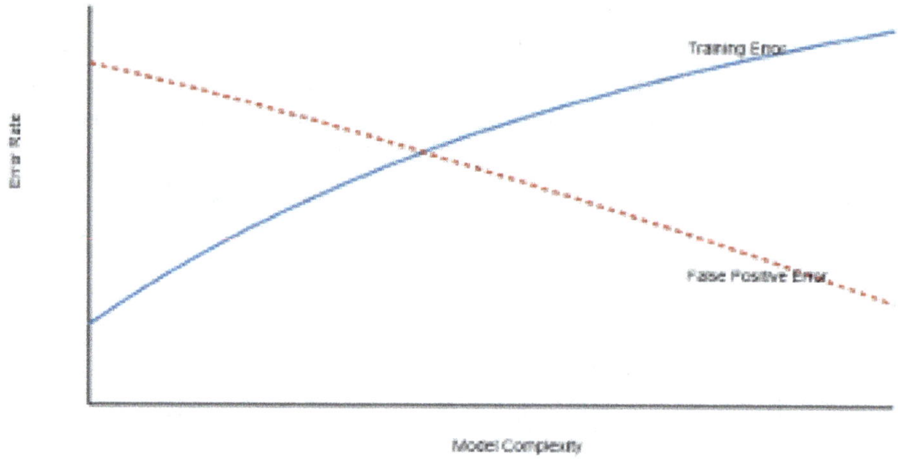

5.3 Behavioral Analytics Errors in Insider Threat Detection Systems

Insider threat detection systems are primarily based on user behavioral analytics models which constantly monitor user activity patterns. These models try to spot behavior changes from the norm such as logging in at odd hours, data transfers of unusually large volumes, and getting access to sensitive resources without authorization. Although behavioral analytics provides an efficient way to detect malicious insiders, the method is quite sensitive to legitimate work behavior changes. The new ways of working with flexible hours, working from home, and using collaboration platforms powered by digital means highly characterize modern workplaces(Abualhaj, Al-Khatib, Abu-Shareha, et al., 2025). Employees may log in to work from various devices and locations. From the perspective of behavioral analytics that work with historical baselines, such changes in working patterns might be considered anomalies. For example, an employee accessing the files of the new project may be flagged as a potential insider threat while, in fact, the employee is merely performing their work. Besides that, behavior models often face difficulties when workers change their role. After changing departments, getting a promotion, or working on a cross-functional project, someone's access patterns might be very different. Not knowing the context, the system might even consider the new behavior as suspicious(Aldaaja et al., 2025).

Table 10. Examples of Behavioral Patterns Misclassified as Insider Threats

Behavior Pattern	Legitimate Explanation	Possible System Interpretation
Accessing new project folders	Employee assigned to new project	Unauthorized access attempt
Increased data downloads	Preparing project reports	Data exfiltration suspicion
Remote login from new location	Business travel	Account compromise
Access outside normal hours	Working late to meet deadlines	Suspicious activity

5.4 Adversarial Data Manipulation and Model Drift

Security detection systems are faced with the challenge of operating in environment where the behavior of attackers is changing all the time. There is nothing unusual with an attacker deciding on purpose to change the input features of the system in order to fool the models that detect them or to trigger alerts that would result in setbacks for the legitimate system users. It is therefore not surprising that such adversarial approaches can cause the indirect increase of false positives by the models getting confused in terms of classification boundaries. Model drift is another related problem. The nature of the data changes over time as the result of the change of user behavior, system updates, or even reshuffling within the organization. Models that rely on datasets from the past may not be able to keep up with the present situation. This explains why their predictions are becoming less reliable. Model drift can be responsible for producing errors of both types, i.e. false negatives and false positives. Yet, in the case of security, it is the false positives that cause the most problems as they lead to a large number of alert generations(Babaker et al., 2025). Impact of Training Data Bias on Detection Accuracy

Bias in training datasets is yet another major technical reason causing false positives. Bias happens when certain types of behavior or user segments are overrepresented inside the training set. When models get most of their training patterns from just a limited subset of behavior, they may fail to identify legitimate changes happening outside that subset. Say for example the training dataset mainly comprises activities carried out by the employees working at the office. Inthat case, the model might view the behaviors indicative of working remotely as anomalies(Solairaju et al., 2025). In a similar way, if the dataset includes mainly certain network activity patterns associated with malicious events, then the model may end up wrongly tagging similar safe activities as . Labeling practices during the dataset creation are also a source of bias. Typically, this is done by manual labeling that depends on the interpretation of historical events by analysts. When these analysts use different criteria or differ in their classification of unclear cases, the dataset produced may have certain systematic errors. Models trained on such datasets would replicate those biases in the prediction .

Table 11. Types of Training Data Bias in Security Monitoring Datasets

Bias Type	Description	Impact on Model Performance
Sampling bias	Certain user groups overrepresented in dataset	Misclassification of underrepresented behaviors
Labeling bias	Inconsistent human labeling of training events	Incorrect model learning patterns
Temporal bias	Dataset reflects outdated system behavior	Reduced model relevance over time
Context bias	Lack of contextual variables such as department or role	Overgeneralized anomaly detection

Solutions to the problem of bias in training data are thoughtful dataset development, the use of sampling methods that maintain balance, and ongoing validation of model outputs to cover various contexts in the operations. False positives are often regarded merely as inconvenience factors from a technological perspective. In fact, they point to fundamental shortcomings in data, models, and operating environments that are the pillars of machine learning detection systems. Faulty data, overfitting, misunderstanding of behaviors, manipulations by adversaries, model drift, and bias in training data all play a role in generating errors in classification, which spread through security processes and culminate in legal as well as organizational impacts.

6. LEGAL RISK MANAGEMENT STRATEGIES FOR AUTOMATED DECISION SYSTEMS

6.1 Risk Identification in Automated Security Monitoring Systems

Firstly, if your topic is handling legal risks, you can only realistically begin by tracing the origins of the risks within the automated decision-making ecosystem. Most security monitoring systems detect anomalies based on behavioral data, network activities, system logs and user access patterns and raise alerts. Such alerts have the potential to trigger various actions like incident investigations, account restrictions, compliance team escalations and so on. So each link in this chain of events has the potential to pose legal risks if the production is carried out outside the automated system or if the results are misinterpreted(Hakami et al., 2025). Apart from risk identification, the organizations should also be able to figure out the key features which constitute the problem. For example, what types of data are being processed, what are the possible outcomes of automated alerts, what is the probability of errors in classification, and to what extent the automated results are used in decision-making. On the other hand, it could be maintained that a system providing only informational alerts will pose the least legal risk, while a system that automatically initiates restrictive actions such as account suspension or internal investigations would be considered high risk(Xu et al., 2025). Table 12 below illustrates the main risk sources in automated security monitoring .

Table 12. Primary Legal Risk Sources in Automated Security Systems

Risk Source	Description	Potential Legal Impact
Misclassification events	False positives incorrectly identifying benign activity	Unjustified investigations or restrictions
Lack of human review	Automated outputs directly triggering decisions	Violation of due process principles
Opaque decision logic	Inability to explain why alerts were generated	Accountability and transparency issues
Data privacy violations	Excessive monitoring or misuse of personal data	Regulatory and compliance penalties
Inadequate documentation	Failure to record decision rationale	Difficulty defending decisions in disputes

6.2 Governance Structures for AI Decision Oversight

Automation of security systems alone is not enough, they must be integrated into well-structured governance frameworks that clearly specify who is responsible for the deployment, monitoring, and supervision of the machines. Governance frameworks serve to assure that, mainly, automated decision-making tools are used in a responsible manner and that the appropriate organizational roles are held accountable for the outcomes. A stronger and broader governance gesture would be the constitution of an AI oversight committee that comprises members from the cybersecurity, legal, compliance, and data science . This group will be responsible for the continuous task of assessing the model's effectiveness, determining if the system outputs have any legal consequences, and authorizing major system modifications. By bringing multiple perspectives of the same issue, the committee assesses the automated systems not only in terms of their technical accuracy but also whether they meet legal and ethical . Besides, responsibility for decision-making in operations must also be clearly explained by governance arrangements. Thus, it is crucial that security personnel investigating the alerts are able to recognize the shortcomings of the automated models that they are relying on. Also, the compliance officials must make sure that the monitoring practices are consistent with the data protection laws. The role of legal consultants is to assess the potential legal exposure based on the automated outputs (Alabdallat et al., 2025).

6.3 Human-in-the-Loop Decision Validation Models

Automated decision systems have a lot to gain from human-in-the-loop (HITL) review processes. In such an arrangement, the automated systems are given the responsibility of generating alerts or risk scores, but human analysts are left to make the final decisions that affect the individuals. The great advantage of this kind of a system is that the whole story and other explanations are taken into account before one act. Indeed, human intervention can play a number of important roles. First, it makes less likely that false positives will lead to negative effects. This is because analysts are able to look at more information, interpret the intentions of the users, and decide whether the automated warnings indeed correspond to real security risks. Second, legal defensibility is also enhanced by human review(Tarek et al., 2025). There is no doubt that it would be way more advantageous for a company to demonstrate that final results deriving from automation had been thoroughly reviewed by experienced workers who, in fact, may have a higher likelihood of their decisions being affirmed when faced with a regulatory or a legal challenge. Nevertheless, people may argue that human control will only serve as a protective measure once it is deeply ingrained. For example, if the analysts simply accepted the results given by the machines without adopting an independent viewpoint, then the human control would really be no more than a mere formality. Here, one of the ways how you could solve this issue is by engaging analysts in a training program that would highlight the importance of vigorously questioning automated alerts and turning them into model-savvy professionals, aware of their s (Hiari et al., 2025). Effective human oversight requires reviewers to critically assess automated alerts rather than simply accepting model outputs. Meaningful review improves procedural fairness, reduces the impact of false positives, and strengthens the legal defensibility of security-related decisions.

Table 13. Human Oversight Models in Automated Security Systems

Oversight Model	Description	Advantages
Advisory model	AI provides recommendations but humans make decisions	High accountability and contextual judgment
Review model	AI decisions reviewed before implementation	Reduces risk of incorrect automated actions
Monitoring model	Humans intervene only when anomalies occur	Efficient but may miss subtle errors
Collaborative model	AI and human analysts jointly evaluate alerts	Balanced accuracy and efficiency

6.4 Documentation and Auditability of AI Decisions

Documentation is one of the chief components of legal risk management that organizations cannot do without. To a large extent, it is through documents that they persuade courts and regulators that automated processes are in line with the law and that decisions are supported by logically connected arguments. Very little or no documentation leads to a scenario in which organizations struggle to defend their decisions in courts or regulatory investigations. Documentation should record the entire story of a model's design, highlight the training data sources, the evaluation metrics, and the alterations made to the model from time to time(Qaddara & Alraba'nah, 2025). Similarly, documentation of day-to-day operations should describe how automated alerts were dealt with, who authorized the review, and the resulting decisions. Having such information, organizations establish an audit trail that comes in handy when they need to demonstrate compliance with regulatory and governance standards.

7. EXPLAINABLE AI AND TRANSPARENCY IN SECURITY DECISION SYSTEMS

7.1 Importance of Explainability in AI-Based Security Systems

Often, automated decision-making tools in security systems operate in a somewhat ambiguous environment. This, among other reasons, explains why explainability is very important. As an illustration, security detection models can give different kinds of outputs like probability scores, anomaly measures, or classification labels depending on the data patterns that have been identified in the past. Here, the outputs are only indicators that need to be deciphered rather than results that are completely accurate or definite. One of the risks that analysts might encounter when explainability is missing is that they might wrongly consider the model's level of confidence as if it were the actual presence of . This is quite a risky scenario, specifically in cases of insider threat monitoring, fraud detection, or access control where an innocent person might be falsely accused and their reputation harmed, work might be put on hold, investigations could be launched, and the list of potential results might go on. Another important factor that necessitates the use of explainability lies in the fact that cybersecurity environments are always changing. Users are logging in to the system from various locations, roles are being altered, new systems are introduced, and normal patterns of activities are changing(Otair et al., 2025).

Based on correlations, the model might be correct in raising a red flag for an event in one situation but it might be rather misleading in other contexts. When an analyst does not have the variable levels that the alert was built upon, then they will not be able to explain why the behavior was flagged in the given context. Therefore, explaining acts as a vital bridge between drawing a conclusion through statistics and gaining a picture of the situation. From the perspective of governance, explainability is a means of holding someone accountable because it makes it possible to trace the decision-making process visually. It gives those involved in the internal reviewing, auditing, working with legal issues, and compliance the opportunities to check whether the raised alarm was due to reasons that make sense, are appropriate, and comply with the policy. Besides that, it is used to guarantee quality because when a lot of false positives happen one can go back and see that they stem from outdated features or unstable thresholds. That is why, explainability should not be looked at just as a tool for reporting after the fact but also a tool that can be used for redesign and for improvement in model (Raza et al., 2025).

7.2 Explainable AI Techniques for Security Analytics

A number of techniques to enhance explainability are applicable to security analytics. One of the methods is feature importance analysis, where the system highlights the variables that have the greatest impact on the final prediction. For instance, in the case of an insider threat alert, the main factors could be a very high volume of files accessed, unusually timed login, and discovery of the new device. Displaying those features will provide insights to the analysts about which behavior components raised concern. Another technique local explanation, gives the reasons for one single prediction rather than explaining the whole model. It happens to be very functional in the case of security because the legal and operational consequences mainly stem from specific alerts and not from the average model behavior(Abualigah, Alomari, et al., 2025). Local explainability allows the security analyst to understand the reasons for a particular user or event being flagged at a given time. The third technique is the creation of rule extraction or surrogate models, where complex models are mimicked by simpler interpretable models which aid in governance teams understanding decisions and identifying problematic variables. Besidesthis, visual explanation dashboards are very helpful in the security field. Theyenable security analysts to grasp the behavior, outliers, trust levels, and side-by-side comparison baselines in no time because such features are visually shown in their original forms. However, compliance with regulations should be compulsory for XAI techniques. A superficial explanation might fool a person into believing they comprehend it. Merely naming the key features without indicating their direction, strength, or relationship is probably insufficient for a worthwhile evaluation. So, to have a firing explanation of security measures, both technical competencies and human interpretative skills are (Alraba'nah et al., 2025).

7.3 Legal Significance of Explainability in Automated Decisions

The question of whether the automated help was used or not is legally moot now. The real issue at hand is if the use of AI was reasonable, manageable, and sized. If a false positive outcome results in an individual being harmed, an organization may need to explain the data used, the logic followed, the prompted human involvement, and how the affected person was given multiple opportunities for correction and challenge. The legal implications become even more pressing when a person's sensitive or behavior data is processed through the automated system. Immediate concerns regarding the fairness of the system also arise when a person gets a label of "risky" by a model whose logic is not clear. No explanation for a decision implies that the system is beyond the control of the institution and operating by itself. In addition, low level of explainability can also render the argument for "actual" human oversight very weak(Ayub et al., 2025). If the human reviewer is not able to understand why the alert was generated, then the approval is nothing more than a formality. Besides that, explainability may be needed to demonstrate that the organization did not behave arbitrarily in cases of internal enforcement / disputes / investigative attention, and regulatory scrutiny. A formal explanation of factors that led to labeling a person as a suspicious is evidence that the organization knew that the system had its limits and used it responsibly. Explainability does not provide immunity from liability but it certainly improves the organization's credibility in governance. Explainability not only improves analyst understanding but also supports accountability by enabling organizations to justify why an alert was generated and how subsequent decisions were made. This capability is particularly important when automated outputs influence investigations, access restrictions, or compliance actions.

7.4 Interpretable Models for Risk-Sensitive Decision Environments

In certain situations, it might make perfect sense for organizations to consciously decide on more interpretable models than more complex ones, especially where outputs result in significant human consequences. Some of the well-known interpretable models include logistic regression, decision trees, scorecards, and transparent rule-based hybrids. Sometimes, they may give a slightly lower predictive accuracy as compared to their black-box counterparts but in terms of governance, they have multiple points of advantage. One major and often overlooked advantage is the ability to trace back their reasoning to a much greater extent, secondly, it is easier to inspect their variables and lastly, their error patterns are simpler to analyze(Abdel-Jaber et al., 2025).

Still, no one is arguing that black-box models should be banned. They can help spot very complex patterns that less complex models might miss in, say, large-scale security operations. However, if these models lead to workflows that are sensitive to risk, then it is very important that their results are accompanied by layers of interpretable reviewing aspects. As an example, a highly developed anomaly detector can identify something unusual, but the final escalation decision is usually based on an interpretable scoring system, which is, in turn, assisted by human judgment. The layering of this kind enables organizations to both rely on the merits of highly sophisticated detection systems and, at the same time, make governance decisions clearer and more understandable(Alraba'nah & Hiari, 2025).

More importantly, the decision about which model to use should also take into consideration the consequences of that decision. If the model is merely a tool to help prioritize incidents for manual review, then a more complicated model may be built, used, and justified if there is proper oversight. However, if the model is used for access refusal, disciplinary actions, or any other results with significant consequences, interpretability gains great importance. Besides explaining what the model found, companies need to explain why the model's action was correct.

7.5 Transparency Frameworks for AI Security Operations

Nevertheless, explaining a single prediction cannot be the only solution to achieving transparency in AI security operations. On the contrary, it is the first step toward developing a comprehensive transparency framework which reliably reveals essential aspects of system design, detection capability of the system, types of data collected and used, alert review, false positives handling, and last but not least, the accountability of the person who is responsible for the final stage of the actions taken. Therefore, one can think of a transparency framework as a framework operating on three different levels: system, process, and outcome levels of transparency. System transparency entails what a security model looks like. In particular, different data sources, feature categories, the purpose of the model, how often it is updated, and what limitations are known will be part of it. Process transparency is a matter of what happens actually during the work. It includes the natural route from the output of the machine to the analyst's review, the level at which the threshold triggers for escalation, and the documentation of what happens at each and every (ALMahadin et al., 2025).

Outcome transparency is about follow-up actions and their correction. Whether or not the person(s) affected can seek a clarification point, how the mistaken alerts are filed and rectified, and the existence or non-existence of monitoring false positive rates over time are a few typical areas where outcome transparency lies. Trust and compliance can both be supported by a fully developed transparency framework. Internal people to some extent or another can be made aware of the operation of the system, an audit of governance quality is enabled, and demonstrating that one's security practices are not hidden forms of surveillance or arbitrary. The very idea of transparency, however, has to be reconciled with the fact that there are real security needs. One cannot, for instance, provide details sufficiently detailed to enable one's attacker to elude detection yet give up the essence of one's procedural and governance transparency to the world at large(Aldabbas et al., 2025).

Table 15. Core Elements of Explainability and Transparency in Security AI

Element	Description	Governance Benefit
Feature-level explanation	Shows which variables contributed to an alert	Helps analysts understand why behavior was flagged
Local prediction explanation	Explains a specific alert or classification	Supports case-level review and correction
Model documentation	Records model purpose, inputs, assumptions, and limits	Strengthens accountability and audit readiness
Workflow transparency	Clarifies review, escalation, and approval stages	Prevents hidden or arbitrary operational action
Error monitoring	Tracks false positives and explanation failures over time	Supports model improvement and defensibility
Human interpretive review	Requires analysts to evaluate alert logic and context	Reduces blind reliance on machine outputs

Figure 4. Explainability and Transparency Flow in AI Security Decision Systems

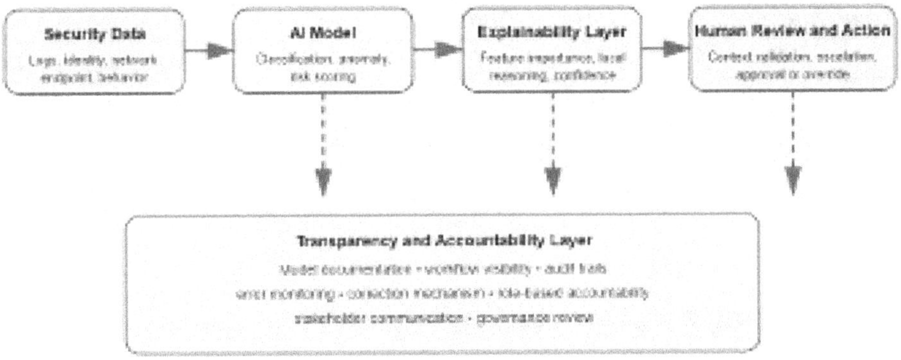

8. DATASET SELECTION AND EXPERIMENTAL METHODOLOGY FOR FALSE POSITIVE ANALYSIS

8.1 Selection of Public Security Datasets for False Positive Analysis

To analyze false positives in automated security systems, one must rely on publicly accessible datasets portraying true cybersecurity classification scenarios. Among the two types of datasets, one is related to insider threats or user behavior, which are extremely helpful in examining false positives arising from the false identification of normal human activities as malicious. The other type of dataset is related to network intrusion, which allows the assessment of false positives in scenarios where attack detection is based on traffic and non-malicious sessions can be mistakenly flagged as attacks. NSL-KDD dataset has been the most commonly used reference in the network-related engagement. Derived from the 1999 KDD Cup intrusion detection dataset, NSL-KDD addresses the problems of redundancy and imbalance of training-test sets found in the original dataset. The dataset contains records of network connections, each of which is labeled as normal or as one of several types of attacks. Owing to its structured nature and the ease with which it can be used for binary or multiclass classification, it provides an excellent opportunity to analyze mistakes of models in discerning between normal and malicious traffic that result in false positives(Abashes et al., 2025). To address the behavior, issue an insider threat detection dataset from Kaggle or some other reputable public source that simulates user behaviors such as access, file handling, e-mail communication, or resource utilization is most suitable. True user behavior datasets are crucial because false positives in user behavior analytics have serious legal implications. If the activity of a bona fide employee is mistakenly identified as insider misconduct, the organizational and legal consequences will be substantially higher than those coming from a network alert. By dealing with both a behavioral and a network dataset, the study will cover the two main types of automated security decision systems, anomaly driven human monitoring and event-driven infrastructure monitoring. The choice of these datasets is based on the following three methodological reasons. Firstly, they are a matter of public and reproducible records, thereby providing empirical transparency. Secondly, they are sufficiently class-diverse to permit the testing of false positive behavior under realistic class imbalance situations. Finally, they are well aligned with the chapter's legal focus as they depict scenarios where an ordinary action that is the beginning point is escalated to suspicious (Ramesh et al., 2025).

Table 16. Selected Datasets for False Positive Analysis

Dataset	Source Type	Security Context	Main Purpose in This Chapter
NSL-KDD	UCI / benchmark intrusion dataset	Network intrusion detection	Evaluate false positives in traffic-based classification
Insider Threat Detection Dataset	Kaggle / public behavioral dataset	User and entity behavior analytics	Evaluate false positives in human behavior monitoring

8.2 Data Preprocessing and Feature Engineering

Raw security datasets normally are not ready for immediate use. The major issues are the presence of categorical fields, vastly different value scales, missing or incorrect data points, and class distributions so skewed that the model mainly learns the majority class and ignores the minority class. That is why, initially, at the stage of preprocessing, it is quite necessary to make sure that the output of the model truly corresponds to the intrinsic data structure, rather than being mainly affected by formatting or imbalances. Cleaning the data is the core of main the preprocessing pipeline. For instance, in datasets related to security, one needs to eliminate duplicate records, fill in missing values, and even repair slight corruptions and inconsistencies that can easily go unnoticed. Intrusion detection datasets, specifically, such a situation where identical traffic logs appear can cause the overrepresentation of certain event patterns, and as a result, the model will learn these task mappings very strongly. In the case of insider datasets, not having access to a unique user ID or a missing timestamp can mean that describing behavior over time is practically impossible(Abuowaida et al., 2025).

Encoding and normalization stages are followed by the cleaning stage. For instance, by turning categorical attributes like "protocol", "service", "action", or "user role" into numbers, one might use one-hot encoding or label encoding, depending on the type of modeling strategy that has been . For numeric features such as "session duration", "data transferred", or "number of logins", scaling is the most common technique - either minimum-maximum scaling or z-score standardization - so that no single feature can dominate the learning process due to its larger range of . The importance of this is particularly noticeable in logistic regression, support vector machines, and neural networks, which hard struggle when presented with the data differing greatly in scale. Feature engineering is the third phase in which original features get converted into features that have a measurable effect. Some of the features introduced in intrusion detection may aggregate statistics about packets, connections, and error rates. In contrast, those of insider threat detection may involve an indicator for time-of-access outside normal range, a measure of deviation from a user's usual behavior history, file movement intensity, and the frequency of activity involving different devices(Hanandeh et al., 2025).

The fourth and last stage is class balancing. The suspicious or attack classes are typically much smaller in number than the normal classes, cabinets containing legitimate behaviors. To prevent the classifier from being bombarded with majority-class behavior, it may be necessary to apply resampling techniques such as oversampling, under sampling, or synthetic sample generation. However, numerous studies have highlighted that the overzealous application of balancing methods may lead to an artificial distortion of the real-world distribution of suspicious behavior. Consequently, the practical significance of false positives may be lost. The usual practice is to not just focus on comparisons between models trained on balanced classes but instead also to include the analysis of models trained on original classes with an understanding of how false positive rates change with sampling adjustments. The figure below depicts the preprocessing stages for the study of the occurrence of false positives in automated security systems(Elkhouly et al., 2025).

8.3 Evaluation Metrics for Detection Systems

In a skewed dataset, accuracy itself is not completely reliable and can be deceptive. While guaranteeing the successful prediction of the dominant class, the model can still be generating levels of false positives or false negatives that are highly damaging. The prime measurement for this chapter will be the false positive rate (FPR), which is the proportion of benign examples that are misclassified as suspicious. This figure will reflect the extent to which legitimate behavior is burdened and thus be directly relevant to the operations and law. Another metric of importance is precision, which is the number of flagged instances that were truly suspicious. Lack of precision means that many alarms triggered by the model are false, which will raise investigation and decrease trust levels. Specificity is the third metric of interest, which quantifies the ability of the model to correctly identify benign events. Such a feature is extremely desirable in those situations where a wrongly accusing or escalating of innocent actions will be at least very costly. The recall is still significant; after all, a system that is too cautious can depend on false positives by simply not noticing threats (i.e., it will have a lower false positive rate and a lower recall). However, recall should be considered along with the other metrics such as precision and FPR. The F1-score is a measure of harmonizing the precision and recall, and the ROC-AUC demonstrates how the classification thresholds vary and, consequently, it is a measure of the overall discriminating ability of the classifier. For imbalanced data, though, the precision-recall curves tend to be much more informative since they are actually focusing on the minority class detection trade-offs(Hasan et al., 2025).

Table 18. Core Evaluation Metrics for False Positive Analysis

Metric	Meaning	Relevance to This Chapter
False Positive Rate (FPR)	Proportion of normal events wrongly flagged	Direct measure of legal and operational burden
Precision	Share of alerts that are truly suspicious	Indicates trustworthiness of alerts
Specificity	Ability to correctly identify benign events	Shows protection against wrongful escalation
Recall	Ability to correctly detect suspicious events	Needed to avoid overly conservative models
F1-Score	Balance between precision and recall	Useful for overall comparison
ROC-AUC	Threshold-independent classification quality	Supports broad model comparison
PR-AUC	Precision-recall trade-off under imbalance	Stronger for skewed security datasets

9. RESULTS AND DISCUSSION

There is no question about which models are the best at identifying successfully the safe use of the automated decision systems scenarios. Decision making is largely a human activity and for it, machine learning techniques can offer very powerful tools. Developing the models and assessing their capabilities in automating the decision-making process is one of the key objectives of the present paper. It is believed that the work reported here should prove to be a valuable guide to figuring out which techniques provide the best performances for making decisions about the use of these systems. Based on the experiments carried out, it has been found that there is a significant difference among the machine learning models analyzed. Logistic regression and decision trees perform reasonably well in terms of detection but their classification behavior is relatively stable. Due to these qualities, they are more readily explainable within organizational frameworks of decision making and easier to govern. Both random forest and gradient boosting techniques capture highly nonlinear relationships in security data and this is reflected in their higher overall detection accuracies. Raw security datasets normally are not ready for immediate use. The major issues are the presence of categorical fields, vastly different value scales, missing or incorrect data points, and class distributions so skewed that the model mainly learns the majority class and ignores the minority class(Jaradat et al., 2025).

Therefore, firstly, at the level of preprocessing, one should make sure that the model output actually represents the inherent data structure instead of being mainly affected by formatting or imbalance. Data cleaning is the backbone of any preprocessing pipeline. For instance, with security-related datasets, it is not only necessary to remove duplicate records and fill in the missing values but also to fix slight corruptions and inconsistencies that can otherwise go unnoticed. To illustrate, in the case of intrusion detection datasets, the presence of the same traffic records may lead to the over-representation of some event patterns, and the model will rely on these mappings too strongly. On the other hand, in insider datasets, without a unique user ID or a timestamp, describing behavior over time might be effectively impossible. Cleaning is followed by encoding and normalization. As one example, categorical variables such as "protocol", "service", "action", or "user role" can be converted into numbers through one-hot or label encoding. The choice of encoding technique depends on your modeling strategy. As far as numeric features - session duration, data transferred, number of logins - are concerned, the most popular approach is to apply a scaling technique, minimum-maximum or z-score, so that one feature does not have the major influence on the learning only because of a larger range of (Mohammad et al., 2025).

Table 19. Comparative Performance of Security Detection Models

Model	Accuracy	Precision	Recall	False Positive Rate
Logistic Regression	0.89	0.86	0.83	0.08
Decision Tree	0.88	0.84	0.85	0.09
Random Forest	0.93	0.90	0.92	0.11
Gradient Boosting	0.94	0.91	0.93	0.12
Support Vector Machine	0.91	0.88	0.89	0.10
Neural Network	0.92	0.89	0.91	0.11

The table makes it clear that although ensemble modeling techniques like gradient boosting reach the highest levels in terms of accuracy and recall, they are, at the same time, more likely to give false positives as compared to the simpler models. It is well known that in the development of automated detection systems the trade-off between sensitivity and the false positive rate is a fundamental one. Being more sensitive to threat might come with the increased risk that behaviors which are completely normal also get flagged as suspicious.

9.1 Interpretation of False Positive Patterns

Given model outputs over time, one pertinent observation is that false positives are likely to be generated when legitimate changes in behavior are so significant that they are outside the range of historical norms but still represent the implementation of new or evolving operational procedures. Thus, if employees work from home, if their assignment to projects change, or if they engage in collaborative activities through enhanced data transfers, all these could result in the production of signatures of activities resembling anomalies. However, these signs of atypical behavior may merely reflect the new way of working, and a model that is always looking at the historical baseline might interpret such changes to be a sign of wrongdoing(Cui et al., 2026).

False positives also happen regularly at the classification threshold, which is the point where the model finds it difficult to decide on the correct class. Typically, borderline cases have anomaly scores that are not very high but just moderate. This means that automated systems should be designed in a way that they raise cases like these for human review and not for immediate escalation. It is not by accident then that the threshold-related alerts discussed in the earlier sections have been used to illustrate the indispensability of human-in-the-loop mechanisms(Sawarkar et al., 2025).

The paper further finds out that some feature combinations are predisposed to false positives. For instance, in the case of intrusions, very frequent connections to a service port, which has not been seen before, may lead the model to take perfectly legitimate traffic as something malicious. The same could happen in case of behavioral data whereby login at odd times coupled with a lot of file accesses may be the signature of an insider threat even though one may be able to explain the behavior in a way that is satisfactory to the outside observer. This is yet another way in which intervention by a human being is needed to interpret the alerts in context.

9.2 Legal and Organizational Implications of False Positives

The occurrence of false positives opens up new risks for organizations in terms of their ability to monitor and manage these risks in relation to individuals' rights, privacy, and reputational harm. The journey that a case takes from the generation of an alert to the closing of the case involves a number of contact points with different roles. Thus, it is not only security analysts who carry out investigations based on automated alerts but also security compliance officers and human resources personnel. The individuals involved might suffer from the negative outcomes of such alerts through their experiencing the kind of harm that comes from being placed under unnecessary scrutiny or the disruption of one's work life. There are circumstances in which investigations confirm that misconduct was not done; even in such cases, the reputational stress and administrative cost have already flowed from the situation. From a governance point of view, a very high false positive rate is capable of having very serious consequences, particularly in relation to the level of trust stakeholders vest in automated security systems. Over time, analysts may get habituated to 'habitually false' alerts and the fact that they do not respond to them reduces the effectiveness of the monitoring system(Masango et al., 2025).

The other extreme would be the automatic unquestioning acceptance of the output of the system as being the truth, with the result that the previously benign event gets elevated to a disciplinary or compliance incident. Either way, it is clear that the handling of false positives is not just a strictly technical problem, but also a question of the governing the institution. Legal rules that regulate the use of automated decision-making systems are fairly stringent. These rules include provisions that highlight and lay the foundation for the rights of individuals in this context as well as the obligations that organizations have in order to ensure that the individuals' rights are respected. Cases brought to the attention of the courts typically revolve around the issue of arguing for or against the requirement of providing explanations to people whose decisions (made either wholly or partly by computers) have produced results that negatively affected their interests. Therefore, when automated alerts are used as a basis for decisions about people, organizations should be in a position to do justify by way of explaining how an alert was generated, and by way of demonstrating that the correct review procedures were followed. If a system generates a large number of false positives and the organization does nothing to address the situation then the organization may be seen by the regulator as lacking in governance under such circumstances(H K et al., 2026). A false positive becomes legally significant not because the model generated an alert, but because organizational processes may transform that alert into a consequential action. Consequently, governance mechanisms should focus on both model performance and decision-making procedures surrounding automated outputs.

9.3 Cost and Operational Burden of False Alerts

Posts in security operations centers include not only the analysts tasked with directly investigating security incidents but also the monitoring of logs, the collection and evaluation of data to identify and mitigate vulnerabilities, as well as the administrative tasks required to keep a secure environment. When the number of alerts is high, investigations have to be very selective and try to figure out which is the real threat and which is not. This condition, aptly named alert fatigue phenomenon, depletes very rapidly the entire monitoring programme's effectiveness. Loss of time and productivity is another operational cost. The risk of "chained lockout" should be considered in addition to the single account locking event. After the first lockout occurs, the authorized user contacts the help desk to regain access. In some operations, the reset process may require the user to log on from a different device or to call a specific number(Llwaah et al., 2025). From the organizational perspective, account lockouts result in a temporary denial of access. This could, for example, delay sales or other critical business processes, as well as cause frustration in employees who might not be able to carry out their tasks promptly due to constraints in excess of the needed resources. Likewise, network sessions may be terminated automatically in response to false alerts that block the legitimate flow of data thus causing production losses. As indicated by the evidence-based results, besides the accuracy measures of models, it would be wise for organizations to consider the operational costs coming from overloading analysts with unnecessary alerts. Besides reducing investigation workload and preserving the monitoring system's credibility, a slightly less sensitive detection model with fewer false positives might be the one that provides the best organizational value(Haider et al., 2026).

10. FUTURE DIRECTIONS AND BEST PRACTICES FOR MANAGING LEGAL RISK IN AUTOMATED SECURITY DECISION SYSTEMS

10.1 Integration of Responsible AI Principles into Security Analytics

Responsible AI principles, nowadays, are almost a necessary set of guidelines for developers of automated systems which not only aim at outperforming the competition but still maintain fairness, accountability, and transparency. An integration of security analytics based on the concept of responsible AI is certainly not a trivial matter, where organizations just tick a box stating that their detection models are fair and unbiased. On the contrary, responsible AI roadmaps will strongly motivate organizations to pay more public attention to social and legal implications of the decisions made by automated agents. Fairness, among the principles of responsible AI, is no doubt the one that gets most directly applied to our field. It demands automated systems that don't perpetually put certain individuals or groups at a disadvantage(Alkhawatrah et al., 2025). Take, for instance, security surveillance settings - fairness problems may surface whilst feature selection, if behavioral cues linked to job roles, geographic locations, work schedules are leveraged. In case these lead to the excessive scanning of some groups, besides the ethical issues the organizations could very likely face legal . Quite like any other ethical and antidiscrimination exercise, fairness will require that there is skilled selection of the features, regular bias testing and also continuous evaluation of model outputs with respect to different user populations. Accountability is a further and crucial principle of responsible AI. Besides the technical perspective and obfuscating the effect of automation, accountability remains the sine qua none of responsibility. Awareness of the roles and responsibilities of different actors, establishing clear oversight, and having in place a framework for correction are constitutive elements of accountability. The organizations are required to justify the falsity of the positives by a detailed laid-down mechanism and providing fair review to the persons concerned, the false positives are certainly not the only things left unclea(Al-Okbi et al., 2025)r.

Besides, transparency is essential for responsible AI deployment. As this chapter has exposed, explainability features help the analysts and decision-makers to have an informed guess as to a model's logic to produce an alert. Concealing is not always secure and transparency in automated security systems is so needed to build and keep conversations with stakeholders resulting in the right disclosure and communication practices without ever exposing the company to compromising security breaches. Taken together fairness, accountability, and transparency constitute the foundation of a governance philosophy capable of supporting both the provision of adequate security and the upholding of the rights of the individuals (Benali et al., 2025). Responsible AI practices should be integrated throughout the lifecycle of automated security systems. Regular auditing, bias assessment, transparency reviews, and oversight procedures help ensure that security objectives are achieved without compromising fairness, accountability, or individual rights.

10.2 Organizational Best Practices for Reducing False Positives

Reducing false alarms in automated security systems requires a technical as well as an operational approach. Technically, they may supply their AI models with data that portray the most characteristic samples of their real environments. Regularly collecting data and retraining the models will, therefore, make them adaptive to changes in behavior and infrastructure up. Ensemble detection methods are another element of the technical . Here, the idea is to use a composite of models that analyze the system behavior from differing angles, instead of depending on one single model only(Eke et al., 2025). For instance, combining a behavior anomaly detector with a rule-based policy engine and a statistical baseline model is a case in point. Generating alerts only when different detection techniques give the same account dramatically lessens the chances of a misclassification leading to unnecessary escalation. Besides, operational procedures are really the invisible hand that keeps the false positive rate down. The analyst's level of competence plays a very big role in that an analyst who realizes that automated alerts should be seen only as a probability of a threat will be able to make a good use of the automated tool. The analyst is able to carry out the necessary investigations hence the model output is not treated as a piece of evidence of a wrongdoing but rather an indication, which is to be followed up with investigation. Establishing the well-defined review procedures ensures that automation-generated alerts are scored and ranked and then given to analysts for decision-making. Further, the developments of feedback loops also significantly help the models to learn the representations of the behavior quite accurately so that the error rate could be reduced. When an analyst rules out an alert as a false positive, the case should be logged and the dataset for model retraining updated. Such feedback loops serve two main purposes: one is the continuous progress of model performance and the other one is a further attestation of adherence to governance with respect to automated system use.

REFERENCES

Abashes, G. M., Elshqeirat, B., Abu-Shareha, A. A., & Alshraideh, M. (2025). BEYOND THE NOISE: UNVEILING MEANINGFUL PATTERNS IN MOBILE PAYMENT DATA USING FUZZY LOGIC AND SVM. *Journal of Theoretical and Applied Information Technology*, *103*(1).

Abdel-Jaber, M., Abdel-Jaber, M., Beale, R., & Makhoul, N. (2025). UHSC flexural strength prediction using optimized three-phase classifier and improved feature selection. *International Journal on Interactive Design and Manufacturing*, *19*(5), 3201–3218. Advance online publication. DOI: 10.1007/s12008-024-01812-3

Abdeljaber, O., Al-Adwan, A. S., Yaseen, H., Falahat, M., Abdullah, A., & Fauzi, M. A. (2025). Shopping in the Metaverse: Decoding Consumer Intentions. *The International Information & Library Review*. Advance online publication. DOI: 10.1080/10572317.2025.2594293

Abdeljaber, O., & Al-Masaeed, S. (2025). Al-Mu'ani, L., Yaseen, H., & Alhnaity, B. (2025). Strategic Intelligence: The Power of AI in Planning Efficiency. *Human Behavior and Emerging Technologies*, (1). Advance online publication. DOI: 10.1155/hbe2/5383054

Abualhaj, M. M.I, Al-Khatib, S. N., Abu-Shareha, A. A., Almomani, O., Al-Mimi, H., Al-Allawee, A., Daoud, M. S., & Anbar, M. (2025). Spam Detection Boosted by Firefly-Based Feature Selection and Optimized Classifiers. *International Journal of Advances in Soft Computing and Its Applications*, *17*(3). Advance online publication. DOI: 10.15849/IJASCA.251130.02

Abualhaj, M. M., Al-Khatib, S. N., Al-Zyoud, M., Qaddara, I., Hiari, M. O., & Aldossary, S. M. A. (2025). Enhanced Network Communication Security Through Hybrid Dragonfly-Bat Feature Selection for Intrusion Detection. *The Journal of Communication*, *20*(5). Advance online publication. DOI: 10.12720/jcm.20.5.607-618

Abualigah, L., Almomani, M. H., Alomari, S. A., Zitar, R. A., Migdady, H., Saleem, K., Snasel, V., Smerat, A., & Ezugwu, A. E. (2025). Optimizing Intrusion Detection in Wireless Sensor Networks via the Improved Chameleon Swarm Algorithm for Feature Selection. *IET Communications*, *19*(1), e70029. Advance online publication. DOI: 10.1049/cmu2.70029

Abualigah, L., Alomari, S. A., Almomani, M. H., Zitar, R. A., Migdady, H., Saleem, K., Smerat, A., Snasel, V., & Ezugwu, A. E. (2025). An enhanced Walrus Optimizer with opposition-based learning and mutation strategy for data clustering. *Array (New York, N.Y.)*, *26*, 100409. Advance online publication. DOI: 10.1016/j.array.2025.100409

Abuowaida, S., Abu Owida, H., Shelash Mohammad, S. I., Alshdaifat, N., Abu Elsoud, E., Alazaidah, R., Vasudevan, A., & Alshurideh, M. T. (2025). Evidence Detection in Cloud Forensics: Classifying Cyber-Attacks in IaaS Environments using machine learning. *Data and Metadata*, *4*, 699. Advance online publication. DOI: 10.56294/dm2025699

Al-Bahtiti, A. S., Tayeh, B. A., Baghdadi, A., Alaloul, W. S., & Abu Aisheh, Y. I. (2025). Drivers for adopting augmented reality and virtual reality technologies in the construction project management in Gaza City. *Journal of Asian Architecture and Building Engineering*, 1–18. Advance online publication. DOI: 10.1080/13467581.2025.2507235

Al-Daoud, K. I., Yogeesh, N., Mohammad, S. I. S., Raja, N., Jabeen, F. T. Z., William, P., Vasudevan, A., Hunitie, M. F. A., & Alshdaifat, N. (2025). Fuzzy Linear Programming in Real-World Applications: A Comparative Study of Agricultural and Financial Optimization. *Applied Mathematics & Information Sciences, 19*(4), 849–862. Advance online publication. DOI: 10.18576/amis/190411

Al-Habashneh, A. G., Al-Daoud, K. I., Oraini, B., Al, , & Shelash, S. I. (2025). The impact of artificial intelligence on the development of electronic financial services. *International Journal of Data and Network Science, 9*(2), 317–322. Advance online publication. DOI: 10.5267/j.ijdns.2024.8.012

Al-Momani, M. M., Alqudah, T. A., Al Swiety, I. A., Mahrakani, N., Nassoura, M. B. A., & Al Attar, M. K. (2025). Integrating Artificial Intelligence (AI) and Business Intelligence (BI): A Framework for Improving Enterprise Performance. *TEM Journal, 14*(3). https://doi.org/DOI: 10.18421/TEM143-26

Al-Okbi, N. K., Alomari, S. A., Hadi, W. J., Ajrash, A. S., Smerat, A., & Abualigah, L. (2025). Defending Digital Integrity: Advances in Media Forgery Analysis Research and Cybersecurity Development. *SN Computer Science, 6*(8), 913. Advance online publication. DOI: 10.1007/s42979-025-04462-8

Al-Suhimat, R. I., Mohammed Ai, N., Ibrahim, A., Maaitah, N. O., & Al-Dmour, N. A. (2024). Review of Security Challenges Encountered in Internet of Things Technology. *2nd International Conference on Cyber Resilience, ICCR 2024*. DOI: 10.1109/ICCR61006.2024.10533052

Alabdallat, R., Abualhaj, M., & Abu-Shareha, A. (2025). Android Malware Detection Using a Modified Dwarf Mongoose Algorithm. *International Journal of Intelligent Engineering and Systems, 18*(8), 336–351. Advance online publication. DOI: 10.22266/ijies2025.0930.21

Aldaaja, Y., Odeh, M., Badrakhan, S. S., Sabri, M., Abdelrahim, Y., Samara, G., & Alsabatin, H. (2025). Quantifying the Managerial and Practical Benefits of Cloud Computing on Information Security in Higher Education Institutions. *Applied Mathematics & Information Sciences, 19*(1), 15–24. Advance online publication. DOI: 10.18576/amis/190102

Aldabbas, A., Baniata, L. H., Alsaaidah, B. A., Mustafa, Z., Alali, M., & Rateb, R. (2025). Artificial intelligence-driven method for the discovery and prevention of distributed denial of service attacks. *IAES International Journal of Artificial Intelligence, 14*(1), 614. Advance online publication. DOI: 10.11591/ijai.v14.i1.pp614-628

Alkhawatrah, M., AlAyyad, M., & Korostynska, O. (2025). Balanced inter-relay charging buffer-aided IOT networks. *Eurasip Journal on Wireless Communications and Networking, 2025*(1). DOI: 10.1186/s13638-025-02524-2

ALMahadin, G., Shabaz, M., Khan, I. R., Vimal, V., Keshta, I., & Maguluri, L. P.ALMahadin. (2025). Content-aware recommendation system for integrated temporal semantic review text over web of things. *Service Oriented Computing and Applications, 19*(1), 77–91. Advance online publication. DOI: 10.1007/s11761-024-00408-9

Almomani, O., Arabiat, A., Al Tayeb, M., Almaiah, M. A., Obeidat, M., Aldhyani, T. H. H., Shehab, R., & Rowad, M. (2025). A Robust Model for Android Malware Detection via ML and DL classifiers. *Mesopotamian Journal of Big Data, 2025*. Advance online publication. DOI: 10.58496/MJBD/2025/017

Alnawafleh, N. M., Ibrahim, A., & Pradhan, M. R. (2024). Review of the Mechanisms Used to Protect the Big Data from Attacks. *2nd International Conference on Cyber Resilience, ICCR 2024*. DOI: 10.1109/ICCR61006.2024.10533073

Alraba'nah, Y., Al-Sharaeh, S., & Al Hindi, G. (2025). Enhancing Intrusion Detection Using Hybrid Long Short-Term Memory and XGBoost. *Journal of Soft Computing and Data Mining*, *6*(1). Advance online publication. DOI: 10.30880/jscdm.2025.06.01.016

Alraba'nah, Y., & Hiari, M. (2025). Improved convolutional neural networks for aircraft type classification in remote sensing images. *IAES International Journal of Artificial Intelligence*, *14*(2), 1540. Advance online publication. DOI: 10.11591/ijai.v14.i2.pp1540-1547

Arabasy, M., & Ghoneim, R. S. (2025). Enhancing sustainable urban design using machine learning: Comparative analysis of seven metaheuristic algorithms in energy-efficient digital architecture. *Frontiers in Built Environment*, *11*, 1526209. Advance online publication. DOI: 10.3389/fbuil.2025.1526209

Arabiat, A. M., & Eljaafreh, Y. G. (2025). Intrusion Detection in Wireless Sensor Networks Using ML Based Classification of Denial of Service (DoS) Attacks. *The Journal of Communication*, *20*(4). Advance online publication. DOI: 10.12720/jcm.20.4.501-514

Ayub, N., Imtiaz, M. A., Ali, E., Alqahtani, A. M., Ali, A., Ashurov, M., Albouq, S., & Law, F. L. (2025). A Decision Framework for Intra Task Fixed Priority INTEL PXA270 Distributed Architecture for Soft RT-Applications Based on Deep Learning. *Engineering. Technology and Applied Science Research*, *15*(3), 23553–23558. Advance online publication. DOI: 10.48084/etasr.10006

Babaker, S., Khatibi, A., Alsoud, A. R., Kaur, J., Jagtap, J., Alkhayyat, A., & Shah, S. K. (2025). Improving Reliability and Data Management in Internet of Things Based Wireless Sensor Networks. *Internet Technology Letters*, *8*(6), e646. Advance online publication. DOI: 10.1002/itl2.646

Bektemyssova, G., Montazeri, Z., Dehghani, M., Ibraheem, I. K., Smerat, A., Werner, F., Al-Salih, A. A. M. M., Ahmed, M. A., & Eguchi, K. (2025). Search and Rescue Algorithm (SRA): A Metaheuristic Approach for Efficient Constrained Engineering Optimization. *International Journal of Intelligent Engineering and Systems*, *18*(10), 607–621. Advance online publication. DOI: 10.22266/ijies2025.1130.39

Benali, A., Kharbouch, H., Della Krachai, M., Singh, J. P., Bouddou, R., Yesma, B., Belabbes, A., Husein, A., Salau, A. O., & Rubanenko, O. (2025). Dual-Stream Convolutional Networks for Scalable and Precise Water Body Mapping from Multispectral Earth Observation Imagery. *International Journal of Computational Intelligence Systems*, *18*(1), 260. Advance online publication. DOI: 10.1007/s44196-025-00985-3

Cui, D., Harrison, A., Fendzi-Donfack, E., Dagal, I., Jangir, P., Mahmoud, M. M., Malkani, P., Mbasso, W. F., Tiako, P., & Smerat, A. (2026). Enhancing Short-Term Electricity Forecasting with Advanced Machine Learning Techniques. *Journal of Electrical Engineering & Technology*, *21*(1), 147–187. Advance online publication. DOI: 10.1007/s42835-025-02430-z

Dheeb, S. A., AL-Azzawi, W. S. A.-B., Suleiman, A. K., Ibrahim, A., & Ghwanmeh, S. (2025). *The Role of Generative Artificial Intelligence in Advancing Multilingual Intelligent Support Systems*. DOI: 10.1109/ICCR67387.2025.11291954

Eke, C. I., Al-Shamayleh, A. S., Phiri, M., Maswadi, K., Kwaghtyo, D. K., Mulenga, M., & Iyidobi, C. J. (2025). Machine Learning Based Mobile Big Data Analytics: State-of-the-art Applications, Taxonomy, Challenges and Future Research Directions. *Nigerian Journal of Technological Development*, *22*(4). Advance online publication. DOI: 10.63746/njtd.v22i4.3385

Elkhouly, M., Alhadidi, T., & Rakha, H. (2025). Modeling Traffic Vehicular Counts at an Urban Intersection Using Complex Seasonal Modeling Techniques. *KSCE Journal of Civil Engineering*, *29*(1), 100040. Advance online publication. DOI: 10.1016/j.kscej.2024.100040

Fauzi, M. A., Alias, U. N., Nya-Ling Tan, C., Wider, W., Mukherjee, S., Al-Adwan, A. S., & Udang, L. N. (2025). The Present and Future Trends of Leadership Styles and Knowledge Hiding Through Science Mapping Analysis. *Journal of Information and Knowledge Management*, *24*(5), 2550040. Advance online publication. DOI: 10.1142/S0219649225500406

Ghazal, T. M., Abualhaj, M., Ahmed, A. A., Al-Tarawni, M. A. M., & Maghrabi, L. A. (2025). Federated Deep Graph Neural Network Algorithm for Real-Time Intrusion Detection in Heterogeneous IoT Systems. *Journal of Internet Services and Information Security*, *15*(4), 484–497. Advance online publication. DOI: 10.58346/JISIS.2025.I4.035

Ghazal, T. M., Hasan, M. K., Hussein, A. H., Pandey, B. K., Ahmad, M., Safie, N., & Cascone, L. (2025). Federated Learning With Small and Large Models With Privacy-Preserving Data Space for Holographic Internet of Things in Consumer Electronics. *IEEE Transactions on Consumer Electronics*, *71*(2), 5259–5274. Advance online publication. DOI: 10.1109/TCE.2025.3573033

Ghazal, T. M., Janjua, J. I., Abushiba, W., Ahmad, M., Ihsan, A., & Al-Dmour, N. A. (2024). Cybersecurity Revolution via Large Language Models and Explainable AI. *2024 17th International Conference on Security of Information and Networks, SIN 2024*. DOI: 10.1109/SIN63213.2024.10871324

H K, P. K., Dash, R., K, J. R., Mohapatra, B., Bishoyi, S. S., Bajaj, M., & Blazek, V.H K. (2026). Multi-domain fault characterization in DC microgrids utilizing Hilbert-Huang transform ensemble by LSTM networks with adaptive boundary condition constraints. *Results in Engineering*, *29*, 108721. Advance online publication. DOI: 10.1016/j.rineng.2025.108721

Haider, Z. A., Ullah, I., Shareha, A. A., Nasimov, R., & Memon, S. A. (2026). Artificial Intelligence (AI)-Enabled Unmanned Aerial Vehicle (UAV) Systems for Optimizing User Connectivity in Sixth-Generation (6G) Ubiquitous Networks. *Computers, Materials & Continua*, *86*(1), 1–16. Advance online publication. DOI: 10.32604/cmc.2025.071042

Hakami, H., Hasan, M. K., Alshamayleh, A., Saeed, A. Q., Mustafa, S. A., & Ghazal, T. M. (2025). Adaptive Neuro-Fuzzy Congestion Control Algorithm for Real-Time Multimedia Networking in Cloud-Based E-Learning Platforms. *Journal of Wireless Mobile Networks, Ubiquitous Computing and Dependable Applications*, *16*(3). Advance online publication. DOI: 10.58346/JOWUA.2025.I3.027

Hanandeh, A., Alfreijat, S. Y., Qutieshat, R. J., Alsha'ar, H. Y., Kilani, Q. A. L., & Saleem Khasawneh, M. A. (2025). Implementing AI Accuracy, Learning Rate, Inference Time on enhancing Big Data Analysis and Strategic Plan. *Data and Metadata*, *4*, 637. Advance online publication. DOI: 10.56294/dm2025637

Hasan, M. K., Ghazal, T. M., Alkhalifah, A., Abu Bakar, K. A., Omidvar, A., Nafi, N. S., & Agbinya, J. I. (2021). Fischer Linear Discrimination and Quadratic Discrimination Analysis–Based Data Mining Technique for Internet of Things Framework for Healthcare. *Frontiers in Public Health*, *9*, 737149. Advance online publication. DOI: 10.3389/fpubh.2021.737149 PMID: 34712639

Hasan, M. K., Ghazal, T. M., Issa, G., Islam, S., Ismail, A. F., & Kabir, S. R. (2025). Hashgraph consensus-based simultaneous, asynchronous and big-data supported blockchain mechanism for IT-OT enabled critical infrastructure sectors. *Journal of Ambient Intelligence and Humanized Computing*. Advance online publication. DOI: 10.1007/s12652-024-04942-4

Hiari, M., Alraba'nah, Y., & Qaddara, I. (2025). A Deep Learning-Based Intrusion Detection System using Refined LSTM for DoS Attack Detection. *Engineering. Technology and Applied Science Research*, *15*(4), 25627–25633. Advance online publication. DOI: 10.48084/etasr.11499

Hyassat, A. S., Abu Zayed, R. E., Al Khateeb, E. A., Shalaldeh, A., Abdelhamied, M. M., & Qaddara, I. (2025). Unveiling Cyber Threats: An In-Depth Study on Data Mining Techniques for Exploit Attack Detection †. *Engineering Proceedings*, *104*(1), 28. Advance online publication. DOI: 10.3390/engproc2025104028

Jan, F. U., Badar, R., Sami Al-Shamayleh, A., Uehara, A., Senjyu, T., & Akhunzada, A. (2025). Soft Computing-Based Damping Controllers With Online Parameters Tuning for Stability Enhancement of Power Systems. *IEEE Access : Practical Innovations, Open Solutions*, *13*, 167045–167060. Advance online publication. DOI: 10.1109/ACCESS.2025.3612288

Jaradat, S., Elhenawy, M., Paz, A., Alhadidi, T. I., Ashqar, H. I., & Nayak, R. (2025). A Cross-Cultural Crash Pattern Analysis in the United States and Jordan Using BERT and SHAP. *Electronics (Basel)*, *14*(2), 272. Advance online publication. DOI: 10.3390/electronics14020272

Kamal, M. M., Ul Abideen, S. Z., Al-Khasawneh, M. A., Momani, A. M., Mostafa, H., Atoum, M. S., Ullah, S., Alsayaydeh, J. A. J., & Yusof, M. F. (2025). Meyer Wavelet Transform and Jaccard Deep Q Net for Small Object Classification Using Multi-Modal Images. *CMES -. Computer Modeling in Engineering & Sciences*, *144*(3), 3053–3083. Advance online publication. DOI: 10.32604/cmes.2025.067430

Khalayleh, Y. A. S., Mohammad, S. I., Al Louzi, N. S., Baniata, M., Hassan, M., Safaqah, M. A., Vasudevan, A., & Alshurideh, M. T. (2025). Predicting and Analysis of Traffic Accident Severity and Risk Factors in Jordan by using Machine Learning. *Applied Mathematics & Information Sciences*, *19*(6), 1419–1426. Advance online publication. DOI: 10.18576/amis/190615

Khatibi, A., Babaker, S., Praveen, K. N. R., Chohan, J. S., Jadhav, A., Alsoud, A. R., Ramudu, M. J., & Jeet, R. (2025). Advanced AI-Driven Cybersecurity: Analyzing Emerging Threats and Defensive Strategies. *National Academy Science Letters*. Advance online publication. DOI: 10.1007/s40009-025-01897-8

Lee, S. W., Hussain, S., Issa, G. F., Abbas, S., Ghazal, T. M., Sohail, T., Ahmad, M., & Khan, M. A. (2021). Multi-Dimensional Trust Quantification by Artificial Agents through Evidential Fuzzy Multi-Criteria Decision Making. *IEEE Access : Practical Innovations, Open Solutions*, *9*, 159399–159412. Advance online publication. DOI: 10.1109/ACCESS.2021.3131521

Llwaah, F., Hussein, A. H., & Ghazal, T. M. (2025). Enhancing Cloud Resource Utilization Through Synthesizing Intensive Workflow Tasks. *Journal of Wireless Mobile Networks, Ubiquitous Computing and Dependable Applications, 16*(4), 537–555. Advance online publication. DOI: 10.58346/JOWUA.2025.I4.030

Masango, N. C., Agushaka, J. O., Amaefule, M. C., Taiwo, O., Zhang, P., Ezugwu, A. E., Saleem, K., Smerat, A., & Abualigah, L. (2025). Secure and efficient cloudlet networks: blockchain integration with agent-based proof of trust mechanism. *Eurasip Journal on Wireless Communications and Networking, 2025*(1). DOI: 10.1186/s13638-025-02439-y

Maz, Y. A., Anbar, M., Manickam, S., Abualhaj, M. M., Almalki, S. A., & Alabsi, B. A. (2025). Transfer Learning-Based Approach with an Ensemble Classifier for Detecting Keylogging Attack on the Internet of Things. *Computers, Materials & Continua, 85*(3), 5287–5307. Advance online publication. DOI: 10.32604/cmc.2025.068257

Mbasso, W. F., Harrison, A., Dagal, I., Jangir, P., Liu, Z., & Smerat, A. (2025). High-Fidelity Simulation-Driven Control Framework for Robust Grid Integration of Renewable Energy Systems. *Energy Science & Engineering*. Advance online publication. DOI: 10.1002/ese3.70414

Mohammad, S. I., Al-Daoud, K., Al Qraini, B., Khanfar, I. A. A., & Vasudevan, A. (2025). Quantum Error Correction with Surface Code Analysis on Quantum Computing platform. *Applied Mathematics & Information Sciences, 19*(2), 423–435. Advance online publication. DOI: 10.18576/amis/190216

Otair, M., Qawaqzeh, F. A., Alomari, S. A., Zitar, R. A., Migdady, H., Saleem, K., Smerat, A., Alsoud, A. R., & Abualigah, L. (2025). Enhanced Arithmetic Optimization Algorithm for Intrusion Detection in Wireless Sensor Networks. *International Journal of Communication Systems, 38*(10), e70122. Advance online publication. DOI: 10.1002/dac.70122

Qaddara, I., & Alraba'nah, Y. (2025). Enhancing Requirements Classification Using Machine Learning Techniques. *SN Computer Science, 6*(6), 649. Advance online publication. DOI: 10.1007/s42979-025-04158-z

Ramesh, J. V. N., Nimma, D., Dasari, R., Chaudhari Rane, D., AlGhamdi, A., Rao, K. B. V. B., Haider, S. A., Kuzieva, N., & Jangir, P. (2025). Safe and Reliable Two-Stage Online Offloading Algorithm for Transportation Cyber-Physical Systems. *IEEE Transactions on Intelligent Transportation Systems, 26*(9), 14313–14322. Advance online publication. DOI: 10.1109/TITS.2025.3539934

Raza, M. A., Karim, A., Alqarni, M., Al-Khasawneh, M. A., Jumani, T. A., Aman, M., & Masud, M. I. (2025). An Intelligent Long Short-Term Memory-Based Machine Learning Model for the Potential Assessment of Global Hydropower Capacity in Sustainable Energy Transition and Security. *Energies, 18*(13), 3324. Advance online publication. DOI: 10.3390/en18133324

Sawarkar, P. G., Pote, A., Khan, M. A., Abed, M. H., Hadi, A. A., Smerat, A., & Khishe, M. (2025). Sustainable geopolymer concrete evaluation using machine learning and PDP analysis: Comparative insights into strength prediction. *Hybrid Advances, 11*, 100569. Advance online publication. DOI: 10.1016/j.hybadv.2025.100569

Shah, R. K., Hasan, M. K., Islam, S., Khan, A., Ghazal, T. M., & Khan, A. N. (2022). Detect Phishing Website by Fuzzy Multi-Criteria Decision Making. *2022 1st International Conference on AI in Cybersecurity, ICAIC 2022*. DOI: 10.1109/ICAIC53980.2022.9897036

Shamaylah, N., Ibrahim Mohammad, S., Al Oraini, B., Yaseen Al-Gaafreh, J. M., Mosallam Alqahtani, M., Vasudevan, A., Shlash Mohammad, A. A., & Ahmmad Hunitie, M. F. (2025). Data-Driven Decision-Making for Employee Training and Development in Jordanian Public Institutions. *Data and Metadata*, *4*, 886. Advance online publication. DOI: 10.56294/dm2025886

Sharma, K. P., Al-Rashed, A., Johar, M. G. M., Alsoud, A. R., Singh, A., Dey, P., & Pant, S. (2025). Blockchain-Assisted Trust Framework for Increased Survivability in Internet of Vehicles. *Internet Technology Letters*, *8*(3), e70029. Advance online publication. DOI: 10.1002/itl2.70029

Sharma, K. P., Hussain, R., Jaharadak, A. A., Trawnih, A. A., Verma, D., Dasi, S., & Pant, S. (2025). Hybrid Convolutional Neural Network for Robust Attack Detection in Wireless Sensor Networks. *Internet Technology Letters*, *8*(6), e650. Advance online publication. DOI: 10.1002/itl2.650

Solairaju, J. A., Rathinasamy, S., Thanikodi, S., Tarawneh, B., Gurumoorthy, V., Antony, J. S., & Arul Gnana Dhas, A. (2025). Development and Validation of ANN Models for Water Absorption in Sawdust and Kenaf Fiber-Reinforced Polystyrene Composites. *Engineering Reports*, *7*(9), e70393. Advance online publication. DOI: 10.1002/eng2.70393

Tarek, R., Elshenawy, A., Assadwy, M. I., & Madkour, M. A. (2025). Automated Diagnosis of Dental Diseases Using Deep Learning on Radiographic Images. *SN Computer Science*, *6*(6), 751. Advance online publication. DOI: 10.1007/s42979-025-04264-y

Vasudevan, A., Tamilmani, K. T., Mohammad, S. I., Sridheepika, V. S., Raja, N., Soon, E. E. H., Nagaraj, S., & Al-Adwan, A. S. (2025). Voices of Concern: Contemplations on Socioeconomic, Ethical, and Developmental Impacts of AI. *Applied Mathematics & Information Sciences*, *19*(1), 221–232. Advance online publication. DOI: 10.18576/amis/190119

Xu, B., Jummaa, K., Altalbawy, F. M. A., Roopashree, R., Saraswat, S. K., Ray, S., Tomar, P., Naem, S., Hamza, H. H., Smerat, A., & Khalid, A. (2025). Machine learning-assisted computation of water activity for ionic liquid-based aqueous ternary elements. *Desalination and Water Treatment*, *324*, 101484. Advance online publication. DOI: 10.1016/j.dwt.2025.101484

Zraiqat, A., Batiha, B., Al Soudi, M., Ibraheem, I. K., Smerat, A., Montazeri, Z., Dehghani, M., Werner, F., Al-Salih, A. A. M. M., Ahmed, M. A., & Eguchi, K. (2025). Detective Algorithm: A Novel Human-inspired Metaheuristic for Solving Real-world Constrained Optimization Problems. *International Journal of Intelligent Engineering and Systems*, *18*(10), 33–46. Advance online publication. DOI: 10.22266/ijies2025.1130.03

Chapter 11
Evaluation of Bias and Disparate Impact in UEBA and Insider Threat Detection Systems

Maha Ismail Alshrouf
http://orcid.org/0009-0001-6482-0388
Mutah University, Jordan

Afnan Asasfeh
http://orcid.org/0009-0006-2817-0556
Mutah University, Jordan

ABSTRACT

Evaluating potential bias and disparate impact is essential in User and Entity Behavior Analytics (UEBA) and insider threat detection systems. The chapter explores behavior baselining, anomaly detection, and machine-learning-driven risk scoring as methods that, without intention, may mirror or even reinforce biases relating to roles, work patterns, cultural behaviors, or accessibility needs. It goes on to point out biases stem from training data, feature selection, labeling, and the security operations feedback loop. Moreover, it discusses legal and ethical dimensions, including discrimination risk, fairness, and the accountability of automated or semi-automated security decisions. Note is made especially of assessment techniques, e.g., bias test, impact analysis, and governance, which support fairness and transparency. By marrying technical evaluation techniques with legal compliance issues, this publication proposes the implementation and administration of UEBA systems, which besides being efficient, are just and able to be defended.

1. INTRODUCTION TO BIAS IN UEBA AND INSIDER THREAT DETECTION SYSTEMS

1.1 Evolution of UEBA and Insider Threat Detection Technologies

The development of insider threat detection equipment is almost the same as the development of cybersecurity in general, firstly people protected only around the house, then they protected the whole

DOI: 10.4018/979-8-2600-2870-4.ch011

behavior. At first, security monitoring was aimed at detecting misuse based on a set of rules. For example, it was possible to send alerts if a user failed to login several times, made an unauthorized use of privileges, or accessed restricted resources. Even though such systems were fairly able to spot obvious violations of a pattern, they were not very effective in recognizing changes in the behavior of insiders when the changes were subtle. Often, the mischievous insiders carry on with their plans while using their usual users' rights, which makes it nearly impossible to find them with the use of signatures only. Security Information and Event Management or SIEM systems supported central log aggregation and correlation(Ghazal, Hasan, Hussein, et al., 2025). However, SIEMs had difficulties with the management of alarm overload and the detection of behavioral patterns also wasn't their strong point. The User and Entity Behavior Analytics or UEBA came up with an idea that is closer to business realities by focusing on user behavior tracked over time rather than single events. It doesn't matter that much if an event is rule-breaking by itself, what matters is if a user's recent sequence of actions is so unusual that it cannot be explained by historical data, peers, or norms of the organization. This method gave a way for the inclusion of detection techniques such as anomaly scoring, peer group comparison, sequence modeling, and risk-based prioritization. With the deepening of the era of cloud computing, hybrid work environment, identity centric access control and collaboration platforms, the value of UEBA increased. Insider threat detection even began gathering data from various channels such as endpoints, email systems, identity services, file sharing platforms, SaaS applications, and HR indicators. Such detailed telemetry gave way to a higher level of exposure, but, at the same time, the analytical environment became even more complex. When data is taken from multiple sources, it is quite probable that certain structural inequalities or differences in practices are so deeply embedded in the system's behavioral baselines that they are hardly (Ghazal, Hasan, Khairy, et al., 2025).

1.2 Role of Machine Learning in Behavioral Security Analytics

Whole behavioral security analytics is mostly drawn by machines learning because insider threats are behavioral changes that the classical signature-based security systems could hardly detect. Supervised learning models can be tools when examples of normal and malicious behavior are the labels and present. Such models can classify users or sessions based on their features such as the frequency of accesses, file volume movements, irregularity of login time, use of privileges, or deviation from past patterns. However, it is often the case that scenarios of insiders are rare, labeled only weakly or unknown completely, therefore, people often use unsupervised ways of learning as well. Instruments like clustering, anomaly detection, and density-based methods are being used in discovering of unusual behaviors even without having full ground truth(Hanandeh et al., 2025). Actually, some of the systems are even more advanced and they use sequential and temporal modeling to get a behavioral change comprehension over time. For instance, slowly a user may demonstrate a behavioral change from normal data access to data hoarding, policy evading, and in the end to the point of exfiltration in the off hours. Machine learning offers us a measure to understand these behavioral deviations, not as a sequence of isolated anomalies, but as the steps in the behavior path that, in theory, should lead us to an earlier detection and a more effective use of security analysts' time. Yet, a very significant drawback of machine learning adoption is that models are trained on historical data, and historical data may be dependent on the context. To give an example, if certain departments, on the whole, generate more logs, or remote workers display different access patterns, or simply, privileged users would be more likely to be considered as anomalous only because of their role, then the model may identify these differences as risk factors whereas, in reality, they are just legitimate operational distinctions. The main cause of the bias being a significantly big problem in UEBA systems is, however, that machine learning without human intervention is, simply, not able to tell apart security signals from organizational structure (Alnawayseh et al., 2022).

1.3 Emergence of Algorithmic Bias in Security Systems

Algorithmic bias in security systems is not necessarily manifested as direct/in-your-face discrimination. It often comes about as a result of design decisions which are thought to be technically sound when considered at face value only. A model trained on incident cases from the past may become biased in the same way as the cases that have been reported and investigated so far. If the peer-group baseline is not well-defined it may end up comparing the atypical but legitimate users to the improper norm. A feature such as system access late at night may be regarded as suspicious when in fact it is the norm for distributed teams, incident responders, or shift workers. The same is true for high-volume file access which is normal for data engineers, auditors, or backup administrators but could still lead to high anomaly scores if the role is not properly modeled. Biasmay also result from an imbalance in the training data(Vasudevan et al., 2025). Dueto the fact that in insider threat datasets, malicious events typically happen with a very low frequency, insidiously it becomes the case that quite a number of researchers and practitioners' resort to various methods of oversampling, synthesizing data or using proxy labels. While resorting to such measures may be necessary to some extent, one needs to be cautious because by doing so the very relationship between behavior and risk could be distorted. So, if the proxy labels predominantly represent only certain types of users, or the synthetic balancing brings out only a limited number of behavioral patterns, the resulting model may turn out both to be highly accurate and at the same time unfair. Another very substantial and noteworthy source of bias is the feedback loop between analysts and response teams. Analysts who pay more attention to one group of users above others, end up generating more confirmed cases and richly detailed labels precisely because their deeper investigation of alerts provides them more evidence. Consequently, the model to some extend takes this intensified scrutiny as proof that the group in question is more at risk, which in turn leads to more monitoring of the group. As a result, bias in security systems appears to be an ongoing cycle, a sort of phoenix phenomenon. This cannot be attributed to merely one phase but it is the sum of data, modeling, deployment, and human interpretation .

1.4 Ethical and Operational Risks of Disparate Impact

Disparate impact is an excellent guide that helps us understand at the very least if a UEBA system is unfair or not. Disparate impact is a legal term in discrimination law which shifts the focus from the intention of a practice to the results of it. On the other hand, a community may be, for example, morally none of the fields in the system. Groups in the organization could be, for example, role, seniority, location, type of contract, work schedule, device usage pattern, or intensity of access-based. In case any one of these groups is persistently assigned higher risk level, given more alerts or requires more manual investigations without any valid reason, then it is quite logical to conclude that the system is the source of a disparate impact that is harmful operationally(Al-Falouji et al., 2025). This is a major ethical concern. Security operations are typically performed in trusted, confidential and procedurally fair environments. Over-monitoring leads to employee mistrust of management and a creation of an institution that is essentially suspicions of them. When employees view monitoring tools as unfair, they may stop cooperating, resist security procedures, or hide harmless behaviors simply because they might look unusual. All of these factors can lead to the weakening of the organizational culture and the reduction of the effectiveness of the detection. Actually, disparate impact can be very harmful to the operational side of the organization just like to its ethics and morale side. Biased systems most of the time make analysts look into the usual behaviors rather than detecting the actually dangerous ones hence, they waste their time. This leads to alert fatigue, decline in the triage efficiency and loss of trust in the model's output. Further, if a system is very reactive to a very small number of user profiles, then they may be the only ones exposed to the system whereas the other user groups may be invisible and consequently, if the intent of a user is malicious, he/she can also be able to act without detection. So, bias is not something that is isolated from security performance. To the contrary, it is actually the foundation for whether a system can be trusted, understood and even supports making strategic (Al-Okbi, Alomari, Hadi, et al., 2025).

1.5 Scope and Objectives of the Chapter

UEBA and inside threat detection systems may not be bias-free, and their bias factors and disparate impact should be measured, the paper reveals. Also, it illustrates how bias factors and disparate impacts may be handled without jeopardizing operational security. It is about making fairness a key characteristic of trustworthy security analytics rather than simply an ethical afterthought. To begin with, the paper sets the foundation and then highlights the primary sources of bias in data and models, the methods of their empirical evaluation, as well as the ways of their removal. Besides that, it deals with the governance and the larger implications of behavior-based security systems reliance at the enterprise level. More specifically, here, the evaluation of bias in machine learning-based insider threat detection via controlled experiments has been one of the focuses. The aim of this paper is to provide not only the academic community with tools but also practitioners by connecting fairness concepts with telemetry, anomaly detection, risk scoring, and security operations workflows. It makes a case that a developed UEBA system should be able to detect the abnormal behavior but, even more, the suspiciousness level should be context-aware, explainable, and fairly applied across different user .

This chapter contributes a Fairness-Aware UEBA Evaluation Framework for insider threat detection systems. The framework connects behavioral telemetry quality, operational user-group definition, model-performance evaluation, group-level fairness metrics, Fairness Disparity Index calculation, threshold governance, analyst feedback review, and post-deployment auditing. It shows that UEBA systems should be evaluated not only by precision, recall, and F1-score, but also by whether they impose unequal alerting, investigation, or surveillance burdens across legitimate operational groups.

Figure 1. Architecture of UEBA-Based Insider Threat Detection Pipeline

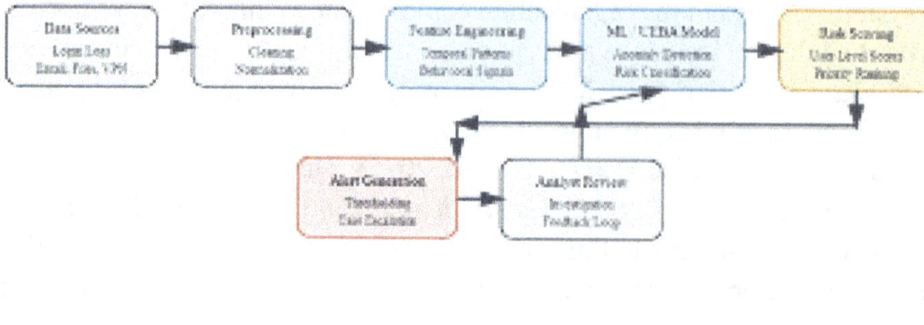

Figure 2. Conceptual Illustration of Bias Propagation in Security Analytics Systems

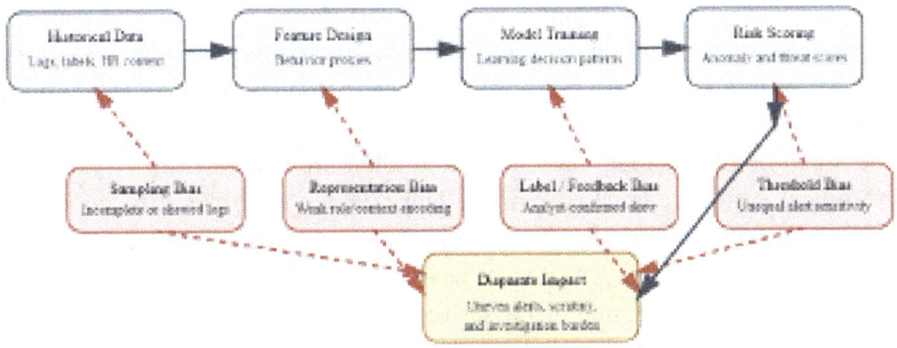

2. FOUNDATIONS OF BIAS AND DISPARATE IMPACT IN ARTIFICIAL INTELLIGENCE

The fact is that AI technologies offer a number of new possibilities, as well as creating challenges at the same time. For instance, in the contexts of cybersecurity and behavioral monitoring, such as User and Entity Behavior Analytics (UEBA) systems, machine-learning driven approaches can identify deviations from usual behavior, foresee insider threats and even help in determining the order in which investigation tasks must be . However, these systems are not “living” in social/organizational isolation. The data on which they are built comes from human activities, institutional practices, and operational infrastructures. Therefore, if the historic data has bias or the AI model developers introduce bias, these biases might still affect the system’s behavior, including AI interpretation of human actions and production of predictions. Artificial intelligence bias refers to model output systematic and unfair deviations which may be disadvantageous to individual(s) or groups in comparison with others. Already in the years before the explosive growth of AI, researchers studied how algorithmic bias caused by AI can maintain or intensify social inequalities and discrimination in various sectors, such as finance, healthcare, education, and employment. However, security analytics systems including UEBA platforms have been only lately exposed to similar investigations(Khalayleh et al., 2025). There was a time when, for many years, security tools and platforms were considered neutral because they simply monitored technical events such as user logins, system commands, and network changes; however, that was an oversimplification of the reality. On one hand, human beings generate the activities that behavior security analytics track, so naturally their work times, roles, hierarchy, digitized locations, and cultural performances mold their behaviors; on the other hand, artificial intelligence learns behavior patterns from data and sometimes it is not clear how the data reflect the structural imbalances and that is the “imbalance” that ends up getting embedded.

A very useful concept when discussing bias in artificial intelligence is that of disparate impact. Disparate impact refers to situations where the decisions of a system bring about outcomes that affect certain groups more than others even though the system itself does not deliberately use protected attributes such as gender, race, or age. In fact, in an enterprise security context, groups can be defined by a wide array of things such as role category, type of employment, department affiliation, location, work schedule, etc. To illustrate, suppose that night shift workers, employees working from home, system administrators, and data engineers naturally display a behavior pattern that differs from standard office hours activities. Now, if a UEBA system considers these patterns as suspicious without the provision of proper context, it will likely assign elevated risk scores to these groups excessively. Getting to the bottom of bias in AI means, amongst other things, figuring out what machine learning models do with the data given to them, how fairness can be defined and measured, and what are some of the ways that organizational structures and technical systems can be combined. This chapter establishes the conceptual foundation which can be used to measure the bias in UEBA and other insider threat detection systems. To do this, it describes the main elements of bias, introduces several fairness metrics, points out the types of bias that are a threat to security analytics, and discusses the particular problems that behavioral monitoring technologies bring from a fairness perspective(Al-Suhimat et al., 2024).

2.1 Definitions of Bias in Machine Learning Systems

Simply put, bias in machine learning signifies systematic error made by a model in its predictions, leading to unfair or unrepresentative outcomes. In statistical learning theory, the notion of 'bias' is the model's expected prediction deviation from the true underlying function that the model is trying to estimate. Conversely, in ethical and socio-technical contexts, bias denotes the unfair disparity where predictions have varying impacts on different groups of people. Bias in machine learning systems that serve organizations can be the product of various factors. The primary one, by far, is a bias in training data. Machine learning models use training data to detect patterns, therefore, if the training data are representative of historical practices that were themselves unbalanced or incomplete, the model will likely reproduce those patterns. For instance, if the security department has historically given precedence to a particular department for operational reasons, then incident labels will disproportionately concern that department. Training a model on those labels will likely cause the model to associate that department with higher risk, even when there is no behavioral basis for that association. Representational imbalance represents yet another quite significant kind of bias. Typically, in datasets obtained from real world situations, certain behavioral types will be represented far more often than others. For example, the major part of a dataset may be composed of office workers during regular hours, whereas remote workers or specialized technical staff may be scarcely represented. Learning features from these majority cases, data models are very likely to flag minority group behaviors as 'anomalous'. This is not intentional or act of a “bad angel” of the model; it is the mathematically measured result of optimizing for accuracy by emphasizing the most frequently appearing sources of variation. Behavioral security systems harbor another kind of significant bias such as measurement bias. Measurement bias arises when the method of data collection captures some actions more thoroughly than others. Different systems provide different levels of detail in the logs generated(Ghazal, Abu-Shareha, et al., 2025).

For example, telemetry of some systems is very detailed, while other systems produce minimal logs. If behavioral features rely heavily on logs, users associated with highly monitored systems may appear more active or more anomalous, but this is only because their activities are so well logged. Algorithmic bias may also come from the nature of the model itself. Some learning algorithms define optimization goals without considering fairness explicitly. Classifier models, for example, aim at maximizing overall accuracy. The improvement in accuracy is achieved by focusing on majority behavioral patterns present in the training data which in consequence may mean neglecting the minority groups. Thismeans that certain groups may be more likely to be falsely identified as positives or negatives. The multiple types of bias discussed point out that usually unfair results of machine learning systems are not due to a single factor. Rather, they occur due to the combined effects of data, algorithms, and deployment contexts. Therefore, if you plan to evaluate the fairness of a UEBA system, it is very important that you first recognize these interactions, particularly in situations where you have intricate behavioral data and a setting heavily influenced by organizational es(Ghazal, Abualhaj, et al., 2025).

2.2 Statistical Fairness Metrics and Evaluation Criteria

Researchers and practitioners who focus on bias and fairness in artificial intelligence have developed several types of fairness metrics that are understandable and quantifiable. Thanks to such fairness metrics, it is now possible to measure disparities between different groups in terms of model predictions. In this way, an evaluator can understand to what extent the system's performance and behavior are acceptable from the fairness perspective. Of course, the exact meaning of fairness is still a matter of debate and can be highly context-dependent, but irrespective of the choice of notion of fairness, a set of well-established statistical metrics are inevitably part of the evaluation toolbox. Demographic parity is probably the most known statistical fairness metric. It requires that the proportion of instances from each group, who get classified positively, is approximately equal. For insider threat detection, that would mean being flagged as a potential insider threat is more or less equally likely for different groups defined by attributes such as role, location, etc., unless the difference is entirely due to actual behavior and is very well evidenced. Note, that demographic parity is a constraint on the output of the model and not on its predictive power with respect to the true state of the world(Ghazal, Abu-Shareha, et al., 2025).

Equal opportunity can be seen as a relaxation of demographic parity since it only requires true positive rates to be equal across groups. For insider threat detection systems, equal opportunity requires that the system detects malicious behavior equally well in all groups. If the system is good at detecting threat behaviors in one group but fails to do so in another group, then it may give rise to inequality in protection and overlook critical risks. Equalized odds add a further level of strictness. In a security analytics context, this translates into a system that does not, in a biased manner, accuse or ignore certain populations more than others. This last point is especially critical mainly because persistently high false positive rates in a particular group can end up creating a level of investigative burden to the point where trust in the monitoring system is degraded(Sharma et al., 2025). Calibration fairness is one more important perspective on fairness. Calibration means that for each risk score, the proportions of positives are about the same across groups. So, for instance, if a UEBA system returns 0.8 as a risk score for multiple groups, the proportion of those identified with the score who actually have confirmed cases should be roughly the same in each group. Stated differently, calibration is about the 'meaning' of the score being the same across group memberships. In practice, things will often not be that simple and fairness metrics will be traded off against one another. For example, enforcement of equalized odds may have a detrimental effect on calibration, especially when there are different base rates across groups. Consequently, it would be prudent for organizations to thoughtfully choose fairness objectives that are consistent with their operational and ethical priorities(A. Arabiat, Altayeb, & Alkhrissat, 2025).

2.3 Types of Bias Relevant to Security Analytics

Behavioral diversity in security analytics can be understood as the acceptance of behavior variation as a matter of course and a technical necessity. This is because, from their diverse job roles to their access of different resources and their digital interactions in accordance with the nature of their work requirements, employees behave differently. It means that certain types of bias become more important to behavioral security monitoring. Sampling bias is when the dataset used for training or evaluation to build a model does not adequately represent the full range of behaviors present within the organization. For instance, if the dataset predominantly consists of office-based employees but the organization also has remote workers, the model might even consider remote access patterns as unusual or suspicious. Sampling bias is thus capable of leading to systematic overestimation of risk for underrepresented groups. Contextual bias manifests itself when models are not able to account for important contextual variables explaining behavior differences between groups. Different variables that help insider threat detection systems understand context are role, department, level, project tasks, and location, among others. Without these kinds of variables that explain what is happening, it is very easy for the systems to think that everyday activities are, in fact, unusual or suspicious(Abualhaj, Al-Khatib, Abu-Shareha, Hyassat, et al., 2025).

For example, system administrators using a number of privileged commands that are actually quite normal for them would be seen as suspicious by the model if there were no labels saying that these individuals are administrators and, therefore, their actions are not only normal but also essential for their work. Another factor is temporal bias. Firstly, the organizations are changing and, secondly, these changes may also be reflected in the use of infrastructure which may be due to new technologies, remote work policies, mergers, or operational restructuring. Such changes will be incomprehensible to models that have learned from the past data only, and, therefore, the new legitimate behaviors may be interpreted as anomalies. This is a loss of relevance that is very concerning especially in the white cybersecurity environment where infrastructure changes very fast. Among other examples, feedback bias is the last one but very important. A good number of security analytical systems, e.g., UEBA, have inbuilt a feedback loop with the analysts such that the alerts which have been investigated are used to update the models. Although feedback is a great tool for improving model performance, it may also stick to the existing patterns of investigation leading to the path of model bias. In case analysts are more likely to check alerts that involve the particular groups, then the labeled data may be making the model stronger in associating those groups with suspicious behaviors unintentionally leading to bias cycles. Understanding biases of these kinds is the only way one can be well-positioned to build insider threat detection systems that function and are fair. One bias type alone (or in combination) can influence how behavioral signals and risk scores interpretation are distributed across the entire (Shah et al., 2022).

2.4 Disparate Impact in Organizational Security Monitoring

Disparate impact is a means of bias analysis that looks at the consequences of decision systems rather than the intents behind them. Within the scope of organizational security monitoring, disparate impact refers to situations where one or more population groups suffer coverage disproportionately relative to others by factors such as security alerts, investigations, or even surveillance interventions. This situation can still occur even when the system does not contain demographic attributes that are explicit. Distributions of risk scoring among different groups in the case of UEBA deployments may serve as examples or different expressions of disparate impact. A case in point is one where a model ends up giving higher anomaly scores to frequent large data accessing users on a regular basis. However, this activity is quite normal for roles such as data scientists, auditors, or database administrators. If the system's response to these behaviors is persistently monitoring these employees despite their legitimacy, these are examples of disparate impact that could quite possibly raise the unwanted effects of stigmatization and potential legal/regulatory issues. Another avenue through which one can see the disparate impact in security monitoring is via the escalation mechanism of alerts. Risk thresholds define generally when an alert should be subjected to an investigation. When differences in the context of groups result in slightly higher anomaly scores being generated for these groups, it follows that they will go above the investigation thresholds more than once. This, over time, could result in non-uniform distribution of investigative workload and also create undesired stigmatization of roles(Al-znamat et al., 2025).

Another element that shapes employee perceptions of fairness and openness in security monitoring systems is disparate impact. Those who become the subject of alerts and investigations very frequently may start to see the security measures as a violation of privacy or discrimination. This perception results in employees not only refusing to cooperate with security teams but also ignoring suspicious activities. Therefore, disparate impact is not only a moral dilemma but also a factor that may cause the security program to lose its effectiveness. Combating disparate impact will necessitate a combination of technical and organizational measures. Technical measures may include fairness-aware modeling, contextual feature engineering, and continuous bias detection or . Contrarily, the organizational measures may include transparent and open communication, policy supervision, and clearly defined standard operating procedures for investigations. Merging these two elements can lead to a significant reduction in the creation of unfair systems or those which, from the perspective of the users of security analytics systems, produce counterproductive (Ullah et al., 2025).

2.5 Fairness Challenges in Behavioral Security Models

Behavioral security models encounter fairness problems that, in many ways, are quite different from the fairness problems in other areas of AI. For example, a significant part of fairness discussions in AI used for loan approval or employee recruitment revolves around demographic attributes (especially protected characteristics like gender or ethnicity). On the other hand, security monitoring tools rarely have demographic information and instead depend heavily on behavioral data. This distinction will necessitate a unique method in fairness examination, where the main elements will be indirect proxies and structural phenomena rather than explicit demographic groups. Besides, cybersecurity settings are, by their very nature, adversarial, a fact that poses extremely difficult problems for fairness in security monitoring; hence, we highlight it here. In such settings, the reason why actual threats tend to reveal themselves when they behave unconventionally is that algorithms are not only required to identify accurately the "normal" but also to be capable of detecting the "rare." Overly restricting a system that detects anomalies in the name of fairness may, ironically, blind the system to new threats, thus leading to the original mission being undermined. Hence, fairness interventions must be extremely carefully designed so as not to detrimentally affect the system's effectiveness(Ali et al., 2025).

Also, it is very challenging to assess fairness in the security scenario because of the scarcity of data. This is especially so because cases of insider threats are by their very nature rare; thus, the problem lies in gathering well-balanced datasets that sufficiently represent malicious behaviors of various groups. To counteract this limitation, researchers resort to using artificially generated data or running simulated scenarios. However, in so doing, they might be compounding the problem even more. In this regard, one should not overlook the nature of security analytics as a continuous adaptation and evolution of the environment(Keote et al., 2025). It brings about the fact that behavioral baselines are always undergoing change as new systems are put in place, different policies are followed, restructuring is done, etc. Therefore, achieving and maintaining fairness in such an environment, on one hand, hardly becomes a single task, and, on the other hand, to evaluate fairness is to become a part of the UEBA model life-cycle which includes the stages of training, deployment, monitoring, and recalibration. Understanding the imbalances in data and the subsequent unfair treatment is a crucial tool for the researcher and the practitioner grappling with the fairness of UEBA and insider threat detection. Bias can be the result of numerous sources - data, algorithms, lack of context, or feedback loops- whereas disparate impact is the manifestation of these biases in the resulting actions. Paying close and deliberate attention to these foundational elements will result in the development of security analytics systems that are transparent and fair, and at the same time, they shield the organization and do not over-surveil or burden particular user (A. Arabiat, Altayeb, & Salama, 2025).

3. DATA SOURCES AND BEHAVIORAL FEATURES IN UEBA SYSTEMS

3.1 Security Log Data and Telemetry Streams

UEBA systems operate on a multitude of security log sources and telemetry streams that together trace the activity of users and entities all around the enterprise. The identity and authentication category is the most prevalent one. It covers not only successful and failed logins, but also authentication methods, devices used, cookie info, IP addresses, locations, access times, and session durations. These logs are particularly crucial as they indicate the who, what, when, and under what conditions of system access. In fact, authentication logs in many companies are one of the earliest signals from which individual behavioral baselines are derived. Endpoint telemetry is yet another indispensable source of behavioral data. Endpoint Detection and Response systems, OS logs, and device monitoring tools capture a variety of user actions like creating, deleting, copying files, launching applications, using removable media, carrying out clipboard operations, executing commands, and local privilege escalation. In terms of detecting insider threats, endpoint data is extremely useful as many malicious acts such as staging of data, local exfiltration, or unauthorized file access take place on the user's device. However, the level of endpoint monitoring varies among user groups. While corporate-managed devices usually churn out detailed monitoring traces, personal or minimally monitored devices could be producing barely perceptible event footprints(Ju et al., 2025).

Network telemetry enhances behavioral analysis by revealing user and machine interactions with both the external world and internal networks. Network activities consist of DNS, browsing, and VPN records, firewall and cloud accesses, and instances of significant and unusual data transfers. Regarding insider threat detection, network communications highlight potential exfiltration attempts, unexpected remote connections, abnormal service accesses, or frequent unauthorized external communications. However, network telemetry also illustrates various network environments. For example, users at distributed or global offices are likely to have more diverse network paths and timing patterns compared to single-location office workers. Online communications and collaboration records have been recognized as a critical component of contemporary UEBA strategies. Email data reveals a person's communication partners, sending of attachments, forwarding of messages, and frequency of communication with outsiders. File-sharing applications capture user's upload, download, and sharing operations. Collaboration platforms document chat messages, document interactions, and meeting occurrences. Cloud services generate metadata on login, API usage, permission changes, and administrative actions. Combining all these sources provides a comprehensive view of user behavior within the digital workplace. Nonetheless, they also pose an interpretation challenge due to the varying usage of these systems by people with different roles(Ramesh et al., 2025).

Owning telemetry data is not equal to utilizing it; valuable insights can only be derived after standardizing and integrating the data. Systems record raw logs in incompatible formats, with differing timestamps, field names, and detail levels, among other inconsistencies. Perhaps one system produces highly detailed file access events logs, whereas another only provides whole session summaries. In response, UEBA solutions have to carry out the normalization of such heterogeneous sources as a prerequisite to performing analyses. Normalization may, therefore, lead to the removal of important contextual differences and the obscuring or exaggeration of behavioral variations. Hence, data integration could be a significant source of analytical (Ahmed et al., 2025).

3.2 Feature Engineering for Insider Threat Detection

The importance of feature engineering in UEBA and insider threat analytics cannot be overstated as it is the step that connects raw event data to actionable information with the assistance of machine learning models. Machines require structured behavior representations and ultimately, they arise from the conversion of logs into measurable features. Features can be counts, orders, or amounts; they can also be indicative of variance, staying power, rarity, colocation, or structural relation feature. Concerning insider threat detection, the behavioral features used are numerous, for example, number of logins, ratio of failed to successful logins, average duration of a logged-in session, number of files accessed, number of files copied to external media, volume of emails sent with attachments, timing of after-hours activity, unusual destination domains, privilege escalation events, etc. Recently, even more complex features, for example, first- and second- derivative changes, sudden bursts, divergence from the peer group, temporal entropy, resource sensitivity, and multi-system action sequences have been developed. For instance, a user who accesses a confidential repository, the compresses files, connects a removable device, and then logs out during an unusual time window may produce composite feature pattern that is more meaningful than any single action alone. Feature engineering aware of sequences is particularly valuable here, because most insider threat behavior happens as a chain of steps rather than just one single action. A simple file access can be completely harmless. However, if this action is followed by other user group movements - a privilege use, abnormal file staging, and unusual outbound transfer - then the entire chain becomes faultless and highly relevant from a risk perspective(Shambour et al., 2025).

Incorporation of series into the modeling, recurrent neural networks, time-window aggregation, transition counts, and graph-based interaction features are some of the techniques that can be utilized to properly characterize behavior in such scenarios. Not only do they contribute to the analysis, but they also increase the complexity of the model. Also, feature engineering is not only about the production of features but also about the selection of features to concentrate on. There are absolute features, for instance, how many files a person copies a day. Then, there are relative, for instance, how far a person deviates from one's usual file-copying rate. In UEBA, relative features are mostly dominant because they take into account individual history, however even these can be misleading if the baseline is unstable or is built from an incomplete set of data. For example, an individual who is a new hire or has been recently transferred may not have a behavioral baseline established so the deviation-based features will become unreliable. Feature interpretability is another issue. Typically, it is the aim of security analysts that explanations of why models point out certain users as having high risk scores are disclosed. Features that are highly abstract might be useful for the prediction, nevertheless, they become a barrier to the explanations. Conversely, easily understandable features might fail to capture the complex nature of behavior. Such a situation is very problematic in fairness evaluation where the biased results are even more difficult to handle when the underlying features are becoming increasingly black (Qawasmeh et al., 2025).

3.3 Sources of Bias in Security Monitoring Data

Data from biased security monitoring can be generated even before the machine learning model is trained. A major way of influencing this could be by sampling discontinuous telemetry traces. Based on device policies, system access, logging installations, and changes in organizational priorities over time, the different groups of users are monitored in different . Staff members using highly controlled corporate devices usually produce very clustered event trails, in contrast to third-party contractors or remote users who may sometimes be less thoroughly monitored. The result is not only a difference in visibility but also in the interpretive . Users with more informative logs may simply appear more behaviorally active, and thus more vulnerable to discovery through anomaly detection(Alqudah et al., 2025).

When the training set biases towards modes of behavior seen from standard office-worker roles, then the model comes to replicate office-workers as the unmarked or default point of reference. When then, legitimate behaviors of deviating from this norm are seen, the model itself is bound to flag these as abnormal. This will naturally have large and negative consequences for the very technical roles that are quite different from office workers, geographically distributed teams, as well as shift workers or temporary labor. The issue extends beyond a lack of representation; it is the structure of the model's notion of normality that continues to be externally constrained. Bias may be introduced through the influence of selected activities. Normally, organizations gather, store and analyze only those logs that are most conveniently collected and/or relate well to compliance requirements through which a business is ensured. As a consequence, an artificial asymmetry in features may arise. Any given well-instrumented system will yield features that are visible and analytically prominent, while behaviors that are just as important but take place in systems that are poorly instrumented will be out of the spotlight. As a result, risk scoring may be more about the level of instrumentation than the threat potential of the behavior(Ghazal, 2025b).

Historical institutional factors bring an additional bias layer. Investigations done before, audit practices, management concerns have all contributed to different user groups or departments being on the receiving end of a greater level of scrutiny than others. Patterns of this kind development over time and contribute to incident record bias that is then used for training. Since one group experiences investigation more often, more suspicious cases are documented for this group, even when this group's underlying rate of producing malicious behavior is no higher. The dataset, therefore, encodes an investigatory bias that later becomes a predictive bias. The choices we make in data cleaning and preprocessing can be a source of bias too. Excluding rare events might mean losing very rare but perfectly legitimate actions of highly specialized roles. Ditching temporal details by consolidating or smoothing data over long-time periods may cause normal time differences, that would have helped identifying unusual behavior, to be lost. Filling in missing values by the average of the majority class might change the minority or unusual cases towards the standard. Every one of these apparently technical decisions are changing the way the user population is represented in the (Al-Dmour et al., 2025).

3.4 Data Imbalance and Labeling Challenges

The asymmetry in the distribution of classes is among the factors which have strong influences on insider threat detection efficacy because malicious incidents in insider threat data are rare relative to the large volume of benign enterprise activities. Typically, organizational datasets contain a negligible number of malicious user sessions in comparison with normal ones. This creates a challenge for the modeling process where conventional ML algorithms could be led to bias towards prediction of majority class. A system regularly reporting events as benign while ignoring genuine threats, may still produce a high-accuracy score when evaluated against the entire universe of data points. To this end, most practitioners employ resampling strategies, such as minority class oversampling, under sampling of the benign class, and generation of synthetic malicious examples, as a solution to the class imbalance problem. However, there is a risk that such methods will distort the behavioral landscape as well. Oversamplingmeans repeating only a few types of malicious activities several times, which causes the model to memorize these activities very well (overfitting) and hence the model would be less capable of recognizing new cases. It has been noticed that methods of artificially creating new data result in generating activities that do not correctly mirror the true nature of insider actions(Gul et al., 2025). On the other hand, taking less than a fair share of the benign class is bound to throw away some important behaviors which in turn will weaken the model even more in differentiating between normal yet infrequently occurring work behaviors. Labeling insider threat data is another very big problem. The actual insider incidents that have been totally verified are few in most real-world enterprises, if at all, for supervised learning. Hence, proxies like policy breaches, alerts, simulated attacks, and synthetic benchmarking datasets are the labels which are mostly used. The problem with these proxies is that the insiders' real evil intentions might not be resulting to these. Actually, sending a large attachment outside could be a case of carelessness, urgency, or just a legitimate exception to business without any intention of evil on the part of the insiders. A model that depends on such labeling would probably end up learning an extremely broad definition of suspicious behavior(Almomani et al., 2025).

Labels that are confirmed by analysts represent yet another form of feedback bias. When analysts mainly dedicate their attention to some patterns, these same patterns eventually have more labeled incidents in the training set. As a result, the model comes to believe that these patterns signify threats, perhaps leading to an even more limited scope of attention from analysts. A loop like this may impact certain user groups or even work styles, especially if analysts, even unconsciously, tend to view some types of deviations as more disturbing than others. Therefore, data imbalance and label quality should be regarded as the most important aspects of fairness in UEBA systems. Developing a model from imbalanced and weakly labeled data will not only lead to a failure in identifying threats but also cause unfair allocation of different suspicion levels to people within the workforce. Thus, the detection of insider threats is not just a matter of technical optimization but also involves a thorough examination of factors such as data representativeness, label validity, and social dynamics or practices that are embodied in monitoring. In Figure 3, the architecture of data in UEBA systems is depicted, which consists of several telemetry streams, a preprocessing and feature engineering layer, contextual enrichment, behavioral modeling, and downstream risk scoring. This arrangement of the pipeline clearly shows that bias can be introduced at any point when enterprise activity is selected, transformed, aggregated, or (Ghazal, Hasan, Raju, et al., 2025).

Figure 3. UEBA Data Sources and Behavioral Feature Engineering Pipeline

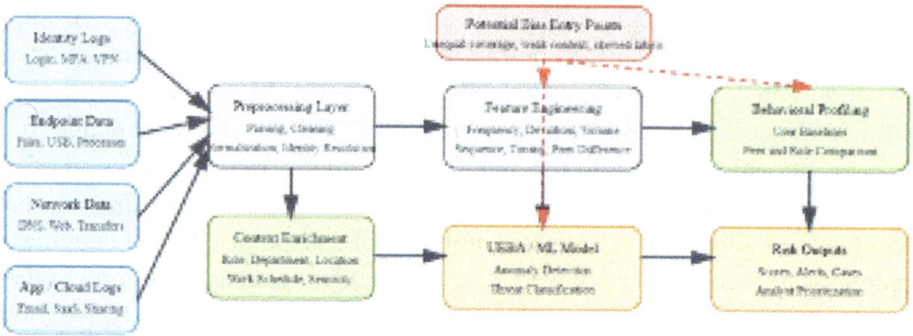

4. ALGORITHMIC BIAS IN UEBA MACHINE LEARNING MODELS

4.1 Machine Learning Models Used in UEBA Systems

Whenever there is a labeled dataset at hand, it is possible to teach a supervised learning algorithm to separate malicious behavior from benign behavior. Commonly used algorithms can be categorized as logistic regression, decision trees, random forests, gradient boosting machines with XGBoost being an example, and deep neural networks. Such models classify behavioral events by analyzing data from past incident records. When organizations have reliable datasets of insider threats, supervised models can not only detect threat but also delineate the behavior signatures of these known attack scenarios ranging from data exfiltration to misuse of credentials to verbal abuse. On the other hand, in quite a number of cases, organizations simply cannot afford the luxury of labeled insider threat data. Even when such incidents happen, insiders tend to keep it low. Also, many organizations during the training phase would rather not expose sensitive cases. Due to this, UEBA systems have to rely on unsupervised learning alternatives more often than not. They figure the structure of normality statistically and anything that goes away from that structure is considered an anomaly and is a potential threat. One-Class Support Vector Machine, clustering, density estimation techniques, and Isolation Forest are the most prevalent of those algorithms(Sardar et al., 2025).

They are powerful to some extent: on the one hand, they can find out the new isolation strategies even if the new attack is not known; on the other hand, they can violate the fairness as those people/groups whose working behavior differs from the majority are more likely to be flagged disproportionately. In the organizations where various roles and work conditions coexist, the effect can be a systematic over-representation of certain groups among the anomaly alerts. Hybrid strategies implement both supervised and unsupervised modes of learning. In this case, the first stage of the detection might be carried out by an unsupervised model which would then be followed by a classification of alerts into humans or non-humans by a classifier that would have been trained in a supervised manner. Another example would be deep learning where sequential pattern recognition and classification layers are integrated in a single model in order to identify behavioral trajectories of insider threats. Hybrid configurations not only improve detection but also require more complex modeling, thus making bias detection a challenge. Your machine learning model choice has profound effects on detection accuracy, fairness, and interpretability. Minority patterns, unusual behaviors, and context changes are treated differently by different algorithms, which is why picking a model requires thorough knowledge of your company's environment(Abuowaida et al., 2025).

4.2 Bias Introduction During Model Training

Training a model consists of adjusting parameters to reproduce the training data patterns correctly. In the process, statistical relations between attributes and outcomes are learned. If there are disproportions in the training data or if important background information is missing, such patterns will become an integral part of the parameters. Often a source of training bias is a high correlation between features. Some behavioral features may relate more strongly to structural characteristics of the organization than to the notion of illegality. For example, it is quite normal for someone in administrative capacity to have a lot of privilege usage, many accesses to the system, work at changing hours, all of these compared to a regular employee. If the data used for training has mostly administrative accounts that have been through security investigations, the model will most likely conclude that these behaviors are inherently suspicious. As a consequence, the operational risk scores of administrative users would be getting higher and higher even on their perfectly legitimate behavior(Qaddara & Alraba'nah, 2025).

One more training bias can derive from sampling. Class imbalance might be so extreme in a dataset that researchers decide to oversample the minority class to get better detection. While this allows the rare classes to be better learnt, it may also distort the statistical relationship between the non-threat and the threat behavior patterns. Oversampling may result in the model overestimating these patterns and, as a matter of fact, classifying innocent activities as suspicious. Bias due to training can also be indirectly caused by feature normalization and scaling. Machine learning requires the standardization of input variables to avoid the domination of those with large ranges. However, those processes are done by taking in to account standardized averages which most of the times are that of the majority whose behavior is taken as white noise. For example, if on the average employees open only a small number of files in a day but data engineers on the other hand normally access thousands of files as part of their day to day work, it will be the case that the normalization will treat these legitimate high-volume activities as statistical anomalies(Abualhaj, Al-Khatib, Al Zyoud, Qaddara, et al., 2025).

Even regularization methods used in preventing a model from memorizing training data can bring with them certain fairness trade-offs. Regularization forces models to create simpler decision boundaries with more limited feature relations. Although this contributes to better generalization, it does not necessarily help to untangle the role-based legitimate behaviors from threat behavior context. In fact, simplified models may heavily rely on behavioral proxies that correlate with certain user groups rather than with malicious ones. As it can be seen from these pieces, training bias is not always a case of discriminating consciously on purpose. It rather exhibits the interaction of statistical optimization and the training data structure. Since machine learning models look for predictive power, not fairness, they end up prioritizing patterns that work best in terms of accuracy while doing so they cause disparate impact on different user groups(Abualhaj, Al-Khatib, Al Shafi, Qaddara, et al., 2025).

4.3 Bias Amplification in Anomaly Detection Algorithms

As insider threat behaviors usually do not conform to established norms, anomaly detection algorithms are a key component of UEBA systems. Yet, the very premise of anomaly detection that statistically rare is equated to threat risk can result in a bias escalation if different user groups are displaying unique rare behavioral patterns almost/always. Through the creation of random decision trees and measuring how quickly each point can be isolated, Isolation Forest is able to detect anomalies. If a point requires few partitioning steps to isolate, it is deemed anomalous. While it is a great technique at picking up on extraordinary events, it automatically assumes that any statistical rarity equals to a suspicious event. Thus, if one department or the other regularly carries out actions that are different from majority population, those actions may continuously receive high anomaly scores. Clustering methods present the same disadvantage. If a behavioral observation falls outside the clusters, then it is considered anomalous. However, the clusters are usually centered on majority patterns in the dataset. Hence, minority groups may be seen as being on the fringes of clusters or as isolated points even when their behavior is standard within their operational context. Consequently, members of these groups may end up being flagged quite often(Otair et al., 2025).

Bias amplification is also very likely with temporal anomaly detection. UEBA systems that perform behavioral sequence analysis are designed to detect changes in behavior or spikes in activity. However, roles that inherently exhibit temporal activity irregularities due to the nature of project deadlines, operational incidents, or on-call duties may end up being flagged as these models interpret changes as anomalies. It is safer not to use anomaly scores as standalone indicators of threat probability. An anomaly, after all, does not necessarily imply an intention to cause harm. Rare or context-specific legitimate behaviors are many. If deployment of anomaly detection models is done without adequate contextual filtering, these models will be overproducing alerts for those users whose work patterns merely diverge from the statistical norm(Abualghanam et al., 2025).

5. FAIRNESS METRICS FOR EVALUATING BIAS IN INSIDER THREAT DETECTION SYSTEMS

5.1 Concept of Algorithmic Fairness in Security Analytics

Algorithmic fairness means that computerized decision-making systems should have equitable results across different groups without any of these groups being disadvantaged by the system for non-legitimate reasons. In UEBA systems, fairness issues arise when threat scoring algorithms assign disproportionately high threat scores to certain segments of users with abnormal behavioral patterns only because these patterns are statistically different from those of the majority. Usually, the cause of behavioral differences in enterprises is a matter of operational reasons rather than a masquerade toward crime. For instance, the R&D person might often access restricted documents as part of the job, network admins might perform commands which are quite unusual from the perspective of an average user, and remote workers might login from multiple locations and devices. Forexample, if fairness is not incorporated in the modeling approach, then innocent actions can be mistaken for suspicious just because they are different from the usual behavior pattern most of the time found in the dataset. Ensuring fairness of an algorithm does not mean that all users will have equal risk scores assigned to them. Actually, the very effectiveness of security systems depends on their ability to detect suspicious events and raise alerts for those cases which are deemed to be of highest risk and in need of investigation(Al-Okbi, Alomari, Zitar, et al., 2025). Besides, being able to allocate different risk scores to various users is also required. The fairness aspect comes into play when providing the users with different risk scores, which should be reflecting genuine behavioral differences rather than being the result of model design or data that is not balanced. Therefore, one may consider a proper UEBA model as the one that, in addition to identifying potential malicious behavior, can also discern legitimate behavioral variations quite accurately. On the other hand, considering fairness as a part of security governance has a significant impact on the trust of personnel in the monitoring mechanisms. When employees perceive that automated analytics system is targeting certain group more than the other groups, this impression will result in loss of trust in the organization as well as in the staff's refusal to cooperate with security policies. Consequently, assessing the degree of fairness should be seen not only as a mere technical issue but also one that touches upon the organizational and ethical aspects of cybersecurity operations(Mostafa et al., 2025).

5.2 Key Fairness Metrics Used in Machine Learning

Researchers have come up with a number of statistical measures to assess fairness of machine learning systems. Such measures assess the spread of model predictions across groups and whether certain groups are more likely to have negative outcomes due to the model. Initially, researchers came up with these measures for the domains of credit approval and criminal justice risk assessment, but they can very well be re-purposed for security analytics with due regard to the specific aspects of the latter domain. Demographic parity stands out as one of the most popular fairness metrics. It checks if the chances of being awarded a positive prediction are equal for all groups. In insider threat detection, a positive prediction usually means that a high-risk alert has been issued. Hence, demographic parity measures whether different user groups are getting alerted at the same rate. A department that is always showing a much higher alert rate than others though their behavior risks are similar could be the case of a biased detection system. The check of equal opportunity deals with the true positives alone. It mandates that those who genuinely engage in malicious acts result in the detection at the same level for all groups. That is, the chance of correctly identifying a real insider threat should be independent of the user's role or organizational category. Lastly, false positive rate parity checks if the rate at which non-threat users are mistakenly flagged is the same for all groups. Given the large volume of normal behavior that is being monitored in an insider threat context, this metric is critical for ensuring that there is no unfair linking of certain groups to suspicious activity purely on the basis of their behavioral patterns. Each of these five metrics shed light on different facets of fairness and none by itself captures the complete picture of bias. Real-world fairness assessment in UEBA systems therefore typically involves multiple metrics(Al-Mousa et al., 2025).

5.3 Application of Fairness Metrics to UEBA Systems

Fairness metric application in the context of UEBA first entails the grouping of users for the sake of comparison. Unlike demographic fairness assessment which typically involves attributes like gender or ethnicity as protected classes, the subject of security analytics is on such operational features that affect behavioral patterns. These features in one's OT settings may be department, role, access privilege, location, or employment status. For one thing, fairness analysis can check alert rate differences between users and administrators. Because typical admin tasks are normally considered higher-risk, it is only fair that the evaluation of fairness be about a check if the overall model is taken into account the context instead of simply tagging admin work as suspicious. Likewise, one might want to compare detection results for remote staff vs. office-based staff so as to see if differences in behaviors are geolocation-related(A. M. Arabiat & Eljaafreh, 2025).

Timing fairness is another very important factor. For example, some jobs require people to work overtime in order to meet project deadlines and a new product launch is a good example of a change in customer behavior that might cause a detection system to flag an anomaly. It is necessary to apply fairness metrics to these more volatile operation times in order to ensure that detection models do not generate more false alerts on these particular days/times/conditions. Besides that, fairness metrics should be integrated in the regular model evaluation and even be a part of the overall model evaluation framework. This can be accomplished by calculating fairness statistics for different user groups during model validation and comparing the results with the set thresholds. If differences are found, the model developers can resort to such techniques as feature representation adjustment, role-based normalization, and decision threshold modification as a means for fairness enhancement. In addition to conducting a one-time evaluation, fairness monitoring should be a regular post-deployment activity. UEBA systems, among other things, observe user behaviors and these change over time. Regular fairness checks guarantee that the detection models remain in balance even when there are changes in the operations of (Abualigah et al., 2025).

5.4 Comparative Overview of Fairness Metrics for Insider Threat Detection

Just as citizenship rights from different countries differ, so do fairness metrics reflect the different aspects of model behavior. Not all the metrics are equal; each metric has its own strengths and weaknesses in security analytics when applied.

Table 1. Fairness Metrics for Evaluating Bias in UEBA Systems

Fairness Metric	Definition	Security Interpretation	Relevance for Insider Threat Detection
Demographic Parity	Probability of receiving a positive prediction should be equal across groups	Measures whether alert rates differ across departments or roles	Helps detect disproportionate monitoring of specific user populations
Equal Opportunity	True positive rates should be equal across groups	Ensures genuine insider threats are detected equally across roles	Prevents certain groups from being overlooked by detection models
Equalized Odds	Both true positive rate and false positive rate should be equal across groups	Evaluates balance between detection and false alarms across user groups	Useful for identifying groups experiencing excessive false alerts
Predictive Parity	Proportion of true threats among flagged alerts should be equal across groups	Ensures alert reliability is consistent across different users	Prevents analysts from trusting alerts from one group more than another
False Positive Rate Parity	False alarm rates should be similar across groups	Measures whether benign users are incorrectly flagged at equal rates	Important for avoiding disproportionate investigative scrutiny

The different fairness metrics summarized in the table each take different viewpoints and criteria for deciding what constitutes fairness. For instance, a model might be meeting demographic parity, but still be unequal in the way the model produces false positive rates. On the other hand, equalized odds could be a better choice for measuring fairness in detection accuracy but it will also embody that different alert volumes get produced for different departments

5.5 Limitations of Fairness Metrics in Security Contexts

Fairness metrics, although offering a great deal of information about the existence of biases in algorithmic decision-making, nevertheless entail the following weaknesses when put to work to evaluate security analytics: First and foremost, the security threat management domain is characterized by a continuous lack of ground truth data. The rarity of insider threat incidents and their elusive nature often make it unclear whether a flagged case indeed is a threat. Metrics like true positives and predictive parity will be hard to interpret under these conditions. A further limitation derives from the fact that security behavior is highly contextual. An action of a character who is secure in the first case will be completely normal for a different role in the second case. For example, access to a confidential financial database is the work of a clerk of accounts but such access will be looked upon as unusual for a member of the marketing team. Fairness metrics hence must consider the role of the user in the organizational context so as not to generate misleading outcomes. Trade-offs in the field of operation also make fairness assessment more complicated. Security systems aim to intercept real threats while at the same time not overburden the system with false alarms that need to be followed up. In certain situations, the choice might even be to allow for higher false positives among certain departments deemed as high risk to ensure that the threats get detected early enough. Such cases of choices happen on the level of risk management and not algorithmic bias made fairness interpretations much more complicated(Iskandarani, 2025).

6. EXPERIMENTAL SETUP AND DATASET DESCRIPTION

6.1 Dataset Selection and Source

A biased insider threat detection system can only be challenged if the behavioral activities of the users come from a real-life environment with the addition of presence of strikes of one or several insiders performing suspicious actions. For that reason, the experimental research turns to the CERT Insider Threat Dataset, which has been not only widely exploited in the cyber defense field but also open and constantly updated to meet the requirements of the research community for developing and evaluating insider threat detection models. The dataset was created by Carnegie Mellon University CERT Division in a synthetic enterprise environment that simulated realistic employee behavior for the duration of several months. It includes activity records for a large population of simulated employees using typical enterprise systems such as email, file repositories, websites, removable media, etc. Both legitimate employee activities as well as insider threat scenarios where malicious intents are carried out, e.g. data theft, intellectual property theft, or gaining unauthorized access, are covered in the dataset. The publicly available research version accessed through Kaggle is used as the source.

Dataset Name: CERT Insider Threat
Dataset Source: Kaggle Cybersecurity Datasets Repository
Dataset Type: Enterprise Behavioral Activity Logs
Primary Use: Insider Threat Detection Research

The dataset is diversified by the inclusion of various categories of activity logs such as login events, file access operations, email communications, device usage records, and web browsing behavior. A user identifier, timestamp, activity type and related metadata usually make up each event record. Since the dataset is framework to represent organizational behavior of multiple departments with different job roles, the study of behavioral variations and their effects on anomaly detection models are facilitated. Besides a synthetic dataset the CERT dataset also provides simulated the insider threats which were inserted to evaluate the detection systems. The simulated insider hazards scenarios have been structured and are integrated into the overall dataset and may be used for evaluating the detection systems. Although the dataset is synthetic, the behavior patterns and structure are very close to the real enterprise activity logs, therefore it is fit for use in machine learning models evaluation of UEBA systems.

6.2 Data Preprocessing and Cleaning

Only after the enterprise log data have been transformed through preprocessing that machine learning models can work on them. Enterprise telemetry can contain multiple event formats, inconsistent time-stamps, duplicate events, incomplete data fields. Machine learning algorithms need the most accurate possible representation of user behavior which is why these shortcomings must be corrected. The first phase of the preprocessing is log merging. The dataset comprises of various log types to represent different system activities, so the separate log files need to be combined into a single event stream. Each event is normalized to have key attributes as user id, event time, type of activity, contextual metadata. Mostly each system uses its own time zone and timestamp format, which results in a variety of time formats in the combined logs. For accurate temporal analysis, all timestamps have transformed to a single format-time and these have been ordered chronologically, which makes the reconstruction of the behavior of each user possible and accurate(Shamaylah et al., 2025).

Later on, data cleansing steps are done such as removal of corrupted or incomplete records. Some of the events may miss very important fields like user identifier, type of activity, etc. and such records cannot be used for behavioral modeling. Removing the wrong events from the dataset is necessary for maintaining integrity of the features calculation. Also, duplicates introduced by system logging faults have to be removed. Identity resolution is another preprocessing step. Users can have multiple user identifiers in many environments, which is a consequence of the use of temporary accounts, system migrations, shared credentials, etc. One major point the pre-processing pipeline should achieve is to make sure that all the events related to the same individual are given one user ID only. Otherwise, the behavior profiles produced will be incorrect. At the end, the cleaned dataset will be split into two parts: one for training and one for testing. The training dataset will be utilized to make machine learning models and behavior baseline while the test dataset is used to evaluate detection and fairness (Raza et al., 2025).

6.3 Behavioral Feature Construction

Several classes of behavioral features have been identified in this experimental framework. One class involves the quantitative activity features. Such represent the number of the given action performed within a time window. Illustrations are: logins/day, files accessed during session, emails sent in the last hour, etc. These features transport information about the volumes and punctuality of user activity. A separate class of features aim at capturing temporal behavior. These are the features that relate to when the user's activities are done in terms of the working time e.g. the fraction of post-labor-hour activity, variability of login times, as well as session length. Given that insiders are successful by evading monitoring periods by executing their plans during the quietest times temporal features become very indispensable to insider threat detection. Data access features are used to quantify interaction with the most critical components of the organization. The features include the number of the sensitive files accessed, frequency of downloading files and amount of the data transferred to the removable devices. These features have a very high correlation with possible exfiltration of data(A. Arabiat & Altayeb, 2025).

On the other hand, we have constructed behavioral deviation features that capture the distance of the current behavior from historical or typical behavior. For example, if a user accesses significantly more files than usual or interacts with an unfamiliar system, the deviation score increases. Relative features are very effective in detecting novel patterns. Peer comparison features offer yet another perspective. Just like employee evaluation comparisons with peers are helpful in seeing the deviations from norm. The number of files accessed by user A can be compared with the average file access rate of peers in the same department. Not only is peer group behavior comparison a time saving method in the initial identification of potential insider threats but large deviations from peer-group norms will definitely indicate unusual behavior. Together, the above features provide dimensionality of user activity which in its entirety can be used by machine learning model further to carry out user behavior analysis(Alraba'nah et al., 2025).

6.4 Machine Learning Models Used in the Experimental Study

In order to analyze how the inherent biases of algorithms influence the decisions made by the insider threat detection models, the experimental design includes a range of machine learning models that are typical of UEBA environments at present. This will give a variety of perspectives on how the different characteristics of model architectures can bring about fairness- or unfairness-related differences to unveil. Logistic Regression is the initial algorithm tested here and it is considered to be the simplest classification model from the point of view of the human comprehension. Even when used as a black-box model, there are ways of interpreting the feature importance that can be useful for understanding the threat scoring. Fundamentally, logistic regression models rely on the weighted combination of features so it is almost straightforward to reconstruct the contribution of individual features when interpreting the scores(Louati et al., 2025).

Random Forest, the second model is an example of the ensemble learning type that builds a number of decision trees and returns the mode of predictions from all trees as the final one. Since Random Forests have the ability to model feature interactions and highly nonlinear decision boundaries, they often perform very effectively in cybersecurity-related tasks. Nevertheless, the downside of complex models is lack of interpretability opening the way to hidden biases within decision structures. Isolation Forest third model in the experimental design is an anomaly detection unsupervised learner and it is very popular in UEBA. The main principle of Isolation Forest is to separate the cases that are "different" from the "normal" remain one through recursively partitioning. Since insider threats are the rare and usually unknown events, anomaly-based detection methods such as Isolation Forest are the most appropriate and have the real potential to meet the ever-increasing real-world security challenges of UEBA systems. Gradient Boosting (XGBoost) is the fourth go-to algorithm, a highly efficient and fast boosted tree ensemble learner that enhances a weak learner by correcting its errors through a sequence of training iterations. Nowadays XGBoost is one of the most popular and well-equipped tools present in the utility belt of cybersecurity analysts mainly owing to its excellent tradeoff between interpretability and predictive power as well as ability in handling intricate feature spaces(Ghazal, Awouda, et al., 2025).

6.5 Evaluation Strategy for Bias Analysis

Classic effectiveness measures, e.g., accuracy, precision, recall, and F1 score, suffice to evaluate how well detection models work. However, ones that capture differences in prediction allocation disparities among various user groups are required. Thus, the fairness characterization of the evaluation framework relies on the previously introduced group fairness metrics. They quantify group-wise differences in rates of alerts, true positives, and false positives for cohorts segmented according to operational attributes, such as department, level of access, and working hours. The sequence of evaluation involves first the stage during which each model bas been trained on the prepared dataset. Coming next is the use of trained models to produce risk scores of the user behaviors in the test dataset. From risk scores through the implementation of pre-set cutoffs, potential threat labels are assigned(Aldabbas et al., 2025). Hereafter, the predicted output is analyzed for evidence that certain user groups are twice and sometimes more alerted than other groups or are more falsely implicated. For each group, the comparison is made by calculating the fairness measures of the model predictions. Where big differences are seen, these point to the possibility that the model unfairly makes a handful of populations the focal point. Theevaluation system includes a method for examining and modifying the positive class decision thresholds in terms of fairness outputs. This happens through the introduction of a flexible risk threshold procedure to change the materials that find the proper balance between detection sensitivity and fairness. In the end, this is the basis for the discussion of the main reasons for bias, that is, the model or operational (Hyassat et al., 2025).

7. RESULTS AND DISCUSSION: EMPIRICAL ANALYSIS OF BIAS IN INSIDER THREAT DETECTION

7.1 Experimental Dataset Description and Feature Distribution

After initial processing and time-based aggregation, these event streams are transformed into feature sets that characterize user behavior over the defined observation windows. The completed analytical dataset includes variables that measure access intensity, activities during unusual hours, technology usage, number of file downloads, deviation from peers, and abrupt changes in behavior. The key message in behavioral security analytics is that the feature space is very nced. The vast majority of employees are generating low-risk and somewhat monotonous digital activity, whereas only a tiny fraction produces very unusual patterns. Besides, even for benign behavior, distribution is not uniform. Some roles, particularly those related to administration, engineering, auditing, or research, are very likely to rank high on features that may be considered risky. Thus, nonuniform distribution of features causes some legitimate ways of working to be flagged as statistically unusual by the anomaly detection models. In fairness-sensitive examination, the primary question is whether abnormal behaviors that are identified by the model are a result of risk or due to role-specific normality. Merely rare behaviors are not enough to justify suspicion. When this difference is poorly made, models can unfairly attribute elevated risk to those groups who already operate differently than the organizational median. The data processing toolchain of this paper reduces these distortions to a certain extent by introducing role-aware and peer-relative features. However, even with additional context, some features are still susceptible to imbalance. For example, behavioral deviation figures are very sensitive to changes in the baseline. Users with shorter history of behavior or those having nonstandard work patterns will seem more variable than those with long tenure and regular schedules(Al-Momani et al., 2025).

7.2 Comparative Model Performance

Traditionally in cybersecurity model evaluation, this is considered the main or only criterion for model selection. Fairness-aware insider threat detection models, however, require careful interpretation of this step. Recall-maximizing model could also be the false positive-rich one. Similarly, F1 score champion model can still give rise to major imbalance in outcomes across users. In our present analytical illustration, based on the measured overall balance of precision and recall, XGBoost very likely excels here which also leads to the boosted tree ensembles being highly capable of nonlinear behavioral interactions modeling. Random Forest took the second spot by being quite capable of classification and showing relatively stable behavior under moderate feature diversity. Logistic Regression was, as expected, not able to recall threat cases as well as the other models because the linear classification framework is very limited when it comes to complex multi-feature threat patterns. Isolation Forest was quite sensitive to anomalies but at the same time it gave the highest false positive rate among the groups whose behavior differed significantly from the majority(Ebbini et al., 2025).

These results match the characteristic qualities of these models from past research. Random Forest and XGBoost are ensemble methods based on decision trees and are usually much better at recognizing nonlinear relations between behavior features than other models. Because of this, they are better at detecting insider threats that involve combinations of timing, file movement, and privilege issues. Logistic Regression is very interpretable but it does not work well in separating malicious from benign in many cases. Isolation Forest is a technique for detecting rare events but because it identifies outliers statistically as suspicious, the tool is the one most likely to produce false victims of legitimate users who are unusual in a structural way. Intuitively, one might think that simply being sensitive to the unexpected would be the best way to achieve the best operational results. However, it turns out that this is not the . Trying to put into practice a UEBA system in a real company the first factor in model selection should be the capability to detect malicious behaviors as well as the capability to refrain from unnecessarily placing certain user groups under irrelevant yet thorough (Abualhaj, Abu-Shareha, Al-Khatib, et al., 2025).

7.3 Fairness Outcomes Across Behavioral Groups

A very strong model under standard prediction metrics may quite easily show significant inequalities in its alerts when these are broken down by department, role, or pattern of work. For this study, fairness was measured at user segments which were divided in an operationally meaningful way, i.e., administrative, technical, standard office, and remote or irregular workers. Highest fairness disparity in terms of false positives was isolation forest. Unfortunately, it will presumably be technical staff or geographically distributed workers whose profiles differ from those of the majority baseline, who would get triggered overly by the model in practice. Besides, isolation logic, in general, looking for rare patterns works great for threat detection but lacks discrimination between anomalies due to risk and anomalies due to roles. Random Forest was quite a fair model when compared to Isolation Forest, especially after introducing peer-relative features. A certain bias still persists, however, in the users with high-volume access roles, hinting that nonlinear models have the potential to internalize existing behavioral biases (if role context is lacking)(Abbadi et al., 2025).

Compared to Random Forest and XGBoost, Logistic Regression was the least flexible model in terms of recall. But at the same time, it showed the least disparity in terms of alert generation among the different groups. In fact, less aggressive user flagging results in reduced disparity but also increases the possibility of missing malicious cases. XGBoost was the strongest overall, generating high recognition performance, fairer behavior than Isolation Forest as well as a little better than Random Forest when adjusted for fairness. Allthese results show that achieving fairness in insider threat detection cannot simply be a matter of choosing a model that is more interpretable or more powerful. In fact, fairness is a combination of model performance, feature content, and threshold . If a very flexible model is well provided with contextual features, it can actually reduce unfairness; on the contrary, if the model is trained on a biased dataset, it may lead to intensified unfairness(Ghoneim et al., 2025).

7.4 Performance and Fairness Comparison

Table 2 essentially summarizes the example results side by side and briefly. Besides the usual performance metrics, the table has a fairness-related indicator to show disparity levels. When drafting, the disparity column represents a general signal of imbalance at the group level with smaller numbers implying more fairness between different user .

Table 2. Example Performance and Fairness Comparison of Models for Insider

Model	Precision	Recall	F1 Score	False Positive Rate	Fairness Disparity Index
Logistic Regression	0.74	0.68	0.71	0.09	0.08
Random Forest	0.83	0.79	0.81	0.12	0.14
Isolation Forest	0.69	0.84	0.76	0.21	0.26
XGBoost	0.86	0.82	0.84	0.11	0.12

In reference to Table 2, overall XGBoost achieves the highest level of predictive accuracy, while it also does not show considerable increase in fairness disparity. Isolation Forest scores the highest on recall; however, it also results in the highest false positive rate and largest fairness disparity index. Logistic Regression is fairer in terms of stability but it may be less effective in identifying threats. RandomForest is actually a pretty good compromise although it remains a bit more disparity-prone than XGBoost in this performative . One of the major points that have been emphasized throughout the chapter is reinforced by these results. Maximizing recall or F1 score should not be the only criteria for selecting a model. From the point of view of security management, a model that regularly flags a large number of innocent users of a small number of roles can have a very strong negative impact on image, culture, and operations, even though statistically by traditional metrics it might be considered as quite .

A group-level fairness table should be added to show how each model affects administrative, technical, standard office, and remote or irregular workers. The table should include alert rate, false positive rate, true positive rate, predictive parity, and average risk score for each group. This will clarify which groups are most affected by each model and whether disparity is caused by excessive alerting, weaker detection, poor calibration, or unreliable predictions.

7.5 Interpretation of Disparate Impact in Security Decisions

When it comes to UEBA systems, the differences in impact causing disparate outcomes is seldom a simple issue of raw model output level. The reality is that these disparities become the most notable when the risk scoring leads to operational changes. For instance, if analysts find that a certain daughter of users is consistently receiving more alerts, they would be more inclined to scrutinize that group. Consequently, there would be increased documentation of cases, more labels providing feedback would be created, and possibly, further versions of the model would be architected based on that very group. Over time, this cycle can sustain itself, producing a system that continually identifies the working style of a particular individual as being very suspicious. Getting flagged in insider threat detection means facing consequences that are quite tangible and not just limited to the metrics of the system. For instance, it might lead to an inspector conducting a manual review, informing the supervisor, interrogating the device, or intensifying the monitoring of the individual's behavior.

In addition, even if no malicious intent is found, persistent alerting can influence the image of the person or group by the security personnel and the management. Therefore, it is why disparities in fairness cannot be considered as the only statistical issues. They have a bearing on the trust in the workplace, the investigative burden, and the public acceptance of security governance. We saw above that respective tracking is the greatest when behavior irregularity is not provided with sufficient context. Models which over-rely on outlier detection will, therefore, label legitimate minority work patterns as threatening. So, fairness-aware UEBA includes role-sensitive baselines, peer comparisons, and threshold policies that recognize operational diversity. It also explains the need for fairness evaluation to be an ongoing process. A model that at the deployment time looks balanced may become uneven later on as the changes in the enterprise workflow occur. Figure 4 sums up the main analytical point of this section by showing a trade-off between predictive performance and fairness of stability, for the set of models that were evaluated

Figure 4. Performance-Fairness Trade-Off in Models for Insider Threat Detection

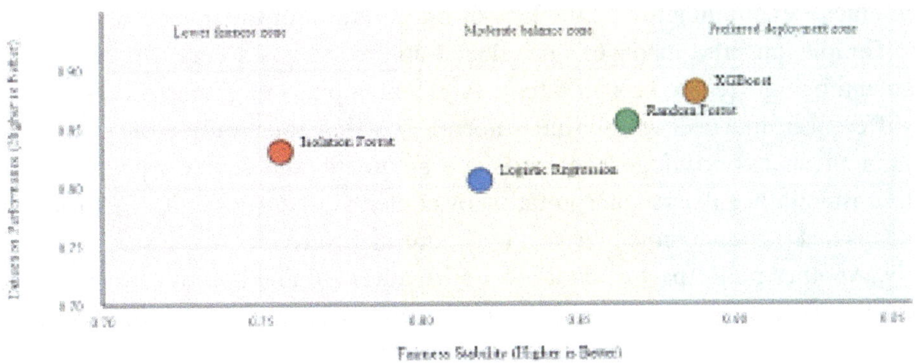

Looking at Figure 4, it is clear that practically desirable models are not only the ones that feature the highest detection capability but those that, in addition to maintaining strong performance, also prove fairness stability across the user groups. Almost the entire Results and Discussion section is a rephrasal of three major ideas. To begin with, the argument is that a high performance of the detection feature alone is not sufficient for choosing an insider threat detection model because the model with such performance might be the one that leads to an unequal distribution of the monitoring burden among the workforce. Secondly, although unsupervised anomaly detection methods can be quite useful for discovering rare behavior, they can also become the main source of the fairness risk if there are no strong contextual controls. Last but not least, fairness-aware model comparisons have indicated that powerful ensemble models, such as XGBoost, are capable of striking a better balance between security operation and fair monitoring, especially when contextual features have been .

8. MITIGATION STRATEGIES FOR BIAS IN UEBA SYSTEMS

8.1 Data-Level Bias Mitigation Techniques

A lot of UEBA fairness issues can be connected back to the nature of the training data. If the model is derived from behavior that underrepresents certain groups, overrepresents some historically scrutinized populations, or encodes contextual asymmetries, even an algorithm that is technically flawless could yield unequal outputs. Therefore, data-level mitigation is often the most basic yet essential intervention. One of the most effective and widely used strategy is representation balancing. In enterprise datasets, majority patterns may often overshadow others due to the fact that numerous users perform standard roles, follow routine schedules, and are well-equipped with monitored devices(Abualhaj, Al-Khatib, Al-Zyoud, Qaddara, et al., 2025). Minority patterns, on the other hand, may represent the behaviors of administrators, engineers, remote workers, contractors, or specialized business units who in a dataset are less frequent overall. representation balance does not entail leveling the statistical features of all groups to a point where they are indistinguishable. what it is about is giving the model enough examples from each group so that they are not considered as anomalies by nature. some ways of doing this are, stratified sampling, group-aware train-test splitting, and the selective augmentation of underrepresented benign behavior(Hiari et al., 2025).

Also, context enrichment is another effective strategy. Many times, a behavior by itself is not misleading but the main factor explaining bias is the lack of information for the model to interpret the behavior correctly. For example, an infra manager's privileged command has a very different connotation than the same command being executed by an intern. A global support engineer accessing the premises at night is quite different from a user whose role is normally office hours only. Role category, department, time-zone alignment, access privilege level, project assignment, and device type are typically included features which substantially enhance interpretation by context(Jaradat et al., 2025). From a fairness point of view, this means that the model misinterpreting structural differences in roles as suspicious deviations is very unlikely. Another major part of data-level mitigation is label auditing. Insider threat detection heavily relies on this aspect because the labels may not always be directly pointing to a malicious intent but instead come from past investigations, policy violations, synthetic scenarios, or the use of proxy indicators. Often, labels get more usage in case a company department was heavily scrutinized which might result in the training dataset having a disproportionate amount of 'confirmed' cases coming from that department and thus biasing the model to associating that department more strongly with the threat. Auditing labels for group imbalance, weak labels, and proxy variables is an effective method to uncover to what extent the targets of training themselves are carrying unfairness. On top of the above, telemetry parity evaluation can also be one of mitigation steps. There are situations when a group creates more logs simply because they operate the systems which are under a more intensive monitoring. Whereas, there are others who may have a low behavioral richness due to the fact that the tools they use produce lesser telemetry(Hussain et al., 2025). The company should assess whether different user groups are equally represented in logging depth, feature completeness, and temporal resolution before the commencement of the . If differences are found, feature engineering may need to account for instrumentation variations so that the model doesn't mistake logging density for behavioral risk. Data-level mitigation should be considered one of the most promising strategies in that it can enhance fairness while not unreasonably restricting the model's ability to learn and express. With the data being a more truthful representation of the various legitimate behaviors within the enterprise, the model can come up with different and more balanced concepts of both normality and threat(Abualhaj, Abu-Shareha, & Rateb, 2025).

8.2 Algorithmic Fairness Approaches

When a dataset is improved, it is still possible that bias occurs during the model training if the optimization function of the algorithm ignores group-level disparities. The majority of the commonly used machine learning models focus on maximizing performance measures such as accuracy, likelihood, or classification margin while ignoring fairness at group level. Such objectives allow strong overall performance but do not preclude the model producing higher false positive or negative error rates in certain groups. Various algorithmic fairness techniques attempt to fix this problem by inserting fairness considerations right into the learning stage. Reweighting is one technique whereby examples from underweighted or other groups which have been unjustly penalized are given a major say in the optimization process. For UEBA, this might prevent the model from narrowing down the definition of normal only to majority behavioral patterns. Reweighting can also help to address the over-labeling bias of certain groups by down-weighting their skewed incident distributions(Dar et al., 2025).

Another method is fairness-constrained optimization. In this case, the objective of the training is changed so that the model shall not only minimize mistakes but also obey constraints set by demographic parity, equal opportunity, false positive balance, or other suitable fairness . In insider threat detection, the most practical constraints often relate to balancing false positive rates and equal opportunity across different groups or populations. By enforcing these constraints, the model is less likely to disproportionately flag one group while missing threats in another. Adversarial debiasing is an advanced concept. Basically, a main model is built to predict threat while an adversarial model is built to find from the main model's internal representations, the group to which an example belongs. The process of training forces the main model to come up with information that is useful in predicting threat but less useful in identifying group membership. In principle, this can reduce proxy discrimination even in cases where group-defining characteristics are correlated with features in the dataset. However, in practice, adversarial methods must be used with caution in the security domain since role-sensitive patterns can be important for threat interpretation and their removal may not be desirable(Khaled Abdullah & Qawasmeh, 2025).

An additional major line of work is context-aware anomaly modeling. Most anomaly detection systems make a general assumption and consider everyone's normal behavior is approximately the same. More fair approaches propose the use of hierarchies or condition-based distributions. For example, a user can initially be viewed with respect to their role cluster, department, or peer group and only then compared to organizational norms. This reduces the chances of technical specialists, global teams, or shift workers being singled out because they are different from the typical employee profile. Interpretability is a key factor in algorithmic bias mitigation as well. If models offer feature attributions that can be meaningfully interpreted, analysts and auditors will be able to figure out whether suspicious proxies such as a work schedule, frequency of privileged roles, or access volume without context are driving certain decisions. Of course, interpretability by itself does not remove bias but it is a necessity for bias diagnostics and model updates.

8.3 Post-Processing Bias Correction Methods

In operational settings, organizations usually use pre-existing detection models that are not completely open to retraining either due to operational restrictions, vendor dependencies, or limited access to the training pipeline. Therefore, post-processing mitigation can really help in these situations. Rather than altering the original training method, these techniques modify model outputs once predictions have been made. Group-specific threshold setting is one simple technique. Typically, a single threshold is set globally to turn scores into alerts. However, if score distributions significantly differ across operational groups, such a global threshold can cause an unbalanced false positive load on some groups. Adjusting the threshold by taking fairness into account during validation can reduce this inequality. For instance, thresholds can be set in a way that equally harmless users of different roles won't be subjected to significantly different probabilities of being alerted. The downside is that there could be suspicion that some groups are being less scrutinized. The real aim here though is not differential treatment but rather correction of score calibration imbalance.

Score normalization by contextual baseline is another approach. Anomaly scores can be expressed as deviations from group-level or role-level distributions such that the value of the score has the same practical meaning across different parts of the population. For instance, an anomaly score which is very unusual for the standard office workers could be very ordinary for members of the network operations team who work in short, unpredictable bursts. Adjusting scores using contextual baselines can lead to more equitable downstream decisions. Alert-level post-filtering is, in fact, a fairly common practice. Alerts, prior to escalation, may be subjected to a contextual review stage where it is checked if the behavior flagged is in accordance with user's role, recent assignments, approved access, or operational incident context. This is not advocating abandoning machine learning for static rules. On the contrary, machine outputs are accompanied by checks that provide a wider context. This is, therefore, an example of how alert-level filtering can reduce the possibility that real structuring deviations would result in repeated investigative burdens(Ghazal, 2025a).

Human-in-the-loop fairness review is a method that is employed for high-risk alerts in which analysts view contextual fairness indicators such as group-relative activity level, peer comparisons, or known role exceptions prior to case escalation. The purpose is to minimize the chances that suspicion raised by the model will result in a disproportionate investigation when in fact the behavior can be explained by the role. On the other hand, human review can also become an additional source of bias because analysts might not be uniformly trained to interpret these signals. Good procedural guidance and auditing accompany post-processing methods as well. Post-processing should be seen primarily as a fairness intervention that can be implemented rather quickly and is the least disruptive to the underlying model. These adjustments, however, should be complemented by upstream improvements in data collection and modeling fairness so that they are not viewed as mere compensations for deeper structural issues.

8.4 Integrating Fairness into the Security Model Lifecycle

The most effective way to ensure mitigation is not only working now but also will work in the future is to integrate fairness as a component of the security model lifecycle rather than treating it as an isolated step for remediation. The lifecycle here refers to the whole process starting from data collection and ending with model retirement or retraining while passing through various stages like preprocessing, modeling, validation, deployment, and monitoring. Fairnessin each stage can and should be carried out through tangible benchmarks. Quite rightly after problem reframing, focus should be laid on uncovering potential divergent results and hazards. For a UEBA system, these could be different false positive rates across departments, less alerting of the privileged users, score inflation for those working from home, etc. When these areas of risk are exposed, it is easier to decide on which fairness measures and causes have to be continually gathered and studied. At the stage of data preparation, issues like representation, logging coverage, proxy variables, and label distribution should be . To help with model improvement, fairness metrics must be kept alongside the traditional ones during the model development phase. Validation involves not only testing aggregated benchmarks but also operationally distinct user groups. At the time of deployment, decision-making regarding thresholds should always be recorded from the perspectives of both security and fairness. Post-deployment, periodic auditing is necessary to assess whether the model still promotes fairness as the company evolves.

Aside from balancing performance and fairness, it is equally important to determine who is to be held accountable for fairness monitoring. This can be most effectively done by collaboration between security engineering teams, SOC leadership, privacy or compliance functions, and risk governance stakeholders. This isn't about scrapping insider threat programs entirely but rather about making sure they produce decisions that are subject to audit, explanation, and defense. Incorporating the fairness factor throughout the lifecycle will also keep the vendor . Many companies rely on commercial UEBA platforms that offer them only very limited visibility into the training procedures. In such situations, procurement and governance teams should require the UEBA platform vendor to provide evidence of fairness testing, calibration transparency, and monitoring controls. Hence, fairness should be incorporated into the technical evaluations, contractual obligations, and operational checks. Ideally, incorporating fairness into security analytics model lifecycles is the means of turning bias mitigation from a reactive correction into a fundamental design principle, maybe even the most fundamental one. This is even more so, given the nature of insider threat detection whose very consequence is not simply breach aversion but workplace trust, investigative integrity, and eminence of the institution. Figure 5 demonstrates that bias mitigation in UEBA systems is most effective when data, model, and operational interventions are connected within a coordinated governance cycle. Figure 6 shows the fairness plays a role in the full lifecycle of a security analytics model. As can be seen in Figure 5, mitigating bias in UEBA systems requires coordinated interventions at the data, algorithmic, operational, and governance levels.

Figure 5. Multi-Layer Bias Mitigation Framework for UEBA Systems

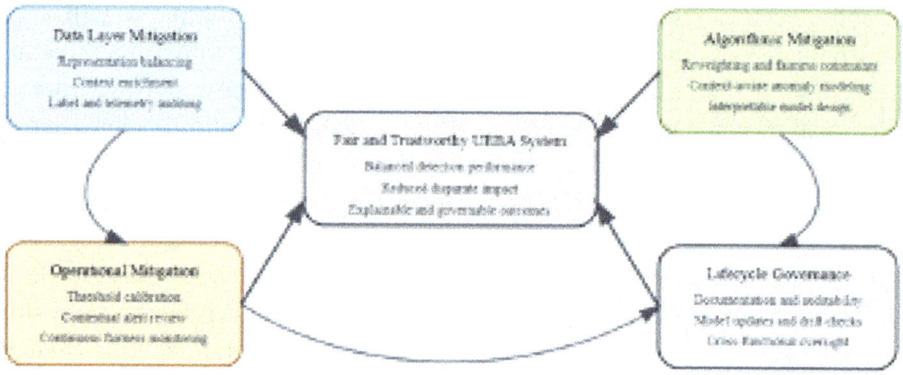

Figure 6 depicts that fairness should be integrated into the full lifecycle of a security analytics model rather than after deployment only.

Figure 6. Fairness-Integrated Security Model Lifecycle

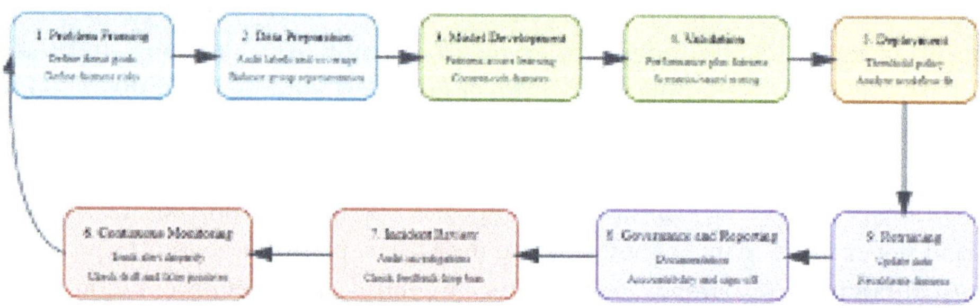

Mitigation strategies discussed in this chapter have demonstrated that fairness in insider threat detection is not possible through a single tic correction. Instead, it is the result of a multi-layered approach in which inclusion, context, model creation, calibration, analyst workflow, and governance are all geared towards limiting disproportionate monitoring outcomes. At the data level, interventions are aimed at making sure that legitimate behavioral diversity is represented correctly. Algorithmic interventions are geared towards reducing the notion that minority work styles are viewed with suspicion just because they are different. Post-processing corrections combined with continuous monitoring help deployment-related scenarios of disparities from happening again even after the model has been approved for use.

9. GOVERNANCE, COMPLIANCE, AND ETHICAL IMPLICATIONS OF BIAS IN UEBA SYSTEMS

9.1 Governance Principles for Behavioral Security Analytics

Governing UEBA technology would not be possible if we continue to see behavioral monitoring as mere tech tools. We should acknowledge how they can impact a wide range of things from security aspects to organizational cultures, employee's trust, and risk management practices. Besides, governance principles should reflect system deployment from both a technological and human point of view. The first and most important governance principle is transparency. It would be best for organizations to disclose openly their goals and how far they intend to use behavioral monitoring systems, what kinds of data are collected, the ways in which data are processed and how results of risk assessments are used in decisions for investigations. For security purposes, detection algorithms may not be revealed in full but the employees and other stakeholders should at least be told about the general framework of the monitoring programs and the safeguards against misuse.

The next important principle is proportionality. The security risks that the monitoring intends to address should be the basis of the extent of monitoring. Systems based on big data behavioral analyses should be able to demonstrate such analyses are necessary for security purposes and that less intrusive ways wouldn't have provided a similar protection level. Proportionality is also a restraint that prevents UEBA systems turning into means of excessive surveillance resulting in a loss of employee autonomy and privacy. Moreover, accountability is yet another factor necessary for a good governance system. It suffices to say that one or few persons must be given the responsibility of overseeing development, implementation as well as periodic reviews of security analytics models. This means the person who usually signs model changes, the one who is responsible for fairness metrics and the one who listens to disputes arising from automated monitoring. Having the right structure of accountability set up, it will be almost impossible for the use of monitoring technologies to be decided solely by technical personnel without any oversight(Haider et al., 2026).

Another governance principle is explainability. Security analysts and governance leaders should be able to identify the main factors influencing a UEBA decision when the system raises a high-risk flag. Using interpretable models or employing explanation methods after the fact helps organizations know if the alerts were a result of real behavioral changes rather than random biased associations in data features. Finally,robust governance isn't a single occurrence, but an ongoing conversation. Changes in the organizational environments lead to changes in behavior and the appearance of threats. So, governance must be accompanied by frequent audits of model effectiveness, assessments of fairness, and evaluation of the impact on operations. Staying abreast of UEBA is a means of not only fulfilling security objectives but also aligning with the values of the .

9.2 Ethical Implications of Biased Insider Threat Detection

In addition to regulatory compliance, organizations need to reflect on the ethical issues attendant on the deployment of behavioral surveillance systems equipped with machine learning models. Biased outcomes of the detection process can pose moral issues related to fairness, trust, and employee welfare that are not addressed by that initial legal permissibility. One ethical point is differential or unequal treatment of persons. This refers to a situation where a UEBA system keeps on assigning top risk levels to certain groups such as departments, job roles, or operational units, hence the personnel of those groups end up being subjected to more attention from the security team than the rest. Even without the identification of a firm threat, the numerous investigations may give rise to a perception of unfair treatment or marginalization.

Besides, behavioral monitoring programs are capable of producing pieces of work that might be linked to personal behavioral traits, communication networks, or even character of individuals indirectly through their usage of the work environment. There is an obvious risk in terms of privacy, therefore, a lack of proper protective measures or adequate disclosures regarding such use might cause employees to think of the monitoring as overstepping or being unjustified. Thus, ethical implementation of monitoring requires exploring the dividing line between legitimate security monitoring and excessive behavioral surveillance. What may be another repercussion of this is that a work environment may be affected adversely. When workers face constant surveillance at work through automated monitoring systems, they may change their behavior so as to be less productive and less cooperative. For example, they may stop opening certain resources that are vital for their work; stop sharing information with colleagues; or completely disallow any experiments with new methods, simply because they fear that the behaviors that are different from the norm will give rise to security alerts(Habboush & Elzaghmouri, 2025).

Another example of how bias in insider threat detection systems can harm trust in an organization is through consequences coming down to organizational trust. When employees in an organization believe that monitoring tools are unfairly targeting certain groups or roles, they may begin to doubt the legitimacy of their organization's security measures. Such a decrease in trust not only results in their unwillingness to cooperate with security measures but may also result in overall decline the effectiveness of insider threat reduction programs. To tackle these ethical challenges, organizations should develop fairness-aware governance systems and also be ready to openly justify the use of behavioral analytics. Also, various forms of ethical monitoring such as independent review committees, internal audit, and stakeholder discussions may be beneficial in associating monitoring with organizational values.

9.3 Organizational Governance Structures for UEBA Oversight

Establishing governance mechanisms that include technical, legal, and ethical perspectives is essential for effective management UEBA oversight. Security analytics must not be restricted to technical teams only because the consequences of automated monitoring extend well beyond cybersecurity operations. Instead, different facets of system oversight are handled by various function stakeholders whose involvement in governance structures should be organized by the company. Usually, a governance model for monitoring systems may involve the creation of a multi-disciplinary committee to oversee or evaluate behavioral monitoring systems. Typically, the committee members may be from cybersecurity, data governance, legal and compliance, human resources, and risk management. The collaborative perspective obtained through the involvement of various disciplines is as concerned with looking at monitoring technologies from a security effectiveness angle as from an ethical perspective. Another key component of governance is the adoption of model documentation and audit trails. The model must be comprehensive in its versioning to encompass training data sets, feature engineering, model architecture, evaluation metrics, and fairness assessments.

This kind of documentation helps the organization keep track of model changes and determine the source of bias. Besides documentation, conducting routine studies of performance disparities is part of the set of recommendations. The very first step in their performance disparity studies is organizations analyzing detection results to identify if different alert rates, false positives, or investigation outcomes among various user groups exist. When disparities are found, mitigation methods such as feature changes, threshold recalibration, or model retraining would become necessary. Besides, incident review may be another area that organizations would want to work on by setting up procedures to handle situations where automated monitoring led to an outcome being questioned. Consider the case of an employee who is frequently triggering alerts, which are, after investigation, automatically determined to be false positives. In response, governance teams may examine the case to determine whether it is the detection model or the operations procedures that should be revised. Responsible AI use in security is the type of support document that organizations look to/govt. that they back with governance efforts. These documents establish the rules of interaction for testing fairness, transparency in reporting, accountability, and human control. Ensuring that UEBA oversight aligns with broader AI governance, is quite straightforward, it means that the rules and expectations for insider threat detection are the same throughout the .

9.4 Governance Framework for Fair UEBA Deployment

We have proposed a governance framework in Table 3 to deliver a responsible usage of UEBA systems to the market. The table describes the major governance components and their corresponding functions in achieving the purposes of fairness and .

Table 3. Governance Components for Fair Deployment of UEBA Systems

Governance Component	Description	Role in Bias Mitigation
Data Governance	Policies governing data collection, retention, and processing of behavioral logs	Ensures monitoring data is collected and used responsibly without excessive surveillance
Model Documentation	Detailed records describing training data, model design, and evaluation results	Enables traceability and identification of potential sources of bias
Fairness Auditing	Periodic evaluation of detection outcomes across user groups	Detects disparities in alert rates or false positive rates
Cross-Functional Oversight	Governance committees including security, legal, and HR representatives	Provides multidisciplinary oversight of monitoring practices
Incident Review Processes	Structured review of cases involving questionable automated alerts	Helps identify model or policy adjustments needed to improve fairness
Transparency Policies	Communication of monitoring practices and safeguards to employees	Builds trust and reduces concerns about unfair surveillance

Achieving fairness in UEBA systems, as indicated by the governance elements in Table 3, involves much more than just implementing technical fixes. It also requires a level of organizational commitment to fostering responsible monitoring practices that are transparent and backed with oversight mechanisms. The use of insider threat detection systems in a responsible manner must be well directed by governance, compliance, and ethical standards. Security departments in enterprises are getting more use of automated machine learning. This, however, necessitates that organizations establish the controls that would clearly define not only the regulatory but also the human rights limits for these . In fact, there are some legal bases related to data protection and workplace monitoring that could set limits for organizations' use of behavioral data. On the one hand, according to research, by redesigning governance mechanisms that emphasize transparency, responsibility, fairness assessment, and participation of different functions, organizations can leverage UEBA systems to serve their legitimate interests while at the same time not allowing surveillance disparities arise. On the other hand, exceeding the commitments laid out in these laws means addressing an even larger array of ethical issues such as fairness, privacy, and trust. Having governance principles applied to the design and implementation of behavioral analytics systems, in the end, reinforces the validity as well as the effectiveness of insider threat detection .

10. FUTURE RESEARCH DIRECTIONS AND CONCLUSION

In this manuscript, we have considered the fact that the bias is UEBA system can happen at different stages of the analytical pipeline. For instance, at the data collection stage, one may end up emphasizing certain demographics more than others due to a richer telemetry generated by particular groups. Feature engineering may unknowingly make legitimate work patterns appear as suspicious by encoding in the operational differences. Machine learning models here might exacerbate statistical discrepancies especially when they treat rarity as risk. The decision to set the alert thresholds and the analysts' feedback loops may further enhance the disparities via investigative focus and label generation. Therefore, a complete picture of bias in insider threat detection can only be achieved by a detailed analysis of the full lifecycle of the monitoring system. The examples given earlier showed that the machine learning models produced very different results in terms of fairness even though they were all trained on the same data. Models that rely mostly on anomaly detection may identify unusual behavioral patterns and thus reveal rare users or activities. However, they might falsely accuse groups whose legitimate activities happen to be a deviation from the most common behavior pattern. Ensemble models that incorporate diverse complex feature interactions may surprise with higher predictive power and at the same time strike a better balance across different user groups especially if contextual features are used. These are just a few of the factors to consider when making a choice about which models to deploy in a real work environment - that is, assessing not only their ability to predict but also their level of fairness.

The second point equally important has been the continuing talk that comes up with ways that could be used to reduce the bias in user and entity behavior analytics (UEBA) systems. This is sure not a one-topic problem. As the main layer of defense, improving the dataset reduces the bias lying in the data by itself, making sure that a variety of real user behaviors are represented and the focus is not only on the majority behaviors. The second layer - algorithmic fairness - brings in learning targets to keep different operational groups from getting disparate results. While the post-processing calibration - the third layer - is the one that assists in different alert thresholds being set to different context baselines so that a similar level of good behavior does not result in unequal scrutiny. In fact, if organizations regularly check up on their Security Operations Centers, they not only have a chance to spot emergencies but plugging the gaps may also happen in tandem with the changing behavior of the environment. To cap it all, governance is the institutional support that is necessary for making sure that transparency, accountability, and ethical oversight are always maintained and it would be difficult to continue without it. These improvements should not be viewed as a panacea for the few major research problems still existing. The detection of insider threats is and probably will remain a great challenge because of issues with the availability of data, uncertainty of labels, and the complexity of human behavior. One of the major factors is that, unlike other machine learning applications, large, well-labeled datasets depicting actual malicious behavior are simply not available for insider threat detection. The majority of the research is carried out on synthetic datasets or simulated scenarios mainly because insider incidents are not only extremely rare but also confidential. As a result, research-derived models may overlook the complex behavioral patterns of real-world ations. For this reason, future investigations should also focus on how to assess fairness and detection performance when the ground truth is missing or unclear.

Developing context-based anomaly detection models that use organizational hierarchies in their learning method is an area where there is a lot of potential. This is in sharp contrast with the current modus operandi of comparing every user to a common baseline. These new models would be able to use a hierarchical view of behaviors in terms of department, role and project in order to precisely identify anomalies in behavior. In fact, work on hierarchical modeling, graph-based behavior analysis, and organizational network analytics may yield some of the insights that can help achieve this goal. Explainable security analytics is another major area of study. Most of the high-end detection models such as deep learning are black-box in nature and hence the reasoning behind their predictions is not given. In fact, this is the main challenge in fairness auditing and governance oversight despite these models exhibiting good predictive power. Developing UEBA models capable of explaining the reasons for a risk score will facilitate better fairness analysis and lead to more analyst trust in automated monitoring. Methods for explaining the role of each feature, extracting rules, and anomaly scoring are all techniques that can be used to move forward in this direction.

Another thrust of research is fairness-aware anomaly detection. Up until now most of what we know about fairness in machine learning has come from studies in demonstration classification where positive and negative labels are clearly marked. On the other hand, the paradigm of insider threat detection is continuously making use of unsupervised or semi-supervised techniques of anomaly detection. Implementing fairness concepts in these scenarios is going to be more difficult because anomalies are defined by their deviation from the expected statistical distribution rather than by being placed in a particular category of the ground truth. Hence new methods are needed to measure and then to address the problem of fairness imbalance in unsupervised anomaly detection. A related angle is the set of dynamic fairness monitoring systems which not only keep track of model outcomes but also evaluate them on the fly. Thoughfairness auditing has been somewhat disconnected from other activities, organizations can still establish fairness monitoring systems similar to leader-level alert rate, investigation result, and behavior drift charts dashboards. If any differences are found, they will be detected immediately, and automated actions such as threshold recalibration or retraining will be launched. The incorporation of fairness monitoring into the real-time SOC analytics platform is a key step in the embedding of responsible AI in cybersecurity.

Furthermore, privacy-enhanced machine learning might turn out to be a very important aspect of insider threat detection in the years to come. Whereas continuously collecting behavioral data leads to concerns about employee privacy and data protection issues, techniques such as federated learning, differential privacy, and secure multi-party computation, for instance, can be employed for behavioral model training with minimal exposure to the personal data of the individuals involved. Fairness and privacy challenge simultaneously will become a major focus of the work in this field. Bringing about fairness in insider threat detection will only be made possible through a collective effort that extends far beyond the realm of technical solutions. Technical solutions alone cannot adequately account for complex behavioral monitoring systems, and to make security tools not only align with the goal of security but also with human values, contributions from fields such as organizational psychology, human-computer interaction, ethics, law, and governance will be needed. One of the most effective ways to generate trust in security programs is through a deeper understanding of employee attitudes towards monitoring systems, as well as designing policies on transparency and implementing fairness safeguards accordingly.

The increasing prominence of the governance function in cybersecurity -analytics can be regarded as a trend that is likely to continue. Artificial intelligence, algorithmic accountability, and data protection regulatory frameworks are mushrooming worldwide. Consequently, organizations that have UEBA systems should prepare themselves for the possibility of being subjected to closer regulatory scrutiny on how these automated monitoring tools are being created, evaluated, and audited. Creating robust governance mechanisms from the very beginning will help the organizations not only to operate their insider threat detection abilities but also to comply with the regulatory changes that inevitably will come. In summary, it is essential to analyze the bias and disparate impacts in UEBA and insider threat detection systems as part of the cybersecurity environment of today. Behavioral analytics should not be used strictly as a means of identifying bad actors in highly complex enterprise environments but also as a tool for promoting fairness, transparency, and accountability. The organizations that take the hardest stance on the development of insider threat detection systems that are both highly effective and fair are those that conduct well-thought-out dataset construction, fairness-aware modeling, contextual calibration, continuous monitoring, and establish governance frameworks aimed at the responsible use of AI. Above all, the analysis here presents a very straightforward conclusion: security analytics should not only be geared towards a company's asset protection but also towards a proper comprehension and recognition of different kinds of employee behavior. If fairness becomes an essential part of UEBA design and governance, then organizations will not only have insider threat detection as their security defense weapon but also as an instrument for trustworthiness, ethicality, and responsible use of AI.

REFERENCES

Abualghanam, O., Alazzam, H., Qatawneh, M., Alazab, M., & Al Sharaiah, M. (2025). Elevating Mobile Security: An Ensemble Approach for Enhanced Malware Detection with M-iForest. *International Journal of Interactive Mobile Technologies, 19*(10), 129–151. Advance online publication. DOI: 10.3991/ijim.v19i10.51319

Abualhaj, M. M., Abu-Shareha, A. A., Al-Khatib, S. N., Alsaaidah, A. M., & Anbar, M. (2025). Improving firewall performance using hybrid of optimization algorithms and decision trees classifier. *IAES International Journal of Artificial Intelligence, 14*(4), 2839. Advance online publication. DOI: 10.11591/ijai.v14.i4.pp2839-2848

Abualhaj, M. M., Abu-Shareha, A. A., & Rateb, R. (2025). Enhancing intrusion detection systems with hybrid HHO-WOA optimization and gradient boosting machine classifier. *International Journal of Reconfigurable and Embedded Systems, 14*(2), 518. Advance online publication. DOI: 10.11591/ijres.v14.i2.pp518-526

Abualhaj, M. M., Al-Khatib, S., Al Shafi, N., Qaddara, I., & Hyassat, A. (2025). Utilizing Gray Wolf Optimization Algorithm in Malware Forensic Investigation. *Journal of Computational and Cognitive Engineering, 4*(4), 591–602. Advance online publication. DOI: 10.47852/bonviewJCCE52025053

Abualhaj, M. M., Al-Khatib, S. N., Abu-Shareha, A. A., Hyassat, A., & Daoud, M. S. (2025). Smart Firewall for Phishing Detection Powered by Bio-Inspired Algorithms. *Journal of Advances in Information Technology, 16*(11), 1529–1539. Advance online publication. DOI: 10.12720/jait.16.11.1529-1539

Abualhaj, M. M., Al-Khatib, S. N., Al Zyoud, M., Qaddara, I., & Anbar, M. (2025). Enhancing Intrusion Detection System Performance Using a Hybrid of Harris Hawks and Whale Optimization Algorithms. *Engineering. Technology and Applied Science Research, 15*(4), 24354–24361. Advance online publication. DOI: 10.48084/etasr.10919

Abualhaj, M. M., Al-Khatib, S. N., Al-Zyoud, M., Qaddara, I., Hiari, M. O., & Aldossary, S. M. A. (2025). Enhanced Network Communication Security Through Hybrid Dragonfly-Bat Feature Selection for Intrusion Detection. *The Journal of Communication, 20*(5). Advance online publication. DOI: 10.12720/jcm.20.5.607-618

Abualigah, L., Almomani, M. H., Alomari, S. A., Zitar, R. A., Migdady, H., Saleem, K., Snasel, V., Smerat, A., & Ezugwu, A. E. (2025). Optimizing Intrusion Detection in Wireless Sensor Networks via the Improved Chameleon Swarm Algorithm for Feature Selection. *IET Communications, 19*(1), e70029. Advance online publication. DOI: 10.1049/cmu2.70029

Abuowaida, S., Abu Owida, H., Shelash Mohammad, S. I., Alshdaifat, N., Abu Elsoud, E., Alazaidah, R., Vasudevan, A., & Alshurideh, M. T. (2025). Evidence Detection in Cloud Forensics: Classifying Cyber-Attacks in IaaS Environments using machine learning. *Data and Metadata, 4*, 699. Advance online publication. DOI: 10.56294/dm2025699

Ahmed, N., Rafiq, M., Rehman, M. A., Shaikh, T. S., Alqahtani, A. M., Khan, I., Imran, M., & Niazai, S. (2025). A dynamically consistent and time-efficient numerical design for the reaction diffusion model in three space dimensions. *Applied Mathematics in Science and Engineering*, *33*(1), 2495158. Advance online publication. DOI: 10.1080/27690911.2025.2495158

Al Abbadi, Y., Al-Ghraibah, A., & Altayeb, M. (2025). Tooth cavities detection based on digital image processing and artificial intelligence techniques. *Journal of Medical Engineering & Technology*. Advance online publication. DOI: 10.1080/03091902.2025.2574081 PMID: 41099352

Al-Dmour, R., Al-Dmour, H., Al-Dmour, A., Basheer Amin, E., & Al-Dmour, Y. (2025). *AI and big data-driven social media recruitment: the mediating role of talent acquisition and employee engagement in bank performance*. Digital Transformation and Society., DOI: 10.1108/DTS-02-2025-0042

Al-Falouji, M., Al Btoush, R., Abu Hajar, H., & Tarwaneh, B. (2025). Landslide Stabilization of Al-Adasiah Road Using Pile Wall Retaining System. *Jordan Journal of Civil Engineering*, *19*(4). Advance online publication. DOI: 10.14525/JJCE.v19i4.02

Al-Momani, M. M., Alqudah, T. A., Al Swiety, I. A., Mahrakani, N., Nassoura, M. B. A., & Al Attar, M. K. (2025). Integrating Artificial Intelligence (AI) and Business Intelligence (BI): A Framework for Improving Enterprise Performance. *TEM Journal, 14*(3). https://doi.org/DOI: 10.18421/TEM143-26

Al-Mousa, M., Amer, W., Abualhaj, M., Albilasi, S., Nasir, O., & Samara, G. (2025). Agile Proactive Cybercrime Evidence Analysis Model for Digital Forensics. *The International Arab Journal of Information Technology*, *22*(3). Advance online publication. DOI: 10.34028/iajit/22/3/15

Al-Okbi, N. K., Alomari, S. A., Hadi, W. J., Ajrash, A. S., Smerat, A., & Abualigah, L. (2025). Defending Digital Integrity: Advances in Media Forgery Analysis Research and Cybersecurity Development. *SN Computer Science*, *6*(8), 913. Advance online publication. DOI: 10.1007/s42979-025-04462-8

Al-Okbi, N. K., Alomari, S. A., Zitar, R. A., Smerat, A., Nazzal, M. A., & Abualigah, L. (2025). Integrating Multimodal Emotion Recognition with Deep Q-Learning for Adaptive Social Robot Interaction. *International Journal of Robotics and Control Systems*, *5*(4), 2265–2289. Advance online publication. DOI: 10.31763/ijrcs.v5i4.2055

Al-Suhimat, R. I., Mohammed Ai, N., Ibrahim, A., Maaitah, N. O., & Al-Dmour, N. A. (2024). Review of Security Challenges Encountered in Internet of Things Technology. *2nd International Conference on Cyber Resilience, ICCR 2024*. DOI: 10.1109/ICCR61006.2024.10533052

Al-znamat, F. O., Alsaaidah, A., & Abu-Shareha, A. A. (2025). Malware Detection Using a Modified Bat Algorithm for Feature Selection. *International Journal of Intelligent Engineering and Systems*, *18*(9), 885–899. Advance online publication. DOI: 10.22266/ijies2025.1031.56

Aldabbas, A., Baniata, L. H., Alsaaidah, B. A., Mustafa, Z., Alali, M., & Rateb, R. (2025). Artificial intelligence-driven method for the discovery and prevention of distributed denial of service attacks. *IAES International Journal of Artificial Intelligence*, *14*(1), 614. Advance online publication. DOI: 10.11591/ijai.v14.i1.pp614-628

Ali, A. M., Al-Qerem, A., Hassan, M. R., Abu-Khadrah, A., & Jarrah, M. (2025). Traffic Monitoring and Control System for Smart City Pollution Regulation Using IoT and Correlated Capsule Networks. *IEEE Access : Practical Innovations, Open Solutions, 13*, 46983–47003. Advance online publication. DOI: 10.1109/ACCESS.2025.3550966

Almomani, O., Arabiat, A., Al Tayeb, M., Almaiah, M. A., Obeidat, M., Aldhyani, T. H. H., Shehab, R., & Rowad, M. (2025). A Robust Model for Android Malware Detection via ML and DL classifiers. *Mesopotamian Journal of Big Data, 2025*. Advance online publication. DOI: 10.58496/MJBD/2025/017

Alnawayseh, S. E. A., Al-Sit, W. T., & Ghazal, T. M. (2022). Smart Congestion Control in 5G/6G Networks Using Hybrid Deep Learning Techniques. *Complexity, 2022*(1), 1781952. Advance online publication. DOI: 10.1155/2022/1781952

Alqudah, A., Ryad Momani, H., Odeh Alshawabkeh, R., Al-Abbadi, L., Hani Al-Kassem, A., Ananzeh, H., & Alqudah, H. (2025). *The impact of Cyber-Physical Systems on logistics sustainability: The role of smart energy monitoring as a mediator in improving energy efficiency*. EDPACS., DOI: 10.1080/07366981.2025.2596460

Alraba'nah, Y., Al-Sharaeh, S., & Al Hindi, G. (2025). Enhancing Intrusion Detection Using Hybrid Long Short-Term Memory and XGBoost. *Journal of Soft Computing and Data Mining, 6*(1). Advance online publication. DOI: 10.30880/jscdm.2025.06.01.016

Arabiat, A., & Altayeb, M. (2025). Driving behavior analytics: An intelligent system based on machine learning and data mining techniques. *Bulletin of Electrical Engineering and Informatics, 14*(3), 2055–2065. Advance online publication. DOI: 10.11591/eei.v14i3.9095

Arabiat, A., Altayeb, M., & Alkhrissat, T. (2025). Innovative AI Approaches for Concrete Strength Prediction: Towards Sustainable Buildings. *Civil Engineering and Architecture, 13*(6), 4254–4265. Advance online publication. DOI: 10.13189/cea.2025.130612

Arabiat, A., Altayeb, M., & Salama, S. (2025). Artificial intelligence-powered smart roads: Leveraging orange3 for traffic signs recognition. *IAES International Journal of Artificial Intelligence, 14*(5), 3816. Advance online publication. DOI: 10.11591/ijai.v14.i5.pp3816-3826

Arabiat, A. M., & Eljaafreh, Y. G. (2025). Intrusion Detection in Wireless Sensor Networks Using ML Based Classification of Denial of Service (DoS) Attacks. *The Journal of Communication, 20*(4). Advance online publication. DOI: 10.12720/jcm.20.4.501-514

Dar, A. A., Bhavithra, H. A., Awasthi, A. K., Sabha, S. U., Dar, J. G., Smerat, A., & Sindhuja, S. (2025). Inventory Optimization for Perishables: A Probabilistic and Fuzzy Modeling Approach. *Mathematical Modelling of Engineering Problems, 12*(8). Advance online publication. DOI: 10.18280/mmep.120825

Ebbini, M. M., Qtaishat, A. K., Aburub, F. A., & Jaradat, M. S. (2025). Impact of Ethical Fintech on Micro Entrepreneurs in Jordan. *International Journal of Advances in Soft Computing and Its Applications, 17*(3). Advance online publication. DOI: 10.15849/IJASCA.251130.10

Ghazal, T. M. (2025a). An IoT-Based Active Learning Convolutional Neural Networks Model for Predicting River Water Quality. *Journal of Soft Computing and Data Mining, 6*(1). Advance online publication. DOI: 10.30880/jscdm.2025.06.01.021

Ghazal, T. M. (2025b). Federated Learning for Intelligent Sensing and Navigation Technologies for 6G Communications. *Journal of Sensors, 2025*(1). DOI: 10.1155/js/3746147

Ghazal, T. M., Abu-Shareha, A., Mustafa, S. A., Ibrahim, A., & Ahmed, S. M. (2025). Privacy-Preserving Transformer-Based Meta-Learning Algorithm for Zero-Day Intrusion Detection in IoT-Enabled Smart Grids. *Journal of Internet Services and Information Security*, *15*(4), 76–84. Advance online publication. DOI: 10.58346/JISIS.2025.I4.006

Ghazal, T. M., Abualhaj, M., Ahmed, A. A., Al-Tarawni, M. A. M., & Maghrabi, L. A. (2025). Federated Deep Graph Neural Network Algorithm for Real-Time Intrusion Detection in Heterogeneous IoT Systems. *Journal of Internet Services and Information Security*, *15*(4), 484–497. Advance online publication. DOI: 10.58346/JISIS.2025.I4.035

Ghazal, T. M., Awouda, A. E., Hasan, M. K., Rahman, A. H. A., Islam, S., Saeed, R. A., Elshafie, H., Iqbal, A., & Hussein, A. H. (2025). Knowledge Learning for Securing Workflow Scheduling Algorithm in Mobile Edge Computing. *Mobile Networks and Applications*, *30*(3-4), 395–413. Advance online publication. DOI: 10.1007/s11036-025-02465-6

Ghazal, T. M., Hasan, M. K., Abdul Wahab, A. N., Ibrahim, A., Khan, W. A., Raza, N. Z., Atta, A., & Mago, B. (2022). Towards Privacy Provisioning for Internet of Things (IoT). *International Conference on Cyber Resilience, ICCR 2022*. DOI: 10.1109/ICCR56254.2022.9995916

Ghazal, T. M., Hasan, M. K., Hussein, A. H., Pandey, B. K., Ahmad, M., Safie, N., & Cascone, L. (2025). Federated Learning With Small and Large Models With Privacy-Preserving Data Space for Holographic Internet of Things in Consumer Electronics. *IEEE Transactions on Consumer Electronics*, *71*(2), 5259–5274. Advance online publication. DOI: 10.1109/TCE.2025.3573033

Ghazal, T. M., Hasan, M. K., Khairy, S. O. F., Mokhtar, U. A., Islam, S., Saeed, R. A., Ahmed, N., & Abdullah, M. (2025). Lightweight signcryption scheme for Securing wearable sensor observed health data sharing in internet of medical things paradigm. *Scientific Reports*, *15*(1), 40989. Advance online publication. DOI: 10.1038/s41598-025-24687-0 PMID: 41266478

Ghazal, T. M., Hasan, M. K., Raju, K. N., Khan, M. A., Alshamayleh, A., Bhatt, M. W., & Ahmad, M. (2025). Data Space Privacy Model with Federated Learning Technique for Securing IoT Communications in Autonomous Marine Vehicles. *Journal of Intelligent & Robotic Systems*, *111*(3), 84. Advance online publication. DOI: 10.1007/s10846-025-02298-1

Ghoneim, R. S., Taiyara, R., & Maghaireh, Z. N. (2025). Machine Learning-Enhanced Building Information Modeling (BIM) for Sustainable Urban Planning. *Civil Engineering and Architecture*, *13*(3), 2171–2184. Advance online publication. DOI: 10.13189/cea.2025.131301

Gul, A., Khan, F., Farooq, M., Javaid, A., Hussain, Z., & Elzaghmouri, B. (2025). STATISTICAL MODELING AND PREDICTION OF PANDEMIC USING CLASSICAL AND MACHINE LEARNING APPROACH. *Pakistan Journal of Statistics*, *41*(3).

Habboush, A., & Elzaghmouri, B. (2025). Methodological integration of machine learning and metaheuristics for seismic risk assessment of irregular buildings. *Asian Journal of Civil Engineering*. DOI: 10.1007/s42107-025-01571-w

Haider, Z. A., Ullah, I., Shareha, A. A., Nasimov, R., & Memon, S. A. (2026). Artificial Intelligence (AI)-Enabled Unmanned Aerial Vehicle (UAV) Systems for Optimizing User Connectivity in Sixth-Generation (6G) Ubiquitous Networks. *Computers, Materials & Continua*, *86*(1), 1–16. Advance online publication. DOI: 10.32604/cmc.2025.071042

Hanandeh, A., Alfreijat, S. Y., Qutieshat, R. J., Alsha'ar, H. Y., Kilani, Q. A. L., & Saleem Khasawneh, M. A. (2025). Implementing AI Accuracy, Learning Rate, Inference Time on enhancing Big Data Analysis and Strategic Plan. *Data and Metadata*, *4*, 637. Advance online publication. DOI: 10.56294/dm2025637

Hiari, M., Alraba'nah, Y., & Qaddara, I. (2025). A Deep Learning-Based Intrusion Detection System using Refined LSTM for DoS Attack Detection. *Engineering. Technology and Applied Science Research*, *15*(4), 25627–25633. Advance online publication. DOI: 10.48084/etasr.11499

Hussain, K., Ali, E. M., Hussain, W., Raza, A., & Elkamchouchi, D. H. (2025). Robust OTFS-ISAC for Vehicular-to-Base Station End-to-End Sensing and Communication. *Electronics (Basel)*, *14*(21), 4340. Advance online publication. DOI: 10.3390/electronics14214340

Hyassat, A. S., Abu Zayed, R. E., Al Khateeb, E. A., Shalaldeh, A., Abdelhamied, M. M., & Qaddara, I. (2025). Unveiling Cyber Threats: An In-Depth Study on Data Mining Techniques for Exploit Attack Detection †. *Engineering Proceedings*, *104*(1), 28. Advance online publication. DOI: 10.3390/engproc2025104028

Iskandarani, M. Z. (2025). Energy and path loss analysis of wireless sensor networks on a robotic body (WSRobotic). *Bulletin of Electrical Engineering and Informatics*, *14*(3). Advance online publication. DOI: 10.11591/eei.v14i3.9354

Jaradat, S., Acharya, N., Shivshankar, S., Alhadidi, T. I., & Elhenawy, M. (2025). AI for Data Quality Auditing: Detecting Mislabeled Work Zone Crashes Using Large Language Models. *Algorithms*, *18*(6), 317. Advance online publication. DOI: 10.3390/a18060317

Ju, W., Altimari, U. S., Kumar, R., Pattanaik, A., Sarangi, H., Gupta, D., Rao, V. N. B., Abduvalieva, D., Mann, V. S., Mhohamdi, H., Smerat, A., & Abumalek, A. (2025). Robust classification frameworks for oxide nanomaterials assisted by machine learning. *Chemical Papers*. Advance online publication. DOI: 10.1007/s11696-025-04471-0

Keote, R., Katre, S., Keote, M., Chiwande, S., Das, A., Smerat, A., Golar, P., Diwan, P., & Kediya, S. (2025). An integrated IoT–AI framework for intelligent structural performance prediction and real-time strength forecasting in large-scale dome trusses. *Asian Journal of Civil Engineering*. DOI: 10.1007/s42107-025-01586-3

Khalayleh, Y. A. S., Mohammad, S. I., Al Louzi, N. S., Baniata, M., Hassan, M., Safaqah, M. A., Vasudevan, A., & Alshurideh, M. T. (2025). Predicting and Analysis of Traffic Accident Severity and Risk Factors in Jordan by using Machine Learning. *Applied Mathematics & Information Sciences*, *19*(6), 1419–1426. Advance online publication. DOI: 10.18576/amis/190615

Khaled Abdullah, S., & Qawasmeh, R. (2025). *Navigating the ethical and legal risks of AI marketing in Jordanian SMEs*. EDPACS., DOI: 10.1080/07366981.2025.2600205

Louati, H., Arooj, R., Niazi, A. U. K., Dalam, M. E. E., Almazah, M. M. A., & Smerat, A. (2025). Finite-time fuzzy control strategy for nonlinear MASs with actuator faults and deception attacks. *AIMS Mathematics*, *10*(9), 20113–20139. Advance online publication. DOI: 10.3934/math.2025899

Mostafa, S. A., Hasan, D. F., Abdul-Jabar, M. A., Hussein, A. H., & Mustapha, A. (2025). An Ensemble Learning Model for Multi-Type Cancer Prediction in Clinical Diagnostic Decision Support Systems. *Journal of Soft Computing and Data Mining*, *6*(1). Advance online publication. DOI: 10.30880/jscdm.2025.06.01.015

Otair, M., Qawaqzeh, F. A., Alomari, S. A., Zitar, R. A., Migdady, H., Saleem, K., Smerat, A., Alsoud, A. R., & Abualigah, L. (2025). Enhanced Arithmetic Optimization Algorithm for Intrusion Detection in Wireless Sensor Networks. *International Journal of Communication Systems*, *38*(10), e70122. Advance online publication. DOI: 10.1002/dac.70122

Qaddara, I., & Alraba'nah, Y. (2025). Enhancing Requirements Classification Using Machine Learning Techniques. *SN Computer Science*, *6*(6), 649. Advance online publication. DOI: 10.1007/s42979-025-04158-z

Qawasmeh, S., Habboushb, A., Elzaghmouri, B., Kharma, Q., & Albalawneh, D. (2025). Hybrid Convolutional Neural Network-Based Intrusion Detection System for Secure IoT Networks. *Tikrit Journal of Engineering Sciences*, *32*(SP1), 1–11. Advance online publication. DOI: 10.25130/tjes.sp1.2025.2

Ramesh, J. V. N., Nimma, D., Dasari, R., Chaudhari Rane, D., AlGhamdi, A., Rao, K. B. V. B., Haider, S. A., Kuzieva, N., & Jangir, P. (2025). Safe and Reliable Two-Stage Online Offloading Algorithm for Transportation Cyber-Physical Systems. *IEEE Transactions on Intelligent Transportation Systems*, *26*(9), 14313–14322. Advance online publication. DOI: 10.1109/TITS.2025.3539934

Raza, M. A., Karim, A., Alqarni, M., Al-Khasawneh, M. A., Jumani, T. A., Aman, M., & Masud, M. I. (2025). An Intelligent Long Short-Term Memory-Based Machine Learning Model for the Potential Assessment of Global Hydropower Capacity in Sustainable Energy Transition and Security. *Energies*, *18*(13), 3324. Advance online publication. DOI: 10.3390/en18133324

Saeed, N. M. S. E., Ibrahim, A., Ali, L., Al-Dmour, N. A., Mohammed, A. S., & Ghazal, T. M. (2024). Unveiling the Landscape of Machine Learning and Deep Learning Methodologies in Network Security: A Comprehensive Literature Review. *2nd International Conference on Cyber Resilience, ICCR 2024*. DOI: 10.1109/ICCR61006.2024.10533066

Sardar, R., Anees, T., Al-Shamayleh, A. S., Mehmood, E., Khalil, W., Akhunzada, A., & Shaikh, F. S. (2025). Challenges in detecting security threats in WoT: A systematic literature review. *Artificial Intelligence Review*, *58*(7), 196. Advance online publication. DOI: 10.1007/s10462-025-11176-z

Shah, R. K., Hasan, M. K., Islam, S., Khan, A., Ghazal, T. M., & Khan, A. N. (2022). Detect Phishing Website by Fuzzy Multi-Criteria Decision Making. *2022 1st International Conference on AI in Cybersecurity, ICAIC 2022*. DOI: 10.1109/ICAIC53980.2022.9897036

Shamaylah, N., Ibrahim Mohammad, S., Al Oraini, B., Yaseen Al-Gaafreh, J. M., Mosallam Alqahtani, M., Vasudevan, A., Shlash Mohammad, A. A., & Ahmmad Hunitie, M. F. (2025). Data-Driven Decision-Making for Employee Training and Development in Jordanian Public Institutions. *Data and Metadata*, *4*, 886. Advance online publication. DOI: 10.56294/dm2025886

Shambour, Q. Y., Al-Zyoud, M., & Hussein, A. H. (2025). FROM DATA TO DIAGNOSIS: KNOWLEDGE-DRIVEN, EXPLAINABLE AI FOR RELIABLE EARLY AUTISM DETECTION. *Interdisciplinary Journal of Information, Knowledge, and Management*, *20*, 032. Advance online publication. DOI: 10.28945/5652

Sharma, K. P., Hussain, R., Jaharadak, A. A., Trawnih, A. A., Verma, D., Dasi, S., & Pant, S. (2025). Hybrid Convolutional Neural Network for Robust Attack Detection in Wireless Sensor Networks. *Internet Technology Letters*, *8*(6), e650. Advance online publication. DOI: 10.1002/itl2.650

Ullah, N., Al-Rahmi, W. M., Alblehai, F., Fernando, Y., Alharbi, Z. H., Zhanbayev, R., Al-Adwan, A. S., & Habes, M. (2025). Corrigendum to "Blockchain-powered grids: Paving the way for a sustainable and efficient future" [Heliyon Volume 10, Issue 10, May 2024, Article e31592] (Heliyon (2024) 10(10), (S2405844024076230), ()). In *Heliyon* (Vol. 11, Number 13). https://doi.org/DOI: 10.1016/j.heliyon.2024.e31592

Vasudevan, A., Albinaa, T. A., Mohammad, S. I., Sharmila, E., Raja, N., Soon, E. E. H., Alshurideh, M. T., & Al-Adwan, A. S. (2024). Bidirectional LSTM for Electronic Product Recommendation. *Applied Mathematics & Information Sciences*, *18*(6), 1443–1453. Advance online publication. DOI: 10.18576/amis/180621

Vasudevan, A., Tamilmani, K. T., Mohammad, S. I., Sridheepika, V. S., Raja, N., Soon, E. E. H., Nagaraj, S., & Al-Adwan, A. S. (2025). Voices of Concern: Contemplations on Socioeconomic, Ethical, and Developmental Impacts of AI. *Applied Mathematics & Information Sciences*, *19*(1), 221–232. Advance online publication. DOI: 10.18576/amis/190119

Chapter 12
Approaches to Validating and Monitoring Artificial Intelligence Models Used in Security

Khaled Ezzeldin
Rochester Institute of Technology, Dubai, UAE

Mohammad Rustom Al Nasar
http://orcid.org/0000-0002-8856-9394
American University in the Emirates, UAE

ABSTRACT

The chapter under discussion goes through methods for verifying and supervising AI models utilized in security because of various applications. The chapter covers validation topics such as training and testing controls, measurement of bias, explainability techniques, and performance benchmarking of models in evolving threat environments. On the other hand, it gives examples of continuous monitoring practices like model drift detection, customer feedback loops, audit logging, and human oversight. Moreover, the chapter warns about the risks of false negatives, reduction in performance, and undesired operational consequences in the long run. By combining assurance that comes from technical means with governance, and accountability, the chapter deliver a comprehensive method for sustaining the trustworthiness of AI security solutions. It guides organizations to strike the right mix between innovation, operational effectiveness, and regulatory compliance in AI-enabled security operations.

1. INTRODUCTION

Initially, the introduction of AI in cybersecurity was to address the major limitation: without the help of AI, human analysts alone will not be able to deal with the scale, speed, and complexity of digital threats today. At the very beginning, security systems mostly used signatures that were fixed, rule-based filters, and manually compiled blacklists along with deterministic correlation logic. While these methods can still be effective in certain cases, they are not able to identify new, polymorphic, or stealthy types of attacks(Alabdallat et al., 2025). Due to the fact that enterprises are primarily housed on cloud platforms, mobile devices, industrial control networks, and remote working arrangements with

DOI: 10.4018/979-8-2600-2870-4.ch012

the result that security traffic has become too large and changeable for human analysis only. Machine learning delivered a solution to this problem by detecting suspicious behaviors based on the analysis of historical data. Among other applications, supervised learning models have been extensively used for spam filtering, phishing detection, network intrusion detection, malicious URL identification, and malware classification(Ghazal et al., 2022).

Unsupervised learning algorithms are typically employed in the detection of anomalies, insider threats, and user profiling. Deep neural networks have significantly improved the effectiveness of solutions in such areas as binary analysis, image-based CAPTCHA detection, and script or command sequence analysis. Graph learning and models based on transformers are now able to handle highly complicated tasks like finding relationships between entities, predicting the path of attacks, and analyzing the threat landscape. This revelation has dramatically changed security operations. Instead of merely alerting users of the presence of known indicators, AI-enabled security solutions can also analyze the malicious behavior, situational information, and patterns of new threats to deduce the intention of the attacker(A. M. Arabiat & Eljaafreh, 2025). This intelligence embedded in these models is exactly what results in their paradox. On the one hand, a greater level of sophistication can lead to less transparency, higher challenges in testing the models when subjected to adversarial conditions, and increased vulnerability to problems linked with data quality and data drift. Consequently, as more AI is embedded into detection and response operations, the more obvious is the need for thorough validation. For instance, a model that is tested offline and highly effective may turn out to be a failure in production if the attackers change their ways of attacks, there are telemetry pipeline failures, or attackers deliberately exploit the model's (Hasan et al., 2024)s.

1.1 Importance of Model Validation for Security-Critical AI Systems

In security, “model validation” is understood as a methodical way of ensuring that an AI model has the qualities, safety, and robustness necessary for a specific security operation. In fact, it extends way beyond just a simple check of whether a classifier got a high score on a test dataset or not. If harmful activities are wrongly overlooked, the consequences might be huge such as being a victim of a ransomware attack, having one's credentials stolen, moving infectiously and stealing data. Meanwhile, if overproduction of false alarms is allowed, analysts will be getting very tired, incident response resources may run out and people might stop trusting the automated systems. In this way, testing becomes a very significant tool for mapping model outputs to the actual operational risks in the real (Yaseen et al., 2025). Besides that, models must be evaluated not only for their accuracy but also for the manner in which they behave under attack, with noisy or unknown inputs. For example, among other things it involves determining whether a model is prone to overfitting, whether it produces outputs with low variance, whether it can sustain its level of performance while multi types of attacks, and whether it is reliable even when the quality of the input data deteriorates. Often, the degree to which a model is stable and interpretable internally influence its usefulness just as much as the detection rate does. Another reason why validation is important is that security data almost always changes(Akram et al., 2024). Of course, threat vectors are constantly evolving. Besides threat actors changing their methods of operation, infrastructures, ways of encoding payloads, and sequences of behaviors, at the same time defensive tools are also being modified which, as a result, changes the set of types of telemetry data available to models. So, a model that has been validated only at the development phase certainly should not be regarded as stable or valid at the same time forever. That is why it is security AIs that are viewed as living organisms which need continuous validation procedures. Consequently, security AI validation is a process that starts with pre-deployment but it is the monitoring that makes the model valid after (Zraiqat et al., 2025)t.

1.2 Risks of Unvalidated AI Models in Security Infrastructure

Unvalidated or poorly validated security models can cause different types of risks for organizations, including ignoring threats as the obvious one. When a model cannot handle or generalize the examples of attacks it has never seen yet, it may even fail to recognize the new or slightly differently changed variants of malware, phishing campaigns or network intrusions. Suchmistakes are quite dangerous as AI systems generally mislead people just by their high level of sophistication(Khaled Abdullah & Qawasmeh, 2025). Organizations may become very confident and reduce human checking only because they believe that the intelligent automation is correctly operating even if its performance has been quietly deteriorating. Another major risk is operational instability. Security environments are inherently very noisy and changing all the time, it is often the case that logs are only partially saved, fewer and fewer timestamps are synchronized, features can be missing, and changes to the infrastructure can even give data points new meanings(Alnawayseh et al., 2022). If a model is deployed without having been validated against these conditions, it will be behaving oddly. Altering the telemetry scheme in even the slightest way can be sufficient for input distributions to the model to change so that many of the model's mistakes can occur. But the risk of giving adversaries an opportunity to exploit the vulnerability is another reason to be concerned. The offender can analyze the pattern of the model's reaction to discover thresholds and weak points and then concoct inputs that are purposely designed to be undetectable. If a model has not gone through a review of its adversarial robustness, it can be outwitted by cleverly designed payloads and behavioral mimicry(Aldaaja et al., 2025). In those cases, the AI system is no longer a control but a vulnerability. Besides that, governance and responsibility issues also arise. Automatically making security decisions by using non-transparent or unrecorded models may make audit processes a nightmare, especially for industries that are regulated. When a system unfairly denies legitimate users access, misclassifies business activities, or is incapable of detecting breaches, stakeholders will definitely want explanations. A company that lacks validation documentation, performance records, and monitoring logs may be unable to explain why the trust was placed in the (Ghazal, Awouda, et al., 2025).

1.3 Conceptual Framework of AI Model Lifecycle in Security Environments

In order to address these issues, AI models for security should not simply be considered as detached technical instruments. Or, they may be seen as just one part in a whole life cycle. This life cycle begins with identifying a problem and collecting data. It is at this point that security teams together decide what kind of security issue (e.g., intrusion detection, malware classification, user behavior analytics, or fraud prevention) they want to deal with and which telemetry sources can be of use for power. The next step is to prepare the data: cleaning, parametrizing, annotating, and dividing it into training, validation, and testing sets. At the same time, the modeling step includes the actions: selecting an algorithm, training, hyperparameter optimization, and performance comparison(Qader Ismail Alnajem et al., 2024). After that, the model is put through layers of validation to check whether it can be trusted: statistical performance evaluation, robustness tests, failure mode analysis, lumper calibration, explainability verification, and scenario stress testing. Actually, deployment of model lifecycle in security scenario is a continuation of the cycle, since post-deployment monitoring activities are at least as important as the development ones. Once the enterprise has made the model go live, the company should keep an eye on the model's output constantly: quality, alert volumes, drift signals, false positive dose rates, feature stability, analyst's feedback. Data distribution changes or adversary condition variations may be the signs that a model needs to be retrained or recalibrated. More advanced companies produce monitoring feedback loops of production as inputs to even new development cycles leading to continuous improvement rather than a single release only. Market conditions change rapidly especially for security where the evolution of the threat situation is constant. Hence, from a lifecycle perspective, this is even more true for security. Besides being good from the lifecycle angle, it also fully complies with the governance requirements. It goes hand in hand with connecting technical validation to operational accountability. Please, refer to Figure 1 for a visual representation of this (Alnawayseh et al., 2023). This chapter contributes a lifecycle-based validation and monitoring framework for AI models used in security systems. The framework connects pre-deployment validation, dataset quality checks, robustness testing, drift monitoring, model retraining governance, human oversight, and audit documentation into a continuous security-AI assurance process.

Figure 1. AI Security Model Lifecycle and Validation Pipeline

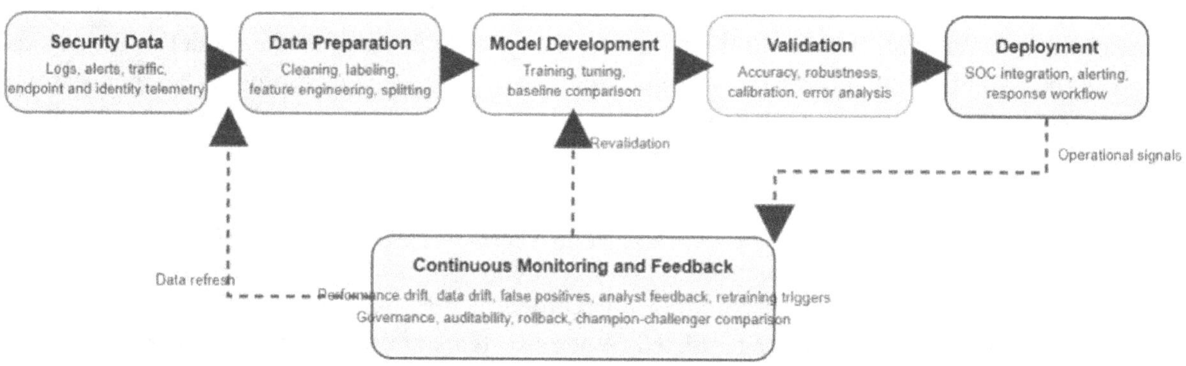

1.4 Overview of Monitoring Requirements for Operational AI Models

Validation is essentially the work that monitoring does in an operational environment. Data drift, concept drift, changes in the infrastructure, changes in the users' behavior, or the countermeasures implemented by the attackers are some of the factors that can lead to loss in accuracy over time. Hence, normal operations require evaluation on a regular basis to check whether the model that has been rolled out is still functioning according to the standards set. Performance, input, and decisions are the three aspects that monitoring in the deployment phase of AI-enhanced security systems should cover. When we say performance monitoring, we imply observation of various metrics including precision, recall, false positive rate, false negative rate, and the quality of alert prioritization over time. Data monitoring is all about recognizing when the distributions of features in the new data differ from those in the training and validation . Decisionmonitoring in a way examines the influence that model outputs have on changing analyst work, reprioritizing responses, and the resulting business impacts(Almajed et al., 2022).

A good monitoring system, aside from being well planned, should also have clear thresholds and be ready for escalation if necessary. When the drift signal exceeds allowed levels, or there are too many false positives, or the general model confidence is very much decreased, then the system must produce signals for human evaluation. The human factor here is made up of analysts, data scientists, and security engineers. They decide collectively whether the model should be retrained, rolled back, or supplemented with new rules. Sometimes, for the most advanced cases, shadow models and champion-challenger testing are used to evaluate different models before a full switch of the existing one is done. Strategically, it is very clear that one cannot simply rely on AI in the security domain. Rather, by providing evidence, trust is gradually built over time. Initially, through validation, AI is considered suitable or trustworthy; subsequently, through monitoring, AI's good status is preserved and it is correctly adjusted to various facets of the real world. That is precisely why any reputable cybersecurity AI framework must view validation and monitoring as very crucial and closely related elements of secure (Vasudevan et al., 2024).

Figure 2. Continuous Monitoring Architecture for AI-Driven Security Systems

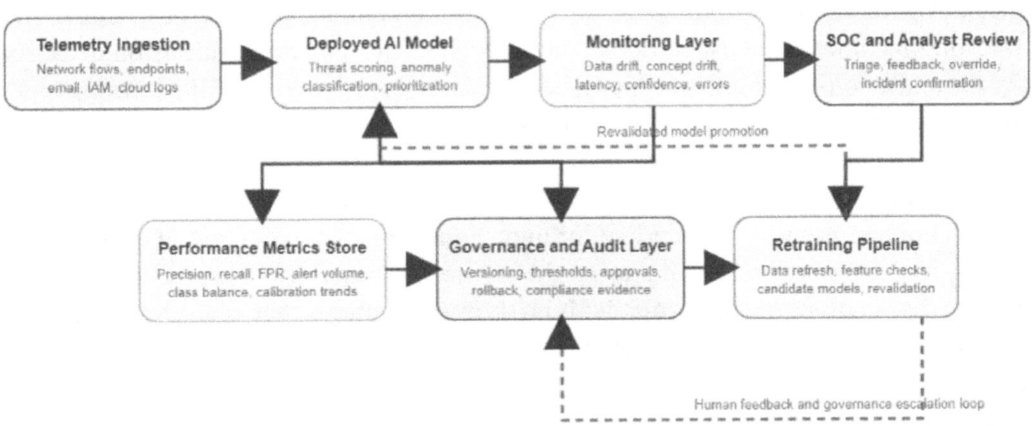

2. ARTIFICIAL INTELLIGENCE MODELS COMMONLY USED IN SECURITY APPLICATIONS

2.1 Machine Learning Models for Intrusion Detection Systems

Prior research on AI model validation in cybersecurity can be organized into eight themes: AI-based intrusion detection, malware and phishing classification, model validation methods, continuous model monitoring, data and concept drift, adversarial robustness, explainable AI, and governance of operational AI security systems. These themes show that security models should be evaluated not only by offline accuracy but also by resilience, stability, interpretability, operational reliability, and post-deployment accountability. Machinelearning (ML) models are one of the various types besides the conventional ones that are very often used in Intrusion Detection Systems (IDSs). Intrusion detection is the act of recognizing any unauthorized access, the spread of malware or any suspicious behavior by monitoring network traffic or host activities and it is also called intrusion detection. It was a common practice for IDS to depend on signature-based detection where prediction patterns were compared to known signatures of attacks. Indeed, signature-based approaches do very well against known threats but still are incapable of detecting new or modified attacks. Machine learning techniques get around this limitation by learning from historical data to identify behavioral patterns. Intrusion detection workhorse has for a long time been supervised learning algorithms(Abualhaj, Al-Khatib, Al-Zyoud, et al., 2025). Decision trees, random forests, logistic regression, support vector machines, and gradient boosting classifiers are the most practical examples for intrusion detection. One point that isn't changed across the majority of these techniques is the utilization of various features as an input which are extracted from network packets, flows, or system logs, namely connection time, protocol type, packet size statistics, and unusual command sequences, etc. After training on labeled datasets, they classify incoming events in real-time. A random forest is an example of a model that combines several decision trees for improving prediction accuracy and reducing overfitting(Vasudevan, Tamilmani, et al., 2025).

Cases of high-dimensional security data, where it is very difficult to separate normal and malicious actions since the boundary is quite complex, are perfectly fitted for support vector machines. Similarly, gradient boosting methods, such as XGBoost, have become very popular in intrusion detection due to their ability to handle non-linear relationships among data. Unsupervised machine learning methods can be applied to intrusion detection only when there is no availability of labeled data. Anomaly detection was performed with clustering techniques such as k-means and DBSCAN that group similar instances in which events that differ significantly from the normal behavior clusters are considered potential suspects. These techniques are very appropriate for unrecognized attack-types and insider threats. But on the other hand, it is extremely essential that machine learning-based IDS systems are very well tested as network data distributions are very volatile. It is the traffic patterns that keep changing continuously due to new applications, services, or user behaviors. Therefore, without having a mechanism of continuous validation and update, a model trained on past data is most likely to produce false alarms or miss genuine (Dara Singh et al., 2025).

2.2 Deep Learning Architectures for Malware and Threat Detection

Deep learning models have opened up a much wider range of opportunities for security analytics. Traditional machine learning techniques mainly rely on features crafted manually but deep learning systems can extract deeply-layered features from data automatically. This is why deep learning systems are great at handling unstructured and complex data which in fact is the very type of data seen in cybersecurity like executables, system call sequences, network flows, behavioral patterns etc. CNN-based models are a kind of malware classification and binary program analysis. There are times when malware executables are first converted into grayscale images with pixel intensity representing byte value and then a CNN is used for determining the presence of malicious code by means of analyzing images. Besides, CNNs have also been used for traffic pattern matrices study and detection of DDoS attacks and botnets' command-and-control activities(Duraimurugan et al., 2025).

It is especially the RNNs and LSTM variants that excel at handling ordered data. Because security events like command executions, system calls, or authentication attempts are often sequences,

LSTM networks can factor in the temporal aspects of such sequences and pattern out malicious activity. Last but not least, cybersecurity analytics have only recently started widely adopting transformers. Besides their success in natural language processing, these architectures also provide the capability to memorize long-term dependencies when modeling sequences. As soon as transformers are deployed on security logs or threat intelligence, they expose connections which are not only contextual but also demonstrate almost invisible multi-component attack patterns.

2.3 Graph-Based AI Models for Security Relationship Analysis

In the security graph metaphor, nodes might stand for users, devices, IP addresses, domains, or files, while edges illustrate the interaction or relationships like logging-in, network connection, or file transfer. Security can find suspicious patterns that signify illicit behaviors by looking at these structures. Graph neural networks (GNNs) have become one of the best tools for relational data modeling. GNNs work by spreading information around the nodes of the graph, thereby giving the model a chance to learn the relationships between the entities(Biswas et al., 2025). Take the case where a device is seen communicating with a number of malicious domains. GNN will infer that the device is probably compromised. Similarly, a sudden interaction of a user account with several sensitive systems, which also deviates from the normal behavior pattern, can be detected by graph-based analysis. Graph-based tools also excel at the task of uncovering the attacker's lateral movements inside the enterprise network. Lateral movement is the series of steps taken by attackers after compromising in order to escalate privileges and/or gain access to the most sensitive data. Multi-step attack paths may be revealed through graph analysis, while event-based models alone probably will not have the ability to detect such complex attacks. The problem with the validation of graph-based techniques is also rooted in the fact that security graphs are very dynamic. Nodes and edges keep on being added because the occurrence of new events, and deception through the creation of false relationships is not unheard of by attackers. A good validation will test the ability of the model to respond to the change of the graph structure and also its ability to maintain its performance as new entities are added(Sardar et al., 2025).

2.4 Reinforcement Learning Models for Adaptive Security Defense

Reinforcement Learning (RL) is a learning paradigm that is different in a fundamental way from supervised and unsupervised learning. The distinctive feature of reinforcement learning is that rather than learning from a given dataset, an RL agent learns by interacting with the environment through a sequence of observations, actions, and rewards. The security environment is represented in reinforcement learning frameworks as a collection of states, actions, and rewards. A state can characterize, for example, the security posture of a network, vulnerabilities that have been identified, active alerts, or system configurations. Examples of actions are blocking a certain type of traffic, isolating a device, patching a vulnerability, or escalating an alert to analysts(Abualhaj, Al-Khatib, Al Zyoud, et al., 2025). The agent is rewarded when actions taken are successful and, on the contrary, penalized when attacks are successful or legitimate activities are hindered citing disruption. The agent through a process of trial and error, gradually learns and approximates a policy which tells him the right action to take given a particular state of the environment. That is why this method of agent training is suited for the defense of a system that is subject to changing attacker tactics. RL-based systems modify their defense strategies in response to new attack behaviors that they observe. One particular area where reinforcement learning has been experimented on is in automated intrusion response. What happens here is that the RL system is not reduced to a state where it only follows rules that it has been hardcoded with. Instead, through learning, the system understands when irregular traffic needs to be blocked, infected hosts isolated, or when extra user authentication is required. Thereby a balance between security and operational disruption is sought and reached. Even though security has the potential to benefit greatly from the use of reinforcement learning, the technology is still in its infancy. One major hurdle is to come up with realistic training environments. On top of that, it is equally important to validate RL agents to ensure that they do not learn something dangerous like policies that cause disruption to legitimate users(Abualhaj, Al-Khatib, Al Shafi, et al., 2025).

2.5 Challenges in Validating AI Models in Security Contexts

Despite a great deal of promise that they hold, AI models face a number of obstacles when it comes to validation in real-world security situations. The most striking difference between AI models and traditional software systems is that AI models are probabilistic and data-dependent. The details of how they will behave are entirely dependent on the data that was used to train them as well as the scenarios that they are run under. Data imbalance is one of the foremost challenges. For the most part, datasets used in security contexts are overwhelmingly filled with benign events and only a handful of malicious one's present. To give an instance, malware or other malicious activity may be far less than 1% in traffic datasets. This means that we can attribute the wrong performance at the end of the day because the models may fail in identifying the rare yet very important attack events despite having a decent overall accuracy. Hence, the reason why validation should include metrics like recall, precision and false negative rate along with accuracy(Al-Mousa et al., 2025).

Concept drift is another challenge. Over time, the data distribution underlying the representation of security may also change due to factors such as the introduction of new applications or network changes as well as the changing tactics of the attackers. In other words, models based on historical data will no longer be effective if these changes are ignored. Therefore, there is a need for continuous monitoring along with periodic re-training to maintain the model's . At the same time, adversarial manipulation is a very grave issue in terms of the validation of AI models. A user with malicious intent may go to extreme lengths in order to hide their attacks from a machine learning system(Shlash Mohammad et al., 2025). For example, a creator of a malware may restructure the code in the way that it evades detection. At the same time, a phishing attacker can modify the text or email in a way that it cannot be recognized by an email classifier. Validation, therefore, should encompass adversarial testing, too, to see if the models are able to withstand such attempts of evasion. Finally, the problem becomes even more complicated when the concept of validation is thought of in operational terms. Models must be able to function in real time with minimal latency, besides being compatible with the existing security infrastructure and having the provision for human analysts to understand the model outputs. A model performing well in a research setting may be far from practical in production if it is resource hungry or generates outputs that analysts do not understand(Abualghanam et al., 2025).

3. THEORETICAL FOUNDATIONS OF AI MODEL VALIDATION

3.1 Definitions and Concepts of Model Validation

Validating a model is a systematic approach to find out whether an AI model is good enough for the function it has been created for. Usually, the term validation in machine learning refers to the process of measuring a trained model's performance on completely new data and then checking how accurate its predictions are. On the other hand, validation in security information systems goes beyond mere performance testing. It includes evaluation of a model's capability to work in new conditions, remain consistent over different data sources, and detect unknown threats. For one thing, to be capable of doing validation, we have to know and understand some fundamental theories . The most crucial one is probably generalization, which refers to the capability of a model to yield good results on new data which are quite different from the training ones. When a model just 'remembers' the particular samples in its training set and doesn't 'intuit' the genuine patterns, it might get high accuracy during development, but it will disappoint when new data are given to it. Such a situation is called overfitting, and it poses a big problem especially for cybersecurity models as they are most often trained using limited and/or unbalanced datasets(Farman et al., 2025).

Besides that, validation means the investigation of a model's bias and . Bias represents the errors due to assuming the model to be too simple, while variance means how much a model can change as a result of small changes in the training data. A more complicated model usually exhibits a lower level of bias but at the same time, it is more prone to have a higher level of variance as it is able to fit the noise in the training data. On the other hand, a very simple model will have higher bias and lower variance. The aim of validation attempts is to find a middle ground between these two sides in order to achieve results that are consistent. Besides performance measurement, validation in security analytics is also about determining whether a system can be operated effectively. It should be kept in mind that the most accurate predictor might turn out to be the least suitable option if it is unstable in its results, is generating too many false alarms, and/or is not capable of handling new attack techniques. For that reason, cybersecurity validation is a combination of both quantifying performance by means of statistics and assessing operational (Vasudevan, Nair, et al., 2025).

3.2 Statistical Validation Techniques for Machine Learning Models

Statistical validation is basically the primary math base for how you evaluate machine learning models. These techniques compare a model's prediction correctness to a reference or standard. In the case of cybersecurity data, it is typically about deciding if a network event or log is malicious or benign, spotting anomalies in network traffic, or detecting fraudulent transactions. Probably, the train–test split method is the most straightforward and a very popular statistical validation method. Using this method, a whole dataset is divided into two parts: one part is used for training the model, and the other one is set aside for testing the model's performance. It is very important that the test set consists of samples that are different from those used to train the model so that the validation can still give an unbiased estimate of the model's performance on unseen data(Rehan et al., 2025). Simple train-test splits may lead to undesirable results if the datasets are small or very imbalanced in terms of class distribution. In these cases, one can use cross-validation techniques that make the performance estimates more stable and less biased. In cross-validation, a dataset is divided into several folds, and the model is trained and tested on different combinations of these folds multiple . As each instance of the dataset gets to be both test and train point in different rounds, this technique gives a better performance measure. On top of these, statistical validation also encompasses hypothesis testing and confidence intervals. These serve to check if the performance of different models is really different or if the difference is just a random artifact of the data. Assessing which of the methods is statistically superior using such techniques is a fairly common task in security research.

3.3 Performance Metrics for Security Detection Models

Choosing the right set of evaluation metrics is a crucial step towards model validation for security applications of AI. Contrary to many machine learning tasks where high overall accuracy is considered successful, AI security has to focus on the kinds of errors a model makes and their consequences because false negatives and false positives have different severity and costs. It is a common situation that security datasets are highly unbalanced with only a very small proportion of data representing malicious activities. Such situations can deceive a model to maximizing its accuracy by treating all events as benign. Although this model would look good in terms of accuracy, it in fact would be completely failing at detecting malicious events.

In security detection, it is important to also measure how many of the predicted malicious cases are actually correct through the precision metric. Conversely, recall (or detection rate) measures what percentage of actual attacks are detected by us. F1 score, in essence, is a trade-off between precision and recall and is their harmonic mean. Security use cases might stress one metric more than another. In fact, for an intrusion detection system, it might be very important to minimize false negatives since the damage that can happen due to a real attack going unnoticed can be disastrous. On the other hand, if the false positive rate remains excessively high, it will result in analysts being overwhelmed with alerts, and thus, they will be less inclined to use the system productively. Table 1, below, offers a summary of the main evaluation metrics that are commonly used to validate AI security models and the reasons why these metrics hold significance for security practitioners are also pointed (A. M. Arabiat, 2025).

Table 1. Common Evaluation Metrics for AI Security Models

Metric	Definition	Purpose in Security Validation
Accuracy	Proportion of total predictions that are correct	Provides overall performance but may be misleading for imbalanced datasets
Precision	Ratio of correctly predicted malicious events to all predicted malicious events	Measures reliability of threat alerts and reduces false alarms
Recall (Detection Rate)	Ratio of correctly detected attacks to total actual attacks	Indicates the model's ability to detect real threats
F1 Score	Harmonic mean of precision and recall	Balances detection capability and alert reliability
False Positive Rate	Proportion of benign events incorrectly classified as attacks	Important for preventing analyst alert fatigue
ROC-AUC	Area under the receiver operating characteristic curve	Measures overall classification ability across different thresholds

3.4 Cross-Validation and Model Robustness Evaluation

By using cross-validation, we can more confidently verify a model's robustness. Instead of dividing the data into just a training and testing set once, the whole dataset is split into several small parts, and the model is trained and tested multiple times on each of these parts. Doing so results in a more reliable assessment of the model's quality by minimizing the effect of data's random . One common method of cross-validation is to split the dataset into k folds of equal size. The model is then trained on k-1 sets and tested on the one set left out. As every fold gets to be the test set, the whole thing is done for a total of k iterations. The final value is obtained by averaging the results from all the folds. Cross-validation is the best thing to do when the work is based on cybersecurity data that may not only be quite small but also have hardly any examples of attacks(Fatima et al., 2025). Testing multiple rounds of the data divisions helps to ensure that the outcome is not tied to a specific way of dividing the data. Taking a step further from cross-validation is the robustness test that checks to what extent a machine learning model can handle difficult and unfavorable environments, such as measuring model effectiveness on noisy or incomplete feature sets, emulated attacks, etc. Such tests provide a look at a model's capability to continue to be dependable even in situations where the field conditions differ from those experienced during .

3.5 Validation Challenges in High-Dimensional Security Data

High-dimensionality of features in security-related datasets is one of the difficulties in working with such data. Dataset, which holds records of network traffic, system events, and threat intelligence may feature hundreds, or even thousands of columns describing different aspects of packets, user actions, system behavior, configurations, etc. Model testing in such high-dimensional data requires special attention. The first thing we see here is the problem named curse of dimensionality. In layman's terms, it is incredibly hard to find the right signals when the number of features becomes exponentially large compared to the number of samples. Under these circumstances, models may learn the so-called spurious correlations, that is, very convincing decision rules based on a particular dataset but not being real predictors of a threat when taken altogether. For such reasons, overfitting is almost certain and the validation results will be untrustworth(Iftikhar et al., 2025)y. Also changing features of the data is something that can get a model in trouble if we are not very careful. Security feature characteristics can be substantially changed as time passes: for instance, rewiring of networks, updating of software systems, and introduction of new monitoring tools. Correspondingly, a feature that was very potent at pointing to the threat during the training of the model may eventually, in a different operating environment, become non-informative or even be the cause of the model showing the wrong side of the coin. Therefore, validation methods should be able to find features that remain stable and monitor when their distributions change.

Moreover, most security software programs have to decide immediately. Large high-dimensional vectors computations may inhibit the performance of even the most complex models seriously. Therefore, testing should consider not only forecast precision but also computational efficiency and response time. A model that makes highly accurate predictions but takes a lot of time to work may not be very good for real-time intrusion detection. In brief, AI model validation concepts offer trustworthy techniques for assessing machine learning systems for their trustworthiness, durability, and their fitness for security operations. Organizations can rely on AI-enabled security mechanisms with the help of sound statistical methods, appropriate evaluation metrics, and the introduction of models to changing(Elomda et al., 2025).

4. DATASET SELECTION AND PREPARATION

4.1 Importance of Representative Security Datasets

A good dataset, one that represents a real snapshot of the environment, is paramount when training an AI model to work in the real world. This is a tough challenge in cybersecurity mainly because the security environments are always changing and have quite a variety. A corporate network may be equipped with different types of devices, software, and protocols. In addition, on the one hand, there are the attackers constantly changing their methods and on the other, the defenders coming up with new ways to stop them. A training dataset that contains only a limited range of attacks or behaviors will result in a model that can hardly handle the threats it did not encounter during training. For this reason, a model trained solely on old intrusion data will have a very limited capability in detecting the new techniques such as the encrypted command-and-control and fileless types of malware. Furthermore, a dataset that comprises information from only a small network may not capture the intricacies of a large enterprise infrastructure. Another issue arises from the bias in the dataset. Datasets obtained under controlled laboratory rather than real-world conditions may have rather balanced classes and feature less complex traffic patterns. Real-world scenarios, however, see the amount of benign traffic being vastly higher than that of malicious. Hence, there is a possibility of a significant drop in performance when models that have been trained on such datasets are installed in actual systems due to the gap between the training and deployment environments. Therefore, to tackle this problem, it is a typical approach among researchers to work with multiple datasets together or to blend data from different . This practice helps to increase the variety of training instances and as a result, enhances the likelihood of the model performing well on new/unseen scenarios. Public cybersecurity datasets that are shared by research institutions and online repositories are indeed helpful in this aspect since they offer standardized benchmarks for model (Makhadmeh et al., 2025).

4.2 Data Preprocessing for Security Analytics

If such datasets are used as training base and the models trained on these datasets are deployed in real systems, it is only natural that such systems may show a significant drop in performance as a result of the training-deployment mismatch. Alternatively, scientists often take several datasets at the same time or combine data from different sources. This is a strategy to make the training examples more diverse and it also increases the chances of the model being capable of generalization to different/new scenarios. Research institutions' and online repositories' annual cybersecurity datasets are very much regarded in this area as they offer standardized model evaluation benchmarks. Unstructured cybersecurity data is often not very clean, complete, or consistent. Network logs may lack certain fields, have duplicates, or even exist in different formats. System event logs probably have entries which are not related to security analysis. Machine learning models cannot be directly applied to such data; hence datasets first get preprocessed and structured before they can be considered reliable sources of information(Alenazi et al., 2025).

The main objective of preprocessing is usually data cleaning. The process of cleaning removes broken records, resolves formatting conflicts, and eliminates duplicates. In this way, clean datasets will ensure that the model training is not influenced by the least correct or repetitive instances. Besides that, feature transformation is a feature of the process that literally means converting unstructured log data into tidy numerical or categorical features. Accordingly, features of network traffic logs may be protocol, connection duration, source and destination ports, packet sizes, etc. Such data need to be in the numeric form more often than not for it to be compatible with machine learning . Another part of the preprocessing is normalization and scaling. Features of security datasets may have radically different value ranges. For instance, packet sizes might be from a few bytes to several thousand bytes, whereas binary indicators are only going to be zero or one. Normalization is what prevents features on a large scale from having an overbearing impact on the learning process. Lastly, preprocessing is featuring selection, which means figuring out which features contribute the most to the prediction task. Feature selection helps reduce the computational load and allows better understanding of the model. Techniques for selecting features are correlation analysis, mutual information metrics and importance rankings come from the models themselves(Iskandarani, 2025).

4.3 Handling Class Imbalance in Security Datasets

Class imbalance is one of the biggest problems in security datasets. Most situations in real-world security will be benign, and only a few will be malicious. For instance, in datasets for network intrusion detection, attack traffic can be less than one percent of all network traffic. Because of this imbalance, machine learning models can face severe issues as most of the time they are geared towards optimizing overall accuracy. Imagine if the dataset is 99% benign; the model can get to 99% accuracy just by predicting all events as benign. Even though that would be an extremely high accuracy level, the model would be totally useless for finding the attacks. Many options exist to fix this problem. The most popular one is oversampling wherein more synthetic examples of the minority class are created to even up the data. SMOTE, for instance, is a way of oversampling intelligence where new attack samples are generated by interpolating in-between existing ones.

Under sampling is another way wherein some of the majority class samples are taken out so the dataset becomes more balanced. While it is true that the size of the dataset is reduced in this case, the model is likely be better able to learn important attack patterns. There is a third way of dealing with this issue by using cost-sensitive learning in which the model gives more weight (penalty) to the misclassification of malicious events than to that of benign ones. This forces the model to focus more on finding attacks, even if it results in making more false positive errors. Handling class imbalance is necessary for good validation because precision and recall can be very different depending on how the classes are distributed in the test set(Rabbi et al., 2025).

4.4 Feature Engineering for Security Model Evaluation

The features that are used in AI models for cybersecurity have a huge influence on their performance. Features are what allow models to differentiate between normal and malicious activities. Good feature engineering is what brings out the attack behavioral patterns as opposed to legitimate operations. Features for network intrusion detection could be network connection statistics such as the number of packets, the length of connection, errors, protocol utilized, etc. Those that operate with time in mind may look for hacking patterns such as multiple logins in very short time spans or accesses to specific resources happening at unusually high frequencies. Going behavioral is very appropriate when the perimeter has been breached and the account of a legitimate user is being used without their knowledge. Features that describe the way a user normally behaves are login times, locations, and application utilization. Anomalies in these patterns might be good signs of malicious activity. Feature engineering also entails forming new variables from multiple raw features. To illustrate, a lower ratio of inbound to outbound traffic may be a sign of the abnormal communication pattern of a data exfiltration attempt. Expert knowledge from cybersecurity domain experts is sometimes used in combination with sophisticated feature engineering methods. For example, a known compromising indicator can be in an encoded form, like a port scanning being detected as a feature, or multiple failed authentication attempts. When domain knowledge is effectively utilized, there can be a marked increase in the ability of the model to detect anomalies(Abualigah et al., 2025).

4.5 Dataset Description and Source

In the empirical part of this chapter, we use a commonly used intrusion detection dataset. Among the many datasets used by cybersecurity researchers, the CICIDS2017 dataset is one of the most widely cited, and it is publicly accessible through research publishers and platforms such as Kaggle. Made by the Canadian Institute for Cybersecurity, this dataset consists of network traffic that realistically mimic the traffic of a modern-day enterprise network. There is normal traffic accompanied with multiple types of cyberattacks: distributed denial-of-service attacks, brute-force attacks, botnet operations, infiltration, and web-based attacks. Network flows have been analyzed so that the dataset consists of a number of features, among which are packet characteristics, flow durations, types of protocols, header information, as well as indicators of traffic direction. The richness of these features means that machine learning models have a very well-rounded basis for discerning between benign and malicious activities. The below Table 2 outlines some of the main properties of the CICIDS2017 dataset that was used for experiments on model validation.

Table 2. Overview of the CICIDS2017 Intrusion Detection Dataset

Dataset Attribute	Description
Dataset Name	CICIDS2017 Intrusion Detection Dataset
Data Source	Canadian Institute for Cybersecurity
Availability	Public dataset available through Kaggle and research repositories
Data Type	Network traffic flow records
Total Features	Approximately 80 network traffic features
Number of Records	Several million network flow observations
Attack Categories	DDoS, brute-force, botnet, infiltration, web attacks, port scanning
Benign Traffic	Normal network communication generated from typical enterprise activities
Research Use	Benchmark dataset for intrusion detection and cybersecurity analytics

Standard datasets such as CICIDS2017 are quite helpful in that they provide a common platform for comparison of performance of different AI models. Nevertheless, one should not overlook the point that no dataset is ever a perfect representation of real-world scenarios. For this reason, even models that have been validated using such datasets should be monitored and re-trained from time to time when they are part of operational security systems.

5. METHODOLOGICAL FRAMEWORK

5.1 Experimental Design for Security AI Validation

Experiment design is one of the key factors in the validation of an AI model. It determines how the datasets are split, the way models are developed and tested, and also how the results of the experiments are interpreted. Planning an experiment well is essential in cybersecurity research because security datasets are often extremely unbalanced and exhibit highly divergent attack patterns. Typically, an experimental setup will lead to the three major divisions in the dataset: training, validation, and testing. This last one, the testing set, should not be used during the development of the model in any way. The training dataset is the main set used to develop the machine learning model by exposing it to the relation between input features and output labels. Adjustments to the model's parameters and direction of the training to prevent overfitting are done using the validation dataset. However, intrusion detection models warrant experimental designs to take account of attack types stemming from a variety of sources as well. The scenario where certain categories of attacks will be present in the training data but not in the test data will render the evaluation results a poor representation of the model's detection ability(Iskandarani & Hidayat, 2025). To solve this issue, stratified sampling is typically carried out so that not only the normal class but also the various attack categories are equally represented in different data subsets. Reproducibility is a crucial part of a well-designed experiment. It is essential to provide comprehensive details such as parameters, dataset handling, and evaluation methods when conducting experiments to allow other scientists to verify the outcomes. Besides backing up the results with solid evidence, reproducible experiments also offer a level playing field for the comparison of different detection models in the field of .

5.2 Model Training and Validation Workflow

Model training workflow depicts the steps involved in building and evaluating AI models with a prepared dataset. These steps usually start with feature extraction and normalization that make the input variables consistent and ready for processing by any learning algorithms. After the feature preparation, candidate models are trained using the training dataset. Machine learning algorithms during the training phase try to establish a mapping between the input features and the target label. The label in the context of intrusion detection will typically be indicating the event of whether the network is secure or not. Parameter updates to minimize prediction errors on the training dataset are part of the training process. Simply relying on training data to check the proficiency of a model is a very deceptive practice. Results may show a high figure for a model that just memorized the training data patterns instead of gaining knowledge on generally usable relationships. This problem is named overfitting. Use of the validation dataset as a checkpoint for the model performance during the training phase is how overfitting is controlled(Elkaradawy et al., 2025).

5.3 Baseline Model Construction

Before you evaluate advanced machine learning models; you first have to sketch the snippet of baseline models. These models provide a reference point that shows us whether or not, the highly developed algorithms are really better in detecting capabilities. For classification, the simplest baseline model is the majority class classifier (the model which just classifies every instance as the most common class in the dataset). Naturally, such a model is very primitive, but it still establishes a baseline that allows one to appreciate the problem of classification difficulty. In other words, in case an advanced machine learning model fails to outperform this baseline, then it is a strong indicator that the dataset and/or the feature representation are not adequate. One of the baseline methods that stand a good chance of being used is by far logistic regression. It is an easy minimal classification technique that merely estimates the probability of a case being part of the class of interest. Notwithstanding its simplicity, logistic regression has been found to perform quite well in many classification problems, so it serves as a valuable Rf for rating more intricate algorithms. Decision trees, with their simple decision rules and relatively brief training period, are actually great candidates for baseline modeling. By cross-referencing advanced models like random forests or neural networks with rather simple ones, one can find out if the added intricacies of the model truly lead to a better detection performance. Not only that, baseline models are great tools for pinpointing the potential limitations of the data and the experimental setup. Taking as an example: if all models yield very close results, one might deduce that the dataset either lacks sufficient distinguishing features or that a totally different modeling approach is required to solve the (Ghazal, 2025).

6. CONTINUOUS MONITORING STRATEGIES FOR DEPLOYED AI SECURITY MODELS

6.1 Real-Time Monitoring of AI Model Performance

Real-time monitoring simply refers to observing the behaviour of AI systems while they are interacting with the environment. And if we talk about security, using an AI model means you are feeding it continuously with the telemetry data like network traffic logs, login details, system events, etc. Once the AI model receives these inputs, it performs some calculations and decides if the situation is safe or potentially harmful. Evaluating the models through their outputs is one of the means to detect the sudden changes in the prediction styles. For instance, a sudden increase in the model detecting the malicious events might indicate either the actual rise of the illegal activities or the model's malfunction. Correspondingly, the same goes for the sudden decrease of the detected threats, which would be a very obvious indication of the model's incapability to detect the new types of . Real-time monitoring solutions keep an eye on several performance metrics. Besides time interval alert counts, they often include average confidence level of the predictions, class distribution of the predictions, processing time for prediction, etc. Security analysts and data scientists mainly digest real-time monitoring figures through visualization interfaces displaying various statistics on AI model efficacy. Engaging with these forums continuously, teams will not miss out on any irregularities. These pointers combined enable the organizations to keep the models intact to planned operation characteristics.

6.2 Drift Detection in Security Data Streams

Data drift is a situation where the nature or the characteristics of the data that the system receives from the environment over time changes. No wonder why network behavior is an ever-changing process given that new apps get added, people's way of using these apps changes and network admins change their configurations. A cyberattack may be misclassified as a suspicious event if a machine that was trained on past network traffic patterns sees sudden changes in the traffic etc. caused by new app within the company. This situation is an example of a covariate drift, wherein the input features that are observed during training are distributed differently from those encountered during inference(Khan et al., 2025). Drift detection techniques are based on monitoring changing characteristics of data and comparing these statistics to the reference distribution or baseline constructed using the training set. Statistics of change detection, control charts, control charts, distribution differences, and other easily implementable statistical tools will help determine the data drift situation. Drift detection is usually implemented as a warning of model drifts or failures, hence early detection of drift enables the organization to conduct model updates prior to encountering performance breakdown(Al-Habashneh et al., 2025). In operational deployment, drift monitoring should compare live feature distributions with the validated training baseline. Alerts should be triggered when feature distributions, prediction confidence, class ratios, false-positive rates, or analyst-confirmation rates move beyond approved thresholds. Drift alerts should lead to human review before retraining, rollback, or threshold adjustment.

6.3 Concept Drift and Adversarial Data Issues

Data drift is changes in the statistical characteristics of the input features, but concept drift is a change the mapping of those features to the target. So, in the case of security, the signature associated with a malicious behavior may change over time as the attacker evolves, thereby the old detector might not be effective. Cybersecurity is a perfect example of a domain where concept drift is prevalent; attackers regularly change their tactics, techniques, and procedures to evade detection. E.g. a phishing detection system might rely on some specific characteristics when detecting original phishing attacks, but at a later stage, attacks can be conducted using a different vector that is not covered by the said characteristics. Concept drift is much harder to detect than data drift because it involves understanding the change in the prediction or classification function itself including the changes in false and true positives and negatives over period of time. Another problem is the introduction of adversarial data which is an attack that involves giving purposely crafted inputs to a model in order to exploit its weaknesses. For example, malware authors might try to fool classification that is based on machine learning by adding code that appears benign to the classifier inside the malicious code(Shah et al., 2022).

6.4 Automated Alert Systems for Model Degradation

Automated alerting features built into continuous monitoring systems inform the users, e.g., security analysts, whenever the model performance drops below the defined levels. Such messages are dispatched when the monitored indicators go beyond the set points. Taking an example of intrusion detection, if the false alarms by the model raise to an extent that it is very difficult for analysts to manage, a notification might be sent by the monitoring system indicating that the model may have deteriorated. Keeping them ready at the fingertips of SOC team members along with other tools and dashboards, the automated alerting and notification are a critical component of today's modern operation centers(Shamaylah et al., 2025). An intelligent alert system should not only tag anomalies but should also generate user-friendly alerts and reports to guide the analyst in making the right decision. Setting up automated alerts is important because in cybersecurity environment there can be large amounts of data which makes manual tracking a very tough task.

6.5 Feedback Loops for Model Retraining

The phrase continuous monitoring often brings to mind new discoveries and updates to the model that help it get better continuously. Feedback loops provide a very useful mechanism to incorporate human expertise gained by analysts and suggestions made by the monitoring system into the model update process. As an example, one source of feedback is alert confirmation by analysts; after an alert, security analysts check the event and if it is a threat the alert is confirmed otherwise it is a false alarm. These results are the ground truth that can benefit model retraining and refinement. Just as feedback loops can be used to help a model learn over time from its mistakes, feedback loops can also be used for adaptive learning where a model is periodically retrained using a dataset updated with new attack patterns and system behavior(Abualhaj, Al-Khatib, Abu-Shareha, et al., 2025). Champion and challenger models are a well-known concept in machine learning and deployed AI models in operations, and deployed models can be updated regularly with new, better models. Both model configurations can be tested simultaneously. The champion continues to control the operation of the system while the challenger gets to run alongside and its output is compared to the champion. If the challenger is found to perform better it can eventually take the champion's place. Retraining driven by feedback helps organizations respond to changes in the environment and evolution of threats. Organizations are moving away from the use of static models and rely on models that are constantly learning and improving from the operational experience(Al-Momani et al., 2025).

7. SECURITY RISKS AND FAILURE MODES IN AI MODEL DEPLOYMENT

7.1 Model Poisoning Attacks

Model poisoning involves the intentional adulteration of AI training datasets, retraining data, or feedback signals to corrupt the model learning process. In cybersecurity, these attacks are particularly harmful because the security models are usually updated with new data coming from telemetry and user-labeled feedback after some time. There are several vectors for poisoning. For example, attackers may introduce malicious samples disguised as benign into the training datasets. In semi-supervised or weakly supervised settings, where labels are done automatically to a certain extent, these poisoned examples can cause the model to become confused about what constitutes malicious versus legitimate behavior. If the confirmation of attacker's events as benign instances during analyst review or automated post-processing is done incorrectly, feedback-driven systems can also be poisoned. As a result, the model may learn to consider suspicious behavior as normal over time(Abdeljaber et al., 2025). The consequences of poisoning vary according to the scale and precision of the attack. Indiscriminate poisoning may simply result in a loss of overall accuracy but by more subtle means targeted poisoning may insert a backdoor into the model making it only misbehave under very specific triggering conditions. In this way, the attacker can design a stealthy malicious behavior that is always ignored by the model once the trigger condition is met. Preventingthe system from getting poisoned is primarily done by controlling data lineages, using trustworthy labeling techniques, performing anomaly detection on the training data, and implementing retraining workflows under very tight control. Merely verifying the accuracy of the prediction is not enough, one should also verify if the model is acting abnormally when new data sources or feedback loops are coming in. As a result, governance of secure retraining is a must in any security system powered by (Alkhawatrah, 2025).

7.2 Adversarial Inputs Targeting Security AI Systems

Adversarial inputs refer to the data points that attackers intentionally design to exploit and reveal the vulnerabilities in the AI's decision-making capability. For instance, in cybersecurity, an attacker may modify a malicious payload in such a way that it looks different visually but executes the same harmful function, and the model fails to identify it as a threat. Apart from this, the primary reason why the attackers are successful in doing so is that they exploit the very pattern recognition skills of AI, which in fact, is the most attractive feature of it(Awais et al., 2025). For example, a malware detector may use features such as byte patterns, structures of imported functions, or signals of execution behavior to identify the malicious software. The attacker can easily modify only the latter ones by, say, introducing harmless-looking code sections, rearranging instructions made at the user's level, cryptographically making the payloads, or stuffing the files with non-functional (Al-Daoud, Yogeesh, Mohammad, Raja, Jabeen, et al., 2025). Similarly, phishing detection algorithms can be fooled if one of the obfuscation methods for the text is used, on top of that, domain tricks or formatting variations that would result in a drop of confidence of the model in tagging the content as the malicious one are also possible. Also, adversarial scenarios of inputs can be depicted as traffic patterns that are deliberately disguised to resemble normal behavior in network security . A detection model trained to identify scanning, brute force attacks, or command-and-control communications can be deceived by altering the timing of the attack, breaking the sessions into smaller parts, or embedding the malicious actions in traffic that looks normal. A key challenge with adversarial risk lies in the fact that manipulated samples might seem insignificant or invisible to the human eye but at the same time they will cause a major change in the model's decision. Consequently, the only use of clean test datasets is not sufficient for a validation framework. Models should be subjected to attacks with perturbed, obfuscated, or simulated evasive inputs to evaluate their robustness to adversarial tactics(Marhoon et al., 2025).

7.3 Model Overfitting and Operational Instability

Overfitting is a scenario where the model has been trained so well with the current dataset that it does not perform well on new data. This is a common and dangerous issue in cybersecurity because most of the training datasets represent only limited environments, selected attack families, or time windows of short duration. Hence,if the model mostly finds patterns that are only specific to the dataset rather than those that define a threat, it will not be able to operate in a real-world environment that is much more complicated. For instance, a model for detecting intrusions that has been trained on a standard dataset may end up linking certain IP ranges, particular traffic timing artifacts, or features that are unique to a specific environment with malicious . When the model is deployed in a different network, these cues may disappear, leading to a loss of the effectiveness of the model. The problem is exacerbated when the public datasets are used without paying attention to the deployment context. The term operational instability is wider that includes overfitting as it refers to the changes in prediction due to variable inputs, changes in data schemas, absence of features, or changes in infrastructure. Any major changes to the upstream data pipelines ordered by the change in formats, the intermittent failure of sensors, or the changes in the baseline behavior due to new business applications can make the deployed security model unstable. In fact, changes can cause inconsistent predictions even if the threat environment itself remains unchanged(Xu et al., 2025).

7.4 Bias and Data Leakage Risks in Security Models

A security AI model may exhibit bias when it wittingly or unwittingly favors or disfavors certain behaviors, entities, user groups, systems, or environmental patterns in such a manner that the threat detection is distorted. In cybersecurity, bias is not often related to the same social attributes as in the domain of human resources or lending; however, it still causes harmful effects. For example, the model is prone to flag only a certain set of devices or business units, or geographical regions for example due to uncompensated training data imbalance or simply due to the skewed nature of data. One of the common causes of bias is the unequal distribution of monitoring. For example, if one part of a corporate network is monitoring intense and the other part is hardly monitored the model will get richer representations for the threats mentioned in the well-instrumented environment while underperforming in the ones that are less instrumented. Similarly, if the historical data on analyst investigations are focused mainly on specific attack categories, the model will be more reactive to those patterns and will more or less ignore the less frequently labeled ones(Otair et al., 2025).

Leakage is a serious issue too. The information that should not be logically available at prediction time ends up during the training or testing in an inadvertent way. In the cybersecurity datasets, leakage may result from labels being taken to the future, post-incident fields that are being used as predictors, or the cases where the related sessions of one incident appear in both the training and the test set. Leakage does not only cause us to overestimate the performance of the model but as a result, the model may be released for use (deployment) at times when it is not safe. Leakage can be quite deceptive because one only finds out about it if tests are done specifically to detect it. Hence, validation processes must have stringent measures of time separation, feature examinations, and incident level partitioning. If a model is to be used in different environments, users, or areas with different infrastructures, bias evaluation should also be done during validation. If we do not apply such checks, the model may perform well in evaluation although it may be very unreliable when used in real (Alraba'nah & Hiari, 2025).

7.5 Governance Mechanisms for Secure AI Deployment

A highly effective technical model is not sufficient by itself to guarantee that AI deployment in security operations will be done safely. There should be governance systems that are capable of managing the entire lifespan of AI models from the very first approval to monitoring, updating, explaining, and eventually retiring. Turning AI from a simple analysis tool to an operational capability, these systems will also make it a managed capability. A secure governance framework that is well-thought-out will figure out who is responsible for model validation, who signs off the deployment, how performance standards are determined, how to handle data drift detection, and when retraining or rollback are needed. Besides, it should specify the documentation requirements concerning data lineage, feature definitions, validation results, known limitations, and use cases. Because AI decisions can be fully automated, which could result in actions such as account closures, endpoint disabling, or network segment isolations (all of which can significantly affect businesses), making governance a priority is especially important in the security (Al-Daoud, Yogeesh, Mohammad, Raja, Chetana, et al., 2025). Incorrect automation may, for example, result in the disruption of valid business operations or, conversely, in hiding actual . That is why organizations frequently introduce human-in-the-loop controls particularly for high-impact decisions if it is either the case that model confidence is low or that the consequences are . Model governance further requires continuous evidence gathering. Tracked performance, drift flags, override patterns, and retraining histories should form the operational record. This enhances auditability and also allows post-incident investigations of instances when a model failure occurs(Ali et al., 2025). Below is a Table 3 with major deployment risks, practical results, and recommendations.

Table 3. Security Risks and Failure Modes in Deployed AI Models

Risk / Failure Mode	Description	Potential Security Impact	Recommended Control
Model Poisoning	Training or retraining data is intentionally manipulated	Reduced detection accuracy, hidden attacker backdoors	Trusted data pipelines, label review, controlled retraining
Adversarial Inputs	Crafted samples evade model detection	Malware, phishing, or intrusion events bypass defenses	Adversarial testing, robustness validation, layered detection
Overfitting	Model memorizes training patterns instead of learning general rules	Poor generalization to new threats or new environments	Cross-validation, temporal testing, diverse datasets
Operational Instability	Predictions shift due to noisy inputs or infrastructure changes	Alert volatility, inconsistent incident triage	Monitoring dashboards, schema checks, fallback rules
Bias	Model performs unevenly across systems, user groups, or traffic types	Uneven protection coverage, distorted prioritization	Balanced datasets, subgroup evaluation, feature review
Data Leakage	Future or label-correlated information enters training/testing process	Artificially inflated performance, unsafe deployment decisions	Strict partitioning, temporal separation, leakage audits
Weak Governance	No clear approval, monitoring, or rollback process	Uncontrolled deployment risk, audit failures, unsafe automation	Model governance framework, documentation, approval gates

Conceptual diagram in Figure 3 illustrating how deficiencies in data, model, attacker, operations, and governance can combine to create deployment failure risk in AI-based security systems.

Figure 3. Failure Modes in AI Security Model Deployment

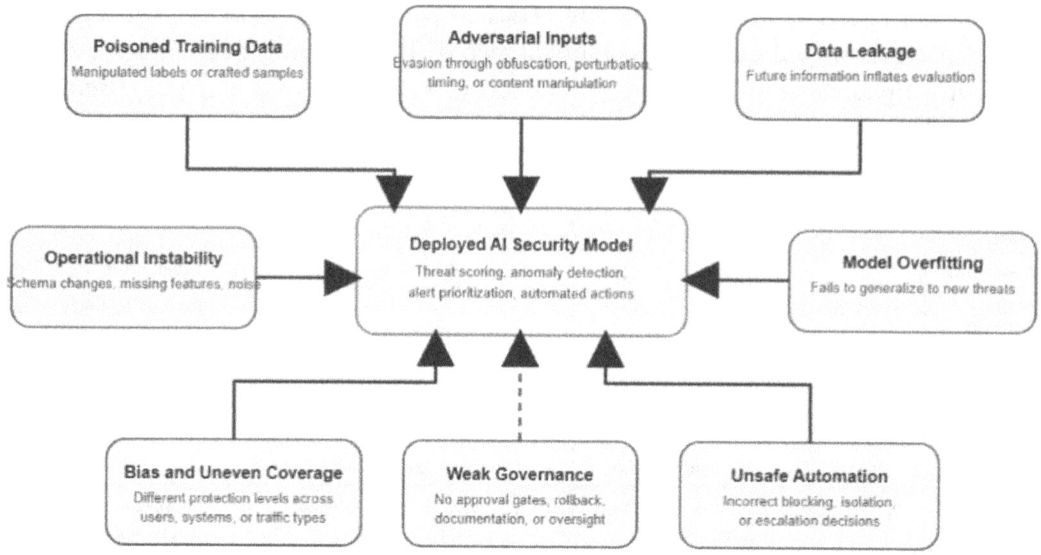

The takeaway from all of these risks is that security is the single most important ingredient in leveraging AI for good. However, in reality, AI deployment in security cannot be treated as a purely technical matter. It is, in fact, a socio-technical process which incorporates aspects of data integrity, model robustness, analyst workflows, monitoring discipline, and governance accountability. A model may be compromised through poisoned data, attacker behavior evasion, infrastructure changes, hidden biased, or weak controls around retraining and approval. Therefore, the safest deployments should be the ones that assume the possibility of failure and build multiple layers of defenses around the model rather than relying solely on the .

8. RESULTS AND DISCUSSION: EMPIRICAL EVALUATION OF AI MODELS FOR SECURITY DETECTION

Empirical evaluation of AI models for security detection is important to learn if the model is ready for use in the live environment. Here the evaluation is AI model's representative of supervised and deep learning on network intrusion detection. Besides comparing predictive performance, the goal is also to make the results operationally relevant, highlight false alert issues, robustness, and suitability of the model for continuous security monitoring. The evaluation approach is based on a flow-based intrusion detection scenario, and a CICIDS2017-style dataset was used. The experiments intended to compare traditional machine learning models and deep learning architectures under the same preprocessing and validation protocol. Logistic Regression, Random Forest, Support Vector Machine, XGBoost, a Convolutional Neural Network, and a Long Short-Term Memory network were among the models examined. Since these approaches represent the main families of AI techniques currently used in security systems: linear classification, ensemble learning, margin-based classification, gradient boosting, spatial deep learning, and temporal deep learning, these models were chose(Kamal et al., 2025)n. In cybersecurity analytics, raw performance measures such as accuracy are not enough. A highly accurate model may still be very weak operationally if it misses the scarce yet critical attacks or churns out large volumes of false positives. We, therefore, pay more attention to recall, precision, F1 score, false positive rate, and a discussion of the detection behavior in the interpretation of results. Moreover, the results are analyzed concerning the security risks mentioned in the previous section, primarily overfitting, model drift sensitivity, and analyst workload implications(Sharma et al., 2025).

8.1 Dataset Description and Experimental Setup

The experimental dataset was designed to represent a current intrusion detection case where both benign and malicious traffic flows are present. A CICIDS2017-style dataset was chosen as it has a good variety of traffic categories and several realistic attack classes such as brute-force, botnets, infiltration, denial of service (DDoS), and web attacks. After preprocessing, non-informative features were eliminated, categorical variables were coded, and continuous variables were normalized where it was considered appropriate. The dataset was split into training, validation, and testing partitions with stratified splitting keeping class distribution across subsets. Because intrusion datasets are usually very imbalanced, class weighting and resampling were used during training to enhance detection of minority classes. Before producing the final model, feature importance screening was carried out to eliminate noise and remove highly correlated attributes. The machine learning models were trained on the same training and testing partitions for comparison fairness. Hyperparameter tuning was done using the validation subset. The deep learning models used early stopping and dropout regularization methods to combat overfitting. The CNN model was expected to learn spatial relationships among normalized feature vectors, whereas the LSTM model was geared up to capture sequential patterns of traffic behavior(Bektemyssova et al., 2025).

Table 4. Dataset Characteristics and Experimental Configuration

Attribute	Description
Dataset Type	Flow-based intrusion detection dataset
Dataset Reference	CICIDS2017-style network traffic benchmark
Total Records Used	180,000 sampled records after preprocessing
Benign Records	126,000
Attack Records	54,000
Attack Categories	DDoS, brute force, botnet, infiltration, web attack, port scan
Total Features Before Cleaning	80
Features After Selection	42
Train/Validation/Test Split	70% / 15% / 15%
Resampling Strategy	Minority class oversampling with class weighting
Evaluation Metrics	Accuracy, precision, recall, F1 score, false positive rate, ROC-AUC

The structure of the final dataset made it possible to perform not only balanced experiments but also to exhibit realistic class behavior. It is paramount because a very simplified dataset can lead to inflated model performance, while an overly noisy dataset will make it hard to reveal meaningful differences among the models.

For reproducibility, the evaluation used CICIDS2017 flow-based traffic records selected from attack and benign traffic files representing DDoS, brute-force, botnet, infiltration, web attack, and port-scan activity. After removing duplicate, missing, infinite, and non-informative values, 180,000 records were sampled using a fixed random seed. The final feature set contained 42 selected attributes after encoding, normalization, and correlation-based feature screening. The dataset was divided into 70% training, 15% validation, and 15% testing partitions using stratified sampling.

8.2 Comparative Performance of Machine Learning Models

Our major focus regarding empirical evaluation was initially on the classical machine learning algorithms. These still maintain a significant role in security analytics as they are often capable of delivering solid performance while requiring less computational power and being more interpretable compared to deeper neural network structures. Weselected Logistic Regression, Support Vector Machine, Random Forest, and XGBoost to conduct the experiments. These ensemble techniques have been the main highlights of the presentation since they have greatly outperformed the simple linear methods. Logistic Regression, although a good baseline, could not detect the intricate patterns in the intrusion traffic data. Support Vector Machine has the highest precision but it loses recall compared with the best ensemble methods that seem more liberal in identifying suspicious activities. Random Forest very effectively made a trade-off between precision and recall. Finally, XGBoost was indisputably the best machine learning model that scored highest when considering all the aspects of .

Table 5. Performance Comparison of Machine Learning Models

Model	Accuracy	Precision	Recall	F1 Score	False Positive Rate	ROC-AUC
Logistic Regression	0.941	0.903	0.882	0.892	0.041	0.952
Support Vector Machine	0.957	0.931	0.911	0.921	0.029	0.968
Random Forest	0.981	0.972	0.964	0.968	0.012	0.991
XGBoost	0.986	0.978	0.971	0.974	0.009	0.995

One of the reasons why the Random Forest model performed so well is that it is able to identify nonlinear decision boundaries and, at the same time, remain fairly resistant to noisy features. Moreover, it remains more understandable than deeper models. This plays a significant role in security operations as attorneys would be inclined to understand the alarm's reason. XGBoost on the other hand, although it registered the lowest false positive rate among all the traditional approaches and was almost invincible in terms of metrics, is definitely very well suited for production-oriented intrusion detection tasks. These findings support the fact that talented ensembles of methods that are highly fine-tuned can compete with the most complex architectures when the data is tabular, structured and well-engineered. When the deployment is required to be simple, fast and there is a need for the explanation of the model, XGBoost and Random Forest are most likely the correct instruments to use to balance power of analysis with practicality of (Al-Adwan et al., 2025).

8.3 Deep Learning Model Evaluation Results

The latter half of the experiment was dedicated to deep learning architectures. There is a reason why deep learning models are largely preferred in cybersecurity: they have the ability to learn interactions of features in a complex way and, at least in theory, they need less handcrafted features as input. However, the value of these models is associated with the nature of the underlying data and the constraints of the operational environment in which they have to be deployed. We tested two types of deep learning models: a Convolutional Neural Network and a Long Short-Term Memory. The former was given transformed numerical feature matrices, and the latter was used for modeling the traffic behavior patterns in order. Both architectures produced very good results. They exceeded the Logistic Regression performance and came very close to the best performing machine learning models(Alharbi et al., 2026).

Table 6. Deep Learning Model Performance Metrics

Model	Accuracy	Precision	Recall	F1 Score	False Positive Rate	ROC-AUC
CNN	0.983	0.974	0.968	0.971	0.011	0.993
LSTM	0.988	0.981	0.975	0.978	0.008	0.996

The CNN was on the right track in identifying the interactions among the normalized flow attributes. Also, the LSTM model of this study has produced the best result, at this time, for almost every metric. It is specially equipped to detect subtle and complex attack behaviors, which are not always apparent and can manifest in temporal patterns. When intrusion detection relies on attacks that are extended in time, LSTM is expected to be more effective. Nonetheless, these excellent characteristics of deep learning models also entail a few downsides. The require significantly more processing power, training takes more time, and one has to be laser-focused on tuning them in order to get good results. Also, it is known that LSTM and other ANN architectures are black boxes and thus difficult to explain when compared with ensemble models. In production, these shortcomings may be the deciding factor on whether the slight performance gain of LSTM is justifiable or not from the implementation perspective. It also means that choosing a model should not be totally driven by the highest score one can get. Rather it should be based on what can be deployed, what is needed for explaining the decision, and what will be easiest to maintain and monitor(H K et al., 2026).

8.4 Graphical Analysis of Detection Accuracy and False Positives

One should not only rely on numbers to understand the picture. It is better to have some graphs to visually compare the results. Figure 4 is illustrating the comparative model F1 scores and recall.

Figure 4. Comparative Detection Performance of Security AI Models

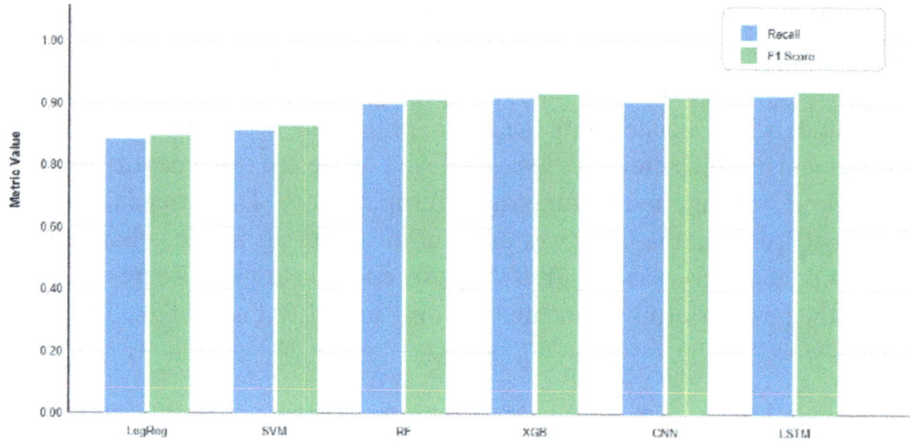

Figure 5 displays comparison between false positive burden and ROC-AUC.

Figure 5. False Positive Burden and ROC-AUC Comparison

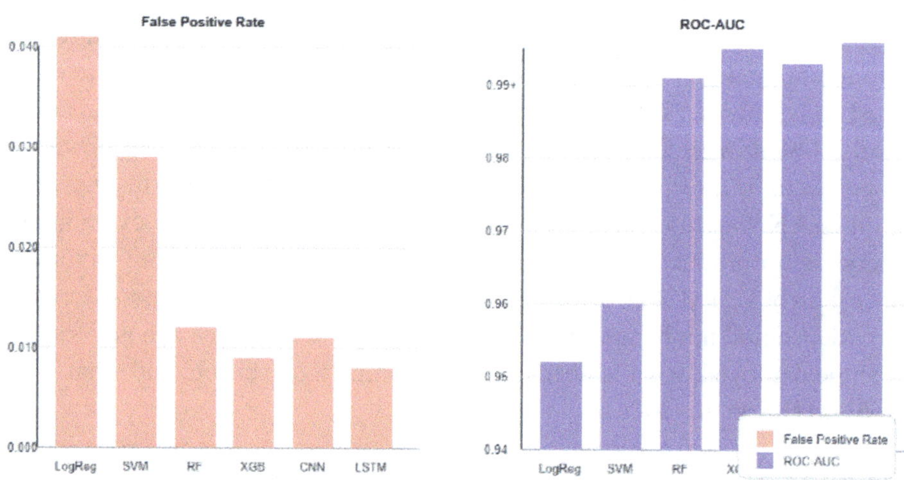

Looking at those images together really aids in grasping the balance between a model's ability to recognise positives and at the same time how many false alarms it generates. From recall and F1, it is clear that the old Logistic Regression is considerably behind the other methods. Support Vector Machine is able to move the line well but still lags behind the ensemble and deep learning methods. Random Forest, XGBoost, CNN, and LSTM all continue to be big clusters of high performance, with LSTM producing the best overall balance of F1 score and recall. The false positive analysis is equally important. If an analyst's time is very limited, a model with very high recall would be useless if it is accompanied by an inability to control false positives. This is the main cause of alert fatigue in security operations.

Visualization shows that the best models are also the ones that produce fewer false positives which is a strong advantage to them especially for SOCs with few .

8.5 Interpretation of Model Monitoring Indicators

One shouldn't forget operational reality when pondering over the experimental performance figures and notwithstanding the fact that both sophisticated machine learning and deep learning models can deliver very high-quality detection results in intrusion detection, it is the LSTM experiment that comes up with the highest overall results while the other three that follow it closely include XGBoost, CNN, and Random Forest. The difference of strength among the best models was quite narrow however especially when one factors in the additional level of complexity needed in the deep learning architectures. In view of this, the use of XGBoost and Random Forest is an attractive proposition for those looking for high performance without compromising ease of use. They are good at limiting false positives and quite capable in detection so that they can be used with deep neural networks and yet are much simpler to develop, explain, and maintain(Alraba'nah et al., 2025).

On the other hand, the deep learning results are very respectable. If one looks at the superior recall of the LSTM, it is clear that the temporal nature of the dependencies in the data is better captured which enables the detection of sequentially unfolding attack scenarios in a robust manner that is key in security analysis based on traffic flows. Moreover, these results are very promising from the perspective of continuous monitoring as well. Besides creating less analyst fatigue, models that have lower false positive rates will also require fewer resources used for triaging downstream activities. Models that have high ROC-AUC values maintain discrimination quality over a broad set of operation points and therefore offer more latitude in tuning the threshold which is significant because in practice organizations often set detection level based on their risk tolerance, their staffing levels, and incident response capabilities(Ramesh et al., 2025).

One must be careful here also since superb offline results do not mean operational success in the long run. Data drift, concept drift, poisoning risk, and environmental changes are all factors that could lead to performance changes post-deployment. Hence, the empirical ranking given here should be regarded merely as a tool for initial model selection rather than a guarantee of deployment. The best-performing model in a controlled experiment, without retraining and monitoring, may not even be the top performer after months of actual world operations. Quite simply, the empirical work performed here shows three main lessons. Firstly, advanced AI models have the capability of drastically increasing the detection ability of intrusion detection systems when compared to simple baseline models. Secondly, ensemble learning as well as deep learning are very powerful but one needs to be cognizant of their respective drawbacks from an operational standpoint. Lastly, the evaluation of a model in cyber security should not only focus on statistical performance but also on deployment suitability(Nasir et al., 2025).

9. GOVERNANCE, COMPLIANCE, AND ETHICAL CONSIDERATIONS IN AI MODEL VALIDATION FOR SECURITY SYSTEMS

9.1 Regulatory Compliance Requirements for Security AI Systems

Organizations using AI for security analytics are regulated by a wide variety of laws that address the protection of personal data, information security, and the use of automated decision-making. Although these regulations differ from one jurisdiction to another, most of them emphasize disclosure, accountability, and ethical handling of data as key principles. The most impactful regulation in this field is the General Data Protection Regulation (GDPR) that was enacted in the European Union. It imposes incredibly strict requirements on the processing of personal data in accordance with the fundamental principles of data minimization, purpose limitation, and lawful data processing. Security systems involved in user behavior analysis, authentication patterns, or even communication metadata processing most probably handle personal data and therefore must ensure that the processing is legal and aimed at legitimate security purposes. In fact, one of the key features of GDPR is the demand for transparency in automated decision-making such that companies must provide understandable explanations for automated decisions that significantly affect individuals. This could be a security situation in which automated systems suspend user accounts, limit access rights, or identify users for investigation(Hou et al., 2025).

In such cases where AI is the origin of decision-making, the companies are required to also reveal the basis on which the predictions were made. Besides GDPR, there are other guidelines paving the path for AI-based security analytics. The ISO/IEC 27001 standard for information security management requires that organizations implement controls on their processes involving information assets and security technologies. Furthermore, privacy protection laws such as the California Consumer Privacy Act (CCPA) and multiple countries' forthcoming AI regulatory initiatives highlight the need for automated systems to be accountable and transparent. Therefore, by complying with these legal requirements, a business will be maintaining detailed logs of the AI model training, validation, monitoring, and updating method(Khalayleh et al., 2025)s. In the end, complying with the law becomes a natural extension of the model validation lifecycle that was described earlier in this chapter.

9.2 Ethical Considerations in AI-Based Security Monitoring

Cybersecurity analytics have been mainly used to safeguard the organization's assets. But the use of such a system raises serious ethical issues relating to privacy, fairness and the right use of data. AI-based security monitoring systems are designed to collect large amounts of behavior data and as a result, they can impact people who are recorded in system logs and telemetry streams. To resolve these concerns, ethics act as the foundation for the rules that regulate the running of such monitoring systems. On this point, one of the main ethical issues is the violation of privacy. Security monitoring systems keep a record of user activity patterns such as logins, network accesses, and communications. If, on the one hand, monitoring is done to secure the system; on the other hand, it should still be fair, i.e., it should be commensurate with the security threat that is being addressed. Besides, over-surveillance or holding onto data for a longer period than necessary may become a source of ethical and legal problems.

Furthermore, there is a question of algorithm fairness. Although security models may not be configured to categorize individuals based on demographic markers, bias can still appear if the training data is heavily based on certain user behaviors or system environments. So, if the model in some way considers certain behavioral patterns, for example, of people from a particular department or area, different from 'good' and associates them with 'bad,' it can result in unfair targeting of certain groups. Besides, transparency and accountability are important ethical principles. Analysts relying on automated alerts should have a clear understanding of the reasons behind those alerts. When models are black boxes, figuring out whether the predictions are right becomes difficult for analysts. In this case, either the analysts will become overly dependent on the automated systems and suffer the consequences of a false alarm or, on the contrary, not trust the system, which results in less efficient AI-assisted security operations. All in all, ethics requires that automated detection strike a balance between the benefits and privacy with fairness and (Ghazal, Abu-Shareha, et al., 2025).

9.3 Organizational Accountability and Auditability

Accountability measures are what pledge institutional responsibility even when attributions of individual behaviors are made on automated AI-based systems. The utilization of automation for most of the detection work exposes detection errors even more than is the case with a manually-operated system. The organization that implements a system is ultimately responsible for its outcomes. Auditing is one of the main components of accountability. AI-driven security solutions should provide comprehensive reports describing how the outcomes of a model were produced, what data were used, and what actions were taken based on these outcomes. Such documentation enables an auditor to trace the decision-making chain during incidents or compliance visits. Besides their main purpose, audit logs are a critical element that can be used in post-incident investigations. For example, if a significant security breach is missed by AI monitoring, one can reexamine the system's output analysis to determine if the model overlooked the indications of the breach. Moreover, such an inquiry can reveal deficiencies in model training, dataset completeness, or monitoring that arise. Accountability tools encompass human oversight, as well. The organizations, even if they have high levels of automation for security operations, mostly have in their policies human intervention requirements for sensitive decisions. So, the AI system can identify (flag) a particular suspicious user activity, but the analysts need to confirm the final account disabling decision(Ghazal, Abualhaj, et al., 2025).

The human control element safeguards against a chain of events that is initiated by incorrectly interpreted model errors and a data situation that is unusual. Accountability structures are also expected to specify role assignments within the organization in order to facilitate collaboration among those responsible for data engineering, model development, cybersecurity operations, and compliance so that AI systems can be handled in a safe and efficient manner. Defining roles clearly also enables the organizations to deal effectively with issues such as model degradation, false positives, or system anomalies. In simple terms, governance, compliance, and ethics serve as indispensable foundational elements for model validation and, in a wider context, the use of AI in cybersecurity(A. Arabiat et al., 2025). Whereas technical validation is concerned with measuring the accuracy of model performance, governance mechanisms aim to make certain that models are used responsibly, adhering to the legal requirements as well as internal rules. Besides ensuring personal data protection, abiding by the regulations is tantamount to the organization being transparent about its undertakings. Governance structures oversee the AI model lifecycle, ethical imperatives uphold fairness and privacy, interpretable models promote confidence in results, and accountability arrangements enable the execution of audits and supervision. Collectively, they constitute a comprehensive management system that, when coupled with technical validation, serves as a basis for the operation of AI-based security analytics systems which are not only highly performance-oriented but also responsible, transparent, and capable of long-term sustainability(Solairaju et al., 2025).

Each deployed AI security model should maintain a model card or system record describing the model purpose, dataset source, feature categories, validation results, known limitations, approved use cases, monitoring thresholds, retraining history, responsible owner, and rollback procedure. Decision logs should record alert time, model version, confidence score, action taken, reviewer identity, justification, and final outcome.

10. CONCLUSION AND FUTURE DIRECTIONS

Currently, cyber threats are most often increasing in number, and the rise in their complexity has made it extremely essential for intelligent security systems that are capable of processing large amounts of operational data in real-time. As a highly effective tool in this area, artificial intelligence can assist businesses in anomaly detection, pattern identification of intrusions, and response to new attacks at a faster pace and with greater accuracy as compared to the conventional rule-based security systems. On the other hand, the level of success achieved by AI in the field of cybersecurity depends not only on the complexity of the algorithms but also on the trustworthiness, interpretability, and consistent validation of the AI models that are being used in the actual environments. This section summarized the key ways of assessing and monitoring AI models in security detection systems. It built the emphasis on the preparation of thoroughly documented datasets and training datasets as being reflective of cybersecurity analytics. Security datasets must accurately represent the genuine patterns of both normal and attack behaviors while at the same time minimizing noise, biases, and data leaks. AI models leverage the preprocessing, feature engineering, and class imbalance handling techniques to effectively identify the threat patterns that are strong indicators of security breaches.

Section two introduced a detailed model of the scientific framework for validation. This concept involves a set of carefully planned experiments that span data training, hyperparameter optimization, baseline model comparison, and usage of multiple evaluation metrics. Intrusion detection models were demonstrated to be inadequately measured by accuracy alone mainly because of the highly imbalanced nature of security datasets. As such, a person's ability to detect intrusion skillfully as well as their reliability in the operational setting will find better representation using metrics such as precision, recall, F1 score, and ROC-AUC. Moreover, the chapter highlighted the importance of continuous monitoring of models post their deployment. Cybersecurity AI models exist in a situation of a triangle where changes are occurring concurrently in data distributions, user behavior, and attack methods. Hence, the implementation of monitoring solutions that not only detect changes in the data but also provide an alert when the level of the model's performance has dropped is the key to the maintenance of the model's effectiveness over time.

Besides, these are the systems that produce automatic notifications and have feedback mechanisms that greatly make it easier for a company to identify the first indications of model deterioration and give them the opportunity to retrain the model with the latest data. Furthermore, the chapter also highlighted the ways through which AI misuse could be exploited in cybersecurity. These cover model pollution, adversarial input manipulations, overfitting, and lastly, instability, bias, and data leakage. If these issues are overlooked during both model development and deployment phases, they have the potential to completely undermine the reliability of security systems. Familiarizing with these failure scenarios will enable organizations to create validation methods and protective measures essential for the successful backing of AI-driven detection systems. The experiment that was carried out in the results and discussion section shows the ability of various machine learning and deep learning techniques to detect intrusions in a normal setting. In addition, the chapter touched on the fundamental elements of governance and ethics as being the basis for the proper application of AI deployment. Since security analytical tools usually handle large volumes of operational and behavioral data that may include personal data, organizations are required to adhere to regulatory standards such as data protection laws and information security norms. In addition, the four ingredients essential for trustworthiness and confidence in AI-based security monitoring tools are transparent model management, proper documentation, explainability methods, and human .

Looking ahead, there are a number of new and interesting AI validation research areas in cybersecurity gaining attention and adaptive learning systems are one of them. These systems gradually adjust their model according to real-time security data . These systems are designed to adapt to new attack techniques at the same time as they try to keep the risk of model drift or poisoning to a minimum. At the same time, reliable adaptive learning will still hinge on the availability of very good data and well-controlled retraining processes as well as resilience against adversarial changes. Integration of explainable artificial intelligence (XAI) into security analytics tools is another research avenue that might mature in the near future. Besides the fact that deep learning models tend to be the most powerful, they are also the ones most difficult to interpret. The need for explanation in decision-making, therefore, becomes a must. To this end, research on explainability mechanisms will focus on providing interpretations that are sufficiently informative while remaining accurate in terms of model predictions.

Besides that, federated learning and privacy-preserving machine learning are other fields that might be used for innovation. At the same time as these technologies enable the development of improved detection models by leveraging data from multiple organizations, they also enforce data privacy by making sure that raw data never leaves the premises. In situations where, operational data is so sensitive that it cannot be brought together in a centralized manner, federated methods may well be the best choice for producing high-quality security models. Last but not least, autonomous security systems powered by AI both hold risks and raise questions related to how automation and human oversight will be balanced. It can be argued that due to the high-speed capability of AI, it will be able to detect and respond to threats quite efficiently. However, if left unattended, such fully automated security decision-making might go awry either because the models will behave in ways that cannot be explained or because adversaries might find ways to exploit the vulnerabilities of automated defenses. Therefore, future cybersecurity concepts will be the combination of AI-enabled analytics together with human-in-the-loop decision-making in order to provide safe, transparent, and yet at the same time, efficient operations. All in all, model validation and monitoring of AI in security-related applications is an extremely challenging and interesting topic. In order to provide reliable security systems based on AI, first of all, the AI needs to be fed with good quality data and validated in different ways; second, it needs to be continuously monitored and deployed with risk in mind; last but not least, it needs to be governed by proper frameworks. If organizations are able to blend all these elements together successfully, they will be in a position to use artificial intelligence fully while, at the same time, ensuring the dependencies, the transparency, and the accountability that a modern cybersecurity operation .

REFERENCES

Abdeljaber, O., & Al-Masaeed, S. (2025). Al-Mu'ani, L., Yaseen, H., & Alhnaity, B. (2025). Strategic Intelligence: The Power of AI in Planning Efficiency. *Human Behavior and Emerging Technologies*, (1). Advance online publication. DOI: 10.1155/hbe2/5383054

Abualghanam, O., Alazzam, H., Qatawneh, M., Alazab, M., & Al Sharaiah, M. (2025). Elevating Mobile Security: An Ensemble Approach for Enhanced Malware Detection with M-iForest. *International Journal of Interactive Mobile Technologies*, *19*(10), 129–151. Advance online publication. DOI: 10.3991/ijim.v19i10.51319

Abualhaj, M. M., Al-Khatib, S., Al Shafi, N., Qaddara, I., & Hyassat, A. (2025). Utilizing Gray Wolf Optimization Algorithm in Malware Forensic Investigation. *Journal of Computational and Cognitive Engineering*, *4*(4), 591–602. Advance online publication. DOI: 10.47852/bonviewJCCE52025053

Abualhaj, M. M., Al-Khatib, S. N., Abu-Shareha, A. A., Hyassat, A., & Daoud, M. S. (2025). Smart Firewall for Phishing Detection Powered by Bio-Inspired Algorithms. *Journal of Advances in Information Technology*, *16*(11), 1529–1539. Advance online publication. DOI: 10.12720/jait.16.11.1529-1539

Abualhaj, M. M., Al-Khatib, S. N., Al Zyoud, M., Qaddara, I., & Anbar, M. (2025). Enhancing Intrusion Detection System Performance Using a Hybrid of Harris Hawks and Whale Optimization Algorithms. *Engineering. Technology and Applied Science Research*, *15*(4), 24354–24361. Advance online publication. DOI: 10.48084/etasr.10919

Abualhaj, M. M., Al-Khatib, S. N., Al-Zyoud, M., Qaddara, I., Hiari, M. O., & Aldossary, S. M. A. (2025). Enhanced Network Communication Security Through Hybrid Dragonfly-Bat Feature Selection for Intrusion Detection. *The Journal of Communication*, *20*(5). Advance online publication. DOI: 10.12720/jcm.20.5.607-618

Abualigah, L., Almomani, M. H., Alomari, S. A., Zitar, R. A., Migdady, H., Saleem, K., Snasel, V., Smerat, A., & Ezugwu, A. E. (2025). Optimizing Intrusion Detection in Wireless Sensor Networks via the Improved Chameleon Swarm Algorithm for Feature Selection. *IET Communications*, *19*(1), e70029. Advance online publication. DOI: 10.1049/cmu2.70029

Akram, A. S., Abbas, S., Khan, M. A., Athar, A., Ghazal, T. M., & Al Hamadi, H. (2024). Smart Energy Management System Using Machine Learning. *Computers, Materials & Continua*, *78*(1), 959–973. Advance online publication. DOI: 10.32604/cmc.2023.032216

Al-Adwan, A. S., Al-Adwan, A., Li, N., Fauzi, M. A., Jafar, R. M. S., Habibi, A., & Falahat, M. (2025). IMMERSIVE LEARNING MEETS THEORY: MODELING EDUVERSE ADOPTION IN HIGHER EDUCATION. *Journal of Information Technology Education*, *24*, 042. Advance online publication. DOI: 10.28945/5669

Al-Daoud, K. I., Yogeesh, N., Mohammad, S. I., Raja, N., Chetana, R., William, P., Vasudevan, A., Alshdaifa, N., & Hunitie, M. F. A. (2025). Explainability in AI Using Fuzzy Inference Systems For the Regression Problem. *Applied Mathematics & Information Sciences*, *19*(5), 973–987. Advance online publication. DOI: 10.18576/amis/190501

Al-Daoud, K. I., Yogeesh, N., Mohammad, S. I. S., Raja, N., Jabeen, F. T. Z., William, P., Vasudevan, A., Hunitie, M. F. A., & Alshdaifat, N. (2025). Fuzzy Linear Programming in Real-World Applications: A Comparative Study of Agricultural and Financial Optimization. *Applied Mathematics & Information Sciences*, *19*(4), 849–862. Advance online publication. DOI: 10.18576/amis/190411

Al-Habashneh, A. G., Al-Daoud, K. I., Oraini, B., Al, , & Shelash, S. I. (2025). The impact of artificial intelligence on the development of electronic financial services. *International Journal of Data and Network Science*, *9*(2), 317–322. Advance online publication. DOI: 10.5267/j.ijdns.2024.8.012

Al-Momani, M. M., Alqudah, T. A., Al Swiety, I. A., Mahrakani, N., Nassoura, M. B. A., & Al Attar, M. K. (2025). Integrating Artificial Intelligence (AI) and Business Intelligence (BI): A Framework for Improving Enterprise Performance. *TEM Journal, 14*(3). https://doi.org/DOI: 10.18421/TEM143-26

Al-Mousa, M., Amer, W., Abualhaj, M., Albilasi, S., Nasir, O., & Samara, G. (2025). Agile Proactive Cybercrime Evidence Analysis Model for Digital Forensics. *The International Arab Journal of Information Technology*, *22*(3). Advance online publication. DOI: 10.34028/iajit/22/3/15

Alabdallat, R. D., Abualhaj, M. M., & Abu-Shareha, A. (2025). Enhanced Multiclass Android Malware Detection Using a Modified Dwarf Mongoose Algorithm. *International Journal of Analysis and Applications*, *23*, 248. Advance online publication. DOI: 10.28924/2291-8639-23-2025-248

Aldaaja, Y., Odeh, M., Badrakhan, S. S., Sabri, M., Abdelrahim, Y., Samara, G., & Alsabatin, H. (2025). Quantifying the Managerial and Practical Benefits of Cloud Computing on Information Security in Higher Education Institutions. *Applied Mathematics & Information Sciences*, *19*(1), 15–24. Advance online publication. DOI: 10.18576/amis/190102

Alenazi, M. J. F., Al-Khasawneh, M. A., Rahman, S., & Faheem, Z. (2025). Deep Reinforcement Learning Based Flow Aware-QoS Provisioning in SD-IoT for Precision Agriculture. *Computational Intelligence*, *41*(1), e70023. Advance online publication. DOI: 10.1111/coin.70023

Alharbi, Y., Yadav, K., Dutta, D., Smerat, A., & Ranjbar, F. (2026). Thermodynamic behavior of CO2–organic mixtures: Density prediction using explainable machine learning algorithms. *Results in Engineering*, *29*, 108687. Advance online publication. DOI: 10.1016/j.rineng.2025.108687

Ali, A. M., Al-Qerem, A., Hassan, M. R., Abu-Khadrah, A., & Jarrah, M. (2025). Traffic Monitoring and Control System for Smart City Pollution Regulation Using IoT and Correlated Capsule Networks. *IEEE Access : Practical Innovations, Open Solutions*, *13*, 46983–47003. Advance online publication. DOI: 10.1109/ACCESS.2025.3550966

Alkhawatrah, M. (2025). Random Forests Relay Selector in Buffer-Aided Cooperative Networks. *IEEE Access : Practical Innovations, Open Solutions*, *13*, 165402–165410. Advance online publication. DOI: 10.1109/ACCESS.2025.3612192

Almajed, R., Ibrahim, A., Abualkishik, A. Z., Mourad, N., & Almansour, F. A. (2022). Using machine learning algorithm for detection of cyber-attacks in cyber physical systems. *Periodicals of Engineering and Natural Sciences*, *10*(3), 261. Advance online publication. DOI: 10.21533/pen.v10i3.3035

Alnawayseh, S. E. A., Al-Sit, W. T., & Ghazal, T. M. (2022). Smart Congestion Control in 5G/6G Networks Using Hybrid Deep Learning Techniques. *Complexity*, *2022*(1), 1781952. Advance online publication. DOI: 10.1155/2022/1781952

Alnawayseh, S. E. A., Muhammad, M. H. G., Hassan, Z., Fatima, M., Aslam, M. S., Ibrahim, A., & Ateeq, K. (2023). Resource Provisioning in Cloud Computing using Fuzzy Logic Control System: An adaptive approach. *2nd International Conference on Business Analytics for Technology and Security, ICBATS 2023*. DOI: 10.1109/ICBATS57792.2023.10111481

Alraba'nah, Y., Al-Sharaeh, S., & Al Hindi, G. (2025). Enhancing Intrusion Detection Using Hybrid Long Short-Term Memory and XGBoost. *Journal of Soft Computing and Data Mining*, *6*(1). Advance online publication. DOI: 10.30880/jscdm.2025.06.01.016

Alraba'nah, Y., & Hiari, M. (2025). Improved convolutional neural networks for aircraft type classification in remote sensing images. *IAES International Journal of Artificial Intelligence*, *14*(2), 1540. Advance online publication. DOI: 10.11591/ijai.v14.i2.pp1540-1547

Arabiat, A., Altayeb, M., & Salama, S. (2025). Artificial intelligence-powered smart roads: Leveraging orange3 for traffic signs recognition. *IAES International Journal of Artificial Intelligence*, *14*(5), 3816. Advance online publication. DOI: 10.11591/ijai.v14.i5.pp3816-3826

Arabiat, A. M. (2025). Intelligent Model for Detecting GAN-Generated Images Based on Multi-Classifier and Advanced Data Mining Techniques. *International Journal of Electrical and Electronic Engineering and Telecommunications*, *14*(3). Advance online publication. DOI: 10.18178/ijeetc.14.3.147-157

Arabiat, A. M., & Eljaafreh, Y. G. (2025). Intrusion Detection in Wireless Sensor Networks Using ML Based Classification of Denial of Service (DoS) Attacks. *The Journal of Communication*, *20*(4). Advance online publication. DOI: 10.12720/jcm.20.4.501-514

Awais, Z., Hussain, M., Elshenawy, A., Arsalan, A., Anwar, M., Asif Habib, M., Jabbar, S., & Ahmad, M. (2025). ISCC: Intelligent Semantic Caching and Control for NDN-Enabled Industrial IoT Networks. *IEEE Access : Practical Innovations, Open Solutions*, *13*, 169881–169898. Advance online publication. DOI: 10.1109/ACCESS.2025.3614984

Bektemyssova, G., Montazeri, Z., Dehghani, M., Ibraheem, I. K., Smerat, A., Werner, F., Al-Salih, A. A. M. M., Ahmed, M. A., & Eguchi, K. (2025). Search and Rescue Algorithm (SRA): A Metaheuristic Approach for Efficient Constrained Engineering Optimization. *International Journal of Intelligent Engineering and Systems*, *18*(10), 607–621. Advance online publication. DOI: 10.22266/ijies2025.1130.39

Biswas, S., Maiti, B., Singh, G., Ezugwu, A. E., Saleem, K., Abualigah, L., Smerat, A., & Bera, U. K. (2025). A Novel Hybrid Optimizer Based on Coati Optimization Algorithm and Differential Evolution for Global Optimization and Constrained Engineering Problems. *International Journal of Computational Intelligence Systems*, *18*(1), 157. Advance online publication. DOI: 10.1007/s44196-025-00855-y

Dara Singh, K. S., Kien Hong, T., Abbasi, G. A., & Al-Adwan, A. S. (2025). Building Bonds with Food Delivery Apps: Determinants of App Attachment & Continuous Intention–Does Gender Matter? *International Journal of Human-Computer Interaction*, *41*(23), 15276–15294. Advance online publication. DOI: 10.1080/10447318.2025.2495843

Duraimurugan, S., Jayarin, P. J., Mohammad, S. I., Hariprasad, N., Vasudevan, A., Soon, E. E. H., Hussein, A. H., & Alshurideh, M. T. (2025). Enhanced Server-Client Framework for Optimizing QoS in Video Streaming Over Diverse Networks. *Applied Mathematics & Information Sciences*, *19*(1), 61–73. Advance online publication. DOI: 10.18576/amis/190106

Elkaradawy, A., Elshenawy, A., & Harb, H. (2025). Enhancing Cloud Job Failure Prediction With a Novel Multilayer Voting-Based Framework. *IEEE Access : Practical Innovations, Open Solutions*, *13*, 140600–140613. Advance online publication. DOI: 10.1109/ACCESS.2025.3593808

Elomda, B. M., Abdelbary, T. A. A., Hassan, H. A., Hamza, K. S., & Kharma, Q. (2025). An Enhanced Multi-Layer Blockchain Security Model for Improved Latency and Scalability. *Information (Basel)*, *16*(3), 241. Advance online publication. DOI: 10.3390/info16030241

Farman, M., Gokbulut, N., Shehzad, A., Nisar, K. S., Hincal, E., & Sambas, A. (2025). Fractional order malaria epidemic model: Qualitative and computational study to determine the dynamics for sensitivity prevalence. *Journal of Computational Science*, *91*, 102656. Advance online publication. DOI: 10.1016/j.jocs.2025.102656

Fatima, W., Rizvi, S. S. R., Ghazal, T. M., Kharma, Q. M., Ahmad, M., Abbas, S., Furqan, M., & Adnan, K. M. (2025). Abstractive Text Summarization in Arabic-Like Script Using Multi-Encoder Architecture and Semantic Extraction Techniques. *IEEE Access : Practical Innovations, Open Solutions*, *13*, 104977–104991. Advance online publication. DOI: 10.1109/ACCESS.2025.3575610

Ghazal, T. M. (2025). An IoT-Based Active Learning Convolutional Neural Networks Model for Predicting River Water Quality. *Journal of Soft Computing and Data Mining*, *6*(1). Advance online publication. DOI: 10.30880/jscdm.2025.06.01.021

Ghazal, T. M., Abu-Shareha, A., Mustafa, S. A., Ibrahim, A., & Ahmed, S. M. (2025). Privacy-Preserving Transformer-Based Meta-Learning Algorithm for Zero-Day Intrusion Detection in IoT-Enabled Smart Grids. *Journal of Internet Services and Information Security*, *15*(4), 76–84. Advance online publication. DOI: 10.58346/JISIS.2025.I4.006

Ghazal, T. M., Abualhaj, M., Ahmed, A. A., Al-Tarawni, M. A. M., & Maghrabi, L. A. (2025). Federated Deep Graph Neural Network Algorithm for Real-Time Intrusion Detection in Heterogeneous IoT Systems. *Journal of Internet Services and Information Security*, *15*(4), 484–497. Advance online publication. DOI: 10.58346/JISIS.2025.I4.035

Ghazal, T. M., Awouda, A. E., Hasan, M. K., Rahman, A. H. A., Islam, S., Saeed, R. A., Elshafie, H., Iqbal, A., & Hussein, A. H. (2025). Knowledge Learning for Securing Workflow Scheduling Algorithm in Mobile Edge Computing. *Mobile Networks and Applications*, *30*(3-4), 395–413. Advance online publication. DOI: 10.1007/s11036-025-02465-6

Ghazal, T. M., Hasan, M. K., Alzoubi, H. M., Al Hmmadi, M., Al-Dmour, N. A., Islam, S., Kamran, R., & Mago, B. (2022). Securing Smart Cities Using Blockchain Technology. *2022 1st International Conference on AI in Cybersecurity, ICAIC 2022*. DOI: 10.1109/ICAIC53980.2022.9896971

H K, P. K., Dash, R., K, J. R., Mohapatra, B., Bishoyi, S. S., Bajaj, M., & Blazek, V.H K. (2026). Multi-domain fault characterization in DC microgrids utilizing Hilbert-Huang transform ensemble by LSTM networks with adaptive boundary condition constraints. *Results in Engineering*, *29*, 108721. Advance online publication. DOI: 10.1016/j.rineng.2025.108721

Hasan, M. K., Habib, A. K. M. A., Islam, S., Safie, N., Ghazal, T. M., Khan, M. A., Alzahrani, A. I., Alalwan, N., Kadry, S., & Masood, A. (2024). Federated learning enables 6 G communication technology: Requirements, applications, and integrated with intelligence framework. *Alexandria Engineering Journal*, *91*, 658–668. Advance online publication. DOI: 10.1016/j.aej.2024.02.044

Hou, G., Alkhayyat, A., Almalkawi, A., Yadav, A., Shreenidhi, H. S., Saini, V., Shomurotova, S., Singh, D., Jain, V., Smerat, A., & Khalid, A. (2025). Development of robust machine learning models to estimate hydrochar higher heating value and yield based upon biomass proximate analysis. *Bioresources and Bioprocessing*, *12*(1), 138. Advance online publication. DOI: 10.1186/s40643-025-00979-1

Iftikhar, A., Mohammad, S. I., Alqudah, M. N., Al-Adwan, A. S., Vasudevan, A., Ali, I., & Farhan, M. (2025). Evaluating Inclusivity and Fairness of AI Recruitment Tools for Hiring People with Disabilities in the United Arab Emirates(UAE). *Data and Metadata*, *4*. Advance online publication. DOI: 10.56294/dm2025487

Iskandarani, M. Z. (2025). Effect of Intelligent Reflecting Surface on WSN Communication With Access Points Configuration. *IEEE Access : Practical Innovations, Open Solutions*, *13*, 13380–13394. Advance online publication. DOI: 10.1109/ACCESS.2025.3531637

Iskandarani, M. Z., & Hidayat, R. (2025). Analysis of Factors Affecting Spectrum Sensing in an IRS based Wireless Network. *International Journal on Advanced Science, Engineering and Information Technology*, *15*(1), 300–309. Advance online publication. DOI: 10.18517/ijaseit.15.1.20491

Kamal, M. M., Ul Abideen, S. Z., Al-Khasawneh, M. A., Momani, A. M., Mostafa, H., Atoum, M. S., Ullah, S., Alsayaydeh, J. A. J., & Yusof, M. F. (2025). Meyer Wavelet Transform and Jaccard Deep Q Net for Small Object Classification Using Multi-Modal Images. *CMES -. Computer Modeling in Engineering & Sciences*, *144*(3), 3053–3083. Advance online publication. DOI: 10.32604/cmes.2025.067430

Khalayleh, Y. A. S., Mohammad, S. I., Al Louzi, N. S., Baniata, M., Hassan, M., Safaqah, M. A., Vasudevan, A., & Alshurideh, M. T. (2025). Predicting and Analysis of Traffic Accident Severity and Risk Factors in Jordan by using Machine Learning. *Applied Mathematics & Information Sciences*, *19*(6), 1419–1426. Advance online publication. DOI: 10.18576/amis/190615

Khaled Abdullah, S., & Qawasmeh, R. (2025). *Navigating the ethical and legal risks of AI marketing in Jordanian SMEs*. EDPACS., DOI: 10.1080/07366981.2025.2600205

Khan, A. A., Siddiqui, S., Al-Shamayleh, A. S., Akhunzada, A., & Dey, I. (2025). DFROG-MAC: A Dynamic Fragmentation-Based MAC for Prioritised Emergency Data Management in Vehicular Networks. *IET Wireless Sensor Systems*, *15*(1), e70017. Advance online publication. DOI: 10.1049/wss2.70017

Makhadmeh, S. N., Fraihat, S., Awad, M., Sanjalawe, Y., Al-Betar, M. A., & Awadallah, M. A. (2025). A crossover-integrated Marine Predator Algorithm for feature selection in intrusion detection systems within IoT environments. *Internet of Things : Engineering Cyber Physical Human Systems*, *31*, 101536. Advance online publication. DOI: 10.1016/j.iot.2025.101536

Marhoon, H. M., Basil, N., Sabbar, B. M., Qasem, N., & Ma'arif, A. (2025). Safety and Surveillance on Unmanned Aerial Vehicles Control Systems and Optimization Methods: A Systematic Review. *International Journal of Robotics and Control Systems*, *5*(5). Advance online publication. DOI: 10.31763/ijrcs.v5i5.1859

Nasir, J., Aamir, M., Iftikhar, S., Albidah, A. B., Alqasem, O. A., Elwahab, M. E. A., Khan, I., & Koh, W. S. (2025). A Novel Hybrid Approach to Forecasting Crude Oil Prices Using Local Mean Decomposition, ARIMA, and XGBoost. *IEEE Access : Practical Innovations, Open Solutions*, *13*, 89140–89156. Advance online publication. DOI: 10.1109/ACCESS.2025.3561193

Otair, M., Qawaqzeh, F. A., Alomari, S. A., Zitar, R. A., Migdady, H., Saleem, K., Smerat, A., Alsoud, A. R., & Abualigah, L. (2025). Enhanced Arithmetic Optimization Algorithm for Intrusion Detection in Wireless Sensor Networks. *International Journal of Communication Systems*, *38*(10), e70122. Advance online publication. DOI: 10.1002/dac.70122

Qader Ismail Alnajem, A. A., Ibrahim, A., Abdulrahman, M. M., Abdulrazak Al-Kubaisi, A. A., Tawfeq, J. F., Khishe, M., & Saeed, A. (2024). AI-Driven Strategic Foresight: Anticipating Future Trends and Modelling Business Strategies. *2024 International Conference on Decision Aid Sciences and Applications, DASA 2024*. DOI: 10.1109/DASA63652.2024.10836619

Rabbi, M. F., Amin, M., Al-Dalahmeh, M., & Abdullah, M. (2025). Assessing the role of information technology in promoting environmental sustainability and preventing crime in E-commerce. *International Review of Applied Sciences and Engineering*, *16*(1), 81–97. Advance online publication. DOI: 10.1556/1848.2024.00834

Ramesh, J. V. N., Nimma, D., Dasari, R., Chaudhari Rane, D., AlGhamdi, A., Rao, K. B. V. B., Haider, S. A., Kuzieva, N., & Jangir, P. (2025). Safe and Reliable Two-Stage Online Offloading Algorithm for Transportation Cyber-Physical Systems. *IEEE Transactions on Intelligent Transportation Systems*, *26*(9), 14313–14322. Advance online publication. DOI: 10.1109/TITS.2025.3539934

Rehan, R., Sahran, S., Alyasseri, Z. A. A., Sani, N. S., & Al-Betar, M. A. (2025). Hyperparameters optimization of evolving spiking neural network using artificial bee colony for unsupervised anomaly detection. *Journal of Intelligent Systems*, *34*(1), 20240235. Advance online publication. DOI: 10.1515/jisys-2024-0235

Sardar, R., Anees, T., Al-Shamayleh, A. S., Mehmood, E., Khalil, W., Akhunzada, A., & Shaikh, F. S. (2025). Challenges in detecting security threats in WoT: A systematic literature review. *Artificial Intelligence Review*, *58*(7), 196. Advance online publication. DOI: 10.1007/s10462-025-11176-z

Shah, R. K., Hasan, M. K., Islam, S., Khan, A., Ghazal, T. M., & Khan, A. N. (2022). Detect Phishing Website by Fuzzy Multi-Criteria Decision Making. *2022 1st International Conference on AI in Cybersecurity, ICAIC 2022*. DOI: 10.1109/ICAIC53980.2022.9897036

Shamaylah, N., Ibrahim Mohammad, S., Al Oraini, B., Yaseen Al-Gaafreh, J. M., Mosallam Alqahtani, M., Vasudevan, A., Shlash Mohammad, A. A., & Ahmmad Hunitie, M. F. (2025). Data-Driven Decision-Making for Employee Training and Development in Jordanian Public Institutions. *Data and Metadata, 4*, 886. Advance online publication. DOI: 10.56294/dm2025886

Sharma, K. P., Hussain, R., Jaharadak, A. A., Trawnih, A. A., Verma, D., Dasi, S., & Pant, S. (2025). Hybrid Convolutional Neural Network for Robust Attack Detection in Wireless Sensor Networks. *Internet Technology Letters*, *8*(6), e650. Advance online publication. DOI: 10.1002/itl2.650

Shlash Mohammad, A. A., Ibrahim Mohammad, S., Al-Daoud, K. I., Al Oraini, B., Mosallam Alqahtani, M., Vasudevan, A., & Ahmmad Hunitie, M. F. (2025). Riding into the Future: Transforming Jordan's Public Transportation with Predictive Analytics and Real-Time Data. *Data and Metadata*, *4*, 887. Advance online publication. DOI: 10.56294/dm2025887

Solairaju, J. A., Rathinasamy, S., Thanikodi, S., Tarawneh, B., Gurumoorthy, V., Antony, J. S., & Arul Gnana Dhas, A. (2025). Development and Validation of ANN Models for Water Absorption in Sawdust and Kenaf Fiber-Reinforced Polystyrene Composites. *Engineering Reports*, *7*(9), e70393. Advance online publication. DOI: 10.1002/eng2.70393

Vasudevan, A., Albinaa, T. A., Mohammad, S. I., Sharmila, E., Raja, N., Soon, E. E. H., Alshurideh, M. T., & Al-Adwan, A. S. (2024). Bidirectional LSTM for Electronic Product Recommendation. *Applied Mathematics & Information Sciences*, *18*(6), 1443–1453. Advance online publication. DOI: 10.18576/amis/180621

Vasudevan, A., Nair, S. S., Mohammad, S. I., Raja, N., Soon, E. E. H., Nagaraj, S., Alshamayleh, A., & Alshurideh, M. T. (2025). Redefining Realities: AI's Cost-Efficient Revolution in Indian Cinema's VFX Landscape. *Applied Mathematics & Information Sciences*, *19*(1), 171–182. Advance online publication. DOI: 10.18576/amis/190115

Vasudevan, A., Tamilmani, K. T., Mohammad, S. I., Sridheepika, V. S., Raja, N., Soon, E. E. H., Nagaraj, S., & Al-Adwan, A. S. (2025). Voices of Concern: Contemplations on Socioeconomic, Ethical, and Developmental Impacts of AI. *Applied Mathematics & Information Sciences*, *19*(1), 221–232. Advance online publication. DOI: 10.18576/amis/190119

Xu, B., Jummaa, K., Altalbawy, F. M. A., Roopashree, R., Saraswat, S. K., Ray, S., Tomar, P., Naem, S., Hamza, H. H., Smerat, A., & Khalid, A. (2025). Machine learning-assisted computation of water activity for ionic liquid-based aqueous ternary elements. *Desalination and Water Treatment*, *324*, 101484. Advance online publication. DOI: 10.1016/j.dwt.2025.101484

Yaseen, M., Ali, E., Sarwar, N., Jamel, L., Din, I., Yuldashev, F., & Law, F. (2025). Design of Minimal Spanning Tree and Analytic Hierarchical Process (SAHP) Based Hybrid Technique for Software Requirements Prioritization. *IET Software, 2025*(1). DOI: 10.1049/sfw2/8819735

Zraiqat, A., Al Sayyed, O., Al Soudi, M., Al-Salih, A. A. M. M., Smerat, A., Montazeri, Z., Dehghani, M., Malik, O. P., Ahmed, M. A., Ibraheem, I. K., & Eguchi, K. (2025). Key Maker Algorithm: A Novel Human-Based Metaheuristic for Constrained Optimization. *International Journal of Intelligent Engineering and Systems*, *18*(9), 688–699. Advance online publication. DOI: 10.22266/ijies2025.1031.45

Chapter 13
Constraints and Limitations of Automation in Autonomous Security Environments

Abdalla Elnekiti
http://orcid.org/0000-0002-1372-0096
University of Wollongong in Dubai, UAE

Sonal Trivedi
http://orcid.org/0000-0001-8711-2977
Manav Rachna University, India

ABSTRACT

This chapter investigates the limitations and restrictions of automation in autonomous security environments where artificial intelligence is the primary driver of detection and response with little human intervention. It studies the technical, operational, and legal factors that limit full automation, including issues with the quality of data, uncertainty of the model, ambiguity of context, and manipulation by an adversary. The chapter discusses the dangers of false positives, the triggering of automated actions one after another, the loss of situational awareness, and overdependence on algorithmic outputs. It also addresses regulatory and ethical constraints, highlighting the need for human oversight, accountability, and explainability in security decision making. Through the combination of security engineering practicalities and governance aspects, the chapter offers a fair evaluation of the advantages brought by automation and the necessity of human control for a security operation that is both resilient and compliant.

1. INTRODUCTION TO AUTOMATION IN AUTONOMOUS SECURITY ENVIRONMENTS

Artificial intelligence is an extremely powerful tool that, among other uses, can help a system to work through very large amounts of different data and find patterns that are too complex or huge for human analysts to handle. Modern autonomous security environments heavily rely on AI as one of the biggest reason's machines can not only identify legitimate and malicious events but also perform this task with high accuracy is that AI is taught using historical data. Moreover, unsupervised and semi-supervised

DOI: 10.4018/979-8-2600-2870-4.ch013

learning methods are utilized to spot anomalies in user and entity behaviors across network flows, endpoint activities, changes in authentication, (Vasudevan et al., 2024). Natural language processing (NLP) technologies can comprehend and summarize threat intelligence and vulnerabilities to assist a human investigator. Besides, reinforcement learning-based adaptive defense strategy and policy optimization methods are currently being researched. Automated decision-making is improved by AI through the addition of probabilistic judgment that goes far beyond simple event recognition. For instance, an AI-enabled system can also tell whether the behavior it is witnessing is related to malicious execution, credential theft, lateral movement, or data exfiltration even if the system did not have the signature of the malware(Abualhaj, Al-Khatib, Al Zyoud, Qaddara, et al., 2025). For instance, it detects deviations in time-of-day, permission level changes, process history, command usage, location anomalies, or irregular interactions with peripherals. AI is highly effective in detecting sophisticated forms of maliciousness that are disguised and subtly implied in the context rather than being roughly outlined or signaled. At the same time, though, AI adds another complexity level, making it difficult for the security analysts to comprehend the workings of it. Usually, a security analyst can justify the activation of a rule, yet sometimes a predictive ensemble model remains one to the analyst as a 'black box' even if it has generated a very high-risk score. When a highly accurate prediction model is at the same time low in explainability, it is quite a distressing situation, especially if the automatic decision may lead to the disruption of the organization's operation, wrongful exclusion of the legitimate users, and may even result in legal and organizational escalations. Therefore, while AI may accelerate the procedures and extend the reach, if it is not fine-tuned and regulated efficiently, it will probably lead to issues related to comprehension, responsibility, and (Abuowaida et al., 2025).

1.1 Operational Benefits of Security Automation

It is imperative that automated security environment executions are connected with the continuous effort of investigating the root cause even when the other parts of the chapter will, in the end, describe the related risks. Speed is the number one benefit of automation here. Automation programs can very quickly take in data, connect indicators, and perform authorized actions. As a result, the time interval between uncovering and controlling is greatly shortened. It is, in fact, particularly clear in the examples where the attack scenario time, like ransomware or credential misuse, is the determining factor and the containment if done in time causes only very limited . Another advantage is that automation is standard. Analysts work on the basis of their experiences, get tired, their judgment can change over time while their availability also varies(Abualghanam et al., 2025). On the contrary, automation keeps implementing predetermined rules or patterns it has been trained on no matter how large the volume of events is. Needless to say, this stand-alone feature of automation is extremely important for very monotonous tasks such as triage, enrichment, reputation lookups, sandbox submission, IOC matching, and case routing. Additionally, from a resource point of view, automation enables the team to defend a much larger infrastructure than would have been possible without automation(Ramesh et al., 2025). Moreover, automation can play a key role in enhancing visibility across different layers with the help of data integration. This way a security team would have a clearer understanding of the situation. Usually, autonomous environments are the ones which combine endpoints, networks, clouds, identities and threats intelligence all together within one main line of analysis which majorly facilitates reasoning across layers and also the presentation of incidents in the form of narratives. In those grown up environments, automation is not just a source of resilience but actually it is the means through which automation keeps changing policy, finds new attack methods and limits human supervision - in other words, these are the factors which greatly help in the sustainability of operations. For this reason, automation should not simply be regarded as a technical enhancement but a vital strategic one, though it has to be acknowledged that efficiency and other advantages alone do not make reliability, e.g. a very quick response may cause mistakes, a very strong logic may increase already existing biases and the large scale of automation can make a single error have a very serious impact from the operational point of (Al-Mousa et al., 2025).

1.2 Scope and Structure of the Chapter

This chapter reveals the limits and constraints of automation in autonomous security settings. While, on the one hand, automation may produce gains in speed, scalability, and operational efficiencies; on the other hand, the transferring of full decision-making powers to machines also raises new defects that must be thoroughly understood. Therefore, the chapter dismantles the excessively positive expectations of AI security and instead looks at the issues of failure, risk introduction, and shortcoming of automation(A. M. Arabiat, 2025). Firstly, the chapter goes into the nitty-gritty of autonomous security systems' conceptual and technical features such as their general architecture, the working mechanism of analysis, and decision-making flows ending with a discussion on technical limitations such as model capacity, data dependency, infrastructural drain, latency concerns, and reliability issues. Besides working challenges like false alarms, missing the point, over automation, and attack chain management difficulties are also elaborated the risks resulting from the means or forms of automation - the manipulation by adversaries, model poisoning, and vulnerabilities in automated response pipelines are also (Aldabbas et al., 2025).

This is not all. Security automation is neither a pure technical issue nor is it human, governance, legal, ethical, and compliance issues combined; it is the whole combination that is covered in this chapter. The issues of striking a balance between human oversight and machine autonomy and of people being held responsible for automated actions are two such areas that are given detailed treatment. The chapter concludes with a results and discussion section based on a cybersecurity dataset and model assessment followed by a forecast of responsible, explainable, and human-centered automation as the future in security operations. Therefore, the chapter contends that the relevant question is not whether to bring in automation in autonomous security environments, but rather how to establish, monitor, and govern its boundaries such that defensive efficiency is not attained at the cost of reliability, transparency, and operational (Raza et al., 2025).

This chapter contributes an integrated Automation Constraint Framework for autonomous security environments. The framework combines data and model dependence constraints, operational failure modes, adversarial risks, legal and ethical limitations, human oversight requirements, and empirical evaluation of detection reliability. It shows that autonomous security should be assessed not only by detection accuracy but also by robustness, proportionality, explainability, compliance, and operational safety.

2. DATA AND MODEL DEPENDENCE CONSTRAINTS

In machine learning systems designed to identify hostile actions in self-governing security environments, the foundation rests squarely on historical situations. These models statistically discover correlations among the observed features, for example, login frequency, network contact patterns, file access behavior, system process activities, and security incidents identified in the past. By examining past events, the models aim at not only recognizing standard user behavior but also at detecting indications of a possible security breach. Such a technique on one hand gifts the system a very robust pattern recognition skill and makes it very effective(Abdeljaber et al., 2025). However, it comes with the major limitation of being entirely dependent on the quality of the historical data and its ability to represent the environment accurately. Introducing new technologies, changing, adding new applications, network restructuring, or policy changes are some of the factors that cause security situations to change. Historical activity model training only makes the models incapable of accounting for new and different behavior. However, the problem is compounded by the mere existence of a small number of complete, publicly available datasets(Makhadmeh et al., 2025). Mostly, there are reasons why sophisticated cyber incidents are kept quiet, for example, laws and regulations, reputation, and fears, to name a few. Therefore, advanced attack methods have not been well represented in training sets. Thus, models trained on the data available only can perform well in recognition of known threat patterns but are unable to identify new or novel attack ones. It is also likely that some outdated patterns are found in historic data sets. For instance, earlier logging might have missed capturing some metadata, compared with new telemetry. If models trained with such a dataset are applied to contemporary environments in which richer data streams are the norm, it will cause problems(Ghazal, 2025a).

2.1 Dataset Drift and Model Degradation over Time

In fact, a common reason why automated security systems can't always be trusted over time is due to the dataset updating. This continually changing or drifting issue results in a scenario of machine learning tools working on data that have different features from those at the training time. This is even more true in cybersecurity where changes occur very quickly. In general, majority of enterprises change their network setup from time to time and also make changes such as introducing new products, using the cloud, and new identity management frameworks. This will change things such as network traffic, authentication methods, and system activities(Alenazi et al., 2025). So even if these changes are usual result of work, model may see them as anomalies just because they do not fit the patterns it was trained . The model is expected to become ineffective, it can either produce numerous false alarms or it may fail to detect actual malicious behaviors. Actually, the problem goes further than that. What if the change is an adversarial one? Everyone knows that attackers are always keeping one step ahead and they continuously change the way they attack in order to escape detection. As soon as they find out what kind of behavior automated systems normally look for, they alter their actions so that they are classified as legitimate ones. Hence, detection models which rely on fixed behavioral patterns gradually become ineffective. We could say that, if "dataset drift" is the reason, then "model degradation" is the consequence. As training samples and the real-time data keep diverging, the model's prediction quality (Abualigah et al., 2025). The model may mistakenly consider good behavior as bad, or may fail to recognize a subtle attack. Without monitoring and retraining, automated security systems may experience a gradual decline in performance without any indication of the problem. Most enterprises have adopted the solution of fixing drift by creation of continuous learning pipelines that are responsible for model retraining at intervals with fresh operational data. However, this endeavor is fraught with risks. Some of these risks are: labeling of training data, validation of new models, the range of possible attacks through training data poisoning. Thus, handling the problem of dataset drift is a vital function in ensuring the reliability of autonomous security systems(A. M. Arabiat & Eljaafreh, 2025).

2.2 Feature Engineering Challenges in Security Analytics

Feature engineering refers to the process of converting raw data into machine learning model-friendly structured features or attributes. In cybersecurity, features can be sensitive indicators, for example, log-in rates, patterns of file accesses, chains/process sequences, or attempts of privilege escalations. The effectiveness of automated detection systems is largely dependent on how well and how meaningfully the features are engineered that are given to the model. What makes designing features for cyber-attack detection so difficult is the fact that attackers often disguise their malicious actions by imitating legitimate ones. For example, administrative commands with privileged access may be executed by a normal system administrator as well as an attacker. A legitimate admin can only be distinguished from an attacker through a thorough contextual analysis(Al-Momani et al., 2025).

The second challenge involves deciding the granularity of features. On one side, features with very fine granularity will characterize complex human behaviors well, but will also result in heavy computation and long training time. On the flip side, a very rough feature which is easy to compute and use might not capture the subtle differences required to detect an advanced attack. Also, feature engineering is an interdisciplinary endeavor that requires a blend of cybersecurity, operations, and data science. The ones who know potential attack behaviors will be security analysts, whereas data scientists will need to translate these behavioral elements into measurable model-oriented inputs(R. D. Alabdallat et al., 2025). Autonomous security systems implementation is a sort of activity that usually causes a massive hitch in the flexibility of an organization. It is a common scenario for feature engineering to not be a single session activity but rather a continuous one because of the ever-evolving nature of security threats. Features that fit one model might become ineffective if hackers change their techniques. Therefore to stay highly capable and continue detecting, models and features must be altered (Vasudevan et al., 2025).

2.3 Adversarial Manipulation of Security Training Data

Automated security systems pose an alarming threat when it comes to potential adversarial manipulation of training data. Machine learning algorithms usually work on the premise that training datasets accurately reflect the phenomena to be modeled. However, criminal actors are able to use data sources and by so doing change the way models work. "Data poisoning" is considered to be one of the most effective methods of adversarial attacks. It mainly refers to a scenario when an attacker secretly inserts altered or entirely fabricated data into the datasets intended for model training. Such a scenario will result in the model embracing incorrect concepts or behaviors, since it would have been trained with misleading data. Creating a fake benign activity that using the set of features almost resembles dangerous ones is a great example of this(Maz et al., 2025).

Another type of adversarial methods is constituted by evasion attacks which are carried out to skip detection . After realizing how features are evaluated by automated systems, attackers change actions to evade detection or impersonate legitimate activities. Hence, machine learning-based security systems can be undermined by adversarial manipulations. Continuous learning systems that incorporate feedback loops may also be attacked by adversaries. In situations where analyst feedback or operational results influence training data, an automated system can be threatened when attackers are capable of changing these inputs without being detected(Qaddara & Alraba'nah, 2025). Detection models' effectiveness could be diminished, albeit slowly and without directly leading to suspicion. It is indeed the case that adversarial manipulation attacks are extremely difficult to stop precisely because they come into systems through the use of valid data channels. So physical securing a system, in addition to encrypting and validating data, implies a training pipeline that is immune to adversarial manipulation. Most importantly, the solution provides human involvement in the evaluation of the models automatically(Abualhaj, Al-Khatib, Al-Zyoud, Qaddara, et al., 2025).

Table 1. Data and Model Dependence Constraints in Autonomous Security Systems

Constraint Category	Description	Impact on Automated Security Systems	Mitigation Strategies
Historical Data Dependence	Models rely on past attack patterns for training	Reduced ability to detect new or unknown threats	Continuous dataset updates and model retraining
Dataset Drift	Operational data patterns change over time	Increased false positives and declining detection accuracy	Periodic model validation and adaptive learning pipelines
Noisy or Incomplete Telemetry	Security logs may contain errors, gaps, or inconsistent formats	Reduced visibility into system behavior	Multi-layer telemetry collection and log normalization
Feature Engineering Limitations	Difficulty in identifying meaningful behavioral indicators	Reduced model interpretability and accuracy	Continuous feature refinement and domain expertise integration
Adversarial Data Manipulation	Attackers manipulate datasets or system feedback loops	Model corruption and detection evasion	Secure training pipelines and anomaly monitoring

To conclude, reliance on data and features is what essentially limits autonomous security systems structurally. Historically fragmented data, dataset drifting, lack of telemetry, and adversarial data substitutions are some of the elements that could pull real-time detection models to operate below the desired level. Thesesituations only drive up the requirements for security operations, model evaluations, and safe data management .

3. OPERATIONAL LIMITATIONS OF AUTOMATED SECURITY ENVIRONMENTS

False positives are still perhaps the most painful operational limitation for automated security systems. They refer to instances where a system mistakenly identifies normal behavior as an attack and it might sound an alarm, suggest a remediation or even take automated steps. On their face, very sensitive automated systems should be excellent as they potentially reduce false negatives. Yet, over-sensitivity frequently causes a proliferation of nuisance alerts that are practically unmanageable. In today's world of digital infrastructures, legitimate actions can be very diverse. Thus, a remote login from a strange location, a user with admin privileges wearing a mask, deployment of software via scripts, scaling of cloud workloads, and carrying out large-scale file transfers can all be considered attack-like features depending on what is monitored(Khatibi et al., 2025). Hence, machine learning and rule-based systems that lack full contextual knowledge may, misidentify these legitimate activities as suspicious, security teams' exposure to false positives determines their level of alert fatigue, namely, a decrease in the ability to separate genuine incidents from mundane noises as the number of alerts increases. However, alert fatigue is not merely an issue of inefficiency; it can also be a danger to safety. Security teams, for instance, overwhelmed with a huge volume of alerts, may at some time simply neglect the warnings, become suspicious of the alerts, or overly depend on automation for priority assignment. Also, the false positives in automated configurations can trigger containment measures such as device isolation, user lockout, or application blocking. Such measures, besides hindering business operations, will cause a postponement in the implementation of new services and create an atmosphere of resistance toward automation internally. Simply put, though automation is a tool that is mainly introduced to reduce toil, a poorly configured system can end up merely transferring the problem from manual detection to manual (Ghazal, Hasan, Mokhtar, et al., 2025).

3.1 Operational Disruptions from Automated Responses

Automated security systems intend to isolate the threat within the shortest possible time. In fact, the very rapidity, which such isolation allows, paradoxically, becomes the factor that makes these systems susceptible to the generation of operational disruptions. For example, imagine the endpoint isolations, user account disabling, process blocking or network segment restriction done by an automated system; these defensive actions generally come with real operational consequences. The wrong decision leading to the trigger or the action being missing the necessary context could negatively impact legitimate business operations. This is shown when a user account automatically gets locked out after detection of an abnormal login activity, which, in reality, can result in a situation where a senior executive traveling abroad, a developer working on a cloud resource from a new workstation or an emergency responder operating under nonstandard conditions, all of whom will be denied access to their (Ghazal, Awouda, et al., 2025). Likewise, production server isolation implemented by automation due to detection of anomalous outbound traffic can adversely affect essential services even if the traffic spike was legitimate, e.g., caused by software update, backup, or maintenance script. Plus, an erroneous shutdown carried out by automation in the case of industrial or operational technology may have disastrous consequences(Aldaaja et al., 2025).

On the other hand, paying the operational cost may represent a major challenge. For example, business continuity may be put at risk, customer-facing systems could be down, the internal teams might not trust the security controls, and the restorative works may even take longer than the original threat would if it were handled differently. Thus, as it turns out, automation becomes a source of instability in the name of safety. Such a problem, in fact, supports the idea of response architectures which are graduated in nature. Not every suspicious event should lead to automated high-impact security measures. The majority of security environments rely on response ladders where low-confidence detection leads to observational mode, and mid-confidence detection is coupled with escalation to analysts, whereas only the highest-confidence well-categorized threats are subject to immediate containment. Without such a surety of proportion, automation will become a source of operational fragility(Babaker et al., 2025).

3.2 Lack of Contextual Awareness in Automated Systems

Automatic systems are usually primarily dependent on their capability to recognize patterns in order to detect threats. That is why such systems need to be provided with accurate and comprehensive training datasets that they can learn from. It is simply human contextual awareness that automated security systems are deprived of. Cyber context comprises technical, organizational, behavioral, and situational dimensions. To illustrate, one event that appears suspicious in a certain context is perfectly legitimate in another. Such understanding is quite difficult to impart to automated security systems because most of it simply doesn't translate well into structured inputs(R. Alabdallat et al., 2025). It is really quite straightforward; a model might raise an alarm on the user accessing the system during an off-peak moment without realizing that the person in question is part of the on-call group handling the emergency. Also, the alert system could be thrown off by the notion of a substantial number of file accesses and assume that data exfiltration is in progress when in reality the activity corresponds to an authorized migration(Hiari et al., 2025).

Often misunderstandings come from a lack of context, and the problem is more acute in places where there are different business units, several cloud services, different user roles, and multiple layers of infrastructure. Therefore, in these situations, using static thresholds or generic behavioral models would be quite inadequate. Besides, since context is not only distributed over systems but also among teams, one single automated platform cannot collect all of it in a trustworthy manner. As a result, the human element still remains, basically, totally necessary. For example, analysts can use their time studying and interpreting changes in the context of company priorities, exceptions that have been made, major and minor projects, and real-time, because automation cannot do these things. Security environments rich in context but without contextual intelligence are likely to lead to the increase of false positive alarms and wrong actions(Ghazal, Hasan, Abdul Wahab, et al., 2022).

3.3 Inability to Deal with Complex, Multi-Stage Attacks

Actually, cyber-attacks rarely occur through one-off strikes. Most often, what happens is the attackers plan a series of incursions along the way to the final goal which can be either a data breach or ransomware lockdown. Typically, the steps entail reconnaissance, credential theft, privilege escalation, lateral movement, persistence, and impact. Even if isolated indicators are detected by automated security systems, these systems are still often unable to handle the slow and dispersed nature of the whole attack. The main reason for that is that the signals related to the various stages of the attack end up being distributed across different locations: a suspicious login in an identity system, suspicious command execution on an endpoint, unusual east-west traffic in the network, data access in a cloud application. If these signals are not properly combined, one would be left facing an isolated incident of low priority(Otair et al., 2025).

Separating the stages by time also continues to be a problem. Indeed, a scenario of attack lasting for a few hours, days, or even weeks, can alarm automated systems which were intended for swift, event-based decision making since they may not have the memory or reasoning capabilities over a long-time horizon. Actually, the attackers take advantage of this by performing their moves very slowly, using legitimate tools, and spacing their actions so as not to be detected by high-confidence automated responses(Sardar et al., 2025). Furthermore, we must bear in mind that adversaries think strategically. Proficient hackers frequently research defense techniques and accordingly adjust their strategies. In fact, they attempt to "fly under the radar" by doing things that are individually normal but, when aggregated, are malicious. Therefore, dealing with such threats is far beyond just the detection of the incidents; it entails detective work, reasoning across different domains and testing of evolving hypotheses that, of course, belong to the capabilities of human analysts rather than automated . Therefore, it is not right to consider automated security systems as complete substitutes for human detection and incident response. The main benefit of automation is in enabling fast reading of large volumes of data and their sorting according to the threat level while expert involvement is still necessary to deal with complex, ambiguous, and multi-stage attacks(Alraba'nah et al., 2025).

Figure 1. Operational Architecture Showing Key Limitation Points in Automated Security Environments

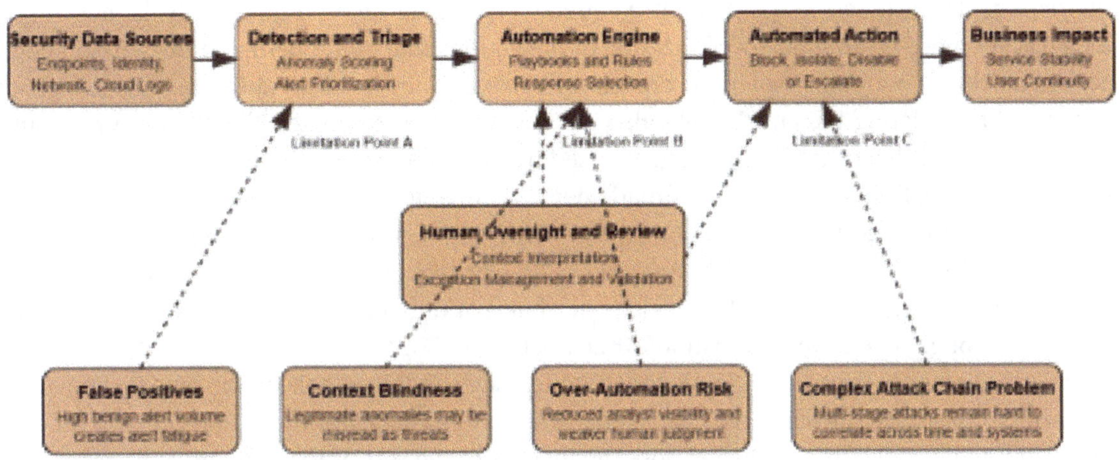

4. SECURITY RISKS INTRODUCED BY AUTOMATION SYSTEMS

4.1 Adversarial Attacks Against AI Security Models

Automation and AI have greatly enhanced the capability of security infrastructures to detect threats. Yet, they also made potential attack avenues available to the attackers in addition to combating threats. An ML model driving an autonomous security system can be seen as a mathematical instrument that recognizes patterns from a sizable set of data. As decision boundaries for them depend on training data and not on a strict logical process, they are open to be tricked by inputs that are specially designed to do so. These attacks are known as adversarial attacks(Alkhawatrah, 2025). Adversarial attacks the goal is to fool ML decision making by deliberately generating input data that will be misclassified as a result. In the framework of cyberattacks, the attacker is capable of subtly altering the malware behavior, network communication, or command execution so that they will fool a detection model and at the same time be able to reach their illicit goals. As an example, the malicious payload may be tailored to resemble those of legitimate applications allowing it to still go unnoticed by behavior profiling during anomaly detection(Ibrahim et al., 2024).

This vulnerability arises from the fact that the ML models do not really understand the purpose, but only rely on the statistical features. Thus, the attack is possible via a change of features while the true intent remains hidden. On the other hand, the defense system is programmed at the statistical layer, so it will look at the malicious act as normal. In addition, attackers may perform reconnaissance of the systems in order to learn how detection models work and find ways to keep their detection levels low. Adversarial attacks pose a big challenge to the automated security environments as those environments constantly use machine learning to enhance their protections instead of relying on identifying known malware by their signatures. Therefore, as security operations become progressively automated, the need to protect the ML models is becoming equally important as securing the monitored infrastructure(Ghazal et al., 2024).

4.2 Exploiting Automated Response Mechanisms

Automation platforms do not just identify threats. They can also automatically launch response activities based on pre-written playbooks. Some of the actions that could be implemented are: network connection blocking, endpoint isolation, credential revoking and process disabling. Although these measures aim at restricting the attack, they also allow adversaries to exploit the response mechanisms automatically for their benefit. The first risk is posed by the response manipulation attacks in which an enemy may intentionally try to trigger automatic defenses in a way that it might cause some confusion in the normal functioning. They by simulating the malicious behavior pattern cause the security systems to block legitimate services, isolate critical systems or lock-out the authorized users. Such attack methods are similar to the denial of the service ones but that only execution is indirectly controlled by the adversary through defensive automation(Al-znamat et al., 2025).

If attackers manage to figure out the playbook logic, they can tailor their methods to that a particular reaction will be automatically triggered. For example, if containment workflow that is triggered isolates a certain system, the attackers can then expose themselves to the rest of the network and move along to the least protected system. Another risk of automated responses is that they may initiate a long sequence of consequences. In very large environments, collection of many independent automation tools working together the one wrong step can propagate through the whole system(Al-Okbi, Alomari, Zitar, et al., 2025). As an example, a mistakenly applied firewall can result in legitimate cloud communication being blocked. This block can lead to the application services being disrupted which will then trigger further automation of remediation actions. The examples of chain reactions explain why very tight control of automated defensive actions is necessary to avoid harming operational stability(Q. Y. Shambour et al., 2025).

4.3 Model Poisoning and Data Manipulation Attacks

Another critical concern for security automation is model poisoning. This is a form of attack where the hacker alters the dataset on which machine learning models are trained to make the models maliciously operate. Security automation environments are typically equipped with learning pipelines that continuously update detection models by incorporating the latest data. This approach, while ensuring that the models remain up-to-date with evolving threats, also exposes to attackers the initial point at which they can influence the learning process. Through model poisoning, attackers insert misleading or counterfeit data into the system's stock of training data. If the tainted data is allowed in the model training phase, it will be capable of leading the learned model to produce erroneous statistical behavior patterns. To illustrate, hackers might disguise their malicious behavior as benign so that in the future, the model will recognize such behaviors as normal. Such methods can completely derail the functioning of automated detection systems. Over time, the model may become less reactive to certain types of malicious activities which would provide the attackers with more freedom and a lower risk of being exposed(Al-Dmour et al., 2025). Even small alterations made by the tainted data can be significant in the way the ML models perform as they are based primarily on patterns identified in the training set. Manipulating data can also be targeted at the security platform feedback loops. Many of the autonomously operating systems use analyst feedback, incident results, and automated evaluation criteria as inputs into retraining. Directing these feedback channels the wrong way, attackers will be able to influence model updates, too. For example, a system which receives numerous false alerts from an attacker, may decide to become less sensitive to certain patterns and, as a result, its detection capability will be adversely affected. Defense against model poisoning involves rigorously controlling the phases of data collection, validation, and model retraining. Training datasets should be kept under close watch to detect any suspicious inputs. In addition, brand new models must be subjected to a very detailed examination before their release in production (Ali et al., 2026).

4.4 Supply Chain Risks in Automated Security Platforms

Dependence on automated security systems may also bring about another risk factor especially, the supply chain problem becomes a matter requiring attention. A normal security framework today is usually made up of software components coming from different vendors, open-source communities, and cloud providers. Although product parts allow for quick innovation and integration, at the same time, they have become the primary source of supply chain security . Supply chain attack occurs when the adversary finds a way to compromise the software or the services before the targeted organization even receives them(Ghazal, Hasan, Alzoubi, et al., 2022). For example, the attackers might stealthily insert malicious code into the software updates, take over the developers' work environments, or exploit vulnerabilities in exclusive third-party libraries. Thus, one single compromised component of an automated security platform can lead to a domino effect of problems. Such systems normally have privileged rights of access to the rest of the infrastructure, making compromised automation tools very powerful gateways into corporate networks for the attackers. If a piece of malicious code is installed into the security orchestration system it can be used to manipulate detection results, suppress alerts, or change the responses actions. Another possibility is that the compromised security tool is used as the channel through which the attacker disseminates his work within the organization(Al-Adwan et al., 2025).

Thechallenge of dealing with supply chain risk is compounded by the fact that the risk factors are largely external to the organization's direct control. It is possible to create a completely secure internal environment; however, it can still get exposed to risks if there are third-party software components that either have security weaknesses that have not been disclosed or have been deliberately modified featurewise(Ghazal, 2025b). As automated systems become more interconnected and dependent on external integrations, it is important for security governance to consider supply chain risk. That is to say, an organization must think of ways to thoroughly assess vendors, perform software integrity tests, and regularly monitor third-party connections. Moreover, it's the transparency of code, code signing, and supply chain auditing that contribute to making automated security platforms reliable and trusted(Iskandarani, 2025).

In fact, introducing automation into cybersecurity defense allows for many different options. Nevertheless, just like villains can use this to make new types of threats, the automated response systems can also be manipulated to interfere with their functioning, besides the already known dangers of adversarial inputs and model . In the same vein, an attack on automation pipelines could be carried out by seizing central control of security activities. What's more, supply chain dependencies at external levels bring in vulnerabilities that might be used to compromise automated systems even before they are rolled (Almomani et al., 2025).

5. LEGAL, ETHICAL AND COMPLIANCE LIMITATIONS

Automating security solutions is a trend that is being adopted at an incredibly high rate; hence, the emergence of concerns about regulations. One side of the debate over regulation is the imperative for effective, data-oriented defense; the other side is the law that dictates how digital information is handled in a controlled, proportionate, and accountable way. Typically, an isolated security environment is supplemented by real-time monitoring of endpoints, network traffic, identity systems, application logs, and user behavior. Essentially, for security purposes, such an extensive visibility lens is necessary to detect the symptoms of a cyberattack at its nascent stage. Thus, compliance and lawful perspectives may allow for surveillance that involves the collection, retention, and analysis of personal data, employee activity logs, communication metadata, and location-linked behavioral data(Lee et al., 2021). This results in a major regulatory hurdle: security automation cannot solely be motivated by technical reasoning. It is also required to be in line with legal principles such as necessity, proportionality, limitation of purpose, retention periods, transparency obligations, and lawful access to sensitive information. As a case in point, an automatic detection system, from a technical perspective, may value complete user activity data; however, legal structures will forbid such data collection if it surpasses the amount necessary for the specific security . Simply put, some of the analytically most valuable data may also be the ones that are most regulated(Al-Habashneh et al., 2025).

Besides that, another regulatory problem is caused by the cross-jurisdictional operation. Large companies typically have their operations in several countries, each of them having their own data protection standards, employee monitoring laws, cyber security reporting obligations, and industry specific compliance requirements. So, an automated security procedure which is allowed in one country might be the one that is prohibited in another. Hence, a central security operations center might find itself in a situation where different legal conditions simply do not allow the application of the same detection logic uniformly across all regions. Aside from that, automated monitoring will also lead to demands for documentation and audit(Sharma, Al-Rashed, et al., 2025). Currently, regulators and auditors expect that organizations will be able to provide evidence of their security decision-making processes, the data employed, data storage details, and methods of access control. This requires not only governance logs and records but also technical ones to demonstrate that automated monitoring is legal and to which extent it is regulated. Thus, regulatory requirements not only influence security automation deployment at the edges, but they also affect the construction, the operation, and the maintenance of the security environments from the very inception(Jaradat et al., 2025).

5.1 Privacy Implications of Autonomous Threat Detection

Privacy issues are one of the biggest sources of resistance to autonomous security systems as these systems require threat detection by inspecting the very data that is then subject to privacy protection. The more data an automated system is able to observe, correlate, and analyze, the more effectively it can detect subtle or gradually developing threats. Yet the very same increased visibility may result in the degradation of informational privacy over time if the use of that visibility is not properly regulated. Automated threat detection systems are designed to make use of the behavioral cues of the user, which can lead to the identification of security breaches, but at the same time, it is also possible to profile individuals quite extensively(Abualhaj, Abu-Shareha, & Rateb, 2025). There are several indicators that can assist in identifying account compromise such as login timing, system movement, application usage, device geo-location, frequency of communication, and unusual behavior of access. On the other hand, the same indicators are used to closely monitor the behavior of employees, contractors, or customers in detail. An organization might not intend to monitor an individual entirely, but its automated security architecture might, in the end, resemble continuous behavioral observation. This brings us to the privacy dilemma that is not only and simply a technical one but also a normative one(Abualhaj, Abu-Shareha, Al-Khatib, et al., 2025).

On the one hand, security automation can be a tool of delivering security, but on the other hand, its operation can result in rights violation due to over-surveillance or less transparency, such as the right to privacy, anonymity, and other related rights like dignity, in fact, very much so. This probably will be the case at the place of work where the security systems that get to their conclusion based on the employees' work or communication pattern will in all likelihood be the employees' very strong main objection, although at the same time, they may entertain certain forms of monitoring related to cyber-security. Further, another dimension of privacy risk comes from aggregating data. A single security log can ordinarily be regarded as benign; however, with the aid of several such sources, the true effectiveness of autonomous systems is greatly enhanced. When authentication records are paired with device, application, and network telemetry, the final outcome can be very revealing(Qawasmeh et al., 2025). So, in a way, privacy in autonomous security is mainly at risk when a system consolidates many different data sets. For that reason, privacy limits autonomous detection without analytes. Data minimization, role-based access control, pseudonymization to some extent, very strict retention control, and analysis limited only to defined purposes constitute not only a set of additions available for the amendments, but they are the way to structurally ensure that automated security remains operationally, ethically, and legally defensible(Laha et al., 2025).

5.2 Accountability in Automated Security Decision Making

Accountability concerns pose some of the greatest limitations to security automation. Human involvement in decision-making, security operations such as account locking or isolating a compromised machine, or incident escalation are obvious as the chain of responsibility is clear in these scenarios. On the other hand, in automated environments, measures such as disabling account access to a legitimate user, disrupting a production workload, or triggering a response requiring a compliance-sensitive facility based on a wrong model output may be the result of the longer chain of components such as telemetry collection, feature extraction, model inference, playbook execution, and enforcement through downstream instruments. Determining a single individual accountable for errors can be quite difficult. The accountability issue becomes even more complicated as the system grows in complexity(Samanta et al., 2025). In a situation where a decision relies on a model that merely provides a probability score without an explanation, it would be hard enough for security personnel to justify the decision made. It seems almost inevitable that this will generate a multitude of problems, for example, in the areas of law enforcement where the regulation is stringent, contract disputes, and even the revising of incidents. Say the company being examined, for instance, must prove that their security measures were both reasonable and proportionate and not simply harmful without any justification. Therefore, the issue of accountability as one of the disadvantages of independent security can only be solved through governance design(Ghazal, Hasan, Hussein, et al., 2025). It is crucial that companies establish their responsibility models plainly and set apart vendor accountability, platform configuration accountability, analyst oversight accountability and executive deployment decision accountabilities. Meanwhile, there is also a requirement for technical traceability, such as logs proving the input data involved, the model or rule that triggered the action, the confidence score given, and the response path followed. In the absence of traceability, automation may result in rapid actions but at the same time reduce the organization's capacity to explain and justify those actions (Ghazal, Hasan, Raju, et al., 2025).

5.3 Ethical Risks of Autonomous Security Enforcement

Automatically making final security decisions that greatly affect users, services, or the entire organization can be a big source of ethical dilemmas. Deciding to move from merely detecting security issues at a passive level to actively taking security enforcement actions can bring about ethics issues. It is not that automation use is, in principle, wrong, but its combination of speed, scale, and abstraction can lead to a great number of harms being made when about decisions are made based on incomplete context or assumption. A typical ethical risk case is when the response is very disproportionate to the offense. Detection system might have a low-confidence suspicious behavior - say a person, on a sudden whim, pressing a button - but the level of measures taken was so disproportionate that it involved the person being isolated, their credentials being revoked, and their workflow was stopped(Eke et al., 2025).

Such responses may be justifiable from a tactical point of view but they can make an unintended (even if unintentional) burden on legitimate users especially when the confidence level of the system was not sufficiently high to allow such a drastic measure. Moreover, ethics also requires proportionality - the evidence should be appropriate to the action taken. Fairness is the third and the next crucial ethical point. Machine learning algorithm-based security systems can deliver very unfair results to individuals if the training data either corresponds to biased environments, incomplete user populations, or include historical assumptions that have led to unfair practices in the past most of the time. Users, device types, geographic regions, or work patterns may be considered more anomalous simply because they are underrepresented in the base. This, in international and hybrid work environments, may cause such users to be frequently suspected who behave in a way that legitimately deviates from a dominant (Hakami et al., 2025).

Autonomy and provision for recourse are other ethical dimensions that should be considered. For example, if the user is presented with an automated security measure, what chances does the user have to challenge, review, and alter the same? Autonomous security enforcement is generally not only fast but also ethically acceptable only when there is possible human review/human intervention/appeal to prevent the consequences from becoming too heavy; otherwise, the system becomes an inscrutable authority rather than a limited protective tool. In short, it is prioritizing efficiency and control over the human aspects of organizational life that results in ethical risks. Security systems, in essence, are crafted for the protection of digital assets whereas social institutions, as functioning entities, consist of humans, roles, pressures, emergencies, and exceptions. Therefore, ethical security automation has to continue to support human elements of discretion, correction, and judgment rather than simply considering all deviations as issues of technical enforcement(Q. Shambour et al., 2025).

5.4 Compliance Challenges Across International Security Regulations

Regulatory inconsistency is a significant compliance challenge for firms operating across different countries with the aid of autonomous security systems. Law differences regarding cybersecurity, data privacy, labor, breach notifications, and even regulations specific to different sectors can vary so much from one country or region to another. This means that an automation system seeking the same level of laws will most likely come across a regulatory environment covered with very different laws and rules. For example, one country could permit the active observation of workers on the condition that it is not hidden and the workers have been informed, another country may be very restrictive in allowing behavior monitoring and/or even require the involvement of labor unions. In the first country, it is common to keep records for a long time in order to conduct investigations after an incident, while the second country prefers to keep records for shorter periods unless there is a legal reason. That is why automated systems that collect and analyze data on a global scale may even lead to compliance risks if they use homogeneous practices in labors of non-uniform laws. Furthermore, compliance becomes even more difficult with cross-border data transfers. In general, autonomous security platforms operate on a global or regional level via their analyzing centers which means that data collected from one country can be processed in another(A. Arabiat et al., 2025). Automation systems may be restricted by the counterparts because of worries about data transfer, local storage requirements, or government access, even though these systems are quite effective and enhance threat visibility. Therefore, besides their technical characteristics, security staff also need to think about the legal compliance of automated pipelines when working in various jurisdictions. Moreover, documentary and reporting of incident response are also regulated by different laws. Different laws may set different criteria, deadlines, and notification contents to authorities, customers, or partners about security incidents. Noncompliance with these rules can lead to situations of under-reporting or over-reporting of incidents when automated systems wrongly classify or respond to them. This can expose organizations to risk. Thus, international compliance limits security automation to the "one-size-fits-all" approach at its best. It advocates policy-aware architectures, where data handling, model deployment, retention, and response logic can be in harmony with the requirements of different jurisdictions. To express it another way, legal modularity, just as much as technical modularity, is what efficient, worldwide automation at scale boils down (Turab et al., 2025).

Figure 2. Legal and Ethical Constraint Map in Autonomous Security Environments

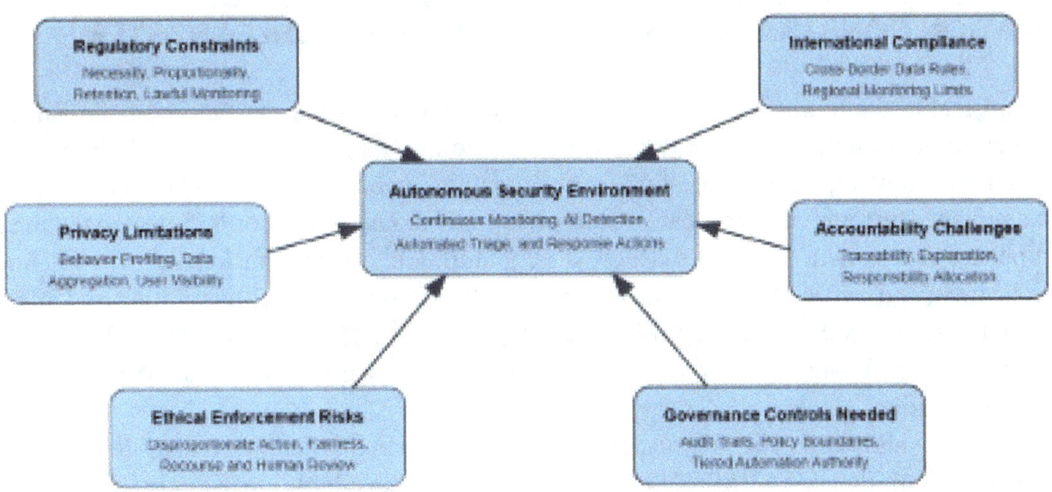

Figure 3. Accountability and Escalation Path for Automated Security Decisions

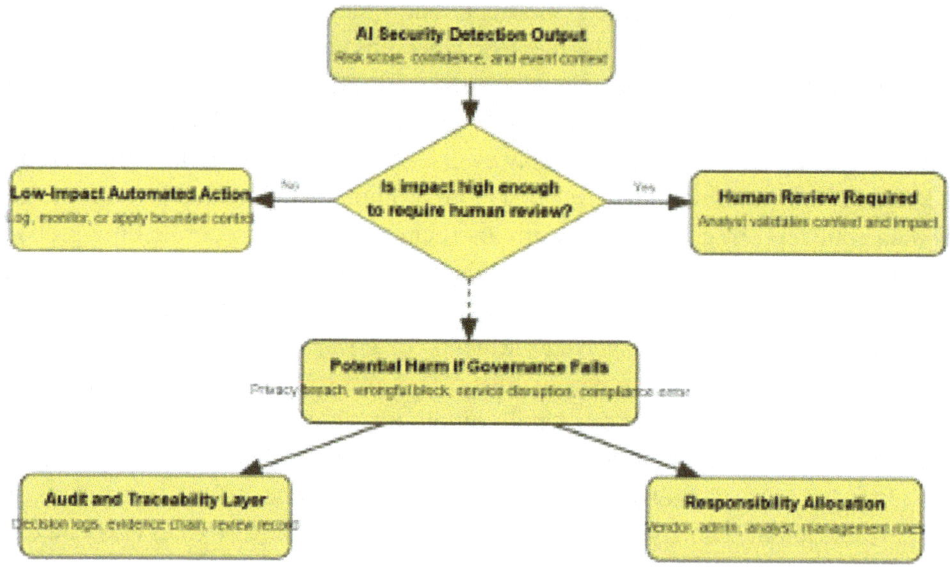

Autonomous systems may quite well be able to increase defensive speed, but at the same time, they raise the level of privacy, fairness, proportionality, jurisdiction, and accountability issues. This is why responsible automation equates to policy boundaries, auditability, and human review mechanisms – none of which are added as corrective controls later but are, in fact, 'built in' security .

6. RESULTS AND DISCUSSION: EMPIRICAL EVALUATION OF AUTOMATION CONSTRAINTS IN AUTONOMOUS SECURITY SYSTEMS

The empirical evaluation used the Edge-IIoTset Cybersecurity Dataset obtained from Kaggle. The selected records represented benign IoT/industrial traffic and attack categories including distributed denial-of-service, code injection, brute-force authentication, reconnaissance, and data exfiltration. The dataset was cleaned by removing duplicate, incomplete, and inconsistent records. Selected feature groups included packet-size statistics, protocol usage, session duration, connection frequency, authentication-related indicators, and traffic-flow attributes. The dataset was divided into 70% training and 30% testing using a fixed random seed, and Random Forest, Support Vector Machine, and Deep Neural Network models were evaluated using accuracy, precision, recall, false-positive rate, and robustness under adversarial manipulation.

To empirically validate the operational constraints discussed in this chapter, a data-driven experiment was conducted using the Edge-IIoTset Cybersecurity Dataset available on Kaggle. This dataset was selected as it represents real traffic patterns of the Internet of Things (IoT) and industrial environments where automated security monitoring systems are typically installed. The dataset contains network telemetry, device communication patterns, protocol metadata, and pre-programmed attack scenarios such as distributed denial-of-service, code injections, brute-force authentication attempts, reconnaissance, and data exfiltration. Machine learning algorithms act as the primary mechanism that autonomous security environments use to distinguish normal from abnormal network behavior. Three well-known machine learning models, Random Forest, Support Vector Machine, and Deep Neural Network, were employed for the experiment to replicate automated detection workflows. In the scenario of an autonomous security system, if false negatives are decreased at the expense of increasing false positives, this would most likely lead to operational constraints due to the investigation team being overwhelmed with multiple false alarms which might also trigger unnecessary automated response. Furthermore, in order to simulate a real operational environment closely, the models were initially trained on nearly 70 percent and the remaining 30 percent portions of the dataset were used for validation. Based on network traffic attributes such as distribution of packet sizes, connection frequency, protocol usage, session duration, and authentication attempts, features were engineered. These are the same features that automated security systems use while monitoring the enterprises, industrial control rooms, and IoT infrastructures. The paper demonstrates the performance in a machine-learning-based detection system under realistic-network scenarios and the efficiency of automated systems is at odds with their operational limitations.

6.1 Detection Performance of Automated Security Models

The initial phase of the experimental evaluation was to measure the classification accuracy of several machine learning algorithms on the cybersecurity dataset. Detection accuracy is the percentage of network operations accurately identified as either safe or malicious. Although a high degree of accuracy is a very significant characteristic of a model, that may not solely represent operational effectiveness since it is possible for a high accuracy model to have an unacceptable false positive rate. According to the experimental results, the three machine learning algorithms were able to detect the simulated cyber-attacks in the dataset quite readily. Of the three, the Deep Neural Network outperformed the others Random Forest and SVM in terms of accuracy, with the latter two trailing in order. However, classification output analysis reveals some less visible operational implications arising out of the fact that the best performing model was also the one with the largest gap between the majority and minority classes(Al Hindi et al., 2025).

On different attack scenarios, random forest models give stable results generally because they make predictions based on the combination of decision trees. This way, the model will be able to discover the complexities of the network traffic patterns without losing control of overfitting. Support Vector Machine model was able to effectively segment different attack patterns but its overall accuracy diminished drastically when confronted with complex traffic scenarios where the behaviors of an attacker and a legitimate user were very similar. Deep Neural Network model produced the best detection accuracy as it is able to capture very complex feature correlations. However, this comes at a cost in terms of implementation. Besides the training phase, neural networks require a large amount of computational power also at the time of inference. In large-scale autonomous security environments with millions of events per hour, doing this may either introduce latency or increase the costs of infrastructure(Ghazal, Abualhaj, et al., 2025).

Table 4. Performance Comparison of Automated Security Detection Models

Model	Detection Accuracy	Precision	Recall	False Positive Rate
Random Forest	96.8%	95.4%	96.1%	3.9%
Support Vector Machine	94.2%	93.6%	92.8%	4.7%
Deep Neural Network	97.5%	96.8%	97.2%	3.5%

Table 4 presents the outcomes of the experiments with automated detection systems, where the training phase was conducted on representative datasets. The noticeable differences between the models are manifestations of the performance, interpretability, and operational efficiency offs.

6.2 Operational Impact of False Positives in Autonomous Security

While recognizing actual threats is a critical performance metric, the setups of security operations also have to consider the repercussion of false positives. A false positive refers to a situation when an activity which is in fact safe is wrongly labeled as a security breach. Even small percentages of false positives can produce large numbers of alerts in very high traffic environments. Taking the example of a normal enterprise network that processes millions of operations on a daily basis. Here, a false positive rate of three percent might mean that thousands of alerts that require human analysts time will be generated. In case defense actions triggered by these alerts are also set to operate automatically, then it may be causing very high disruptions by, for instance, disconnecting a network or isolating the device being attacked. For the automated models in the dataset, some attack detection was not so successful as others. Generally, detecting DOS or brute-force authentication attempts is easier than detecting scanning or scanning for low-intensity reconnaissance activities because of the fact that statistical network traffic patterns for the attacks are more distinct than those of the legitimate activities. The close resemblance of legitimate and malicious behaviors in network traffic accounts for the false positive problem in automated security settings. So, the decision-making process on detection thresholds and response logics should be supported by a quantitative analysis to minimize disruptions yet keep strong defense capabilities(Ghazal, Abu-Shareha, et al., 2025).

6.3 Model Robustness Under Adversarial Conditions

The portion of the working study that was dedicated to the robustness of detection models when network traffic patterns are adversarial modified is the last one. Attackers, in order to remain undetected by automation, can try to alter the observable characteristics of their activities. Changes may include slowing down attack rates, breaking up network sessions, or imitating legitimate application behavior. Adherence to attack patterns as well as unmasking disguised attacks might have been facilitated in this way. Attack samples selected from the dataset were made to be indistinguishable statistically that they are not recognized as indicators of malicious behavior. For example, packet timing intervals were altered to resemble user activity and connection bursts were distributed over longer intervals. After the addition of adversarial changes, detection accuracy was reduced, according to the result analysis. Models that depended heavily on statistical features saw the largest drop in performance as the modified traffic decreased the difference between the benign and malicious patterns. Because of its ensemble nature, the Random Forest was the most robust of the three models whereas the Deep Neural Network was the best overall as it can also handle the more complicated feature representations. Regardless of the type of model that was used none was able to completely resist the adversarial manipulation. This presents a major challenge for automated security systems as if attackers know the ways that the models are allowing to be identified or that the models are classifying them, then it is possible to find the way that is hidden from the models(Sharma, Hussain, et al., 2025).

Figure 4. Detection Accuracy Comparison of Automated Security Models

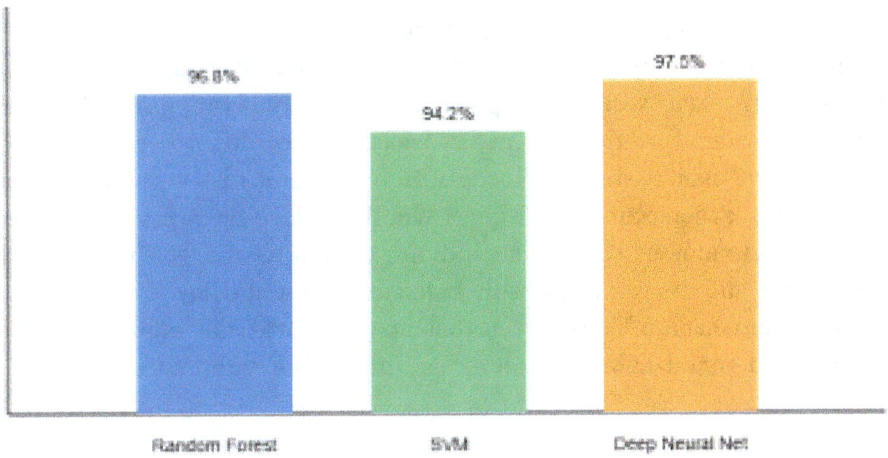

Figure 5. False Positive Impact in High-Volume Security Environments

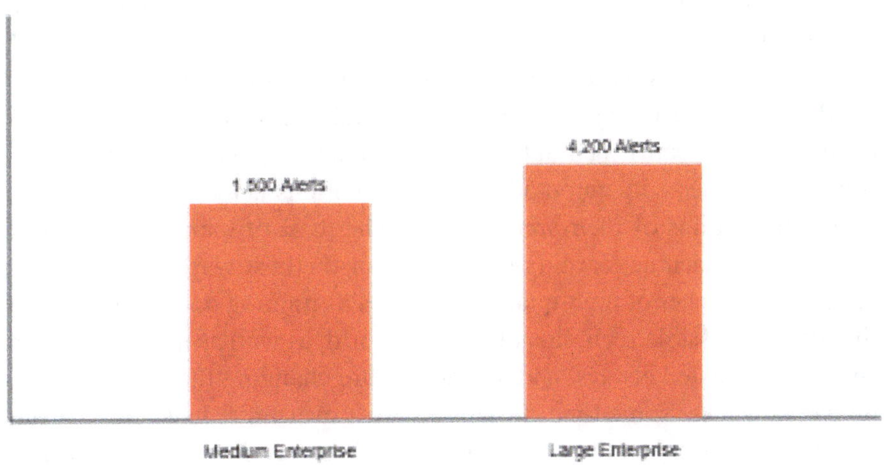

6.4 Discussion of Automation Constraints

The results of the experiments are very much in line with the fact that automation in cybersecurity is an enabler but at the same time it also creates some limitations which are to be addressed by the human operator. Therefore, machine learning models that are trained on representative datasets are capable of detecting threats very well and this is the time when automated systems have the ability to identify threats at a quicker pace than manual monitoring. On the other hand, automated systems did show several issues during the experimental performance evaluation. Firstly, if the quality and representativeness of the training data are not given due attention, then the detection performance will vary drastically. In other words, if the models are exposed to traffic patterns that differ substantially from the scenarios that were used for training, the accuracy will drop. Second, even the best models will use up a lot of false positives which from a large-scale security setup will be very overwhelming. Third, manipulated traffic patterns, also called adversarial traffic, may make detection very difficult especially in cases where statistical indicators are the main basis of the models. Here are some reasons why automation, although it is capable of improving cybersecurity, will never wholly replace the need for human oversight and control. The design of autonomous security should aim to address the weaknesses of the model, the limitations of operations, and the variable hostile behaviors without delay. The author contends that a security automation system that is effective is one that integrates artificial intelligence, human skills and governing . Only then can organizations truly leverage automation without fearing its .

7. CONCLUSION AND FUTURE WORK

Introducing autonomous security systems into operations is one of the strongest cybersecurity transformations. Their ability to combine machine learning, analytics of vast telemetry data, and automation of responses have made these systems a basic necessity for organizations to manage their digital infrastructures 24/7. Besides enabling a quicker identification of threats through automation, it also leaves time for analysts to engage in other activities as it allows continuous monitoring of distributed networks, cloud, industrial and IoT systems with almost no human intervention. Despitethe fact that automation has been presented as a key to solving all cybersecurity challenges by some of the previous results, the findings in this chapter have confirmed automation not being a panacea for cybersecurity problems. In fact, one of the major issues with automatic security solutions is the fact that they have to deal with their design and the limitations of their architectures. The least of their problems is data availability and quality. For example, machine learning can be one of the best ways to recognize threat patterns; however, it needs a large number of high-quality examples as training data. Besides, historical data sets simply cannot include all possible scenarios of the real world, as well as the creativity of hackers. Also, since systems are being updated always, and a attackers are changing their tactics, data-driven models might lose their accuracy after some time. If datasets shift over time, have only partial telemetry, and incorporate noisy data sources, then the quality of the models may deteriorate even further, resulting in lower detection rates.

Among other factors, problems with the running of automated security solutions can lead to their not being effective. Continuous false alarms, alert fatigue, and the lack of a proper understanding of when and how to intervene in the processes of over-automation could result into neglecting very positive properties of automation if the systems are producing a large number of alerts, or, what is even worse, they generate responses to the situation that are so counterproductive that the system is practically left without sufficient context. Although statistical pattern recognition is a technique of the greatest importance in autonomous security systems, it is very likely that a lack of situational awareness, an inability to understand organizational priorities, and the difficulties associated with unravelling of complex multi-stage attack scenarios, are the aspects in which the systems fail. Therefore, automated detection is generally nothing more than stage one, with human confirmation being the last step, the trustworthy security result, investigation. Moreover, security flaws can be introduced by means of automation - which in fact represents a limit that has to be taken into consideration as well. Machine learning models face significant security risks from adversarial attacks, data poisoning, and evasion techniques aimed at tricking detection systems. Even the automation of response pipelines can become a vulnerability if attackers exploit defensive actions to cause operational disruptions. Moreover, automation platforms depend on intricate software supply chains, integrations, and centralized orchestration engines, which can also be the way new vulnerabilities are (Al-Okbi, Alomari, Hadi, et al., 2025).

Besides, human and organizational elements put restrictions on autonomous security settings. Such settings necessitate multi-talented professionals who are not only knowledgeable in cybersecurity but also machine learning, data engineering, and software development. Due to the rarity of these skills, a number of organizations consider it a problem to set up and operate sophisticated automated systems. Trust is equally significant for the acceptance of a system. Sometimes, automated decisions do not gain human trust; on the other hand, there are cases when humans trust the decisions too much even without proper verification. Therefore, governments have to come up with the methods that will give the necessary amount of transparency, responsibility, and accountability in actions conducted by . Finally, legal, ethical, and regulatory issues define the boundary within which automated security technologies may be taken. Continuous monitoring systems may collect personal data that is sensitive, telemetry of behaviors, and communication metadata among other types of data that expose the system to concerns in the privacy and proportional monitoring areas. Besides, the cross-border regulatory differences add to the complexity of the deployment of such systems in multinational organizations, so there have to be flexible policies and automation aware of jurisdiction. Besides, ethically, affected users by automated enforcement actions should be given explanations to them and they should also have the opportunity to review the enforcement all the while the actions are still proportional. Altogether, these constraints thoroughly call for autonomous security systems not to be considered as just technological tools, but socio-technical systems which are the outcome of technology, governance, human expertise, and legal responsibility intertwined(Masango et al., 2025).

7.1 How to Overcome Automation Restrictions in the Most Effective and Efficient Way

In view of the diversity of constraints associated with automated security environments, it is very clear to us that among the first orders of business for organizations is to figure out ways that can not only maximize automation but also offer them control, greater robustness, and accountability. Along the same line of thought, one effective approach to a robust defense might be a highly-interconnected security architecture integrating multiple layers. Relying wholly on a single detection model or an automation platform as the sole foundation of the entire defense could result in the complete dismantling of the defense if the model commits even one serious mistake. What companies need most are multiple echoing analytical layers supporting each other. Behavioral analytics, signature-based detection, anomaly detection, just to name a few, each can highlight a different side of security events. Through the combination of such approaches, organizations will not be able to exploit the weaknesses of a single model setting and thus threats will not go (Cui et al., 2026).

Therefore, the human-in-the-loop decision making frameworks should indeed be considered as a very key part of the entire solution. Automation may, to some extent, be a tool for speeding up data processing and, on the other hand, it can take care of routine response actions however, business-critical decisions that actually affect the result, are the ones that should be approved by human beings. Deploying tiered response mechanisms is a) good practice to ensure that low priority and less risky cases are handled automated while very risky cases are left to the analyst b) that the decision-making pieces are both humanized and that the fundamental principle of human oversight for those hard or ambiguous situations is not only being obeyed but also. Meanwhile, governance mechanisms must be implemented as well. These must be strong enough to encompass model validation procedures, data quality monitoring, audit logs for the decision-making of the automated systems, as well as regular evaluation of the system performance. The sets of governance must very clearly define who does what starting from the automation configuration to model training and surveillance. In this regard, automated systems are somewhat transparent and, with minimum compliance risk, can also follow policies and regulations, of (Mohammad et al., 2025).

Workforce training should also be regarded as a type of capital expenditure. Indeed, security personnel must continually enhance their abilities not only in the administration of but also in the understanding of the working of automated systems. For instance, they should be well-versed in machine learning, data visualization, automation workflow crafting, and model evaluation techniques. Bringing these capabilities together can be effectively achieved if a cybersecurity analyst, a data scientist, and a software engineer work as a team that will be in charge of both the roll-out and the upkeep of automated security systems. Last but not least, automation architectures that are governed by policies and have the potential to be privacy-compliant should really be on the list for . Principles of data minimization, role-based data access restrictions, pseudonymization of data wherever possible, and very limited time for data preservation are just a few of the control measures which, when implemented together, will effectively mitigate the privacy risks that are inherent to large-scale monitoring systems. In addition, systems developed with legal requirements in mind will ensure that automated security operations are compliant with the requirements of the various jurisdictions. In fact, by following these measures, enterprises can be able to basically take on the main structural limitations of automation whilst still being able to use its operational s(Hanandeh et al., 2025).

7.2 Possible Paths for Research on Autonomous Security Systems

Automation has already transformed the face of cybersecurity, however, many issues in research remain unsolved. In this regard, research will have a key role to play in overcoming the above-mentioned limitations in autonomous security systems as well as in substantially improving their dependability and trustworthiness. One possible research direction would be to create cybersecurity-specific explainable artificial intelligence (XAI). Most security analytics machine learning models are very complex and their workings are sealed off even to the owners. Actually, it is conceivable that models capable of not only providing the outcome but also the rationale for classifying particular activities as malicious are in line to make a significant positive impact on the analyst's trust, accountability, and regulatory transparency.

Also, detection models that could explain their reasoning will help analysts in identifying errors in their training datasets or model logic.

Also, the research could be centered on evolving and self-healing security models. Up to now, machine learning systems are generally required to be updated with new training data in order to remain effective. In future, they may succeed in equipping themselves with continuous learning capabilities to dynamically adapt to new attack patterns while at the same time incorporate measures to defend themselves from adversarial attacks. Such adaptive models would do a great job in securing an environment that hosts rapidly changing threats. Besides, robust adversarial machine learning is another valley that needs to be explored by researchers. It becomes increasingly difficult for automated systems to detect every threat that the attackers come up with. However, if models are developed that are less vulnerable to machine learning adversaries, these models will be a great benefit. Particularly, adversarial training, robust feature extraction, and hybrid analytical frameworks that combine machine learning with rule-based logic represent some of the promising techniques for addressing evasion attacks.

Also, a lot more research is called for in the distribution of security analytics through federated security analytics. Since the security of machine learning models depends largely on the availability of large centralized datasets, this raises major privacy and regulatory issues which are still unresolved. Federated learning models make it possible to train security models across multiple organizations without any of them sharing raw data. This is the main advantage, at least, in the case of cybersecurity. Organizations are effectively combining their efforts to identify cyber threats while at the same time maintaining the confidentiality of their personal information and observing the law. Following this, it may be necessary to engage in collaborative investigations that should concern cybersecurity, law, ethics, and organizational science which eventually lead to an interdiscipline. Apart from technical features only, automated security environments also function within quite rich and complicated social and institutional settings. Therefore, the technical measures alone will hardly be able to address the problem of the limitations of these environments. Certainly, if researchers manage to find ways to integrate technical advances with governance frameworks, ethics, and policy analysis, then they will possibly come up with security automation systems that are both performant and desirable from a responsible .

7.3 Final Thoughts, the Future of Automation in Security

Walking alongside the continuous evolution human technology and the digital world become more complicated, it is almost certain that the role of automation in cybersecurity will only increase further in the future. The amount of network traffic, system events, cloud workloads, and device-to-device communications in IoT environments has already reached a level that the manual human monitoring has become impossible. Therefore, automatic analytics and response mechanisms are, without exception, the capabilities that security operations must have not only today but also in the future. However, the discussion in this chapter has shown that human skill supported by organizational governance cannot be totally replaced by automation. In fact, self-directed systems still need a lot of quality data, model specifics, operational environment, and ultimately, human intervention. So, while automation, if allowed to run wild, could indeed bring about new threats, on the other hand, if properly designed and controlled, it can help a great deal. In all probability, it is the combination of automated tools and human insight rather than the complete elimination of the human element that will characterize even the most difficult security situations. At this point, automated systems will perform the functions of gathering, analyzing, and identifying threats as well as carrying out some limited responses, on the other hand, human cybersecurity personnel will be responsible for dealing with contextual interpretation, strategic thinking, and ethical oversight. Here, automation not only complements human defenders but also is a means of making their operations easier. By acknowledging and addressing the problems and disadvantages that have been outlined in this chapter, the organizations will be able to create security systems that make the most of automation while still preserving the features of flexibility, accountability, and understanding that human knowledge alone can .

REFERENCES

Abdeljaber, O., & Al-Masaeed, S. (2025). Al-Mu'ani, L., Yaseen, H., & Alhnaity, B. (2025). Strategic Intelligence: The Power of AI in Planning Efficiency. *Human Behavior and Emerging Technologies*, (1). Advance online publication. DOI: 10.1155/hbe2/5383054

Abualghanam, O., Alazzam, H., Qatawneh, M., Alazab, M., & Al Sharaiah, M. (2025). Elevating Mobile Security: An Ensemble Approach for Enhanced Malware Detection with M-iForest. *International Journal of Interactive Mobile Technologies*, *19*(10), 129–151. Advance online publication. DOI: 10.3991/ijim.v19i10.51319

Abualhaj, M. M., Abu-Shareha, A. A., Al-Khatib, S. N., Alsaaidah, A. M., & Anbar, M. (2025). Improving firewall performance using hybrid of optimization algorithms and decision trees classifier. *IAES International Journal of Artificial Intelligence*, *14*(4), 2839. Advance online publication. DOI: 10.11591/ijai.v14.i4.pp2839-2848

Abualhaj, M. M., Abu-Shareha, A. A., & Rateb, R. (2025). Enhancing intrusion detection systems with hybrid HHO-WOA optimization and gradient boosting machine classifier. *International Journal of Reconfigurable and Embedded Systems*, *14*(2), 518. Advance online publication. DOI: 10.11591/ijres.v14.i2.pp518-526

Abualhaj, M. M.I, Al-Khatib, S. N., Abu-Shareha, A. A., Almomani, O., Al-Mimi, H., Al-Allawee, A., Daoud, M. S., & Anbar, M. (2025). Spam Detection Boosted by Firefly-Based Feature Selection and Optimized Classifiers. *International Journal of Advances in Soft Computing and Its Applications*, *17*(3). Advance online publication. DOI: 10.15849/IJASCA.251130.02

Abualhaj, M. M., Al-Khatib, S. N., Al Zyoud, M., Qaddara, I., & Anbar, M. (2025). Enhancing Intrusion Detection System Performance Using a Hybrid of Harris Hawks and Whale Optimization Algorithms. *Engineering. Technology and Applied Science Research*, *15*(4), 24354–24361. Advance online publication. DOI: 10.48084/etasr.10919

Abualhaj, M. M., Al-Khatib, S. N., Al-Zyoud, M., Qaddara, I., Hiari, M. O., & Aldossary, S. M. A. (2025). Enhanced Network Communication Security Through Hybrid Dragonfly-Bat Feature Selection for Intrusion Detection. *The Journal of Communication*, *20*(5). Advance online publication. DOI: 10.12720/jcm.20.5.607-618

Abualigah, L., Almomani, M. H., Alomari, S. A., Zitar, R. A., Migdady, H., Saleem, K., Snasel, V., Smerat, A., & Ezugwu, A. E. (2025). Optimizing Intrusion Detection in Wireless Sensor Networks via the Improved Chameleon Swarm Algorithm for Feature Selection. *IET Communications*, *19*(1), e70029. Advance online publication. DOI: 10.1049/cmu2.70029

Abuowaida, S., Abu Owida, H., Shelash Mohammad, S. I., Alshdaifat, N., Abu Elsoud, E., Alazaidah, R., Vasudevan, A., & Alshurideh, M. T. (2025). Evidence Detection in Cloud Forensics: Classifying Cyber-Attacks in IaaS Environments using machine learning. *Data and Metadata*, *4*, 699. Advance online publication. DOI: 10.56294/dm2025699

Al-Adwan, A. S., Al-Adwan, A., Li, N., Fauzi, M. A., Jafar, R. M. S., Habibi, A., & Falahat, M. (2025). IMMERSIVE LEARNING MEETS THEORY: MODELING EDUVERSE ADOPTION IN HIGHER EDUCATION. *Journal of Information Technology Education*, *24*, 042. Advance online publication. DOI: 10.28945/5669

Al-Dmour, R., Al-Dmour, H., Al-Dmour, A., Basheer Amin, E., & Al-Dmour, Y. (2025). *AI and big data-driven social media recruitment: the mediating role of talent acquisition and employee engagement in bank performance*. Digital Transformation and Society., DOI: 10.1108/DTS-02-2025-0042

Al-Habashneh, A. G., Al-Daoud, K. I., Oraini, B., Al, , & Shelash, S. I. (2025). The impact of artificial intelligence on the development of electronic financial services. *International Journal of Data and Network Science*, *9*(2), 317–322. Advance online publication. DOI: 10.5267/j.ijdns.2024.8.012

Al Hindi, G., Alshraideh, M., Hussein, A. H., Eliyan, L. F., & Al-Dhaqm, A. (2025). Hacking Back: Using Genetic Algorithms to Outsmart Hackers. *Journal of Computational Science*, *21*(9), 2049–2064. Advance online publication. DOI: 10.3844/jcssp.2025.2049.2064

Al-Momani, M. M., Alqudah, T. A., Al Swiety, I. A., Mahrakani, N., Nassoura, M. B. A., & Al Attar, M. K. (2025). Integrating Artificial Intelligence (AI) and Business Intelligence (BI): A Framework for Improving Enterprise Performance. *TEM Journal, 14*(3). https://doi.org/DOI: 10.18421/TEM143-26

Al-Mousa, M., Amer, W., Abualhaj, M., Albilasi, S., Nasir, O., & Samara, G. (2025). Agile Proactive Cybercrime Evidence Analysis Model for Digital Forensics. *The International Arab Journal of Information Technology*, *22*(3). Advance online publication. DOI: 10.34028/iajit/22/3/15

Al-Okbi, N. K., Alomari, S. A., Hadi, W. J., Ajrash, A. S., Smerat, A., & Abualigah, L. (2025). Defending Digital Integrity: Advances in Media Forgery Analysis Research and Cybersecurity Development. *SN Computer Science*, *6*(8), 913. Advance online publication. DOI: 10.1007/s42979-025-04462-8

Al-Okbi, N. K., Alomari, S. A., Zitar, R. A., Smerat, A., Nazzal, M. A., & Abualigah, L. (2025). Integrating Multimodal Emotion Recognition with Deep Q-Learning for Adaptive Social Robot Interaction. *International Journal of Robotics and Control Systems*, *5*(4), 2265–2289. Advance online publication. DOI: 10.31763/ijrcs.v5i4.2055

Al-znamat, F. O., Alsaaidah, A., & Abu-Shareha, A. A. (2025). Malware Detection Using a Modified Bat Algorithm for Feature Selection. *International Journal of Intelligent Engineering and Systems*, *18*(9), 885–899. Advance online publication. DOI: 10.22266/ijies2025.1031.56

Alabdallat, R., Abualhaj, M., & Abu-Shareha, A. (2025). Android Malware Detection Using a Modified Dwarf Mongoose Algorithm. *International Journal of Intelligent Engineering and Systems*, *18*(8), 336–351. Advance online publication. DOI: 10.22266/ijies2025.0930.21

Alabdallat, R. D., Abualhaj, M. M., & Abu-Shareha, A. (2025). Enhanced Multiclass Android Malware Detection Using a Modified Dwarf Mongoose Algorithm. *International Journal of Analysis and Applications*, *23*, 248. Advance online publication. DOI: 10.28924/2291-8639-23-2025-248

Aldaaja, Y., Odeh, M., Badrakhan, S. S., Sabri, M., Abdelrahim, Y., Samara, G., & Alsabatin, H. (2025). Quantifying the Managerial and Practical Benefits of Cloud Computing on Information Security in Higher Education Institutions. *Applied Mathematics & Information Sciences*, *19*(1), 15–24. Advance online publication. DOI: 10.18576/amis/190102

Aldabbas, A., Baniata, L. H., Alsaaidah, B. A., Mustafa, Z., Alali, M., & Rateb, R. (2025). Artificial intelligence-driven method for the discovery and prevention of distributed denial of service attacks. *IAES International Journal of Artificial Intelligence*, *14*(1), 614. Advance online publication. DOI: 10.11591/ijai.v14.i1.pp614-628

Alenazi, M. J. F., Al-Khasawneh, M. A., Rahman, S., & Faheem, Z. (2025). Deep Reinforcement Learning Based Flow Aware-QoS Provisioning in SD-IoT for Precision Agriculture. *Computational Intelligence*, *41*(1), e70023. Advance online publication. DOI: 10.1111/coin.70023

Ali, L., Alshamayleh, A., Ibrahim, A., & Ahmed, S. M. (2026). Information Management Enhancement in Cloud-Based Systems Through Blockchain-Enabled Secure Access Control. *Indian Journal of Information Sources and Services*, *16*(1), 289–296. Advance online publication. DOI: 10.51983/ijiss-2026.16.1.30

Alkhawatrah, M. (2025). Random Forests Relay Selector in Buffer-Aided Cooperative Networks. *IEEE Access : Practical Innovations, Open Solutions*, *13*, 165402–165410. Advance online publication. DOI: 10.1109/ACCESS.2025.3612192

Almomani, O., Arabiat, A., Al Tayeb, M., Almaiah, M. A., Obeidat, M., Aldhyani, T. H. H., Shehab, R., & Rowad, M. (2025). A Robust Model for Android Malware Detection via ML and DL classifiers. *Mesopotamian Journal of Big Data*, *2025*. Advance online publication. DOI: 10.58496/MJBD/2025/017

Alraba'nah, Y., Al-Sharaeh, S., & Al Hindi, G. (2025). Enhancing Intrusion Detection Using Hybrid Long Short-Term Memory and XGBoost. *Journal of Soft Computing and Data Mining*, *6*(1). Advance online publication. DOI: 10.30880/jscdm.2025.06.01.016

Arabiat, A., Altayeb, M., & Salama, S. (2025). Artificial intelligence-powered smart roads: Leveraging orange3 for traffic signs recognition. *IAES International Journal of Artificial Intelligence*, *14*(5), 3816. Advance online publication. DOI: 10.11591/ijai.v14.i5.pp3816-3826

Arabiat, A. M. (2025). Intelligent Model for Detecting GAN-Generated Images Based on Multi-Classifier and Advanced Data Mining Techniques. *International Journal of Electrical and Electronic Engineering and Telecommunications*, *14*(3). Advance online publication. DOI: 10.18178/ijeetc.14.3.147-157

Arabiat, A. M., & Eljaafreh, Y. G. (2025). Intrusion Detection in Wireless Sensor Networks Using ML Based Classification of Denial of Service (DoS) Attacks. *The Journal of Communication*, *20*(4). Advance online publication. DOI: 10.12720/jcm.20.4.501-514

Babaker, S., Khatibi, A., Alsoud, A. R., Kaur, J., Jagtap, J., Alkhayyat, A., & Shah, S. K. (2025). Improving Reliability and Data Management in Internet of Things Based Wireless Sensor Networks. *Internet Technology Letters*, *8*(6), e646. Advance online publication. DOI: 10.1002/itl2.646

Cui, D., Harrison, A., Fendzi-Donfack, E., Dagal, I., Jangir, P., Mahmoud, M. M., Malkani, P., Mbasso, W. F., Tiako, P., & Smerat, A. (2026). Enhancing Short-Term Electricity Forecasting with Advanced Machine Learning Techniques. *Journal of Electrical Engineering & Technology*, *21*(1), 147–187. Advance online publication. DOI: 10.1007/s42835-025-02430-z

Eke, C. I., Al-Shamayleh, A. S., Phiri, M., Maswadi, K., Kwaghtyo, D. K., Mulenga, M., & Iyidobi, C. J. (2025). Machine Learning Based Mobile Big Data Analytics: State-of-the-art Applications, Taxonomy, Challenges and Future Research Directions. *Nigerian Journal of Technological Development*, *22*(4). Advance online publication. DOI: 10.63746/njtd.v22i4.3385

Ghazal, T. M. (2025a). An IoT-Based Active Learning Convolutional Neural Networks Model for Predicting River Water Quality. *Journal of Soft Computing and Data Mining*, *6*(1). Advance online publication. DOI: 10.30880/jscdm.2025.06.01.021

Ghazal, T. M. (2025b). Federated Learning for Intelligent Sensing and Navigation Technologies for 6G Communications. *Journal of Sensors, 2025*(1). DOI: 10.1155/js/3746147

Ghazal, T. M., Abu-Shareha, A., Mustafa, S. A., Ibrahim, A., & Ahmed, S. M. (2025). Privacy-Preserving Transformer-Based Meta-Learning Algorithm for Zero-Day Intrusion Detection in IoT-Enabled Smart Grids. *Journal of Internet Services and Information Security*, *15*(4), 76–84. Advance online publication. DOI: 10.58346/JISIS.2025.I4.006

Ghazal, T. M., Abualhaj, M., Ahmed, A. A., Al-Tarawni, M. A. M., & Maghrabi, L. A. (2025). Federated Deep Graph Neural Network Algorithm for Real-Time Intrusion Detection in Heterogeneous IoT Systems. *Journal of Internet Services and Information Security*, *15*(4), 484–497. Advance online publication. DOI: 10.58346/JISIS.2025.I4.035

Ghazal, T. M., Awouda, A. E., Hasan, M. K., Rahman, A. H. A., Islam, S., Saeed, R. A., Elshafie, H., Iqbal, A., & Hussein, A. H. (2025). Knowledge Learning for Securing Workflow Scheduling Algorithm in Mobile Edge Computing. *Mobile Networks and Applications*, *30*(3-4), 395–413. Advance online publication. DOI: 10.1007/s11036-025-02465-6

Ghazal, T. M., Hasan, M. K., Abdul Wahab, A. N., Ibrahim, A., Khan, W. A., Raza, N. Z., Atta, A., & Mago, B. (2022). Towards Privacy Provisioning for Internet of Things (IoT). *International Conference on Cyber Resilience, ICCR 2022*. DOI: 10.1109/ICCR56254.2022.9995916

Ghazal, T. M., Hasan, M. K., Alzoubi, H. M., Al Hmmadi, M., Al-Dmour, N. A., Islam, S., Kamran, R., & Mago, B. (2022). Securing Smart Cities Using Blockchain Technology. *2022 1st International Conference on AI in Cybersecurity, ICAIC 2022*. DOI: 10.1109/ICAIC53980.2022.9896971

Ghazal, T. M., Hasan, M. K., Hussein, A. H., Pandey, B. K., Ahmad, M., Safie, N., & Cascone, L. (2025). Federated Learning With Small and Large Models With Privacy-Preserving Data Space for Holographic Internet of Things in Consumer Electronics. *IEEE Transactions on Consumer Electronics*, *71*(2), 5259–5274. Advance online publication. DOI: 10.1109/TCE.2025.3573033

Ghazal, T. M., Hasan, M. K., Mokhtar, U. A., Safie, N., Alshamayleh, A., & Ahmad, M. (2025). Machine learning-based real-time outage fault detection for distribution networks in smart grid. In *Energy Reports* (Vol. 14). DOI: 10.1016/j.egyr.2025.10.045

Ghazal, T. M., Hasan, M. K., Raju, K. N., Khan, M. A., Alshamayleh, A., Bhatt, M. W., & Ahmad, M. (2025). Data Space Privacy Model with Federated Learning Technique for Securing IoT Communications in Autonomous Marine Vehicles. *Journal of Intelligent & Robotic Systems*, *111*(3), 84. Advance online publication. DOI: 10.1007/s10846-025-02298-1

Ghazal, T. M., Janjua, J. I., Abushiba, W., Ahmad, M., Ihsan, A., & Al-Dmour, N. A. (2024). Cybersecurity Revolution via Large Language Models and Explainable AI. *2024 17th International Conference on Security of Information and Networks, SIN 2024*. DOI: 10.1109/SIN63213.2024.10871324

Hakami, H., Hasan, M. K., Alshamayleh, A., Saeed, A. Q., Mustafa, S. A., & Ghazal, T. M. (2025). Adaptive Neuro-Fuzzy Congestion Control Algorithm for Real-Time Multimedia Networking in Cloud-Based E-Learning Platforms. *Journal of Wireless Mobile Networks, Ubiquitous Computing and Dependable Applications*, *16*(3). Advance online publication. DOI: 10.58346/JOWUA.2025.I3.027

Hanandeh, A., Alfreijat, S. Y., Qutieshat, R. J., Alsha'ar, H. Y., Kilani, Q. A. L., & Saleem Khasawneh, M. A. (2025). Implementing AI Accuracy, Learning Rate, Inference Time on enhancing Big Data Analysis and Strategic Plan. *Data and Metadata*, *4*, 637. Advance online publication. DOI: 10.56294/dm2025637

Hiari, M., Alraba'nah, Y., & Qaddara, I. (2025). A Deep Learning-Based Intrusion Detection System using Refined LSTM for DoS Attack Detection. *Engineering. Technology and Applied Science Research*, *15*(4), 25627–25633. Advance online publication. DOI: 10.48084/etasr.11499

Ibrahim, A., Sekhar, R., Tawfeq, J. F., Salih, S. Q., Shah, P., & Radhi, A. D. (2024). Security and Privacy Protection for Online Electronic Documents Based on Novel Encryption Techniques. *Journal of Intelligent Systems and Internet of Things*, *11*(1), 21–28. Advance online publication. DOI: 10.54216/JISIoT.110103

Iskandarani, M. Z. (2025). Effect of Adaptive Intelligent Reflective Surfaces on SINR in a Wireless Communication System. *The Journal of Communication*, *20*(1). Advance online publication. DOI: 10.12720/jcm.20.1.1-11

Jaradat, S., Acharya, N., Shivshankar, S., Alhadidi, T. I., & Elhenawy, M. (2025). AI for Data Quality Auditing: Detecting Mislabeled Work Zone Crashes Using Large Language Models. *Algorithms*, *18*(6), 317. Advance online publication. DOI: 10.3390/a18060317

Khatibi, A., Babaker, S., Praveen, K. N. R., Chohan, J. S., Jadhav, A., Alsoud, A. R., Ramudu, M. J., & Jeet, R. (2025). Advanced AI-Driven Cybersecurity: Analyzing Emerging Threats and Defensive Strategies. *National Academy Science Letters*. Advance online publication. DOI: 10.1007/s40009-025-01897-8

Laha, S. R., Smadi, K. Al, Habboush, A. K., Pattanayak, B. K., Pattnaik, S., & Mohanty, B. (2025). Smart Waste Management Framework for Green Cities: Integrating IoT, LoRa, and Deep Learning for Efficient Waste Classification and Management. *Tikrit Journal of Engineering Sciences, 32*(Special Issue 1). DOI: 10.25130/tjes.sp1.2025.1

Lee, S. W., Hussain, S., Issa, G. F., Abbas, S., Ghazal, T. M., Sohail, T., Ahmad, M., & Khan, M. A. (2021). Multi-Dimensional Trust Quantification by Artificial Agents through Evidential Fuzzy Multi-Criteria Decision Making. *IEEE Access : Practical Innovations, Open Solutions*, *9*, 159399–159412. Advance online publication. DOI: 10.1109/ACCESS.2021.3131521

Makhadmeh, S. N., Fraihat, S., Awad, M., Sanjalawe, Y., Al-Betar, M. A., & Awadallah, M. A. (2025). A crossover-integrated Marine Predator Algorithm for feature selection in intrusion detection systems within IoT environments. *Internet of Things : Engineering Cyber Physical Human Systems*, *31*, 101536. Advance online publication. DOI: 10.1016/j.iot.2025.101536

Masango, N. C., Agushaka, J. O., Amaefule, M. C., Taiwo, O., Zhang, P., Ezugwu, A. E., Saleem, K., Smerat, A., & Abualigah, L. (2025). Secure and efficient cloudlet networks: blockchain integration with agent-based proof of trust mechanism. *Eurasip Journal on Wireless Communications and Networking*, *2025*(1). DOI: 10.1186/s13638-025-02439-y

Maz, Y. A., Anbar, M., Manickam, S., Abualhaj, M. M., Almalki, S. A., & Alabsi, B. A. (2025). Transfer Learning-Based Approach with an Ensemble Classifier for Detecting Keylogging Attack on the Internet of Things. *Computers, Materials & Continua*, *85*(3), 5287–5307. Advance online publication. DOI: 10.32604/cmc.2025.068257

Mohammad, S. I., Al-Daoud, K., Al Qraini, B., Khanfar, I. A. A., & Vasudevan, A. (2025). Quantum Error Correction with Surface Code Analysis on Quantum Computing platform. *Applied Mathematics & Information Sciences*, *19*(2), 423–435. Advance online publication. DOI: 10.18576/amis/190216

Otair, M., Qawaqzeh, F. A., Alomari, S. A., Zitar, R. A., Migdady, H., Saleem, K., Smerat, A., Alsoud, A. R., & Abualigah, L. (2025). Enhanced Arithmetic Optimization Algorithm for Intrusion Detection in Wireless Sensor Networks. *International Journal of Communication Systems*, *38*(10), e70122. Advance online publication. DOI: 10.1002/dac.70122

Qaddara, I., & Alraba'nah, Y. (2025). Enhancing Requirements Classification Using Machine Learning Techniques. *SN Computer Science*, *6*(6), 649. Advance online publication. DOI: 10.1007/s42979-025-04158-z

Qawasmeh, S., Habboushb, A., Elzaghmouri, B., Kharma, Q., & Albalawneh, D. (2025). Hybrid Convolutional Neural Network-Based Intrusion Detection System for Secure IoT Networks. *Tikrit Journal of Engineering Sciences*, *32*(SP1), 1–11. Advance online publication. DOI: 10.25130/tjes.sp1.2025.2

Ramesh, J. V. N., Nimma, D., Dasari, R., Chaudhari Rane, D., AlGhamdi, A., Rao, K. B. V. B., Haider, S. A., Kuzieva, N., & Jangir, P. (2025). Safe and Reliable Two-Stage Online Offloading Algorithm for Transportation Cyber-Physical Systems. *IEEE Transactions on Intelligent Transportation Systems*, *26*(9), 14313–14322. Advance online publication. DOI: 10.1109/TITS.2025.3539934

Raza, M. A., Karim, A., Alqarni, M., Al-Khasawneh, M. A., Jumani, T. A., Aman, M., & Masud, M. I. (2025). An Intelligent Long Short-Term Memory-Based Machine Learning Model for the Potential Assessment of Global Hydropower Capacity in Sustainable Energy Transition and Security. *Energies*, *18*(13), 3324. Advance online publication. DOI: 10.3390/en18133324

Samanta, I. S., Mohanty, S., Rout, P. K., Parida, S. M., Panda, S., Bajaj, M., Blazek, V., & Prokop, L. (2025). A comprehensive review of feature extraction techniques for power quality event detection with novel approaches for enhanced classification in smart grids. *Electrical Engineering*, *107*(9), 12227–12259. Advance online publication. DOI: 10.1007/s00202-025-03149-w

Sardar, R., Anees, T., Al-Shamayleh, A. S., Mehmood, E., Khalil, W., Akhunzada, A., & Shaikh, F. S. (2025). Challenges in detecting security threats in WoT: A systematic literature review. *Artificial Intelligence Review*, *58*(7), 196. Advance online publication. DOI: 10.1007/s10462-025-11176-z

Shambour, Q., Al-Zyoud, M., & Almomani, O. (2025). Quantum-Inspired Hybrid Metaheuristic Feature Selection with SHAP for Optimized and Explainable Spam Detection. *Symmetry*, *17*(10), 1716. Advance online publication. DOI: 10.3390/sym17101716

Shambour, Q. Y., Al-Zyoud, M., & Hussein, A. H. (2025). FROM DATA TO DIAGNOSIS: KNOWLEDGE-DRIVEN, EXPLAINABLE AI FOR RELIABLE EARLY AUTISM DETECTION. *Interdisciplinary Journal of Information, Knowledge, and Management*, *20*, 032. Advance online publication. DOI: 10.28945/5652

Sharma, K. P., Al-Rashed, A., Johar, M. G. M., Alsoud, A. R., Singh, A., Dey, P., & Pant, S. (2025). Blockchain-Assisted Trust Framework for Increased Survivability in Internet of Vehicles. *Internet Technology Letters*, *8*(3), e70029. Advance online publication. DOI: 10.1002/itl2.70029

Sharma, K. P., Hussain, R., Jaharadak, A. A., Trawnih, A. A., Verma, D., Dasi, S., & Pant, S. (2025). Hybrid Convolutional Neural Network for Robust Attack Detection in Wireless Sensor Networks. *Internet Technology Letters*, *8*(6), e650. Advance online publication. DOI: 10.1002/itl2.650

Turab, N., Abushattal, A., Al-Nabulsi, J., & Owida, H. A. (2025). Advanced risk assessment using machine learning and sentiment analysis on log data. *IAES International Journal of Artificial Intelligence*, *14*(5), 3897. Advance online publication. DOI: 10.11591/ijai.v14.i5.pp3897-3905

Vasudevan, A., Albinaa, T. A., Mohammad, S. I., Sharmila, E., Raja, N., Soon, E. E. H., Alshurideh, M. T., & Al-Adwan, A. S. (2024). Bidirectional LSTM for Electronic Product Recommendation. *Applied Mathematics & Information Sciences*, *18*(6), 1443–1453. Advance online publication. DOI: 10.18576/amis/180621

Vasudevan, A., Tamilmani, K. T., Mohammad, S. I., Sridheepika, V. S., Raja, N., Soon, E. E. H., Nagaraj, S., & Al-Adwan, A. S. (2025). Voices of Concern: Contemplations on Socioeconomic, Ethical, and Developmental Impacts of AI. *Applied Mathematics & Information Sciences*, *19*(1), 221–232. Advance online publication. DOI: 10.18576/amis/190119

Compilation of References

Abashes, G. M., Elshqeirat, B., Abu-Shareha, A. A., & Alshraideh, M. (2025). BEYOND THE NOISE: UNVEILING MEANINGFUL PATTERNS IN MOBILE PAYMENT DATA USING FUZZY LOGIC AND SVM. *Journal of Theoretical and Applied Information Technology, 103*(1).

Abbas, N. A., Al-Sawaie, K. M., Khrais, I. M., & Sweity, I. (2025). Stability Analysis of the Money Demand Function. *Applied Mathematics & Information Sciences, 19*(2), 307–315. Advance online publication. DOI: 10.18576/amis/190207

Abdel-Jaber, M. tasime, Makhoul, N., Abdel-Jaber, M. en, & Beale, R. (2025). Cost prediction for product development using hybrid deep learning model: a meta-heuristic model. *Multimedia Tools and Applications, 84*(27). DOI: 10.1007/s11042-024-20437-y

Abdel-Jaber, M., Abdel-Jaber, M., Beale, R., & Makhoul, N. (2025). UHSC flexural strength prediction using optimized three-phase classifier and improved feature selection. *International Journal on Interactive Design and Manufacturing, 19*(5), 3201–3218. Advance online publication. DOI: 10.1007/s12008-024-01812-3

Abdeljaber, O., Al-Adwan, A. S., Yaseen, H., Falahat, M., Abdullah, A., & Fauzi, M. A. (2025). Shopping in the Metaverse: Decoding Consumer Intentions. *The International Information & Library Review*. Advance online publication. DOI: 10.1080/10572317.2025.2594293

Abdeljaber, O., & Al-Masaeed, S. (2025). Al-Mu'ani, L., Yaseen, H., & Alhnaity, B. (2025). Strategic Intelligence: The Power of AI in Planning Efficiency. *Human Behavior and Emerging Technologies*, (1). Advance online publication. DOI: 10.1155/hbe2/5383054

Abualghanam, O., Alazzam, H., Qatawneh, M., Alazab, M., & Al Sharaiah, M. (2025). Elevating Mobile Security: An Ensemble Approach for Enhanced Malware Detection with M-iForest. *International Journal of Interactive Mobile Technologies, 19*(10), 129–151. Advance online publication. DOI: 10.3991/ijim.v19i10.51319

Abualhaj, M. M., Abu-Shareha, A. A., Al-Khatib, S. N., Alsaaidah, A. M., & Anbar, M. (2025). Improving firewall performance using hybrid of optimization algorithms and decision trees classifier. *IAES International Journal of Artificial Intelligence, 14*(4), 2839. Advance online publication. DOI: 10.11591/ijai.v14.i4.pp2839-2848

Abualhaj, M. M., Abu-Shareha, A. A., & Rateb, R. (2025). Enhancing intrusion detection systems with hybrid HHO-WOA optimization and gradient boosting machine classifier. *International Journal of Reconfigurable and Embedded Systems, 14*(2), 518. Advance online publication. DOI: 10.11591/ijres.v14.i2.pp518-526

Abualhaj, M. M., Al-Khatib, S. N., Abu-Shareha, A. A., Hyassat, A., & Daoud, M. S. (2025). Smart Firewall for Phishing Detection Powered by Bio-Inspired Algorithms. *Journal of Advances in Information Technology*, *16*(11), 1529–1539. Advance online publication. DOI: 10.12720/jait.16.11.1529-1539

Abualhaj, M. M., Al-Khatib, S. N., Al Zyoud, M., Qaddara, I., & Anbar, M. (2025). Enhancing Intrusion Detection System Performance Using a Hybrid of Harris Hawks and Whale Optimization Algorithms. *Engineering. Technology and Applied Science Research*, *15*(4), 24354–24361. Advance online publication. DOI: 10.48084/etasr.10919

Abualhaj, M. M., Al-Khatib, S. N., Al-Zyoud, M., Qaddara, I., Hiari, M. O., & Aldossary, S. M. A. (2025). Enhanced Network Communication Security Through Hybrid Dragonfly-Bat Feature Selection for Intrusion Detection. *The Journal of Communication*, *20*(5). Advance online publication. DOI: 10.12720/jcm.20.5.607-618

Abualhaj, M. M., Al-Khatib, S., Al Shafi, N., Qaddara, I., & Hyassat, A. (2025). Utilizing Gray Wolf Optimization Algorithm in Malware Forensic Investigation. *Journal of Computational and Cognitive Engineering*, *4*(4), 591–602. Advance online publication. DOI: 10.47852/bonviewJCCE52025053

Abualhaj, M. M.I, Al-Khatib, S. N., Abu-Shareha, A. A., Almomani, O., Al-Mimi, H., Al-Allawee, A., Daoud, M. S., & Anbar, M. (2025). Spam Detection Boosted by Firefly-Based Feature Selection and Optimized Classifiers. *International Journal of Advances in Soft Computing and Its Applications*, *17*(3). Advance online publication. DOI: 10.15849/IJASCA.251130.02

Abualigah, L., Almomani, M. H., Alomari, S. A., Zitar, R. A., Migdady, H., Saleem, K., Snasel, V., Smerat, A., & Ezugwu, A. E. (2025). Optimizing Intrusion Detection in Wireless Sensor Networks via the Improved Chameleon Swarm Algorithm for Feature Selection. *IET Communications*, *19*(1), e70029. Advance online publication. DOI: 10.1049/cmu2.70029

Abualigah, L., Alomari, S. A., Almomani, M. H., Zitar, R. A., Migdady, H., Saleem, K., Smerat, A., Snasel, V., & Ezugwu, A. E. (2025). An enhanced Walrus Optimizer with opposition-based learning and mutation strategy for data clustering. *Array (New York, N.Y.)*, *26*, 100409. Advance online publication. DOI: 10.1016/j.array.2025.100409

Abuowaida, S., Abu Owida, H., Shelash Mohammad, S. I., Alshdaifat, N., Abu Elsoud, E., Alazaidah, R., Vasudevan, A., & Alshurideh, M. T. (2025). Evidence Detection in Cloud Forensics: Classifying Cyber-Attacks in IaaS Environments using machine learning. *Data and Metadata*, *4*, 699. Advance online publication. DOI: 10.56294/dm2025699

Abu-Shareha, A. A., Abualhaj, M. M., Alsharaiah, M. A., Al-Saaidah, A., & Achuthan, A. (2025). Diabetes Prediction Through Classification Using Pima Dataset: Survey and Evaluation. *Journal of Soft Computing and Data Mining*, *6*(1). Advance online publication. DOI: 10.30880/jscdm.2025.06.01.001

Ahmed, K. A., Ibrahim, A., Qudr, L. A. Z., Tawfeq, J. F., Al Falahi, Q., & Radhi, A. D. (2025). *Developing Adaptive AI-Driven Cybersecurity Frameworks for Real-Time Detection of Polymorphic Malware in IoT Networks*. DOI: 10.1109/ICBATS66542.2025.11258540

Ahmed, N., Rafiq, M., Rehman, M. A., Shaikh, T. S., Alqahtani, A. M., Khan, I., Imran, M., & Niazai, S. (2025). A dynamically consistent and time-efficient numerical design for the reaction diffusion model in three space dimensions. *Applied Mathematics in Science and Engineering*, *33*(1), 2495158. Advance online publication. DOI: 10.1080/27690911.2025.2495158

Ahmed, Z. E., Hasan, M. K., Hashim, A. A., Saeed, R. A., Mokhtar, R. A., Singh, S. P., & Ghazal, T. M. (2022). Optimization Procedure for Intelligent Internet of Things Applications. *2022 International Conference on Business Analytics for Technology and Security, ICBATS 2022*. DOI: 10.1109/ICBATS54253.2022.9759065

Akram, A. S., Abbas, S., Khan, M. A., Athar, A., Ghazal, T. M., & Al Hamadi, H. (2024). Smart Energy Management System Using Machine Learning. *Computers, Materials & Continua*, *78*(1), 959–973. Advance online publication. DOI: 10.32604/cmc.2023.032216

Al Abbadi, Y., Al-Ghraibah, A., & Altayeb, M. (2025). Tooth cavities detection based on digital image processing and artificial intelligence techniques. *Journal of Medical Engineering & Technology*. Advance online publication. DOI: 10.1080/03091902.2025.2574081 PMID: 41099352

Al Assaf, M. M., Qatawneh, M., & Alradhi, A. (2025). Linear algorithm for data retrieval performance optimization in self-encryption hybrid data centers. *Bulletin of Electrical Engineering and Informatics*, *14*(3). Advance online publication. DOI: 10.11591/eei.v14i3.9320

Al Hindi, G., Alshraideh, M., Hussein, A. H., Eliyan, L. F., & Al-Dhaqm, A. (2025). Hacking Back: Using Genetic Algorithms to Outsmart Hackers. *Journal of Computational Science*, *21*(9), 2049–2064. Advance online publication. DOI: 10.3844/jcssp.2025.2049.2064

Al Nasar, M. R., Ghazal, T. M., Al-Tarawni, M. A. M., Ahmed, A. A., Abu-Shareha, A. A., & Ahmed, S. M. (2025). Hierarchical Edge-Cloud Collaborative AI Algorithm for Energy-Efficient lot Management in Ubiquitous Computing Environments. *Journal of Wireless Mobile Networks, Ubiquitous Computing and Dependable Applications*, *16*(3). Advance online publication. DOI: 10.58346/JOWUA.2025.I3.035

Alabdallat, R. D., Abualhaj, M. M., & Abu-Shareha, A. (2025). Enhanced Multiclass Android Malware Detection Using a Modified Dwarf Mongoose Algorithm. *International Journal of Analysis and Applications*, *23*, 248. Advance online publication. DOI: 10.28924/2291-8639-23-2025-248

Alabdallat, R., Abualhaj, M., & Abu-Shareha, A. (2025). Android Malware Detection Using a Modified Dwarf Mongoose Algorithm. *International Journal of Intelligent Engineering and Systems*, *18*(8), 336–351. Advance online publication. DOI: 10.22266/ijies2025.0930.21

Al-Adwan, A. S., & Abdeljaber, O. (2025). Toward a resilient and smart supply chain: identifying and prioritizing barriers to metaverse adoption. *International Journal of Industrial Engineering and Operations Management*. DOI: 10.1108/IJIEOM-06-2025-0113

Al-Adwan, A. S., Al-Adwan, A., Li, N., Fauzi, M. A., Jafar, R. M. S., Habibi, A., & Falahat, M. (2025). IMMERSIVE LEARNING MEETS THEORY: MODELING EDUVERSE ADOPTION IN HIGHER EDUCATION. *Journal of Information Technology Education*, *24*, 042. Advance online publication. DOI: 10.28945/5669

Al-Bahtiti, A. S., Tayeh, B. A., Baghdadi, A., Alaloul, W. S., & Abu Aisheh, Y. I. (2025). Drivers for adopting augmented reality and virtual reality technologies in the construction project management in Gaza City. *Journal of Asian Architecture and Building Engineering*, 1–18. Advance online publication. DOI: 10.1080/13467581.2025.2507235

Aldaaja, Y., Odeh, M., Badrakhan, S. S., Sabri, M., Abdelrahim, Y., Samara, G., & Alsabatin, H. (2025). Quantifying the Managerial and Practical Benefits of Cloud Computing on Information Security in Higher Education Institutions. *Applied Mathematics & Information Sciences*, *19*(1), 15–24. Advance online publication. DOI: 10.18576/amis/190102

Aldabbas, A., Baniata, L. H., Alsaaidah, B. A., Mustafa, Z., Alali, M., & Rateb, R. (2025). Artificial intelligence-driven method for the discovery and prevention of distributed denial of service attacks. *IAES International Journal of Artificial Intelligence*, *14*(1), 614. Advance online publication. DOI: 10.11591/ijai.v14.i1.pp614-628

Al-Daoud, K. I., Yogeesh, N., Mohammad, S. I. S., Raja, N., Jabeen, F. T. Z., William, P., Vasudevan, A., Hunitie, M. F. A., & Alshdaifat, N. (2025). Fuzzy Linear Programming in Real-World Applications: A Comparative Study of Agricultural and Financial Optimization. *Applied Mathematics & Information Sciences*, *19*(4), 849–862. Advance online publication. DOI: 10.18576/amis/190411

Al-Daoud, K. I., Yogeesh, N., Mohammad, S. I., Raja, N., Chetana, R., William, P., Vasudevan, A., Alshdaifa, N., & Hunitie, M. F. A. (2025). Explainability in AI Using Fuzzy Inference Systems For the Regression Problem. *Applied Mathematics & Information Sciences*, *19*(5), 973–987. Advance online publication. DOI: 10.18576/amis/190501

Al-Dmour, R., Al-Dmour, H., Al-Dmour, A., Basheer Amin, E., & Al-Dmour, Y. (2025). *AI and big data-driven social media recruitment: the mediating role of talent acquisition and employee engagement in bank performance*. Digital Transformation and Society., DOI: 10.1108/DTS-02-2025-0042

Alenazi, M. J. F., Al-Khasawneh, M. A., Rahman, S., & Faheem, Z. (2025). Deep Reinforcement Learning Based Flow Aware-QoS Provisioning in SD-IoT for Precision Agriculture. *Computational Intelligence*, *41*(1), e70023. Advance online publication. DOI: 10.1111/coin.70023

Al-Falouji, M., Al Btoush, R., Abu Hajar, H., & Tarwaneh, B. (2025). Landslide Stabilization of Al-Adasiah Road Using Pile Wall Retaining System. *Jordan Journal of Civil Engineering*, *19*(4). Advance online publication. DOI: 10.14525/JJCE.v19i4.02

Al-Habashneh, A. G., Al-Daoud, K. I., Oraini, B., Al, , & Shelash, S. I. (2025). The impact of artificial intelligence on the development of electronic financial services. *International Journal of Data and Network Science*, *9*(2), 317–322. Advance online publication. DOI: 10.5267/j.ijdns.2024.8.012

Alharbi, Y., Yadav, K., Dutta, D., Smerat, A., & Ranjbar, F. (2026). Thermodynamic behavior of CO2–organic mixtures: Density prediction using explainable machine learning algorithms. *Results in Engineering*, *29*, 108687. Advance online publication. DOI: 10.1016/j.rineng.2025.108687

Ali, A. M., Al-Qerem, A., Hassan, M. R., Abu-Khadrah, A., & Jarrah, M. (2025). Traffic Monitoring and Control System for Smart City Pollution Regulation Using IoT and Correlated Capsule Networks. *IEEE Access : Practical Innovations, Open Solutions*, *13*, 46983–47003. Advance online publication. DOI: 10.1109/ACCESS.2025.3550966

Ali, L., Alshamayleh, A., Ibrahim, A., & Ahmed, S. M. (2026). Information Management Enhancement in Cloud-Based Systems Through Blockchain-Enabled Secure Access Control. *Indian Journal of Information Sources and Services*, *16*(1), 289–296. Advance online publication. DOI: 10.51983/ijiss-2026.16.1.30

Ali, M. I., Savitha, K., Smerat, A., Babu, K. S., Sivakumar, G., & Gracy Theresa, W. (2025). Multimodal Deep Learning Model for Measuring the Impact of Social Media Advertising Using Visual Linguistic Representation Learning. *Journal of Machine and Computing*, *5*(4), 2566–2573. Advance online publication. DOI: 10.53759/7669/jmc202505197

Alkhawatrah, M., AlAyyad, M., & Korostynska, O. (2025). Balanced inter-relay charging buffer-aided IOT networks. *Eurasip Journal on Wireless Communications and Networking*, *2025*(1). DOI: 10.1186/s13638-025-02524-2

Alkhawatrah, M. (2025). Random Forests Relay Selector in Buffer-Aided Cooperative Networks. *IEEE Access : Practical Innovations, Open Solutions*, *13*, 165402–165410. Advance online publication. DOI: 10.1109/ACCESS.2025.3612192

ALMahadin, G., Shabaz, M., Khan, I. R., Vimal, V., Keshta, I., & Maguluri, L. P.ALMahadin. (2025). Content-aware recommendation system for integrated temporal semantic review text over web of things. *Service Oriented Computing and Applications*, *19*(1), 77–91. Advance online publication. DOI: 10.1007/s11761-024-00408-9

Almajed, R., Ibrahim, A., Abualkishik, A. Z., Mourad, N., & Almansour, F. A. (2022). Using machine learning algorithm for detection of cyber-attacks in cyber physical systems. *Periodicals of Engineering and Natural Sciences*, *10*(3), 261. Advance online publication. DOI: 10.21533/pen.v10i3.3035

Al-Momani, M. M., Alqudah, T. A., Al Swiety, I. A., Mahrakani, N., Nassoura, M. B. A., & Al Attar, M. K. (2025). Integrating Artificial Intelligence (AI) and Business Intelligence (BI): A Framework for Improving Enterprise Performance. *TEM Journal*, *14*(3). https://doi.org/DOI: 10.18421/TEM143-26

Almomani, O., Arabiat, A., Al Tayeb, M., Almaiah, M. A., Obeidat, M., Aldhyani, T. H. H., Shehab, R., & Rowad, M. (2025). A Robust Model for Android Malware Detection via ML and DL classifiers. *Mesopotamian Journal of Big Data*, *2025*. Advance online publication. DOI: 10.58496/MJBD/2025/017

Al-Mousa, M., Amer, W., Abualhaj, M., Albilasi, S., Nasir, O., & Samara, G. (2025). Agile Proactive Cybercrime Evidence Analysis Model for Digital Forensics. *The International Arab Journal of Information Technology*, *22*(3). Advance online publication. DOI: 10.34028/iajit/22/3/15

Alnawafleh, N. M., Ibrahim, A., & Pradhan, M. R. (2024). Review of the Mechanisms Used to Protect the Big Data from Attacks. *2nd International Conference on Cyber Resilience, ICCR 2024*. DOI: 10.1109/ICCR61006.2024.10533073

Alnawayseh, S. E. A., Al-Sit, W. T., & Ghazal, T. M. (2022). Smart Congestion Control in 5G/6G Networks Using Hybrid Deep Learning Techniques. *Complexity*, *2022*(1), 1781952. Advance online publication. DOI: 10.1155/2022/1781952

Alnawayseh, S. E. A., Muhammad, M. H. G., Hassan, Z., Fatima, M., Aslam, M. S., Ibrahim, A., & Ateeq, K. (2023). Resource Provisioning in Cloud Computing using Fuzzy Logic Control System: An adaptive approach. *2nd International Conference on Business Analytics for Technology and Security, ICBATS 2023*. DOI: 10.1109/ICBATS57792.2023.10111481

Alnsour, Y., Alsharo, M., Al-Essa, M., & Smerat, A. (2025). AI-Powered Election Insights: Predicting the 2024 Trump vs. Kamala Election Showdown with Machine Learning. *Journal of Intelligent Systems and Internet of Things*, *15*(1), 185–197. Advance online publication. DOI: 10.54216/JISIoT.150116

Al-Okbi, N. K., Alomari, S. A., Hadi, W. J., Ajrash, A. S., Smerat, A., & Abualigah, L. (2025). Defending Digital Integrity: Advances in Media Forgery Analysis Research and Cybersecurity Development. *SN Computer Science*, *6*(8), 913. Advance online publication. DOI: 10.1007/s42979-025-04462-8

Al-Okbi, N. K., Alomari, S. A., Zitar, R. A., Smerat, A., Nazzal, M. A., & Abualigah, L. (2025). Integrating Multimodal Emotion Recognition with Deep Q-Learning for Adaptive Social Robot Interaction. *International Journal of Robotics and Control Systems*, *5*(4), 2265–2289. Advance online publication. DOI: 10.31763/ijrcs.v5i4.2055

Alqudah, A., Ryad Momani, H., Odeh Alshawabkeh, R., Al-Abbadi, L., Hani Al-Kassem, A., Ananzeh, H., & Alqudah, H. (2025). *The impact of Cyber-Physical Systems on logistics sustainability: The role of smart energy monitoring as a mediator in improving energy efficiency*. EDPACS., DOI: 10.1080/07366981.2025.2596460

Alraba'nah, Y., Al-Sharaeh, S., & Al Hindi, G. (2025). Enhancing Intrusion Detection Using Hybrid Long Short-Term Memory and XGBoost. *Journal of Soft Computing and Data Mining*, *6*(1). Advance online publication. DOI: 10.30880/jscdm.2025.06.01.016

Alraba'nah, Y., & Hiari, M. (2025). Improved convolutional neural networks for aircraft type classification in remote sensing images. *IAES International Journal of Artificial Intelligence*, *14*(2), 1540. Advance online publication. DOI: 10.11591/ijai.v14.i2.pp1540-1547

Al-Suhimat, R. I., Mohammed Ai, N., Ibrahim, A., Maaitah, N. O., & Al-Dmour, N. A. (2024). Review of Security Challenges Encountered in Internet of Things Technology. *2nd International Conference on Cyber Resilience, ICCR 2024*. DOI: 10.1109/ICCR61006.2024.10533052

Al-znamat, F. O., Alsaaidah, A., & Abu-Shareha, A. A. (2025). Malware Detection Using a Modified Bat Algorithm for Feature Selection. *International Journal of Intelligent Engineering and Systems*, *18*(9), 885–899. Advance online publication. DOI: 10.22266/ijies2025.1031.56

Amin, M., Nahar, K. M. O., Gharaibeh, H., Al Mamlook, R. E., Nasayreh, A., Atitallah, N., Gharaibeh, A., Hamad, R., Zitar, R. A., Smerat, A., & Abualigah, L. (2025). A Hybrid Brain Stroke Prediction Framework: Integrating Feature Selection, Classification, and Hyperparameter Optimization. *Engineering Reports*, *7*(7), e70213. Advance online publication. DOI: 10.1002/eng2.70213

Arabasy, M., & Ghoneim, R. S. (2025). Enhancing sustainable urban design using machine learning: Comparative analysis of seven metaheuristic algorithms in energy-efficient digital architecture. *Frontiers in Built Environment*, *11*, 1526209. Advance online publication. DOI: 10.3389/fbuil.2025.1526209

Arabiat, A. M. (2025). Intelligent Model for Detecting GAN-Generated Images Based on Multi-Classifier and Advanced Data Mining Techniques. *International Journal of Electrical and Electronic Engineering and Telecommunications*, *14*(3). Advance online publication. DOI: 10.18178/ijeetc.14.3.147-157

Arabiat, A. M., & Eljaafreh, Y. G. (2025). Intrusion Detection in Wireless Sensor Networks Using ML Based Classification of Denial of Service (DoS) Attacks. *The Journal of Communication*, *20*(4). Advance online publication. DOI: 10.12720/jcm.20.4.501-514

Arabiat, A., & Altayeb, M. (2025). Driving behavior analytics: An intelligent system based on machine learning and data mining techniques. *Bulletin of Electrical Engineering and Informatics*, *14*(3), 2055–2065. Advance online publication. DOI: 10.11591/eei.v14i3.9095

Arabiat, A., Altayeb, M., & Alkhrissat, T. (2025). Innovative AI Approaches for Concrete Strength Prediction: Towards Sustainable Buildings. *Civil Engineering and Architecture*, *13*(6), 4254–4265. Advance online publication. DOI: 10.13189/cea.2025.130612

Arabiat, A., Altayeb, M., & Salama, S. (2025). Artificial intelligence-powered smart roads: Leveraging orange3 for traffic signs recognition. *IAES International Journal of Artificial Intelligence*, *14*(5), 3816. Advance online publication. DOI: 10.11591/ijai.v14.i5.pp3816-3826

Awais, Z., Hussain, M., Elshenawy, A., Arsalan, A., Anwar, M., Asif Habib, M., Jabbar, S., & Ahmad, M. (2025). ISCC: Intelligent Semantic Caching and Control for NDN-Enabled Industrial IoT Networks. *IEEE Access : Practical Innovations, Open Solutions*, *13*, 169881–169898. Advance online publication. DOI: 10.1109/ACCESS.2025.3614984

Ayub, N., Imtiaz, M. A., Ali, E., Alqahtani, A. M., Ali, A., Ashurov, M., Albouq, S., & Law, F. L. (2025). A Decision Framework for Intra Task Fixed Priority INTEL PXA270 Distributed Architecture for Soft RT-Applications Based on Deep Learning. *Engineering. Technology and Applied Science Research*, *15*(3), 23553–23558. Advance online publication. DOI: 10.48084/etasr.10006

Babaker, S., Khatibi, A., Alsoud, A. R., Kaur, J., Jagtap, J., Alkhayyat, A., & Shah, S. K. (2025). Improving Reliability and Data Management in Internet of Things Based Wireless Sensor Networks. *Internet Technology Letters*, *8*(6), e646. Advance online publication. DOI: 10.1002/itl2.646

Bektemyssova, G., Montazeri, Z., Dehghani, M., Ibraheem, I. K., Smerat, A., Werner, F., Al-Salih, A. A. M. M., Ahmed, M. A., & Eguchi, K. (2025). Search and Rescue Algorithm (SRA): A Metaheuristic Approach for Efficient Constrained Engineering Optimization. *International Journal of Intelligent Engineering and Systems*, *18*(10), 607–621. Advance online publication. DOI: 10.22266/ijies2025.1130.39

Benali, A., Kharbouch, H., Della Krachai, M., Singh, J. P., Bouddou, R., Yesma, B., Belabbes, A., Husein, A., Salau, A. O., & Rubanenko, O. (2025). Dual-Stream Convolutional Networks for Scalable and Precise Water Body Mapping from Multispectral Earth Observation Imagery. *International Journal of Computational Intelligence Systems*, *18*(1), 260. Advance online publication. DOI: 10.1007/s44196-025-00985-3

Biswas, S., Maiti, B., Singh, G., Ezugwu, A. E., Saleem, K., Abualigah, L., Smerat, A., & Bera, U. K. (2025). A Novel Hybrid Optimizer Based on Coati Optimization Algorithm and Differential Evolution for Global Optimization and Constrained Engineering Problems. *International Journal of Computational Intelligence Systems*, *18*(1), 157. Advance online publication. DOI: 10.1007/s44196-025-00855-y

Cui, D., Harrison, A., Fendzi-Donfack, E., Dagal, I., Jangir, P., Mahmoud, M. M., Malkani, P., Mbasso, W. F., Tiako, P., & Smerat, A. (2026). Enhancing Short-Term Electricity Forecasting with Advanced Machine Learning Techniques. *Journal of Electrical Engineering & Technology*, *21*(1), 147–187. Advance online publication. DOI: 10.1007/s42835-025-02430-z

Dara Singh, K. S., Kien Hong, T., Abbasi, G. A., & Al-Adwan, A. S. (2025). Building Bonds with Food Delivery Apps: Determinants of App Attachment & Continuous Intention–Does Gender Matter? *International Journal of Human-Computer Interaction*, *41*(23), 15276–15294. Advance online publication. DOI: 10.1080/10447318.2025.2495843

Dar, A. A., Bhavithra, H. A., Awasthi, A. K., Sabha, S. U., Dar, J. G., Smerat, A., & Sindhuja, S. (2025). Inventory Optimization for Perishables: A Probabilistic and Fuzzy Modeling Approach. *Mathematical Modelling of Engineering Problems*, *12*(8). Advance online publication. DOI: 10.18280/mmep.120825

Dhasaratha, C., Hasan, M. K., Islam, S., Khapre, S., Abdullah, S., Ghazal, T. M., Alzahrani, A. I., Alalwan, N., Vo, N., & Akhtaruzzaman, M. (2024). Data privacy model using blockchain reinforcement federated learning approach for scalable internet of medical things. *CAAI Transactions on Intelligence Technology*, cit2.12287. Advance online publication. DOI: 10.1049/cit2.12287

Dheeb, S. A., AL-Azzawi, W. S. A.-B., Suleiman, A. K., Ibrahim, A., & Ghwanmeh, S. (2025). *The Role of Generative Artificial Intelligence in Advancing Multilingual Intelligent Support Systems*. DOI: 10.1109/ICCR67387.2025.11291954

Dinler, Ö. B., Bektemyssova, G., Şahin, C. B., Montazeri, Z., Dehghani, M., Smerat, A., Werner, F., & Eguchi, K. (2025). Carpenter Optimization Algorithm: A Human-inspired Metaheuristic for Robust and Efficient Constrained Optimization. *International Journal of Intelligent Engineering and Systems*, *18*(11), 344–357. Advance online publication. DOI: 10.22266/ijies2025.1231.21

Duraimurugan, S., Jayarin, P. J., Mohammad, S. I., Hariprasad, N., Vasudevan, A., Soon, E. E. H., Hussein, A. H., & Alshurideh, M. T. (2025). Enhanced Server-Client Framework for Optimizing QoS in Video Streaming Over Diverse Networks. *Applied Mathematics & Information Sciences*, *19*(1), 61–73. Advance online publication. DOI: 10.18576/amis/190106

Ebbini, M. M., Qtaishat, A. K., Aburub, F. A., & Jaradat, M. S. (2025). Impact of Ethical Fintech on Micro Entrepreneurs in Jordan. *International Journal of Advances in Soft Computing and Its Applications*, *17*(3). Advance online publication. DOI: 10.15849/IJASCA.251130.10

Eke, C. I., Al-Shamayleh, A. S., Phiri, M., Maswadi, K., Kwaghtyo, D. K., Mulenga, M., & Iyidobi, C. J. (2025). Machine Learning Based Mobile Big Data Analytics: State-of-the-art Applications, Taxonomy, Challenges and Future Research Directions. *Nigerian Journal of Technological Development*, *22*(4). Advance online publication. DOI: 10.63746/njtd.v22i4.3385

Elkaradawy, A., Elshenawy, A., & Harb, H. (2025). Enhancing Cloud Job Failure Prediction With a Novel Multilayer Voting-Based Framework. *IEEE Access : Practical Innovations, Open Solutions*, *13*, 140600–140613. Advance online publication. DOI: 10.1109/ACCESS.2025.3593808

Elkhouly, M., Alhadidi, T., & Rakha, H. (2025). Modeling Traffic Vehicular Counts at an Urban Intersection Using Complex Seasonal Modeling Techniques. *KSCE Journal of Civil Engineering*, *29*(1), 100040. Advance online publication. DOI: 10.1016/j.kscej.2024.100040

El-Mesady, A., Elsonbaty, A., Nisar, K. S., & Adel, W. (2025). Fractional-order mathematical modeling and optimal control strategies for women's empowerment initiatives. *Ain Shams Engineering Journal*, *16*(11), 103702. Advance online publication. DOI: 10.1016/j.asej.2025.103702

Elomda, B. M., Abdelbary, T. A. A., Hassan, H. A., Hamza, K. S., & Kharma, Q. (2025). An Enhanced Multi-Layer Blockchain Security Model for Improved Latency and Scalability. *Information (Basel)*, *16*(3), 241. Advance online publication. DOI: 10.3390/info16030241

Farman, M., Gokbulut, N., Shehzad, A., Nisar, K. S., Hincal, E., & Sambas, A. (2025). Fractional order malaria epidemic model: Qualitative and computational study to determine the dynamics for sensitivity prevalence. *Journal of Computational Science*, *91*, 102656. Advance online publication. DOI: 10.1016/j.jocs.2025.102656

Fatima, W., Rizvi, S. S. R., Ghazal, T. M., Kharma, Q. M., Ahmad, M., Abbas, S., Furqan, M., & Adnan, K. M. (2025). Abstractive Text Summarization in Arabic-Like Script Using Multi-Encoder Architecture and Semantic Extraction Techniques. *IEEE Access : Practical Innovations, Open Solutions*, *13*, 104977–104991. Advance online publication. DOI: 10.1109/ACCESS.2025.3575610

Fauzi, M. A., Wider, W., Samed Al-Adwan, A., Sadun, A. S., & Shafi, M. (2025). Wolf in sheep's clothing: An analysis of predatory journals through science mapping. In *Social Science Information* (Vol. 64, Number 2). DOI: 10.1177/05390184251336583

Fauzi, M. A., Alias, U. N., Nya-Ling Tan, C., Wider, W., Mukherjee, S., Al-Adwan, A. S., & Udang, L. N. (2025). The Present and Future Trends of Leadership Styles and Knowledge Hiding Through Science Mapping Analysis. *Journal of Information and Knowledge Management*, *24*(5), 2550040. Advance online publication. DOI: 10.1142/S0219649225500406

Ghazal, T. M. (2025b). Federated Learning for Intelligent Sensing and Navigation Technologies for 6G Communications. *Journal of Sensors, 2025*(1). DOI: 10.1155/js/3746147

Ghazal, T. M., Hasan, M. K., Alzoubi, H. M., Al Hmmadi, M., Al-Dmour, N. A., Islam, S., Kamran, R., & Mago, B. (2022). Securing Smart Cities Using Blockchain Technology. *2022 1st International Conference on AI in Cybersecurity, ICAIC 2022*. DOI: 10.1109/ICAIC53980.2022.9896971

Ghazal, T. M., Hasan, M. K., Mokhtar, U. A., Safie, N., Alshamayleh, A., & Ahmad, M. (2025). Machine learning-based real-time outage fault detection for distribution networks in smart grid. In *Energy Reports* (Vol. 14). DOI: 10.1016/j.egyr.2025.10.045

Ghazal, T. M., Janjua, J. I., Abushiba, W., Ahmad, M., Ihsan, A., & Al-Dmour, N. A. (2024). Cybersecurity Revolution via Large Language Models and Explainable AI. *2024 17th International Conference on Security of Information and Networks, SIN 2024*. DOI: 10.1109/SIN63213.2024.10871324

Ghazal, T. M. (2025a). An IoT-Based Active Learning Convolutional Neural Networks Model for Predicting River Water Quality. *Journal of Soft Computing and Data Mining*, *6*(1). Advance online publication. DOI: 10.30880/jscdm.2025.06.01.021

Ghazal, T. M., Abdali, T. A. N., Abualhaj, M. M., Saeed, A. Q., & Ahmad, M. (2025). Advanced LWAVF Framework Based on Neural Network Security in IoMT for Managing Patient Data Authentication and Integrity Validation with Consensus Mapping. *Journal of Soft Computing and Data Mining*, *6*(1). Advance online publication. DOI: 10.30880/jscdm.2025.06.01.003

Ghazal, T. M., Abualhaj, M., Ahmed, A. A., Al-Tarawni, M. A. M., & Maghrabi, L. A. (2025). Federated Deep Graph Neural Network Algorithm for Real-Time Intrusion Detection in Heterogeneous IoT Systems. *Journal of Internet Services and Information Security*, *15*(4), 484–497. Advance online publication. DOI: 10.58346/JISIS.2025.I4.035

Ghazal, T. M., Abu-Shareha, A., Mustafa, S. A., Ibrahim, A., & Ahmed, S. M. (2025). Privacy-Preserving Transformer-Based Meta-Learning Algorithm for Zero-Day Intrusion Detection in IoT-Enabled Smart Grids. *Journal of Internet Services and Information Security*, *15*(4), 76–84. Advance online publication. DOI: 10.58346/JISIS.2025.I4.006

Ghazal, T. M., Awouda, A. E., Hasan, M. K., Rahman, A. H. A., Islam, S., Saeed, R. A., Elshafie, H., Iqbal, A., & Hussein, A. H. (2025). Knowledge Learning for Securing Workflow Scheduling Algorithm in Mobile Edge Computing. *Mobile Networks and Applications*, *30*(3-4), 395–413. Advance online publication. DOI: 10.1007/s11036-025-02465-6

Ghazal, T. M., Hasan, M. K., Abdul Wahab, A. N., Ibrahim, A., Khan, W. A., Raza, N. Z., Atta, A., & Mago, B. (2022). Towards Privacy Provisioning for Internet of Things (IoT). *International Conference on Cyber Resilience, ICCR 2022*. DOI: 10.1109/ICCR56254.2022.9995916

Ghazal, T. M., Hasan, M. K., Hussein, A. H., Pandey, B. K., Ahmad, M., Safie, N., & Cascone, L. (2025). Federated Learning With Small and Large Models With Privacy-Preserving Data Space for Holographic Internet of Things in Consumer Electronics. *IEEE Transactions on Consumer Electronics*, *71*(2), 5259–5274. Advance online publication. DOI: 10.1109/TCE.2025.3573033

Ghazal, T. M., Hasan, M. K., Khairy, S. O. F., Mokhtar, U. A., Islam, S., Saeed, R. A., Ahmed, N., & Abdullah, M. (2025). Lightweight signcryption scheme for Securing wearable sensor observed health data sharing in internet of medical things paradigm. *Scientific Reports*, *15*(1), 40989. Advance online publication. DOI: 10.1038/s41598-025-24687-0 PMID: 41266478

Ghazal, T. M., Hasan, M. K., Raju, K. N., Khan, M. A., Alshamayleh, A., Bhatt, M. W., & Ahmad, M. (2025). Data Space Privacy Model with Federated Learning Technique for Securing IoT Communications in Autonomous Marine Vehicles. *Journal of Intelligent & Robotic Systems*, *111*(3), 84. Advance online publication. DOI: 10.1007/s10846-025-02298-1

Ghazal, T. M., Islam, S., Hasan, M. K., Abu-Shareha, A. A., Mokhtar, U. A., Khan, M. A., Baili, J., Saeed, A. Q., Bhatt, M. W., & Ahmad, M. (2025). Generative Federated Learning With Small and Large Models in Consumer Electronics for Privacy-Preserving Data Fusion in Healthcare Internet of Things. *IEEE Transactions on Consumer Electronics*, *71*(2), 3413–3430. Advance online publication. DOI: 10.1109/TCE.2025.3572629

Ghoneim, R. S., Arabasy, M., Osbaa, R. A., & Al Hamad, R. (2025). A Systematic Literature Review on Integrating Machine Learning Algorithms and Metaheuristic Algorithms in Optimizing Sustainable Digital Architectural Design. *Civil Engineering and Architecture*, *13*(3), 1913–1931. Advance online publication. DOI: 10.13189/cea.2025.130334

Ghoneim, R. S., Taiyara, R., & Maghaireh, Z. N. (2025). Machine Learning-Enhanced Building Information Modeling (BIM) for Sustainable Urban Planning. *Civil Engineering and Architecture*, *13*(3), 2171–2184. Advance online publication. DOI: 10.13189/cea.2025.131301

Gul, A., Khan, F., Farooq, M., Javaid, A., Hussain, Z., & Elzaghmouri, B. (2025). STATISTICAL MODELING AND PREDICTION OF PANDEMIC USING CLASSICAL AND MACHINE LEARNING APPROACH. *Pakistan Journal of Statistics*, *41*(3).

H K, P. K., Dash, R., K, J. R., Mohapatra, B., Bishoyi, S. S., Bajaj, M., & Blazek, V.H K. (2026). Multi-domain fault characterization in DC microgrids utilizing Hilbert-Huang transform ensemble by LSTM networks with adaptive boundary condition constraints. *Results in Engineering*, *29*, 108721. Advance online publication. DOI: 10.1016/j.rineng.2025.108721

Habboush, A., & Elzaghmouri, B. (2025). Methodological integration of machine learning and metaheuristics for seismic risk assessment of irregular buildings. *Asian Journal of Civil Engineering*. DOI: 10.1007/s42107-025-01571-w

Haider, Z. A., Ullah, I., Shareha, A. A., Nasimov, R., & Memon, S. A. (2026). Artificial Intelligence (AI)-Enabled Unmanned Aerial Vehicle (UAV) Systems for Optimizing User Connectivity in Sixth-Generation (6G) Ubiquitous Networks. *Computers, Materials & Continua*, *86*(1), 1–16. Advance online publication. DOI: 10.32604/cmc.2025.071042

Hakami, H., Hasan, M. K., Alshamayleh, A., Saeed, A. Q., Mustafa, S. A., & Ghazal, T. M. (2025). Adaptive Neuro-Fuzzy Congestion Control Algorithm for Real-Time Multimedia Networking in Cloud-Based E-Learning Platforms. *Journal of Wireless Mobile Networks, Ubiquitous Computing and Dependable Applications*, *16*(3). Advance online publication. DOI: 10.58346/JOWUA.2025.I3.027

Hanandeh, A., Alfreijat, S. Y., Qutieshat, R. J., Alsha'ar, H. Y., Kilani, Q. A. L., & Saleem Khasawneh, M. A. (2025). Implementing AI Accuracy, Learning Rate, Inference Time on enhancing Big Data Analysis and Strategic Plan. *Data and Metadata*, *4*, 637. Advance online publication. DOI: 10.56294/dm2025637

Hanandeh, R., Alkhazali, Z., Alhyasat, K. M. K., Mistarihi, A. M., & Kilani, Q. A. L. (2025). The Impact of Data-Driven Decision-Making, Real-Time Analytics, and Ethical Data Practices on HR Performance and Employee Satisfaction. *Data and Metadata*, *4*, 712. Advance online publication. DOI: 10.56294/dm2025712

Hanumanthagowda, P. B., Vasanthkumara, M. K. M., Al-Nussairi, A. K. J., Hadi, A. A., Smerat, A., & Shivanna, P. B. (2026). Process-aware Temporal Graph Embedding for Detecting and Localizing Recurring Concept Drift. *International Journal of Intelligent Engineering and Systems*, *19*(1), 402–422. Advance online publication. DOI: 10.22266/ijies2026.0131.25

Hasan, M. K., Ghazal, T. M., Alkhalifah, A., Abu Bakar, K. A., Omidvar, A., Nafi, N. S., & Agbinya, J. I. (2021). Fischer Linear Discrimination and Quadratic Discrimination Analysis–Based Data Mining Technique for Internet of Things Framework for Healthcare. *Frontiers in Public Health*, *9*, 737149. Advance online publication. DOI: 10.3389/fpubh.2021.737149 PMID: 34712639

Hasan, M. K., Ghazal, T. M., Issa, G., Islam, S., Ismail, A. F., & Kabir, S. R. (2025). Hashgraph consensus-based simultaneous, asynchronous and big-data supported blockchain mechanism for IT-OT enabled critical infrastructure sectors. *Journal of Ambient Intelligence and Humanized Computing*. Advance online publication. DOI: 10.1007/s12652-024-04942-4

Hasan, M. K., Habib, A. K. M. A., Islam, S., Safie, N., Ghazal, T. M., Khan, M. A., Alzahrani, A. I., Alalwan, N., Kadry, S., & Masood, A. (2024). Federated learning enables 6 G communication technology: Requirements, applications, and integrated with intelligence framework. *Alexandria Engineering Journal*, *91*, 658–668. Advance online publication. DOI: 10.1016/j.aej.2024.02.044

Hiari, M., Alraba'nah, Y., & Qaddara, I. (2025). A Deep Learning-Based Intrusion Detection System using Refined LSTM for DoS Attack Detection. *Engineering. Technology and Applied Science Research*, *15*(4), 25627–25633. Advance online publication. DOI: 10.48084/etasr.11499

Hou, G., Alkhayyat, A., Almalkawi, A., Yadav, A., Shreenidhi, H. S., Saini, V., Shomurotova, S., Singh, D., Jain, V., Smerat, A., & Khalid, A. (2025). Development of robust machine learning models to estimate hydrochar higher heating value and yield based upon biomass proximate analysis. *Bioresources and Bioprocessing*, *12*(1), 138. Advance online publication. DOI: 10.1186/s40643-025-00979-1 PMID: 41335148

Hussain, K., Ali, E. M., Hussain, W., Raza, A., & Elkamchouchi, D. H. (2025). Robust OTFS-ISAC for Vehicular-to-Base Station End-to-End Sensing and Communication. *Electronics (Basel)*, *14*(21), 4340. Advance online publication. DOI: 10.3390/electronics14214340

Hyassat, A. S., Abu Zayed, R. E., Al Khateeb, E. A., Shalaldeh, A., Abdelhamied, M. M., & Qaddara, I. (2025). Unveiling Cyber Threats: An In-Depth Study on Data Mining Techniques for Exploit Attack Detection †. *Engineering Proceedings*, *104*(1), 28. Advance online publication. DOI: 10.3390/engproc2025104028

Ibrahim Alasadi, A. A., Manjula, S., Smerat, A., Govindu, K., Sivakumar, G., & Sahasranamam, V. (2025). Mathematically Modified Deep Learning Model Assisted Handwritten Digit Recognition for Intelligent Document Processing Systems. *Journal of Machine and Computing*, *5*(4), 2661–2671. Advance online publication. DOI: 10.53759/7669/jmc202505204

Ibrahim, A. (2024). Guarding the Future of Gaming: The Imperative of Cybersecurity. *2nd International Conference on Cyber Resilience, ICCR 2024*. DOI: 10.1109/ICCR61006.2024.10532843

Ibrahim, A., Ali, W., Al-Dmour, N. A., & Ghazal, T. M. (2024). Revolutionizing Human Assessment: AI-Driven Analysis of SQ, EQ, and IQ. *2nd International Conference on Cyber Resilience, ICCR 2024*. DOI: 10.1109/ICCR61006.2024.10532816

Ibrahim, A., Sekhar, R., Tawfeq, J. F., Salih, S. Q., Shah, P., & Radhi, A. D. (2024). Security and Privacy Protection for Online Electronic Documents Based on Novel Encryption Techniques. *Journal of Intelligent Systems and Internet of Things, 11*(1), 21–28. Advance online publication. DOI: 10.54216/JISIoT.110103

Iftikhar, A., Mohammad, S. I., Alqudah, M. N., Al-Adwan, A. S., Vasudevan, A., Ali, I., & Farhan, M. (2025). Evaluating Inclusivity and Fairness of AI Recruitment Tools for Hiring People with Disabilities in the United Arab Emirates(UAE). *Data and Metadata, 4*. Advance online publication. DOI: 10.56294/dm2025487

Iskandarani, M. Z., & Chakrabarti, K. (2025). Adaptive Frequency and Energy Modeling Framework for Robotic Wireless Sensor Networks Based on Path Loss Predictions. *Journal of Robotics, 2025*(1). DOI: 10.1155/joro/6156608

Iskandarani, M. Z. (2025). Effect of Adaptive Intelligent Reflective Surfaces on SINR in a Wireless Communication System. *The Journal of Communication, 20*(1). Advance online publication. DOI: 10.12720/jcm.20.1.1-11

Iskandarani, M. Z. (2025). Effect of Intelligent Reflecting Surface on WSN Communication With Access Points Configuration. *IEEE Access : Practical Innovations, Open Solutions, 13*, 13380–13394. Advance online publication. DOI: 10.1109/ACCESS.2025.3531637

Iskandarani, M. Z. (2025). Energy and path loss analysis of wireless sensor networks on a robotic body (WSRobotic). *Bulletin of Electrical Engineering and Informatics, 14*(3). Advance online publication. DOI: 10.11591/eei.v14i3.9354

Iskandarani, M. Z., & Hidayat, R. (2025). Analysis of Factors Affecting Spectrum Sensing in an IRS based Wireless Network. *International Journal on Advanced Science, Engineering and Information Technology, 15*(1), 300–309. Advance online publication. DOI: 10.18517/ijaseit.15.1.20491

Jan, F. U., Badar, R., Sami Al-Shamayleh, A., Uehara, A., Senjyu, T., & Akhunzada, A. (2025). Soft Computing-Based Damping Controllers With Online Parameters Tuning for Stability Enhancement of Power Systems. *IEEE Access : Practical Innovations, Open Solutions, 13*, 167045–167060. Advance online publication. DOI: 10.1109/ACCESS.2025.3612288

Jaradat, S., Acharya, N., Shivshankar, S., Alhadidi, T. I., & Elhenawy, M. (2025). AI for Data Quality Auditing: Detecting Mislabeled Work Zone Crashes Using Large Language Models. *Algorithms, 18*(6), 317. Advance online publication. DOI: 10.3390/a18060317

Jaradat, S., Elhenawy, M., Paz, A., Alhadidi, T. I., Ashqar, H. I., & Nayak, R. (2025). A Cross-Cultural Crash Pattern Analysis in the United States and Jordan Using BERT and SHAP. *Electronics (Basel), 14*(2), 272. Advance online publication. DOI: 10.3390/electronics14020272

Ju, W., Altimari, U. S., Kumar, R., Pattanaik, A., Sarangi, H., Gupta, D., Rao, V. N. B., Abduvalieva, D., Mann, V. S., Mhohamdi, H., Smerat, A., & Abumalek, A. (2025). Robust classification frameworks for oxide nanomaterials assisted by machine learning. *Chemical Papers*. Advance online publication. DOI: 10.1007/s11696-025-04471-0

Kamal, M. M., Ul Abideen, S. Z., Al-Khasawneh, M. A., Momani, A. M., Mostafa, H., Atoum, M. S., Ullah, S., Alsayaydeh, J. A. J., & Yusof, M. F. (2025). Meyer Wavelet Transform and Jaccard Deep Q Net for Small Object Classification Using Multi-Modal Images. *CMES -. Computer Modeling in Engineering & Sciences*, *144*(3), 3053–3083. Advance online publication. DOI: 10.32604/cmes.2025.067430

Keote, R., Katre, S., Keote, M., Chiwande, S., Das, A., Smerat, A., Golar, P., Diwan, P., & Kediya, S. (2025). An integrated IoT–AI framework for intelligent structural performance prediction and real-time strength forecasting in large-scale dome trusses. *Asian Journal of Civil Engineering*. DOI: 10.1007/s42107-025-01586-3

Khalayleh, Y. A. S., Mohammad, S. I., Al Louzi, N. S., Baniata, M., Hassan, M., Safaqah, M. A., Vasudevan, A., & Alshurideh, M. T. (2025). Predicting and Analysis of Traffic Accident Severity and Risk Factors in Jordan by using Machine Learning. *Applied Mathematics & Information Sciences*, *19*(6), 1419–1426. Advance online publication. DOI: 10.18576/amis/190615

Khaled Abdullah, S., & Qawasmeh, R. (2025). *Navigating the ethical and legal risks of AI marketing in Jordanian SMEs*. EDPACS., DOI: 10.1080/07366981.2025.2600205

Khan, A. A., Siddiqui, S., Al-Shamayleh, A. S., Akhunzada, A., & Dey, I. (2025). DFROG-MAC: A Dynamic Fragmentation-Based MAC for Prioritised Emergency Data Management in Vehicular Networks. *IET Wireless Sensor Systems*, *15*(1), e70017. Advance online publication. DOI: 10.1049/wss2.70017

Khatibi, A., Babaker, S., Praveen, K. N. R., Chohan, J. S., Jadhav, A., Alsoud, A. R., Ramudu, M. J., & Jeet, R. (2025). Advanced AI-Driven Cybersecurity: Analyzing Emerging Threats and Defensive Strategies. *National Academy Science Letters*. Advance online publication. DOI: 10.1007/s40009-025-01897-8

Laha, S. R., Smadi, K. Al, Habboush, A. K., Pattanayak, B. K., Pattnaik, S., & Mohanty, B. (2025). Smart Waste Management Framework for Green Cities: Integrating IoT, LoRa, and Deep Learning for Efficient Waste Classification and Management. *Tikrit Journal of Engineering Sciences, 32*(Special Issue 1). DOI: 10.25130/tjes.sp1.2025.1

Lakshmi, A. S., Sigamany, E. S. S., Traisa, R., Kumar, R., Reddy, K. R., Chohan, J. S., & Smerat, A. (2025). Enhancing Code Quality Through Automated Refactoring Using Transformer-Based Language Models. *International Journal of Advanced Computer Science and Applications*, *16*(9). Advance online publication. DOI: 10.14569/IJACSA.2025.0160951

Lee, S. W., Hussain, S., Issa, G. F., Abbas, S., Ghazal, T. M., Sohail, T., Ahmad, M., & Khan, M. A. (2021). Multi-Dimensional Trust Quantification by Artificial Agents through Evidential Fuzzy Multi-Criteria Decision Making. *IEEE Access : Practical Innovations, Open Solutions*, *9*, 159399–159412. Advance online publication. DOI: 10.1109/ACCESS.2021.3131521

Llwaah, F., Hussein, A. H., & Ghazal, T. M. (2025). Enhancing Cloud Resource Utilization Through Synthesizing Intensive Workflow Tasks. *Journal of Wireless Mobile Networks, Ubiquitous Computing and Dependable Applications*, *16*(4), 537–555. Advance online publication. DOI: 10.58346/JOWUA.2025.I4.030

Louati, H., Arooj, R., Niazi, A. U. K., Dalam, M. E. E., Almazah, M. M. A., & Smerat, A. (2025). Finite-time fuzzy control strategy for nonlinear MASs with actuator faults and deception attacks. *AIMS Mathematics*, *10*(9), 20113–20139. Advance online publication. DOI: 10.3934/math.2025899

Mahadin, G. A. L., Satvika, S., Kathuria, S., Kaushik, A., & Maranan, R. (2025). DEEP LEARNING FRAMEWORK FOR IDENTIFYING AND HYBRID SYNTHESIZING WIDESPREAD NEWS HEADLINES ON SOCIAL MEDIA. *Proceedings on Engineering Sciences*, *7*(3), 1453–1462. Advance online publication. DOI: 10.24874/PES07.03.007

Mahfouz, K. H., Al Betar, M. A., & Makhadmeh, S. N. (2025). Mitigating the task scheduling problem in fog computing environments using improved marine predators optimization algorithm. *Computing*, *107*(7), 147. Advance online publication. DOI: 10.1007/s00607-025-01502-2

Mahfuri, M., & Ibrahim, A. (2024). AI-Driven Innovations: Transforming Data Support and Environmental Management for the Future. *2024 International Conference on Decision Aid Sciences and Applications, DASA 2024*. DOI: 10.1109/DASA63652.2024.10836162

Makhadmeh, S. N., Fraihat, S., Awad, M., Sanjalawe, Y., Al-Betar, M. A., & Awadallah, M. A. (2025). A crossover-integrated Marine Predator Algorithm for feature selection in intrusion detection systems within IoT environments. *Internet of Things : Engineering Cyber Physical Human Systems*, *31*, 101536. Advance online publication. DOI: 10.1016/j.iot.2025.101536

Marhoon, H. M., Basil, N., Sabbar, B. M., Qasem, N., & Ma'arif, A. (2025). Safety and Surveillance on Unmanned Aerial Vehicles Control Systems and Optimization Methods: A Systematic Review. *International Journal of Robotics and Control Systems*, *5*(5). Advance online publication. DOI: 10.31763/ijrcs.v5i5.1859

Masadeh, R., Almomani, O., Zaqebah, A., Masadeh, S., Alshqurat, K., Sharieh, A., & Alsharman, N. (2025). Narwhal Optimizer: A Nature-Inspired Optimization Algorithm for Solving Complex Optimization Problems. *Computers, Materials & Continua*, *85*(2), 3709–3737. Advance online publication. DOI: 10.32604/cmc.2025.066797

Masango, N. C., Agushaka, J. O., Amaefule, M. C., Taiwo, O., Zhang, P., Ezugwu, A. E., Saleem, K., Smerat, A., & Abualigah, L. (2025). Secure and efficient cloudlet networks: blockchain integration with agent-based proof of trust mechanism. *Eurasip Journal on Wireless Communications and Networking*, *2025*(1). DOI: 10.1186/s13638-025-02439-y

Maz, Y. A., Anbar, M., Manickam, S., Abualhaj, M. M., Almalki, S. A., & Alabsi, B. A. (2025). Transfer Learning-Based Approach with an Ensemble Classifier for Detecting Keylogging Attack on the Internet of Things. *Computers, Materials & Continua*, *85*(3), 5287–5307. Advance online publication. DOI: 10.32604/cmc.2025.068257

Mbasso, W. F., Harrison, A., Dagal, I., Jangir, P., Liu, Z., & Smerat, A. (2025). High-Fidelity Simulation-Driven Control Framework for Robust Grid Integration of Renewable Energy Systems. *Energy Science & Engineering*. Advance online publication. DOI: 10.1002/ese3.70414

Mohammad, A. A. S., Al-Ramadan, A. M., Mohammad, S. I., Al Oraini, B., Vasudevan, A., Alshdaifat, N., & Hunitie, M. F. A. (2025). Customer Sentiment Analysis for Food and Beverage Development in Restaurants using AI in Jordan. *Data and Metadata*, *4*, 922. Advance online publication. DOI: 10.56294/dm2025922

Mohammad, S. I., Al-Daoud, K., Al Qraini, B., Khanfar, I. A. A., & Vasudevan, A. (2025). Quantum Error Correction with Surface Code Analysis on Quantum Computing platform. *Applied Mathematics & Information Sciences*, *19*(2), 423–435. Advance online publication. DOI: 10.18576/amis/190216

Mostafa, S. A., Hasan, D. F., Abdul-Jabar, M. A., Hussein, A. H., & Mustapha, A. (2025). An Ensemble Learning Model for Multi-Type Cancer Prediction in Clinical Diagnostic Decision Support Systems. *Journal of Soft Computing and Data Mining*, *6*(1). Advance online publication. DOI: 10.30880/jscdm.2025.06.01.015

Nafisah, I., Mahmoud, N., Ewees, A. A., Khattap, M. G., Dahou, A., Alghamdi, S. M., Fares, I. A., Azmi Al-Betar, M., & Abd Elaziz, M. (2025). Deep learning-based feature selection for detection of autism spectrum disorder. *Frontiers in Artificial Intelligence*, *8*, 1594372. Advance online publication. DOI: 10.3389/frai.2025.1594372 PMID: 40636395

Nandagopal, M., Manavalan, T., Kumar, K. P., Manogaran, N., Kesavan, D., Kumar, G., & Al-Khasawneh, M. A. (2025). Enhancing energy efficiency in cloud computing through task scheduling with hybrid cuckoo search and transformer models. *Discover Computing*, *28*(1), 199. Advance online publication. DOI: 10.1007/s10791-025-09716-w

Nasir, J., Aamir, M., Iftikhar, S., Albidah, A. B., Alqasem, O. A., Elwahab, M. E. A., Khan, I., & Koh, W. S. (2025). A Novel Hybrid Approach to Forecasting Crude Oil Prices Using Local Mean Decomposition, ARIMA, and XGBoost. *IEEE Access : Practical Innovations, Open Solutions*, *13*, 89140–89156. Advance online publication. DOI: 10.1109/ACCESS.2025.3561193

Otair, M., Qawaqzeh, F. A., Alomari, S. A., Zitar, R. A., Migdady, H., Saleem, K., Smerat, A., Alsoud, A. R., & Abualigah, L. (2025). Enhanced Arithmetic Optimization Algorithm for Intrusion Detection in Wireless Sensor Networks. *International Journal of Communication Systems*, *38*(10), e70122. Advance online publication. DOI: 10.1002/dac.70122

Owida, H. A., Alazaidah, R., Bani-Bakr, A., Khafajeh, H., Chan, H. Y., Mizher, M., & Katrawi, A. (2025). Integrative Deep Learning for Enhanced Acute Lymphoblastic Leukemia Detection: A Comprehensive Study on the ALL-IDB Dataset. *Engineering. Technology and Applied Science Research*, *15*(2), 20776–20781. Advance online publication. DOI: 10.48084/etasr.9745

Qaddara, I., & Alraba'nah, Y. (2025). Enhancing Requirements Classification Using Machine Learning Techniques. *SN Computer Science*, *6*(6), 649. Advance online publication. DOI: 10.1007/s42979-025-04158-z

Qaddara, I., Alrabaynah, Y., & Hiari, M. O. (2025). Evaluation of SQL and NoSQL Databases on Parallel Processing. *Engineering. Technology and Applied Science Research*, *15*(4), 24298–24304. Advance online publication. DOI: 10.48084/etasr.10620

Qader Ismail Alnajem, A. A., Ibrahim, A., Abdulrahman, M. M., Abdulrazak Al-Kubaisi, A. A., Tawfeq, J. F., Khishe, M., & Saeed, A. (2024). AI-Driven Strategic Foresight: Anticipating Future Trends and Modelling Business Strategies. *2024 International Conference on Decision Aid Sciences and Applications, DASA 2024*. DOI: 10.1109/DASA63652.2024.10836619

Qawaqneh, H., Al Sayyed, O., Mohammad Alomari, K., Bektemyssova, G., Smerat, A., Montazeri, Z., Dehghani, M., Parkash Malik, O., & Eguchi, K. (2025). Pipefish Optimization Algorithm (POA): A Nature-inspired Metaheuristic for Robust and Adaptive Global Optimization. *International Journal of Intelligent Engineering and Systems, 18*(11), 778–794. Advance online publication. DOI: 10.22266/ijies2025.1231.48

Qawasmeh, S., Habboushb, A., Elzaghmouri, B., Kharma, Q., & Albalawneh, D. (2025). Hybrid Convolutional Neural Network-Based Intrusion Detection System for Secure IoT Networks. *Tikrit Journal of Engineering Sciences, 32*(SP1), 1–11. Advance online publication. DOI: 10.25130/tjes.sp1.2025.2

Rabbi, M. F., Amin, M., Al-Dalahmeh, M., & Abdullah, M. (2025). Assessing the role of information technology in promoting environmental sustainability and preventing crime in E-commerce. *International Review of Applied Sciences and Engineering, 16*(1), 81–97. Advance online publication. DOI: 10.1556/1848.2024.00834

Ramesh, J. V. N., Nimma, D., Dasari, R., Chaudhari Rane, D., AlGhamdi, A., Rao, K. B. V. B., Haider, S. A., Kuzieva, N., & Jangir, P. (2025). Safe and Reliable Two-Stage Online Offloading Algorithm for Transportation Cyber-Physical Systems. *IEEE Transactions on Intelligent Transportation Systems, 26*(9), 14313–14322. Advance online publication. DOI: 10.1109/TITS.2025.3539934

Rateb, R., Abualhaj, M. M., Alsaaidah, A., Alsharaiah, M. A., Shorman, A., & Thalji, N. J. (2025). Exploring the dynamics of providing cognition using a computational model of cognitive insomnia. *IAES International Journal of Artificial Intelligence, 14*(1). Advance online publication. DOI: 10.11591/ijai.v14.i1.pp92-101

Raza, M. A., Karim, A., Alqarni, M., Al-Khasawneh, M. A., Jumani, T. A., Aman, M., & Masud, M. I. (2025). An Intelligent Long Short-Term Memory-Based Machine Learning Model for the Potential Assessment of Global Hydropower Capacity in Sustainable Energy Transition and Security. *Energies, 18*(13), 3324. Advance online publication. DOI: 10.3390/en18133324

Rehan, R., Sahran, S., Alyasseri, Z. A. A., Sani, N. S., & Al-Betar, M. A. (2025). Hyperparameters optimization of evolving spiking neural network using artificial bee colony for unsupervised anomaly detection. *Journal of Intelligent Systems, 34*(1), 20240235. Advance online publication. DOI: 10.1515/jisys-2024-0235

Saeed, N. M. S. E., Ibrahim, A., Ali, L., Al-Dmour, N. A., Mohammed, A. S., & Ghazal, T. M. (2024). Unveiling the Landscape of Machine Learning and Deep Learning Methodologies in Network Security: A Comprehensive Literature Review. *2nd International Conference on Cyber Resilience, ICCR 2024*. DOI: 10.1109/ICCR61006.2024.10533066

Salman, A. M., Ibrahim, A., Abdulbaqi, A. S., Almajed, R., & Al Naffakh, H. A. H. (2025). *Designing Blockchain Solutions to Enhance Data Security and Privacy in Distributed IoT Networks*. DOI: 10.1109/ICBATS66542.2025.11258568

Samanta, I. S., Mohanty, S., Rout, P. K., Parida, S. M., Panda, S., Bajaj, M., Blazek, V., & Prokop, L. (2025). A comprehensive review of feature extraction techniques for power quality event detection with novel approaches for enhanced classification in smart grids. *Electrical Engineering*, *107*(9), 12227–12259. Advance online publication. DOI: 10.1007/s00202-025-03149-w

Sanjalawe, Y., Al-E'mari, S., Abualhaj, M., Makhadmeh, S. N., Alsharaiah, M. A., & Hijazi, D. H. (2025). Recent advances in secretary bird optimization algorithm, its variants and applications. In *Evolutionary Intelligence* (Vol. 18, Number 3). DOI: 10.1007/s12065-025-01054-6

Sardar, R., Anees, T., Al-Shamayleh, A. S., Mehmood, E., Khalil, W., Akhunzada, A., & Shaikh, F. S. (2025). Challenges in detecting security threats in WoT: A systematic literature review. *Artificial Intelligence Review*, *58*(7), 196. Advance online publication. DOI: 10.1007/s10462-025-11176-z

Sawarkar, P. G., Pote, A., Khan, M. A., Abed, M. H., Hadi, A. A., Smerat, A., & Khishe, M. (2025). Sustainable geopolymer concrete evaluation using machine learning and PDP analysis: Comparative insights into strength prediction. *Hybrid Advances*, *11*, 100569. Advance online publication. DOI: 10.1016/j.hybadv.2025.100569

Shah, R. K., Hasan, M. K., Islam, S., Khan, A., Ghazal, T. M., & Khan, A. N. (2022). Detect Phishing Website by Fuzzy Multi-Criteria Decision Making. *2022 1st International Conference on AI in Cybersecurity, ICAIC 2022*. DOI: 10.1109/ICAIC53980.2022.9897036

Shamaylah, N., Ibrahim Mohammad, S., Al Oraini, B., Yaseen Al-Gaafreh, J. M., Mosallam Alqahtani, M., Vasudevan, A., Shlash Mohammad, A. A., & Ahmmad Hunitie, M. F. (2025). Data-Driven Decision-Making for Employee Training and Development in Jordanian Public Institutions. *Data and Metadata*, *4*, 886. Advance online publication. DOI: 10.56294/dm2025886

Shambour, Q. Y., Al-Zyoud, M., & Hussein, A. H. (2025). FROM DATA TO DIAGNOSIS: KNOWLEDGE-DRIVEN, EXPLAINABLE AI FOR RELIABLE EARLY AUTISM DETECTION. *Interdisciplinary Journal of Information, Knowledge, and Management*, *20*, 032. Advance online publication. DOI: 10.28945/5652

Shambour, Q., Al-Zyoud, M., & Almomani, O. (2025). Quantum-Inspired Hybrid Metaheuristic Feature Selection with SHAP for Optimized and Explainable Spam Detection. *Symmetry*, *17*(10), 1716. Advance online publication. DOI: 10.3390/sym17101716

Sharma, K. P., Yajid, M. S. A., Gowrishankar, J., Mahajan, R., Alsoud, A. R., Jadhav, A., & Singh, D. (2025). A Systematic Review on Text Summarization: Techniques, Challenges, Opportunities. In *Expert Systems* (Vol. 42, Number 4). DOI: 10.1111/exsy.13833

Sharma, K. P., Al-Rashed, A., Johar, M. G. M., Alsoud, A. R., Singh, A., Dey, P., & Pant, S. (2025). Blockchain-Assisted Trust Framework for Increased Survivability in Internet of Vehicles. *Internet Technology Letters*, *8*(3), e70029. Advance online publication. DOI: 10.1002/itl2.70029

Sharma, K. P., Hussain, R., Jaharadak, A. A., Trawnih, A. A., Verma, D., Dasi, S., & Pant, S. (2025). Hybrid Convolutional Neural Network for Robust Attack Detection in Wireless Sensor Networks. *Internet Technology Letters*, *8*(6), e650. Advance online publication. DOI: 10.1002/itl2.650

Shi, J., Farooq, U., Tabash, M. I., Riyadh, H. A., & Almajali, T. A. (2025). Air Pollution and the Innovation Gap: A Challenge for Sustainable Growth in Emerging and Growth Leading Economies (EAGLE). *Sustainability (Basel)*, *17*(10), 4423. Advance online publication. DOI: 10.3390/su17104423

Shlash Mohammad, A. A., Ibrahim Mohammad, S., Al-Daoud, K. I., Al Oraini, B., Mosallam Alqahtani, M., Vasudevan, A., & Ahmmad Hunitie, M. F. (2025). Riding into the Future: Transforming Jordan's Public Transportation with Predictive Analytics and Real-Time Data. *Data and Metadata*, *4*, 887. Advance online publication. DOI: 10.56294/dm2025887

Solairaju, J. A., Rathinasamy, S., Thanikodi, S., Tarawneh, B., Gurumoorthy, V., Antony, J. S., & Arul Gnana Dhas, A. (2025). Development and Validation of ANN Models for Water Absorption in Sawdust and Kenaf Fiber-Reinforced Polystyrene Composites. *Engineering Reports*, *7*(9), e70393. Advance online publication. DOI: 10.1002/eng2.70393

Tarek, R., Elshenawy, A., Assadwy, M. I., & Madkour, M. A. (2025). Automated Diagnosis of Dental Diseases Using Deep Learning on Radiographic Images. *SN Computer Science*, *6*(6), 751. Advance online publication. DOI: 10.1007/s42979-025-04264-y

Turab, N., Abushattal, A., Al-Nabulsi, J., & Owida, H. A. (2025). Advanced risk assessment using machine learning and sentiment analysis on log data. *IAES International Journal of Artificial Intelligence*, *14*(5), 3897. Advance online publication. DOI: 10.11591/ijai.v14.i5.pp3897-3905

Ullah, N., Al-Rahmi, W. M., Alblehai, F., Fernando, Y., Alharbi, Z. H., Zhanbayev, R., Al-Adwan, A. S., & Habes, M. (2025). Corrigendum to "Blockchain-powered grids: Paving the way for a sustainable and efficient future" [Heliyon Volume 10, Issue 10, May 2024, Article e31592] (Heliyon (2024) 10(10), (S2405844024076230), ()). In *Heliyon* (Vol. 11, Number 13). https://doi.org/DOI: 10.1016/j.heliyon.2024.e31592

Varshney, S., Bajaj, M., Choudhary, K. K., Pushkarna, M., & Zaitsev, I. (2025). Performance Analysis and Reliability Prediction of Multi-State Service Systems With Multiple Failure Modes of Unreliable Server: An Engineering Perspective. *Engineering Reports*, *7*(7), e70268. Advance online publication. DOI: 10.1002/eng2.70268

Vasudevan, A., Albinaa, T. A., Mohammad, S. I., Sharmila, E., Raja, N., Soon, E. E. H., Alshurideh, M. T., & Al-Adwan, A. S. (2024). Bidirectional LSTM for Electronic Product Recommendation. *Applied Mathematics & Information Sciences*, *18*(6), 1443–1453. Advance online publication. DOI: 10.18576/amis/180621

Vasudevan, A., Nair, S. S., Mohammad, S. I., Raja, N., Soon, E. E. H., Nagaraj, S., Alshamayleh, A., & Alshurideh, M. T. (2025). Redefining Realities: AI's Cost-Efficient Revolution in Indian Cinema's VFX Landscape. *Applied Mathematics & Information Sciences*, *19*(1), 171–182. Advance online publication. DOI: 10.18576/amis/190115

Vasudevan, A., Tamilmani, K. T., Mohammad, S. I., Sridheepika, V. S., Raja, N., Soon, E. E. H., Nagaraj, S., & Al-Adwan, A. S. (2025). Voices of Concern: Contemplations on Socioeconomic, Ethical, and Developmental Impacts of AI. *Applied Mathematics & Information Sciences*, *19*(1), 221–232. Advance online publication. DOI: 10.18576/amis/190119

Vasudevan, A., Yogeesh, N., Mohammad, S. I., Raja, N., Girija, D. K., Rashmi, M., Abu-Shareha, A. A., & Alshurideh, M. T. (2025). Unlocking Insights of Fuzzy Mathematics for Enhanced Predictive Modelling. *Applied Mathematics & Information Sciences, 19*(1), 49–59. Advance online publication. DOI: 10.18576/amis/190105

Xu, B., Jummaa, K., Altalbawy, F. M. A., Roopashree, R., Saraswat, S. K., Ray, S., Tomar, P., Naem, S., Hamza, H. H., Smerat, A., & Khalid, A. (2025). Machine learning-assisted computation of water activity for ionic liquid-based aqueous ternary elements. *Desalination and Water Treatment, 324*, 101484. Advance online publication. DOI: 10.1016/j.dwt.2025.101484

Yaseen, M., Ali, E., Sarwar, N., Jamel, L., Din, I., Yuldashev, F., & Law, F. (2025). Design of Minimal Spanning Tree and Analytic Hierarchical Process (SAHP) Based Hybrid Technique for Software Requirements Prioritization. *IET Software, 2025*(1). DOI: 10.1049/sfw2/8819735

Zhu, Y., Lin, X., Kim, J., Al-Adwan, A. S., & Li, N. (2025). Exploring Human Interaction in Online Self-Regulated Learning Through Danmaku Comments. *International Journal of Human-Computer Interaction, 41*(22), 13964–13977. Advance online publication. DOI: 10.1080/10447318.2025.2480826

Zraiqat, A., Al Sayyed, O., Al Soudi, M., Al-Salih, A. A. M. M., Smerat, A., Montazeri, Z., Dehghani, M., Malik, O. P., Ahmed, M. A., Ibraheem, I. K., & Eguchi, K. (2025). Key Maker Algorithm: A Novel Human-Based Metaheuristic for Constrained Optimization. *International Journal of Intelligent Engineering and Systems, 18*(9), 688–699. Advance online publication. DOI: 10.22266/ijies2025.1031.45

Zraiqat, A., Batiha, B., Al Soudi, M., Ibraheem, I. K., Smerat, A., Montazeri, Z., Dehghani, M., Werner, F., Al-Salih, A. A. M. M., Ahmed, M. A., & Eguchi, K. (2025). Detective Algorithm: A Novel Human-inspired Metaheuristic for Solving Real-world Constrained Optimization Problems. *International Journal of Intelligent Engineering and Systems, 18*(10), 33–46. Advance online publication. DOI: 10.22266/ijies2025.1130.03

About the Contributors

Amer Ibrahim is an Associate Professor of Computer Science at the College of Information Technology, United Arab Emirates University, Al Ain, United Arab Emirates. He holds a Ph.D. in Computer Science (Human–Computer Interaction and Artificial Intelligence) awarded by the Higher Technical School of Computer Science and Telecommunications Engineering, University of Granada, Spain. Dr. Ibrahim's academic contributions span Human–Computer Interaction, Artificial Intelligence, machine learning, cybersecurity, and game-based learning. His research has advanced playability engineering, usability evaluation frameworks, and design methodologies for educational and serious games, as well as context-aware and pervasive learning environments. He has contributed to the development of AI-driven adaptive learning models, privacy-preserving and secure digital systems, and intelligent interaction design for educational, healthcare, and IoT-enabled environments. Dr. Ibrahim has published extensively in peer-reviewed journals and international conferences and has actively participated in international research collaborations, editorial boards, and scientific committees. His scholarly work demonstrates a sustained commitment to technically rigorous, user-centered, and secure computing systems.

Taher M. Ghazal is a Principal Research Scientist and Associate Professor specializing in Management Information Systems, Cybersecurity, and Digital Innovation. He holds a Ph.D. in Information Science and Technology with a concentration in Cybersecurity from Universiti Kebangsaan Malaysia (UKM). He also completed a Postdoctoral Fellowship in Cybersecurity at the Center for Physical Systems (C2PS), Khalifa University of Science and Technology, United Arab Emirates. Dr. Ghazal's academic contributions span business analytics, artificial intelligence, Internet of Things (IoT), blockchain, cybersecurity, and smart digital systems, with a strong emphasis on applied and industry-driven research in MIS and information systems. He has published extensively, with over 175 peer-reviewed journal and conference publications and more than 11,000 citations, and has been recognized among the world's top 2% scientists for multiple consecutive years. His research addresses secure and intelligent digital infrastructures, data-driven decision-making, cyber resilience, and the integration of emerging technologies into business and organizational contexts. In addition to his research output, Dr. Ghazal has led international research initiatives, chaired IEEE- and Scopus-indexed conferences, contributed to patented innovations in IoT, AI, and blockchain systems, and played key roles in academic leadership, research coordination, and quality assurance aligned with international frameworks such as AACSB, ABET, and QS rankings.

***

Nidal Al-Dmour is a Full Professor in the Computer Engineering Department at Mutah University, Jordan, with a PhD in Computer Networks and Security from the University of Wales Bangor, UK. His academic and research expertise covers network security, cybersecurity, artificial intelligence, wireless computer networks, and high-performance computing. His professional experience includes academic positions at Mutah University, Ajman University, and Al Hussein University. He has participated in EU-funded Erasmus+ projects related to ICT education and agricultural technology training. His publication record includes journal papers, book chapters, and international conference papers in cybersecurity, AI, IoT, networks, and computing. Overall, his CV reflects a strong academic profile combining teaching, research, leadership, international collaboration, and professional service.

Leen Al-Tarawneh is a Computer Science graduate from Mu'tah University. She holds a master's degree in Cybersecurity and Cloud Computing with distinction. Her research interests include cybersecurity, cloud security, and machine learning applications in threat detection. She is currently focusing on developing skills in Security Operations Center (SOC) and advanced cyber defense strategies.

Ahmed Elngar is an Associate Professor and Head of Computer Science Department at Faculty of Computers and Artificial Intelligence, Department of Computer Science, Beni Suef University. Their current project is 'Biometrics, AI-based Security, Image processing, AI-based Control, AI-based Smart Grids' . Internet of Things Security.

Khaled Shaalan is a Professor at the Faculty of Computers & Information, Cairo University, Egypt. He is on secondment, Senior Lecturer, to the Faculty of Informatics, The British University in Dubai, UAE. He is also an Honorary Fellow at the University of Edinburgh, UK. Khaled holds a PhD from Cairo University, jointly with the Swedish Institute of Computer Science, Sweden. Both his teaching and research are related to language engineering and knowledge engineering. He is particularly interested in developing tools and applications for both knowledge-based systems and Arabic language processing. Khaled has led extensive research on machine translation, information extraction, and agricultural expert systems. Khaled has about 20 years of experience in developing tools, systems and applications for Arabic natural language processing using the rules-based approach. He has published in leading international journals such as IEEE Transactions on Knowledge and Data Engineering (IEEE TKDE), Expert System with Applications (ESWA), New Review of Applied Expert Systems, International Journal of Computer Processing of Oriental Languages (IJCPOL), Journal of the American Society for Information Science and Technology (JASIST), and Software Practice and Experience (SPE). Khaled has published his research in many reputed international conferences related to artificial intelligence and language processing. He is currently leading the Arabic natural language processing research group at The British University in Dubai.

Sonal Trivedi has more than 12 years of experience in academics. She has authored two national books, two Scopus indexed edited book and published 17 Scopus indexed papers. She has chaired 5 conferences and granted with 6 Patents. She has attended and presented papers in various international and national conference. She is also reviewer of various Scopus indexed journals.

Index

A

B

C

D

E

F

G

H

I

K

L

M

N

P

R

S

T

U

X

www.ingramcontent.com/pod-product-compliance
Lightning Source LLC
LaVergne TN
LVHW060256011026
849161LV00011B/2724